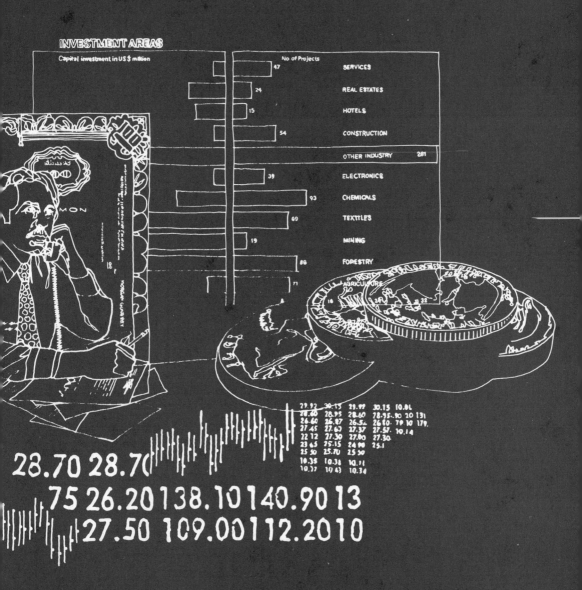

Introduction to

FINANCIAL MANAGEMENT

Introduction to
FINANCIAL
MANAGEMENT

O. Maurice Joy

The School of Business
The University of Kansas

1977

Richard D. Irwin, Inc.   Homewood, Illinois   60430

Irwin-Dorsey Limited   Georgetown, Ontario   L7G 4B3

ISBN 0-256-01880-4
Library of Congress Catalog Card No. 76–13079

Printed in the United States of America

to BETSY
for her birthday

PREFACE

The title of this text, *Introduction to Financial Management,* conveys its orientation and its intended use as the main text in the beginning college course in financial management. I am aware, however, that the title is not particularly self-explanatory. *Introductory* may imply any of several different levels of difficulty and, to the new student, the words *financial management* are largely devoid of meaning.

First, let me try to explain what I mean by introductory. I expect the book to be used in either a beginning undergraduate or MBA business finance course. Its level of difficulty is essentially predicated on the assumption that students have taken an introductory financial accounting course and are familiar with high school algebra. Some simple statistical concepts are developed in the text and a preparatory course in statistics would be useful, but is not essential. No previous finance background is presumed.

For those who will take no more finance, the book is intended to cover adequately the practical aspects of the subject of financial management, to provide a reference book in which it is relatively easy to find things long after the course is over, and to impart at least the flavor of the deeper financial management issues. For those who plan to pursue advanced study, my intent is to provide an adequate background for subsequent finance courses, to introduce conceptual problems that will be encountered later at a more elegant level, and to whet the appetite.

Let us consider next what the words *financial management* mean. Financial management refers in this book to the financial decisions business firms make. The book particularly emphasizes financial decision making by *corporations.* In general, firms face three major kinds of financial management decisions: the investment decision (what assets to buy), the financing decision (how to pay for these assets), and the dividend decision (how to distribute profits to the stockholders). One of the book's goals is to provide a thorough treatment of these decision-making areas.

A major concern in an introductory text such as this is how deeply to explore theory questions. Any author must be cognizant of the tradeoff between the richness and the difficulty of the material presented. A particularly rich, high quality presentation will necessarily be a more difficult one. It will involve more theory, more abstraction and (usually) a higher level of mathematical exposition. Conversely, a less difficult book will contain less of these qualities. I am aware that many business students approach theory discussions apprehensively. They view the study and practice of business from a purely practical perspective and consider attempts to introduce theoretical constructs as "academic" exercises. This is, however, a naïve viewpoint. The pragmatic financial practitioner, for example, who will be most successful will be well grounded in the fundamental concepts of financial management; and these concepts necessarily involve financial management theories. Consequently, I view theory and the development of a theoretical framework as an indispensable element of the study of financial management, even at the introductory level. Accordingly, there is an appreciable amount of financial theory contained in this book. However, in presenting those theoretical constructs used in this text, I have purposely attempted to keep the presentation at a relatively simple level. In addition, I have attempted to relate the theory closely to "real world" problems by use of examples and illustrations. That is, I have tried to make the theory understandable, meaningful, and relevant.

One of the principal themes of this book is that all financial management decisions are related to the goal of the firm and this relationship must be constantly kept in mind in discussing financial management problems. Accordingly, the text emphasizes the integrated whole of financial management decisions and constantly relates these different parts to the whole. This is in contrast to many financial management texts that present separate, almost unrelated blocks of techniques and analysis. Furthermore, the book includes up-to-date concepts and practices of modern financial management and (hopefully) is clearly written. All major points are amplified by use of student-tested illustrations and examples. In addition to the theoretical aspects of the subject matter, considerable attention is paid to the institutional aspects of financial management that relate to the factual and descriptive circumstances and arrangements of transacting business financial affairs.

The book's organization is somewhat different than some of the current standard financial management texts. The first two parts establish the goal of the firm, review financial statement information, and introduce the fundamental concepts of financial management: the time value of money, risk, and valuation principles. We draw on these fundamental concepts throughout the text. The other major organizational difference is that many of the traditional "profit planning" topics are not bunched together, but rather are found in those sections that seem (to me) most pertinent. Cash budgeting, for example, is covered in the working capital management section, and financial forecasting is introduced in the long- and intermediate-term financing section.

Part Three analyzes long-run investment decisions, decisions that are the primary key to the ultimate success of the firm. Parts Four and Five deal with the long-run financing decisions and dividend policy decisions faced by the firm.

Once the long-run decisions have been analyzed, we turn our attention in Parts Six and Seven to the short-run investment and financing decisions. These day-to-day operating decisions help determine the efficiency with which the firm pursues its long-run objectives. In addition, they serve the purpose of making certain that the firm avoids problems of bankruptcy and insolvency so that it may live to enjoy the fruits of its long-run decisions.

In the final part of the book we investigate the topics of business combinations, which deal with major external expansion opportunities, and financial distress, which deals with business contraction and failure.

Many professors and former students made helpful comments on the book. I am particularly grateful for assistance from Marc Choate, Gary Emery, Larry Gibbons, Glenn Johnson, Larry Meeker, Rich Parenteau, Burr Porter, Keith Smith, and Howard Stettler.

December 1976   O. Maurice Joy

CONTENTS

section four **CAPITAL STRUCTURE AND DIVIDEND POLICY**

INTRODUCTION

FINANCIAL MANAGEMENT DECISION MAKING

This book is concerned with the financial management decisions that business firms make. Because this is an introductory text our initial task is to provide meaning for the words "financial management decisions." In performing this task we will see that business firms make many different kinds of financial management decisions, some of which are of a repetitive nature and some of which are episodic. However, most of these decisions have one thing in common: They have a financial dimension that must be evaluated. In this introductory chapter we will explore the nature and scope of financial management, we will briefly discuss the major forms of business organization, we will set up an appropriate financial management decision framework, and we will identify the goal for this framework. Once these preliminaries are concluded we will spend considerable time in later chapters in analyzing how financial decisions should be made by the firm.

FINANCIAL MANAGEMENT BY BUSINESS FIRMS

A business firm is an organization established for the primary purpose of making a profit for its owners. In the U.S. economy there are several million business firms, ranging from the very small with only a few thousand dollars in assets to giant corporations with several billion dollars of assets. Business firms play a dominant role in a free enterprise economy as exists in the United States, and the economic health of our country is inextricably entwined with the economic well-being of U.S. business firms. It is therefore of paramount importance that business firms be efficient users and efficient allocators of the scarce resources available to them.

In fact, a good way to describe what financial management is all about is to relate it to economics, which is a sort of "mother science" to finance. Essentially, economics is the study of how scarce resources should be

3

allocated among competing uses of those resources. Financial management as practiced by business firms is frequently called *business finance*
or *corporate finance* and is a kind of applied economics in that it is the
study of how business firms allocate their scarce financial resources
among competing uses. As we will see in further detail below, a business
firm's principal financial activities include investment in new assets,
raising funds to pay for these assets, and disbursing profits. Financial
management theory embraces the study of how these crucial activities
may best be carried out.

Business finance, investment analysis, and money and capital markets

A large portion of the wide array of topics covered under the title
finance has traditionally been categorized in three broad subheadings:
business finance, investment analysis, and *money and capital
markets.* Our purpose in this text is to study business finance, but the
three areas are so interrelated that we necessarily become involved in
the other two as well. Business firms are primary production agents in
the economy. Because of economies of scale and specialization of labor,
firms can perform many economic production tasks much more efficiently
than individual entrepreneurs can. It would be extremely difficult, for
example, for an individual to manufacture automobiles alone. By employing many people, some with very specialized tasks, an automobile
manufacturer can produce cars much more efficiently. And this is only
one isolated example. If you contemplate the vast array of industrial and
consumer products that can be more efficiently produced by firms, the
desirability of these business firm–production agents is apparent.

Firms need to acquire funds, however, to engage in these production
activities. A large part of these funds comes from cash flows generated
by the firms themselves, but another large part of these funds is provided
by investors. To obtain funds from these investors, firms issue financial
securities – stocks, bonds, and the like – that provide the investors with
claims on the firm's assets and income. The analysis of these (and other)
financial securities is called *investment analysis.*[1] This important area
of finance is mainly concerned with the evaluation of financial securities
from the perspective of investors. The marketplace where firms issue
financial securities and where investors buy and sell financial securities
is very well developed and complex in the United States and typically
involves "middlemen" such as investment bankers and stockbrokers.
The study of these marketplaces is the study of *money and capital
markets.*

The relationship among these closely related subjects is shown in
Figure 1–1. To make investments in physical, productive assets, business
firms must have capital. Much of this capital is obtained by issuing
financial securities to investors. Firms issue securities in return for capital funds through the money and capital markets. Firms also disburse

---

[1] An example of "other" financial securities is the financial securities issued by governments, such as U.S. Treasury bills and state and local bonds.

profits back to investors as shown in Figure 1–1. While this book is directed toward business finance we will also find ourselves heavily involved in the areas of investment theory and money and capital markets. The ties between investors and business finance are very important because, as we show later in this chapter, the goal of the firm will be related to *investor* wants and desires. That is, since investors own the financial assets that control the physical assets that comprise the firm, investment theory and much of the theory of business finance are merely two sides of the same coin and necessarily go hand in hand.

FIGURE 1–1
Relationships among investment analysis, money and capital markets, and business finance

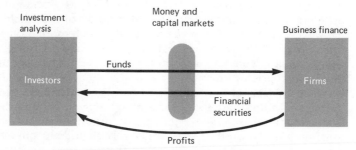

BUSINESS ORGANIZATION FORMS

One of the first decisions that any new firm faces is the choice of organizational form for the business. Although the principles of financial management that we study in this text are generally applicable to any business organization form, each form presents certain advantages and disadvantages to the owners. Therefore, financial managers need to understand the implications of the differences among the three major organizational forms: proprietorship, partnership, and corporation.

Proprietorship

In a proprietorship there is only one owner. The owner receives all profits and suffers all losses. The owner shares control with no one and is personally liable for all debts incurred by the business. This means that business creditors can look to the proprietor's personal assets to satisfy business-related claims. The proprietor thus has unlimited liability. In essence, the proprietor's personal and business assets are viewed as the same by the law.

Despite this disadvantage of unlimited liability most U.S. businesses are proprietorships. Firms are frequently categorized into one of five industry types: (1) manufacturing, (2) agricultural, forestry, and fisheries, (3) transportation, (4) wholesale and retail trade, and (5) services. Except in manufacturing, where there are slightly more corporations and partnerships than proprietorships, there are vastly many more proprietorships than partnerships and corporations. How-ever, proprietorships are typically small, and while they are more numer-ous than the other forms of business, corporations are much more im-portant in the U.S. economy in terms of the amount of assets owned.

Advantages One advantage of proprietorships is the ease and flexi-bility of organization. There are no articles of incorporation to secure as with a corporation and there are only minimal organization costs. Another important advantage is the control feature. The proprietor is in complete control of the business and is not required to make compromise decisions with other owners. The proprietor also receives all profits. An important aspect of proprietorships is their tax treatment. Proprietor-ships, unlike corporations, pay no federal income tax. Proprietorship profits are income to the owner and are taxed as personal income. This avoids the double taxation that corporate stockholders incur—where the firm's profits are taxed and then dividends to stockholders are taxed. However, personal income tax rates vary much more with an individual's income level than do corporate tax rates, and in some instances the double taxation on corporate profits may result in less tax than single tax-ation of proprietor profits.

Disadvantages One of the foremost disadvantages of proprietorships is the unlimited liability feature noted above. Another disadvantage is that small businesses—typified by proprietorships—have difficulty raising external capital. They are largely excluded from major segments of the capital market (see Chapter 12). A disadvantageous tax feature of proprietorships is that certain fringe-benefit expenses that are tax de-ductible from the corporation's standpoint—such as medical and in-surance expenses—are not tax deductible. It is also frequently hard to transfer ownership of a proprietorship because, unlike many corporations whose ownership claims are bought and sold in an organized securities market (see Chapter 12), there is no ready supply of buyers. This illiquidity feature reduces the value of the proprietor's ownership.

Partnerships

A partnership is basically a proprietorship with more than one owner. The partnership may be a *general* partnership where all partners have un-limited liability, or it may be a *limited* partnership where some partners liability is limited to the capital contributed to the organization.[2]

Advantages Because the primary difference between proprietorships and partnerships is the number of owners, most of the advantages and disadvantages noted in the proprietorship section above apply here, too. Recall that these advantages pertain mainly to ease and flexibility of organization and the tightness of control. The same tax advantages apply here; and in addition, partnerships may provide a better opportunity for specialization of labor—where one partner has primary marketing re-sponsibilities, another has primary financial management and account-ing responsibilities, and so on.

---

[2] A limited partnership must have at least *one* general partner, however.

Disadvantages All the previously noted disadvantages of proprietorships—unlimited liability, difficulty in raising capital, the nontax deductibility of certain expenses, and the limited marketability of the ownership equity—also hold here. There are other disadvantages caused by a partnership arrangement. Partners may have difficulty in agreeing on decisions, and many partnerships begun in harmony are dissolved with considerable rancor. Partnerships usually require compromise among principals, and frequently this cannot be arranged. Furthermore, when a partner dies or withdraws from the partnership the organization is legally terminated, and it may be very difficult to arrange a settlement satisfactory to all parties. Avoidance of this problem requires considerable forethought and planning.

Corporations

Corporations are legal entities that are regarded as something separate and apart from their owners. A corporation's assets are owned by it rather than its owners, and a corporation's liabilities are obligations of the corporation, not the owners. Thus a principal feature of a corporation is the limited liability of the owners. The owners have claims on the firm through their ownership of the firm's stock. This also means, however, that unless the stockholders are the principal officers of the firm, the policies of the firm will not be established by the stockholders. It is as if the corporation were an artificial person, able to buy assets, raise funds, and perform all those other activities that proprietors and partners can do.

Because corporations are the dominant form of U.S. business in terms of sales and assets, our orientation in this book is toward *corporate* finance. This does not mean that the financial management principles we study are inappropriate for the other two forms of business. But it does mean that we will emphasize the concept of stockholder wealth maximization, which is most visibly applicable to corporations with widely held common stock that can be publicly traded in auction-type stock markets.

Advantages One of the primary advantages of corporations is the limited liability of its owners. If the firm should fail, the stockholders will not be liable for the firm's debt: The most that a stockholder can lose is the investment in the firm. Another advantage is the ability of the corporation to raise new capital other than from the original owners. Small corporations may have as much difficulty in raising money from the capital markets as proprietorships and partnerships, but medium-sized and larger corporations will have access to these markets where capital is raised at advantageous rates. Ownership shares are also more easily traded in a corporation, particularly if the firm's shares are traded on a major stock exchange. This ease of transferability makes the owner's investment much more liquid.

Disadvantages The main disadvantage of incorporation is the potential loss of control of the owner. Many corporations are effectively controlled by a few (or even one) owners, but the hallmark of the large U.S. corporations is the diffusity of ownership, and many U.S. companies have hundreds of thousands of stockholders. The control of any one owner in such a situation is usually nil. While not everyone's preferences in this arrangement can be satisfied, we presume that management will perform its duties in such a way that investors collectively will view the firm favorably. The response of stockholders who do not approve of the firm's policies will be to sell the stock or attempt to overthrow the management (see Chapter 13). But the fact remains that for most large U.S. firms, ownership and control are effectively separated. For newly organized, smaller businesses there are also some relatively minor disadvantages of incorporation. It is more difficult and costly to organize a corporation because a state charter must be obtained, with all the attendant red-tape difficulties.

FUNDAMENTAL FINANCIAL MANAGEMENT DECISIONS

We now turn to a consideration of the types of financial management decisions that firms face. Our discussion from here on will emphasize the corporate form of organization. While there are many *specific* kinds of financial management decisions that the firm makes, we can classify them into three major groups:

1. *Investment decisions:* What assets should the firm acquire?
2. *Financing decisions:* How should these assets be financed?
3. *Dividend decisions:* How should profits be distributed to investors?

These are the fundamental financial management decisions the firm must consider.

Investment decisions

The term "investment decision" refers to an extremely wide range of decisions. At one extreme the firm must decide in what industry (or industries) it wishes to operate. That is, in what line(s) of business the firm will be. Once the line of business is established the firm will be making investment decisions about individual assets. The size of these potential investments will vary considerably. An oil company may investigate the economic merits of drilling a new $30,000 developmental oil well and simultaneously evaluate a proposed multimillion dollar shale oil venture in Colorado. The scale of these investments is quite different, but both proposals require investment decisions. A vigorous, growing firm will continually search for new investments and will necessarily make a large number of investment decisions.

Financing decisions

Once the firm has committed itself to new investments it must select the best means of financing these commitments. Since firms regularly make new investments the need for financing and hence the necessity of making the financing decision are ongoing. Therefore the firm will be continually planning for new financing needs. A large portion of these needs will be predictable as the firm replaces old assets with new and implements previously established investment plans. From time to time financing needs may be unexpectedly large. The firm may, for example, decide to acquire or merge with another company, and this can create an unforeseen need for funds. At the other extreme, the firm may be perilously close to failing and have a desperate need for financing to stay alive. Both the regular ongoing need for funds and the episodic need are examples of the kinds of decisions subsumed under the title "financing decision." As we will see later in the text, the financing decision is not only concerned with how best to finance new assets, but is also concerned with the best overall mix of financing for the firm.

Dividend decisions

Another issue facing the firm is the disbursement of profits back to investors who supplied capital to the firm. In later chapters we discover that some capital suppliers receive *fixed* income payments from the firm. Examples of these investors are bond holders and preferred stockholders. Because these income payments are fixed, there is (in normal times) no real decision to make regarding payment to these investors. However, the dividends paid to the owners of the firm — the common stockholders — are discretionary, and the crucial profit disbursement decision is actually the question of how much in dividends to pay to the firm's stockholders. That is, is there a best dividend payout ratio? We address this issue in a later chapter.

Planning and control functions

Decision making requires more than merely making decisions as they arise. Good decision making necessarily entails careful attention to planning and control duties. In the financial management decision context the firm should continually plan for future investment, financing, and dividend decisions, and the firm should have a control or monitoring system to evaluate how well these decisions are turning out. The planning and control functions are thus important components of all three basic financial management decision areas.

In normal times these functions insure an orderly progression and integration of financial management decisions; in times of stress they prepare the firm for and protect it against possible adverse financial contingencies and emergencies that may arise. In Chapter 2 we will study financial statements, which are important in both planning and control contexts. We will also study other planning and control issues throughout the text.

A FINANCIAL MANAGEMENT DECISION FRAMEWORK

We have now identified the firm's fundamental financial management decisions: the investment, financing, and dividend decisions. How should the firm actually make these decisions? Before we can answer this question we must have a framework to give the problems perspective. This financial management decision framework is constructed to help the firm make good financial management decisions and has three parts: (1) a goal, (2) the identification of important variables and constraints, and (3) some decision rules.

The goal of the firm

The first part of this framework is the goal of the firm. It is impossible to work toward some objective or goal if we fail to define what that goal is. Intuitively we know that the firm would follow radically different courses of action if its goal were welfare-oriented rather than profit-oriented. Clearly then, what we need first is a goal; and the identification of this goal will strongly influence the way the firm addresses the investment, financing, and dividend decisions.

There are several important things to keep in mind in establishing a goal. First, the notion of a goal implies that some decision maker or group of decision makers is striving for some objective. Acknowledging a goal is merely a way of formalizing this simple idea, and formalizing the idea opens the door for investigating ways to achieve the goal. It permits quantification of the underlying problem. While this may sound abstract, it is really very commonplace. You have a goal in regard to studying financial management, for example. You may never have expressed it (that is, it is an *implicit* goal), but it's there nonetheless. It may range from maximizing your grade, or your comprehension of the material, to minimizing the total number of pages read. But you do have a goal, which means that you are striving toward some objective. The firm has a goal also, and we are interested in identifying what it is.

The second point is that this goal is an abstraction and may not be perfectly realistic. That is, the goals we talk about are much more simple than they are in reality. There's a reason for this difference. In the "real world" things are very complex. We observe, for example, that there are many differences between any two people's tastes and preferences. As an economic unit the firm operates on behalf of many people, and if we tried to set up a goal that perfectly described all things that were important to all these individuals we would have great difficulty in doing so because the resultant goal would be extremely complex with many variables in it. Since it is a hopeless task to describe perfectly the firm's goal, we simplify. We sort through all the things that appear to be important, picking only the *most* important items that appear common to *most* individuals and then state the goal in much simplified terms. We call this process *abstraction,* and in the financial theory of the firm we pick the *one* objective that seems most important and state the firm's goal in terms of that one item. This process invariably disturbs many students and businessmen because it appears unrealistic. But this is the nature of abstraction, and furthermore, just because something *appears* at first glance to be unrealistic doesn't necessarily mean it is. If we find one objective that is so important that it seems to dominate all other considerations, then the abstracted objective must be very important. We will see below that it *is* possible to identify such an objective.

Common stockholder orientation Financial theory envisions the firm as an entity that owes primary loyalty to the firm's owners. There are several other major groups of individuals associated with the firm: employees (both labor and management), creditors, customers, and suppliers. While the firm is obviously interested in the welfare of these other groups, it is a fairly well-accepted doctrine that the financial goal of the firm should be *owner*-oriented; more specifically, the goal should be *common stockholder*-oriented.

Most businesses begin as small owner-entrepreneur operations where the firm's and owner's interests clearly coincide. As the scale of production in the United States has grown to what is now popularly called "big business," large corporations financed by money raised outside the firm have supplanted the smaller owner-entrepreneur business as the dominant form of business organization in terms of economic importance, but the concept of ownership is still clear. The common stockholder is the residual claimant on the firm's income stream in normal times and residual claimant on the firm's assets if the firm should fail and be dissolved.[3] The stockholder has supplied the equity base for the firm's operations, and to the stockholder go the lion's share of the losses when the firm does poorly. It is as if the original owner-entrepreneur had sold the business to several thousand or several million investors who are now the owners. And, in fact, this is exactly what has happened.

So, who owns the firm? The stockholders! And whose goal is implied when we talk about the financial goal of the firm? The stockholders' goal![4] By stockholders we actually mean *common* stockholders. While the preferred stockholder is *legally* an owner also, this person is in front of (has preference to) the common stockholder both in receiving dividends (income claims) and in receiving proceeds from the dissolution of the company (asset claims). Consequently, the preferred stockholder's position is not a residual position like the common stockholder's.

Stockholder utility maximization Equating the stockholders' and the firm's goals is tantamount to asserting that the firm should act so as to enhance the stockholders' welfare. This means that we must next decide what aspects of the stockholders' welfare are most important. Technically, we want to identify what is of paramount importance to stockholders and suitably phrase the stockholder-firm goal. Moreover, we would like the goal to be both quantifiable and operational. To quantify means to express numerically. We want a goal that can be expressed in numbers so we can measure how well the firm is achieving this goal. Also, we want a goal that is operational; that is, the goal should be ex-

---

[3] Residual claimant status means that the common stockholder is last in line for receipt of any money paid from the firm. Prior claimants are employees (wages and salaries), creditors (interest on and repayment of debt), suppliers (bills), and governments (taxes). Any residual left over may be paid out to the stockholders as dividends in normal times or as a liquidating payment in case of failure.

[4] While this statement is generally accepted in finance, there are some forceful objections. We cover some of these objections below.

plicitly tied to variables that the firm has some control over through its operations.

Our direction in this search for a quantifiable goal comes from economics. Traditional economic theory maintains that the goal of *any* individual is to maximize personal utility (happiness or satisfaction).[5] Individuals receive utility or pleasure from doing things that please them, and they act, somehow, as if they were employing all their talents and resources to maximize the utility they receive from the sum total of all their activities. Unfortunately, it is very difficult to quantify or operationalize utility maximization. An individual's utility is a function of many things, and we know that different people have different tastes and preferences. Since it is impossible to completely enumerate all the many things that are important to people, we abstract from reality and select only the most important things.

Stockholder wealth maximization Financial theory asserts that the closest single substitute for a stockholder's utility is wealth. If the firm operates so as to maximize the stockholders' wealth, then the individual stockholders can use this wealth to maximize their own utility. Some will buy new clothes, some new cars, some will save, and so on. But the main point is that by maximizing stockholder wealth the firm is acting consistently with the principle of maximizing stockholder utility. Now we have taken a giant step toward quantifying and operationalizing the goal because stockholder wealth can be directly related to the price of the firm's common stock.

A stockholder's current wealth in the firm is the product of the number of shares owned times the current stock price per share.

$$\begin{matrix} \text{Stockholder's current} \\ \text{wealth in firm} \end{matrix} = \begin{pmatrix} \text{Number of} \\ \text{shares owned} \end{pmatrix} \times \begin{pmatrix} \text{Current stock} \\ \text{price per share} \end{pmatrix}$$

In symbols:[6]

$$W_0 = NP_0$$

That portion of the stockholder's wealth that is entrusted to the firm will be maximized if the firm always acts in a fashion that will keep the product of the number of shares owned times the stock price as large as possible. Given the number of shares that any stockholder owns, the higher the stock price the greater the stockholder's wealth. The firm may occasionally alter the number of shares of stock owned by the investor through stock splits and stock dividends (see Chapter 11), but for any given number of shares, stock price maximization is consistent with stockholder wealth maximization.

In summary, we started with the standard economic premise of utility maximization and have proceeded to substitute wealth for utility. We adopt in this book the concept that the firm should maximize stockholder

---

[5] Technically, economics asserts that individuals seek to maximize *expected* utility. However, the distinction between these two ideas is not important enough at this stage for us to elaborate.

[6] The zero subscripts on W and P emphasize that these are *current* (time zero) values. See Chapter 3.

wealth. This, in turn, implies that the firm should maximize its current stock price, given the number of shares outstanding:

$$\text{Max utility} \rightarrow \text{Max stockholders' wealth} \rightarrow \text{Max } P_0$$

There are alternative ways to state this goal, such as the maximization of the stockholder's equity, but they refer to the same idea. The firm is presumed to act in the best interests of the stockholder-owner and makes those decisions that are consistent with the concept of maximization of the stockholder's wealth.

Criticism of stockholder wealth maximization The goal of stockholder wealth maximization is a normative goal; it is a prescriptive idea. It indicates what the firm should be striving toward. However, some financial practitioners and theorists do not agree with the selection of stockholder wealth maximization as the firm's goal. These criticisms of the stockholder wealth maximization goal mainly take two forms: (1) The goal is not descriptive of what firms *actually* do, and (2) maximizing stockholder wealth is not what the firm *ought* to do because it is not necessarily socially desirable.

These criticisms are challenging and are the bases of important intellectual debates. However, an introductory text is probably not the place to air these issues. Suffice it to say that there is clearly ample justification for selection of the stockholder wealth maximization goal. It is widely accepted in financial and economic literature, and we take it in this text as the accepted goal of the firm. Throughout this book we will build a decision framework oriented toward this goal.

Identification of important variables and constraints

The second part of our financial management decision framework is the identification of important variables. This refers to the need to identify (1) the variables that are important for making decisions, (2) the relationships these variables have to each other and to the goal, and (3) any constraints that may exist.

Given the goal of stockholder wealth maximization we will find that there are two important concepts, risk and return, that will determine stock price and, thus, stockholder wealth. The concept of return refers to the profits that the firm can earn for the stockholder, and the concept of risk refers to the quality or uncertainty of these profits. We will see in subsequent chapters that returns have a strong identifiable time dimension as investors would prefer to receive a dollar of profit today rather than waiting a year. We will also see that risk can be identified with probability concepts. Notice that the firm's goal plays an important role here because the identification of variables is directed toward finding variables that are related to the goal.

The last part of this identification process is to identify any constraints that may exist. There are, for instance, a large number of legal constraints on the firm's activities; the firm should not increase stockholder's wealth by selling products through false advertising, or the like. Many activities that are profitable are legally and morally restricted, and the firm should obviously not become involved in such activities.

The important point in this section is that once having chosen a goal we must identify what variables are important in light of the goal, what the relationships of the variables are to each other and the goal, and what constraints exist, if any.

Decision rules

The last part of the decision framework is the development of decision rules that permit the identified important variables to be systematically analyzed, with the result that the decision made by the firm will be consistent with the firm's goal. Decision rules are simply ways of using the relevant variables in a problem to make choices that are consistent with the stipulated goal. In the context of financial management decisions the firm should employ investment, financing, and dividend decision rules that will help maximize stock price and stockholder wealth.

Financial management process

This proposed financial management decision framework underlies the study of financial management in this text. We have so far only identified the major financial management decision areas and the goal that the firm should work toward and the important concepts of risk and return. In the remainder of the book we will provide flesh to the skeleton. As an overview to what financial management is all about, consider Figure 1–2, which is a diagram that integrates the scope and activities of financial management.

The firm's planning activities are quite varied. They include choice of organizational form, long-range planning, and contingency planning. Planning also includes providing specific guidelines and direction about investment, financing, and dividend decisions. The result of these planning activities is a set of financial management decision policies. Implementing these policies over time causes the firm to acquire certain

FIGURE 1–2
Financial management process

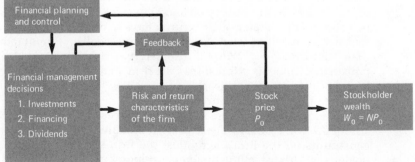

risk and return (profitability) characteristics. These characteristics determine stock price and stockholder wealth. Notice also that there are feedback provisions. The firm monitors itself as part of its control function, and this monitoring includes supervision of the implementation of the financial management decisions and observation of the firm's risk and return characteristics and stock price. If things begin to go badly the firm should pick this up early and take corrective action.

QUESTIONS

1. Under what circumstances might a firm want to organize as a proprietorship? A partnership? A corporation?

2. Discuss possible interrelationships among the three basic types of financial management decisions.

3. Some critics of the financial theory of the firm have argued that the goal of "stockholder wealth maximization" is not descriptive of actual, real world, corporate behavior where, in general, firms do not appear to attempt to singlemindedly maximize stockholder wealth. In attacking this goal on descriptive reality grounds, these critics point out that firms do many things that obviously are not necessarily oriented toward stockholder wealth maximization, such as making philanthropic contributions, providing recreational facilities for employees, maintaining pollution control standards above minimum required levels, and so on. How would you defend the stockholder wealth maximization goal against this kind of complaint?

4. An important part of the financial management decision framework is concerned with identifying legal and moral constraints that would restrict the actions of the firm as it pursues its goal. What kinds of legal and moral constraints exist today?

SELECTED BASIC REFERENCES

Anthony, R. N. "The Trouble with Profit Maximization," *Harvard Business Review* (November–December 1960), pp. 126–34.

Donaldson, G. "Financial Goals: Management vs. Stockholders," *Harvard Business Review* (May–June 1963), pp. 116–29.

Gibson, G. D. "Selecting the Form of Entity for a Small Business," *Business Lawyer* (November 1962), pp. 100–113.

Maer, C. M., Jr., and R. A. Francis. "Whether to Incorporate," *Business Lawyer* (April 1967), pp. 571–76.

Solomon, E. *The Theory of Financial Management.* New York: Columbia University Press, 1963, chapters 1 and 2.

SELECTED ADVANCED REFERENCES

Baumol, W. J. *Business Behavior, Value and Growth.* New York: The Macmillan Co., 1959, chapters 6 through 8.

Fama, E. F., and M. H. Miller.   *The Theory of Finance*. New York: Holt, Rinehart, Winston, Inc., 1972, chapter 1.

Friedman, M.   "The Methodology of Positive Economics," in *Essays in Positive Economics*. 5th ed. Chicago: The University of Chicago Press, 1966.

Lewellen, W. G.   "Management and Ownership in the Large Firm," *Journal of Finance* (May 1969), pp. 299–322.

2

FINANCIAL STATEMENTS

In developing the subject of financial management we will continually utilize financial information. Much of this information is reported in the firm's financial statements, and the purpose of this chapter is to present this information in its customary form. To a large extent this presentation is a review of financial accounting and provides the necessary accounting background for understanding the remainder of the text. We will also perform some simple analyses on this basic accounting information.

FINANCIAL ANALYSIS BY INTERESTED GROUPS

Many diverse groups of people are keenly interested in the information found in the firm's financial statements: They study the statements carefully, interpreting the information that relates to their particular interest in the company. The object of all these analyses is some sort of evaluation of the firm's performance.

Stockholder analysis

From the discussion in Chapter 1 we saw that the firm is an agent of the common stockholders. These stockholders (and potential stockholders) use the firm's financial statements to help assess what the future holds for the firm. In the next three chapters we will construct a valuation framework for the common stockholder, but it suffices here to note that the stockholders are interested in assessing the risk and return characteristics of their investment. The firm's financial statements provide some information regarding this assessment.

Creditor analysis

Creditors (and potential creditors) also analyze the financial statement with an eye to risk and return estimation. Their analysis is directed toward the firm's creditworthiness and centers on the firm's debt position. Short-term creditors are primarily concerned with the firm's liquidity, where liquidity refers to the firm's ability to pay bills as they arise. The firm's liquidity position is the best measure of how readily short-term loans can be paid off. Similarly, long-term creditors are interested in the firm's ability to pay the scheduled interest and principal payments on the firm's long-term debt. The degree of confidence that long-term debt holders have in the firm's ability to "service the debt" strongly influences the ability of the firm to raise long-term debt capital to finance its investments.

Management analysis

The firm's management also analyzes the financial statement. While management has an advantage over outsiders such as creditors and stockholders because it has *internal* reports at its disposal, the financial statements contain considerable information about the strengths and weaknesses of the firm both in the financial and nonfinancial (operating) areas that management (and outsiders) can use. How efficiently the firm uses its assets, how it finances its assets, how risky the firm is, and how profitable the firm has been are all questions that can be roughly determined from the firm's financial statement. Management can use this information in monitoring the firm's activities, in insuring that its policy decisions are implemented by subordinate units within the firm, and through projections based on the financial statement, in planning for the future.

Other analyses

Government agencies and labor unions may also be interested in the firm's performance because of relationships these organizations have with the firm. Many industries are regulated by government agencies (for example, the air transport industry is regulated by the Civil Aeronautics Board), and the rate of return allowed companies in these industries is based on information like that displayed in the financial statements. Similarly, labor unions frequently use financial statements to "show" that the firm's strong profitability position justifies wage increases.

Thus, many diverse groups analyze the firm's financial statements for different reasons. Some of these reasons coincide with those of other groups, some are peculiar to a particular group. There is a great deal of information presented in the firm's financial statements, and this chapter will be divided into two main parts: financial ratios and the statement of changes in financial position. We will also briefly address earnings and dividends as a prelude to developing the basic valuation theme used in subsequent chapters.

MARTIN MATTRESSES

Possibly the easiest way to explore the subject of financial statements is to take an example set of statements and work through them. In

FIGURE 2–1

MARTIN MATTRESSES
Balance Sheet

Assets	Year ended December 31, 19+8	Year ended December 31, 19+7
Current Assets:		
Cash and marketable securities	$ 4,000,000	$ 3,000,000
Accounts receivable—net	6,900,000	6,100,000
Inventory	8,300,000	7,900,000
	$19,200,000	$17,000,000
Property, Plant, and Equipment—at cost:		
Land	$11,000,000	$ 9,000,000
Plant and equipment	43,500,000	40,000,000
	$54,500,000	$49,000,000
Less accumulated depreciation	22,400,000	20,400,000
	$32,100,000	$28,600,000
Total Assets	$51,300,000	$45,600,000
Liabilities and Owners' Equity		
Current Liabilities:		
Accounts payable	$ 6,700,000	$ 5,700,000
Notes payable	4,900,000	4,400,000
Taxes payable	1,100,000	1,000,000
	$12,700,000	$11,100,000
Long-Term Debt:		
Mortgage note—6%	$10,000,000	$10,000,000
Bonds—4%	10,000,000	10,000,000
	$20,000,000	$20,000,000
Total Liabilities	$32,700,000	$31,100,000
Owners' Equity:		
Preferred stock—5% ($100 par)	$ 2,000,000	$ —
Common stock ($10 par)	11,000,000	10,000,000
Capital in excess of par value	2,500,000	1,500,000
Retained earnings	3,100,000	3,000,000
Total Owners' Equity	$18,600,000	$14,500,000
Total Liabilities and Owners' Equity	$51,300,000	$45,600,000

Figures 2–1 and 2–2 the *balance sheet* and *statement of income and retained earnings* for a hypothetical company, Martin Mattresses, a large manufacturer of bedsprings and mattresses, are presented. Later in the chapter we will present Martin's *statement of changes in financial position.* These three statements will be used to illustrate some uses of financial statement analysis. The statements are purposely oversimplified so we can focus on the main points of investigation and not get bogged down in details. The reporting year for Martin is 19+8,

FIGURE 2–2

MARTIN MATTRESSES
Statement of Income and Retained Earnings

	Year ended December 31, 19+8	Year ended December 31, 19+7
Income:		
Net sales...	$65,400,000	$65,000,000
Cost of goods sold	53,200,000	52,500,000
Gross margin	$12,200,000	$12,500,000
Operating expense:		
Selling...	$ 4,000,000	$ 4,100,000
General and administrative (Note A)	4,700,000	4,400,000
	$ 8,700,000	$ 8,500,000
Net operating income	$ 3,500,000	$ 4,000,000
Other expense and losses:		
Interest expense..	1,000,000	1,000,000
Net income before taxes.................................	$ 2,500,000	$ 3,000,000
Income taxes	1,200,000	1,400,000
Net income	$ 1,300,000	$ 1,600,000
Earnings per common share:		
Earnings before extraordinary items.................	$1.09	$1.60
Net earnings	$1.09	$1.60
Retained Earnings:		
Retained earnings at beginning of year	$ 3,000,000	$ 2,400,000
Net income	1,300,000	1,600,000
	$ 4,300,000	$ 4,000,000
Deduct—Cash dividends:		
Preferred..	$ 100,000	$ —
Common..	1,100,000	1,000,000
Retained earnings at end of year	$ 3,100,000	$ 3,000,000

Note A: Included in general and administrative expense are $2,000,000 depreciation in 19+8 and $1,900,000 depreciation in 19+7.

and the reports also show—as most accounting statements do—the previous year's results.

To provide perspective to the analysis, we presume that Martin has recently changed management and the new management is interested in assessing the firm's position with respect to profitability and risk. This assessment requires an evaluation of the company in comparison to its industry competitors and an evaluation of the trend in the company's performance. We initially focus on the calculation of key financial ratios described below and the comparison of these ratios with the bedspring and mattress industry ratios. Later we analyze the time trend of the company and industry ratios. Financial statements are also used to project the future financing needs of the company. These *pro forma* analyses are deferred until Chapter 12, when we discuss financing needs.

FINANCIAL RATIOS

The principal idea in analyzing financial ratios is that there are several key ratios, obtainable from the firm's financial statements, that reveal the financial and nonfinancial health of the firm. In general we will look at four categories of ratios, each attempting to measure a particular aspect of the firm's position and performance:

1. Liquidity ratios.
2. Activity ratios.
3. Leverage ratios.
4. Profitability ratios.

Liquidity ratios reflect the firm's ability to meet scheduled short-term obligations; activity ratios measure how well the firm is managing various classes of assets (like inventory and fixed assets); leverage ratios show how much debt the firm has used to finance its investments; profitability ratios are designed to reflect the profitability of the firm.

Ratio analysis information provides a current "snapshot" of the firm's position with respect to liquidity, activity, capital structure, and profitability. The *trend* of these ratios, over time, tells the story of what has been happening in the firm in recent years. More and more frequently, annual financial statements provide enough information to make the ratio calculations for a five- to ten-year period. For those reports that don't provide this information, the individual annual reports may be laid side by side to obtain the same information.

Industry comparisons require a source of industry data. There are several sources, but probably the best known sets of ratios are provided by Dun and Bradstreet and Robert Morris Associates. They publish comprehensive industry ratio data. Dun and Bradstreet, for example, survey 125 retailing, wholesaling, manufacturing, and construction industries and report 14 financial ratios.

Liquidity ratios

For the firm to remain "alive" it must be able to pay its bills as they become due. Liquidity ratios measure the extent to which the firm can meet its immediate obligations. In a profitable, ongoing firm, liquidity reflects the ability of the firm to generate cash inflow per unit of time that is sufficient to make the required cash outflow (payments) per unit of time. Liquidity ratios also reflect the firm's ability to meet short-run financial contingencies that might arise. The firm's current liabilities ($12,700,000 on Martin's 19+8 balance sheet) show those bills that will mature within the coming year that the firm has already incurred, and the current assets show—to varying degrees—the liquid assets available to meet these obligations. There are two commonly used liquidity ratios: the *current ratio* and the *quick ratio*.

Current ratio The current ratio relates current assets to current liabilities. Current assets include cash, bank balances, marketable securities (like stocks and bonds), accounts receivable, and inventory. Current

liabilities include accounts payable, bank loans, that part of the long-
term debt to be paid off during the coming year, taxes payable, and other
accrued expenses.

$$\text{Current ratio} = \frac{\text{Current assets}}{\text{Current liabilities}} \qquad (2\text{--}1)$$

$$\text{Martin's current ratio} = \frac{\$19{,}200{,}000}{\$12{,}700{,}000} = 1.5$$

$$\text{Industry average} = 1.9$$

Relatively high values of the current ratio are interpreted as an indication that the firm is liquid and in good position to meet its current
obligations. Conversely, relatively low values of the current ratio are
interpreted as an indication that the firm may not be able to easily meet
its current obligations. Martin's current ratio is considerably below its
industry average. Bearing in mind that industry averages are not necessarily magic numbers, we see that Martin's liquidity might be too low.

The current ratio supposedly measures liquidity because it relates
the firm's pending need for cash to pay short-term liabilities to the firm's
present cash and near-cash position. The firm's near-cash is represented
by marketable securities, accounts receivable, and inventory. One
shortcoming of the current ratio as a measure of liquidity, however, is
that it does not differentiate between the liquidity of the near-cash
assets. The current ratio implicitly assumes that inventory is as liquid
as marketable securities, for example. The quick ratio attempts to correct
for this.

Quick ratio   Inventory is typically the least liquid component of current assets; the quick ratio is the same as the current ratio only with
inventory subtracted from the numerator.

$$\text{Quick ratio} = \frac{\text{Current assets} - \text{Inventory}}{\text{Current liabilities}} \qquad (2\text{--}2)$$

$$\text{Martin's quick ratio} = \frac{\$10{,}900{,}000}{\$12{,}700{,}000} = 0.9$$

$$\text{Industry average} = 1.1$$

Like the current ratio, the quick ratio or acid-test ratio is meant to
reflect the firm's ability to pay its short-term obligations, and the higher
the quick ratio the more liquid the firm's position. Martin's quick ratio is
below the industry average, which corroborates the current ratio comparison. There are two distinct dangers in having too low a liquidity
position. One is the danger of not being able to pay obligations as they
come due. Assuming that marketable securities can be sold at approximately their face value, and that the net receivables figure represents
what Martin will soon collect from its customers, the company almost
has enough cash and near-cash to meet pending obligations dollar for
dollar. Even if there is a temporary lack of funds to pay obligations due,
the firm can arrange new short-term credit (see Chapters 19 and 20).
However, the second danger of having too low a liquidity position is that

short-term lenders may perceive the firm as being unable to meet its obligations and will not advance new credit. This would be particularly unfortunate in a situation where the firm needs the credit to pay current obligations.

On balance, it appears that Martin's liquidity position is somewhat low. This does not necessarily mean that Martin's liquidity position is too low, as there may be extenuating circumstances that are not reflected in the ratios. Martin may, for example, have tried to be very aggressive in managing its current assets. Alternatively, the industry average may be too high. But the low liquidity of Martin relative to industry competitors raises a red flag that indicates Martin's new management should investigate this area and give consideration to improving the firm's liquidity position.

Activity ratios

Activity ratios attempt to measure how efficiently the firm is managing its assets. These ratios are called "turnover" ratios because they show how rapidly the assets are being converted (turned over) into sales. Although generalizations can be misleading, high turnover ratios are usually associated with good asset management and low turnover ratios with bad asset management. There are several activity ratios, each directed toward a specific type of asset management.

Inventory turnover   Inventory turnover shows how efficiently the firm's inventory is being managed. It is a rough measure of how many times per year the inventory level is replaced (turned over) and is defined as sales over inventory.

$$\text{Inventory turnover} = \frac{\text{Sales}}{\text{Inventory}} \qquad (2\text{--}3)$$

$$\text{Martin's inventory turnover} = \frac{\$65,400,000}{\$\ 8,300,000} = 7.9$$

$$\text{Industry average} = 8.0$$

There are alternative ways to calculate inventory value. Many analysts prefer to average the inventory figures to partially overcome the fact that the ending inventory figure is only a one-day snapshot.[1] Also, since sales usually carry a markup over inventory costs, many analysts prefer to use cost of goods sold in the numerator rather than sales. However, cost of goods sold is occasionally not shown on the income statement, and industry averages are usually defined by business services in terms of sales rather than cost of goods sold.

Generally, higher than average inventory turnovers are suggestive of good inventory management, and lower than average inventory turnovers are suggestive of ineffective inventory management. Low inventory turnovers may be caused by the firm keeping excessive inventory levels or by the presence of damaged or obsolete inventory that is difficult

---

[1] Martin's average inventory = ($8,300,000 + $7,900,000)/2 = $8,100,000. Therefore, inventory turnover = $65,400,000/$8,100,000 = 8.1.

to sell. Low inventory turnovers may also be caused by unexpectedly low sales levels. On the other hand, inventory turnovers that are *too high* may indicate a future trouble spot. Abnormally high inventory turnovers may indicate that inventory levels are so low that stockouts will occur and future sales will be impaired. The general rule is that ratios that are extremely divergent from industry norms on *either side* warrant further investigation, and this applies to the inventory turnover ratio as well as to other ratios. Martin's inventory turnover is approximately equal to the industry average, indicating that the firm's inventory management practices are about in line with the company's competitors.

Collection period   The collection period attempts to measure how efficient the firm's collection policy is by calculating how long it takes to collect the firm's accounts receivables.

$$\text{Collection period} = \frac{(\text{Receivables})(365)}{\text{Sales}} \qquad (2\text{-}4)$$

$$\text{Martin's collection period} = \frac{(\$6,900,000)(365)}{\$65,400,000} = 39 \text{ days}$$

$$\text{Industry average} = 45 \text{ days}$$

The definition, as shown, is too mechanical to be very intuitive. The collection period figure really means this: Assuming all sales are made on credit, how many days worth of sales are tied up in receivables? To answer this question we calculate the following:

$$\text{Sales per day} = \frac{\text{Sales}}{365}$$

$$\text{Collection period} = \frac{\text{Receivables}}{\text{Sales per day}} = \frac{(\text{Receivables})(365)}{\text{Sales}}$$

The collection period supposedly measures the *quality* of the firm's receivables: The shorter the collection period the better the quality of the receivables since a short collection period means that the firm's customers are prompt payers. A more refined definition of collection period would use *credit sales* in the denominator rather than sales in (2-4). However, it is usually very difficult to ascertain credit sales from a company's income statement, and industry averages calculated by business services use sales rather than credit sales.

Excessively long collection periods may indicate that the firm's receivables policy is not very effective. An important benchmark associated with the collection period is the duration of the credit terms granted to the firm's customers. These terms state within what period payment is due. If the collection period is substantially longer than the stated credit terms, the receivables are not being managed well in relation to the firm's credit policy. Unfortunately, the credit terms are not listed on the firm's financial statements.

Conversely, collection periods shorter than the industry average are usually viewed as an indication that the firm's receivables policy is fairly effective. Martin's collection period is very low relative to the industry average. However, this is an example of where a ratio may be too good. A collection period that is this low in relation to the industry norm may mean that Martin's credit policy is too restrictive. If Martin were to relax its credit policy by selling on credit to customers that it now refuses credit terms to, it might increase its sales significantly, which may more than offset the resultant increased collection period. Such a relaxation, however, would require the firm to finance the increased accounts receivables.

A more complete look at how the firm is managing its receivables could be seen by an "aging schedule" that shows the percentage of receivables that have been outstanding (uncollected) for 20 days, 30 days, etc. The aging schedule shows the percent of the accounts receivable that are long past due, but unfortunately, this schedule can't be determined from the financial statement either. More information than is shown on the financial statement is needed to prepare this schedule.[2]

Fixed assets turnover The fixed assets turnover ratio is sales divided by fixed assets. This ratio is a measure of how well the firm uses its long-term (fixed) assets and shows how many dollars of sales are supported by one dollar of fixed assets.

$$\text{Fixed assets turnover} = \frac{\text{Sales}}{\text{Fixed assets}} \qquad (2\text{--}5)$$

$$\text{Martin's fixed assets turnover} = \frac{\$65,400,000}{\$32,100,000} = 2.0$$

$$\text{Industry average} = 2.2$$

In general, higher than average fixed assets turnover ratios are supposed to reflect better than average fixed asset management, and relatively low fixed assets turnover ratios are supposed to reflect relatively poor fixed asset management. However, since book values of fixed assets may be considerably different than the market value of these assets, the fixed assets turnover may be deceptively low or high. For example, a firm with a relatively old but still serviceable plant that has been almost fully depreciated will have a lower book value of fixed assets than a competitor with a new plant, and for similar sales levels the older plant will tend to have a higher fixed assets turnover even though both firms may be utilizing their fixed assets at about the same efficiency. Martin's fixed assets turnover is slightly below the industry average, which, with the above warning in mind, indicates the firm may not be utilizing its long-term assets as well as other members of its industry.

Total assets turnover Total assets turnover is defined as sales divided by total assets.[3] This ratio indicates how many dollars of sales are supported by one dollar of total tangible assets and is a measure of the firm's total assets management.

---

[2] The use of aging schedules is covered in Chapter 18.

[3] More precisely, total assets turnover is defined as sales divided by total *tangible* assets.

$$\text{Total assets turnover} = \frac{\text{Sales}}{\text{Total assets}} \qquad (2\text{–}6)$$

$$\text{Martin's total assets turnover} = \frac{\$65,400,000}{\$51,300,000} = 1.3$$

$$\text{Industry average} = 1.4$$

In principle, high total assets turnover ratios are supposed to indicate successful asset management, and low ratios unsuccessful asset management. However, since total assets turnover is a composite of all the firm's tangible assets, both current and fixed, all the problems discussed in the inventory turnover, collection period, and fixed assets turnover analysis are imbedded in the total assets turnover. As with other ratios, the key point to remember here is to be wary of extremely high or low ratios. Extreme values should raise a red flag in the analyst's mind and cause him to deepen his explorations beyond simple ratio analysis. Martin's total assets turnover ratio is slightly below the industry average fixed assets turnover.

Leverage ratios

Leverage ratios indicate to what extent the firm has financed its investments by borrowing. We will see in a later chapter (Chapter 14) that use of debt financing increases the risk of the firm, so leverage ratios reflect the financial risk posture of the firm; the more extensive the use of debt, the larger the firm's leverage ratios and the more risk present in the firm. While there are many leverage ratios we will only look at two: the *debt-equity ratio* and *times interest earned.*

Debt-equity ratio The debt-equity ratio is the ratio of the total debt in the firm, both long-term and short-term, to equity, where equity is the sum of common and preferred stockholders' equity.

$$\text{Debt-equity ratio} = \frac{\text{Total debt}}{\text{Equity}} \qquad (2\text{–}7)$$

$$\text{Martin's debt-equity ratio} = \frac{\$32,700,000}{\$18,600,000} = 1.8$$

$$\text{Industry average} = 0.8$$

A high ratio means that the firm has liberally used debt (has borrowed) to finance its assets, and a low ratio means the firm has paid for its assets mainly with equity money (preferred stock, common stock, and retained earnings). Any ratio over 1.0 means the firm has used more debt than equity to finance its investments. Martin obviously has been much more aggressive than most of its industry competitors in using debt financing. Debt-equity ratios may vary considerably within an industry, but many analysts feel that a radical departure from the industry norm is dangerous, and Martin may well have difficulty in raising new long-term debt. This would restrict the firm's future financing mobility. There are several variants of the debt-equity ratio. One is the *long-term* debt-equity ratio, which has only the long-term debt in the numerator. Some firms have no long-term debt, only short-term debt and equity: They are called "all equity" companies. Another common form of the debt-equity ratio is the debt to total assets ratio, which indicates the percentage of assets financed by debt. Another version of the debt-equity ratio includes the preferred stock as debt rather than equity. This redefinition of debt views the debt-equity ratio squarely from the common stockholder's perspective.

All these debt ratios reflect the *capital structure* of the firm: what percent of the firm's capital is in equity and what percent in debt. All reflect the firm's financial risk posture, which investors are very interested in: The higher the percentage of the firm's total capital that is provided by creditors, the more financial risk in the firm.

Times interest earned Times interest earned is the sum of net income before taxes and interest expense divided by interest expense. It is supposed to measure how ably the firm can meet its interest obligations.

$$\text{Times interest earned} = \frac{\text{Net income before taxes} + \text{Interest expense}}{\text{Interest expense}}$$

$$(2-8)$$

$$\text{Martin's times interest earned} = \frac{\$2,500,000 + \$1,000,000}{\$1,000,000} = 3.5$$

$$\text{Industry average} = 6.6$$

Times interest earned is one of several *debt service* ratios. These ratios describe how well the firm can service its debt, that is, how easily the firm can pay its interest obligations as they come due. Times interest earned is a kind of "interest coverage" ratio that shows how many times the interest payments are "covered" by funds that are *normally* available to pay the interest expenses. We emphasize normally available because there are other financial resources that are also available to meet interest expenses. Referring back to Figure 2-2, if we think of the progression down the income statement, starting with income and then proceeding through the payment of expenses in the priority they come due, notice that the times interest earned formula measures the ratio of income available to pay interest to the amount of interest owed.

Martin's times interest earned is considerably lower than the industry average, which reinforces the discussion above regarding the company's debt-equity ratio: Martin has used much more debt than its typical industry competitor. Martin's creditors and potential creditors may not be too happy with this situation, particularly in bad economic times. The degree to which they are displeased will affect Martin's future borrowing possibilities. If long-term lenders become too wary of the firm's ability to service its long-term debt it will become very hard for Martin to get debt money except at very high interest rates and/or with restrictive covenants (agreements between the firm and lender that protect the lender by restricting the firm's financial freedom).

There are other, related, debt service ratios. A commonly used ratio is the *fixed charge coverage* ratio. Fixed charges include *all* expenses that the firm is obligated by contract to pay. This ratio simply acknowledges that the firm may have more fixed charges other than interest, such as repayment of debt principal, sinking fund payments, lease payments, rent, etc.

Profitability ratios

As the name indicates, these ratios tell a story about the firm's profitability. It's especially important to emphasize here, however, that this story relates to the *past* profitability of the firm, as the profitability ratios describe the profitability of events that have already taken place. This point is important to keep in mind because it's very tempting to overemphasize the importance of these profitability ratios in an evaluation context. Investors are continually bombarded with statements to the effect that firm XYZ earned 10 percent on its equity last year and *therefore* will earn 10 percent or higher this year. This book is not an investments text so we don't directly address questions like this. However, there is very little evidence that past profitability results foretell *future* profitability. So we must be careful in attaching too much importance to these profitability numbers from the investors' standpoint. They tell a profitability story, but it's about where the firm has been rather than where it's going.

Profit margin   Profit margin relates net income to the firm's sales level. It shows what percent of every sales dollar the firm was able to convert into net income.

$$\text{Profit margin} = \frac{\text{Net income}}{\text{Net sales}} \qquad (2\text{-}9)$$

$$\text{Martin's profit margin} = \frac{\$1,300,000}{\$65,400,000} = 2.0 \text{ percent}$$

$$\text{Industry average} = 2.3 \text{ percent}$$

The profit margin is an important ratio because it describes how well a dollar of sales is "squeezed" by the firm into profit. In Martin's case, on average, each dollar of sales is processed into two cents profit. However, Martin's profit margin is lower than the industry average, which raises the question: Why? The profit margin numerator, net income, is sales less *all* expenses, including interest expense. Martin has used debt more aggressively than most of its competitors and has larger interest expenses. It may well be that except for interest expenses Martin is doing better than the industry average. Many analysts prefer to call Equation (2-9) *net* profit margin and then define *gross* profit margin as the quantity sales less cost of goods sold divided by sales.

Return on assets   Return on assets relates net income to total tangible assets. The intent of this ratio is to measure how profitably the firm has used its assets.

$$\text{Return on assets} = \frac{\text{Net income}}{\text{Total assets}} \qquad (2\text{-}10)$$

$$\text{Martin's return on assets} = \frac{\$1,300,000}{\$51,300,000} = 2.5 \text{ percent}$$

$$\text{Industry average} = 3.2 \text{ percent}$$

Martin's return on assets is considerably lower than the industry average, which suggests that the firm is not utilizing its assets as profitably as many of its competitors.

DuPont Analysis. This low return on assets should be cause of some concern for the firm. The *DuPont Analysis* system is an integrative approach to explaining and investigating differences in return on assets ratios. Return on assets[4] is equal to the product of total assets turnover and profit margin:

$$\text{Return on assets} = (\text{Total assets turnover})(\text{Profit margin}) \quad (2\text{--}11)$$

$$\text{Martin's return on assets}[5] = (1.3)(2.0 \text{ percent}) = 2.6 \text{ percent}$$

$$\text{Industry average} = (1.4)(2.3 \text{ percent}) = 3.2 \text{ percent}$$

This breakdown of the return on assets formula emphasizes that Martin is behind the industry in both asset utilization and profit margin. Martin needs to find out why its total assets turnover ratio is below the industry average. It may be that the firm has excessive fixed assets relative to its sales potential, or it may be that the firm is not aggressive enough in its sales effort. In any event, the firm should investigate this area. As mentioned previously, the firm also should explore why its profit margin is lower than the industry average.

While the return on assets ratio does crudely reflect how well the firm uses its assets in total, there are some difficulties associated with it. First, since a large part of many firm's total assets are fixed assets and since book values and market values of fixed assets may be widely divergent, there may be differences between some firms' return on assets simply because of the degree to which the assets have been depreciated. This problem was discussed in the fixed assets turnover analysis. Another major problem is that net income is heavily influenced by capitalization and income tax changes. Some analysts prefer a definition of return on assets that uses net operating income instead of net income.

Return on equity Return on equity indicates what kind of rate of return was earned on the book value of the owner's equity.

$$\text{Return on equity} = \frac{\text{Net income}}{\text{Equity}} \quad (2\text{--}12)$$

$$\text{Martin's return on equity} = \frac{\$1,300,000}{\$18,600,000} = 7.0 \text{ percent}$$

$$\text{Industry average} = 5.7 \text{ percent}$$

Martin's return on equity is larger than the industry average. It might seem puzzling that the firm's return on equity is better than the industry average when Martin's profit margin and return on assets are both less than the industry average. This is due to Martin's aggressive use of debt. We saw previously that debt financing causes net income to decline

---

[4] $\text{Return on assets} = \left(\dfrac{\text{Sales}}{\text{Total assets}}\right)\left(\dfrac{\text{Net income}}{\text{Sales}}\right) = \dfrac{\text{Net income}}{\text{Total assets}}$

[5] The discrepancy between this calculated 2.6 percent return and the previously calculated 2.5 percent is due to rounding.

because of interest expenses, but debt financing means the firm issues less equity, which keeps the denominator of (2–12) low. This results in a high return on equity. Alternatively stated, the firm is borrowing money at a fixed cost, earning more on the borrowed money than the cost of borrowing and passing the profit on to the equity holders. We can see this effect from Equation (2–13), which is an alternative way to calculate return on equity:

Return on equity[6] = (Return on assets)(Debt-equity ratio + 1)   (2–13)

Equation (2–13) illustrates that as the firm's use of debt financing increases (as the debt-equity ratio increases), and assuming the return on assets does not decrease, return on equity will increase. This use of debt financing is called *financial leverage* (see Chapter 10) and is intended to increase profit/share for the owners. However, we will see later that it also increases owners' risk.

Notice that the net worth denominator in Equation (2–12) includes preferred stock and that the net income numerator in (2–12) includes any preferred dividends. Many analysts prefer to calculate *return on common equity*, which excludes preferred from the denominator and deducts preferred payments from net income. Return on common equity is one measure of how well the firm is doing in its attempts to maximize shareholder wealth. It is not the best measure, however. The best measure is the increase in the market value of the company's common stock, since that is shareholder wealth.

Summary of ratios

At this point we may summarize the ratios and attempt to draw some rough conclusions from them. One of the main points to understand about ratio analysis is that all the information that would be needed for a *conclusive* judgment about what's going on in the company is not available in the financial statements. Such conclusions may require information that only management has. So usually the best an outside analyst can do with ratio analysis is to identify those areas where something *unusual* is happening. In fact, most analysts use ratio analysis to identify the trouble or potential trouble spots of the firm: to raise red warning flags. We have taken the perspective of Martin's new management making a cursory investigation of Martin's activities. The trouble spots we have identified will impel the firm's new management to investigate those areas more thoroughly. Also, as we have noted throughout this chapter, ratio analysis is most meaningful when a comparison of company and industry results is made. We have been comparing Martin's ratios to its industry average, and the firm's ratios and the companion industry averages are shown in Figure 2–3.

First of all, as evidenced by current and quick ratios, Martin's liquidity seems to be relatively low. This may be because the firm is purpose-

---

[6] Martin's 19+8 return on equity = (2.5 percent)(1.8 + 1) = 7 percent. Notice this calculation agrees with Martin's return on equity calculated from (2–12).

fully aggressive in its working capital management. However, creditors and even the stockholders may not like a relatively low liquidity position.

Second, Martin's lower than average total assets turnover indicates the firm does not appear to be managing its assets as well as it should be. Martin's inventory turnover and fixed asset turnover are both low. On the other extreme, Martin's collection period is quite a bit faster than the industry average, which is indicative of a very high receivables turnover and a tight credit policy. This policy may be unduly restricting sales and could be a contributing factor to the firm's low turnover ratios. These questions certainly warrant investigation.

FIGURE 2-3
Ratio summary for Martin Mattresses

Ratio	Martin	Industry average
Current	1.5	1.9
Quick	0.9	1.1
Inventory turnover	7.9	8.0
Collection period	39 days	45 days
Fixed assets turnover	2.0	2.2
Total assets turnover	1.3	1.4
Debt/equity	1.8	0.8
Times interest earned	3.5	6.6
Profit margin	2.0%	2.3%
Return on assets	2.5%	3.2%
Return on equity	7.0%	5.7%

Martin obviously has used debt financing more liberally than most of its industry competitors. This extra debt has several effects on the firm. It makes the firm riskier. It also decreases the profit margin because of the requirement of paying interest payments that reduce net income. This reduction of profit margin also causes the firm's return on assets to decline, since return on assets equals total asset turnover times profit margin. However, the firm's return on equity is increased by the debt financing. Martin's profit margin and return on assets are less than the industry average, but the company's return on equity is greater than average. Both long-term lenders and common stock investors may feel that the company's financing policies include too much debt, and the firm's new management should give some thought to this question.

In summary, Martin's new management has several things to investigate, and this investigation will entail analysis of information that is not shown on the firm's financial statements. These topics will be covered later in the book.

Analysis of time trends

Another important dimension of ratio analysis is the investigation of trends in ratios over time. Ratios for any one year may mislead the analyst because they are high or low for some peculiar and temporary reason. Trend analysis of the ratios adds considerable depth to the study because it looks at several years and will help distinguish between isolated instances of suspicious ratios and pervasive deterioration of ratios that indicate the firm is in trouble.

While time trends of the company's ratios are informative by themselves, it is frequently more informative to compare the company ratio trends with the industry average ratio trends. This comparison illustrates how well the firm has been doing across time relative to its industry competitors and may also help explain the trends in the company's ratios. If the company's profit margin is declining over time, for example, analysts would be very interested in knowing whether this decline is mainly because of declining industry profit margins or whether the firm is not competitive with other industry members. The comparison of industry and company ratio trends will facilitate this analysis. Martin's ratios for the past several years along with companion industry averages are shown in Figure 2–4.

Martin's liquidity ratios have been lower than the industry average for several years. This would suggest that Martin has been purposely more aggressive in managing its liquidity than most members of its industry. Since Martin has maintained its somewhat low liquidity position relative to the industry average over several years and has been successful in acquiring creditor funds this would indicate that creditors are not overly concerned with Martin's liquidity position, although the company may be paying more for borrowing than other companies in the industry.

The company's inventory turnover and collection period have been fairly constant over the past few years. Martin's inventory turnover has fluctuated around the industry average, and the firm's receivables policy has been historically tighter than the industry average. Notice also that Martin's fixed assets turnover ratio has been declining, which is partly explained by the decline in the industry fixed assets turnover ratio. The lower fixed asset utilization has contributed to declining total assets turnover both in Martin's case and in the industry average. However, Martin's deterioration in these ratios has been more severe than that in the industry average. These trouble spots deserve more thorough analysis, and Martin should investigate whether its recent plant and equipment expansions are generating commensurate sales increases.

Martin's debt usage is considerably higher than the industry average but has been for some time. This evidence, together with the previous trend analysis of liquidity ratios indicates that Martin has been very aggressive with respect to its financing policies. Many financial analysts would argue that Martin has been too aggressive.

Both Martin's and the industry's profit margins have been fluctuating, but in the past three years the company has fallen behind the industry. Part of this is due to Martin's larger interest payments, but notice that

FIGURE 2–4
Trend analysis

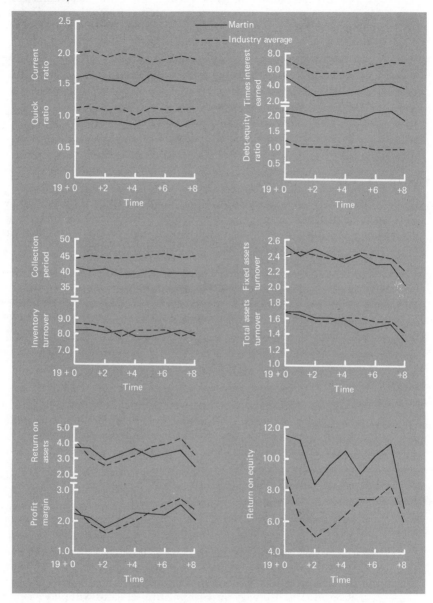

Martin used to have a higher margin than the industry despite its greater debt usage. This difficulty is further highlighted by Martin's poorer than average return on assets relative to the industry the past three years. The combination of Martin's worse than average performance in both profit margin and total assets turnover has caused the company to fall behind the industry in return on assets. These difficulties clearly warrant further investigation. Martin's return on equity has historically been higher than the industry average, which reflects the company's heavy reliance on debt financing. Notice, however, that both Martin's and the industry's returns are down considerably in 19+8.

In summary, there are disappointing trends in several of the company's ratios. Martin's fixed assets turnover ratio is trending downward faster than the industry average, and this has caused Martin's total assets turnover ratio to decline faster than the industry's average. Also, Martin's profit margin has been below the industry's for the past few years and, together with an inferior total assets turnover, has caused Martin's return on assets to slip below the industry average.

EARNINGS AND DIVIDENDS

The statement of income and retained earnings (Figure 2–2) provides two of the most interesting and useful items of information available to common stockholders: earnings and dividends. As with many financial variables, earnings and dividends have more meaning when reported on a per-share basis.

	Earnings per share	*Dividends per share*
19+8............................	$1.09	$1
19+7............................	$1.60	$1

Earnings per share (*EPS*) were $1.09 in 19+8, down from $1.60 the previous year. Despite this decrease the firm paid the same dividend per share (*DPS*), $1. Notice also (from the retained earnings statement) that even though the dividend per share stayed the same, the total dollar dividends increased by $100,000 because there were 100,000 new shares issued, and these new shares also received the $1 per share dividend. Another point to notice is the *EPS* was reduced by this additional common outstanding. That is, the *EPS* for 19+8 of $1.09 was determined by dividing $1,200,000 available for common ($1,300,000 − $100,000) by 1,100,000 shares. If the firm had not issued new common, but rather obtained the $2,000,000 from operations, *EPS* would have been $1,200,000/1,000,000 = $1.20. This reduction of *EPS* caused by broadening the equity base is called *dilution of EPS*.

EPS and *DPS* are very important numbers and will play a central role in our study of financial management. In particular, the projections (predictions) of *future EPS* and *DPS* will be very important. To the extent that past performance is also important we can analyze the recent history of Martin's *EPS* and *DPS* time trends, as we did with the company's financial ratios.

As Figure 2–5 shows, the *EPS* time series has fluctuated, which demonstrates the residual nature of *EPS*. That is, *EPS* represents the common stockholder's claim on the firm's income, and since all other income claims are honored first, *EPS* represents what's left – the residual. *EPS* rose from 19+0 to 19+3, but there seems to have been a declining trend in *EPS* from 19+3 to 19+8. Since *EPS* reflects the profitability of the firm from the common stockholder's viewpoint, this decline is an obvious concern to the company and stockholders.

The dividend per share series has been much steadier, reflecting Martin's dividend policy. Typically, firms have fairly stable *DPS* patterns across time, and Martin's case is no exception. Martin raised dividends from $0.80 per share to $1 per share in 19+3, but the current *EPS* of $1.09 are now barely covering this dividend level. If the earnings picture worsens further in the future, Martin may well *reduce DPS*. Later in the

FIGURE 2–5
EPS and DPS Time Trend

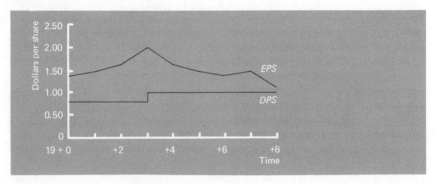

book (Chapter 11) we will investigate how firms establish their dividend policy and the effect of this policy on stockholder wealth.

STATEMENT OF CHANGES IN FINANCIAL POSITION

As an agent for the stockholder, the firm continually makes investments, finances those investments, and returns dividends to the stockholders. The statement of changes in financial position is a relatively new financial accounting requirement and describes how the firm performed these activities over the accounting period. Many companies have voluntarily presented such statements for some time, but starting in 1972, all profit-oriented businesses are required to present a statement of changes in financial position in their annual report.

The rationale for requiring a statement of changes in financial position is to provide information to interested parties (stockholders, creditors, etc.) regarding the firm's financial transactions. A traditional part of financial analysis of the firm's financial statements by these interested parties has been funds-flow analysis where the financial analyst traces how the firm procured financing and where it used these financial resources. Such "where got–where gone" analyses used the firm's income statement and balance sheet. Many transactions, however, were hidden from the analyst's investigation because of the nature of the construction of the income statement and balance sheet. Transactions that do not involve cash or working capital (such as a long-lived asset acquired in exchange for stock) may only be reflected in footnotes or not at all. The statement of changes in financial position rectifies this by explicitly showing significant changes in the investment and financing posture of the firm.

Either one of two formats may be used in presenting the statement of changes in financial position: cash or working capital. Under either approach we can identify potential sources and uses of financial resources as falling into one of two categories: those that directly affect cash or working capital, and those that do not.

Cash or working capital transactions versus exchange transactions

The classification of sources and uses of cash or working capital is as follows:

Sources of cash or working capital	Uses of cash or working capital
1. From operations.	1. In operations.
2. Sale of long-lived assets.	2. Purchase of long-lived investments.
3. Issuance of securities.	3. Retirement or reacquisition of securities.
	4. Payment of dividends.

Most investment and financing decisions result in transactions involving either cash or working capital. For example, when the firm buys a new plant or equipment (both are long-lived assets) it may sell bonds to finance the investment. There is clearly a matchup between investment needs and financial resources, but there is an intermediate step as the financing proceeds flow through cash or working capital into payment for the investment. Similarly, when the firm expands inventory (using financial resources in operations) it may finance this expansion by increasing accounts payable (providing financial resources from operations). This transaction also results in a working capital change.

But some investment and financing transactions will result in changes in the firm's financial position that are *not* reflected in changes in the firm's cash or working capital levels. Examples of these *exchange transactions* are long-lived assets (such as land) exchanged for the firm's stock, or debt retired in exchange for preferred stock. The statement of changes in financial position clearly reveals these exchange transactions.

The statement of changes in financial position for Martin Mattresses is shown in Figure 2–6 along with an accompanying schedule of working capital changes (Figure 2–7). Martin's statement of changes is in a working capital format (as opposed to a cash format). This statement details both the sources and uses of working capital for Martin with special emphasis on the distinction between *operations* and *other* (nonoperations) sources and uses of working capital and changes in financial position that did not affect working capital.

FIGURE 2–6

MARTIN MATTRESSES
Statement of Changes in Financial Position

	Year ended Dec. 31, 19+8	Year ended Dec. 31, 19+7
Sources of financial resources:		
Working capital provided from operations:		
Net income..	$1,300,000	$1,600,000
Items that (increased) decreased net income, but did not affect working capital:		
Depreciation	2,000,000	1,900,000
	$3,300,000	$3,500,000
Working capital provided from other sources:		
Sale of common stock................................	2,000,000	—
Financial resources provided, not affecting working capital:		
Preferred stock issued to acquire land..........	2,000,000	—
Total financial resources provided............	$7,300,000	$3,500,000
Use of financial resources:		
Working capital applied		
Additions to plant and equipment..................	$3,500,000	$2,000,000
Dividends on common stock	1,100,000	1,000,000
Dividends on preferred stock	100,000	—
	$4,700,000	$3,000,000
Financial resources applied, not affecting working capital:		
Land acquired with preferred stock	2,000,000	—
Total financial resources used	$6,700,000	$3,000,000
Increase (decrease) in working capital...............	$ 600,000	$ 500,000

FIGURE 2–7

MARTIN MATTRESSES
Schedule of Working Capital Changes

	Increase (decrease)	
	Year ended Dec. 31, 19+8	Year ended Dec. 31, 19+7
Current assets:		
Cash and marketable securities.............	$1,000,000	$ (200,000)
Accounts receivable—net....................	800,000	900,000
Inventory..	400,000	400,000
Total current assets...................	$2,200,000	$1,100,000
Current liabilities:		
Accounts payable.............................	$1,000,000	$ 300,000
Notes payable	500,000	500,000
Taxes payable	100,000	(200,000)
	$1,600,000	$ 600,000
Increase in working capital..................	$ 600,000	$ 500,000

Working capital provided from operations in Martin's case is the sum of net income and depreciation. In 19+8 this amounted to $3.3 million. Outside funds of $4 million were provided from sale of common stock and also from preferred stock that was issued to acquire land. In total, Martin "generated" $7.3 million of financial resources during the year. As the bottom half of Figure 2-6 shows, Martin used $6.7 million in 19+8 and increased its working capital by $600,000. Financial resources were used to expand plant and equipment and pay dividends, and land was acquired for the preferred stock issued. Because the statement of changes in financial position results in a bottom line net change in working capital, a companion statement of working capital changes (Figure 2-7) is also presented by the company to show how the *composition* of working capital changed. These changes in working capital components are the differences between current asset and liability accounts of the balance sheet shown in Figure 2-1. Notice that the net increase in working capital for 19+8 of $600,000 shown on the bottom line of Figure 2-7 agrees with the bottom line of Figure 2-6.

Investment, financing, and dividend decisions

From Figures 2-6 and 2-7 we can deduce what investment, financing, and dividend decisions Martin made during the year 19+8. A summary of these decisions is shown in Figure 2-8.

Investment decisions relate to changes in assets levels. Typically we think of investment decisions as increases in asset levels, but the firm may also decrease investment in an asset, which is a kind of "disinvestment" decision. A disinvestment would be reflected in a negative entry under investment decisions in Figure 2-8. Martin had no net decreases in any asset accounts for 19+8. Similarly, financing decisions relate to internally generated funds and to changes in liability and/or equity levels. The firm engages in financing when it increases any of these levels and "disfinances" when it decreases any of these accounts. A disfinancing decision would be reflected in a negative entry under financing decisions in Figure 2-8. Martin had none. The dividend actions of Martin in 19+8 are also shown in Figure 2-8. Notice also that there is a basic identity implied in Figure 2-8, as the net investment expenditures plus dividend payments equal the net financing performed by the firm. That is:

$$\text{Investments} + \text{Dividends} = \text{Financing}$$

Figure 2-8 summarizes the major financial management decisions the firm made in 19+8. Martin invested $7.7 million and paid out dividends of $1.2 million to common and preferred stockholders. The firm raised financial resources of $8.9 million. Looking at the *matching* of investment and financing decisions, two things stand out. First, Martin's inventory and accounts receivable expansion were almost completely financed by increasing accounts payable. Second, a large portion of the investment in fixed assets was financed by issuing new common and preferred stock. These and other deductions refer, of course, to events that are already history. What plans Martin has for the future will not be reflected in financial statements like these. We can, however, infer some of what has gone on at Martin. The company is expanding as evidenced by the increase in assets, and Martin financed this expansion by a combination of internally generated funds, new equity issues, and increased short-term liabilities. The firm has *not* used new long-term debt financing.

FIGURE 2–8
Summary of Martin's investment, financing, and dividend decisions for 19+8

Investment decisions:	
Increase cash and marketable securities	$1,000,000
Increase accounts receivable	800,000
Increase inventory	400,000
Increase land	2,000,000
Increase plant and equipment	3,500,000
Total investments	$7,700,000
Financing decisions:	
Financing from operations	$3,300,000
Increase accounts payable	1,000,000
Increase notes payable	500,000
Increase taxes payable	100,000
Issue common stock	2,000,000
Issue preferred stock	2,000,000
Total financing	$8,900,000
Dividend decisions:	
Preferred dividends	$ 100,000
Common dividends	1,100,000
Total dividends	$1,200,000

SUMMARY

In this chapter we have reviewed the information presented in the firm's financial statements. These financial statements are of interest to a broad array of interested parties: stockholders, creditors, management, government agencies, labor unions, and others.

One of the most frequent means of processing the information presented in the financial statements is through financial ratio analysis. There are four main categories of financial ratios. *Liquidity* ratios essentially measure the short-term solvency of the company. *Activity* ratios reflect the firm's success in managing its assets. *Leverage* ratios indicate how much debt the firm has used to finance its investments. *Profitability* ratios measure how profitable the firm's activities have been. Within each category we looked at several ratios.

1. Liquidity ratios

    $a.$ Current ratio $= \dfrac{\text{Current assets}}{\text{Current liabilities}}$

    $b.$ Quick ratio $= \dfrac{\text{Current assets} - \text{Inventory}}{\text{Current liabilities}}$

2. Activity ratios

    $a.$ Inventory turnover $= \dfrac{\text{Sales}}{\text{Inventory}}$

    $b.$ Collection period $= \dfrac{(\text{Receivables})(365)}{\text{Sales}}$

    $c.$ Fixed assets turnover $= \dfrac{\text{Sales}}{\text{Fixed assets}}$

    $d.$ Total assets turnover $= \dfrac{\text{Sales}}{\text{Total assets}}$

3. Leverage ratios

    $a.$ Debt-equity ratio $= \dfrac{\text{Total debt}}{\text{Equity}}$

    $b.$ Times interest earned $= \dfrac{\text{Net income before taxes} + \text{Interest expense}}{\text{Interest expense}}$

4. Profitability ratios

    $a.$ Profit margin $= \dfrac{\text{Net income}}{\text{Net sales}}$

    $b.$ Return on assets $= \dfrac{\text{Net income}}{\text{Total assets}}$

    $c.$ Return on equity $= \dfrac{\text{Net income}}{\text{Equity}}$

Ratio analysis is most effective when a firm's ratios are calculated for several years (trend analysis) and are compared against industry averages. Most annual reports now present enough prior years information to permit a trend analysis, and there are several business information services, for example, Dun and Bradstreet and Robert Morris Associates, that provide the necessary comparative industry data. The analyst should also keep in mind that ratio analysis can, at best, indicate potential trouble areas. Ratios that are either too high or too low may indicate such areas. Since ratios employ financial information that relates to past events, these conclusions may not relate very strongly to the firm's present and future posture.

We also investigated the firm's historical earnings per share and dividend per share data. In addition, the statement of changes in financial position that accompanies the firm's income and retained earnings statement and balance sheet was analyzed. The firm's financial statements were used to construct a summary of the financial management decisions the firm made.

QUESTIONS

1. Which of the financial ratios of a company would you most likely refer to in each of the following situations? Why?
    a. You sell raw materials to the company on credit.
    b. You are contemplating the purchase of $100,000 of the company's bonds.
    c. You are a union leader preparing for upcoming wage negotiations.
    d. You are contemplating the purchase of $100,000 of the company's common stock.

2. Financial ratios are based on historical data. Of what use are they in developing expectations about the future?

3. In comparing financial ratios of different companies, what factors other than major industry classification may be important?

4. In each of the following give an example of how a supposedly "good" ratio value might, in fact, be indicating a trouble spot.
    a. Inventory turnover is considerably higher this quarter than any other time in the history of the company.
    b. The firm's current ratio is substantially higher than the industry average.
    c. Return on equity is significantly higher than the industry average.

5. Distinguish between financing and disfinancing operations.

6. In what ways might common stockholders redefine return on equity and the debt-equity ratio to reflect their unique residual ownership position?

7. Suppose that a firm is interested in comparing its ratios with its industry average but finds that none of the financial ratio industry services carry data on the industry. What could the firm do to accomplish the comparison?

8. Discuss what the statement of changes in financial position attempts to explain.

PROBLEMS

1. Midwest Public Service Company has current liabilities of $5,500,000; a current ratio of 2.2; a quick ratio of 1.3; and sales of $44,550,000. What is its inventory turnover ratio?

2. **You are given the following information about Emery Mfg. Co.:**

Net sales	$2,000,000
Cost of goods sold	1,662,000
Gross margin	$ 338,000
Operating expenses:	
Selling	$ 46,000
General and administrative	50,000
	$ 96,000
Net operating income	$ 242,000
Other expenses and losses:	
Interest expense	12,000
Net income before taxes	$ 230,000
Income taxes	110,000
Net income	$ 120,000

Assets

Current assets:	
Cash and marketable securities	$ 50,000
Accounts receivable — net	100,000
Inventory	450,000
	$ 600,000
Property, plant and equipment — at cost:	
Land	200,000
Plant and equipment	400,000
	$ 600,000
Less accumulated depreciation	200,000
	$ 400,000
Total Assets	$1,000,000

Liabilities and Owners' Equity

Current liabilities:	
Accounts payable	$ 200,000
Notes payable	65,000
Taxes payable	35,000
	$ 300,000
Long-term debt	
Mortgage bonds — 8%	100,000
Total Liabilities	400,000
Owners' Equity:	
Common stock ($1 par)	$ 300,000
Capital in excess of par value	50,000
Retained earnings	250,000
Total Owners' Equity	$ 600,000
Total Liabilities and Owners' Equity	$1,000,000

	Industry average
Current ratio	2.0
Quick ratio	1.0
Inventory turnover	6.67
Collection period	25 days
Fixed assets turnover	5.0

	Industry average
Total assets turnover	2.0
Debt-equity ratio	1.0
Times interest earned	18.0
Profit margin	5 percent
Return on assets	10 percent
Return on equity	20 percent

a. Calculate Emery's financial ratios and compare them with the industry averages. Comment on Emery's strengths and weaknesses suggested by your analysis.

b. The profit margin and return on assets for this company are both higher than industry norms. How do you explain the fact that return on equity is not also higher than the industry norm?

3. Whistlestop Freight Co.'s latest annual report is shown below.

a. Use this report to calculate the following ratios for the year 19+9 for Whistlestop.

	Industry average (19+9)
Current	1.40
Quick	1.05
Inventory turnover	11.08
Collection period	50 days
Fixed assets turnover	3.56
Total assets turnover	1.96
Debt-equity ratio	.75
Times interest earned	14.20
Profit margin	4.2 percent
Return on assets	8.2 percent
Return on equity	14.3 percent

b. In comparison to the stated industry averages for 19+9, list what appear to be operating and financial weaknesses for Whistlestop.

WHISTLESTOP FREIGHT CO.
Annual Report (thousands of dollars)

Assets	19+9	19+8	Claims	19+9	19+8
Cash	$ 770	$ 1,050	Notes payable	$ 1,972	$ 600
Accounts receivable	7,235	5,389	Accounts payable	5,266	3,630
Inventory	4,645	3,731	Accrued expenses	820	910
Net plant and equipment	13,777	11,295	Long-term debt	5,631	5,199
			Preferred stock	100	100
			Common stock	500	500
Total			Retained earnings	12,138	10,526
assets	$26,427	$21,465	Total claims	$26,427	$21,465

	19+9	19+8
Sales	$46,240	$39,490
Cost of goods sold	38,205	32,556
Gross margin	$ 8,035	$ 6,934
Operating expenses:		
Selling	$ 3,995	$ 3,238
Depreciation	793	620
	$ 4,788	$ 3,858
Net operating income	$ 3,247	$ 3,076
Interest expense	335	346
Net income before taxes	$ 2,912	$ 2,730
Income taxes	1,173	1,178
Net income	$ 1,739	$ 1,552

4. **Fill in the missing blanks of the balance sheet below given the following financial data:**

Return on equity	25 percent
Fixed assets turnover	2 times
Profit margin	10 percent
Inventory turnover	5 times
Collection period	18.25 days
Current ratio	3.0
Net income	$100,000

Cash and securities	$50,000	Current liabilities	
Accounts receivable		Long-term debt	
Inventory		Common Stock	
Net plant and equipment	_____	Retained earnings	100,000
Total assets		Total claims	

5. **Ben Wright recently inherited 1,000 shares of the common stock of the Windfall Power Co. from his proverbial rich uncle. Although Ben recognizes his good fortune in receiving this stock, he has become concerned about the return on equity for Windfall. He has the following information:**

WINDFALL POWER CO.

Total assets	$37,800,000	Total liabilities	$17,010,000
		Total owner's equity	$20,790,000
Sales	$98,280,000		
Net income	$ 2,948,400		

	Industry norms
Return on equity	19 percent
Debt-equity ratio	0.9
Return on assets	10 percent
Total assets turnover	2.5
Profit margin	4 percent

a. **Calculate the return on equity for Windfall and explain its departure from the industry norm. Hint: Equations (2–13) and (2–11) are helpful in this explanation.**

  b. Suppose Windfall brings their debt-equity ratio into line with the industry norm. To what level will the profit margin have to be raised so that return on equity equals the industry norm?

6. Given the abbreviated balance sheet shown below for Central Systems Co., find the return on equity if the company's return on assets is:

  a. 5 percent.
  b. 10 percent.

Total assets...	$2,000,000
Current liabilities	$ 200,000
Bonds (8%)...	800,000
Preferred stock (6%)	500,000
Common stock ($100 par)	500,000
Total claims...	$2,000,000

  c. If Central Systems Co. pays out half of its earnings as dividends, determine earnings per share and dividends per share in (*a*) and (*b*).

7. Given the following statement of changes in financial position and companion schedule of working capital changes for Schugart-Southwest, Inc., prepare a summary of the company's investment, financing, and dividend decisions for the year.

Sources of financial resources:	
Net income	$ 5,010,000
Depreciation..	2,420,000
New common stock issued	5,000,000
Sale of plant and equipment..	2,620,000
Total	$15,050,000
Uses of financial resources:	
Common dividends	$ 2,500,000
Repayment of long-term debt.......................................	15,000,000
Total	$17,500,000
Increase (decrease) in working capital	(2,450,000)
Changes in working capital:	
Increase (decrease) in current assets	
Cash and securities...	$ (1,150,000)
Receivables	(640,000)
Inventory..	100,000
Total	$ (1,690,000)
Increase (decrease) in current liabilities	
Accounts payable..	520,000
Taxes payable	240,000
Total	$ 760,000
Increase (decrease) in working capital	(2,450,000)

SELECTED BASIC REFERENCES

Bierman, H., Jr. "Measuring Financial Liquidity," *Accounting Review* (October 1960), pp. 628–32.

Foulke, R. A. *Practical Financial Statement Analysis.* 6th ed. New York: McGraw Hill, Inc., 1968.

Helfert, E. A. *Techniques of Financial Analysis.* 3d ed. Homewood, Ill.: Richard D. Irwin, Inc., 1972, chapter 2.

Horrigan, J. C. "A Short History of Financial Ratios," *Accounting Review* (April 1968), pp. 284–94.

Jaedicke, R. K., and R. T. Sprouse. *Accounting Flows: Income, Funds and Cash.* Englewood Cliffs, N.J.: Prentice-Hall, Inc., 1965, chapter 7.

SELECTED ADVANCED REFERENCES

Altman, E. I. "Financial Ratios, Discriminant Analysis and the Prediction of Corporate Bankruptcy," *Journal of Finance* (September 1968), pp. 589–609.

Benishay, H. "Economic Information in Financial Ratio Analysis," *Accounting and Business Research* (Spring 1971), pp. 174–79.

Pinches, G. E., K. A. Mingo, and J. K. Caruthers. "The Stability of Financial Patterns in Industrial Organizations," *Journal of Finance* (May 1973), pp. 389–96.

section two

FUNDAMENTAL FINANCIAL MANAGEMENT CONCEPTS

3

TIME VALUE OF MONEY

The goal of the firm is maximization of stockholder wealth. Given this choice of goal, the firm should be aware of what things are important to investors so that when the firm makes financial management decisions, these decisions will have accounted for those concepts that the stockholder (and potential stockholders) deem important. Financial theory asserts that investors require compensation for two things when they buy (or hold) stock. First, they require compensation for their time value of money; second, they require compensation for risk bearing. In this chapter we only take up the time value of money concept. Risk is deferred until Chapter 4.

Stock ownership represents a current sacrifice for the stockholder. Rather than buying more food or clothes or another car, the stockholder has entrusted his money to the firm's management. In return for this sacrifice of current consumption the stockholder expects to get some future benefit, either as dividends, or increased stock price when the stock is sold, or both. However, the expected benefit is a *future* one while the sacrifice (foregone consumption) is a *current* one. It seems plausible that most people would prefer current consumption rather than waiting for future consumption, and consequently, investors expect to be rewarded for their patience by receiving a rate of return on their investment that reflects the duration of the consumption deferral. This leads us directly to a study of the rate of return of waiting: the time value of money.

The basic time value of money concept is straightforward: Money received in the future is not as valuable as money received today. We will use this simple concept to develop techniques to make sums of money that are available at different points in time equivalent to one another. This process of making dollars time equivalent is necessary because of the opportunity to earn interest on money. Suppose, for example, you can earn 6 percent interest on money you keep in your savings account. Now,

49

if a rich relative offers you a choice between a gift of $100 today or $100 a year from now, which alternative is more attractive? To formally answer this question we must make the two sums of money time equivalent. If you had the $100 today you could put it in your savings account and earn 6 percent interest for a year. The interest would be $6 ($100 × 0.06) and you would have $106 at the end of the year. So, if you earn 6 percent interest, the choice between $100 now or one year later is the same as a choice between $106 next year or $100 next year. Any rational person would, of course, prefer the larger amount.

In this example, the 6 percent interest rate represents the time value of money. Money has time value because of the opportunity to invest money received at earlier dates at some interest rate, in this case 6 percent. So the time value of money concept really means that the sooner one receives money the better, because of investment opportunities. Since money does have time value we must make comparisons between sums of money that occur in *different* time periods on a time equivalent basis. That is, we must convert the sums of money to a common point in time just as we did with the example above where we converted the $100 gift today into $106 one year later. In this chapter we will develop techniques for doing this.

The purpose of this chapter, then, is to examine the relationship between dollar values at different time periods. In particular, we want to make very clear the manner in which dollars in one period are converted into (or measured in terms of) equivalent dollars in another period. We convert present dollars into future dollars and future dollars into present dollars. Numerical tables are used to simplify this time transfer of dollars. Most of this discussion, and especially the use of the tables, is based on the assumption that dollars are paid or received only at the *end* of the time period (where a time period is usually a year). The purpose of this assumption is to simplify the analysis; it in no way affects the principles involved.

FUTURE VALUE

We start with a simple idea that relates to the example described above regarding the investment of $100 placed in a savings account at 6 percent interest for one year. After one year, $6 interest is paid and the savings account has increased to $106. This $106 is the *future value* at the end of one year of the original $100 investment. We found this future value by performing the following calculations:

Future value at end of period 1 = Original sum of money
$$+ \text{(Interest rate)(Original sum of money)}$$
$$= \$100 + (0.06)(\$100)$$
$$= \$106$$

Now let's generalize this problem using some symbols:
Let V_0 = Sum of money at time zero (that is, original sum of money), V_1 = Future value at end of period 1, and i = Interest rate (or time value of money) per period.

Then

$$V_1 = V_0 + iV_0$$
$$= V_0 (1 + i) \tag{3-1}$$

Notice what this formula does. It takes an original sum of money and converts it to a future value. The subscripts indicate what time period the money is in: V_0 refers to a sum of money *today* and V_1 refers to a sum of money one period in the future.

Time scale technique

At this point it's useful to introduce the *time scale,* which is a visual aid that will help illustrate time value of money concepts. Time scales are diagrams that show the time equivalence of money sums. The time scale for the example is shown in Figure 3–1.

FIGURE 3–1
Future value time scale ($i = 6$ percent)

The time scale here merely shows that at 6 percent interest, $100 grows to $106 after one year. That is, $100 today has a future value after one year of $106, if the interest rate is 6 percent per year.

Compounding

In the example we have been considering we only looked at the future value after one period. More generally, we need to develop a procedure for calculating future values over longer periods. What would the original sum of $100 be worth after two years, assuming that neither the principal nor the interest is withdrawn at the end of one year? The key to answering this question is to understand that the second year's interest is paid on both the original principal *and* the interest earned in the first year. Paying interest on interest is called *compounding.* Since we already know the future value of the original $100 at year one ($106), we can easily find the future value at the end of year 2, V_2:

$$V_2 = V_1 (1 + i) \tag{3-2}$$
$$= \$106 (1.06)$$
$$= \$112.36$$

Therefore, if the interest rate is 6 percent, $100 now (in the present) is equivalent to (or has a future value of) $112.36 after two years. The meaning of equivalence is worth reemphasizing. The statement that

$100 now is equivalent to $112.36 after two years does not mean that $100 *equals* $112.36. Equivalence simply means these two sums have the same time value. That is, when $i = 6$ percent, $100 today is equivalent to (may be converted into) $112.36 two years from now.

The future value of $112.36, calculated in two steps above (finding V_1 and then finding V_2), can be calculated more directly. Using Equations (3–1) and (3–2),

$$V_1 = V_0 (1 + i)$$

and

$$V_2 = V_1 (1 + i)$$

and substituting the value of V_1 in (3–1) into (3–2) gives us:

$$V_2 = [V_0 (1 + i)] (1 + i)$$
$$= V_0 (1 + i)^2 \qquad (3\text{–}3)$$

For our example:

$$V_2 = \$100 (1.06)^2$$
$$= \$100 (1.1236)$$
$$= \$112.36$$

To find the future value at the end of three years (V_3):

$$V_3 = V_0 (1 + i)^3 \qquad (3\text{–}4)$$

For our example:

$$V_3 = \$100 (1.06)^3$$
$$= \$119.10$$

We could continue for four years, five years, etc., but the generality should be becoming apparent. The future value of a current sum of money at period n is V_n:

$$V_n = V_0 (1 + i)^n \qquad (3\text{–}5)$$

For example, the future value of $100 ten years from now at 6 percent interest per year is

$$V_{10} = \$100 (1.06)^{10}$$
$$= \$179.10$$

We interpret this answer the same as before. If the interest rate is 6 percent, $100 will grow into $179.10 at the end of ten years. Stated differently, if $i = 6$ percent per year the future value at the end of ten years of a present sum of $100 is $179.10.

Compound factors and tables

All we need know to find future value from (3–5) are the original sum V_0, the interest rate i, and the future value date n. However, actually using (3–5) to calculate future values requires that the quantity $(1 + i)$ be raised to the power n. As n becomes large (as in the ten-year example), the task of calculating $(1 + i)^n$ becomes very tedious. Fortunately such tasks are not required. Let us define a new term called the *compound factor*. The compound factor for i percent interest and n periods, $CF_{i,n}$, is:

$$CF_{i,n} = (1 + i)^n$$

Calculations for many combinations of i and n have already been performed and the results provided in numerical tables. Consequently, to find the value of $(1.06)^{10}$, for example, one need only look up the value of $CF_{.06,10}$ in the compound factor table.

A compound factor table for a fairly wide range of interest rates and periods is presented in Table A in the back of the book. A portion of Table A is reproduced as Figure 3–2. It shows compound factors for all

FIGURE 3–2
Compound factor table*

	Percent (i)				
Period (n)	2	4	6	8	10
1	1.020	1.040	1.060	1.080	1.100
2	1.040	1.082	1.124	1.166	1.210
3	1.061	1.125	1.191	1.260	1.331
4	1.082	1.170	1.262	1.360	1.464
5	1.104	1.217	1.338	1.469	1.611
6	1.126	1.265	1.419	1.587	1.772
7	1.149	1.316	1.504	1.714	1.949
8	1.172	1.369	1.594	1.851	2.144
9	1.195	1.423	1.689	1.999	2.358
10	1.219	1.480	1.791	2.159	2.594

* For a more complete set of compound factors see Table A in the back of the book.

combinations of interest rates 2, 4, 6, 8, and 10 percent and of periods one through ten. The number in the 4 percent column and the period 6 row, for example, is $CF_{.04,6} = 1.265$. And it is easy to verify that $(1.04)^6 = 1.265$. Similarly, the number in the 10-percent column and period 10 row is $CF_{.10,10} = 2.594$. In finding compound factors notice that one only needs the values of i and n.

Equation (3–5) may now be rewritten to accommodate the use of the compound factors. Since

$$CF_{i,n} = (1 + i)^n$$
$$V_n = (V_0)(CF_{i,n}) \tag{3–6}$$

That is,

$$\begin{array}{c} \text{Future value in} \\ \text{period } n \end{array} = \left(\begin{array}{c} \text{Original sum} \\ \text{at time zero} \end{array} \right) \left(\begin{array}{c} \text{Compound factor for } i \text{ percent} \\ \text{per period and } n \text{ periods} \end{array} \right)$$

The compound factor then is simply the number that is multiplied times the original sum of money to get future value. Therefore, for $V_0 = \$2,000$, $i = 8$ percent per year and $n = 5$ years, $V_5 = (\$2,000)(1.469) = \$2,938$. That is, the future value in five years of $2,000 invested at 8-percent interest is $2,938. Similarly, if $V_0 = \$100,000$, $i = 4$ percent and $n = 5$ years, $V_5 = (\$100,000)(1.217) = \$121,700$.

Future value of a series of payments

So far we have considered only the future value of a single payment made at time zero (that is, right now). In many instances we may be interested in the future value of a *series* of payments represented by R_1, R_2, R_3, etc. If we think of the future value of this series of payments

FIGURE 3–3
Time scale for future value of series of payments

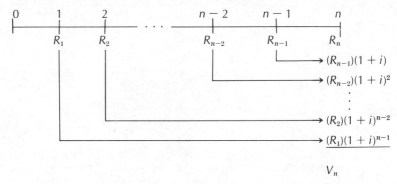

as the sum of the individual future values of the separate payments we can follow the same procedures used with single payments. The future value at period n is V_n:

$$V_n = (R_1)(1 + i)^{n-1} + (R_2)(1 + i)^{n-2} + \cdots + (R_{n-1})(1 + i) + R_n \quad (3\text{--}7)$$

In looking at this expression, notice that the first payment, R_1, compounds (receives interest) for $n - 1$ periods; the second payment, R_2, compounds for $n - 2$ periods, and so on.[1] The next to the last payment, R_{n-1}, compounds for only one period, and the last payment, R_n, receives no interest since the payment is made on the future value date. Figure 3–3 shows the compounding periods for each payment.

Suppose, for example, that we are required to find the future value at the end of five years of the following set of payments: $R_1 = \$1,000$, $R_2 = \$2,000$, $R_3 = \$1,000$, $R_4 = \$500$, and $R_5 = \$2,500$. The interest rate is 6 percent per year. The future value of this series of payments is:

---

[1] The mathematical notation "$+ \cdots +$" in Equation (3–7) means "and so on."

$$V_5 = (R_1)(1.06)^4 + (R_2)(1.06)^3 + (R_3)(1.06)^2 + (R_4)(1.06)^1 + R_5$$
$$= (\$1,000)(CF_{.06,4}) + (\$2,000)(CF_{.06,3}) + (\$1,000)(CF_{.06,2})$$
$$+ (\$500)(CF_{.06,1}) + \$2,500$$
$$= (\$1,000)(1.262) + (\$2,000)(1.191) + (\$1,000)(1.124) + (\$500)(1.060)$$
$$+ \$2,500$$
$$= \$1,262 + \$2,382 + \$1,124 + \$530 + \$2,500$$
$$= \$7,798$$

Figure 3–4 shows the time scale for this example. The $1,000 put in at the end of the first year (at $n = 1$) compounds for four years and has a future value of $1,262 at 6 percent interest. Similarly, the $2,000 payment at $n = 2$ compounds for three years at 6 percent to $2,382, and so on. The last payment of $2,500 comes at the future value date and therefore has future value at $n = 5$ of $2,500. The future value of the entire stream of payments is the sum of the individual future values, $7,798.

FIGURE 3–4

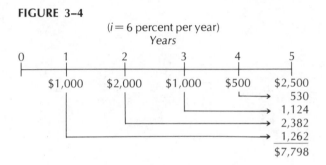

($i = 6$ percent per year)
Years

Future value of an annuity

A special class of future value problems pertains to a series of equal payments. Streams of equal payments are called *annuities*. That is, an annuity is a series of equal payments lasting for some specified duration. Since the payments are equal, $R_1 = R_2 \ldots R_n = R$; payment in any period equals $\$R$.[2] The future value of this series of equal payments is:

$$V_n = (R)(1 + i)^{n-1} + (R)(1 + i)^{n-2} + \cdots + (R)(1 + i)^1 + R$$
$$= (R)[(1 + i)^{n-1} + (1 + i)^{n-2} + \cdots + (1 + i)^1 + 1] \qquad (3\text{–}8)$$

The expression within the bracket in Equation (3–8) is called the *annuity compound factor* (*ACF*). It is the factor that, when multiplied times the amount of the annuity, gives its future value.

$$V_n = (R)(ACF_{i,n}) \qquad (3\text{–}9)$$

---

[2] We assume the payments start at the *end* of each period so the first payment comes at $n = 1$. Such annuities are called *deferred annuities*. If the annuity began at the *beginning* of the period (with the first payment at $n = 0$) it would be called an *annuity due*.

As with compound factors, annuity compound factors have been tabu-larized. The annuity compound factor table (Table B) is in the back of the text. An abbreviated version of Table B is presented in Figure 3–5 for interest rates of 2, 4, 6, 8, and 10 percent and periods one through ten. The entry in the table for six periods and 8 percent is 7.336. Consequently, the future value of a six-year annuity of $10,000 per year at an interest rate of 8 percent per year is $73,360 ($10,000 times 7.336).

FIGURE 3–5
Annuity compound factor table*

| | Percent (i) | | | | |
Period (n)	2	4	6	8	10
1	1.000	1.000	1.000	1.000	1.000
2	2.020	2.040	2.060	2.080	2.100
3	3.060	3.122	3.184	3.246	3.310
4	4.122	4.246	4.375	4.506	4.641
5	5.204	5.416	5.637	5.867	6.105
6	6.308	6.633	6.975	7.336	7.716
7	7.434	7.898	8.394	8.923	9.487
8	8.583	9.214	9.897	10.637	11.436
9	9.755	10.583	11.491	12.488	13.579
10	10.950	12.006	13.181	14.487	15.937

* For a more complete set of annuity compound factors see Table B in the back of the book.

PRESENT VALUE

Present value is the exact opposite or mirror image of future value. While future value shows how much a sum can become at some future date, present value shows what the value is today (at present) of future sums of money. Suppose, for example, you have a chance to buy a U.S. government bond that can be sold back to the U.S. government in one year for a guaranteed $1,000. There are no interest payments to consider: You buy the bond today and you get back $1,000 one year later. If your time value of money is 8 percent per year, what would you be willing to pay for the bond *today*? Alternatively stated, the question is: What is the present value of $1,000 to be received one year from now if the time value of money is 8 percent per year? Equation (3–5) was used to convert present sums (values) into future values. This equation may be rear-ranged to solve for V_0, present value:

$$V_0 = \frac{V_n}{(1 + i)^n} \tag{3–10}$$

Substituting in the numbers from the example, you would be willing to pay for the bond (its present value):

$$V_0 = \frac{\$1,000}{(1.08)^1} = \$926$$

Present value is a concept that converts future sums of money into equivalent, *present* (current) sums of money. Given a future amount and the time value of money, the current equivalent amount is called the present value of the future amount. The effect of finding a present value is to move the future amount back in time (to time zero) to find today's dollar amount that is equivalent to the future amount. Figure 3–6 shows the time scale view of the present value concept for the example.

This process of reducing future sums by moving them back in time is called *discounting*, and *i* is called the *discount rate*. Discounting is the exact opposite of compounding and refers to the shrinking of sums of money as they are brought back to the present. Why are present values (such as the $926 in the example above) less than their future values (the $1,000)? Because the present sum could be invested at the rate *i* percent and accumulated to the larger future value.

FIGURE 3–6
Present value time scale (*i* = 8 percent per year)

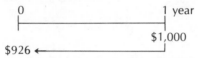

Discount factors and tables

As with compounding, Equation (3–10) becomes very tedious to work with when *n* is large. Therefore, discount tables have been developed to ease the computational work. Discount tables are tables of *discount factors*. The discount factor for *i* percent interest and *n* periods is $DF_{i,n}$.

$$DF_{i,n} = \frac{1}{(1 + i)^n}$$

Discount factors for a wide range of *i* and *n* combinations are presented in Table C in the back of the text. A portion of Table C is presented in Figure 3–7. It shows discount factors for all combinations of discount rates 2, 4, 6, 8, and 10 percent and periods one through ten. As with the compound tables, finding the discount factor requires knowledge of only *i* and *n*.

The discount factor is multiplied by the future sum to convert the sum to a present value.

$$\text{Present value} = \left(\begin{matrix}\text{Future sum at} \\ \text{period } n\end{matrix}\right)\left(\begin{matrix}\text{Discount factor for } i \text{ percent} \\ \text{per period and } n \text{ periods}\end{matrix}\right)$$

$$V_0 = (V_n)(DF_{i,n}) \tag{3-11}$$

For example, if the time value of money is 6 percent per year, the present value of $500 to be received ten years in the future is $279 ($500 × 0.558). This present value represents what the future income of $500 in year ten is worth today. A rational investor who can earn 6 percent per year on his own money would be indifferent between receiving $279 now or $500 ten

FIGURE 3–7
Discount factor table*

	Percent (i)				
Period (n)	2	4	6	8	10
1	0.980	0.962	0.943	0.926	0.909
2	0.961	0.925	0.890	0.857	0.826
3	0.942	0.889	0.840	0.794	0.751
4	0.924	0.855	0.792	0.735	0.683
5	0.906	0.822	0.747	0.681	0.621
6	0.888	0.790	0.705	0.630	0.564
7	0.871	0.760	0.665	0.583	0.513
8	0.853	0.731	0.627	0.540	0.467
9	0.837	0.703	0.592	0.500	0.424
10	0.820	0.676	0.558	0.463	0.386

* For a more complete set of discount factors see Table C in the back of the book.

years from now because the amounts are time equivalent. For if the investor had the $279 today he could invest it at 6 percent and have $500 in ten years. This equivalence is what is implied when we say that the present value of the future $500 payment is $279.

Present value of a series of payments

We are now ready to consider the present value of several sums of money, each occurring at a different point in time. The series of sums is represented by R_1, R_2, R_3, etc., where the subscripts indicate in what time period the sum is located. The present value of such a series of payments is simply the sum of the individual present values of the separate payments.

$$V_0 = \frac{R_1}{(1+i)} + \frac{R_2}{(1+i)^2} + \cdots + \frac{R_{n-1}}{(1+i)^{n-1}} + \frac{R_n}{(1+i)^n} \qquad (3\text{--}12)$$

The first payment is discounted one period, the second payment two periods, etc. This process is also shown in Figure 3–8.

At this point it is convenient to introduce some elementary mathematical notation. Equation (3–12) may be written more compactly by using a mathematical symbol that means "to sum up" or "add together." This symbol is Σ. Therefore:

$$V_0 = \sum_{t=1}^{n} \frac{R_t}{(1+i)^t} \qquad (3\text{--}13)$$

This expression is merely an elegant way of writing what present value is in terms of payments, R_t, discount factors, $1/(1+i)^t$, and duration, n.

FIGURE 3–8
Time scale for present value of series of payments

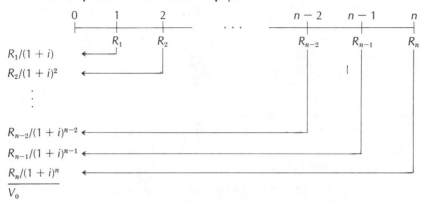

This is a somewhat general form of the present value formula. It could be further generalized by allowing the time value of money to change in each period also (in addition to the payments, R_t), but we will not pursue that issue here. The problems dealt with in this book assume that i is constant from period to period. To find the present value of a series of future payments we can apply (3–13). To put the problem in a more practical perspective, (3–13) is equivalent to:

$$V_0 = (R_1)(DF_{i,1}) + (R_2)(DF_{i,2}) + \cdots + (R_{n-1})(DF_{i,n-1}) + (R_n)(DF_{i,n})$$

$$= \sum_{t=1}^{n} (R_t)(DF_{i,t}) \qquad (3\text{–}14)$$

As (3–14) shows, the present value of a series of payments is simply the sum of the present value of each individual payment. The present value of each individual payment is merely the payment times the appropriate discount factor. If the time value of money is 6 percent per year, we can easily find the present value of the following series of yearly payments: $R_1 = \$1,000$, $R_2 = \$2,000$, $R_3 = \$1,000$, $R_4 = \$500$, and $R_5 = \$2,500$.

$$V_0 = \sum_{t=1}^{5} \frac{R_t}{(1.06)^t} = \sum_{t=1}^{5} (R_t)(DF_{i,t})$$

In expanded form this is:

$$
\begin{aligned}
V_0 &= (\$1,000)(0.943) + (\$2,000)(0.890) + (\$1,000)(0.840) \\
&\qquad + (\$500)(0.792) + (\$2,500)(0.747) \\
&= \$943 + \$1,780 + \$840 + \$396 + \$1,868 \\
&= \$5,827
\end{aligned}
$$

The present value of this series is $5,827. A time scale for the example is shown in Figure 3–9.

FIGURE 3–9
(i = 6 percent)

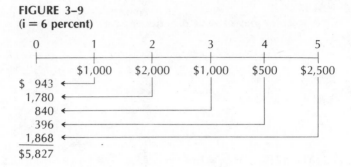

Present value of an annuity

We have previously defined an annuity as a series of equal payments of R dollars in each time period. The present value of an annuity is:

$$V_0 = \frac{R}{1+i} + \frac{R}{(1+i)^2} + \cdots + \frac{R}{(1+i)^{n-1}} + \frac{R}{(1+i)^n}$$

$$= R\left[\frac{1}{1+i} + \frac{1}{(1+i)^2} + \cdots + \frac{1}{(1+i)^{n-1}} + \frac{1}{(1+i)^n}\right]$$

$$= R\left[\sum_{t=1}^{n} \frac{1}{(1+i)^t}\right] \tag{3–15}$$

The expression within the bracket in (3–15) is called the *annuity discount factor (ADF)*. The product of the annuity discount factor and the annuity payment is the present value of the annuity at the stated time value of money:

$$V_0 = (R)(ADF_{i,n}) \tag{3–16}$$

FIGURE 3–10
Annuity discount factor table*

	Percent (i)				
Period (n)	*2*	*4*	*6*	*8*	*10*
1	0.980	0.962	0.943	0.926	0.909
2	1.942	1.886	1.833	1.783	1.736
3	2.884	2.775	2.673	2.577	2.487
4	3.808	3.630	3.465	3.312	3.170
5	4.713	4.452	4.212	3.993	3.791
6	5.601	5.242	4.917	4.623	4.355
7	6.472	6.002	5.582	5.206	4.868
8	7.325	6.733	6.210	5.747	5.335
9	8.162	7.435	6.802	6.247	5.759
10	8.983	8.111	7.360	6.710	6.145

* For a more complete set of annuity discount factors see Table D in the back of the book.

These factors have also been tabularized and are presented in some detail in Table D in the back of the book. An abbreviated version of Table D is shown in Figure 3–10 for the same combinations of i and n as other tables presented earlier. If $i = 4$ percent per year, the present value of a \$10,000 six-year annuity is $V_0 = \$10,000 \times 5.242 = \$52,420$.

Present value of an infinite life annuity

A casual look at Table D in the back of the text shows that as the length of time the annuity is received increases, the annuity discount factors increase, but as length gets *very* long, this increase in the annuity factors slows down. In fact, as annuity life becomes *infinitely* long ($n \to \infty$), the annuity discount factor approaches an upper limit. It may be shown that this limit is $1/i$. The present value for an infinite life annuity is therefore:

$$V_0 = (R)(ADF_{i,\infty}) = \frac{R}{i} \qquad (3-17)$$

If, for example, the discount rate is 15 percent per year, the present value of an infinite annuity of \$300 per year is \$300/0.15 = \$2,000.

It is true, of course, that most realistic problems do not have payments that last forever, but the assumption of infinite life frequently leads to answers that are very close approximations of the more precise answer and are helpful computational timesavers. Moreover, the generalizations we can make from this simplified present value are still very valid. The determinants of present value are R and i, and notice that as R increases, present value increases, and as i increases, present value decreases.

Time and discount rate effects on present value

Present value is directly related to the discount factor. Since $V_0 = (V_n)\,(DF_{i,n})$, as the discount factor increases (decreases), present value also increases (decreases). So those factors that affect the discount factor also affect present value in the same direction. There are two things that affect discount factors and, consequently, present values of future sums: the time distance the future sum is removed from the present, n, and the discount rate, i.

Recall that the discount factor equals $1/(1 + i)^n$. As time (n) increases, the denominator of the discount factor becomes larger and, therefore, the discount factor (and present value) gets smaller. Four-percent discount factors for 5, 10, 15, 20, and 25 periods show this decline:

Time, n (years)	5	10	15	20	25
4 percent discount factor	0.822	0.676	0.555	0.456	0.375

Similarly, as the discount rate (i) increases, the denominator of the discount factor increases and the discount factor (and present value) decreases. Ten-period discount factors for 2, 4, 6, 8, and 10 percent illustrate this point:

Discount rate, i (percent)	2	4	6	8	10
Ten-period discount factor	0.820	0.676	0.558	0.463	0.386

This analysis indicates two things. First, the more distant a sum of money is from today, the less its present value. This is intuitively true because the basic tenet of present value is that future sums of money are less valuable than current sums, and this tenet is consistent with the idea just expressed that the more distant the sum the less valuable it is. Second, the greater the discount rate the less a future sum of money is

FIGURE 3–11
Time and discount rate effects on present value

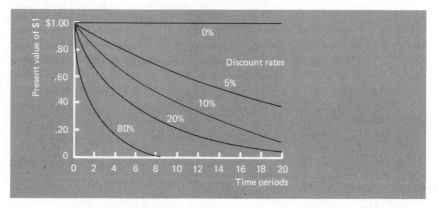

worth today. This point is not as obvious as the first, but the basic explanation is that the discount rate represents an opportunity cost of not having use of the future sum today. The opportunity cost idea merely means that if the future sum *were* available today, a rate of return equal to the discount rate could be earned on the money. Consequently, because investors with high opportunity costs forego high rates of return due to the unavailability of the money, the higher the investor's discount rate the less valuable a future sum of money is.

Figure 3–11 shows some examples of the relationship between the present value of one dollar and both time and the discount rate. As discussed above, as time increases, present value decreases, and as the discount rate increases, present value decreases. One exception to the increasing time–decreasing present value rule is the zero-percent discount rate case. When $i = 0$ percent the future sum equals its present value no matter what time period the future sum occurs. A person with a zero-percent discount rate – if there are any in the world – basically doesn't believe in the time value of money. He would as soon wait ten years to receive money as have it today. Notice also in Figure 3–11 that for very large discount rates, present value drops off extremely quickly. A person with an 80-percent discount rate, for example, views one dollar in period four as being worth only about $0.10 today.

Determining discount rates

Up to now we have assumed the discount rate, i, was given. We will spend considerable time later in the text, however, in finding discount rates. The preliminaries to these tasks are introduced here. The crux of present value problems is "given a future value, V_n, and the discount rate, i, find the present value, V_0." Suppose, instead, we knew both present and future values, but not the discount rate. How would we find this unknown rate? To begin, recall the basic present value formula:

$$V_0 = \frac{V_n}{(1 + i)^n} = (V_n)(DF_{i,n})$$

Solving for the discount factor, we get:

$$DF_{i,n} = \frac{V_0}{V_n} \tag{3-18}$$

Consequently, to find the discount rate that makes future and present values time equivalent we need only find (in Table C) that rate that corresponds with the discount factor and is consistent with the stated time period, n. For example, if $V_0 = \$200$ and $V_9 = \$400$, $DF_{i,9} = \$200/\$400 = 0.50$ and from Table C we find the discount rate to be 8 percent per period.

Now consider the case of an annuity of $\$R$ per period. Given the size and duration of the annuity and its present value, how would we find the unknown discount rate? Recall that the present value of an annuity is:

$$V_0 = \sum_{t=1}^{n} \frac{R}{(1 + i)^t} = (R)(ADF_{i,n})$$

Therefore:

$$ADF_{i,n} = \frac{V_0}{R} \tag{3-19}$$

and the procedure is the same as before except that we use Table D. If, for example, a $300 annuity lasts eight years and has present value of $1,500, $ADF_{i,8} = \$1,500/\$300 = 5.0$, and from Table D, the discount rate is found to be approximately 12 percent per year.

A more difficult problem arises when there is a series of unequal payments. Suppose the present value of future receipts of $100 in year one, $200 in year two, and $400 in year three is $500. What interest rate is implied by these numbers? Since there are several payments we can't use Table C and since the payments are not equal we can't use Table D. However, we can set the problem up:

$$V_0 = \frac{\$100}{1 + i} + \frac{\$200}{(1 + i)^2} + \frac{\$400}{(1 + i)^3}$$
$$= (\$100)(DF_{i,1}) + (\$200)(DF_{i,2}) + (\$400)(DF_{i,3})$$

Even though there is no direct easy solution we can find i by trial and error. First, we choose a trial discount rate, say $i = 20$ percent. The present value of the series of payments at $i = 20$ percent is:

$$V_0 = (\$100)(0.833) + (\$200)(0.694) + (\$400)(0.579)$$
$$= \$83.30 + \$138.80 + \$231.60$$
$$= \$453.70$$

But this calculated present value does not equal the known present value of $500. So let's try another discount rate. We observe that the calculated present value of $453.70 is too low so we choose a new trial discount rate that will raise the calculated present value. Since present value increases as the discount rate decreases, let's try 15 percent.

$$V_0 = (\$100)(0.870) + (\$200)(0.756) + (\$400)(0.658)$$
$$= \$87.00 + \$151.20 + \$263.20$$
$$= \$501.40$$

This calculated present value is not exactly equal to $500, but it's very close. Obviously, the correct discount rate is approximately 15 percent. The technique illustrated by this example will be used both in investment and financing decision work problems later on. In the investment decision work we will refer to such derived discount rates as "internal rates of return," and in financing decision work we will refer to these derived discount rates as the "cost of capital."

SOLVING FOR ANNUITY PAYMENTS

So far we have considered both future value and present value concepts. Future value techniques move money sums forward in time and present value techniques bring future sums back to the present. In both instances we investigated the special case of annuities. In addition to finding the future value or present value of an annuity we may instead be interested in calculating what annuity is required to accumulate to a future sum or what annuity is created by a present sum. The former question is called the *sinking fund problem* and the second question is called the *capital recovery problem.*

Sinking fund problems

The sinking fund problem refers to this question: What equal payment, R, compounded at i percent per period, is required to provide a future sum, V_n, n periods from now? An annuity of $\$R$ per period for n periods is being set up to provide a future sum of money. The periodic payments receive interest and the question is how large should R be? An example of this problem is when the firm borrows money and is required to make sinking fund payments each period to have enough money accumulated at the designated date (period n) to pay back the original loan. The answer to the question can be found by recalling Equation (3–9) which solves for future value given the annuity payment:

$$V_n = (R)(ACF_{i,n}) \tag{3–9}$$

Solving for the annuity payment, R, we get

$$R = \frac{V_n}{ACF_{i,n}} \qquad (3\text{-}20)$$

Assume the firm borrows $1.2 million and the loan agreement stipulates that the loan principal must be paid off three years from now. The firm's time value of money is 8 percent per year. What annual payment must the firm make to insure that the needed $1.2 million is available at the designated date?

$$R = \frac{\$1,200,000}{ACF_{.08,3}} = \frac{\$1,200,000}{3.246} = \$369,686$$

The firm must deposit $369,686 at the end of every year for three years to have accumulated $1,200,000 at the designated repayment date. This annual deposit is called a sinking fund payment.

Capital recovery problems

The capital recovery problem refers to a different question: What equal payment, R, is required to exactly recover a present sum, V_0, with interest i percent per period over n periods? The calculation is again directed toward finding an annuity, but the annuity is one that will exactly recover a *present* sum with interest.[3] If, for example, the firm borrows $400,000 at 6 percent interest per year and is required to pay off this loan with ten equal annual payments, what is the size of the required annual payment? The answer to the capital recovery problem is most readily seen by recalling Equation (3-16):

$$V_0 = (R)(ADF_{i,n}) \qquad (3\text{-}16)$$

Rearranging this equation, we get

$$R = \frac{V_0}{ADF_{i,n}} \qquad (3\text{-}21)$$

For the example

$$R = \frac{\$400,000}{ADF_{.06,10}} = \frac{\$400,000}{7.36} = \$54,348$$

The firm must pay $54,348 every year. By paying this amount the firm is repaying the principal of the loan ($400,000) and also paying interest at 6 percent per year on the declining balance of the loan. Alternatively stated, the lender is recovering his capital and is also making 6 percent per year on his capital.

INTEREST PERIODS LESS THAN A YEAR

Compound factors, annuity compound factors, discount factors, and annuity discount factors all have one thing in common: They are de-

---

[3] This kind of problem is faced most frequently by firms that lend money. For example, when a savings and loan institution makes a mortgage loan on a house the monthly payment is set up to allow the savings and loan company to recover their initial lending, V_0, with interest, by requiring the homeowner to pay back $\$R$ per month.

termined completely by the number of interest periods, n, (that is, the number of compounding or discounting periods) and the time value of money per period, i. Notice in particular that the definition of n and i do not specify the *length* of the time period. In working examples through-out the chapter we have focused on n in years and i in percent per year and this focus will be reinforced through most of the book. Frequently, however, the interest period is less than a year and we must take care to acknowledge this fact in setting up and working problems.

Some of the most common interest periods less than a year are monthly, quarterly, and semiannual periods. The key to correctly hand-ling such problems is to always keep in mind the generality of the defini-tions of n and i: They are *per interest period* concepts. Looking at a specific example, we must determine two critical things: How many interest periods are there and what is i per period? Suppose, for example, that the firm is considering putting $1 million into a short-term savings account that pays 8-percent interest compounded quarterly. The firm expects to leave the money in this account for five years. How much will be in the account at the end of the five years? Asked differently, what is the future value of the $1 million? We know, of course, that $V_n = (V_0)$ $(CF_{i,n}) = (\$1,000,000)(CF_{i,n})$, but what are i and n? We emphasize first that n is *not* five and i is *not* 8 percent. The interest period is a quarter in this example, and n (the *number* of interest periods) is 20 (5 years $\times$ 4 times per year). Also, the 8 percent represents what is called a *nominal interest rate*. That is, it is a *stated annual rate*. To find the interest rate per period, we divide the *nominal rate* by the number of interest periods per year.[4] Since in the example the compounding is performed quarterly, there are four compounding periods per year. Therefore $i = 0.08/4 = 0.02$ (2 percent per quarter) and:

$$V_{20} = (\$1,000,000)(CF_{.02,20})$$
$$\doteq (\$1,000,000)(1.486)$$
$$= \$1,486,000$$

We can also express these ideas more formally:

$$i = \frac{\text{Stated annual interest rate}}{\text{Number of interest periods per year}}$$

$n = $ (Number of interest periods per year) $\times$ (Number of years)

As another example consider the problem of finding the present value of $2,000 due in five years if the time value of money is 6 percent, com-pounded semiannually. In this case, $i = 0.06/2 = 0.03$ and $n = (2)(5) = 10$. Therefore

$$V_0 = (\$2,000)(DF_{.03,10}) = (\$2,000)(0.744) = \$1,488$$

The main thing to remember in problems such as these is that neither the procedures nor the future and present value formulas have changed,

---

[4] Introductory finance students are often confused by expressions such as "8-percent interest, compounded quarterly." This expression does not mean the interest rate per quarter is 8 percent. The 8 percent is a yearly rate called the nominal rate. To find the quarterly interest rate we divide the nominal rate by four, the number of quarters in a year. The effect of compounding quarterly is to make the effective (or true) annual rate higher (in our ex-ample, 8.24 percent).

but we must be especially careful in determining n and i. The key to working problems where the interest period is less than a year is to set the problem up where n is the number of interest periods and i is the interest rate per period.[5]

SUMMARY

In making financial management decisions that will please the stockholders and be consistent with the firm's goal of stockholder wealth maximization the firm must be aware of the things that investors deem important. One of the important things that investors require is compensation for their time value of money. That is, investors require a rate of return for making a current sacrifice of consumption expenditures, and this return is called their time value of money. The basic tenet of the time value of money is that money received in the future is not as valuable as money received today. Development of the time value of money concept permits comparison of sums of money that are available at different points in time.

Future value

Finding future values refers to compounding money forward into the future to determine the money's value at a specified future date. The future value, V_n, of a present sum of money, V_0, compounded for n periods at i percent per period is:

$$V_n = (V_0)(1 + i)^n$$

The quantity $[(1 + i)^n]$ is called the compound factor, $CF_{i,n}$, for n periods and i percent interest per period and has been tabulated as Table A in the back of the text. Restating the future value formula in terms of the compound factors, we get

$$V_n = (V_0)(CF_{i,n})$$

The future value of a series of payments is merely the sum of the individual future values of the separate payments:

$$\begin{aligned} V_n &= (R_1)(1 + i)^{n-1} + (R_2)(1 + i)^{n-2} + \cdots + (R_{n-1})(1 + i) + R_n \\ &= (R_1)(CF_{i,n-1}) + (R_2)(CF_{i,n-2}) + \cdots + (R_{n-1})(CF_{i,1}) + R_n \end{aligned}$$

In the special case where all payments are equal the series is called an annuity and the future value of the annuity is:

$$V_n = (R)(ACF_{i,n})$$

where $ACF_{i,n}$ is the annuity compound factor for n periods and i-percent interest per period and R is the amount of the annuity payment. The $ACF_{i,n}$ factors are found in Table B in the back of the text.

---

[5] Another problem to note: What do you do when the tables do not include those values needed to work a given problem? Answer: Learn how to use a slide rule or calculator, or be content with an approximate answer.

Present value

Present value is the exact opposite of future value and refers to discounting money back to the present to determine what future sums are worth today. If the time value of money is i percent, the present value of a sum of money to be received n periods from now is:

$$V_0 = \frac{V_n}{(1 + i)^n}$$

The quantity $[1/(1 + i)^n]$ is called the discount factor, $DF_{i,n}$, for n periods and i percent discount rate and has been tabulated as Table C in the back of the book. Since $DF_{i,n} = 1/(1 + i)^n$:

$$V_0 = (V_n)(DF_{i,n})$$

The present value of a series of payments is equal to the sum of the present values of the individual payments:

$$V_0 = \sum_{t=1}^{n} \frac{R_t}{(1 + i)^t} = \sum_{t=1}^{n} (R_t)(DF_{i,t})$$

If the series is an annuity,

$$V_0 = (R)(ADF_{i,n})$$

If the annuity has an infinite life:

$$V_0 = \frac{R}{i}$$

We also briefly explored the effects that time and the discount rate had on present value. The more distant a future sum the less its present value is, and the larger the discount rate used the smaller the present value is.

In the last part of the chapter, we also investigated some other topics related to the chapter's central theme of determining future and present values. We discussed how to find the implied discount rate if both future and present values were known. We also discussed how to determine annuity payments given the time value of money and either (a) a future sum of money or (b) a present sum of money. Problem (a) is called the *sinking fund problem* and (b) the *capital recovery problem*. Finally, we briefly studied problems where the interest period was less than one year. We saw that this consideration did not affect the general solution procedures developed throughout the chapter.

Future value and present value have been emphasized about equally in this chapter. However, the central theme in this book is valuation, and this concept will be shown (in Chapter 5) to be a present value concept. Consequently, ensuing chapters will emphasize present value principles much more than future value principles.

QUESTIONS

1. As a new financial analyst for a manufacturing company, you are interested in applying correct financial analysis techniques to your job. Your supervisor graduated from business school in 1947 and is not aware of some of the recent developments in finance. Describe how you would convince him that money has "time value."

2. Define the following terms and phrases:
   a. Annuity.
   b. Discount rate.
   c. Future value.
   d. Discount factor.
   e. Annuity discount factor.
   f. Sinking fund.
   g. Nominal interest rate.

3. Two investors are contemplating buying a U.S. Treasury bill (see Chapter 17) that promises to pay the owner of the bill $10,000 in 90 days. Investor A has a time value of money of 8 percent and investor B has a time value of money of 10 percent.
   a. Which investor would be willing to pay more for the bill? Why?
   b. Suppose the bill were for 180 days; what would this change in maturity do to the price that either investor would be willing to pay?

4. Assume that an American chemical company has just purchased and paid for mineral rights to bauxite deposits in Africa. Under terms of the contract, the company may not have access to the bauxite until after the African government completes further geological exploration of the area. Other things equal, what would the following conditions imply about the present value of the company's bauxite holdings? Explain your answers.
   a. During the interim for exploration, the firm's time value of money decreases.
   b. Because of weather difficulties and government planning priorities the exploration is delayed for several months.
   c. Further exploration reveals that the deposit is not as large as originally thought.
   d. Because of a change of governments in the African country, the company is advised that, while it still has the right to extract the bauxite, the rate at which the mineral may be extracted will not be as fast as originally agreed upon.

5. What relationship exists between discount factors and annuity discount factors?

6. Given the following nominal interest rates, compounding frequencies, and lengths of time involved, find the interest rate per period, i, and the number of interest periods, n, in each case:

Part	Nominal interest rate (percent)	Compounding frequency	Time (years)
a	12	Quarterly	4
b	8	Semiannually	8
c	10	Yearly	10
d	20	Daily	3
e	6	Monthly	6

7. Suppose that you are contemplating investing in one of two different bonds, A and B, that offer expected rates of return (or yields) of 10 and 6 percent, respectively.

    a. What factors might cause this discrepancy in yields?

    b. Under what conditions might you prefer to purchase Bond B?

PROBLEMS

1. If you place $1,000 in a savings account, what will be the amount in the account after three years, assuming no withdrawals, if it earns 7 percent annual interest?

2. Suppose $1,000 were deposited in a savings account at the end of each year for the next four years. If the account earns 8 percent annually and there are no withdrawals, what will be the value of the account:

    a. At the end of the four-year period?

    b. At the end of five years?

    c. At the end of four years if an additional $1,000 were deposited at the *beginning* of the four-year period?

3. If you need $2,000 five years from now, how much money must you put in a savings account today if it will earn 6 percent annual interest?

4. Your favorite aunt has offered you your choice of the following two gifts. She will give you $1,000 one year from now or $1,250 three years from now. Which would you choose if your opportunity cost is 10 percent? 20 percent? Is there any inconsistency in these answers?

5. Congratulations! You have won the Reader's Digress Sweepstakes. You have the choice of receiving $12,000 a year for the next 15 years, first payment to be received today, or $100,000 in cash. If your opportunity cost is 10 percent, which should you choose?

6. As a reward for excellence in academics, you have been promised a cash gift of $1,000 four years from today. How much is this gift worth to you today if your opportunity cost is 6.25 percent?

7. Calculate the present value and then the future value at the end of period six for each of the following cash flow streams. Assume an interest rate of 8 percent:

Period	1	2	3	4	5	6
a	$200	$200	$200	$200	$300	$300
b	150	150	150	150	150	150
c	150	180	210	70	125	90
d	300	300	−100	75	200	300

8. Burley and Bright Tobacco, Ltd., manufacture and sell a popular chewing tobacco, Cud. The company receives about $20,000 cash flow each year from the product after all expenses, including taxes. Harris Cigars has recently offered to buy the product (with trademark) from Burley and Bright for $130,000. Assuming Burley and Bright's discount rate is 15 percent, should they sell the product if they think its estimated life expectancy is:
    a. 15 years?
    b. 25 years?
    c. Indefinitely long?

9. Mr. Jones is 60 years old and a life insurance agent is trying to interest him in an annuity that would pay $1,000 per year (payable once a year) for 15 years. What would be the maximum amount that Mr. Jones would pay for the annuity, assuming his time value of money is 8 percent and the first payment begins:
    a. In one year?
    b. In five years?
    c. Suppose that Mr. Jones buys the annuity and begins receiving the payments. Immediately after receiving the eighth payment, Mr. Jones attempts to sell the remainder of the annuity to a third party. What is the minimum price Mr. Jones would accept if his time value of money is unchanged?
    d. What minimum price would he accept if he decided instead to sell the remainder of the annuity immediately *before* the eighth payment?

10. A firm is attempting to arrange a loan from a bank to purchase some equipment. The firm has talked to four different banks and gotten loan terms from each. Calculate the rate of return the firm would be paying in each case:
    a. Bank A loans $10,000 today to the firm; the firm pays the bank $15,385 at the end of five years.
    b. Bank B loans $9,500 today to the firm; the firm pays the bank $12,925 at the end of four years.
    c. Bank C loans $10,000 today; the firm pays the bank $3,000 per year at the end of each year for four years.
    d. Bank D loans $10,000 today; the firm pays $2,000 per year the first three years and then $4,000 per year for two more years (all payments at year end).

11. Fielitz Mining Co. is establishing a sinking fund to pay off a $100,000 loan that matures on May 20, 19+9. Payments to the sinking fund must be made annually for ten years on May 20; the first payment is

due in 19+0 and the last in 19+9. Fielitz is required to make *equal* annual payments, and the company anticipates that money paid to the sinking fund will earn 8 percent per year. Determine the amount of the annual sinking fund payment.

12. Cohan Food Processing is negotiating a $700,000 loan from a life insurance company. The insurance company wants to be paid in equal annual payments at the end of each year. Determine the size of the annuity payment under the following interest rate and length of loan conditions?
    a. Interest rate is 7 percent and loan is for five years.
    b. Interest rate is 8 percent and loan is for eight years.
    c. Interest rate is 10 percent and loan is for four years.
    d. In general, what effects do interest rate and length of loan have on the size of the annuity payment?

13. A plastics company receives semiannual royalty checks of $50,000 on a processing patent; the patent has six more full years to run before expiring.
    a. If all future royalty checks are put in a savings account that pays 6 percent interest compounded semiannually, how much will be in the savings account at the expiration of the patent? Assume that the next royalty check will be received in six months.
    b. What is the present value of the series of royalty checks?

14. Nichols Coal Co., Inc., strip mines low-grade coal in Kentucky, and estimates that its operations there will be profitable for about ten more years. At that time the supply of economically recoverable coal will be depleted and the company will need to close its Kentucky operations. Nichols anticipates that it will need about $5 million at that time to fill and reforest land that has been damaged by mining. To insure that it has sufficient funds to do this, Nichols has decided to set aside a certain amount of cash each quarter in a sinking fund. The company estimates that it can earn about 8 percent compounded quarterly on this sinking fund.
    a. What should be the amount of the quarterly sinking fund payment?
    b. What is the present value of the $5 million fill and reforestation costs that will occur in ten years?
    c. How much money will have accumulated in the sinking fund at the end of two years? Five years?
    d. If, at the end of five years, the firm were to put in a lump sum amount of money in lieu of making further sinking fund payments, how large a lump sum would be required?

15. Your finance professor makes you the following offer: He will give you $500 at the end of every six months for the next five years if you agree to pay him back $500 every six months for the following ten years.
    a. Should you accept this offer if your opportunity cost (discount rate) is 18 percent, compounded semiannually?

b. Should you accept if your opportunity cost is 8 percent semi-annually?

c. At what semiannual interest rate would you be indifferent to acceptance of the offer?

SELECTED BASIC REFERENCES

Dean, J. "Measuring the Productivity of Capital," *Harvard Business Review* (January–February, 1954), pp. 120–30.

McLean, J. G. "Measuring the Return on Capital—Relating Calculations to Uses," *NAA Bulletin* (September 1960), pp. 120–30.

Osborn, R. *The Mathematics of Investment.* New York: Harper & Brothers, 1957.

SELECTED ADVANCED REFERENCES

Jeynes, P. H. "The Depreciation Annuity," 1956 *AIEE Transactions,* Part II. (February 1957), pp. 1398–1415.

Taylor, G. A. *Managerial and Engineering Economy.* Princeton, N.J.: D. Van Nostrand Co., Inc., 1964, chapters 3 and 4.

4

RISK CONCEPTS

In the previous chapter we examined the concept of the time value of money. The reason for the investigation was that investors require compensation (a rate of return) in exchange for foregoing current consumption by letting the firm use their money. This compensation is called the time value of money. Implicit in that work was the assumption of certainty. That is, the outcome resulting from any decision is known with certainty. We found, for example, that $100 invested for one year at a guaranteed rate of return of 10 percent would accumulate to $110 at the end of the year. In fact, the decisions of the financial manager are never made under conditions of certainty. There is always a chance that the result of his actions will be either better or worse than he anticipated when he made the decision. Thus the financial manager must make his decisions under conditions that we refer to as "risk" or "uncertainty."[1] Investors require compensation when they invest money in ventures where the returns are not certain. Investing in such ventures exposes the investors to risk, and the required compensation to induce investors to enter these risky investments is over and above the compensation they require for time value of money considerations. Investors require a rate of return on their investment that reflects (1) their time value of money and (2) their risk aversion. The former is called the *price of time* and the latter the *price of risk*.

The previous chapter developed the price of time concepts and in this chapter we develop the price of risk concepts. First, we further develop the notion of uncertainty and introduce some very simple probability ideas. Then we examine two probability-based measures of risk and select *covariance* (explained in detail later) as the appropriate measure of risk in financial management decision making.

---

[1] For some purposes it is important to distinguish between risk and uncertainty. The technical nature of the distinction is explained below.

THE MEANING OF RISK AND UNCERTAINTY

In contrast to the certainty examples in the last chapter, suppose Mr. Jones, the financial manager, can invest $1 million and that the return from the investment will be an unknown amount, X, at the end of the year. Before the manager can decide to make the investment, he must obtain some "information" regarding the possible values of X. Assume that he conducts an investigation and decides that the actual value of X will be determined by the general level of economic activity during the year. After looking at several forecasts of economic activity he concludes that there are three possible values for X: $800,000, $1,000,000, $1,200,000, each with a one-third chance of occurrence.[2] He now knows the possible values for X, and he knows how likely each value is to occur. *But,* he still does not know what X will be at the end of the year. In other words, he does not have complete certainty concerning the outcome of his decision, and his decision must be made under conditions of risk or uncertainty.

At this point we can distinguish between the concepts of risk and uncertainty. Risk refers to situations where we "know" all possible outcomes (the X's) and the chances of occurrence associated with each outcome. If we're flipping a coin, for example, we know there are only two outcomes (heads or tails) and the chances of occurrence of each are one half for a fair coin. Uncertainty refers to situations where we "don't know" all possible outcomes and/or associated chances of occurrence but can only estimate them. If we're investing in a stock, for example, we will not know all possible rates of return and associated chances of occurrence. Realistically, financial management decisions are thus made under conditions of uncertainty, but financial management decision techniques are based on the assumption that conditions of risk exist. There is a growing tendency in finance to use the terms "risk" and "uncertainty" interchangeably with no distinction between them and we will also follow this practice in this book.

Let us adopt the following definitions:

1. The outcome, X, of a decision made in the absence of certainty is a *random variable*. (A random variable is a variable that has chances associated with its outcomes.)
2. *Risk* and *uncertainty* are terms used to describe any situation in which the outcome of a decision is a random variable.

In connection with our discussion of risk and uncertainty, two important facts must be remembered. First, some risk is present in almost any decision that the financial manager makes. The risk may be smaller in a decision to invest $10,000 in an asset that is similar to other assets the firm has and is familiar with than in a decision to invest $10 million in a revolutionary process for extracting gold from seaweed. But some risk is present in almost every decision. The only way that a financial manager can avoid risk in his decisions is to resign his position. Even this drastic action, however, will not isolate the manager from risk because

---

[2] We'll explain fully what chance of occurrence means below.

risk is a pervasive fact of life. Resigning only substitutes the risk of not being able to find a new job (or some other risk) for the risk of making an incorrect financial decision for the firm.

The second fact is that since risk cannot be avoided, the best strategy for one who wants to account for the effect of risk is to recognize it formally, measure it as best he can, and then make choices on the basis of decision rules that incorporate the measure of risk as an integral part of the rule. The remainder of this chapter is devoted to defining and developing the concept of risk. Later chapters develop decision rules that include risk considerations.

Probability concepts

In the example problem used above to discuss risk, the result of the decision was described as a random variable, X, with three possible outcomes. Moreover, each possible outcome was considered to be as likely to occur as either of the other two possible outcomes. Since, by assumption, one of the values of X must occur, we can express the idea of "equally likely" outcomes by the statement that each possible outcome has an "equal chance" (in the example, one in three) of being the true result. Consider another case in which only two outcomes are possible— the drilling of a wildcat oil well. Although the amount of oil in the ground can vary, we can think of the primary consideration as being "Is there oil, yes or no?" Suppose that a geological investigation concludes that the "odds are three-to-one against finding oil." This statement is equivalent to saying there is a 75 percent chance that oil will not be found and, therefore, a 25 percent chance that oil will be found. In both of these examples, the notion of risk has been expressed in terms of *chances of occurrence*. Our next step is to convert from chances to probabilities. This is made easy by recognizing that the concept of probability is nothing more than a formalization of the idea of relative chance of occurrence. But this formalization is important; it allows us to develop a measurable concept of risk.

We can begin by recognizing that a 25 percent chance is the same as a 0.25 probability, and a 75 percent chance is the same as a 0.75 probability. Therefore, if the odds against finding oil are three-to-one, then the probability of finding oil is 0.25. With this background, we can adopt a formal definition of probability.

Probability — a probability is a number, p_i, that represents the chance that the random variable X will have the outcome X_i.

If we let X_1 represent the outcome "no oil" in our drilling decision and X_2 represent the other outcome "oil," then $p_1 = 0.75$ and $p_2 = 0.25$.

In addition to our definition, we need to recognize several facts about probabilities. For example, no possible outcome of a decision can have less than a zero chance of occurrence. That is, a chance of −10 percent has no meaning. Similarly, no outcome can have more than a 100 percent chance of occurrence. All chances must fall between 0 and 100 percent inclusive. Since zero percent means zero probability and 100 percent means a probability of one, the corresponding rule for probabilities is

that all probabilities must fall between zero and one, inclusive. Therefore, we have:

Rule 1 — All probabilities are between zero and one. That is, $0 \leq p_i \leq 1$
for all i.

In the oil drilling example, the probabilities 0.25 and 0.75 are both
between 0 and 1.

We also assume that in all cases, all possible outcomes are identified.
If there are five possible outcomes of an investment, for example, each
one must be identified and assigned a probability. Suppose the outcomes
of such an investment can be described as follows:

Possible outcome	Dollar value	Probability
X_1.........................	−10	0.10
X_2.........................	0	0.15
X_3.........................	10	0.25
X_4.........................	20	0.40
X_5.........................	30	0.10
		1.00

There are five possible outcomes,[3] and each has an associated probability
of occurrence. Since, by assumption, there are no other possible outcomes of this investment, one of these five values must occur. That is,
there is a 100 percent chance that the actual outcome will be one of the
five listed above. Thus, the probabilities must add up to one.

Rule 2 — The sum[4] of the probabilities of all possible outcomes is one.
That is,

$$\sum_{i=1}^{N} p_i = 1.00$$

where N is the number of possible outcomes of X. (For the example,
$N = 5$.)[5]

---

[3] Notice that while Rule 1 says that all *probabilities* must be nonnegative ($p_i \geq 0$), the
outcomes (X_i) are not similarly restricted. Thus $X_1 = -\$10$ (representing a loss of \$10) is a
permissible outcome.

[4] Recall from Chapter 3 that the symbol Σ means "sum" or "add together."

[5] Notice again that while Rule 2 says that the *probabilities* must sum to one

$$\sum_{i=1}^{N} p_i = 1.0$$

the sum of the *outcomes*

$$\sum_{i=1}^{N} X_i$$

is not restricted.

We have purposely ordered the outcome values so that X_1 is the smallest value and X_N is the largest value. This procedure is useful and will be maintained throughout this text.

Probability distributions

We will, on occasion, find it useful to talk in terms of probability distributions. Intuitively, the easiest notion of probability distributions to grasp is the idea that a probability distribution is a description of the assignment of probabilities to individual outcomes. The listing of the five separate dollar outcomes and their associated probabilities in our last example represents a probability distribution. In many cases, however, there are special mathematical rules or formulas that specify how the probabilities are to be assigned to the outcomes. In order to encompass all cases we adopt the following definition:

Probability distribution — a complete description of the outcomes of a random variable and the associated probabilities.

A probability distribution may be in the form of a complete enumeration of outcomes and probabilities (as in the example above) or it may be in

FIGURE 4–1
A discrete probability distribution

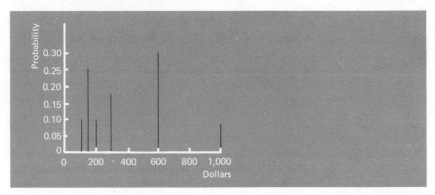

the form of a mathematical description. In either event, if all possible outcomes and probabilities are described we have a probability distribution.

The graph of the probability distribution yields a picture of the outcomes and associated probabilities that helps in understanding the risk concepts we'll investigate below. Figure 4–1 provides an example of the graph of a probability distribution with six possible outcomes. The dots on the figure indicate both the outcome — plotted on the horizontal axis — and the probability associated with the outcome — plotted on the vertical axis. Notice that the graph and the following written description of the probability distribution both contain the same information (that is, they agree).

Possible outcome	Dollar value	Probability
X_1	100	0.10
X_2	150	0.25
X_3	200	0.10
X_4	300	0.17
X_5	600	0.30
X_6	1,000	0.08
		1.00

A probability distribution of the type just presented is referred to as a *discrete* probability distribution. The word "discrete" refers to the fact that probabilities are assigned to specific individual points (or X values). A different class of probability distributions, called *continuous* probability distributions, assigns probabilities to an interval between two points of a continuous graph. Figure 4–2 shows an example of a continuous probability distribution. Continuous probability distributions are extremely useful in both portraying and analyzing problems dealing with

FIGURE 4–2
A continuous probability distribution

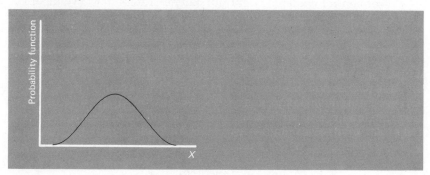

uncertainty. However, in this book we will emphasize discrete probability distributions. Except for special continuous distributions, like the "normal," corresponding general analysis of continuous probability distributions would require calculus.

SUMMARY FEATURES OF PROBABILITY DISTRIBUTIONS

Rather than work with complete probability distributions it is frequently desirable to limit the analysis to a summary feature of the probability distribution. By summary feature we mean some property or characteristic of the function that conveys or describes something important about the distribution. We will investigate some summary features of probability distributions and associate some of these features with important finance concepts. To assist in this investigation consider the two following example investment prospects. Each prospect has a distribution of rates of return (X = rate of return) for the coming year as shown:

A		B	
X_i (percent)	p_i	X_i (percent)	p_i
20	0.10	20	0.20
30	0.80	40	0.60
40	0.10	60	0.20
	1.00		1.00

We will use these two example distributions in the sections below.

Central tendency: Expected value

One summary feature of a probability distribution relates to the idea of central tendency. Central tendency refers to the value of the random variable that the outcomes tend to cluster around. There are several measures of central tendency, but finance emphasizes the importance of a particular measure called *expected value*. It is also called the *arithmetic mean;* it is an average:

$$\text{Expected value} = \mu = \sum_{i=1}^{N} p_i X_i \qquad (4\text{--}1)$$

Now let's calculate the expected value of each of these distributions:

$$\mu_A = (0.10)(20) + (0.80)(30) + (0.10)(40)$$
$$= 2 + 24 + 4$$
$$= 30 \text{ percent}$$

$$\mu_B = (0.20)(20) + (0.60)(40) + (0.20)(60)$$
$$= 4 + 24 + 12$$
$$= 40 \text{ percent}$$

The expected value or average of these distributions of rates of return are 30 and 40 percent, respectively. These numbers represent the weighted "center" of the outcomes. The outcomes have, in fact, been weighted by their probabilities and averaged. If the firm repetitively acquired assets that had rate of return distributions like A's, the average rate of return for these investments would be 30 percent.

If the random variable, X_i, is in units of dollars or (as in the example) rates of return, μ represents expected dollar return or expected rate of return, respectively. Other things equal, investors are presumed to prefer distributions with large values of μ. That is, investors desire large expected profits and large expected rates of return. In the example above, the expected rate of return of B is greater than A's expected rate of return. Other things equal, B is more attractive to investors than A. This does not mean, however, that offered the choice of the two prospects, at the same price, investors would necessarily choose B over A. The meaning of "other things equal" requires here that the two distributions be alike in all other important features. In reality other things are not usually equal. Obviously the two example distributions are not alike; investors may perceive, for example, that B is riskier than A. We turn now to a discussion of dispersion that will lead us to a formal consideration of risk.

Dispersion: Variance and standard deviation

In contrast to central tendency is the notion of dispersion. Dispersion refers to spread or scatter in the probability distribution. Just as central tendency identifies a number that X values tend to center on, dispersion measures how spread out or scattered the X values are. There are several dispersion measures, but finance has traditionally measured dispersion by *variance* and *standard deviation*.

Variance Variance is a dispersion measure based on the weighted dispersion of possible outcomes around the expected value with probabilities serving as weights.

$$\text{Variance} = \sigma^2 = \sum_{i=1}^{N} p_i(X_i - \mu)^2 \tag{4-2}$$

Using the same example as before (recall that $\mu_A = 30$ percent and $\mu_B = 40$ percent), we get

$$\sigma_A^2 = (0.10)(20 - 30)^2 + (0.80)(30 - 30)^2 + (0.10)(40 - 30)^2$$

$$= (0.10)(100) + (0.80)(0) + (0.10)(100)$$

$$= 10 + 0 + 10$$

$$= 20$$

$$\sigma_B^2 = (0.20)(20 - 40)^2 + (0.60)(40 - 40)^2 + (0.20)(60 - 40)^2$$

$$= (0.20)(400) + (0.60)(0) + (0.20)(400)$$

$$= 80 + 0 + 80$$

$$= 160$$

An examination of these calculations shows the way in which both the spread of possible outcomes and the probabilities of these outcomes are measured by the variance. Deviations from expected value, $X_i - \mu$, are squared, and this squaring process magnifies large deviations more than it does small deviations. With prospect A, for example, $X_3 - \mu = 10$ is a smaller deviation than $X_3 - \mu = 20$ for prospect B. The smaller deviation is only 100 when squared, but the large deviation squared is 400, a large difference. Therefore, the greater the spread of possible outcomes, the larger the variance. In addition, the dispersion of the probabilities affects σ^2. If high probabilities are concentrated near the mean, then the smaller deviations receive most of the probability weight while the extreme deviations receive less probability weight. Using prospect *B* as an example, most of the probability weight (60 percent) falls right *on* the mean (zero deviation) while less probability weight falls out at the extreme values of $X = 20$ percent and $X = 60$ percent. The result of heavy probability weighting at the center of the distribution is a relatively smaller variance.

The variances in the example are thus 20 and 160, respectively. These numbers represent a kind of index number that describes how dispersed from the expected value the *X* observations are. The larger the variance, the more dispersion evident in the distribution.

Standard deviation   A close relative of variance that is commonly used to represent dispersion is the standard deviation. The standard deviation is simply the positive square root of the variance:

$$\text{Standard deviation} = \sigma = \sqrt{\sigma^2} = \sqrt{\sum_{i=1}^{N} p_i(X_i - \mu)^2} \qquad (4\text{--}3)$$

For example distributions *A* and *B*:

$$\sigma_A = \sqrt{20} = 4.5 \text{ percent}$$

$$\sigma_B = \sqrt{160} = 12.7 \text{ percent}$$

The popularity of the standard deviation as a measure of dispersion stems from its interpretation in connection with the *normal* probability function. If the probability function is normal, for example, then the chances are approximately two out of three that any *X* value will fall within one standard deviation of the expected value of the distribution. Similar statements can be made regarding other multiples of the standard deviation. Obviously, the standard deviation conveys considerable probability information when the distribution is normal.

For purposes of comparing dispersion, standard deviation and variance give identical results because the standard deviation is simply the positive square root of the variance. Thus if the variance of distribution *A* is greater than the variance of distribution *B*, the standard deviation of distribution *A* is also greater than the standard deviation of distribution *B*. The example distributions we have worked on illustrate this. Therefore, in measuring dispersion, variance and standard deviation are interchangeable measures, and although we will mainly allude to standard deviation in later work, we could as well use variance instead.

Comovement: Correlation and covariance

In discussing expected value and standard deviation concepts we have focused on a single random variable, *X*, and its probability distribution. We turn next to considering *two* random variables and how these random variables move together: their comovement. The comovement concept is extremely important in finance in the development of a theory of risk.

Correlation coefficient   Comovement refers to the association of movement between two variables. There are, of course, many ways that two variables may be associated, but the simplest form of association is a *linear* (straight line) relationship. The *correlation coefficient* is a statistic that describes how much linear comovement exists between two random variables, say X_A and X_B:

$$\text{Correlation coefficient between } X_A \text{ and } X_B = \rho_{AB}.$$

The correlation coefficient indicates the degree to which two random variables move together (linearly) and may be positive ($\rho_{AB} > 0$), negative ($\rho_{AB} < 0$) or zero ($\rho_{AB} = 0$). If correlation is *positive*, generally speaking, when X_A values are relatively large, X_B values are also relatively large. The two variables tend to be large at the same time and small at the same time. Rates of return on common stocks are a good example of positively correlated random variables. When rates of return are relatively high on

FIGURE 4–3
Correlation coefficient plots

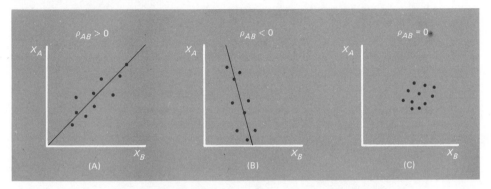

Stock A (say, Ford Motor Co.) they are usually relatively high on Stock B (say, General Electric). If X_A and X_B are positively correlated, then values of X_A and X_B, when plotted against one another, suggest a roughly linear, positively sloping, straight-line graph as shown in Figure 4–3A.

If ρ_{AB} is *negative*, relatively large values of X_A are associated, in general, with relatively small values of X_B. Thus when X_A is high, X_B is low: The variables move opposite to one another. An example of negatively correlated random variables are interest rates and the volume of new housing construction activity. When interest rates climb, building activity declines, and when interest rates go down, building activity increases. An example of negatively correlated variables is shown in Figure 4–3B.

When $\rho_{AB} = 0$, the variables are *uncorrelated*. They are not linearly related, and movements in one variable appear unrelated to movements in the other variable. Although some experimenters claim otherwise, sunspot activity and stock-market rates of return are uncorrelated. Uncorrelated variables have a plot as indicated in Figure 4–3C.

The *sign* of the correlation coefficient indicates something about the *direction* of the comovement, whether it is positive or negative. The *absolute value* of the correlation coefficient indicates the *relative strength* of the comovement. The range of values that ρ_{AB} can assume is $-1.0 \le \rho_{AB} \le +1.0$.

That is, ρ_{AB} can be no larger than $+1.0$ and no smaller than -1.0. The closer ρ_{AB} gets to either $+1.0$ or -1.0 the stronger the association between the two variables. When $\rho_{AB} = +1.0$ the variables exhibit *perfect positive* correlation. When $\rho_{AB} = -1.0$ the variables exhibit *perfect negative* correlation. The geometrical meaning of $\rho_{AB} = +1.0$ and $\rho_{AB} = -1.0$ is illustrated in Figure 4–4. When $\rho_{AB} = +1.0$ the straight-line relationship between X_A and X_B observations is such that all X_A and X_B points fall precisely on the line of association (see Figure 4–4B). For variables with

FIGURE 4–4
Geometric meaning of perfect correlation

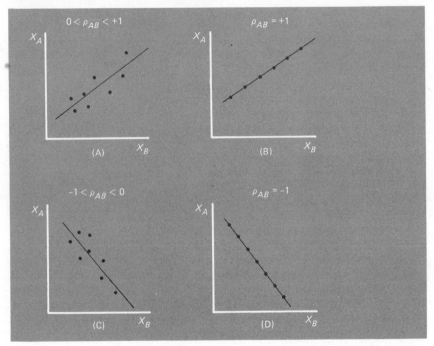

a positive, but less precise association, ρ_{AB} is still positive, but the X_A, X_B points no longer fall precisely on the straight line. This is shown in Figure 4–4A. Thus, $0 \leq \rho_{AB} \leq +1.0$ indicates a positive relationship, but not a perfect one. Similarly, when $-1 < \rho_{AB} < 0$, we say that the two random variables are negatively correlated, but not perfectly so, and when $\rho_{AB} = -1$ the X_A, X_B points fall precisely on a negatively sloping straight line. Such instances are illustrated in Figure 4–4D and 4–4C, respectively.

Covariance   Covariance is also a measure of comovement. As its name indicates, covariance indicates how two variables covary. However, covariance is a more inclusive measure of comovement than correlation:

$$\text{Covariance between } X_A \text{ and } X_B = \text{Cov}_{AB} = \rho_{AB}\sigma_A\sigma_B$$

Thus, in addition to accounting for the direction of the relationship and the strength of the relationship between variables A and B (indicated by ρ), covariance also reflects something about the dispersion of each variable (indicated by σ_A and σ_B).

We will see below that covariance is an extremely important concept in finance. It is associated with a particular formulation of risk, and the concept will be used repetitively in the remainder of the text. If the correlation between the two example prospects A and B previously discussed were +0.8 (recall that $\sigma_A = 4.5$ percent and $\sigma_B = 12.7$ percent), the covariance between rates of return on the two prospects would be: $\text{Cov}_{AB} = (0.8)(4.5)(12.7) = 45.7$. We'll return to covariance in developing the notion of risk below.

FINANCIAL RISK CONCEPTS

We are now ready to apply these probability-based ideas to a consideration of risk. We will see that there are two main risk concepts in corporation finance, one relating to investor's total risk and the other relating to the risk involved in financial management decisions made by the firm on behalf of its investors. We will define these below as *total risk* and *financial management risk,* respectively.

Total risk

Standard deviation plays an important role in finance because of its association with a particular kind of risk. Specifically, standard deviation[6] is associated with a concept called "total" risk or "portfolio" risk.

Other things equal, investors prefer for their investments to have as little risk as possible in them. Faced with two investments that are equal in all other respects (such as the same expected return), a rational investor is presumed to prefer the less risky alternative. He is *risk averse.*

Consider an investor whose total wealth is committed to one asset, say some shares of one common stock. He knows that the rate of return on his investment, X, is a random variable with a set of possible outcomes, X_i, with probabilities associated with these outcomes, p_i. The investor's expected return on his total wealth is

$$\mu = \sum_{i=1}^{N} p_i X_i$$

Now, finance asserts that the "total" risk this investor faces is determined by the dispersion in the distribution of rates of return of his total wealth, and that dispersion is adequately portrayed by the standard deviation. Recall that:

$$\sigma = \sqrt{\sum_{i=1}^{N} p_i (X_i - \mu)^2}$$

---

[6] We use the standard deviation to develop this section, but the discussion and conclusions also apply to variance.

Since the investor has all of his wealth tied up in one asset, the standard deviation of rate of return of that one asset represents his total risk.

Typically, however, an investor's wealth is not all lumped into one asset. Investors are observed to spread their investments over several assets. In short, they *diversify* their investments. To keep the example simple, suppose the total wealth of an investor is spread across two assets, both stocks: Stock A and Stock B. The rate of return on Stock A, X_A, is a random variable with outcomes, X_{Ai}, and associated probabilities, p_{Ai}. Similarly, for Stock B, the rate of return, X_B, is a random variable with outcomes, X_{Bi}, and associated probabilities, p_{Bi}. The expected rates of return for the two stocks are:

$$\mu_A = \sum_{i=1}^{N} p_{Ai} X_{Ai}$$

$$\mu_B = \sum_{i=1}^{N} p_{Bi} X_{Bi}$$

and the standard deviations of rate of return are:

$$\sigma_A = \sqrt{\sum_{i=1}^{N} p_{Ai}(X_{Ai} - \mu_A)^2}$$

$$\sigma_B = \sqrt{\sum_{i=1}^{N} p_{Bi}(X_{Bi} - \mu_B)^2}$$

Now if the investor puts part of his money in Stock A (fraction W_A) and part in Stock B (fraction W_B),[7] what would be the expected rate of return and standard deviation of rate of return on the investor's *total* investment or wealth?

Notice first that the investor has a portfolio or group of stocks. What we're asking is equivalent to asking what are the expected rate of return and standard deviation of rate of return on the investor's portfolio? The portfolio is the investor's entire wealth, which in this example is committed to some combination of two stocks. Let's define expected rate of return on the *portfolio* as μ_P and the standard deviation of the rate of return on the *portfolio* as σ_P. For the portfolio expected rate of return:

$$\mu_P = W_A \mu_A + W_B \mu_B \tag{4-4}$$

That is, the expected rate of return on the portfolio (of total wealth) is the weighted average of the expected rates of return of the two stocks that make up the portfolio. The portfolio's expected rate of return is thus a function of the expected rates of return of the two stocks (μ_A and μ_B) and the proportion's of wealth committed to each stock (W_A and W_B).

The standard deviation of portfolio rate of return, σ_P, is:

$$\sigma_P = \sqrt{W_A^2 \sigma_A^2 + W_B^2 \sigma_B^2 + 2W_A W_B \text{Cov}_{AB}} \tag{4-5}$$

The standard deviation of the portfolio rate of return is the square root of the sum of the weighted variances of the two stocks plus twice the weighted covariance. Recall that Cov_{AB} equals $\rho_{AB}\sigma_A\sigma_B$. Therefore

---

[7] Since all of the investor's wealth is put in the two stocks, $W_A + W_B = 1$.

$$\sigma_P = \sqrt{W_A^2\sigma_A^2 + W_B^2\sigma_B^2 + 2W_AW_B\rho_{AB}\sigma_A\sigma_B} \qquad (4\text{-}6)$$

This equation looks pretty formidable, but some simple examples will show that it is manageable.

Suppose an investor has decided to place all of his wealth into two stocks, *A* and *B*, that have the following summary information:

Stock	μ (percent)	σ (percent)	ρ
A..................	20	10	
			+0.6
B..................	10	5	

Now suppose an investor puts 50 percent of his wealth in stock *A* ($W_A =$ 0.50) and 50 percent in stock *B* ($W_B = 0.50$). We can now determine the expected rate of return and standard deviation of rate of return of the *portfolio:*

$$\mu_P = (0.5)(20) + (0.5)(10) = 15 \text{ percent}$$

$$\begin{aligned}\sigma_P &= \sqrt{(0.5)^2(10)^2 + (0.5)^2(5)^2 + 2(0.5)(0.5)(0.6)(10)(5)}\\ &= \sqrt{25.0 + 6.25 + 15.0} = \sqrt{46.25}\\ &= 6.8 \text{ percent}\end{aligned}$$

By constructing a portfolio composed of 50 percent of Stock *A* and 50 percent of Stock *B* the resultant portfolio expected rate of return is 15 percent and the portfolio standard deviation of rate of return is 6.8 percent. Choosing different values of W_A and W_B leads to different μ_P and σ_P results. As W_A ranges from its lower limit of zero to its upper limit of one, μ_P and σ_P both change. For the example problem:

W_A	W_B	μ_P (percent)	σ_P (percent)
0.....................	1.00	10.0	5.0
0.25..................	0.75	12.5	5.6
0.50..................	0.50	15.0	6.8
0.75..................	0.25	17.5	8.3
1.00	0	20.0	10.0

The point is, as the portfolio weights are changed the portfolio's expected return and standard deviation also change. Figure 4–5 shows all possible μ_P and σ_P results for portfolios composed of these two stocks.

It's worth reemphasizing that σ_P, the portfolio standard deviation of rate of return, is assumed to be an adequate measure of *total* risk for investors. Consequently, the larger σ_P the riskier an investor's portfolio. Other things equal, investors will prefer portfolios with low σ_P values.

To acquire such portfolios, however, the investor must accept a lower expected return, μ_P. This is what is meant by a risk-return *tradeoff*. To procure a larger expected return an investor must expose himself to a larger risk. Looking again at Figure 4–5 indicates this is so. Higher expected rates of return, μ_P, are associated with higher values of risk, σ_P, and similarly, lower expected rates of return are associated with lower values of risk. Consequently, to obtain a high expected rate of return an investor must expose himself to greater risk. Also, an investor

FIGURE 4–5
Risk-return tradeoff

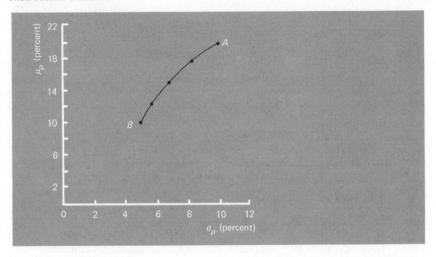

who attempts to construct a portfolio with a low degree of risk will have a low expected rate of return.

Well-diversified portfolios

In the previous section we developed portfolio risk (σ_P) and return (μ_P) measures for portfolios with two assets. Obviously, most investors own more than two assets, and we should be able to expand our definitions of μ_P and σ_P to account for this. Unfortunately, the definitions get rather cumbersome. For *three* assets (A, B, and C):

$$\mu_P = W_A\mu_A + W_B\mu_B + W_C\mu_C \tag{4-7}$$

$$\sigma_P = \sqrt{W_A^2\sigma_A^2 + W_B^2\sigma_B^2 + W_C^2\sigma_C^2 + 2W_AW_B\text{Cov}_{AB} + 2W_AW_C\text{Cov}_{AC} + 2W_BW_C\text{Cov}_{BC}} \tag{4-8}$$

The subscripts refer to the three assets and the definitions are intuitive expansions of Equations (4–4) and (4–5). The portfolio expected return, μ_P, is now the weighted average of the expected return of the three assets. Portfolio standard deviation, σ_P, is the square root of the sum of the weighted variances and covariances of the three assets. Since there are three assets there are three covariance terms, one for each pair of assets.

This situation is substantially more complicated than with only two assets, and for *many* assets the calculation formula gets extremely cumbersome. In addition, most investors do own many assets rather than two or three. They own many assets because of the appeal of diversification. Diversification refers to spreading one's wealth across many assets, and most investors are observed to do this. Very few people are willing to risk putting all their eggs in one basket. Rather than develop cumbersome expressions for μ_P and σ_P for these more realistic examples, finance theory takes a simplified view of the world and says that the average investor's expected rate of return and standard deviation of rate of return may be expressed in terms of a general wealth or *market index*.

X_m = Rate of return on a market index of wealth (such as the Dow Jones Industrial Average), a random variable with outcomes X_{mi} and associated probabilities p_{mi}

$$\mu_m = \text{Expected market return}$$

$$\sigma_m = \text{Standard deviation of market return}$$

This simplification obviously presumes several things. It presumes that investors hold well-diversified portfolios (in the Dow Jones Average case, all the stocks used in that particular stock index) and it presumes that the index is general enough to represent all kinds of assets. Both of these assumptions are gross oversimplifications, yet they are not so wild as to lead to conclusions about investor behavior that are greatly at odds with observed behavior. Investors do appear to hold very well-diversified wealth portfolios including stocks, bonds, real estate, furniture, cars, jewelry, etc., and the choice of an index can always be made that is roughly consistent with these holdings. Moreover, this simplification of assuming that an investor's expected rate of return and standard deviation of rate of return can be roughly equated with μ_m and σ_m, respectively, permits us to make very powerful statements regarding the risk involved in the firm's financial management decisions. We turn to this task now.

Covariance as a measure of financial management risk

The standard deviation of rate of return on an investor's portfolio of total wealth is the appropriate measure of total risk for investors. However, portfolios are composed of a group of individual assets. How do we measure the risk associated with a single asset within the portfolio? To answer this question we need a few more definitions. Let

$$X_j = \text{Rate of return from owning asset } j$$

$$\mu_j = \text{Expected rate of return on asset } j$$

$$\sigma_j = \text{Standard deviation of rate of return on asset } j$$

Now suppose an investor currently owns a well-diversified portfolio of assets that does not include asset j. Employing our simplification developed above, the expected rate of return and standard deviation of rate of return of the investor's current portfolio are $\mu_p = \mu_m$ and $\sigma_p = \sigma_m$. That is, because the investor's present portfolio is well-diversified, his portfolio expected rate of return equals the expected rate of return on the market index and his portfolio risk equals the risk associated with the market index.

Let us further suppose that the investor is considering including asset j in his portfolio. If he chooses to do this he must specify the portfolio weights for his new portfolio: W_m equals the percent of total wealth in the market index, and W_j equals the percent of total wealth placed in the new asset. Of course, $W_j + W_m = 1.0$. The expected rate of return and standard deviation of rate of return on the investor's *new* portfolio are, respectively:

$$\mu_P' = W_j\mu_j + W_m\mu_m \tag{4-9}$$

and

$$\sigma_P' = \sqrt{W_j^2\sigma_j^2 + W_m^2\sigma_m^2 + 2W_jW_m\rho_{jm}\sigma_j\sigma_m} \tag{4-10}$$

This formulation is nothing new. Both the new expected return, μ_P', and the new standard deviation of return, σ_P', are just like our previous Equations (4–4) and (4–6). The primary difference is that the investor's well-diversified holdings are succinctly expressed by the market index. Now, a basic tenet of a well-diversified holding is that no one risky asset comprises a large part of the investor's portfolio. Consequently, the portfolio weight for the new asset, W_j, should be relatively small compared to W_m. At this point we're ready for an example to illustrate the main point: *The new asset's contribution to portfolio risk lies not in the degree of dispersion of rates of return of the new asset, but rather in the covariability of the rates of return of the new asset with the market index.* That is, the risk associated with asset j is measured by its covariance with the market index rather than its own variance. Consider the following example:

$$\mu_j = 15\% \qquad \mu_m = 10\%$$
$$\sigma_j = 30\% \qquad \sigma_m = 20\% \qquad \rho_{jm} = +0.8$$
$$W_j = 0.10 \qquad W_m = 0.90$$

$$\mu_P' = (0.10)(15) + (0.90)(10) = 10.5 \text{ percent}$$

and

$$\sigma_P' = \sqrt{(0.10)^2(30)^2 + (0.90)^2(20)^2 + 2(0.10)(0.90)(0.8)(30)(20)}$$
$$= \sqrt{9.0 + 324.0 + 86.4}$$
$$= \sqrt{419.4}$$
$$= 20.5 \text{ percent}$$

The calculation of interest is σ_p', and the primary point the calculation shows is the relative contributions to total portfolio risk made by the addition of a single new asset. The weighted variance term $(W_j^2\sigma_j^2)$ is inconsequentially small (9.0) and effectively contributes nothing to portfolio risk (σ_p'). This is because the weight of the new asset is small (0.10 in the example), and when squared (0.01 in the example) it becomes even smaller. Nor are these results peculiar to the example chosen. So long as portfolios are well-diversified, an individual asset's weight will be small, and this smallness will be exaggerated by the squaring process. In fact, the value of W_j in the example is very large relative to what it would normally be. That is, very few investors are willing to commit even 10 percent of their wealth to one asset. More common values would probably be 0.01 or 0.02 or thereabouts.

On the other hand, the covariance term in the equation did contribute significantly to portfolio risk. The covariance term, 86.4, is almost ten times as large as the variance term. Of course there are some instances where the covariance term may also be small. Recall that covariance equals $\rho_{jm}\sigma_j\sigma_m$. Obviously the correlation coefficient between the asset's returns and the market's returns strongly influences covariance. If ρ_{jm} is relatively small, the covariance is correspondingly small. If ρ_{jm} is *negative*, the covariance term is negative and the covariance is subtractive in Equation (4–10). Thus, covariance may either have large or small positive effects on portfolio risk, or large or small negative effects or a zero effect, depending on the correlation coefficient. But in any event, it is *only* covariance of the asset's returns with the market index that substantially affects portfolio risk. The asset's own variance (σ_j^2) is *always* insignificant as long as the squared weight (W_j^2) is small.

The conclusion of this analysis is that for individual components of an investor's portfolio, the relevant measure of risk is not the component's variance (or standard deviation) but its covariance with some general wealth or market index. That is, the contribution of the component to total (portfolio) risk is through the covariance of the component's returns with the "market's" returns. We have only illustrated and not attempted to formally prove this conclusion because of the elementary nature of this text. But this conclusion is an extremely important finding in finance.

Beta as a measure of covariance

We have now seen that covariance is the appropriate measure of financial management risk. However, covariance is not a very intuitive concept. The notion of a covariance of 40, for example, lacks meaning to most people. Fortunately, we can relate covariance to an equivalent concept that does have some intuitive meaning. This is done through the *beta* concept. The beta of a risky asset is defined as the covariance of the rates of return of that asset with the market index divided by the variance of the market index rates of return:

$$\text{Beta of asset } j = \beta_j = \frac{\text{Cov}_{jm}}{\sigma_m^2} \qquad (4-11)$$

Notice that beta is directly related to covariance; the larger Cov_{jm} is, the larger β_j will be. Beta relates the asset's covariance to the variance of the market index and is a kind of *relative* covariance. Beta also has a strong intuitive meaning: β_j expresses the risk of asset j in terms of the sensitivity of asset j's rates of return *relative* to the market's rates of return. This can be graphically shown by Figure 4–6.

Figure 4–6 depicts a straight-line relationship between the rate of return on the market index, R_m, and the rate of return on asset j, R_j. This straight-line relationship means that as R_m changes, R_j also changes and emphasizes the comovement or association between R_j and R_m that lies at the heart of the covariance and beta concepts. Figure 4–6 also geo-

FIGURE 4–6
Graphical representation of β_j

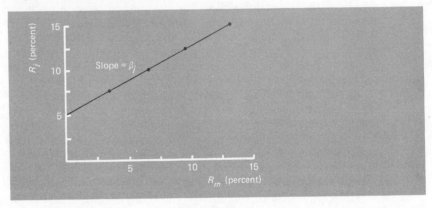

metrically depicts β_j: Beta is the slope of the straight line that relates R_j and R_m:[8]

$$R_j = \alpha + \beta_j R_m \qquad (4\text{--}12)$$

where

α = intercept of the straight line and β_j = slope of the straight line.

Beta thus captures the relevant covariance risk concept by relating the rate of return on an asset to the market index rate of return. The greater an asset's beta, the greater its financial management risk. Figure 4–7 shows beta graphs for three different assets: A, B, and C. Asset A is the riskiest of the three since its slope is the greatest. This means that as the market index rate of return, R_m, changes, R_A will change more than either R_B or R_C. Since $\beta_A = 2.0$, $\beta_B = 1.5$, and $\beta_C = 0.5$, a 1-percent fluctuation in R_M will cause a 2-percent change in R_A, a 1.5-percent change in R_B, and only a 0.5-percent change in R_C. R_A is, therefore, more sensitive to R_m fluctuations; R_A has a higher covariance with R_m than either R_B

---

[8] This is actually a simplification of the linear relationship between R_j and R_m. In reality, the points will not fall directly on the straight line, which requires (4–12) to have an error term, u: $R_j = \alpha + \beta_j R_m + u$.

FIGURE 4–7
Comparison of betas

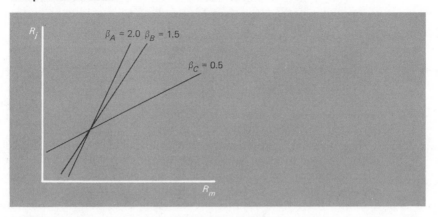

or R_C. Similarly, asset C is the least risky of the three assets whose returns are depicted in Figure 4–7 because its β is lowest.

Financial theory asserts that there is a linear relationship between an asset's risk and its required rate of return. That is, there is a linear risk-return tradeoff. The risk associated with an asset (asset $_j$) is represented by β_j and the required or expected rate of return is represented by μ_j. This linear risk-return tradeoff is shown in Figure 4–8. The expected return of an asset is shown as being linearly related to its risk, and if an investor seeks a relatively high rate of return asset (such as asset A from Figure 4–7) he must expose himself to more risk. Conversely, if an investor seeks a relatively low risk asset (such as C) he will expect a lower rate of return. Figure 4–8 describes the tradeoff between risk and return.

Figure 4–8 also shows that an important benchmark for betas is 1.0,

FIGURE 4–8
Linear risk-return tradeoff

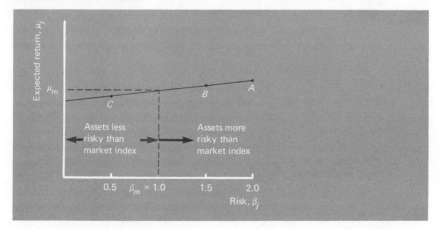

which is the beta for the market index. Any asset whose beta is greater than 1.0 (such as A and B) is said to be riskier than the market, and any asset whose beta is less than 1.0 (such as C) is said to be less risky than the market. This benchmark provides some relative meaning to the beta risk concept.

The notion that beta describes the risk of an asset comes from the development of the covariance idea. Given that investors hold diversified portfolios, the risk associated with an asset is large when the comovement—measured by beta—of the asset's return and the market index returns is large. Assets with low betas have less risk because their returns are only loosely related to an investor's other holdings.

The firm makes financial management decisions that affect only that portion of the investor's wealth entrusted to the firm. Consequently, the firm's financial management decisions contribute to an investor's total risk only to the extent that the rates of return, resulting from the firm's actions covary with the rates of return of an investor's current holdings, which are presumed to be represented by a market index. For example, a new investment undertaken by the firm has the effect of adding a new asset to the investor's portfolio, and the relevant measure of risk associated with that investment is the covariance between the rates of return of the investment and a market or wealth index. Similarly, when the firm decides on a financing plan for the investment, the relevant measure of risk is also covariance with the market index. Last, when the firm selects a dividend policy, the appropriate measure of risk associated with this selection is covariance of rates of return with the market index.

Because covariance is the appropriate measure of risk associated with all three of the firm's financial management decision areas, we equate covariance with financial management risk. Thus, when the firm makes a financial management decision, the risk involved in that decision emanates from the covariance concept. While the mathematics may appear difficult, the conclusion of covariance importance is significant purely in a qualitative sense. What the "covariance equals risk" finding for financial management decisions emphasizes is that the risk in such decisions cannot be determined by considering the decision in isolation. The comovement of the rates of return associated with the decision with the "market's" returns is the crucial thing.

Risk of failure

We have emphasized that risk can be equated with the covariance (beta) concept. However, there is one dimension of risk that covariance does not capture: the risk of default or failure. For the firm as a unit, the risk of default refers to the firm not being able to meet its obligations as they become due and going bankrupt. For an individual asset we might describe default risk as the risk that the profitability of the asset is below some specified critical level. In either case we can describe default risk by a probability statement:

$$\text{Prob}(x < x_c) = p_c \qquad (4\text{--}13)$$

where

x = profitability outcome, x_c = profitability failure level, and p_c = probability of failure.

Suppose, for example, that a proposed investment project has a probability function of rate of return as follows:

x_i
(percent) p_i
−10 ....0.2
20 ....0.5
30 ....0.3

Suppose, further, that we define failure here as the situation where the project has a negative rate of return. The probability of failure is $\text{Prob}(x < 0) = 0.2$.

Investors are said to be risk averse and this notion seems to mean more than that they will require large expected rates of return for risky – in the beta sense – investments. Many investors are observed to shy away from investments that are too risky in the risk of failure sense. That is, there are x_c and p_c combinations that will impel investors to reject risky investment proposals. Firms behave similarly. If the consequences (outcomes) of an investment or financing plan are too unfavorable in the risk of failure sense, firms will reject the plan.

While our main emphasis in this book will be on covariability (beta) risk, we must also keep in mind this second dimension of risk, the risk of failure. The risk of failure plays a particularly important role in working capital management (see Chapters 16–18) where the firm must be especially careful to keep enough liquid assets to avoid failure in the short run.

SUMMARY

When investors make an investment they expect to make a rate of return that compensates them for two things: their time value of money and risk exposure. In the previous chapter we investigated time value of money concepts; in this chapter we investigated risk concepts. Risk or uncertainty – using the terms synonymously – is present in almost all financial management decision problems and alludes to the fact that future consequences of present decisions are not known with certainty.

A *probability distribution* is a complete description of all possible outcomes and associated probabilities, but it is usually easier to work with summary features of probability distributions, and we investigated three important such summary features.

1. Central tendency

Central tendency indicates a measure of average outcome. There are several measures of central tendency, but we associated central tendency with *expected value*:

$$\text{Expected value} = \mu = \sum_{i=1}^{N} p_i X_i$$

2. Dispersion

Dispersion indicates scatter or spread in the probability distribution. There are also several measures of dispersion, but we associated dispersion with two related concepts: *variance* and *standard deviation:*

$$\text{Variance} = \sigma^2 = \sum_{i=1}^{N} p_i(X_i - \mu)^2$$

$$\text{Standard deviation} = \sigma = \sqrt{\sum_{i=1}^{N} p_i(X_i - \mu)^2}$$

3. Comovement

Comovement indicates how *two* random variables are related, that is, how they move together. A simple measure of linear comovement is the *correlation coefficient:*

Correlation coefficient between X_A and $X_B = \rho_{AB}$.
If $\rho_{AB} > 0$, X_A and X_B are *positively* correlated.
If $\rho_{AB} < 0$, X_A and X_B are *negatively* correlated.
If $\rho_{AB} = 0$, X_A and X_B are uncorrelated.
The limits of ρ_{AB} are

$$-1.0 < \rho_{AB} < +1.0$$

Covariance is a more inclusive measure of comovement.

$$\text{Covariance between } X_A \text{ and } X_B = \text{Cov}_{AB} = \rho_{AB}\sigma_A\sigma_B$$

The three summary features above play prominent roles in financial risk concepts. *Total* or *portfolio* risk is defined as the standard deviation of the rate of return on an investor's total portfolio of wealth. Since investors usually hold well-diversified portfolios of assets (including stocks, bonds, savings accounts, cars, real estate, furniture, jewelry, etc.), this diversified portfolio is approximated by a wealth or *market index.* The expected rate of return on this market index, μ_m, and the standard deviation of rate of return on this market index, σ_m, are thus approximations of the expected rate of return and the risk associated with average investors' portfolios. μ_m = expected rate of return on well-diversified portfolios, and σ_m = total risk associated with well-diversified portfolios.

For financial management decisions made by the firm the appropriate measure of risk is the covariance of the rates of return associated with these decisions with this market index, Cov_{jm}:

$$\text{Cov}_{jm} = \rho_{jm}\sigma_j\sigma_m$$

A more intuitive measure of covariance is *beta:*

$$\text{Financial management risk} = \beta_j = \frac{\text{Cov}_{jm}}{\sigma_m^2}$$

The beta for the market index is 1.0, and β_j's greater (less) than 1.0 are said to be riskier (less risky) than the market. The qualitative implication of equating financial management risk and beta is that the risk involved in financial management decisions cannot be determined by considering the decision in isolation. Rather, the important risk consideration is the relationship of the decision involved with the "market." This effectively ties the decision back to investors' well-diversified holdings.

Another important risk measure is the risk of failure. This type of risk focuses on outcomes that are very undesirable. The combination of undesirable outcomes and their associated probabilities may lead the firm to reject investment and financing plans that are too risky in the risk of failure sense.

QUESTIONS

1. Define the following (without using equations):
   a. Probability.
   b. Probability distribution.
   c. Expected value.
   d. Variance.
   e. Standard deviation.
   f. Correlation coefficient.
   g. Covariance.
   h. Total or portfolio risk.
   i. Financial management or covariance risk.
   j. Beta.
   k. Risk-return tradeoff.
   l. Failure risk.

2. Some financial analysts argue that investment alternatives whose returns are negatively correlated with market index rates of return are—other things equal—very desirable investments. Explain this idea.

3. Among Anderson Alloys' stockholders are two completely •different investor types: Mr. Bold and Mr. Cautious. Mr. Bold has almost every penny of his wealth (except for a few clothes) invested in Anderson Alloys. Mr. Cautious holds a well-diversified portfolio of assets and consequently has only a small portion of his total wealth invested in Anderson Alloys. Both of these investors are presumed by financial theory to associate the risk involved with holding Anderson stock with the variability of rates of return of the stock, but they are presumed to have different perceptions of the kind of variability that is important.

   Identify risk measures advocated by finance theory for these investors and contrast these risk measures, justifying why each is appropriate for the particular investor.

4. Explain why an investment's covariance with a market index is assumed to be a better measure of the investment's risk than the investment's variance.

5. In what situation would the variance of an individual asset's rates of return be an appropriate measure of the asset's risk?

6. Other things equal—what would be the effect on the beta of the Z Co. stock if:
   a. the variance of the market index rate of return increased?
   b. the standard deviation of rate of return on Z's stock decreased?
   c. the correlation between rates of return of Z stock and the market index increased?

PROBLEMS

1. A firm is considering some investments that offer the following rate of return probability function: (rate of return $= X$)

A		B		C	
X_i (percent)	p_i	X_i (percent)	p_i	X_i (percent)	p_i
−20	0.1	−10	0.4	−30	0.4
0	0.2	40	0.6	10	0.4
10	0.4			50	0.2
20	0.2				
40	0.1				

   a. Find the expected rate of return of each investment.
   b. Find the standard deviation of rate of return of each investment.
   c. Which is most profitable? Explain your answer.
   d. Which is riskiest? Explain your answer.

2. The Ziliox Computer Co. is considering two alternative financing plans to raise capital next year. One plan involves issuing common stock and the other plan involves issuing bonds. The two plans have different effects on the firm's earnings per share. Ziliox's finance staff has determined the following information about its earnings per share under the two alternatives and about the earnings per share of the "market":

	Stock plan	Bond plan	Market
μ	$1.50 per share	$2 per share	$4 per share
σ	$0.25 per share	$1 per share	$1 per share
ρ (with market).....	0.8	0.7	1.0

   Assuming that high earnings per share are good:
   a. Which plan is preferable from the standpoint of expected return?
   b. Which plan involves more risk? Explain your answer.

3. An investor has three securities in which to invest capital: two risky common stocks and a riskless government bond. The investor also estimated the following data:

	Expected rate of return (percent)	Standard deviation of rate of return (percent)
Security 1	6	0
Security 2	10	25
Security 3	15	36

The correlation coefficient between securities is as follows: between 1 and 2, 0; between 1 and 3, 0; and between 2 and 3, 0.8.

Find the expected rate of return and standard deviation of rate of return of portfolios with the following weights:

a. $W_1 = 0, W_2 = 0.5, W_3 = 0.5$
b. $W_1 = 0.6, W_2 = 0, W_3 = 0.4$
c. $W_1 = 0.4, W_2 = 0.3, W_3 = 0.3$

4. You have the opportunity to invest in one of three investment prospects: A, B, or C. You have determined the rate of return, X, of each prospect under the assumptions of a "bad," a "normal," and a "good" economic climate. You have also estimated the probability of each economic climate occurring. A summary of these estimates is shown below along with estimated correlation coefficients, ρ, that describe how the rate of return of each prospect is correlated with "market index" rates of return.

		Rates of return		
Economic climate	Probability	A	B	C
Bad.........................	0.4	−10%	0%	5%
Normal...................	0.5	0	10	7
Good	0.1	200	15	10
ρ..		0.5	0.7	0.8

a. Rank the prospects on the basis of expected rate of return.
b. Rank the prospects on the basis of covariance risk.
c. If you define "failure" as the situation where you realize less than an 8 percent rate of return, rank the prospects on the basis of failure risk.

5. Given the following information regarding the distributions of rates of return of a proposed project and the market index:

p_i	Project rate of return (percent)	Market rate of return (percent)
0.20.....................	−20	0
0.20.....................	30	10
0.20.....................	40	15
0.40.....................	50	20

a. Find the expected rate of return of each.
b. Find the beta of the project if $\rho = 0.97$.

6. Parenteau Optical, Inc., has just completed some financial planning analysis that indicated that the estimated beta on the firm's stock is about 1.8.

   a. Is Parenteau's stock more risky, less risky, or equally risky relative to the market index? Explain your answer.

   b. If the estimate of beta is reasonably accurate and the coming year is a good economic year, would Parenteau's stockholders expect to do better, worse, or about the same as the market index? Explain your answer.

   c. If Parenteau estimates that the correlation between rates of return on its stock and the market is 0.7, and also estimates the distribution of rates of return on the company's stock (ROR) is as shown, what standard deviation of market index rates of return is implied by Parenteau's analysis?

ROR_i (percent)	p_i
0	0.3
10	0.4
20	0.3

7. You have acquired the following information about the rate of return (ROR) of two investment alternatives. In the covariance risk sense, what must the value of ρ_{BM} be to make the two investments equally risky?

A		B	
ROR_i (percent)	p_i	ROR_i (percent)	p_i
20	0.5	0	0.5
40	0.5	60	0.5

   $\rho_{AM} = 0.5$

8. Jay B. Hawk is considering the purchase of a strategically located apartment complex in a midwestern university town. He plans to purchase the property, hold it for one year, and then sell it, hoping for a profit. Hawk feels that his return will depend upon the level of enrollment at the university. If enrollment expands next year, the need for additional housing will increase the demand for his property. Hawk estimates that his rate of return will be directly tied to the student enrollment level. Specifically, he thinks that for every 200 student enrollment increase (decrease) that occurs, he will make (lose) 1 percent in rate of return.

   a. Given the following distribution of possible enrollment changes and their associated probabilities, what expected rate of return should Hawk make on this investment?

Enrollment change	Probability
−2,000	0.10
0	0.10
1,200	0.50
2,000	0.20
4,000	0.10

b. Suppose this investment represents Hawk's total wealth. Calculate the appropriate measure of his total risk.

c. Hawk defines failure as earning a return of less than 3 percent. If he will tolerate at most a 15-percent probability of failure, will this investment be acceptable from a risk of failure standpoint?

9. Rob N. Hood is considering the addition of one new asset to his present portfolio. The latter is fairly well-characterized by the expected return of 10 percent and the standard deviation of 15 percent associated with the market portfolio. The three competing assets he is considering are described as follows:

Surewood Estates is a planned living community complete with a well-stocked hunting preserve. Its expected return, standard deviation, and correlation with the market index are 12 percent, 33 percent, and +0.9, respectively.

The Little John Manufacturing Co. produces plumbing fixtures for recreational vehicles. It has an expected return of 11 percent, a standard deviation of 30 percent, and has a +0.8 correlation with the market index.

Finally, Nottingham Nursing Homes provides custodial care for those in their retirement years. Its expected return, standard deviation, and correlation coefficient are 9 percent, 12 percent, and +1.0, respectively.

Mr. Hood intends to invest 10 percent of his wealth in one of these three alternatives, keeping 90 percent in his current well-diversified portfolio.

a. Calculate portfolio expected rates of return and total risk measures for all three prospective portfolios.

b. Identify best choices assuming Mr. Hood wants to: (1) maximize expected portfolio return, (2) minimize total risk.

c. If Mr. Hood wanted to avoid the calculation of total risk, but still wanted to determine which prospective investment was least risky, what could he have calculated instead?

d. Explain why this alternate calculation suggested in (c) is a legitimate shortcut to determining which asset is least risky.

10. Financial theory asserts that any two assets that have the same risk must have the same expected return, and vice versa. Grube Market Advisors, Ltd., a Kansas City market research firm has lost some of the financial data they recently prepared but can make use of the risk-return idea expressed above to overcome their missing data problem. Fill in the missing elements of the following table, assuming that $\beta_A = 5\beta_C$ and that $\sigma_m = 20$ percent.

Stock	μ_j (percent)	σ_j (percent)	ρ_{jm}	β_j
A...............	18	40	—	—
B...............	—	—	0.5	2.0
C...............	10	20	—	—
D	10	10	0.8	0.4

11. A newly formed company, Bi-Product Utility, Inc., has basically all of its assets, $100 million in two investments. The first is a waste processing plant that uses the refuse and sewage of the city of Ecoburg to produce methane gas. This asset costs $30 million. The second investment is a power generating station that uses methane gas to generate the electricity used by Ecoburg. The power station costs $70 million. For obvious reasons, Bi-Product anticipates that the rate of return on its stock will be primarily influenced by the size of the population of Ecoburg, which will determine how profitable the two investments are. Bi-Product estimates that the rate of return per dollar of investment on the waste processing plant and the power generating station will be 1 percent and 1.5 percent per 100,000 population, respectively. The correlation of rates of return between the two investments is 1.0. Demographic studies indicate that the average population of Ecoburg over the next ten years will have the following distribution.

Average population	Probability
300,000	0.05
400,000	0.2
500,000	0.5
600,000	0.2
700,000	0.05

Calculate expected portfolio rate of return and total risk if:
a. An investor has all of his wealth in Bi-Product stock.
b. An investor is well-diversified and only has 5 percent of his wealth in Bi-Product stock. Assume also that the expected rate of return on the market index is 9 percent, the standard deviation of market index rates of return is 20 percent, and $\rho_{\text{Bi-Product, } m} = 0.5$.

SELECTED BASIC REFERENCES

Francis, J. C., and S. H. Archer. *Portfolio Analysis.* Englewood Cliffs, N.J.: Prentice-Hall, Inc., 1971, chapters 1 and 2.

Modigliani, F., and G. A. Pogue. "An Introduction to Risk and Return," *Financial Analysts Journal* (March – April 1974), pp. 68–80.

Sharpe, W. F. *Portfolio Theory and Capital Markets.* New York: McGraw Hill, 1970, chapters 1, 2, 3 and 4.

SELECTED ADVANCED READINGS

Fama, E. F., and M. H. Miller. *The Theory of Finance*. New York: Holt, Rinehart, Winston, Inc., 1972, chapters 6 and 7.

Lintner, J. "Security Prices, Risk, and Maximal Gains from Diversification," *Journal of Finance* (December 1965), pp. 587–615.

Sharpe, W. F. "Captial Asset Prices: A Theory of Market Equilibrium under Conditions of Risk," *Journal of Finance* (September 1964), pp. 425–42.

VALUATION AND FINANCIAL MANAGEMENT DECISIONS

Once the firm is charged with the goal of maximizing stockholder wealth the obvious question that arises is "How does the firm go about doing this?" That portion of any stockholder's wealth that is currently invested in the common stock of the firm, W_0 (where the zero subscript represents the present time), is equal to the number of shares that stockholder owns times the price per share:

$$W_0 = N \times P_0$$

where

W_0 = current stockholder's wealth in the firm; N = number of shares owned; and P_0 = current price per share in the firm.

Obviously the stockholder's wealth in the firm can be affected by two things: changes in the number of shares that the stockholder owns and changes in the price per share of the stock. We assume in this chapter that the number of shares that the stockholder owns is constant so that the only determinant of that person's wealth in the firm is the stock price.[1] Our emphasis in this chapter then is on the firm's stock price.

To maximize stock price we must first understand what determines stock price. We must decide which variables (factors) influence stock price. The firm must understand what variables are related to its goal (and how) before it can decide how to go about carrying out this goal. In searching for the variables that determine stock price the firm needs to take the perspective of the investor since it is investors who collectively determine the price of the stock. The basic issue then is one of

---

[1] If the firm should arbitrarily change the number of shares the stockholder owns by say, *splitting* the stock or by issuing a stock dividend (see Chapter 11) the price of the stock will adjust proportionately to keep the stockholder's wealth the same. Thus, a 2–1 split would give the stockholders twice as much stock, but each share would only be worth half as much as before the split, other things equal.

valuation: how investors determine the value of the stock. This is the first step in a chain that will tie the firm's goal to the three fundamental financial management decision areas – investment, financing, and dividend policy – that we identified in Chapter 1. As an introduction to evaluating the stock we first briefly look at valuation from a general perspective.

VALUATION CONCEPTS

From a financial viewpoint, the basis for value in *any* asset, whether physical (such as a machine) or financial (such as stock), is the expected future cash benefits that will be paid to the owner of the asset over the asset's life. If you decide to buy a share of stock, for example, what are you willing to pay for it? Traditional theory suggests that the amount you are willing to pay is determined by what you expect to receive in the future in return for "giving up" (paying) the purchase price of the stock. The return that the asset buyer receives encompasses both recapture of the original investment and a return on the investment, and is typically spread out over time. The process of establishing the price of an asset involves estimating these future cash benefits and then discounting them back to the present as described in Chapter 3. A prospective buyer or seller of an asset estimates what the expected future cash benefits will be at each point in the future and then discounts these back to today at an appropriate discount rate. The resultant present value represents the *value* of the asset to the potential buyer or seller. That is, the asset's value is derived from the discounted expected cash flows[2] the asset is expected to earn, and the valuation process is based on the present value techniques we developed in Chapter 3.

$$V_0 = \frac{C_1}{1+k} + \frac{C_2}{(1+k)^2} + \cdots + \frac{C_n}{(1+k)^n} = \sum_{t=1}^{n} \frac{C_t}{(1+k)^t} \qquad (5\text{--}1)$$

where

V_0 = value of asset at time zero; C_t = expected cash flow in period t; k = discount rate; and n = life of the asset.

If, for example, the cash flow from an asset is expected to be \$100/year for ten years and the discount rate is 10 percent:

$$V_0 = \sum_{t=1}^{10} \frac{100}{(1.10)^t} = (100)(ADF_{.10,10}) = (100)(6.145)$$
$$= \$614.50$$

An investor who uses a 10 percent discount rate would value an asset that promised \$100/year for ten years as being "worth" \$614.50. However, an investor with a different discount rate and/or a different opinion

---

[2] The word "expected" in the phrase "expected cash flow" refers to an expected value as defined in Chapter 4. That is, C_t is the expected value of all possible cash flows in period t. We introduce no special mathematical notation to underscore this point, but emphasize that C_t is indeed a mathematical average of the cash flows in period t. We are also careful to use the word "expected" throughout this chapter to remind the reader of this point. A more careful mathematical notation is used in Chapter 9.

of what the future cash payments are would evaluate the asset differently. This conflict leads us to a discussion of *market value*.

Market values

Prospective buyers and sellers individually estimate what an asset's future expected cash flows will be and discount these at their own discount rates to arrive at value (to them) for the asset. To the prospective buyer of the asset, his calculated present value represents the maximum price he would pay to acquire the asset (he would, of course, pay less); to the prospective seller, his calculated present value represents the minimum price at which he would sell the asset (he would, of course, accept a higher price). In well-established markets there are many potential buyers and sellers of the asset, each evaluating the future expected cash flows associated with the asset and discounting these at his own appropriate rate. The result of the interaction between all these buyers and sellers is a kind of concensus price called the *market value* of the asset. This price occurs at the intersection of the demand and supply schedules of potential buyers and sellers. Market value is thus the price at which transactions take place between marginally satisfied buyers and sellers. We simplify this process by referring to such prices as "market values." For financial assets (like many stocks) where there are large numbers of competing buyers and sellers, an individual buyer or seller has little influence on the asset's price and is essentially a "price taker." That is, an individual cannot personally influence the market price of the asset, and if he desires to either buy or sell the asset he must do so at the "given" market price.

Thus, market value stems from the cash flows expected by investors (who, in aggregate, we call the "market") and the discount rate applied to these cash flows. We now turn to applying these general valuation concepts to the firm's financial assets.

COMMON STOCK VALUATION

Common stock is merely a particular kind of asset, so we can evaluate common stock using the general valuation principle discussed above. The first task is to identify what the variables in Equation (5-1) are when the asset is common stock. Let's develop this idea by progressive steps.

One-period valuation model

Suppose an investor plans to buy a share of stock, hold it one year and then sell. How would this investor value the share of stock? What price would that person be willing to pay for it? The cash income the investor will receive from purchasing the stock is the dividend (if any) paid during the year plus the sale price at the end of the year.[3] Adopting valuation Equation (5-1) to this scenario:

$$P_0 = \frac{D_1}{1 + k_e} + \frac{P_1}{1 + k_e} \qquad (5\text{-}2)$$

----

[3] For simplicity we assume the dividend is paid at the *end* of the year.

where

P_0 = current price (or value) of the stock; D_1 = expected dividend in year one; P_1 = expected price of stock at end of year one; and k_e = discount rate.[4]

If, for example, the expected dividend was $0.70 per share, the expected future price was $20 per share and the investor's discount rate was 15 percent, the value of the share to the investor would be:

$$P_0 = \frac{\$0.70}{1.15} + \frac{\$20}{1.15} = \$18$$

By buying the stock for $18 today, and anticipating a $0.70 dividend and a selling price of $20 next year, the investor is expecting to earn the 15 percent rate of return he requires. This shows why the discount rate is often called the *required rate of return*. It's the expected rate of return the investor is requiring on his investment.

Two-period valuation model

Suppose now that the investor plans to hold the stock for *two* years before selling. The expected dividend in the second year is $0.75, the expected price at the end of the second year is $22, and the discount rate is 15 percent. The value of the stock today to the investor would be:

$$P_0 = \frac{D_1}{1 + k_e} + \frac{D_2}{(1 + k_e)^2} + \frac{P_2}{(1 + k_e)^2} \tag{5-3}$$

$$P_0 = \frac{\$0.70}{1.15} + \frac{\$0.75}{(1.15)^2} + \frac{\$22}{(1.15)^2} = \$17.80$$

where

D_2 = dividend expected in year two; and P_2 = price of stock expected at end of year two.

By buying the stock for $17.80, anticipating a $0.70 dividend next year, a $0.75 dividend the following year, and a selling price of $22, the investor is requiring a 15 percent rate of return. Alternatively stated, if the investor's required rate of return is 15 percent, the present value of an expected income stream of $0.70 in year one and $22.75 in year two is $17.80.

n period valuation model

We could slowly add more years to the example, but the general idea should be evident. For an investor who plans to hold the stock for *n* periods and then sell, the value of the stock is:

$$P_0 = \frac{D_1}{1 + k_e} + \frac{D_2}{(1 + k_e)^2} + \cdots + \frac{D_n}{(1 + k_e)^n} + \frac{P_n}{(1 + k_e)^n}$$

$$P_0 = \sum_{t=1}^{n} \frac{D_t}{(1 + k_e)^t} + \frac{P_n}{(1 + k_e)^n} \tag{5-4}$$

---

[4] The e subscript on the discount rate means it is a discount rate for the firm's *equity* (stock).

If, for example, an investor expects a $2 dividend for each of ten years and a selling price of $50 at the end of ten years and the discount rate is 10 percent, the present value of the stock is:

$$P_0 = \sum_{t=1}^{10} \frac{\$2}{(1.10)^t} + \frac{\$50}{(1.10)^{10}} = (\$2)(ADF_{.10,10}) + (\$50)(DF_{.10,10})$$
$$= (\$2)(6.15) + (\$50)(0.386)$$
$$= \$12.30 + \$19.30 = \$31.60$$

Given the expected dividend stream and expected price of $50 in year ten, the current price of the stock to an investor with a 10 percent required rate of return is $31.60.

Dividend valuation model

There is one last generalization to make in deriving a stock valuation formula. Many investors don't contemplate selling their stock in the near future, but are very long-term holders. Abstractly, we can say:[5]

$$P_0 = \sum_{t=1}^{\infty} \frac{D_t}{(1 + k_e)^t} \tag{5-5}$$

Equation (5–5) is a more general form of the stock valuation model. It is often referred to as the *dividend valuation model* because it shows the current value (price) of the stock as being determined by the discounted future expected dividends the firm will pay to its stockholders. Notice the similarity of (5–5) with the general valuation Equation (5–1). The value of the stock is its current *price* (P_0); the expected cash flows to the stockholder are expected future dividends (D_t), and the discount rate applied to the dividends is called the *required rate of return on equity* (k_e). The time duration in (5–5) is $n = \infty$, indicating the firm is a going concern and there is no forseeable termination date on the stock.

The same points about *market value* we discussed earlier in this chapter will hold for common stock valuation. P_0 is the current *market* price of the stock, D_t represents expected dividends in year t, and k_e represents the market's required rate of return.

There are a couple of points about (5–5) that invariably bother students. First is the issue of firms that pay no *current* dividend. Does this mean that the current price of the stock is zero? The answer is no because the current price of the stock depends on *future* expected dividends. In addition, even if the expected dividends in the next 10 or 20 years were zero this doesn't mean $P_0 = 0$. The current price of the stock is determined by expectations of *all* future dividends not just the near ones. Only if a stock were expected never to pay dividends would $P_0 = 0$ in (5–5). A second confusing point is how can valuation equation (5–5) hold for short-term stockholders? That is, how can (5–5) be consistent with Equations (5–2), (5–3), and (5–4)? The stock price at any future time, say n, can be expressed as the sum of dividends from $n + 1$ to ∞. So,

$$P_n = \sum_{t=n+1}^{\infty} \frac{D_t}{(1 + k_e)^t}$$

---

[5] Recall that $n = \infty$ stands for an infinitely long time (see Chapter 3).

When this expression is substituted for P_n in (5–4), (5–4) becomes (5–5). Similarly, P_2 in Equation (5–3) equals

$$\sum_{t=3}^{\infty} \frac{D_t}{(1 + k_e)^t}$$

and (5–3) also becomes (5–5). The same is true for the one-period evaluation model, Equation (5–2). Equations (5–2) through (5–4) are thus all consistent with the dividend valuation model (5–5).

Special cases of common stock valuation

In developing present value techniques in Chapter 3 we saw that in certain instances the present value calculations could be vastly simplified. The dividend valuation equation expresses the current stock price as the present value of the future expected dividends, so some of these same simplifications are possible here.

No growth case Some companies have future dividend patterns that are anticipated to be very stable with little expectations of growth. This implies a *constant* or *no growth* future dividend stream where $D_1 = D_2 \ldots D_\infty = D$. Notice there are two conditions implied here: (1) constant cash flows (2) forever. When these conditions occur, Equation (5–5) mathematically reduces to a much simpler form:

$$P_0 = \frac{D}{k_e} \qquad (5\text{–}6)$$

The current stock price equals the (constant) dividend divided by the required rate of return. If, for example, dividends are expected to be constant at \$1.50 per share forever and the required rate of return on equity is 10 percent, $P_0 = 1.50/0.10 = \$15$ per share. Technically, this simplification of the more complex valuation Equation (5–5) is only valid when the assumptions of constant dividends and an infinite time horizon are both strictly satisfied. Although there are few instances where these two conditions strictly hold, (5–6) is still very useful because it frequently gives good approximations even when the two assumptions are not met. On the other hand, there are many situations where (5–6) is *not* a good approximation of (5–5). In general, as n gets smaller and/or the expected dividend stream departs from constancy, the approximation becomes worse.

Constant growth case Many companies have expected dividend streams that can be roughly described as growing at a constant rate for long periods of time. For these companies (5–5) can be mathematically reduced to:

$$P_0 = \frac{D_1}{k_e - g} \qquad (5\text{–}7)$$

where

D_1 = expected dividend in year one; and g = expected percent growth in dividends (expressed as a fraction).

There are several assumptions imbedded in deriving (5–7) from (5–5).

First, the expected dividend growth is constant from year to year.[6] Second, the constant growth is forever ($n = \infty$), and third, $k_e > g$. If this last condition were not true we could get some nonsense results about P_0 from using (5–7). As with the previous no growth case, at first glance the first two assumptions of the constant growth case may appear unrealistic. But they are only abstractions from reality, and (5–7) is actually an extremely useful valuation formula that affords good approximations in many situations where the assumptions are not strictly met. We will make extensive use of (5–7) in the cost of capital work in Chapter 8. If, for example, the "market" expects a firm to pay a $0.20 dividend next year, anticipates that dividends will grow at 5 percent per year for the forseeable future, and the "market's" required rate of return is 10 percent, the price of the stock is:

$$P_0 = \frac{D_1}{k_e - g} = \frac{\$0.20}{0.10 - 0.05} = \$4$$

Changes in the expected dividend stream and the discount rate

Equation (5–5) shows that the current market price of the firm's common stock (P_0) is determined by the expected dividend payments (D_t) and the discount rate applied to those payments (k_e). Consequently, changes in P_0 are caused by changes in D_t and k_e.[7] As the expected dividend payments increase (decrease), other things equal, P_0 increases (decreases). Conversely, as k_e increases (decreases), other things equal, P_0 decreases (increases). Suppose, for example, a firm is expected to pay a $3.10 per share dividend for the forseeable future and the stock's required rate of return (k_e) is 16 percent. What is the current market price of the stock? Since the problem indicates a constant dividend for a long period of time, Equation (5–6) is appropriate:

$$P_0 = \frac{D}{k_e} = \frac{\$3.10}{0.16} = \$19.38$$

Now suppose that because of financial management decisions the firm makes, investors' expectations change such that the expected dividend is $3.50 (for the forseeable future) and the required rate of return simultaneously increases to 17 percent. Applying (5–6) again, we get

$$P_0 = \frac{D}{k_e} = \frac{\$3.50}{0.17} = \$20.59$$

Before the expected dividends and discount rate changed the market price of the stock was $19.38. After both the expected dividends and discount rate increased, the *net* effect on the market price of the stock was

---

[6] This means $D_t = (1 + g)D_{t-1}$.

[7] By changes in P_0 we actually mean major changes. P_0 fluctuates continually as buyers and sellers transact. The changes we refer to are not these minor fluctuations.

an increase to \$20.59. In this case the increased expected dividends overpowered the increase in k_e, but if k_e had risen to 19 percent while D was rising to \$3.50, the stock price would have dropped to \$18.43. There are many combinations of k_e and expected dividend changes that could occur. In the example above, the two effects were opposing one another. This is a common situation for reasons described below. Occasionally, only one of the two variables may change and there will be no offsetting effect. If the discount rate had stayed at 16 percent in the example while D increased to \$3.50, P_0 would have increased to \$21.85.

Impact of financial management decisions on stock price

Equation (5–5), the dividend valuation model, is very important because it identifies the two variables that the firm should be most concerned with as it makes its financial management decisions. Every decision the firm makes and everything the firm does should be considered from the standpoint of the potential effect on the stock price through Equation (5–5). That is, since the goal of the firm is to maximize

FIGURE 5–1
Effect of the firm's financial management decisions on stock price

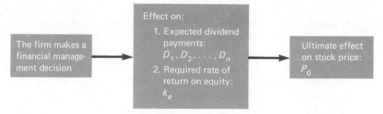

stockholder wealth and since (5–5) shows that stock price and, hence, stockholder wealth is determined by the expected dividend payments and the discount rate applied to these payments, the firm should carefully consider what impact its financial management decisions have on the expected dividend stream and k_e. It is the financial management decisions made by the firm that cause the expected dividend stream and k_e to change and hence cause P_0 to change. The process is shown schematically in Figure 5–1.

The firm makes a financial management decision, and as a result of the decision either the expected dividend stream changes and/or the required rate of return on equity changes, and therefore the stock price changes. Good financial management decisions are those that would be expected to increase P_0, and poor financial management decisions are those that would be expected to decrease P_0.

We have established that making P_0 as large as possible is consistent with the firm's goal and that the variables that determine P_0 are the expected dividend stream and the discount rate investors apply to these payments. We have also asserted that the firm's financial management decisions affect k_e and the expected dividend stream, and consequently affect P_0. In Chapter 1 we identified the three major financial management decision areas as (1) investment decisions, (2) financing decisions, and (3) dividend decisions. Which investments the firm chooses, how it finances these investments, and how dividends are distributed are the main determinants of the stock's discount rate (k_e) and the expected dividend stream and, consequently, P_0. The majority of this book, in fact, is aimed at determining how these decisions affect stock price through the expected dividend stream and the discount rate.

Determinants of expected dividends and the required rate of return on equity

We indicated above that the expected dividend stream and the discount rate were determined by the financial management decisions taken by the firm. In this section we investigate this idea in more detail. In general, both the expected dividend payments and the discount rate are functions of the risk and return associated with the firm's stock.

Expected dividend stream   In the long run the expected dividend stream is mainly determined by the firm's investment policy. Dividends are paid out of earnings, and the larger the expected earnings are, other things equal, the larger the expected dividend payments will be. The firm's earnings are determined by the profitability of the firm's investments, which depend on how well the firm chooses its investments. But this latter issue – choosing investments – is simply the investment decision aspect of financial management. The chain is complete: The firm makes investment decisions that establish the firm's profitability, and this expected profitability determines the expected dividends anticipated by investors. It's very important to keep in mind the role that expectations play here. The current stock price depends on how the firm's current investment actions affect investors' expectations.

The firm's financing decisions also influence the expected dividend stream. Whether or not the firm uses debt (borrows) and how much debt is used affects the size of the expected earnings and, therefore, the level of expected dividends. The firm's dividend policy – how much of each dollar of earnings to pay out as dividends – also has an effect on the expected dividend stream. There is considerable controversy, however, as to the exact impact that financing and dividend decisions have on the profitability of the firm, and the main determinant of the expected dividend stream is the firm's investment policy.

Required rate of return   The required rate of return on the stock is the rate of return that the "market" requires from holding the stock. It is a discount rate. We saw in Chapters 3 and 4 that investors require compensation for both their time value of money and risk exposure. Worded differently, investors require compensation for the price of time *and* the price of risk. We account for both of these requirements in the discount rate applied to the firm's expected dividends. That is, the discount rate,

k_e, is a function of investors' time value of money and risk attitudes.[8] It merits emphasizing once more that not all investors have the same required rate of return, and we are clearly oversimplifying when we equate k_e with "the" required rate of return. Alternatively, k_e might be called the equilibrium rate of return or the rate of return required by marginal investors.

Riskless rate of return   At the very minimum, investors require a return on their investment that compensates them for their time value of money. If an investor could buy shares of a stock where there were no risk involved, the discount rate for such a stock would be a function only of the time value of money and this rate is called the *risk free* or *riskless* interest rate. This rate is usually associated with U.S. government securities, which are said to be risk free. Actually, even for government securities there is some risk present. *Inflation* risk is present because interest received with certainty sometime in the future may not have the purchasing power it's expected to have. We ignore inflation risk in defining the risk free rate. For a riskless stock, $k_e = i$, where i is this risk free rate, that is, the interest rate on government securities.

Risk premiums   In reality, common stock investments are subject to varying degrees of risk. Expected dividend streams are uncertain because the firm's revenues and expenses are uncertain. Because of this uncertainty, investors require a *risk premium* when they invest in common stock. This risk premium is in the form of a required rate of return in excess of the risk free rate and means that $k_e = i + r$ where r is the risk premium. This premium is a function of the risk in the firm's stock that is relevant to investors' portfolios.

Assuming that investors hold well-diversified portfolios, in Chapter 4 we identified financial management risk with the concept of covariance with a suitable market index. Beta was found to be a good intuitive measure of covariance. We will see in Chapter 8 that

$$k_e = i + a\,\beta_e$$

where

i = risk free interest rate; a = a constant; and β_e = a measure of the covariance between rates of return of the market index and the firm's common stock.

At this stage it is not particularly important as to why or how this definition comes about. The important thing here is that the definition clearly shows k_e as being determined by two things: (1) the risk free interest rate, i, and (2) a term that describes the size of the risk premium. The risk premium on the firm's stock is thus determined by the covariance between rates of return of the market index and the firm's stock. This covariance risk premium is, in turn, determined by the firm's financial management policies. *Business risk* is the covariability caused by

---

[8] Some financial theorists object to the conceptual notion that the discount rate is a function of risk. They prefer to think of discount rates as being only a time value of money concept, and they advocate a different method for incorporating risk into the analysis. We discuss this alternate approach in Chapter 9.

the kinds of investments the firm makes, and *financial risk* is the extra covariability caused by the firm's financing and dividend policies. Business and financial risk interact together to determine β_e. We explore these topics more fully in Chapter 10.

OTHER VALUATION PROCESSES

Because the firm's goal is to maximize stockholder's wealth, our valuation emphasis has been focused on the firm's common stock. However, we can apply the basic valuation concepts introduced at the beginning of this chapter to other financial assets as well. In doing so, we set the stage for the cost of capital work later in the book. The same general ideas of valuation apply here as with common stock.

Bond valuation

More generally, we could call this debt valuation, since the features that distinguish bonds from other forms of debt are primarily nonfinancial in nature. A bond's market value is its current price, and the future cash payments to the bondholders are contractual obligations in the form of interest payments and principal repayments. The bond's discount rate is the market's required rate of return on the bonds. Since bonds have a contractual or "promised" payment stream to the bondholders, there is less risk for a firm's bondholders in comparison to its stockholders.[9] The possibility of bankruptcy causes bondholders to require a risk premium (over the risk free interest rate) to hold bonds that are not absolutely free of default risk. This risk premium causes the required rate of return on the bond to exceed the risk free interest rate. However, the required rate of return on a firm's bonds will always be less than the required rate of return on the firm's stock because the bonds are safer than the stock.[10] The firm's bondholders are always paid before its stockholders. Differences in required rates of return *among* bonds of different companies is caused by differences in default risk.

Adapting the general valuation Equation (5–1) to bonds:

$$B_0 = \frac{F_1}{(1 + k_i)} + \frac{F_2}{(1 + k_i)^2} + \cdots + \frac{F_n}{(1 + k_i)^n} = \sum_{t=1}^{n} \frac{F_t}{(1 + k_i)^t} \qquad (5\text{–}8)$$

where

B_0 = current market price of the bond (recall that the subscript zero refers to *current* time); F_t = expected interest plus principal repayment in year t; k_i = market discount rate applied to expected income flows (F_1, $F_2, \ldots, F_n$) associated with the bond; and n = maturity of bonds (number of periods remaining before retirement of bonds).

If, for example, a \$1,000 face value bond is expected to pay a 6 percent annual interest rate, will be retired in 20 years, and the "market" discounts the income flows associated with the bond at 5 percent, then

---

[9] This presumes the bond is held until its maturity, when the bond is retired. See Chapter 14.

[10] In terms of the symbols we have developed: $i < k_i < k_e$.

$$B_0 = \frac{\$60}{1.05} + \frac{\$60}{(1.05)^2} + \cdots + \frac{\$60}{(1.05)^{20}} + \frac{\$1,000}{(1.05)^{20}}$$

$$B_0 = (\$60)(ADF_{.05,20}) + (\$1,000)(DF_{.05,20})$$
$$= (\$60)(12.462) + (\$1,000)(.377)$$
$$= \$1,124$$

If the bonds were perpetuities ($n = \infty$) and the periodic payment were constant ($F_1 = F_2 \ldots F$), then (5–8) would reduce down to simpler form:

$$B_0 = \frac{F}{k_i} \tag{5–9}$$

This, of course, is analogous to Equation (5–6) in the common stock valuation case. If the bonds paid $60 each year, *forever*, and $k_i = 5$ percent, then

$$B_0 = \frac{\$60}{0.05} = \$1,200$$

The main point is that there is no fundamental difference between this valuation process and the valuation process involved in the firm's stock. Future expected cash flows are discounted at the "market" rate to find current market value. This current market value is a present value.

Preferred stock valuation

Preferred stock is something of a hybrid security with features that are part equity and part debt in nature.[11] Preferred stockholders receive dividends, which are discounted at the required rate of return on the preferred. This discount rate is determined in a manner similar to determining the common stock's discount rate, being a function of the risk free rate of interest and a covariance determined risk premium. However, preferred stock has a preferred or prior claim over the common stock on the firm's income in normal times and on the firm's assets in bankruptcy (hence the name, *preferred* stock). Therefore preferred stock is safer than the common. This is another way of saying there is less covariability between expected market index and preferred stock rates of return. Since a firm's preferred stock is less risky than its common it has a lower required rate of return than the common. But the preferred is riskier than the firm's bonds (the bonds have *first* claim to the firm's income and assets), and the required rate of return on the preferred is therefore greater than that of the bonds.[12]

Adapting valuation Equation (5–1) to preferred stock, we get

$$p_0 = \sum_{t=1}^{n} \frac{d_t}{(1 + k_p)^t} + \frac{p_n}{(1 + k_p)^n} \tag{5–10}$$

where

---

[11] See Chapter 13 for a dicsussion of preferred stock.

[12] That is: $i < k_i < k_p < k_e$.

p_0 = current market price of preferred stock; p_n = redemption price;[13] d_t = expected preferred dividend in year t; k_p = market discount rate applied to expected preferred stock dividends; and n = maturity of preferred stock.

If the preferred has no maturity date ($n = \infty$) and the future dividends are expected to be constant ($d_1 = d_2 \ldots d_n$) then (5–10) reduces to:

$$p_0 = \frac{d}{k_p} \qquad\qquad (5\text{--}11)$$

If, for example, a preferred stock is expected to pay a $7 dividend, the market discount rate is 7 percent, and there is no maturity date, the present value of the preferred stock (its current market value) is:

$$p_0 = \frac{\$7}{0.07} = \$100$$

SUMMARY

Understanding the valuation process is fundamental to appreciating how the firm goes about fulfilling its goal. Valuation is a present value concept that involves estimating future income payments and discounting those payments at a required rate of return. Because the goal of the firm is to maximize stock price we have emphasized the valuation of common stock. The value of the stock may be expressed as a function of the expected future dividends and a discount rate called the required rate of return on equity:

$$P_0 = \sum_{t=1}^{\infty} \frac{D_t}{(1 + k_e)^t}$$

This valuation model is called the *dividend valuation model* and clearly shows how P_0 depends on the expected future dividends and the discount rate applied to these dividends. Changes in these latter two variables cause stock price (and, consequently, stockholder wealth) to change. An increase in expected dividends would cause P_0 to increase and a decrease in expected dividends would cause P_0 to decrease. Likewise, an increase in k_e would cause P_0 to decrease, and a decrease in k_e would cause P_0 to increase.

The financial management decisions that the firm makes determine the risk-return characteristics of the firm, which establish the expected dividend stream and k_e and, ultimately, P_0. Thus, the firm should strive to make those financial management decisions that will have a positive effect on P_0 via the expected dividend stream and k_e. That is, the firm should attempt to develop financial management policies that are consistent with investor preferences.

QUESTIONS

1. According to valuation theory, what general factors determine stock price?

---

[13] Actually preferred stock usually has no maturity date, and the use of p_n in (5–10) implies either an expected future call or sale date. See Chapter 13 for a more thorough discussion.

2. Briefly explain the following terms and phrases:
   a. Price taker.
   b. Market value.
   c. Dividend valuation model.
   d. Required rate of return.
   e. Riskless rate of return.
   f. Risk premium.

3. Other things equal, what would be the qualitative effect on the stock price of the XYZ Co. if (explain your answer):
   a. The firm's future earnings prospects decline?
   b. The covariance between market index rates of return and XYZ stock rates of return increases?
   c. The correlation between market index rates of return and XYZ stock rates of return decreases?
   d. The standard deviation of XYZ stock's rate of return distribution increases?
   e. The firm's required rate of return on equity increases?

4. Under what conditions could the following valuation models be justifiably used?
   a. $P_0 = D_1/(k_e - g)$
   b. $P_0 = D/k_e$

5. Explain why the required rate of return on common stock for a firm is greater than its required rate of return on preferred stock.

6. "Many stocks do not pay current dividends, therefore it is not valid to evaluate them using the dividend valuation model." Comment on this statement.

7. Suppose that an investor possesses "inside information" (information that the general public does not have) about new investments the firm recently made that will dramatically increase earnings. Use equation (5–5) to explain how knowledge of this information is valuable to the investor.

8. Suppose you own stock in a privately held corporation where there is no public market for the stock and hence no readily observable market value for the stock. How might you go about determining the market value of the stock?

9. While reading the financial pages one morning you notice that Tollefson Citrus, Inc., has just invested heavily in new orchards in a very arid part of Texas where there is also little irrigation water. Tollefson's executives believe the new orchards will eventually be very profitable and will cause the company's earnings to increase substantially in the future. However, the next day you also observe that Tollefson's stock price drops five points in unusually heavy trading. Explain this drop in stock price using the dividend valuation model.

PROBLEMS

1. An asset with an expected life of four years has the following expected cash incomes, C_t:

t	C_t
1	$ 1,000
2	1,000
3	2,000
4	10,000

   Assuming an appropriate discount rate is 15 percent, calculate the asset's theoretical market value.

2. A stock is expected to pay a $0.50 dividend in year one, a $0.75 dividend in year two, and a $1.00 annual dividend thereafter for the foreseeable future. How much would you pay for such a stock if your required rate of return is 12 percent per year?

3. A 10 year, 4-percent, $1,000 bond pays interest semiannually. The first payment is due in six months. What will be the price of the bond if it yields 6 percent compounded semiannually?

4. XYZ Co. has a $1,000 bond that will mature in 20 years. The coupon rate is 8 percent, and the bond pays interest semiannually.
   a. If the market price of the bond is $699, what is its required rate of return?
   b. The ABC Co. also has a $1,000 bond outstanding that matures in 20 years and pays a 10-percent coupon, interest paid semiannually. If this bond is viewed by investors as being equally risky as the XYZ Co. bond, what should the market price of the ABC bond be?
   c. If interest rates stay the same, what should the market prices of the bonds be ten years from now?
   d. If required rates of return for bonds like XYZ and ABC changed to 16 percent compounded semiannually and maturity is 20 years away, what would the current market prices of these bonds be?

5. A common stock is currently expected to pay a constant $2 dividend, and the "market" discounts these future expected dividends at a 10-percent rate.
   a. What is the market value of the stock?
   b. What will be its market value if:
      (1) The dividend expectations change to a constant $2.50 per year and nothing else changes?
      (2) The dividend expectations do not change from $2, but the required rate of return on the stock increases to 12 percent?
      (3) The dividend expectations change to a constant $3 per year and k_e rises to 20 percent?
      (4) k_e remains at 10 percent, but the firm must omit dividends for the next five years? Assume that dividend expectations for years six and later stay at $2 per year.

6. The Stengel Co. has outstanding an issue of common stock, an issue of preferred stock, and an issue of mortgage bonds.

    The company's common stock sells for $50 per share and is expected to pay a dividend next year of $1.60 per share. Investors expect these dividends to grow at an annual rate of 7 percent.

    Stengel's preferred stock was issued in perpetuity and pays an annual dividend of $3. Its current market price is $35.

    Stengel's $1,000 face value mortgage bonds mature in 30 years. They pay on annual interest rate of 9 percent and currently are selling for $1,248.

    a. What implied required rates of return are investors demanding on each of these securities?

    b. From investors' standpoint, which set of securities is the riskiest of the three? Least risky? Explain how you reached your conclusions.

    c. Determine the price of each security if required rates of return increase by 50 percent in each case.

7. Sam Jackson is considering an investment in the common stock of Terrell Telegraph Co., producers of glass insulators for telegraph poles. The company currently pays a dividend of $1.85 at the end of each year, and since the market for its product is limited, Jackson does not expect this dividend to grow. Further, Jackson has determined that, due to his time value of money and the riskiness of this stock, he should require a rate of return of 12 percent per year.

    a. What maximum price would Jackson pay for the stock?

    b. Suppose Jackson buys the stock at the price determined in (a), but after five years decides to sell it. What is the minimum price that he would accept at that time if his expectations and discount rate have not changed?

8. The common stock of Gaumnitz Realty Company is expected to pay a dividend next year of $2.20, and currently sells for $55. If the required rate of return on this investment is 14 percent, what implied growth rate are investors expecting?

9. The M. B. Hay Co. is a conservatively managed company. The expected next period common dividend is $2 per share, expected dividend growth is about 6 percent per year, and the required rate of return on the stock is 9 percent. However, the board of directors, in response to stockholder pressure, replaces the management of the company with a team of recent business school graduates who have been well-trained in finance. This new management team is considering alternate financial policies that would be expected to have results as shown below. Determine the anticipated effect on stock price of each plan and identify the best plan. Explain why the identified plan is best.

    Plan A: Adopt a set of investment opportunities that will increase the expected dividend growth rate to 8 percent and the required rate of return to 10 percent.

Plan B: Adopt a set of investment opportunities that will increase the expected dividend growth rate to 9 percent and the required rate of return to 13 percent.

Plan C: Adopt new investment and financing plans that will reduce the expected dividend growth rate to 5 percent and the required rate of return to 8 percent.

Plan D: Eliminate some relatively unprofitable investments the firm owns, and rearrange the firms capital structure. The result is that the expected dividend growth rate becomes 10 percent and the required rate of return is 14 percent.

SELECTED BASIC REFERENCES

Baumon, W. S. "Investment Returns and Present Value," *Financial Analysts Journal* (November–December 1969), pp. 107–18.

Wendt, P. F. "Current Growth Stock Valuation Methods," *Financial Analysts Journal* (March–April 1965), pp. 3–15.

Williams, J. B. *The Theory of Investment Value*. Cambridge: Harvard University Press, 1938, pp. 55–75.

SELECTED ADVANCED REFERENCES

Gordon, M. J., and E. Shapiro "Capital Equipment Analysis: The Required Rate of Profit," *Management Science* (October 1956), pp. 102–10.

Malkiel, B. G. "Equity Yields, Growth and the Structure of Share Prices," *American Economic Review* (December 1963), pp. 467–94.

Mao, J. C. T. "The Valuation of Growth Stocks: The Investment Opportunities Approach," *Journal of Finance* (March 1966), pp. 95–102.

Miller, M. H., and F. Modigliani "Dividend Policy, Growth, and the Valuation of Shares," *Journal of Business* (October 1961), pp. 411–33.

LONG-TERM INVESTMENTS

6

CAPITAL BUDGETING AND CASH FLOW PRINCIPLES

In this group of chapters we investigate how the firm should make its long-term investment decisions. The general setting for this decision harkens back to the discussion of the goal of the firm: The stockholders have entrusted the firm with their money and they expect the firm to invest this money wisely. It is very important in this section to keep in mind that the firm's investment decisions should be made in a manner that is consistent with the goal of stockholder wealth maximization. Accordingly, just as investors should evaluate the firm's stock through procedures developed in Chapter 5, the firm should evaluate long-term (longer than one year) investment projects through procedures developed in this section's chapters.

NATURE OF LONG-TERM INVESTMENTS

By definition, long-term investments are investments whose expected lives exceed one year. There are many ways to categorize long-term investments, but most may be placed in either one of two categories:

1. Revenue expansion investments.
2. Cost reduction investments.

Revenue expansion investments

The basic feature of revenue expansion proposals is the expected addition to or expansion of the firm's revenues. These projects are expected to bring in new revenue, thereby increasing the firm's revenue. Revenue expansion investments are generally of two types: expansion of present operations and new product line development.

Expanding present operations refers to adding additional capacity to existing product lines. If, for example, a greeting card company increases its plant size to increase its card production capacity, it is expanding its present operations. Development of a new product line is also income expansionary but represents a new kind of production activity within the firm. As an example, if the same greeting card company invests in new plant and equipment to produce candles, which the firm has not manufactured before, this represents new product line development. Similarly, acquisition of another company may represent either expansion of present operations or new product line development, depending on the nature of the acquisition. If the greeting card company buys another greeting card company (and if the government allows the acquisition — see Chapter 21), this also represents expansion of present operations. But a purchase of a candle manufacturer would represent new product development. In either case, the investment is expected to bring in additional revenue to the firm and therefore expand the firm's total revenues.

Cost reduction investments

Cost reduction investments typically add no additional revenues to the firm. As the name implies, the purpose of the investment is to reduce costs. This cost reduction will, of course, eventually show up as increased earnings for the firm, but the firm's revenues will not increase. The most common type of cost reduction investment is the *replacement* proposal. Assets wear out or become outdated, and the firm must continually decide whether to replace them. Frequently, this decision does not affect the firm's revenues, but only involves replacing an old asset with a new asset that has lower operating costs. A decision to replace the printing equipment used in the manufacturing of greeting cards with a newer, more efficient machine represents a cost reduction decision.

Other considerations

A fundamental difference between income expansion and cost reduction investments concerns the relative uncertainty involved in the decisions. Frequently, the revenues and costs associated with an income expansion project are estimated with less certainty than the cost savings associated with a cost reduction investment. This is because the firm often has a better "feel" for potential cost savings because it can examine past production and cost data. It may be particularly hard to estimate revenues and costs for new product line revenue expansion proposals because the investment may be in some area where the firm has absolutely no expertise.

Also, some investments clearly *both* expand income and reduce costs. If, for example, the firm is considering replacing an old machine with a new and bigger machine, there may be both revenue and cost effects. But this and other issues will cause no real problems in the ensuing analysis.

Data requirements

To make long-term investment decisions that are consistent with the firm's goal, the firm must perform three tasks in evaluating a new investment proposal:

1. Estimate cash flows.
2. Estimate a discount rate or cost of capital.
3. Apply a decision rule to determine if an investment is "good" or "bad."

The firm's long-term investment decision is logically a valuation problem, and valuation problems require estimation of cash flows and discount rates, and identification of decision rules that correctly evaluate these cash flows and discount rates. In this chapter we concern ourselves only with the first element: estimating cash flows. The fact that cash flows are usually not known with certainty is an unfortunate and important fact of life, but in developing the principles of cash flow estimation in this chapter we ignore this very important uncertainty concept for awhile. We'll explore the effect of uncertainty on long-term investment decisions in Chapter 9. In the remainder of this chapter we will only be concerned with defining and estimating cash flows.

CASH FLOW AFTER TAX

When the firm makes a long-term investment decision it is performing a valuation of a long-term asset or *project*. Chapter 5 discussed the fact that the basis for financial value in any asset is the income received from ownership of the asset during its life. As we will argue below, the proper income stream for valuing long-term projects is the yearly *cash flow after tax stream* associated with the project.

Cash flow refers to cash revenues minus cash expenses. That is, as opposed to income statement profits, which have noncash charges such as depreciation expenses included, cash flows represent the *cash* transactions associated with a financial management decision. Since taxes are a cash expense, the term *cash flow after tax* specifically indicates it is the cash flow the firm receives or pays out after all cash expenses, including taxes, have been accounted for.

By definition, long-term investment projects last more than one year, and for *each* year there is an expected cash flow after tax associated with the project:

Cash flow after tax in year $t = CFAT_t =$ cash revenues$_t$ − cash expenses$_t$

$$(6-1)$$

That is, the cash flow after tax in year t for the project equals all *cash* revenues associated with the project in year t minus all *cash* expenses (including tax) in year t associated with the project. In some years cash revenues will exceed cash expenses and cash flow after tax will be *positive*. This represents a net cash inflow to the firm in that year. In other years (most typically at time of investment, $t = 0$), cash expenses will exceed cash revenues and cash flow after tax will be *negative*. A negative cash flow after tax represents a cash outflow from the firm in that year. Thus, we have the following cash flow conventions:

When cash revenues$_t$ > cash expenses$_t$, $CFAT_t$ is positive.
When cash revenues$_t$ = cash expenses$_t$, $CFAT_t$ is 0.
When cash revenues$_t$ < cash expenses$_t$, $CFAT_t$ is negative.

Why use cash flows?

There are two compelling reasons for using cash flows in evaluating investment projects as opposed to using income statement type "earnings" flows, which include noncash flows such as depreciation:

1. Cash flows are a theoretically better measure of the net economic benefits or costs associated with a prospective project.
2. Use of cash flows avoids accounting ambiguities.

Regarding the first point, the firm is really interested in estimating the economic value of a proposed investment project. This economic value is related to the economic outflows (costs) and inflows (benefits) associated with the project. Only cash flows describe the cash transactions that the firm will experience if the project is accepted. The firm must pay for a purchased asset with cash, and this cash outlay represents a foregone opportunity to use the cash in other productive economic alternatives. Consequently, the firm should measure the future *net* benefits (revenues minus costs) in cash terms also. Now, if accounting practices were attuned to reporting cash transactions there would be no problem. But standard financial accounting practices are oriented more toward allocating investment costs across useful economic life than in ascribing costs at point of incurrence. Thus, when the firm makes a new investment, traditional accounting procedures spread out the initial investment by capitalizing it over the life of the asset and then reducing future net benefits by subtracting an annual depreciation charge. But this accounting treatment does not reflect the original need for cash at the time of investment, nor does the accounting treatment reflect the actual size of the net cash inflows or outflows in later years. Only cash flows reflect the actual cash transactions associated with the project, and since investment analysis is concerned with the question: Are future economic inflows sufficiently large to warrant the initial investment?, only the cash flow method is appropriate for investment decision analysis.

A related second reason that cash flows are superior to net income flows pertains to accounting ambiguities in determining net income. There are many ways to value inventory, allocate costs, and choose a depreciation schedule to calculate net income, all of which are permissible under generally accepted accounting practices. Thus, different net income numbers could be developed for the same project depending upon the accounting procedures followed. But there is only *one* set of cash flows associated with the project. The firm pays the initial investment and has a single stream of future cash flows. There are far fewer ambiguities in the cash flow stream. This more pragmatic reason reinforces the need to use cash flows rather than ambiguous net income flows.

Determining cash flows after tax

The basic concept in determining cash flow after tax is expressed in the following definition:

$$\text{Cash flow after tax} = \text{Cash flow before tax} - \text{Tax} \qquad (6\text{-}2)$$

Furthermore,

$$\text{Cash flow before tax} = \text{Cash revenues} - \text{Operating cash expenses}$$
$$(6\text{-}3)$$

Operating cash expenses are cash expenses other than tax. Acknowledging that long-term projects last more than one year and that each year has a cash flow:

$$CFAT_t = CFBT_t - \text{Tax}_t \qquad (6\text{-}4)$$

$CFAT_t$ is cash flow after tax in year t, $CFBT_t$ is cash flow before tax in year t, and Tax_t is tax in year t. Equation (6-4) is the foundation for cash flow determination. We first determine cash flows without tax considerations and then deduct tax charges to arrive at cash flows after tax.

Before we turn to actual methods used to calculate $CFBT_t$, Tax_t, and consequently, $CFAT_t$ numbers, the analysis will be easier to understand if we first recognize that the cash flow after tax stream (the totality of yearly $CFAT$ numbers) has three distinct parts:

1. Initial investment.
2. Operating cash flows.
3. Termination cash flows.

The initial investment is an outlay of cash that takes place at $t = 0$. Operating cash flows are cash flows associated with the normal operation of the project that occur after the initial investment from $t = 1$ to the end of the asset's life at $t = n$. Termination cash flows represent the cash flows, if any, that the firm receives upon abandonment of the project at $t = n$.

Initial investment Potentially, the initial investment has several components. Foremost of these is the *gross investment* in the asset, which is its purchase price plus any installation and freight costs. It is this gross investment that provides the basis for depreciation as explained later in this chapter. In addition to gross investment, usually new investment in long-term assets creates the need for increased investment in *net working capital*, which is the difference between current assets and current liabilities. The reason that increased long-term investment causes increased short-term investment is explained in detail in Chapter 12. Any additional net working capital increases are added to gross investment. There may also be *opportunity costs* that should be charged against (added to) the investment. These costs arise because of foregone opportunities the firm may have availed itself of in lieu of making the proposed investment. If, for example, a firm uses some land it owns to store surplus equipment, the company should be aware of the opportunity cost of selling the land or using the land for some other purpose. If there are relevant opportunity costs associated with an investment proposal, they should be properly accounted for.

Tax considerations associated with the initial gross investment are relatively uncomplicated as the major tax consideration for analysis purposes is the investment tax credit. This topic is discussed more fully below in the tax section, but the effect of the investment tax credit is to create a negative income tax, which reduces the after tax cost of purchasing new assets. The investment tax credit is only applied to the gross investment, as defined above.

Finally, there may be initial period cash *inflows* associated with a new investment. Most typically, these result from the sale of older equipment being replaced. This kind of transaction can have complicated tax considerations. The tax calculation is highly dependent on the *adjusted basis*[1] of the asset at time of salvage, and we investigate different adjusted basis–salvage value relationships below in the tax section.

Operating cash flows   Operating cash flows are more difficult to calculate because the tax calculations are more complex. But basically the idea is the same as before: Calculate cash flows before tax, calculate tax payments, and then net the two to get cash flows after tax. In calculating operating *CFAT* numbers a tabular approach is very useful in helping to understand the problem. As an example of this procedure, consider the following calculations associated with year six of a hypothetical investment project:

	(1)	(2)	(3) = (2)–(1)	(4)	(5) = (3)–(4)	(6) = $T \times$ (5)	(7) = (3)–(6)
Year	Cash revenues	Cash expenses	CFBT	Deprecia-tion	Taxable income	Tax*	CFAT
6	$500	$300	$200	$100	$100	$40	$160

* T = tax rate. The example assumes the tax rate is 40 percent, i.e., $T = 0.40$.

This short example illustrates the way operating *CFAT* numbers (in this case *CFAT* in year six) are constructed. First, operating cash expenses are netted from cash revenues to get *CFBT*. Next, depreciation charges (discussed in detail below) are deducted from *CFBT* to arrive at taxable income. Taxable income is the base by which the firm's tax rate is multiplied to determine tax. That is, the estimated tax bill in year six associated with this proposed project ($40) is taxable income ($100) times the tax rate (0.40). The effect of being able to deduct noncash charges (such as depreciation) for tax purposes, is to make taxable income less than *CFBT*. Thus, depreciation deductions shield income from taxation, creating a tax shield. Finally, *CFAT* = *CFBT* − Tax.

Frequently, cash expenses are denoted as *fixed* or *variable* operating costs. Fixed operating costs are those cash expenses that will be unaffected by the project's production levels. On the other hand, variable operating costs are those cash expenses that are directly related to the project's production levels. Consequently, as production levels fluctuate,

---

[1] Adjusted basis is the book value of the asset for tax purposes. This concept is explained more fully in the tax section below.

variable operating costs will also fluctuate, but fixed operating costs will not.

Termination cash flows When an asset's economic life is terminated there is frequently still some value left in the asset. The asset may still be useable in its current form. For example, a pump on a depleted oil well may be useable on another oil well that is not depleted. If the firm transfers the pump and saves the purchase price of another pump or if the firm sells the pump to another firm there is a cash inflow created. In the transfer case this cash inflow is in the form of a cost saving, and in the case of a sale the cash inflow is in the form of a revenue. But in either case there is a salvage $CFBT$ created. Alternatively, if the asset is worn out there may be some *scrap value* associated with it. If, for example, the pump is worn out and beyond repair it may still have value as scrap metal. The sale of the asset as scrap creates a salvage $CFBT$ in the year of abandonment. Additionally, the firm will recover any increased net working capital that was committed to the project in the initial time period.

DEPRECIATION METHODS

Depreciation calculations enter into the investment decision, not because we are interested in the net income stream associated with a project—we are only interested in the $CFAT$ stream—but because depreciation is a deduction from annual operating $CFBT$ to arrive at taxable income. There are two main types of depreciation schedules: straight-line and accelerated. Accelerated depreciation allows higher depreciation in the earlier years of the life of the project and lower depreciation in later years. This causes $CFAT$'s to be higher in the project's early years and lower in later years. Since money has time value, this transfer of $CFAT$ from later years to early years makes projects more desirable. This explains why the tax laws permit accelerated depreciation: to encourage investment. There are several kinds of accelerated depreciation methods in use today, but the most commonly used are the *sum-of-years'-digits* and the *doubling declining balance methods*. In this part of the chapter we will investigate how to calculate a project's depreciation schedule under the following methods:

1. Straight-line depreciation.
2. Sum-of-years'-digits depreciation.
3. Double declining balance depreciation.

In all three cases we are interested in the complete depreciation schedule. That is, we will calculate depreciation for each year of the life of the asset. Regardless of which of these three methods we use, the depreciation in any year, say year t, is:

$$\text{Depreciation}_t = (\text{Depreciation factor}_t)\,(\text{Depreciation base}_t) \quad (6\text{--}5)$$

The subscripts refer to the year, and Equation (6–5) indicates that any year's depreciation deduction equals the depreciation factor for that year times the depreciation base for that year. The depreciation base is the depreciable cost on which depreciation is calculated for year t. It is the foundation or base for making a depreciation deduction in year t. The depreciation factor is the fraction of the depreciation base that converts depreciable cost into a yearly depreciation deduction. The specification of different depreciation factors and bases (described below) provides the distinction among the three depreciation methods. For any chosen method, the enumeration of all calculated yearly depreciations is the depreciation schedule for that method.

Straight-line depreciation

In straight-line depreciation, the depreciation base for *all* years is the original cost of the asset less its estimated salvage value. Both the original cost of the asset and the salvage value are on a before tax basis. In the straight-line method this depreciation base is depreciated in equal yearly amounts, hence the depreciation factor is $1/n$, where n is the number of years over which the asset is depreciated. Therefore:[2]

$$\text{Depreciation}_t = \left(\frac{1}{n}\right) (\text{original cost} - \text{salvage}) \qquad (6\text{--}6)$$

To reemphasize, the depreciation base is original cost less estimated salvage and the depreciation factor is $1/n$. Neither the depreciation base nor the depreciation factor change during the asset's life under the straight-line method so that depreciations for all years are equal. If, for example, an asset with an expected life of five years costs \$55,000 and its estimated salvage value is \$5,000, the depreciation charges are as follows:

Year	Depreciation factor	×	Depreciation base (dollars)	=	Depreciation (dollars)
1	0.2		50,000		10,000
2	0.2		50,000		10,000
3	0.2		50,000		10,000
4	0.2		50,000		10,000
5	0.2		50,000		10,000
					50,000

Sum-of-years'-digits depreciation

In this method the depreciation base in each year is the same as in the straight-line method – original cost less estimated salvage. However, the depreciation factor changes each year. The depreciation factor for

---

[2] Current tax laws permit the firm to ignore for depreciation purposes that portion of the salvage that does not exceed 10 percent of the asset's original cost. Consequently, a more precise definition of depreciation base would replace "salvage" in Equation (6–6) with "excess salvage over 10 percent of original cost." We ignore this refinement in this book.

any year is the number of useful years remaining divided by the sum of the years' digits. Therefore,

$$\text{Depreciation}_t = \left(\frac{y}{\Sigma t}\right) (\text{original cost-salvage}) \qquad (6\text{--}7)$$

where

y = number of years remaining
Σt = sum-of-years'-digits.

By applying this method to the previous example, where original cost = \$55,000, estimated salvage = \$5,000, and life = five years:

Sum-of-years'-digits = 1 + 2 + 3 + 4 + 5 = 15

Year	Depreciation factor	×	Depreciation base (dollars)	=	Depreciation (dollars)
1	$5/15$		50,000		16,667
2	$4/15$		50,000		13,333
3	$3/15$		50,000		10,000
4	$2/15$		50,000		6,667
5	$1/15$		50,000		3,333
					50,000

In comparison to the straight-line method, the same \$50,000 of original cost less salvage is recovered, but it is recovered more quickly by accelerating depreciation charges in the early years of the project's life. This latter point is the essence of accelerated depreciation.

Double declining balance depreciation

The double declining balance method is also called the *twice straight-line* method. The double declining balance depreciation factor for any year is always two times, or double, the straight-line depreciation factor. Since the straight-line depreciation factor is $1/n$, the double declining balance depreciation factor is $2/n$. In the example above, where the project has an estimated life of five years, the depreciation factor in each year is $(2/5) = 0.4$. Unlike the other two methods above, the depreciation base in this method (as its name implies) declines each year. The depreciation base in each year is the asset's adjusted basis (original cost less accumulated depreciation)[3] at the end of the previous year. The asset's original cost rather than cost minus salvage is the depreciation base for the first year, and the depreciation base is reduced in each subsequent year by the amount of the depreciation taken the previous year. Each

---

[3] Notice that salvage is not deducted from original cost as in the other two methods.

year's depreciation charge is thus the product of the constant depreciation factor and the declining depreciation base:

$$\text{Depreciation}_t = \left(\frac{2}{n}\right)(\text{Adjusted basis}_{t-1}) \qquad (6-8)$$

By applying this method to the same example where original cost is $55,000, salvage value is $5,000 and the project life is estimated to be five years, the depreciation factor each year is 0.4, and the depreciation schedule is determined as follows:

Year	Depreciation factor	×	Depreciation base (dollars)	=	Depreciation (dollars)
1	0.4		55,000		22,000
2	0.4		33,000		13,200
3	0.4		19,800		7,920
4	0.4		11,880		4,752
5	0.4		7,128		2,128*
					50,000

* Depreciation in year 5 equals $7,128 − $5,000 = $2,128, rather than $7,128 × 0.4 = $2,851. This is because the firm is not permitted to depreciate the asset below its salvage value ($5,000).

The first year's depreciation base is the $55,000 original cost (there is no salvage netting as in the other two methods), and the first year's depreciation is therefore $22,000. This depreciation charge reduced the next year's depreciation base to $33,000, which consequently reduces the depreciation charge for the next year to $13,000, and so on. Notice that the depreciation in the last year is not determined using the depreciation Equation (6–8). No matter what depreciation method the firm chooses, it may not depreciate the asset below salvage value. The firm may only take $2,128 depreciation the last year.

When an asset has no estimated salvage value the double declining balance method will be unable to completely recover the original cost of the asset. This is because the yearly depreciation is based on a fraction of the declining book value of the asset. To allow the firm to completely deduct all the depreciation charges legally allowed, tax laws permit the firm to "switch" from the double declining balance method to the straight-line method whenever the straight-line depreciation is greater than the calculated double declining balance depreciations.[4] The alternative straight-line depreciation charge is made each year on the basis of the *remaining* depreciation base and the *remaining* asset life. Suppose that the example five-year, $55,000 asset had no estimated salvage.

---

[4] Under a new, more liberal, set of depreciation guidelines called the *asset depreciation range* system, the firm has more latitude in changing depreciation methods. Under this system, salvage value is also ignored in Equations (6–6) and (6–7) for calculating depreciation charges.

Double declining balance depreciation schedules *without* and *with* switching are as follows:

Year	Double declining balance depreciation	
	Without switching (dollars)	With switching (dollars)
1	22,000	22,000
2	13,200	13,200
3	7,920	7,920
4	4,752	5,940
5	2,851	5,940
	50,723	55,000

In the example the permissible straight-line depreciation, if the switch were made in year two, would be $\frac{1}{4} \times \$33,000 = \$8,250$. The double declining balance depreciation is \$13,200 and so no switch would be made. In year three, straight-line depreciation would be $\frac{1}{3} \times \$19,800 = \$6,600$, which is less than \$7,920, so the firm would not switch. But in year four, straight-line depreciation would be $\frac{1}{2} \times \$11,880 = \$5,940$, which is more than \$4,752, so the switch would be made, and depreciation would be \$5,940 for each of the last two years.

TAX CONSIDERATIONS

Tax considerations of capital investment decisions are both very important and very complex. To complicate matters, tax laws and tax rates periodically change, and procedures that are relevant in one year become no longer relevant. Moreover, some industries have specialized tax aspects associated with the kind of assets companies within that industry regularly invest in. Mining companies, for example, are permitted depletion allowances on the mineral revenues they produce while non-extractive industries have no such allowances. Because of the enormous complexity and diversity of tax laws and because the tax laws change so frequently, we only investigate very general aspects of tax considerations. Mainly, we will look at only those tax considerations that have not been changed frequently and are applicable to almost all U.S. corporations. It's worth reemphasizing that the tax considerations in this chapter are only the main ideas and there are many complexities we have omitted.

Investment tax credit

Since the early 1960s the *investment tax credit* has been used to encourage investment by U.S. corporations. The investment tax credit allows a firm to reduce its federal tax liability in any year by a stated fraction of the new capital investment the company makes in that year. As with other tax matters Congress may change the investment tax credit.

If the government wishes to stimulate corporate capital spending it will encourage Congress to allow firms to take investment tax credits, and if the government wishes to cool off the economy by discouraging excess capital spending it will attempt to eliminate the investment tax credit by encouraging Congress to suspend it.

In recent years the United States has had a 10-percent investment tax credit. Under a 10-percent investment tax credit, if the firm makes a new gross investment of $10,000, the firm receives a $1,000 (0.10 × $10,000) tax credit against its corporate tax liability for the year.[5] Actually, this is an oversimplification, as the qualifying base the 10-percent credit is applied to depends on the estimated life of the asset. If the estimated life is less than three years, none of the cost qualifies; one third of the cost ($3,333 in the example above) qualifies if estimated life is between three and five years (leading to a tax credit of 0.10 × $3,333 = $333 in the example); two thirds of the cost qualifies if estimated life is between five and seven years; and the entire cost qualifies if estimated life is seven years or more. For our purposes we will ignore these refinements and assume that when the investment tax credit rule is in effect, the qualifying investment base is 100 percent of cost regardless of the asset's estimated life.

Unlike depreciation, which is an offset (deduction) against income prior to calculating taxes, the investment tax credit is a *direct* offset against the firm's tax liability. So the investment credit reduces the after tax cost of investing in an asset, and this tax subsidy from the government makes investments financially more attractive to firms.

Taxing operating cash flows

We have previously discussed how operating cash flows after tax are determined. Operating cash flows represent *ordinary income*, that is, income that the firm receives from its usual business operations. Ordinary income is taxed at the firm's *ordinary tax rate*. The present corporate ordinary income tax rate schedule for the firm as a whole is:

Level of ordinary taxable income	Tax rate (percent)
0 to $25,000	20
$25,000 to $50,000	22
Over $50,000	48

This schedule shows that the first $50,000 of ordinary taxable income is taxed at much lower rates than the rest of the firm's taxable income. In previous years, the 48-percent tax rate was applied to all taxable income in excess of the $25,000 level. Because of this tax advantage associated with lower incomes many firms used to establish separate corporate units whose taxable income level did not exceed $25,000. In 1969 the tax laws were tightened to prevent firms from taking advantage of

---

[5] Essentially, there is a *negative* $1,000 tax on the initial investment.

this tax loophole by limiting to one the number of commonly owned firms that could claim the lower tax rate.

In analyzing a prospective project the analyst must decide which rates the taxable income created by the project will be subject to. For very small firms this may be a problem, but for the kinds of firms to which this text is directed, we assume that the 48 percent rate holds.

Occasionally, the estimated taxable income for the year will be negative for a proposed project. If the firm as a *whole* is profitable, then its taxable income is reduced by the negative taxable income on the project. In evaluating projects we will assume the firm as a whole is profitable. The effect of this assumption is that negative project taxable incomes create negative income tax liabilities (just as the investment credit tax does). The interpretation of the negative income tax for the project in any year is that the firm's *total* income tax liability is reduced by the loss on the project. Mechanically, we handle negative taxable incomes just like positive taxable incomes, preserving the algebraic sign of the answer. If, for example, *CFBT* is $100 for a particular year for a proposed project, depreciation is $200, and the firm's tax rate is 48 percent, the project's taxable income for the year will be −$100, and the income tax associated with the project will be −$48. *CFAT* for the project that year will be $148 [$100 − (−$48)]. Notice that we are mechanically doing nothing new, but we are careful to preserve the negative sign on taxable income and income tax calculations.

Taxing salvage proceeds

A complete investment analysis of a proposed project requires estimation of the termination date of the project if it is accepted and the salvage value of the project. Moreover, if the investment decision is a replacement decision, the salvage value of the asset being replaced must be accounted for also. With either situation, when an asset is abandoned the tax treatment of its salvage value depends on the relationship between the salvage value and the asset's *adjusted basis*. Adjusted basis is the cost of the asset for tax purposes; it is defined as original cost minus accumulated depreciation taken for tax purposes. Depending on the relationship between the asset's salvage value and adjusted basis, the salvage proceeds may be subject to no tax at all, or ordinary income tax rates, or a combination of ordinary and capital gains tax rates. For tax computation work it is important that we distinguish between depreciable personal property—such as machinery—and depreciable real estate because tax laws are more complicated on real estate. Technically, the discussion below pertains only to personal property assets.

Suppose that a proposed project originally costs $25,000 and its estimated salvage is $5,000 in year ten. Suppose further that estimated accumulated depreciation for tax purposes is $20,000 after ten years. The estimated adjusted basis at the end of year ten is therefore $5,000 ($25,000 − $20,000). Since the estimated salvage value equals the estimated adjusted basis there is no expected tax liability created by the salvage proceeds. The $5,000 salvage value will be received by the firm tax free since the firm is only recovering its undepreciated investment.

Now consider the possible sale of an old asset in a replacement situation. Suppose, for example, the old asset originally cost $30,000 and accumulated depreciation is $20,000. The current adjusted basis of the asset is therefore $10,000. If the old asset can be sold (salvaged) for $10,000, there is no tax on this sale since salvage value equals adjusted basis. However, if the asset is sold for some value above adjusted basis but not exceeding the original cost, say $15,000, the difference between salvage value and adjusted basis is taxed at the firm's ordinary income tax rate. In the example, the $5,000 difference between the $15,000 salvage value and the $10,000 adjusted basis would be taxed at the 48-percent ordinary income tax rate. This difference is taxed at the firm's ordinary rate because it represents recapture of depreciation. The Internal Revenue Service argues that the firm took too much depreciation and taxes the gain over adjusted basis at the ordinary income tax rate. If the asset were sold for *more* than the *original cost*, say $35,000, the difference ($20,000) between original cost ($30,000) and current adjusted basis ($10,000) is taxed as ordinary income since it represents recapture of depreciation, and the difference between salvage value and original cost ($35,000 − $30,000 = $5,000) is taxed as capital gains. The maximum capital gains tax rate is 30 percent. If the asset were sold for less than its adjusted basis, say $5,000, the loss on the asset is treated as an ordinary income loss and is handled the same as a negative operating cash flow that we discussed above. In the example, the adjusted basis is $10,000 and the salvage is $5,000, so the loss is $5,000. This leads to a negative taxable income on salvage of −$5,000 and a negative income tax of −$2,400 (0.48 × −$5,000).

We may summarize the tax treatment of salvage with the following example, which is worked for several illustrative salvage values below.

Original cost = $50,000; accumulated depreciation = $20,000; ordinary tax rate = 48 percent; and capital gains tax rate = 30 percent.

Case	Salvage value (dollars)	Adjusted basis (dollars)	Taxable income (dollars)		Tax rate	Income tax (dollars)
a 30,000		30,000	Ordinary	0	× 0.48 =	0
			Cap. gains	0	× 0.30 =	0
				0		0
b 40,000		30,000	Ordinary	10,000	× 0.48 =	4,800
			Cap. gains	0	× 0.30 =	0
				10,000		4,800
c........... 53,000		30,000	Ordinary	20,000	× 0.48 =	9,600
			Cap. gains	3,000	× 0.30 =	900
				23,000		10,500
d 20,000		30,000	Ordinary	−10,000	× 0.48 =	−4,800
			Cap. gains	0	× 0.30 =	0
				−10,000		−4,800

In case (*a*) there is no tax because salvage value is not above the asset's adjusted basis. In case (*b*) the $10,000 excess of salvage over adjusted basis is classified as ordinary income and therefore taxed at the 48-percent rate. In case (*c*) the first $20,000 salvage over adjusted basis is taxed at 48 percent and the remaining $3,000 is taxed at the lower capital gains rate. In case (*d*), where salvage is *less* than adjusted basis, the $10,000 book loss is "taxed" at the ordinary rate, leading to a negative income tax.

SIMPLIFIED CFAT WORK SHEETS

At this point we may now summarize the *CFAT* analysis by combining the three parts: initial investment, operating cash flows, and termination cash flows, including the tax considerations. We utilize simplified work sheets designed to determine cash flows after tax. These *CFAT* work sheets will be extended in the next chapter to include economic analysis of the cash flows to decide whether the project is acceptable or not. The first *CFAT* work sheet is basically designed to handle revenue expansion projects and is illustrated by the example given below.

A proposed project—purchase of some new equipment—costs $24,000, and the installation costs are $1,000. There is a 10-percent investment tax credit allowed, and the firm will use straight-line depreciation for tax calculation purposes. Increased net working capital needs are $2,000. The project is expected to generate cash revenues of $22,000 per year, and operating cash expenses are estimated to be $10,000 the first year, increasing by $2,000 per year thereafter as the machine wears out. Estimated salvage value at the end of five years is $5,000. The ordinary tax rate is 40 percent, and the capital gains tax rate is 30 percent.

Given these estimated before tax costs and revenues, the complete *CFAT* stream is determined by using the *CFAT* work sheet shown in Figure 6–1.

The complete *CFAT* stream therefore, looks like this:

t	0	1	2	3	4	5
CFAT	−24,500	8,800	7,600	6,400	5,200	11,000

The next *CFAT* work sheet illustrates cash flow determination associated with a cost savings type of project. It is illustrated with the following example. A textile company is considering replacing some of its older dying equipment. This equipment originally cost $600,000, and its accumulated depreciation is $300,000. The firm anticipates it could operate this equipment for another six years at which time it would have salvage value of $50,000. Depreciation for this older equipment is $50,000 per year; operating costs are expected to be $75,000 per year; and its current salvage value is estimated to be $300,000. Replacement equipment would cost $750,000 and operating costs would be $50,000 per year. The company anticipates it will operate this new equipment for six years and then sell it for $150,000. The company uses straight-line

FIGURE 6–1
Revenue expansion CFAT work sheet

Initial investment				CFBT	10-percent investment credit	CFAT
Gross investment:				−$25,000	$2,500	−$22,500
Increased net working capital:						− 2,000
					$CFAT_0$ =	−$24,500

Operating cash flows

Year	Cash revenues	Cash expenses	CFBT	Deprecia- tion*	Taxable income	Tax†	CFAT (CFBT-Tax)
1......	$22,000	$10,000	$12,000	$4,000	$8,000	$3,200	$8,800
2......	22,000	12,000	10,000	4,000	6,000	2,400	7,600
3......	22,000	14,000	8,000	4,000	4,000	1,600	6,400
4......	22,000	16,000	6,000	4,000	2,000	800	5,200
5......	22,000	18,000	4,000	4,000	0	0	4,000

Termination cash flows

Year	Salvage	Adjusted basis	Taxable income		×	Tax rate	=	Tax	CFAT
5.........	$5,000	$5,000	Ordinary	0	×	0.40	=	0	$5,000
			Cap. gains	0	×	0.30	=	0	
				0				0	

Recovery of net working capital:	2,000
	$7,000

* $Depreciation_t = 0.20 \times (\$25,000 - \$5,000)$.
† $Tax_t = (0.4)(Taxable\ income_t)$.

depreciation for tax purposes. No investment credit is allowed on this new investment. The firm's ordinary tax rate is 40 percent, and no increase in net working capital is anticipated.

Given this information we can construct the *CFAT* stream for this proposed replacement. In constructing this stream we *net* the cash flows between the replacement opportunity and the status quo position. That is

$$\Delta CFAT = CFAT_{Replacement} - CFAT_{Status\ quo}$$

This netting process will be apparent after studying the Replacement *CFAT* work sheet in Figure 6–2.

The complete $\Delta CFAT$ stream looks like this:

t	0	1	2	3	4	5	6
CFAT	−450,000	35,000	35,000	35,000	35,000	35,000	155,000

All cash flows are netted and represent the effect of making the replacement of the old equipment with the new. The after tax initial investment is reduced by after tax salvage proceeds from the immediate

FIGURE 6–2
Replacement CFAT work sheet

Initial Investment
  New equipment:

	CFBT	Investment credit	CFAT
	−$750,000	0	−$750,000

  Old equipment:

	Adjusted	Taxable		Tax			
Salvage	basis	income	×	rate	=	Tax	CFAT
$300,000...	$300,000	0		−		0	+$300,000
							$\Delta CFAT = -$450,000

Operating cash flows

	ΔCFBT (operating cost		ΔTaxable	(T = 0.4)	
Year	savings)	ΔDepreciation*	income	ΔTax	ΔCFAT
1	$25,000	$50,000	−$25,000	−$10,000	$35,000
2	25,000	50,000	− 25,000	−$10,000	$35,000
3	25,000	50,000	− 25,000	−$10,000	$35,000
4	25,000	50,000	− 25,000	−$10,000	$35,000
5	25,000	50,000	− 25,000	−$10,000	$35,000
6	25,000	50,000	− 25,000	−$10,000	$35,000

Termination cash flows

		Adjusted	Taxable		Tax			
	Salvage	basis	income	×	rate	=	Tax	CFAT
New equipment...	$150,000	$150,000	0		−		0	$150,000
Old equipment...	50,000	0	$50,000		0.40		$20,000	30,000
							$\Delta CFAT =$	$120,000

* Depreciation per year for the new equipment is (1/6)($750,000 − $150,000) = $100,000.

sale of the old equipment. As compensation for this new investment, operating cash flows increase by $35,000 per year. This increase in operating cash flows is composed of a cost savings of $25,000 per year and a depreciation tax shield that lowers taxes by $10,000 per year. Last, there is an increase in salvage value if the new equipment is purchased. Notice that three salvage values are pertinent: (1) the *current* sale of the *old* asset, (2) the *future* sale of the *new* asset, and (3) the loss of *future* salvage proceeds of the *old* asset caused by selling the old asset now.

SUMMARY

Estimating cash flows is an essential part of evaluating long-term investment proposals, and we investigated the main features of cash flow estimation in this chapter. The basic principles developed in this chapter apply to both *revenue expansion* investments and *cost reduction* investments.

To begin with, the financial analyst is interested in estimating the *cash flow after tax stream* associated with the proposed projects:

Cash flow after tax in year $t = CFAT_t = $ Cash revenues$_t$ − Cash expenses$_t$

$$= CFBT_t - \text{Tax}_t$$

where

$CFBT_t = $ cash flow before tax in year t and Tax$_t = $ tax in year t.

This $CFAT_t$ stream has three distinct parts:

1. Initial investment.
2. Operating cash flows.
3. Termination cash flows.

In formulating cash flows we analyzed three depreciation methods:

1. Straight-line.
2. Sum-of-the-years'-digits.
3. Double declining balance.

The latter two are *accelerated* depreciation methods. In all three cases the depreciation for year t was:

Depreciation$_t = $ (Depreciation factor$_t$)(Depreciation base$_t$)

Applying this definition to the three depreciation methods, we studied:

Method	Depreciation factor	Depreciation base
Straight-line	$\frac{1}{n}$	Original cost − Salvage
Sum-of-years'-digit	$\frac{y}{\Sigma t}$	Original cost − Salvage
Double declining balance	$\frac{2}{n}$	Previous year's adjusted basis

We also investigated some of the less complicated tax considerations involving initial investment, operating cash flows, and termination proceeds associated with proposed investments.

Proper evaluation of long-term investment proposals is crucial to the firm's operations, for successful investment in productive assets means the firm will prosper. An important part of this evaluation is the estimation of cash flows. We have assumed here that we were *given* the cash revenues and operating costs and initial investment. Given these entities we have calculated the $CFAT$ stream. The important task of actually estimating these "given" revenues and costs is an art that can best be taught by real world experience and analysis and, accordingly, we leave that task for the student's future.

QUESTIONS

1. In the absence of corporate taxation, write the equation for cash flow after tax in terms of cash revenues, cash expenses, and depreciation.

2. Explain the distinction between revenue expansion and cost reduction type investments.

3. Regardless of the depreciation method chosen for an asset, depreciation in any year is the product of the depreciation factor times the depreciation base. Describe and contrast the depreciation factors and bases of the three depreciation methods presented in this chapter.

4. Suppose the investment tax credit were raised from 10 to 15 percent. What effect should this have on:
   a. The initial cost of a new asset?
   b. The depreciation schedule of a new asset?
   c. The estimated salvage value of a new asset?

5. Financial analysts appropriately argue that only those costs that are *cash* costs should be included in a cash flow analysis. However, depreciation, which is a noncash cost, is a prominent part of the cash flow analysis. How do you explain this paradox?

6. Typically, a firm has considerable latitude in establishing depreciation schedules for new assets. In what sense may we say that a particular depreciation schedule is an "optimal" schedule?

7. An older piece of machinery will soon be sold for scrap. Of what importance is the asset's adjusted basis at the time of scrapping?

8. Explain why it is more appropriate to use cash flows in evaluating investment projects rather than earnings.

9. Haddaway Industries is in the middle of preparing cash flow estimates for a proposed foundry in Alabama. During this preparation phase several events occur that might make Haddaway's analysts want to change some of their cash flow estimates. Evaluate the impact of the following events on each of the three distinct parts of the *CFAT* schedule (initial investment, operating cash flows, and termination cash flows):
   a. Congress lowers the ordinary income tax rate.
   b. The labor union representing foundry workers wins a new wage contract that will cause labor costs associated with the new venture to increase.
   c. Depreciation guidelines are liberalized so that more depreciation can be taken in the early years of an investment.
   d. The investment tax credit feature of new investments is revoked. However, this revocation does not apply to new investments that are begun within the next 15 months.

10. Suppose that the firm is considering replacing an old machine with a new one. The firm does not anticipate that any new revenues will

be created by the replacement since demand for the product generated by either machine is the same. However, in the *CFAT* work sheet used in evaluating the proposal, the analyst shows positive *CFBT*'s in the operating cash flow section. What creates operating *CFBT*'s in this situation?

PROBLEMS

1. A freight company has decided to purchase some new trucks for its fleet. The cost of the trucks is $5,000,000. Determine the depreciation schedule for this investment under the following conditions.

Case	Estimated life (years)	Estimated salvage (dollars)	Depreciation method
a.	6	0	Straight-line
b.	5	0	Sum of years
c.	5	0	Double declining: no switch
d.	5	0	Double declining: with switch
e.	6	2,000,000	Straight-line
f.	4	1,000,000	Sum of years

2. An old piece of equipment originally cost $200,000. Assuming the ordinary income tax rate is 48 percent and the capital gains tax rate is 30 percent, determine the amount of tax owed and the *CFAT* the firm will receive from sale of the equipment in the following situations:

Case	Sale price of equipment (dollars)	Adjusted basis of equipment (dollars)
a.	200,000	100,000
b.	200,000	0
c.	100,000	100,000
d.	150,000	180,000
e.	50,000	100,000
f.	300,000	180,000
g.	400,000	50,000

3. Young Widgets Co. is investigating the possibility of diversifying into a new product line, the manufacturing of carbon-treated zwidgets. Equipment for this investment would cost $10,000 and would last four years; its expected salvage value is zero. The firm expects to sell 10 million zwidgets per year at a price of $0.80 per 1,000. Expected operating costs are $0.40 per 1,000. No investment tax credit may be taken, and the ordinary income tax rate is 52 percent. A $2,000 increase in working capital at the beginning of the project will be re-required.

Determine the CFAT schedule assuming:

a. Straight-line depreciation is used.

    b.   Sum-of-the-years'-digits depreciation is used.

    c.   Double declining balance depreciation is used, but the company switches to straight-line when the time is appropriate.

4.   McEnally Minerals, a U.S. firm, is contemplating purchase of mineral deposits in a foreign country where there are no taxes. However, the U.S. government is discouraging foreign investment and has recently passed a law that effectively puts a 100 percent tax on taxable income earned on new investment in foreign countries. To further discourage foreign investment by U.S. firms, no investment tax credit is permitted and the only depreciation method allowed on foreign investments is straight-line. The investment will cost McEnally $10 million initially. McEnally can sell the mineral for $200 per ton and its operating costs will be $100 per ton. There is no salvage anticipated at the expiration of the project's life in ten years, and McEnally anticipates that it can sell 20,000 tons in each of the first two years of operation, 30,000 tons in each of the next three years, and 10,000 tons per year thereafter to termination of the project. Increased net working capital needs amount to 20 percent of the gross investment.

    Determine the relevant cash flow stream for this proposed investment.

5.   The Cohour Publishing Co. is trying to decide if it should replace some of its older printing machinery. The cost of new machinery is $150,000; its estimated life is five years, and the machinery's estimated salvage at the end of its life is zero. The new machinery is expected to produce cash operating cost savings of $25,000 per year during its life in comparison to the older machinery. If the new machine is purchased, the old machinery can be resold today for about $40,000. The old machinery cost $100,000 five years ago and was expected to have a ten-year life. Estimated salvage of the old machinery in five years is zero. Tax rates are 45 percent on ordinary income and 30 percent on capital gains. No investment tax credit can be taken on the new machinery, and the firm uses the sum-of-years'-digits for new equipment purchases. The firm is taking straight-line depreciation on the old machine.

    Determine the replacement cash flow after tax schedule.

6.   Dolphins Plastic is considering replacing some molding equipment used to make party cups. The presently used (two-year-old) equipment originally cost $75,000, has a current adjusted basis of $55,000, and can be sold today for $60,000. If this equipment is retained, it will have scrap value of $5,000 in five years, at which time the equipment will be unusable to Dolphins. This old equipment is depreciated on a straight-line basis. New replacement machinery costs $90,000, and an additional $10,000 must be spent for freight charges and for installation costs. Annual savings in labor and materials costs attributable to the replacement are estimated to be about $30,000 per year. The new machinery is also expected to last about five years and will have an estimated salvage value of $25,000 at that time. The ordi-

nary income tax rate is 40 percent and the capital gains income tax rate is 20 percent.

Prepare a replacement cash flow schedule for this proposed investment using the following depreciation schedule for the new equipment:

a. Straight-line depreciation and a 10-percent investment tax credit.

b. Sum-of-the-years'-digits and no investment tax credit.

7. The Balkan Amusement Park is considering the addition of a new ride to its attractions. The ride, called "The Turkish Delite," costs $200,000. Site preparation and installation will add another $20,000. The company expects that net working capital must also be increased by $2,000 to support the project. The ride, new to the area, is expected to generate cash revenues of $60,000, $80,000, $75,000, $60,000, and $40,000 per year over it's five year life. Balkan estimates that routine operating costs will be $10,000 for the first year of operation and will increase by 5 percent per year thereafter. Due to state law, Balkan will have to make certain operating repairs on pulleys and structural parts at the end of the second and fourth years at expected costs of $5,000 and $7,500, respectively. The company uses straight-line depreciation and estimates the salvage value of the ride to be zero. The ordinary tax rate is 40 percent, and no investment tax credit is permitted.

Determine the *CFAT*'s associated with this proposed project.

8. The Team Tractor Company is planning to introduce a new model loader-backhoe tractor. The company estimates that the necessary retooling and production line modification will require an investment of $1,200,000. Further, working capital will need to be increased by $80,000.

The marketing department has projected the demand for this tractor for the next eight years, at which time it will be replaced by a new model.

Year	Unit sales
1	40
2	48
3	54
4	56
5	53
6	51
7	47
8	41

The company plans to price the tractor at a price high enough to provide a reasonable rate of return, but not so high as to make the product uncompetitive. Marketing has estimated these selling prices to be $10,000/unit for the first year with an 8-percent increase in price in each of the next two years, and then a 3-percent increase in price for each of the remaining five years.

The production manager has forecasted production costs as follows. Regardless of the production level, there will be $300,000 in cash operating costs each year (these are fixed costs of production). Additionally, each unit will cost $3,000 per year in the first year, but this variable production cost will decrease by 5 percent per year after the first year. The company uses sum-of-the-year'-digits depreciation and expects the salvage value of the production equipment to be $300,000 at the end of the life of the project. If ordinary tax rates are 40 percent, and the project qualifies for a 10-percent investment tax credit, determine the *CFAT* schedule.

SELECTED BASIC REFERENCES

Bierman, H., Jr., and S. Smidt. *The Capital Budgeting Decision.* 4th ed. New York: Macmillan Publishing Co., Inc., 1975, chapters 6 and 7.

Johnson, R. W. *Capital Budgeting.* Belmont, Calif.: Wadsworth Publishing Co., Inc., 1970, chapter 2.

Osteryoung, J. *Capital Budgeting: Long-Term Asset Selection.* Columbus, Ohio: Grid, Inc., 1974, chapter 2.

SELECTED ADVANCED REFERENCES

Bodenhorn, D. "A Cash Flow Concept of Profit," *Journal of Finance.* (March 1964), pp. 16–31.

Haley, C. W., and L. D. Schall. *The Theory of Financial Decisions.* New York: McGraw-Hill Book Co., 1973, pp. 195–204.

7

INVESTMENT DECISION CRITERIA

In making long-term investment decisions the firm needs to: (1) estimate project cash flows, (2) estimate an appropriate discount rate or cost of capital for the project, and (3) formulate decision criteria that allow the firm to make investment choices consistent with the firm's goal of shareholder wealth maximization. In Chapter 6 we investigated how to calculate project cash flows, and in Chapter 8 we will develop cost of capital principles. Our concern in this chapter will be with formulating investment decision criteria. Too many investment decision criteria have been proposed in the financial literature to investigate them all. Instead, we will look at those criteria that either best resolve the investment decision—that is, are normatively correct—or are most frequently used by practitioners.[1]

CAPITAL BUDGETING DECISIONS

Long-term investment decision making is frequently referred to as capital budgeting: The firm is allocating or budgeting financial resources to new investment proposals. Basically, there are three kinds of capital budgeting decisions that may confront the firm: the accept-reject decision, the mutually exclusive choice decision, and the capital rationing decision. These three problems are defined below, and we will address all in more detail later in the chapter.

Accept-reject decisions

The accept-reject decision is the fundamental decision of whether to invest in a proposed project or not. Every asset the firm acquires must

---

[1] Recall that normative refers to the way things *should* be done.

first successfully pass the accept-reject decision, so this is easily the most common and most important capital budgeting problem the firm encounters. The problem is defined as: "Given a proposed project, should the firm invest in it?" If the answer is *yes*, the firm accepts (invests in) the project; if *no*, the firm rejects (does not invest in) the project. If, for example, the proposal is a revenue expansion opportunity to open a new plant, the accept-reject decision will determine whether the proposal is implemented. Likewise, a cost reduction proposal to replace an old machine with a new one involves an accept-reject decision on the new machine.

Mutually exclusive choice decisions

Mutually exclusive projects are competing alternatives, only one of which may be chosen. If, for example, a paperbox company frees up extra plant space and is deliberating between using the space for installing more cutting equipment or using the space for storing extra raw material, obviously both alternatives cannot be accepted. The alternatives are mutually exclusive and only one may be chosen. Likewise, if the same company is considering buying a new folding machine and there are three competing makes, each with different initial investment and operating costs, the three machines represent mutually exclusive alternatives – only one of which may be selected. The mutually exclusive choice decision is defined as: "Given a set of competing investment alternatives, only one of which may be selected, which should the firm invest in?" It is important to always bear in mind that possibly *none* of the mutually exclusive alternative proposals should be accepted. If evaluation of all the individual competing proposals results in a reject decision in each instance, none of the proposals should be accepted. In the folding machine example above, if all three machines, when evaluated on an accept-reject basis, lead to reject decisions the firm should not buy a new folding machine. Choice of alternatives involves a ranking decision, and the selection rule will be to choose that *acceptable* proposal that is ranked best. As we will see, "best" refers back to the goal of the firm.

Capital rationing decisions

Capital rationing refers to the situation where the firm has more acceptable investments than it has funds to finance. This amounts to having a budget constraint in one or more time periods during which the firm is choosing investments. The capital rationing problem is defined as: "Given a set of investment alternatives and a budget constraint, which *group* of investments should the firm select?" This problem is concerned with the selection of a group of assets rather than one asset as in the accept-reject and mutually exclusive choice decisions considered above. Consequently, it is more difficult to resolve this decision, except in simplified situations.

INVESTMENT DECISION CRITERIA

What we seek are decision criteria and rules that will enable the firm to resolve the three investment decision problems posed above. Decision criteria are evaluation techniques or yardsticks that indicate how attractive a potential investment is. A decision rule is a way of using the decision criteria to make investment decisions. There are many investment decision criteria, but we will investigate only a few. Among this group, however, are both the most frequently used and the generally recognized "good" criteria, where "good" means consistent with the goal of shareholder wealth maximization. Basically, we can divide investment decision criteria into two broad categories: discounted cash flow (*DCF*) criteria and nondiscounted cash flow (non-*DCF*) criteria.

DCF and non-DCF criteria

DCF refers to *discounted cash flow* and provides the distinction between the two sets of criteria: *DCF* methods use discounted cash flows in some fashion and non-*DCF* methods do not.

We will investigate two non-*DCF* and three *DCF* criteria, and one of the main issues in this investigation is: Which of these criteria are good and which bad? A criterion is good or bad depending on how well it relates to the firm's goal. The firm should only select those investments the stockholders would make themselves had they the opportunity to make the decision. Now, what things would the stockholders require of any potential investment? We discussed in Chapters 3, 4, and 5 that investors require compensation for their time value of money (the price of time) and for risk exposure (the price of risk). Consequently, any proposed investment decision technique should account for time value and risk considerations in the analysis. In the discussion in this chapter we only focus on the time value of money concept; we defer risk considerations to the next two chapters. With that deferral in mind we note that for an investment decision criterion to be good it must, at the very least, account for the fundamental concept of the time value of money. Criteria that do not fulfill this basic requirement are suspect and can cause the firm to accept projects where there is not adequate compensation for investors' time value of money.

An example CFAT stream

In presenting the five capital budgeting criteria below, an example will facilitate the analysis. Suppose the firm is considering investment in a new piece of machinery. The machinery costs $10,000 after all tax considerations, and its estimated life is four years. Estimated cash flows after tax are $4,000 per year in each of the first two years and $3,000 per year in each of the last two years. The firm estimated these cash flows using procedures developed in the previous chapter. The complete stream of estimated cash flows after tax is therefore:

t	CFAT (dollars)
0	−10,000
1	4,000
2	4,000
3	3,000
4	3,000

We will use this example in defining the five decision criteria below. For each technique we will also describe its associated accept-reject rule. Mutually exclusive and capital rationing problems will be deferred to later sections of the chapter.

Payback

Payback is one of the best-known non-*DCF* criteria and is defined as the number of years it takes the project to recover the initial investment:

$$\text{Payback} = \text{Number of years to recover initial investment} \quad (7\text{-}1)$$

Since the initial investment in the example is $10,000, the payback period is the number of years it takes for the project to recover $10,000. Looking at the example *CFAT* stream after time zero:

$$\text{Payback} = 2\frac{2}{3} \text{ years}^2$$

In using payback in the accept-reject decision the firm states a minimum or *required* payback standard, which describes the accept-reject decision rule for the project. Projects with expected payback less than or equal to this standard are accepted and projects with expected paybacks greater than this standard are rejected. Therefore:

If payback ≤ required payback   accept the project.
If payback > required payback   reject the project.

If required payback is three years, the example project will be accepted. If, however, the firm's payback standard is two years, the project will be rejected. Sometimes the standard is related to the estimated life of the project. The firm may require, for example, that the project reach payback by no later than one half of its estimated life. In the example, the required payback would be two years and the project would be rejected.

The payback criterion has two glaring deficiencies. First, it does not account for the timing of the cash flows that occur *within* the payback period. Suppose the estimated *CFAT* stream in the example had been:

---

[2] This assumes the *CFAT* accumulates in a *steady* inflow. Thus, in year three, $1,000 flows in every one third of the year.

	CFAT
t	(dollars)
0	−10,000
1	6,000
2	2,000
3	3,000
4	3,000

The prepayback *CFAT*'s are rearranged ($2,000 has been shifted from year two to year one), but payback is still $2\frac{2}{3}$ years. Clearly though, this alternative *CFAT* stream is more desirable to investors because it provides the firm with an accelerated *CFAT* stream. Payback ignores the timing of prepayback period cash flows. Second, payback completely ignores the postpayback cash flows. Suppose the estimated *CFAT* stream were:

	CFAT
t	(dollars)
0	−10,000
1	4,000
2	4,000
3	3,000
4	10,000

In this instance there is a very large cash inflow in period four, after payback, but payback is still $2\frac{2}{3}$ years. Payback ignores these postpayback cash flows.

In summary, payback does not account for the timing of the prepayback cash flows and it completely ignores the postpayback cash flows. These deficiencies seriously jeopardize the use of payback to evaluate projects. The advantages payback offers are that it can be easily and quickly calculated and it is a readily understood concept. Also, it provides a kind of rough and ready risk screen. If long-lived projects are risky partly because it is so difficult to estimate cash flows that are far distant in the future, requiring fairly short payback periods insures the firm will not invest in many extremely risky projects. Of course, as we have discussed before, if the firm wishes to make high returns it will necessarily have to make some risky investments. Use of payback may effectively block many profitable but risky opportunities.

Average rate of return

Average rate of return (*ARR*) is another non-*DCF* method and has many alternative definitions (and names). One frequently encountered definition is average cash flow after tax divided by initial investment:

$$\text{Average rate of return} = ARR = \frac{\left(\sum_{t=1}^{n} CFAT_t\right)/n}{\text{Initial investment}} \qquad (7\text{-}2)$$

This is also often called the average return on investment. There are other variants of the definition: Sometimes financial analysts use *average* initial investment in the denominator. In addition, oftentimes average *net income* is used in place of average cash flows after tax in the numerator. When net incomes are used the resultant rate of return is usually called the *accounting* rate of return. Of course, the use of net income flows is inconsistent with the cash flow concepts developed in the previous chapter.

For the example problem:

$$ARR = \frac{(\$4,000 + \$4,000 + \$3,000 + \$3,000)/4}{\$10,000}$$

$$= 35 \text{ percent}$$

After calculating average rate of return the firm would next compare it against a *required* average rate of return. If the calculated average rate of return is greater than the required rate the project is accepted, if the calculated average rate of return is less than the required rate the project is rejected. (If the two rates are exactly equal the firm is indifferent as to whether the project is accepted or not.) The investment rule is therefore:

If ARR > required ARR accept the project.

If ARR < required ARR reject the project.

If the example's ARR of 35 percent is greater than the required ARR, the firm will accept the example project, and if not, the firm will reject the example project.

The average rate of return fails to meet, however, the minimum requirement that any good investment yardstick must: It does not account for the timing of the cash flows. Suppose the example project's $CFAT$ stream had been rearranged as follows:

t	CFAT (dollars)
0	−10,000
1	10,000
2	2,000
3	1,000
4	1,000

Cash flows after the investment total $14,000 just as in the original example project, but most of the $14,000 has been pushed up to year one. However, the average rate of return is still 35 percent even though this altered $CFAT$ stream is more desirable because it is accelerated. By definition, ARR *averages* cash flows across time, thus ignoring their timing and, consequently, is not a good investment criterion. Despite this major shortcoming, average rate of return is widely used today, although its usage is declining as the level of capital budgeting sophistication gradually increases. The two advantages that ARR does offer are ease of calculation and understandability. But it is not a good investment evaluation technique.

Net present value

We studied present value techniques in Chapter 3. Net present value (*NPV*) merely refers to netting the initial investment, which is negative, and the present value of the subsequent *CFAT*'s, most of which usually will be positive.

$$NPV = \sum_{t=0}^{n} \frac{CFAT_t}{(1 + k)^t} \tag{7-3}$$

where *k* is the discount rate or required rate of return or cost of capital.
For the example problem,

$$NPV = -\$10,000 + \frac{\$4,000}{1 + k} + \frac{\$4,000}{(1 + k)^2} + \frac{\$3,000}{(1 + k)^3} + \frac{\$3,000}{(1 + k)^4}$$

Recall that $1/(1 + k)^t$ is the discount factor for *k* percent in period *t* ($DF_{k,t}$). If *k* = 10 percent, the net present value of the proposed project is found as follows:

t	*CFAT* (dollars)	×	*DF*	=	$PV_{.10}$ (dollars)
0...................	−10,000		1.000		−10,000
1...................	4,000		0.909		3,636
2...................	4,000		0.826		3,304
3...................	3,000		0.751		2,253
4...................	3,000		0.683		2,049
				$NPV_{.10} =$	1,242

If net present value is positive the firm will accept the project; if negative, the project will be rejected. (If net present value is zero the firm is indifferent to accepting or rejecting the project.) That is:

If *NPV* > 0,   accept the project.
If *NPV* < 0,   reject the project.

Since the example proposal has *NPV* > 0 it should be accepted. Notice that the net present value method does explicitly account for the timing of the cash flows. If the *CFAT* stream were accelerated, the project's *NPV* would increase. If the timing of the *CFAT* schedule were changed in *any* way, the project's *NPV* would reflect the change. So the *NPV* method meets the requirement of properly accounting for cash flow timing.

Actually, the *NPV* method of evaluating prospective investments does much more than meet the minimum requirement of accounting for the time value of money. *The* NPV *method is logically consistent with the firm's goal of maximizing stockholder wealth or maximizing stock price.* Recall from Chapter 5 that the current market price of the firm's stock, P_0, is the present value of the expected future dividends:

$$P_0 = \sum_{t=1}^{\infty} \frac{D_t}{(1 + k_e)^t}$$

where k_e is the firm's cost of equity capital or required rate of return on equity, and D_t is the expected dividend in period t. In comparison, the net present value of a proposed investment is:

$$NPV = \sum_{t=0}^{n} \frac{CFAT_t}{(1 + k)^t}$$

Thus, the *NPV* evaluation of a new project is logically tied to the firm's goal of shareholder wealth maximization. If a proposed project has $NPV > 0$, the market value of the firm's stock should be increased by the firm's acceptance of the project. Similarly, if the firm were to accept a project with $NPV < 0$, the market value of the firm's stock would be expected to decrease. This also explains why the firm is said to be indifferent about accepting a project with $NPV = 0$. The firm expects to make its required rate of return on the project, but there is no expected *increase* of the value of the firm's stock; hence the firm is indifferent to the acceptance of the project.

As a very simplified illustration of this relationship between the *NPV* evaluation of a new investment proposal and the firm's stock price, consider a firm with 100 shares of stock outstanding, where the market price is $10 per share; hence a *total* market value of the stock of $1,000. If the firm has the opportunity to invest in a new project whose $NPV = \$50$, the total market value of the stock would be expected to increase $50 to $1,050 and the stock price would be expected to rise to $10.50 per share. Acceptance of this new project because its $NPV > 0$ is thus consistent with the firm's goal.

So the *NPV* evaluation technique is more than just a good investment criterion. For accept-reject problems the *NPV* always provides theoretically correct decisions, and we will see that for mutually exclusive choice problems the *NPV* method is the best decision criterion.

Perhaps the only drawback to using the *NPV* method is that it is not as easily understood by businessmen as the rate of return concept. Most businessmen intuitively understand the concept of rate of return and must be educated to get the same intuitive grasp of the *NPV* method. This education barrier has no doubt retarded the adoption of the superior *NPV* method, but there also seems to be a steady increase in the usage of the *NPV* technique over the years.

Internal rate of return

The internal rate of return *(IRR)* is usually thought of as the rate of return the project earns. It is defined as that discount rate that will make the net present value of the project equal to zero:

$$\sum_{t=0}^{n} \frac{CFAT_t}{(1 + IRR)^t} = 0 \qquad (7\text{--}4)$$

The left-hand side of Equation (7–4) is the net present value of the project when discounted at the rate $k = IRR$. So the IRR is a discount rate, but it is that particular discount rate that will make the present value of the future cash flows equal the initial investment. Actually calculating the IRR requires procedures we investigated in Chapter 3 in determining discount rates. Unless the $CFAT$ inflow stream is constant, the usual solution procedure used is a trial-and-error procedure. In the trial-and-error procedure we pick a discount rate and check to see if the net present value of the project is zero at that discount rate.

For the example problem we must solve the following equation for IRR:

$$-\$10{,}000 + \frac{\$4{,}000}{(1 + IRR)} + \frac{\$4{,}000}{(1 + IRR)^2} + \frac{\$3{,}000}{(1 + IRR)^3} + \frac{\$3{,}000}{(1 + IRR)^4} = 0$$

In a trial-and-error solution it behooves us to make a judicious first guess at what IRR is. If the $CFAT$ stream were a constant \$4,000 in all four years, the IRR would be approximately 22 percent.[3] Since the $CFAT$ stream tails off to \$3,000/year in the last two years let's try a slightly lower guess, say 20 percent.

$$-\$10{,}000 + \frac{\$4{,}000}{(1.20)} + \frac{\$4{,}000}{(1.20)^2} + \frac{\$3{,}000}{(1.20)^3} + \frac{\$3{,}000}{(1.20)^4} \overset{?}{=} 0$$

$$-\$10{,}000 + (\$4{,}000)(0.833) + (\$4{,}000)(0.694) + (\$3{,}000)(0.579) \\ + (\$3{,}000)(0.482) \overset{?}{=} 0$$

$$-\$10{,}000 + \$3{,}332 + \$2{,}776 + \$1{,}737 + \$1{,}446 \overset{?}{=} 0$$

$$-\$10{,}000 + \$9{,}291 = -\$709 < 0$$

The question marks in the equations signify that we are asking the question: Does the left-hand side equal zero? The left-hand side of this equation does not equal zero, so we choose a new rate. As the discount rate decreases NPV goes up. Since we got a negative NPV at 20 percent, we will choose a lower discount rate, say 15 percent. This will hopefully make NPV positive and we can then interpolate to get the IRR.

$$-\$10{,}000 + \frac{\$4{,}000}{(1.15)} + \frac{\$4{,}000}{(1.15)^2} + \frac{\$3{,}000}{(1.15)^3} + \frac{\$3{,}000}{(1.15)^4} \overset{?}{=} 0$$

$$-\$10{,}000 + \$3{,}480 + \$3{,}024 + \$1{,}974 + \$1{,}716 \overset{?}{=} 0$$

$$-\$10{,}000 + \$10{,}194 = \$194 > 0$$

We now have a bracket on the IRR and we can interpolate to get the answer: $IRR = 16.1$ percent.

After calculating IRR the firm would then compare it against a *required rate of return* or *cost of capital* to determine the acceptability of the project. If the IRR is greater than the required rate, the project is accepted, and if the IRR is less than the required rate, the project is rejected. (If the IRR and the required rate of return are equal, the firm is indifferent as to whether it accepts or rejects the project.)

---

[3] If $CFAT$ is \$4,000/year in each of the four years: $-\$10{,}000 + \$4{,}000\,ADF_{IRR,4} = 0$. Then solving for ADF, $ADF = \$10{,}000/\$4{,}000 = 2.5$ and IRR ≈ 22 percent. If this calculation seems mysterious, review the material in Chapter 3 on determining discount rates.

Let k = the required rate of return or cost of capital.

If $IRR > k$,   accept the project.

If $IRR < k$,   reject the project.

If the calculated IRR of 16.1 percent of the example project is greater than k, the project will be accepted, but if 16.1 percent is less than k, the project will be rejected. Assuming the cost of capital is 10 percent the project will be accepted.

It should be obvious that the IRR does explicitly take into account the timing of the $CFAT$ stream. Any change in the amount of timing of the cash flows will result in a change in the IRR. So this criterion meets the minimum requirement of a good investment yardstick.

Simple and nonsimple investments Unfortunately, there are also some problems in using the IRR investment criterion. The IRR may give unreliable investment decision signals if the cash flow stream is somewhat out of the ordinary. We can envision two different types of project cash flow streams: *simple* and *nonsimple*. In simple cash flow patterns there are cash *outflows* (*minus CFAT* numbers) early in the life of the project followed by a series of expected cash *inflows* (*plus CFAT* numbers) in subsequent years. If we made a series out of the *signs* of the $CFAT$ stream we would have a series composed of negative signs followed by positive signs. If there were an initial investment followed by a stream of expected cash inflows beginning in year one and ending in year five this series of signs would look like $-+++++$. If the investment required an initial outlay in time zero and a further net outlay in time one followed by a stream of expected net cash inflows for seven years, the series of signs would look like $--++++++++$. These two example series have one thing in common: Both have net cash *outlays* in the initial time periods, net cash *inflows* in the last time periods, and only *one* sign change from $-$ to $+$. Thus the projects have one or more *investments* into the project followed by an uninterrupted series of *returns* from the project. Such projects are called *simple* investments.

Nonsimple investments have more than one change of sign in the series of net cash flow signs. Suppose a proposed project has an initial investment at $t = 0$, a series of net cash inflows, and a final net cash flow that is negative (an outflow). This sequence might arise with a logging operation where there is an initial land purchase cost followed by a series of net cash inflows, concluded by a reforestation cost at the end of the project. The cash flow stream would have a series of signs that looked like this: $-+++++-$. Notice there is more than one sign change: There are two changes. Anytime there is more than one sign change the investment is nonsimple. Other examples of nonsimple investments are the following: $-++-+-$, $-+++--$, $-+-+-$, and $-++++-++-$. There are many more, but the common characteristic is that after the first positive sign there is one or more subsequent negative signs. That is, there are net cash outflows interspersed in the series of cash inflows.

Net present value profile One way of assessing the impact of nonsimple cash flows on the reliability of the IRR method of project evaluation is to compare it to the NPV method, which was shown to be a theoretically correct evaluation technique for accept-reject projects. If projects are *simple* the *IRR* method will always give an accept-reject decision that agrees with the *NPV* method. We can illustrate why with the help of a *net present value profile*. A net present value profile is a graph of the net present value of a project discounted at different discount rates. It is a picture of the relationship between the *NPV* of a project and discount rate. Figure 7–1 shows the net present value profile of the example project we have been using throughout this chapter.

FIGURE 7–1
Net present value profile of a simple project

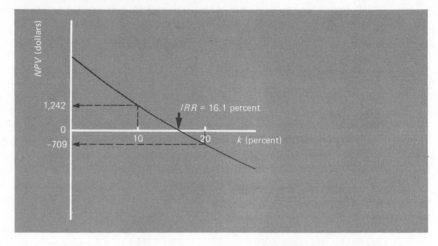

t	$CFAT$ (dollars)
0	−10,000
1	4,000
2	4,000
3	3,000
4	3,000

When $k = 10$ percent the example project's $NPV = \$1,242$. By the *NPV* criterion the project should be accepted. Now notice that as k increases the project's *NPV* decreases. This is shown in Figure 7–1 by the declining net present value profile. At some point the profile cuts the horizontal axis of the graph. By definition the intersection of the net present value profile and the horizontal axis is the project's *IRR*. Why? Because at $k = IRR$ the project's $NPV = 0$ (by definition), and the horizontal axis represents the zero *NPV* line. In the example the *IRR* = 16.1 percent. We can now readily see why the *IRR* and *NPV* methods always agree for simple projects. The *NPV* of the project for all costs of capital less than (to the left of) the *IRR* is positive, indicating the project should be accepted. But similarly, anytime the *IRR* is greater than the cost of capital, the project should be accepted. Thus when *IRR* > k in Figure 7–1, the *NPV* and *IRR* method both indicate the project should be accepted.

Likewise, when $IRR < k$ (as, for example when $k = 20$ percent), the IRR rule rejects the project, and Figure 7–1 shows $NPV < 0$ when $IRR < k$, and the NPV rule would also reject the project. Finally when $k = IRR$, both rules would indicate indifference. The result of this analysis is that for *simple* projects, NPV and IRR give identical accept-reject decisions. They agree.

Multiple rates of return For nonsimple investments the two criteria may not agree. One problem is that for nonsimple cash flow patterns there may be *more than one IRR*. That is, there may be *multiple* internal rates of return. Suppose, for example, that a proposed logging invest-

FIGURE 7–2
Net present value profile of a nonsimple project

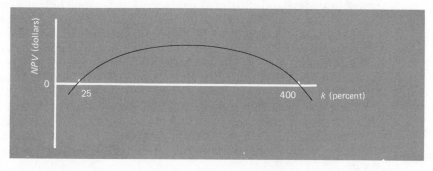

t	CFAT (dollars)
0	− 80,000
1	500,000
2	−500,000

ment has the *CFAT* stream shown in Figure 7–2. There is an initial investment, a large cash inflow in year one, and an equally large cash outflow in the second year as the firm is required to restore the land and reforest. This is a nonsimple cash flow stream since there is more than one sign change. Figure 7–2 shows there are two *IRR*'s: 25 and 400 percent. From looking at the NPV profile in Figure 7–2 it is clear that if the project's cost of capital is between 25 and 400 percent, the NPV of the project is positive and the project should be accepted. If the cost of capital is less than 25 percent (a very likely possibility) or greater than 400 percent (an unlikely possibility), the project should be rejected because its $NPV < 0$.

Applying the IRR criterion to this proposal leads to difficulties. Suppose the cost of capital, k, equals 15 percent. Both IRR's are greater than 15 percent and the IRR rule says that if $IRR > k$, accept. But Figure 7–2 shows that at $k = 15$ percent the project's $NPV < 0$. So the IRR gives an incorrect signal and the firm would be accepting a project with negative net present value. Now suppose $k = 30$ percent. If the analyst discovers $IRR = 25$ percent in his trial-and-error procedure he will erroneously conclude the project is unacceptable because $IRR < k$. Of course, if the analyst instead found $IRR = 400$ percent he would reach a correct decision, but this is unlikely because most discount tables don't go up to 400 percent.

There are instances where nonsimple investments only have one unique IRR, but this requires a laborious check. And if the check indicates there are multiple rates of return the situation is not very hopeful. In comparison, the NPV method is unambiguous and straightforward. There is no requirement to check for the number of sign changes nor for the possibility of multiple rates. The conclusion is that the net present value criterion is superior to the IRR method for evaluating projects on an accept-reject basis.

However, IRR appears to have one clear advantage over NPV: It is easier to understand. Business executives and nontechnical people understand the concept of a rate of return much more readily than they understand the concept of NPV. They may not understand the *formal* definition of IRR – see equation (7–4) – but they do understand the general meaning; it seems to be a culturally acquired concept, whereas NPV is not. One practical difficulty with using IRR – apart from theoretical difficulties we discussed above – is that it is more tedious to calculate. NPV requires only one pass through the discount tables, but most IRR calculations require at least two trials because IRR is usually a trial-and-error procedure. Of course, with the increased business usage of computers on routine problems this objection will be less important in the future.

Profitability index

The profitability index (PI) is defined as the present value of future cash flows divided by the initial investment:

$$\text{Profitability index} = PI = \frac{\sum_{t=1}^{n} CFAT_t/(1 + k)^t}{\text{Initial investment}} \qquad (7\text{–}5)$$

The numerator is the present value (using the cost of capital, k) of the future cash flows from the project and the denominator is the initial cost of the project. Since the future cash flows are typically positive this criterion is also called the *benefit-cost ratio*. It is also sometimes called the *present value per dollar of outlay*.

In the original example problem, if $k = 10$ percent,

$$PI = \frac{\$4,000/1.10 + \$4,000/(1.10)^2 + \$3,000/(1.10)^3 + \$3,000/(1.10)^4}{\$10,000}$$

$$PI = \frac{\$3,636 + \$3,304 + \$2,253 + \$2,049}{\$10,000} = \frac{\$11,242}{\$10,000}$$

$$PI = 1.12$$

If PI exceeds one, the project is acceptable; if it is less than one, it is not acceptable (and if PI equals one, the firm is indifferent about the project). Therefore:

If $PI > 1$,   accept the project.

If $PI < 1$,   reject the project.

Since the example project's PI is greater than one, it should be accepted. Like the NPV and IRR methods this technique explicitly accounts for the time value of money and satisfies this minimum requirement any good investment criterion should have. It is very closely related to the NPV technique and will give the same accept-reject decision as that resulting from the NPV analysis. The example problem illustrates this for a simple project: Both criteria indicate the project should be accepted. However, in some problems that involve ranking mutually exclusive projects the NPV and PI methods will disagree. In those instances NPV will be shown below to be a better evaluation technique. On the other hand, in the situation of capital rationing PI is often a better evaluation technique than NPV. These points are discussed below.

PI also suffers the same disadvantage as NPV. People have no intuitive feel for PI numbers, and it is more difficult to understand. Because it is more difficult to understand it is harder for financial analysts (those who actually prepare the investment proposals) to explain to senior executives (those who approve financial outlays) why an investment is good just because its PI is greater than one.

RANKING MUTUALLY EXCLUSIVE PROJECTS

Except for the problems in using the IRR method on nonsimple projects, the three DCF criteria (NPV, IRR, and PI) provide good guidance on accept-reject type decisions because they account for the time value of money. In this portion of the chapter we investigate how these decision criteria compare in evaluating mutually exclusive projects. In comparing these three criteria we will first contrast NPV and IRR, and then NPV and PI. In both comparisons NPV will be shown to be a better technique for evaluating mutually exclusive projects.

Decision rules

Before comparing the three criteria we must first identify the decision rule each criterion uses to pick the best among several mutually exclusive projects.

NPV   The NPV decision rule is to accept that proposal with the largest *positive* NPV. This requires calculating the NPV of each alternative proposal, checking to see if its NPV is positive, and then investing in the project with the largest positive NPV. If none of the proposals has a positive NPV, none will be accepted.

IRR   The IRR rule is to accept that proposal with the largest *acceptable IRR*,[4] where an acceptable IRR is one greater than the cost of capital, k. This procedure entails calculating each project's IRR and accepting that project whose IRR is both largest and is greater than the

---

[4] Actually this is a naive IRR decision rule. A more sophisticated IRR rule can be specified that will surmount the ranking problems that this naive IRR will be shown to have. This more sophisticated IRR decision rule can be found in more advanced texts.

cost of capital. If none of the competing proposals has an *IRR* greater than *k*, all will be rejected.

PI The *PI* decision rule is to take the project with the largest *acceptable PI*, where an acceptable *PI* is greater than one. If none of the mutually exclusive projects has a *PI* greater than one, none would be accepted.

NPV versus IRR

It was pointed out above that difficulties arise with the *IRR* method when cash flow patterns are nonsimple. In this comparison between *IRR* and *NPV* methods we will only consider simple investments. Even for this less general group of investments *NPV* is a better mutually exclusive ranking technique.

In many instances *NPV* and *IRR* will give consistent rankings, but at times conflicts in rankings between the two will occur. Consider two mutually exclusive investment proposals, *A* and *B*, with cash flow after tax streams and *NPV* and *IRR* results as shown:

t	*A*	*B*
0	−$35,000	−$35,000
1	20,000	5,000
2	15,000	10,000
3	10,000	15,000
4	5,000	25,000
NPV (at *k* = 9 percent)	$ 7,230	$ 7,285
IRR	20 percent	16 percent

At a 9-percent cost of capital the *NPV* of *B* is greater than the *NPV* of *A*, indicating *B* is the better project. However, the *IRR* of *A* is larger than the *IRR* of *B* indicating *A* is better, and a conflict in rankings exists. Why does this conflict arise? Conflicts can occur in two situations. First, the projects may have different initial investments: This is called the *size disparity problem*. The *IRR*, which is the discounted rate of return on the declining initial investment, ignores the relative sizes of the initial investments, where the *NPV* does not. Notice, however, that the conflict in the example above is not caused by the size disparity problem, since the initial investments of *A* and *B* are equal. The conflict in *IRR* and *NPV* rankings of *A* and *B* are attributable to the *time disparity problem*, which occurs when the postinitial investment time patterns of cash inflows of competing alternatives are different. Actually, the time disparity problem may be thought of as a special case of the size disparity problem where the size disparity occurs *after* the initial investment. In either the size or time disparity problem cases, the *IRR* ignores the differential cash flows between the competing alternatives and makes no explicit assumption about their reinvestment. In contrast, NPV explicitly assumes reinvestment of differential flows at the discount rate k.

The conflict between NPV and IRR rankings can be further shown by comparing net present value profiles of the two investment proposals. Figure 7–3 shows the net present value profiles for projects A and B on the same graph.

FIGURE 7–3
Net present value profiles of mutually exclusive projects A and B

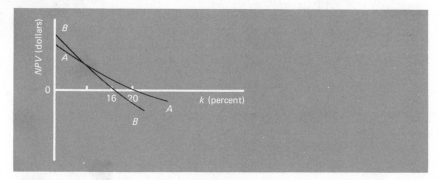

Both projects are simple so both have only one IRR. On the basis of IRR comparisons A is the better project, but the net present value profile clearly shows that, at some costs of capital, project A is better and that, at some discount rates, project B is better. Since the cost of capital is stated to be 9 percent in the example, project B is definitely a better project *at that rate*. If the cost of capital had been 14 percent, then the NPV method would point to A as a better project. However, the IRR decision here is to *always* take project A over B since A's IRR is higher. This criterion ignores the fact that different costs of capital affect the competing projects differently.

When choosing among mutually exclusive projects the firm should always take the one with the largest positive net present value, where net present value is found using the appropriate cost of capital. Therefore, the NPV method is better than the IRR method. The NPV method is better for reasons discussed earlier in the chapter where net present value was defined. The goal of the firm is to maximize stockholder wealth, and we saw that projects with positive NPV increase stock price and, hence, stockholder wealth. When faced with mutually exclusive projects, each having positive NPV, the one with the largest NPV will have the most beneficial effect on stockholder wealth. And the NPV method, by definition, selects the project with largest net present value. Because the firm's goal is a net present value formulation it should not be surprising that the best operational investment criterion is the NPV method. So long as the firm accepts the mutually exclusive investment proposal with the largest positive net present value it will be acting consistently with the firm's goal of maximizing stockholder wealth because the project with the largest positive net present value will cause stock price and stockholder wealth to increase more than any of the other projects will.

NPV versus PI

Because *NPV* and *PI* are so closely related, for most mutually exclusive choice problems *NPV* and *PI* will select the same best alternative. However, in some situations it is possible to get a conflict of rankings. Consider the following two mutually exclusive investment opportunities with *CFAT* streams as shown:

t	Project C	Project D
0	−$1,000	−$700
1	800	600
2	800	600
$NPV_{.15}$	$ 301	$276
$PI_{.15}$	1.3	1.4

Notice that both projects are acceptable if the cost of capital is 15 percent as both have $NPV > 0$ and $PI > 1$. However, when ranked by *NPV*, project C is more attractive while project D is better when ranked by *PI*. A conflict in *NPV* and *PI* rankings can only occur when the initial investments of the two proposals are not the same, which is the situation with projects C and D. Because the *NPV* method *nets* the original cost from the present value of the future cash flows while the *PI* method *divides* the present value of future cash flows by original cost, projects with different initial investments (different *scales* of investment) may have different rankings under the two evaluation methods. This is illustrated by this example.

When there is a conflict in rankings which project should the firm accept? The *NPV* technique is superior and project C is a better project (at least when $k = 0.15$). The reason the *NPV* method is superior is the same as was given in comparing *NPV* and *IRR* techniques. The best project will add the most new value to stockholder wealth, and this is the project that has the highest positive net present value. Since the *NPV* method, by definition, always selects the project with highest positive net present value, the *NPV* method is a better mutually exclusive choice evaluation technique than *PI*. If there were never any situations where *NPV* and *PI* gave conflicting results the firm could use the *PI* method with the assurance it would always choose the correct alternative. But since there are instances where *PI* does not select the correct investment (as in projects C and D) there is some danger to using the *PI* method. The *NPV* technique, on the other hand, always leads to the correct choice for mutually exclusive investments.

CAPITAL RATIONING

Capital rationing refers to the situation where a budget or funds constraint is imposed on the firm and the firm may not invest in all acceptable projects. Given the set of projects that are acceptable, what subset of projects should the firm select? In this situation the firm is still trying to maximize stockholder's wealth, so it should invest in that *group* of projects that collectively have the largest net present value. But this group must be selected without violating the stated budget constraint. The question becomes how to identify that best group of projects out of the larger set of acceptable proposals. That is, what investment criterion will identify this optimum group? Let us answer this question with an example.

Consider the group of investment alternatives shown in Figure 7–4, all of which are acceptable, but because of a $200,000 budget constraint on this period's spending, not all of which may be accepted.

FIGURE 7–4
Capital rationing example ($200,000 budget constraint and k = 10 percent)

Project	Initial investment (dollars)	PV of future cash flows* (dollars)	NPV (dollars)	PI	IRR (percent)
A	$ 50,000	$ 65,000	$15,000	1.30	35
B	50,000	61,000	11,000	1.21	19
C	50,000	58,000	8,000	1.16	15
D	50,000	56,000	6,000	1.12	22
E	100,000	150,000	50,000	1.50	40
F	100,000	120,000	20,000	1.20	21

$$* \; PV \text{ of future cash flows} = \sum_{t=1}^{n} \frac{CFAT_t}{(1+k)^t}$$

If the projects are ranked separately by *NPV*, *IRR*, and *PI* and then a cutoff is made where the $200,000 budget constraint is met (that is, a budget line is drawn when the firm fully expends the $200,000 budget), the resultant rankings and project selections would be as shown in Figure 7–5.

The *NPV* method selects projects *E* and *F* because they have the largest *NPV*. The net present value of this group of assets is $70,000. The *IRR* method selects *E*, *A*, and *D* with a resultant group net present value of $71,000, and the *PI* method selects projects *E*, *A*, and *B* with a combined net present value of $76,000.

This example illustrates two main points. First, the *NPV* method is not the best selection criterion when the firm is operating under capital rationing conditions. Second, the *PI* method *is* the best selection criterion. The reason that the *PI* method is best in this situation is because that by placing a constraint on the firm's goal of wealth maximization the goal has been changed subtly. The firm is now placed in the position of maximizing wealth per dollar of investment. But basically, this is the definition of *PI*. *PI* is present value per dollar of investment, and ranking projects by their *PI* is thus consistent with the altered goal of the firm. This also helps explain why the *IRR* method is superior to the *NPV* method in this example. The *IRR* is more similar to present value per dollar of investment than *NPV* is.

The result of this analysis is that when the firm is faced with *one-period* capital rationing (a budget constraint in *one* time period) the *PI* method is the best selection technique and will lead to selection of the optimal group of projects. Problems arise, however, when the initial in-

FIGURE 7–5
Project selection under capital rationing

Ranking	NPV method	PI method	IRR method
1	E*	E*	E*
2......... Budget	F*	A*	A*
line			
3	A	Budget B*	Budget D*
		line	line
4	B	F	F
5	C	C	B
6	D	D	C
NPV of group of projects selected	= $70,000	$76,000	$71,000

* Project included in budget.

vestment of the projects available are such that the investment budget cannot be completely expended. In such cases the *PI* method may no longer be best. These instances are referred to as project *indivisibility* problems. Fractions of projects may not be purchased, only *whole* projects. If, for example, project *A* cost $55,000 rather than $50,000 the proposed selection of the *PI* and *IRR* methods could not be implemented and the *NPV* method would have selected the best group. In general, when indivisibilities exist there is no way of knowing which of the three methods will work best. In addition, if the firm must budget in *several* time periods (multiperiod capital rationing) none of the three techniques may select the optimal group of projects. Multiperiod capital rationing problems are best handled by linear programming techniques.

Last, financial theorists argue that capital rationing is an irrational thing for the firm to impose on itself. If, in the example problem in Figure 7–4, the firm had accepted all six investments, the net present value of the group would be $110,000, $34,000 more than the group of three projects selected by the best criterion, the *PI* method. This $34,000 is the opportunity cost of rationing capital. By drawing a budget line at $200,000 the firm is passing up the chance to increase total stockholder's wealth by $34,000. This underscores what we have discussed before: If a project has a positive net present value it should be accepted because it will enhance the stockholder's wealth.

SUMMARY

In this chapter we have investigated the topic of investment decision logic. Given a proposed investment with estimated cash flows and an estimated cost of capital, what techniques should be used to evaluate the proposed project so that investment choices made are consistent with the firm's goal?

Three different kinds of long term investment or capital budgeting decision problems were identified:

1. *Accept-reject decision:* Should the firm invest in a new project?
2. *Mutually exclusive rankings:* Which of the competing proposals (if any) should the firm invest in?
3. *Capital rationing:* Without violating the stipulated budget constraint, which set of available investment proposals should the firm select?

Five different investment decision criteria or methods were defined. Each could broadly be categorized as either a discounted cash flow (*DCF*) or a nondiscounted cash flow (non-*DCF*) technique. The distinction is meant to be self-explanatory. Only the *DCF* techniques employ discounting in some fashion and hence explicitly account for the crucial time value of money concept.

1. Non-*DCF* methods

$$\text{Payback} = \text{The number of years before the initial investment is recovered.}$$

$$\text{Average rate of return } (ARR) = \frac{\left(\sum_{t=1}^{n} CFAT_t\right)/n}{\text{Initial investment}}$$

2. *DCF* methods

$$\text{Net present value } (NPV) = \sum_{t=0}^{n} \frac{CFAT_t}{(1+k)^t}$$

$$\text{Internal rate of return } (IRR) : \sum_{t=0}^{n} \frac{CFAT_t}{(1+IRR)^t} = 0$$

$$\text{Profitability index } (PI) = \frac{\sum_{t=1}^{n} \frac{CFAT_t}{(1+k)^t}}{\text{Initial investment}}$$

In analyzing the five evaluation methods discussed in the chapter we accumulated a list of good and bad features of each. This list is summarized in the accompanying table.

Method	Good features	Bad features
Payback	1. Easily understood 2. Easy to calculate 3. Provides a crude risk screen	1. Doesn't account for the time value of money of pre-payback cash flows 2. Completely ignores post-payback cash flows
ARR	1. Easily understood 2. Easy to calculate	1. Doesn't account for the time value of money of any of the cash flows
NPV	1. Relatively easy to calculate 2. Best method for mutually exclusive ranking problems 3. Tied for best method for accept-reject decision problems (with *PI*)	1. Hard to understand 2. May not work well in capital rationing problems
IRR	1. Easily understood 2. Has intuitive economic meaning 3. Works OK on *simple* accept-reject problems, which are most common type of investment problems	1. Can be tedious to calculate 2. May not work well on non-simple accept-reject problems (multiple rates) or mutually exclusive choices or capital rationing problems
PI	1. Relatively easy to calculate 2. Best method for one-period capital rationing problems 3. Tied for best method for accept-reject decision problems (with NPV)	1. Hard to understand 2. May not work well in some mutually exclusive choice situations

Assessing which criteria work best in which situations we reached these conclusions:

1. *Accept-reject decision:* The NPV and PI methods tie for best. They always give the correct and identical accept-reject decisions.
2. *Mutually exclusive choice decision:* The NPV technique is best. It always identifies the correct alternative.
3. *Capital rationing:* The PI method is best for simplified one-period budget problems when there are no difficulties with completely expending the budget. Multiperiod capital rationing problems are best resolved with linear programming methods.

QUESTIONS

1. Define the following terms and phrases:
   a. Payback.
   b. Average rate of return.
   c. Net present value.

      d. Internal rate of return.

      e. Profitability index.

      f. Simple investments.

      g. Capital rationing.

2. Under what condition would the internal rate of return and net present value always give a similar accept-reject decision on a project?

3. Following are *CFAT* schedules for several different investments. Indicate which investments are *simple* and which are *nonsimple:*

	0	1	2	3	4	5	6
				$CFAT_t$			
a	−100	20	40	60	80		
b	−200	−20	100	100	100	100	
c	−25	10	−10	20	30	30	
d	−100	0	0	50	50	50	50
e	−50	10	10	10	20	0	60
f	−85	0	0	−15	50	60	70
g	−250	75	100	0	−50	100	100

4. Suppose that a capital budgeting project has two internal rates of return, 40 and 70 percent. Furthermore, the project's *NPV* at a 50 percent discount rate is +$2,000. Would this project be acceptable if the cost of capital is (justify your answer): (*a*) 20 percent? (*b*) 65 percent? (*c*) 75 percent?

5. What role, if any, does the accept-reject decision play in making mutually exclusive investment decisions?

6. Given the net present value profiles of the three mutually exclusive investments (*A, B,* and *C*) shown, what investment decision should the firm make if the cost of capital, *k*, is equal to: (*a*) k_1? (*b*) k_2? (*c*) k_3? (*d*) k_4?

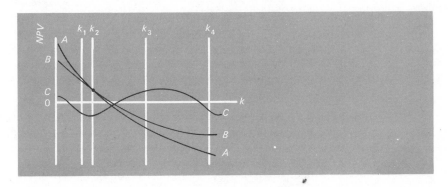

7. For most investment decisions that the firm faces, net present value is either a superior decision criterion, or is at least as good as competing techniques. In what investment situation is the profitability index *better* than net present value? Be careful to *completely* enumerate the conditions associated with this situation.

8. In evaluating a project by the *NPV* criterion, given the cost of capital k, if $NPV > 0$, the project is accepted, and if $NPV < 0$, the project is rejected.
   a. What decision should the firm take if $NPV = 0$? Explain your answer.
   b. What is the analogous *IRR* situation?

9. In some respects, mutually exclusive choice problems are similar to capital rationing problems. List these similarities, then list the major dissimilar characteristic of the two types of decisions.

PROBLEMS

1. Nettie and Sons, Inc., has the chance to purchase an asset that costs $1 million and returns $150 thousand per year for ten years. Both costs and returns are on an after tax basis. Assuming that the firm's required return is 10 percent, determine the following:
   a. Payback.
   b. ARR.
   c. IRR.
   d. NPV.
   e. PI.
   f. Should Nettie and Sons purchase the asset? Why?

2. The Meeker Co. has an ordinary tax rate of 60 percent. The company is considering investing in a project that costs $10,000. No investment tax credit is allowed, no increase in net working capital is required, and estimated salvage value is zero. The firm uses straight-line depreciation, and the proposed project has before tax operating cash flows as follows:

Year	1	2	3	4	5
CFBT	2,000	2,000	3,000	3,000	5,000

Determine:
   a. Payback.
   b. Average rate of return.
   c. Internal rate of return.
   d. Net present value at 10 percent.
   e. Profitability index at 10 percent.

3. Proposals A and B are mutually exclusive investment alternatives that the firm is considering. Their after tax cash flow patterns are shown below. The firm's cost of capital is 5 percent.
   a. Calculate each project's internal rate of return.
   b. Calculate each project's net present value.

c. Determine which project the firm should take and justify your choice.

Year	Proposal A (dollars)	Proposal B (dollars)
0	−70,500	−70,500
1	40,000	10,000
2	30,000	20,000
3	20,000	30,000
4	10,000	50,000

4. Sterling Tennisworld, Inc., has four million shares of common stock outstanding, currently selling for $15 per share. The company is considering undertaking some new investments that are listed below along with accompanying initial investment costs and estimated profitability indices.

Investment prospect	Cost	PI
A: Expand clothing lines	$2,000,000	1.5
B: Open up European retail outlets	3,000,000	1.3
C: Begin producing aluminum rackets	800,000	1.7
D: Increase tennis ball production	1,500,000	1.4
E: Increase advertising budget	1,000,000	1.8

a. Which investment will add the most value to stockholders wealth? Justify your answer.
b. In theory, what would Sterling's stock price be if the company undertakes all five investments?

5. Sharp Steel Co. is considering two alternate milling processes for a new plant facility. Process A will require an initial investment of $1,500,000 and yearly operating costs of $100,000. Process B will require an initial investment of $1,000,000 and yearly operating costs of $200,000. The life of the equipment used in either process will be ten years with no salvage anticipated. Depreciation is straight line. Regardless of the process chosen the anticipated revenues are $300,-000 per year. The firm's tax rate is 40 percent and its cost of capital is 30 percent. No investment tax credit is permitted and no increase in net working capital is anticipated.

Determine what investment decision Sharp Steel Co. should make. Support your recommendation with appropriate calculations.

6. The Mallory Cable Company has been examining the possibility of replacing their present storage facilities with an automated access warehouse. The present warehouse was purchased 20 years ago at a cost of $425,000. At that time it was estimated that the facilities would have a useful life of 40 years and a salvage value of $25,000. This warehouse could be sold today for $200,000. The prospective new warehouse costs $600,000, has a useful life of 20 years, and will

have a zero salvage value. If this warehouse is acquired, it is estimated that operating costs will be reduced by $85,000 per year over the asset's life. The company's tax rate is 48 percent and the investment tax credit is 10 percent. The company's cost of capital is 12 percent and straight-line depreciation is used.

Determine if Mallory should make the replacement. Support your conclusion with net present value calculations.

7. Vivian, Ltd., a novelty and toy manufacturer, is interested in expanding its product lines. One new venture under consideration is the production of high-quality plastic whistles. It would cost Vivian about $50,000 initially to purchase equipment to manufacture the whistles. However this cost would be reduced by a 10-percent investment tax credit. The production equipment would last five years; estimated salvage at project's end is zero. Vivian estimates it can sell whistles for $2 each. Regardless of the level of production, Vivian will incur cash costs of $20,000 each year if the project is undertaken. Additionally, it will cost the company about $1.60 more to manufacture each whistle. Vivian estimates it will sell about 100,000 whistles per year. Sum-of-the-years'-digits depreciation will be used; the ordinary tax rate is 40 percent. No increased net working capital is required.

   a. Calculate the project's net present value at 0, 10, 20, 30, and 40-percent discount rates.
   b. Sketch a net present value profile for the proposal.
   c. Calculate that particular discount rate that, for all discount rates *below* it, the project will be economically desirable, and for all discount rates *above* it, the project will be economically undesirable. What is the name of this particular discount rate?

8. As the financial analyst for the Ozark Can Company, you have been requested to evaluate the following prospective investments which are *not* mutually exclusive. The company's cost of capital is 8 percent.

Project	Description
I	Replace data processing equipment. Cost, $300,000. Expected life, 6 years. Expected *CFAT*, $72,680 per year.
II	Develop nonpolluting container. Cost, $100,-000. Expected life, 5 years. Expected *CFAT*, $27,047 per year.
III	Install safety program. Cost, $100,000. Expected life, 3 years. Expected *CFAT*, $46,566 per year.
IV	Develop plastic can. Cost, $200,000. Expected life, 4 years. Expected *CFAT*, $69,444 per year.
V	Convert to metric system. Cost, $200,000. Expected life, 7 years. Expected *CFAT*, $36,496 per year.
VI	Add 6,000 square feet of manufacturing space. Cost, $300,000. Expected life, 8 years. Expected *CFAT*, $57,421 per year.

   a. Which projects would you recommend if the company has un-
       limited funds? [Note, round off present values to nearest thou-
       sands of dollars here and in (b)]. What is their total net present
       value?
   b. Which projects would you recommend if the company must limit
       capital expenditures this year to $600,000? What is their total
       net present value?
   c. How much do the firm's stockholders lose from the capital ra-
       tioning constraint?

9. Myers Milling Co. is considering the following investment proposals
    which are not mutually exclusive. The company has only $100,000
    to invest this year; the cost of capital is 12 percent.

Project	Description
A	Install new milling controls. Cost, $35,000. Expected life, 6 years. Expected CFAT, $9,535 per year.
B	Replace conveyor belts. Cost, $45,000. Expected life, 4 years. Expected CFAT, $16,299 per year.
C	Purchase patent rights to new milling process. Cost, $20,000. Expected life, 2 years. Expected CFAT, $11,400 in year one, $13,325 in year two.
D	Extend loading dock 50 feet. Cost, $25,000. Expected life, 5 years. Expected CFAT, $8,114 per year.
E	Add two grain storage bins. Cost, $55,000. Expected life, 3 years. Expected CFAT, $27,500 in year one, $24,729 in year two, and $21,254 in year three.

   Select the best set of investments by ranking the proposals according to:
   a. PI.
   b. NPV.
   c. Determine the net present value of *all* feasible combinations of
       projects, where feasible means that the total costs of the projects
       do not exceed the budget limitation. (Hint: this requires an enu-
       meration of all combinations. There are ten two-project combina-
       tions, ten three-project, five four-project and one five-project
       combinations.) Identify the infeasible combinations.
   d. Which set of projects is best, given the budget constraint? What
       is their net present value?

SELECTED BASIC REFERENCES

Bierman, H., Jr., and S. Smidt *The Capital Budgeting Decision.* 4th ed. New
    York: Macmillan Publishing Co., Inc., 1975, chapters 2 and 3.

Lorie, J. H., and L. J. Savage "Three Problems in Rationing Capital," *Journal of Business* (October 1955), pp. 229–39.

Solomon, E. *The Theory of Financial Management*. New York: Columbia University Press, 1963, chapter 10.

SELECTED ADVANCED REFERENCES

Fama, E. F., and M. H. Miller *The Theory of Finance*. New York: Holt, Rinehart and Winston, Inc., 1972, chapter 3.

Hirshleifer, J. "On the Theory of Optimal Investment Decision." *Journal of Political Economy* (August 1958), pp. 329–52.

Schwab, B., and P. Lusztig "A Comparative Analysis of the Net Present Value and Benefit-Cost Ratio as Measures of the Economic Desirability of Investments," *Journal of Finance* (June 1969), pp. 507–16.

8

THE COST OF CAPITAL

In the first part of Chapter 6 we stated that there were three necessary tasks to be performed when making long-term investment decisions:

1. Estimation of cash flows.
2. Estimation of an appropriate discount rate or cost of capital for the proposal.
3. Selection of investment criteria.

Chapter 6 was devoted to cash flow estimation principles and Chapter 7 to selection of investment criteria. These topics were developed under the assumption that the firm knew the appropriate cost of capital, k, to use. In this chapter we turn our attention to the calculation of k. In doing so we will find the task is no easy matter because the concept of the cost of capital is not particularly intuitive and the array of choices of the *appropriate* k to use is confusing. There is also disagreement about several aspects of cost of capital theory. Cost of capital theory has been a hotly debated topic in the study of financial management for many years and many of the debated issues are still unresolved today. Therefore it is frequently hard to make definitive statements that all finance scholars and practitioners would readily agree to. The result of all this is that the cost of capital subject is somewhat difficult to understand. So we will try to take it step by step, slow and easy.

AN OVERVIEW

Let's begin by looking at the cost of capital from two slightly different perspectives. *Operationally*, what is the cost of capital? We can answer this by building on our work in the previous chapter. It is a cutoff or hurdle rate applied to investment projects the firm is considering. If a project's net present value is positive, using the cost of capital as the discount rate, the project should be accepted. If a project's net present value is negative, using the cost of capital as the discount rate, the project should be rejected. The cost of capital then is the hurdle discount rate that, when applied to a project's cash flow stream, will determine whether the project is worthwhile or not.

Now, what should this hurdle rate represent in an *economic* sense? It should represent the cost of acquiring the funds used in paying for the project. Thus, the cost of capital should reflect what it costs the firm to raise new capital for the proposed investment. In fact, this is where the name comes from: "the cost of (raising new) capital." If a project is expected to earn a 10-percent internal rate of return, the firm should accept the project only if new funds cost *less* than 10 percent.

FIGURE 8–1
Cost of capital as a cutoff or hurdle rate

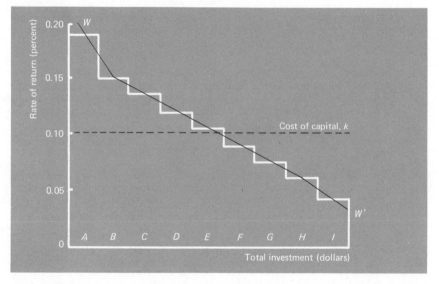

Notice also that the operational and economic concepts of cost of capital both imply that the cost of capital is a *marginal* cost. Marginal cost is a microeconomic concept that, in this case, means the cost (in percent) of raising an *additional* dollar of funds.

Figure 8–1 illustrates this idea. There are several investment opportunities, projects A through I, available to the firm. These are portrayed in Figure 8–1 in an ordered fashion, starting in the upper left-hand corner with the project that offers the highest internal rate of return (A) and going down to the lower right-hand corner with the project that offers the lowest internal rate of return (I). The internal rates of return for these projects are shown by extending the top of each rectangle over to the left-hand axis. Project B's *IRR*, for example, is 15 percent. The total or cumulative dollar investment that would be required to invest in them in a sequential fashion, proceeding from best to worst project, is shown on the bottom axis. The schedule of project internal rates of return represents a *demand schedule* for funds from all the various projects. In fact, by connecting a line through all the project rates of return, we get the demand schedule $W - W'$. Also shown in Figure 8-1 is the cost of capital cutoff, k. In effect this is a *supply schedule* of funds. This supply schedule depicts the rates of return the firm must pay to acquire the funds necessary to make any given level of investment. In Figure 8-1 the supply curve is drawn as perfectly horizontal, although many economists argue that the curve slopes upward as total investment increases.

All projects with $IRR < k$ should be rejected and all projects with $IRR > k$ should be accepted. As Figure 8-1 shows, projects A through E should be accepted and projects F through I should be rejected. If any more projects were to become available we can compare them to k just as was done with projects A through I. In fact, that is exactly what the investment decision is all about, comparing a project's IRR with k.

TWO COST OF CAPITAL APPROACHES

Investment capital is provided to the firm by investors, and logically, the cost of capital should reflect the time value of money and risk attitude of these investors. In developing ways to calculate the cost of capital we will investigate two computational methods. One, the *weighted average cost of capital* is a well-known, traditional method of calculating k. The second method, the *risk adjusted cost of capital* is much newer and therefore less familiar. It emanates from the so-called *capital asset pricing model*, which is a financial model that theoretically describes the way that assets are priced in capital markets. The weighted average cost of capital is better understood by the finance community, but we will see that it has some difficulties associated with it that seriously limit its use in investment problems. The risk adjusted cost of capital approach surmounts these problems but is much less understood by the financial community.

We will study both approaches. We will look first at the weighted averave cost of capital method. This requires a slow building process where we investigate the specific costs of the several components of the weighted average cost of capital. Later, we will study the risk adjusted cost of capital approach, which will relate a project's cost of capital to its risk.

EXPLICIT COSTS OF CAPITAL

Each source of capital has an explicit cost of capital—namely, the cost to the firm of raising funds from that particular source of capital. This cost is not stated in dollar terms, but rather in percentage terms.

To help understand the concept of cost of capital consider the following general process that occurs when the firm obtains new capital. Assume, for illustration purposes, that the firm is acquiring *external* capital, that is, capital from outside the firm, as from the sale of new common stock or new bonds or new preferred stock. The firm sells the securities to investors, usually through an investment banker (we study the role of investment bankers in the capital market in Chapter 12).

The sale price of the securities less all floatation costs[1] associated with issuing the securities represent the *net cash proceeds* the firm receives from issuing the securities. In return for receiving these net sale proceeds the firm is expected to make future cash payments to investors who either originally bought the securities or who subsequently buy the securities from another investor. These expected future cash payments will vary in form with the kind of financial instrument involved. Bonds, for example, will involve interest payments and principal repayment, and common and preferred stocks will involve dividends. But the process is the same in any case: The firm receives cash now in exchange for the expectation that the firm will pay future cash payments to the capital provider.

Definition of k

The rate of return or discount rate that equates the net cash proceeds the firm receives with the present value of future expected payments from the firm to the capital suppliers is called the cost of capital:

Cost of capital (for *any* **source of capital)** = **That discount rate,** k**, that equates the net cash proceeds received by the firm** *from* **the capital source with the present value of the expected future cash payments made** *to* **the capital source.**

Mathematically, this definition may be written as:

$$C_0 = \frac{C_1}{(1+k)} + \frac{C_2}{(1+k)^2} + \cdots + \frac{C_n}{(1+k)^n}$$

More succinctly:

$$C_0 = \sum_{t=1}^{n} \frac{C_t}{(1+k)^t} \tag{8-1}$$

where

C_0 = net cash proceeds received by the firm from the capital source at $t = 0$; C_t = the expected cash payment from the firm to the capital source in year t; n = the expected duration or life of the financial instrument; and k = the cost of capital.

Notice the similarity in the definition of cost of capital and the definition of the internal rate of return: The cost of capital is the internal rate of return the firm pays to procure financing.

Sources of long-term capital

Up to now we have only talked in generalities. We have defined the cost of capital for any source of capital and now we need to be more spe-

---

[1] Floatation costs are composed of *underwriting costs* (costs that investment bankers charge the firm for selling securities for the firm) and other legal fees and registration costs involved when securities are issued. Floatation costs are discussed in detail in Chapter 12.

cific. Bear in mind that we are concerned here with *long-term* capital sources. While the firm also uses short-term sources of capital, our concern here is with how the firm finances its long-term investments. This is done primarily with long-term capital.

There are three broadly defined sources of capital the firm can turn to: debt, equity, and hybrid (part debt–part equity) securities.

1. Debt*
2. Equity
   a. Common stock*
   b. Retained earnings*
3. Other
   a. Preferred stock*
   b. Convertible securities
   c. Warrants
   d. Leases

In developing specific costs of capital we will only investigate those sources marked with an asterisk (*). They represent the most frequently used sources of capital and illustrate well the mechanics of calculating k.

Cost of debt

The cost of debt calculation is basically the same whether the debt is in any one of several forms of bonds or bank loans. The peculiarities that distinguish one form of debt from another are primarily nonfinancial, and we can analyze the explicit cost of debt as if there were just one kind of debt. The distinguishing characteristics of the various debt instruments are covered in Chapter 12. Equation (8–1) is the building block. However, we need to identify the components of Equation (8–1) in terms of debt instruments.

First, C_0 represents the initial proceeds, net of floatation costs that the firm receives from the sale of the debt. Let B_0 equal the expected sale price in dollars per bond and let f equal the total floatation costs expressed as a percent of B_0. If, for example, $B_0 = \$1,000$ and $f = 2$ percent, floatation costs are $20 and net cash proceeds equal $980. Thus, the net cash proceeds from a debt issue, C_0, are:

$$C_0 = B_0(1 - f)$$

Cash outflows or payments to debt holders are composed of two kinds of payments, interest payments and repayment of principal. These two components have different tax treatments. Interest payments made by the firm are tax deductible. Consequently, if the tax rate is 48 percent, every dollar of interest paid by the firm doesn't actually cost a dollar, but only $0.52. Why? Because the firm gets to deduct $0.48 from their taxes for each dollar of interest paid. Thus, if the firm's total interest payments are $10,000 this year and the tax rate is 48 percent, the effective or out of pocket interest payments are not $10,000, but $(1 - 0.48)(\$10,000) = \$5,200$. If the tax rate were 30 percent, the effective interest payments would be $(1 - 0.30)(\$10,000) = \$7,000$. This does not mean that the debt holders don't receive the full $10,000 interest payments, for they do. It simply means that the firm pays less income tax because of the tax deductibility of interest charges. By paying less income tax the firm reduces its after tax or effective interest payments. For any tax rate, T, and any interest payment, I, the after tax interest payment is $(1 - T)I$. Adding the subscript t to the interest payment to show what *year* the payment is made, we see that the after tax interest payment in year t equals $(1 - T)I_t$.

Repayments of principal, however, are *not* tax deductible. So there are no tax advantages for repayment of principal, and each before tax dollar spent in repaying principal results in a one dollar after tax cash outflow. If we define the dollar amount of the principal repayment in any year as B_t, the after tax cash repayment is also B_t.

The total annual after tax dollar payments the firm makes to the debt holders is the sum of the principal payments and after tax interest payments. This sum is the after tax cash flow going from the firm to the debt holders and represents the annual *fixed charges* associated with the debt:

$$C_t = B_t + (1 - T)I_t$$

where

C_t = after tax cash outflow in year t; B_t = principal repayment in year t; T = tax rate; and I_t = interest payment in year t.

We will identify the cost of debt as k_i. We can now rewrite Equation (8-1) for the debt case, and k_i is the discount rate that will make the following equation hold:

$$B_0(1 - f) = \frac{B_1 + (1 - T)I_1}{1 + k_i} + \frac{B_2 + (1 - T)I_2}{(1 + k_i)^2} + \cdots + \frac{B_n + (1 - T)I_n}{(1 + k_i)^n}$$

$$B_0(1 - f) = \sum_{t=1}^{n} \frac{B_t + (1 - T)I_t}{(1 + k_i)^t} \tag{8-2}$$

This equation is different from (8-1) only in that its components are specifically identified as being *debt* components: The cash flows are fixed charges (principal repayments plus after tax interest payments) and the discount rate that makes (8-2) hold is k_i, the cost of *debt*.

An approximation formula We are interested in calculating k_i from Equation (8-2). For most realistic problems this would require a trial-and-error solution of Equation (8-2). However, for debt issues that are reasonably long-lived, say 20 years or more, and that have constant interest payments ($I_1 = I_2 \ldots I_n$), we can considerably reduce the mathematical work through an approximation or short-cut formula that can be mathematically derived from Equation (8-2)

$$k_i = \frac{(1 - T)I}{(1 - f)B_0} \tag{8-3}$$

where I is the constant annual interest payment.

Suppose, for example, Butterfield Bread Co. is planning to issue new $1,000 face value, 20-year bonds. The bonds are expected to sell at $1,000 and the floatation cost is 2 percent. The bonds will carry a 6-percent annual coupon (the firm will pay 6-percent interest on face value each year) and the firm will redeem the bonds at the end of 20 years. The firm's tax rate is 48 percent. What is k_i?

Annual interest payments are $0.06 \times \$1,000 = \$60$ per year for each bond.[2] By definition, k_i is the discount rate that makes Equation (8–2) hold:

$$(\$1,000)(0.98) = \sum_{t=1}^{20} \frac{(0.52)(\$60)}{(1 + k_i)^t} + \frac{\$1,000}{(1 + k_i)^{20}}$$

Since life is fairly long (20 years) and the interest payments are constant we can avoid a detailed trial-and-error solution by employing shortcut Equation (8–3):

$$k_i = \frac{(0.52)(\$60)}{(\$1,000)(0.98)} = 0.032 = 3.2 \text{ percent}$$

Butterfield's cost of debt is 3.2 percent. We will see as we proceed through this chapter that debt has the lowest explicit cost of any source of capital available to the firm. This is partly because of the tax deductibility of interest payments. The explicit cost of debt is also low relative to other sources because, from the investor's viewpoint, debt is the safest financial asset the firm can issue. The debtholders are paid before any other long-term source of capital holders (such as preferred or common stockholders) and the debt also has prior claim on the firm's assets in case of bankruptcy.[3] Because there is less risk in buying debt compared to other financial instruments, investors will accept a lower rate of return on the debt: They impose a lower required rate of return on debt relative to other financial instruments. But investor's required rate of return is a synonym for cost of capital. Hence, lower risk means a lower cost of capital to the firm. Therefore, even without the tax deductibility feature of interest payments, debt has a lower specific cost of capital than any other long-term source of capital.

Even in instances where interest payments are not constant, shortcut Equation (8–3) can provide useful approximations of k_i. There are situations where (8–3) does not provide a good approximation of k_i, but when the debt is issued at a price reasonably close to face value (the usual situation) and the life of the debt is fairly long, (8–3) gives very useful approximations of k_i.

Cost of preferred stock

We will use the same approach here as was used in the debt case, emphasizing the conceptual notion of the cost of preferred stock and leaving the institutional and legal aspects and features of preferred stock to a later chapter (Chapter 13). Equation (8–1) is the foundation for determining the cost of preferred, and our first task is to identify the components of this general equation with the corresponding preferred stock components.

---

[2] Coupon rates are nominal (stated annual) rates. Typically, interest payments are made semiannually, but we ignore that refinement here.

[3] The relative safety features of debt are discussed in more detail in Chapter 14.

Let p_0 equal the expected sale price of the preferred stock in dollars per share and let f equal the total floatation costs expressed as a percent of p_0. Then the net cash proceeds received from the sale of preferred stock is

$$C_0 = p_0(1 - f)$$

Cash payments from the firm to preferred stock owners are in the form of preferred dividends and repayment of preferred stock principal if the preferred is retired (frequently it is never retired so there is no principal repayment). There are stipulated dividend rates on the preferred stock certificate of ownership, usually as a percent of the preferred's par value, and these percentage rates determine what the cash payments will be. We will designate these expected dividend payments with the symbol d and use the subscript t to denote the year in which they will be paid so that expected payment to preferred holders in year t is d_t. Unlike interest payments, preferred dividend payments are not tax deductible – preferred dividends are paid out of *after* tax earnings – so that a dollar paid as preferred stock dividends actually results in a dollar after tax cash outflow from the firm. Similarly, the principal repayment (p_n) is not tax deductible.[4]

The explicit cost of preferred we will denote as k_p. This is the discount rate that equates the net proceeds of the sale of the preferred stock with the present value of the future dividends and principal repayments. Therefore, we can rewrite (8–1) for the preferred stock case:

$$p_0(1 - f) = \frac{d_1}{1 + k_p} + \frac{d_2}{(1 + k_p)^2} + \cdots + \frac{d_n}{(1 + k_p)^n} + \frac{p_n}{(1 + k_p)^n}$$

$$p_0(1 - f) = \sum_{t=1}^{n} \frac{d_t}{(1 + k_p)^t} + \frac{p_n}{(1 + k_p)^n} \qquad\qquad (8\text{–}4)$$

Equation (8–4) is the equation of interest for finding the cost of preferred stock, k_p. There are complicating features that have been left out of Equation (8–4). The preferred may be convertible preferred, which gives the investor the privilege of converting his preferred stock into common stock at some future date. In addition, some preferred stocks have participating provisions that allow the preferred stockholders to share earnings with the common stockholders in very profitable years. These features, which are discussed in Chapter 13, make Equation (8–4) more complex, but the nature of the definition of k_p does not fundamentally change.

An approximation formula Ignoring these complications, we see that the expected dividends, d_t, will be constant and the life of the preferred stock will be fairly long. Under these conditions, there is a shortcut or approximation formula to find k_p rather than using definitional Equation (8–4). This approximation formula is also derived from (8–4).

---

[4] Typically, preferred stock has no maturity date. The use of p_n implies some expected "call" date when the preferred stock will be retired. See Chapter 13.

$$k_p = \frac{d}{p_o(1 - f)} \qquad (8\text{-}5)$$

where d is the constant annual dividend payment.

Suppose, for example, that Butterfield plans to issue new $100 par preferred stock. Expected sale price is $100, floatation costs are 3 percent of the expected sale price, and the dividend rate is stated as 8 percent of par. The preferred has no expected call date: It will be a permanent part of the firm's capital structure. What is k_p?

Annual expected dividends are $0.08 \times \$100 = \$8$ per share. By definition, k_p is the discount rate that makes Equation (8–4) hold:

$$(\$100)(0.97) = \sum_{t=1}^{\infty} \frac{\$8}{(1 + k_p)^t}$$

Using the shortcut Equation (8–5), we get

$$k_p = \frac{\$8}{(\$100)(0.97)} = 0.082 = 8.2 \text{ percent}$$

In comparison to Butterfield's previously calculated cost of debt (3.2 percent) the cost of preferred is higher. This is because the preferred dividends are not tax deductible like interest payments are, and because the preferred stock is a riskier investment for an investor than debt. Because the preferred is riskier, investors impose a higher required rate of return in compensation for this extra risk. Except for floatation costs, the specific cost of capital and the required rate of return are the same thing so that a higher required rate of return necessarily means a higher cost of capital.

Cost of equity

This is the last source of capital we consider, and actually there are two sources of equity capital: common stock and retained earnings. Common stock equity refers to proceeds from the sale of new common stock. Retained earnings are equity funds raised within the firm by keeping a portion of current earnings, so this source of equity is provided by the current stock owners in the form of foregone dividends.

Common stock The process of determining the cost of common stock is no different than the process used in getting the cost of debt or preferred stock. We use Equation (8–1) as before.

Let P_0 equal the expected sale price in dollars per share and let f equal the floatation costs expressed as a percent of P_0. Then the net cash proceeds from the sale of new common stock are:

$$C_0 = P_0(1 - f)$$

Cash payments from the firm to the stockholders are paid as common dividends. Similar to preferred stock dividends, dividends paid to common stock are *not* tax deductible – they are paid out of after tax earnings. Since these dividends are not tax deductible, every dollar paid as common dividends results in a one dollar expense *after* tax. Consequently, the cost of external equity is already on an after tax basis. Unlike the dividends on preferred stock, however, there is no stipulated dividend rate or percent return on common shares. Investors estimate the dividend rate by what is being paid on *current* shares and through any pronouncements the company makes during the promotion of the new issue. Once this new stock is issued, it will have the same rights, privileges, dividends, price, risk, etc., as the current stock, unless the new stock is some special form of common (see Chapter 13).

Let the dividend paid to common in year t be denoted as D_t. This is the cash payment from the firm to the stockholder in year t.

We will call the cost of common stock k_e. This is the discount rate that equates the net proceeds of the sale of the common stock with the present value of the future expected dividends paid to the new shares of common stock. Equation (8-1) can now be adapted for this specific cost of capital. k_e is the discount rate in Equation (8-6):

$$P_0(1 - f) = \frac{D_1}{1 + k_e} + \frac{D_2}{(1 + k_e)^2} + \cdots + \frac{D_\infty}{(1 + k_e)^\infty}$$

$$P_0(1 - f) = \sum_{t=1}^{\infty} \frac{D_t}{(1 + k_e)^t} \tag{8-6}$$

Equation (8-6) is the general equation of concern for finding k_e. Except for floatation costs, (8-6) is the *dividend valuation model* discussed in Chapter 5 that relates the current price of the firm's stock, P_0, to the present value of the future expected dividends [see Equation (5-5)]. k_e is the internal rate of return or discount rate that will make Equation (8-6) hold. Solving for k_e from (8-6) requires, in general, a trial-and-error solution. As always, we are interested in knowing what simplifications could be made that would provide an easier method for solving for k_e. We look at two such instances: *no growth* stocks and *constant growth* stocks.

No growth firms. There are times in the life cycle of firms when the expected future dividend stream may be relatively constant or flat for lengthy periods of time. This might occur because the firm has heavy investment commitments in a mature industry that has little hopes of earnings and dividend growth for some time. Such was the case with American steel companies in the 1960s. If *future* dividends are expected to be the same as *current* dividends for a long time[5] the firm is called a *no growth* firm, meaning no growth in expected dividends. For no growth firms the cost of common stock can be approximated by Equation (8-7), which is derived from (8-6):

$$k_e = \frac{D}{P_0(1 - f)} \tag{8-7}$$

where D is the constant expected dividend.

Assume, for example, that Butterfield is currently paying a $5 per share dividend on its common stock, which is currently priced at $50 per share. The market (investors at the margin) expects this $5 per share

---

[5] Actually, the assumption is that expected future dividends are constant *forever*.

dividend to be maintained indefinitely. What is k_e if floatation costs are estimated to be 5 percent of current market price?

$$k_e = \frac{\$5}{(\$50)(0.95)} = 0.105 = 10.5 \text{ percent}$$

Except for floatation costs, the cost of external equity for no growth firms is the dividend yield (dividend/price) of the firm's stock. It may seem unrealistic to assume no growth in expected dividends forever, but for many firms Equation (8-7) provides a good approximation of their cost of common stock. In addition, this formulation provides a convenient stepping stone to the next model, which *does* have growth in its expected dividend stream.

Constant growth firms. Many firms' expected dividend streams may be characterized as growing at an approximately constant rate. If we assume that dividends are growing at a constant rate, g percent per year, forever, Equation (8-6) may be simplified (we omit the mathematical derivation again) to:

$$k_e = \frac{D_1}{P_0(1-f)} + g \tag{8-8}$$

where

D_1 is next year's expected dividend (dollars per share) and g is growth rate (percent per year) in dividends.

This shortcut approach to estimating k_e is called the *constant growth model*.

If Butterfield's current stock price is $50 per share, next year's expected dividend is $5 per share, expected growth in dividends is 6 percent per year and floatation costs are 5 percent of current stock price, what is k_e?

$$k_e = \frac{\$5}{(\$50)(0.95)} + 0.06 = 0.105 + 0.06 = 0.165 = 16.5 \text{ percent}$$

The constant growth model presumes a growth rate in expected dividends at rate g percent *forever*. While this assumption may also seem extremely unrealistic it is nonetheless a very useful assumption. Many firms have expected dividend growth rates that are constant for several years, and for such firms, Equation (8-8) provides good approximations of k_e. Of course, if future dividends are expected to grow at substantially different rates, the financial analyst may prefer to resort back to Equation (8-6) to get a better estimate of k_e.

Retained earnings Most firms regularly retain part of their earnings for investment purposes. These retained earnings are a source of *internal* equity funds. They are *preemptively* provided since it is the firm that decides what percent of earnings to pay out as dividends and what percent to retain. The firm is implicitly saying that, in its judgment, a certain portion of the firm's current earnings should be retained for investment rather than being paid out as dividends. While the question of what percent of each dollar *should* be retained is a controversial issue, we leave that issue aside until Chapter 11 and only address here the question of calculating the cost of retained earnings. In performing this task we will see that contrary to many executives' view, retained earnings are not free.

Rather than establish a definitional equation for the cost of internal equity, and identifying all the component parts of the equation as we have done for the other capital sources, we can considerably shorten the analysis by noting that internally provided equity (retained earnings) and externally provided equity (new common stock) are basically the same thing. And, except for floatation costs, the costs of internal and external equity are *equal!* The cost of equity capital is simply another way of saying the required rate of return that common stockholders require or expect on their investment. So it should certainly seem reasonable that an investor would require the same return on additional investment in the firm in the form of retained earnings as he would require on an investment in new common stock.

There is another way of explaining why the costs of retained earnings and common stock are equal. By retaining earnings, the firm is denying its stockholders the use of these retentions. Now, what could the stockholders do with the retained earnings if the firm didn't keep them? One option is to reinvest them back in the firm by buying more common stock in the firm. What kind of return would the investor require on this additional investment? The cost of common stock, k_e! So by keeping part of each dollar of earnings, the firm denies the stockholders the chance to make a return of k_e percent on the retained part of the earnings. Consequently, the firm must "make it up" to the stockholders by returning k_e percent on the retained earnings. Thus, the cost of retained earnings is an opportunity cost.

Let k'_e = the cost of retained earnings. The primary factor that makes k_e and k'_e different is floatation costs. Consequently, we can define k'_e as:

$$P_0 = \sum_{t=1}^{\infty} \frac{D_t}{(1 + k'_e)^t} \tag{8-9}$$

Since $k'_e = k_e$ except for floatation costs, Equation (8–9) is identical to Equation (8–6) except that there are no floatation costs in the left-hand side of (8–9) like there are in the left-hand side of (8–6). In both equations the left-hand side represents the *net* proceeds the firm receives in new equity money. However, the firm incurs no floatation costs from retaining earnings, and therefore, retained earnings have a lower cost of capital than new common stock. This is one of the reasons the firm retains earnings; Going to the market incurs floatation costs.[6]

Earnings are retained because the firm has opportunities to invest in projects that will cause growth in its future earnings and dividends. If this growth is assumed (as before) to be at a constant rate g forever, the shortcut method for finding k'_e is:

---

[6] We are ignoring here the problems caused by the existence of different income tax rates for different investors. Investors with relatively high income tax rates may prefer that the firm retain a relatively large percentage of its earnings to take advantage of lower capital gains tax rates. These issues are discussed in Chapter 11.

$$k_e' = \frac{D_1}{P_0} + g \tag{8-10}$$

Notice there are no floatation costs and (8-10) is different from its external equity counterpart [Equation (8-8)] only in that respect. If Butterfield's current stock price is $50 per share, next year's expected dividend is $5 per share, and the expected growth in dividends is 6 percent per year, what is k_e'?

$$k_e' = \frac{\$5}{\$50} + 0.06 = 0.16 = 16 \text{ percent}$$

In comparison with the previously determined cost of external equity of 16.5 percent, k_e' is lower than k_e because there are no floatation costs.

There are two last points to note about k_e and k_e'. First, they are the most difficult explicit costs of capital to accurately estimate. The difficult part is estimating future expected dividends. When the firm calculates the cost of debt, the future expected interest payments and principal repayments are contractual obligations and may therefore be estimated with a very high degree of accuracy. And, while future preferred dividends are not contractual obligations, they are fixed by terms stated on the preferred instrument and therefore may also be estimated with some confidence. Common stock dividends, however, are not contractual obligations and are paid at the discretion of the firm. Predicting what future dividends will be is a most difficult task. Future dividend payments depend on the future earnings stream, and it is extremely difficult to estimate what future earnings will be. Generally speaking, the firm's earnings prospects will follow the economy's trends, but there may be times when the firm does not follow the general economic trend. Moreover, it is equally difficult to predict future economic trends. All in all, it is very hard to predict future earnings, and it is therefore difficult to estimate the future dividends required to calculate k_e and k_e'.

The second point to note about k_e and k_e' is their relative size compared to the previously calculated cost of debt (3.2 percent) and cost of preferred (8.2 percent) for the example company, Butterfield Bread. It is no accident that k_e and k_e' are much larger than k_i and k_p. Part of the reason that k_e and k_e' are greater than k_i is that dividend payments are not tax deductible. We have also stressed before that, except for floatation costs, the cost of capital represents the "market's" required rate of return. Since common stock is the riskiest financial instrument the firm has, investors will only buy it and/or hold it if they are compensated for the increased risk exposure with a higher expected rate of return. Thus, equity has a higher cost of capital than other sources of capital.

WEIGHTED AVERAGE COST OF CAPITAL

We have now looked at several sources of long-term capital and demonstrated how to calculate the cost of capital of each. Recall that the reason for investigating the subject of cost of capital was to determine the proper discount rate to use in evaluating investment proposals. How do the various specific costs of capital derived above relate to the investment decision discount rate? One approach to determining the appropriate discount rate for investments is to use the *weighted average cost of capital*. That is, the specific costs of capital are averaged by a weighting process described below, and this weighted average discount rate is the discount rate used in evaluating investments. An explanation of the weighting scheme requires a brief explanation of *capital structure*.

Capital structure

The overall picture of what kinds of long-term capital a firm has used to finance its long-term investments is revealed by looking at the firm's balance sheet. The composition or proportionate usage of these long-term sources of capital is called the *capital structure* of the firm. Some firms have no long-term debt or preferred stock, but most U.S. corporations have a mixture of sources of long-term capital. This mixture is shown in the firm's balance sheet. Butterfield's balance sheet is shown in Figure 8–2.

FIGURE 8–2

BUTTERFIELD BREAD CO.
Balance Sheet

Current assets	$25,000,000	Current liabilities	$20,000,000
Net plant and			
equipment.............	45,000,000	Mortgage bonds	20,000,000
Total	$70,000,000	Preferred stock	10,000,000
		Net worth:	
		Common stock.......	10,000,000
		Retained earnings ...	10,000,000
		Total	$70,000,000

We are interested in the long-term sources of capital that Butterfield is now employing: debt, preferred, and equity. From Butterfield's balance sheet we can prepare the following capital structure chart:

Source of long-term capital	Book value	Percent of total capital provided by capital source
Debt............................	$20,000,000	40
Preferred stock...............	10,000,000	20
Common stock	10,000,000	20
Retained earnings............	10,000,000	20
Total capital	$50,000,000	100

Butterfield's capital structure is 40 percent debt, 20 percent preferred stock, 20 percent common stock, and 20 percent retained earnings. These percentages are the capital proportions that each source of capital has supplied. Together with the cost of capital figures the firm has estimated, these percentages determine the firm's weighted average cost of capital.

Definition of k_o

$$\begin{array}{l}\text{The weighted}\\\text{average cost}\\\text{of capital}\end{array} = k_o = \sum \left(\begin{array}{l}\text{Percent of the total}\\\text{capital structure}\\\text{supplied by each}\\\text{source}\end{array} \times \begin{array}{l}\text{Cost of capital}\\\text{for each source}\\\text{of capital the}\\\text{firm is using}\end{array}\right)$$

In the Butterfield case, there are only four sources of capital being used: debt, preferred, common stock, and retained earnings. In such a case the weighted average cost of capital k_o would be written as:

$$k_o = w_i k_i + w_p k_p + w_e k_e + w'_e k'_e \tag{8-11}$$

where

w_i = percent of the firm's total capital that is debt; w_p = percent of the firm's total capital that is preferred; w_e = percent of the firm's total capital that is common stock; w'_e = percent of the firm's total capital that is retained earnings; k_i = cost of debt; k_p = cost of preferred stock; k_e = cost of common stock; and k'_e = cost of retained earnings.

Given the capital structure chart we prepared above and the costs of capital we estimated earlier in the chapter we can calculate Butterfield's weighted average cost of capital k_o:

	Weight, w	Cost of capital, k	w × k
Debt	0.40	0.032	0.013
Preferred stock	0.20	0.082	0.016
Common stock	0.20	0.165	0.033
Retained earnings	0.20	0.160	0.032

$$k_o = 0.094 = 9.4 \text{ percent}$$

This example illustrates the concept of the weighted average cost of capital: It is an average of the individual explicit costs of capital with each component (source) weighted by the percentage of the total capital in the firm that is supplied by that source. In the example above, Butterfield's capital structure was 40-percent debt, and that is the weighting factor that is multiplied times the cost of debt to get the portion of the weighted average cost of capital that is attributable to the use of debt. And so on for the other three sources of capital in the example.

Of course, in reality, most firms use more than four sources of capital in financing their investments. But this poses no real problem. The generalized form of Equation (8-11) is:

$$k_o = w_1 k_1 + w_2 k_2 + \cdots + w_m k_m = \sum_{a=1}^{m} w_a k_a \tag{8-12}$$

where

k_a = explicit cost of capital of the ath source; w_a = proportion of the total capital of the firm supplied by the ath source; and m = number of long-term capital sources in firm's capital structure.

Comparing the simpler definition in Equation (8-11) with this general definition of k_o, we see that $m = 4$, because there were four capital sources in the Butterfield example. For sources other than these we can apply our general definition of the cost of capital (8–1) or an appropriate short-cut formula and find the cost of that capital source. The percent of the firm's total capital than the source supplies may also be found, and Equation (8–12) is then employed to find k_o.

k_o as a marginal discount rate

At the beginning of this chapter we stressed that the appropriate discount rate to use in the investment decision was a *marginal* rate, a discount rate that reflects what it costs the firm to raise an incremental dollar to pay for an incremental dollar's worth of new investment. This is what the weighted average cost of capital represents. It's the percentage cost to the firm of raising an incremental dollar in the *same proportions* that the firm has in the past. Since Butterfield's present capital structure is 40-percent debt, 20-percent preferred stock, 20-percent common stock, and 20-percent retained earnings, the weighted average cost of capital shows what it will cost the firm to raise another (incremental) dollar composed of $0.40 debt, $0.20 preferred stock, $0.20 common stock, and $0.20 retained earnings. This cost, k_o, is then used as a discount rate in the investment decision.

Market value and book value weights

The weights (w_a's) that are used in the weighted average cost of capital formulas may be calculated in two different ways. One way – the way we worked the Butterfield example – uses *book value* weights. This means that the w_a's are determined by dividing the book value of each capital source by the sum of the book values of all the long-term capital sources. Under the *market value* weight approach, the w_a's would be determined by dividing the market value of each capital source by the sum of the market values of all the sources. The market value of any capital source is the price per security times the number of securities outstanding. In the Butterfield case, the market value of the debt, for example, would be the current price of the outstanding bonds times the number of bonds currently outstanding. If the bonds have $1,000 face value we can determine the number of bonds outstanding by referring back to the balance sheet in Figure 8–2. There are ($20,000,000/$1,000=) 20,000 bonds outstanding. If the current market price of these outstanding bonds is $800 per bond, the market value of the outstanding bonds is $800 × 20,000 = $16,000,000. If the market values and book values of the various sources are considerably different, the weights calculated under the two methods may be considerably different.

The question is, which is the *correct* weighting system? There is not total agreement among finance scholars, but there seems to be a preference for market weights on the premise that since the costs of capital that are multiplied times these weights are determined by market forces (that is, these costs are market costs), for consistency the weights should be market weights. This is a compelling reason. However, because market weights are determined by market prices, which may fluctuate quite a bit, market weights fluctuate (change) much more so than book weights. Also, it is frequently difficult to determine market values for some kinds of financial instruments. That is, book value information is frequently much easier to obtain. In addition, using k_o implies that the firm will raise new capital in approximately the same proportions that it has raised capital in the past, and book weights reflect the firm's historical use of long-term capital sources better than market weights. For these reasons we will use book weights in this text even though there are compelling reasons (described above) for using market weights.

When to use k_o

At first glance, the weighted average cost of capital appears to answer the question we first started out to resolve: What discount rate is appropriate for the investment decision? However, k_o is appropriate only under certain conditions. The weighted average cost of capital, k_o, is an appropriate discount rate under the following two conditions:

1. The firm intends to finance future projects with new long-term capital that is raised in approximately the same proportions as its present capital structure.
2. Projects under consideration have approximately the same amount of risk that the firm – viewed as a composite project – has.

The first condition is tantamount to assuming the firm will keep the same capital structure in the future as it currently has. Actually, a k_o can be calculated that does not require this condition, but it would involve calculations that are considerably different than those we engaged in above.

The second condition is not so easily dismissed. One of the fundamental concepts we develop in the next chapter is that the discount rate applied to the income stream of an asset is a function of the risk inherent in the asset. Use of k_o as the discount rate for project evaluation implicitly assumes that all projects are equally risky in comparison with the firm as a whole. In Chapter 4 terminology, use of k_o presumes that all projects have the same covariance with a market index as does the firm. It may be that many projects do have roughly the same risk as the firm has. A greeting card company, for example, repetitively brings out new or updated card lines with cash flow streams that are about as risky as previously introduced lines. But it is clear that many projects will not be equally risky as the firm's other assets. For these projects we need to develop a more flexible concept of cost of capital or required rate of return that explicitly relates the required rate of return to project risk. We turn to this task now.

RISK ADJUSTED COST OF CAPITAL

In the valuation chapter (Chapter 5) we noted that the required rate of return for any asset was equal to the risk free interest rate plus a risk premium that reflects the risk inherent in the asset.

Let $k_j^* =$ risk adjusted cost of capital or required rate of return associated with asset j. Then

$$k_j^* = i + r_j \qquad (8\text{-}13)$$

where

$i =$ risk free interest rate, and $r_j =$ risk premium associated with asset j. Thus k_j^* is a function of the price of time (i) and the price of risk (r).

Perfect markets and rational investors

Now assume that capital markets are *perfect* and investors are *rational*. The assumption that markets are perfect implies a world where there are no taxes, no floatation costs, perfect information concerning the distribution of future asset rates of return, and that there are many buyers and sellers of assets with no one buyer or seller able to influence prices. Finance typically describes rational investors as preferring more wealth than less wealth and preferring less risk than more. In Chapter 4 we associated wealth preference with preference for assets with high expected values of rate of return, and risk avoidance with preference for assets with low values of covariance of rate of return with a market index. The assumptions of perfect markets and rational investors describe an ideal world and are never fully satisfied in the real world. However, the assumptions provide the basis for determination of risk adjusted required rates of return that are useful approximations even in the real world. That is, even if the assumptions are not completely realistic, the results of the theory that the assumptions underlie are remarkably useful. And this practical usefulness implies that perhaps the assumptions of perfect markets and rational investors are not all that unrealistic. Indeed, there is considerable evidence to support these assumptions.

If we assume that capital markets *are* perfect and that investors *are* rational, it may be shown that the risk premium for an asset is equal to:[7]

$$r_j = (\mu_m - i)\,\beta_j \qquad (8\text{-}14)$$

where

$r_j =$ risk premium for asset j; $\mu_m =$ expected rate of return of the "market" or "market index"; $i =$ risk free interest rate;   d $\beta_j =$ the beta measure of covariance between asset j and market ind x rates of return.

These terms were all encountered in Chapter 4, and you may wish to review them at this time.

Definition of k_j^*

Having established the value of the risk premium for a risky project or asset we can now relate the risk adjusted cost of capital for an asset to its risk:

Risk adjusted cost of capital for asset $j = k_j^* = i + (\mu_m - i)\,\beta_j$ (8-15)

---

[7] This omitted derivation may be found in the advanced readings referenced at the end of this chapter.

The risk adjusted cost of capital or risk adjusted discount rate for a proposed project or asset is the sum of the risk free interest rate and the risk premium associated with the degree of risk in the project. Moreover, this risk premium is a function of covariance with the market, which is the appropriate financial management risk measure established back in Chapter 4.

Notice that Equation (8–15) indicates there is a straight-line relationship between cost of capital (k_j^*) and risk (β_j). If we plotted k_j^* against β_j we would have a straight-line graph as shown in Figure 8–3. The intercept of the k_j^* axis is the risk free interest rate and the slope of the market line is ($\mu_m - i$). Figure 8–3 shows that, as project risk increases, the project's cost of capital, k_j^*, also increases. Basically, the straight line describes a risk-return tradeoff that exists in perfect capital markets. The

FIGURE 8–3
Risk adjusted cost of capital (k_j*) as a function of risk (β_j)

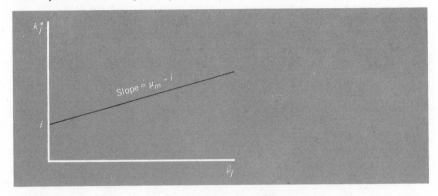

riskier the project the greater the discount rate that will be applied to the project's expected cash flows by the "market" (investors at the margin). Similarly, the less risky the project the smaller the discount rate applied to the project's expected cash flows. If a proposed project had $\beta_j = 0$, there would be no risk associated with the project, and the appropriate cost of capital for evaluating the project would be the risk free interest rate ($k_j^* = i$).

Suppose the firm is considering investment in proposed project A (new equipment) and has collected the following relevant information. The expected market index rate of return is 10 percent and the risk free interest rate is 5 percent. Project A's estimated beta is 1.2. What is the appropriate discount rate, k_A^*, for evaluation of this project?

From the stated problem we know the following items:

$$\mu_m = 0.10, \ i = 0.05, \text{ and } \beta_A = 1.2$$

The risk adjusted cost of capital for project A, k_A^*, is given by (8–15):

$$k_A^* = i + (\mu_m - i) \beta_A$$
$$= 0.05 + (0.10 - 0.05) (1.2)$$
$$= 0.05 + 0.06 = 0.11 = 11 \text{ percent}$$

Given the stated estimations, the appropriate discount rate for project A is 11 percent. Of course, if the β_A estimate had been different, k_A^* would necessarily be different also.

Now consider other independent investment projects the firm is analyzing. The market parameters (μ_m and i) estimated in the example above will also apply to these projects. The determination of appropriate discount rates for these other projects will proceed as above with Equation (8–15). The following list shows the estimated β_j and calculated k_j^* values for several such projects:

Project	β_j	k_j^*
B	0.8	0.09
C	1.0	0.10
D	1.5	0.125

These values of β_j and k_j^* are all shown in Figure 8–4.

FIGURE 8–4
k_j^* versus β_j

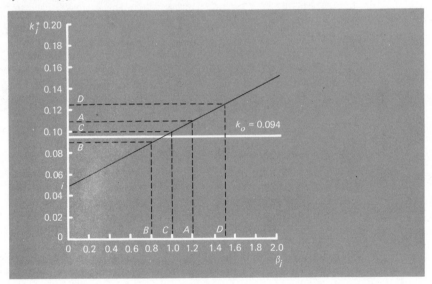

As Figure 8–4 shows, each project has its own risk adjusted cost of capital, which is determined by market parameters (μ_m and i) common to *all* projects and the financial management risk (β_j) peculiar to the project. Thus all project risk and risk adjusted cost of capital values fall on the same straight line. In effect, this straight-line converts the financial management risk of projects into a risk adjusted cost of capital for *each* project. Each project has its own cost of capital and this cost of capital reflects the financial management risk inherent in the project.

k_o VERSUS k_j^*

Superimposed on Figure 8–4 is Butterfield's weighted average cost of capital, $k_o = 0.094$, which we previously determined. By showing k_o in this figure we can better appreciate the limitations of k_o. The use of k_o as a cost of capital for evaluating projects ignores the fact that different projects have different degrees of risk and therefore have different costs of capital.[8] Using k_o on the four projects described above we overstate the cost of capital for project B and understate the cost of capital for projects A, C, and D.

SUMMARY

We began this chapter by asking: How does the firm determine what the discount rate for investment decisions, k, is? We looked at two approaches to answering this question: one uses weighted average cost of capital, k_o, and the other a risk adjusted cost of capital, k_j^*.

Weighted average cost of capital, k_0

To calculate k_o we must first calculate costs of capital for all long-term sources of capital the firm is currently using and their percentage weights. Getting the weights is the relatively easier task and we used *book* weights derived from the firm's balance sheet. Getting the cost of capital is more difficult. The general definition for *any* source of capital is that discount rate, k, that equates the net cash proceeds received by the firm from the capital source, with the present value of the expected future payments to the capital source:

$$C_0 = \sum_{t=1}^{n} \frac{C_t}{(1+k)^t}$$

We then proceeded to derive costs of capital for several of the most frequently used long-term capital sources, developing convenient approximation formulas for each:

$$\text{Cost of debt} = k_i = \frac{(1-T)\,I}{(1-f)\,B_0}$$

$$\text{Cost of preferred stock} = k_p = \frac{d}{p_0(1-f)}$$

$$\text{Cost of common stock} = k_e = \frac{D_1}{P_0(1-f)} + g$$

$$\text{Cost of retained earnings} = k_e' = \frac{D_1}{P_0} + g$$

We then defined the weighted average cost of capital:

$$\text{Weighted average cost of capital} = k_o = \sum_{a=1}^{m} w_a k_a$$

---

[8] Actually, it is possible to reformulate k_o to account for risk differences. This reformulation converts k_o to k_j^*. This is shown in some of the advanced readings referenced at the end of the chapter.

Risk adjusted cost of capital, k_j^*

The risk adjusted cost of capital method acknowledges that different investment projects have different degrees of risk, and determines a discount rate for each project that is dictated by its inherent financial management risk. This risk, β_j, is measured by the covariance of returns of the project with the returns of the "market." This concept of risk directly relates back to the definition of financial management risk developed in Chapter 4:

$$k_j^* = i + (\mu_m - i)\beta_j$$

In comparison with k_o, k_j^* has the advantage that it can be used to evaluate projects that do not have the same degree of risk as the firm.

QUESTIONS

1. Define the following terms and phrases:
   a. Explicit cost of capital.
   b. k_i.
   c. k_p.
   d. k_e.
   e. k_e'.
   f. k_o.
   g. Capital structure.
   h. Risk adjusted cost of capital.
   i. g.
   j. Floatation costs.

2. a. Discuss how the average cost of capital is used in (enters into) long-term investment (capital budgeting) problems.
   b. Explain what impact an increase in the firm's average cost of capital would have on the amount of new investment the firm undertakes, other things equal.

3. Explain why:
   a. The cost of debt is usually considered the cheapest source of financing available to the firm.
   b. The cost of preferred stock is less than the cost of equity.
   c. The cost of internal equity (retained earnings) is less than the cost of external equity (common stock).
   d. The cost of retained earnings is not zero.

4. The calculation of *any* explicit cost of capital requires the firm's financial staff to estimate both the net proceeds the firm will receive from the capital source (investors) and the expected future payments the firm will make to the investors. Despite the similarity of estimation problems, it is well-recognized that the cost of equity (both internal and external) is the most difficult cost to estimate. Breifly explain why this is so.

5. The weighted average cost of capital may be computed using "book" or "market" weights.

      a. Briefly describe how each set of weights is calculated.

      b. Compare the advantages and disadvantages of using book weights rather than market weights in calculating the firm's weighted average cost of capital.

6.   Other things equal, explain how the following events would affect the firm's average cost of capital:

      a. The corporate income tax rate is increased.

      b. The firm begins to make substantial new investment in assets that are considerably riskier than the firm's presently owned assets.

      c. Floatation costs of issuing new securities decline.

      d. Moody's bond rating service lowers its rating of the firm's bonds because, in Moody's opinion, these bonds are now riskier.

7.   Describe what effects the following events might have on companies preferences for raising new capital from the issuance of common stock.

      a. Congress allows common dividends to be tax deductible.

      b. The price of the company's common stock is low because of a depressed stock market.

      c. Floatation costs associated with new common stock increases significantly because the stock market is going through a period of substantial fluctuations.

      d. The firm's investment bankers informally advise the firm's financial officers that an influential group of New York investment analysts feel that the firm's debt level is getting excessively high in comparison to the firm's industry competitors.

8.   The Vice President for Finance of Barron Industries is being closely quizzed by some other members of Barron's Board of Directors at a board meeting. The firm's financial staff, which is headed by the Finance Vice President, has provided the Board with a current estimate of the firm's average cost of capital of 12 percent. This estimate is predicated on the firm maintaining its present capital structure, which, incidentally, the Board plans to do. However, a finance staff member has just completed a presentation concerning a new proposed investment that the finance staff has thoroughly analyzed. The staff's recommendation is to accept the project even though its expected rate of return is only 10 percent. Equally puzzling, the Vice President for Marketing remarks that one of his division's pet projects, which had an expected return of 15 percent, was rejected last week by the finance staff.

     If we accept the estimates of future cash flows for both of these proposals as being reasonably accurate, how might the Finance Vice President explain the fact that a project with an expected rate of return less than k_o is being recommended for acceptance, and a project with an expected rate of return greater than k_o was rejected?

9.   Other things equal, what effect would the following events have on the risk adjusted cost of capital for a proposed purchase of mineral rights to a new iron ore deposit in Minnesota:

    a. The covariance between the project and market index rate of return increases.

    b. The expected rate of return on the market index decreases.

    c. Several of the firm's competitors are attempting to acquire the same mineral rights before the firm can.

10. In determining what discount rate to use in capital budgeting analysis, what advantage does k_j^* offer in comparison to k_o? Any disadvantages?

PROBLEMS

1. Calculate the explicit costs of debt for each of the following situations:
   a. The company issues $1,000 face value bonds with maturity of 30 years. The bonds are sold for $1,000 each.
   1. The bonds pay 8-percent interest anually, floatations costs are 2 percent, and the marginal tax rate is 40 percent.
   2. The bonds pay 8-percent interest annually, floatation costs are 2 percent, and the marginal tax rate is 50 percent.
   3. The bonds pay 8-percent interest annually, floatation costs are 4 percent, and the marginal tax rate is 40 percent.
   4. The bonds pay $100 interest annually, floatation costs are 2 percent, and the marginal tax rate is 40 percent.

   b. The company issues $1,000 face value bonds with maturity of 40 years, floatation costs are $30 per bond, and the marginal tax rate is 45 percent. The bonds pay X percent interest annually and are sold for $Y, where
   1. X = 7 percent, Y = $900 per bond.
   2. X = 8 percent, Y = $800 per bond.
   3. X = 6 percent, Y = $1,100 per bond.

2. If the Suzanne Sportswear Co. can issue $100 par preferred stock at $60 per share and the company's marginal tax rate is 40 percent, find the explicit cost of preferred stock in each of the following situations:
   a. The stock pays an annual dividend of $4 per share and floatation costs are 4 percent of sale price.
   b. The stock pays an annual dividend of $4 per share and floatation costs are $3 per share.
   c. The stock pays an 8-percent dividend and floatation costs are 4 percent of the sale price.
   d. Rework part (*a*) assuming the stock sells for $50 per share.

3. Assuming that the Sudekum Ice Cream Co. can sell new common stock at $75 per share, find the company's costs of internal and external equity for the following situations:
   a. Stockholders expect the next dividend to be $3 and that these dividends will grow at 10 percent per year. Floatation costs are 6 percent of sale price.

b. Stockholders expect the next dividend to be $3 per share and that these dividends will grow at 7 percent per year. Floatation costs are $4.50 per share.

c. Stockholders expect the next dividend to be $3 per share and that these dividends will grow at 10 percent per year. Floatation costs are 3 percent of sale price.

d. Stockholders expect the next dividend to be $2 per share and that these dividends will grow at 10 percent per year. Floatation costs are 6 percent of sale price.

e. Stockholders expect the next dividend to be $6 per share and that these dividends will not grow. Floatation costs are 10 percent of sale price.

f. Rework (b) assuming that the stock sells for $90 per share.

4. KC Chemicals, Inc., has obtained the following information about the cost of new long-term financing:

Source	Net proceeds to firm
Bonds, $1,000 par (7 percent)	$980 per bond
Preferred stock, $100 par (8 percent)	$95 per share
Common stock	$20 per share

The firm expects earnings to be $3 per share for the foreseeable future, and all earnings are paid out to dividends. The firm's tax rate is 40 percent. The firm's most recent balance sheet (in millions of dollars) is:

Assets		Claims	
Current assets	$200	Current liabilities	$100
Net fixed assets	400	Long-term debt	200
		Preferred stock	100
		Common stock	200
Total assets	$600	Total claims	$600

a. Find the explicit costs of capital of all the long-term capital sources.

b. Assuming that KC Chemicals will finance its future long-term investments in about the same capital proportions as it has in the past, calculate the firm's weighted average cost of capital.

5. Sara's International Dance Studios, Inc., currently has the following capital structure:

5-percent debt	$20,000,000
7-percent preferred	5,000,000
Common equity:	
Stock	10,000,000
Retained earnings	15,000,000
Total	$50,000,000

New \$1,000 bonds may be sold at face value with an 8-percent coupon. New preferred may be sold at par (\$100) with a 9-percent dividend. Both would be placed with private investors so that there would be no floatation costs. Sara's common stock is currently selling for \$25 per share. Earnings per share have grown steadily at a 10 percent rate in the past ten years, and dividends are expected to approximate this growth rate in the future. Expected earnings next year are \$2.50 per share. From every dollar of earnings Sara pays out \$0.40 in dividends. Floatation costs on new stock issued would be \$5 per share. The firm's tax rate is 40 percent.

Find the weighted average cost of capital assuming that the company's future capital structure will be approximately the same as its present structure.

6. The Rasch Equipment Co. is in the process of preparing its capital budget for the coming year. The company uses its average cost of capital as the discount rate for evaluating investment proposals, and a Rasch financial analyst has obtained the following data to be used in calculating k_o.

RASCH EQUIPMENT COMPANY
Balance Sheet
December 31, 19+0

Assets		*Claims*	
Current assets		Current liabilities	
Cash and securities......\$	125,000	Accounts payable..... \$	200,000
Receivables	175,000	Notes payable	60,000
Inventory...................	300,000	Taxes payable	40,000
	600,000		300,000
Land	400,000	Mortgage bonds.......	300,000
Plant and equipment....	300,000	Preferred stock	150,000
		Common stock........	400,000
		Retained earnings.....	150,000
Total assets \$1,300,000		Total claims... \$1,300,000	

Anticipated external financing information:
30 year, \$1,000 face value bonds: Sale price = \$1,000, 8-percent coupon, 2-percent floatation costs
Preferred stock: Sale price = \$30 per share, \$3 per share annual dividend, 4-percent floatation costs
Common stock: Sale price = \$10 per share, 6-percent floatation costs

Rasch's marginal tax rate is 40 percent and the expected common dividend growth is 6 percent per year. Next year's expected dividend = \$0.75 per share. Assuming that the company is satisfied with its present capital structure and intends to maintain it, determine Rasch's weighted average cost of capital.

7. The OMJ Corporation is currently analyzing a proposed new investment. Additional after tax cash flows anticipated from the new in-

vestment would be $17,000 per year for 20 years. The investment would cost $110,000 (after tax) at the outset. OMJ is an all equity firm; the stock is currently selling for $22 per share. OMJ intends to remain all equity. Furthermore, OMJ maintains a policy of paying out all earnings as dividends. The company expects a future earnings stream (without the new investment) of $3 per share. If equity floatation costs are $2 per share:

a. Determine k_e and k_o for OMJ.
b. Use k_o in the net present value method to determine whether OMJ should make the proposed investment.

8. As a financial analyst for the Bahr Barber Supply Company, you have been given the assignment of determining the company's average cost of capital. Toward that end, the following financial information has been collected.

The company's present book value capital structure is:

Debt ($1,000 par)	$ 4,000,000
Preferred stock ($100 par).........	1,000,000
Common equity ($10 par).........	5,000,000
	$10,000,000

All three of these securities are traded in the capital markets. Recent prices are:
Debt: $1,317 per bond
Preferred stock: $120 per share
Common stock: $22 per share

Anticipated External Financing Opportunities
$1,000 par bonds: 30-year maturity, 7-percent coupon, 4-percent floatation costs, sale price = $1,000.
$100 par preferred stock: 8-percent dividend rate, 5-percent floatation costs, sale price = $100.
Common stock: $3.20 per share floatation costs, sale price = $22.

Furthermore, next year's expected common dividend is $1 per share, the anticipated growth rate in dividends is 8 percent per year, and the firm pays out all of its earnings in dividends. The company's marginal tax rate is 40 percent. In recognition of the fact that the explicit cost of capital can be weighted according to two different weighting schemes:

a. Determine the average cost of capital using *book value* weights.
b. Determine the average cost of capital using *market value* weights.
c. Briefly explain why the k_o calculated in (b) is greater than the k_o calculated in (a).

9. The company's financial economists have estimated that the expected rate of return for the market for the next ten years is about 14 percent. They have also observed the following market yields on different ten-year bonds: 8 percent on Government bonds, 9 percent on high-grade corporate bonds, 12 percent on low-grade corporate bonds. Given this information, determine the risk adjusted cost of

capital for each of the following proposed ten year new investments whose beta risk measures are as shown:

Project	1	2	3	4	5	6	7
Beta	1.2	1.4	1.0	0.8	0	−0.5	−1.0

10. The Mycroft Construction Company builds single family dwellings. The company recently became interested in the condominium industry and is making preliminary plans to enter this market. Mycroft is presently in the process of evaluating a proposed condominium project and must determine a cost of capital at which to discount the cash flows associated with this investment. The company's average cost of capital is known to be 11 percent. However, since this project is considerably different from the firm's present investments, management has decided to use a risk adjusted cost of capital.

   a. What would be the risk adjusted cost of capital for this project if the expected rate of return and standard deviation of rate of return of the market are 0.10 and 0.13, respectively, the risk free interest rate is 0.06 and the covariance between the market and the condominium project rates of return is 0.0338?

   b. What would be the risk adjusted cost of capital for this project if its correlation with the market is +0.89, its standard deviation of rate of return is 0.013, the risk free interest rate is 6 percent, and the distribution of market returns is as follows:

Probability	0.2	0.2	0.3	0.2	0.1
Market return (percent)	7	10	12	13	14

   c. What *potential* error might Mycroft make if it discounted the project's cash flows at the firm's average cost of capital rather than at: (1) the risk adjusted rate determined in part (*a*)? (2) the risk adjusted rate determined in part (*b*)?

SELECTED BASIC REFERENCES

Lo Cascio, V. R. "The Cost of Capital in an Uncertain Universe," *Financial Executive* (October 1970), pp. 70–78.

Robichek, A. A., and J. G. McDonald. "The Cost of Capital Concept: Potential Use and Misuse," *Financial Executive* (June 1965), pp. 20–35.

Solomon, E. *The Theory of Financial Management.* New York: Columbia University Press, 1963, chapter 3.

SELECTED ADVANCED READINGS

Haley, C. W., and L. D. Schall. *The Theory of Financial Decisions.* New York: McGraw-Hill Book Co., 1973, chapter 13.

Lewellen, W. G. *The Cost of Capital:* Dubuque, Iowa, Kendall/Hunt Publishing Co., 1976.

Modigliani, F., and M. Miller. "Taxes and the Cost of Capital: A Correction," *American Economic Review* (June 1963), pp. 433–44.

Tuttle, D. L., and R. H. Litzenberger. "Leverage, Diversification and Capital Market Effects on a Risk Adjusted Capital Budgeting Framework," *Journal of Finance* (June 1968), pp. 427–43.

9

INVESTMENT DECISIONS UNDER RISK

In the previous three chapters we have systematically investigated the three related parts of long-term investment decisions: estimating cash flows, estimating an appropriate discount rate or cost of capital, and establishing investment criteria. Except for the work in the last chapter on estimating discount rates we have ignored a very real fact of life: risk. In this chapter we further consider risk in investment analysis, completing our work on long-term investment decisions.

Recall from Chapter 4 that the outcome of a decision made in the absence of certainty is called a random variable. A random variable has probabilities assigned to its outcomes, and risk and uncertainty are terms used to describe any situation where the outcome is a random variable. So by investment decisions under risk, we mean investment decisions where the outcomes are random variables.

EXPECTED CASH FLOWS

The two major investment evaluation techniques of risky projects both involve expected cash flow principles, so we turn first to the task of defining and calculating expected cash flows.

Economic influences

Consider the annual cash flows that any new project generates. The *CFAT* in each year is, to some degree, dependent on how the general economy does. Other things equal, if the economy does well it is more likely that any new project will do well also, since rising economic activity creates a favorable climate for investment success. Similarly, average or normal economic years typically lead to average years for investments, and bad overall economic years typically lead to poor results for investments. There are, of course, exceptions to these generalities.

Certain industries may do poorly even in economic booms and other industries may do well even in recession years. However, the *CFAT* from most assets is, in any year, related to the overall market (economic) return. This is another way of saying that rates of return on most assets are positively correlated with general economic conditions.

A natural starting point for projecting results from a proposed risky investment is to relate the project's annual *CFAT* to the overall economic activity. We may pose many possible outcomes and associated probabilities for the general economic outlook, but at the simplest level we can think of the outcomes as "bad," "average," and "good." A "bad" year connotes recession, an "average" year implies normal economic activity, and a "good" year connotes an economic boom. We may also attach probabilities to these qualitative outcomes. For example:

State of economy	Probability
Bad	0.2
Average	0.6
Good	0.2

This is a very simple conceptual framework that views the economic future as having only three qualitative outcomes with stated probabilities; yet it is a beginning toward making investment decisions under risk. We could make the state of economy outcomes more exhaustive (have more finely shaded outcomes, such as "very bad," "fairly bad," etc.), or we could quantify what a bad state of the economy means (a 10-percent drop in GNP), but we will let these issues pass. The real intent here is to illustrate how the financial analyst might develop future annual *CFAT* results for a new project: He looks to the general economy and relates the project to it. For each state of the economy the analyst can posit a companion estimated *CFAT*. For example,

State of economy	Probability	CFAT (dollars)
Bad	0.2	20,000
Average	0.6	25,000
Good	0.2	30,000

If the economy is average the analyst estimates the project will provide a *CFAT* = \$25,000. There are, of course, some necessary preliminary steps in getting this \$25,000 *CFAT*. The analyst begins with cash revenues and expenses and works through an analysis described in Chapter 6. The example only shows the bottom line, \$25,000 *CFAT* result, but the intermediate work was also performed. If the economy is bad, the analyst estimates the project's *CFAT* will drop to \$20,000, and if the economy is good the analyst estimates that *CFAT* will be \$30,000.

Expected value

Now recall from Chapter 4 that:

$$\mu = \sum_{i=1}^{N} p_i X_i \qquad (9\text{--}1)$$

where

μ = expected value; X_i = the ith possible outcome; p_i = the probability of the ith outcome occurring; and N = number of possible outcomes.

Applying this definition to the example, we get

$$\mu = (0.2)(\$20,000) + (0.6)(\$25,000) + (0.2)(\$30,000)$$
$$= \$4,000 + \$15,000 + \$6,000$$
$$= \$25,000$$

The expected cash flow of the project for the example year is $25,000. Notice that determining expected cash flows involves a marrying of ideas involved in Chapters 4 and 6. Expected refers to *expected value* and cash flows refers to *cash flows after tax (CFAT)*.

Multiyear projects

The analyst will estimate *CFAT* outcomes for *each* year of a proposed project's life. Suppose a firm is considering an investment that is expected to last three years. The *CFAT* in each year has been related to the economy by the analyst, and the resultant estimation schedule of possible *CFAT*'s and associated probabilities is shown in Figure 9–1.

The anticipated initial investment is $50,000, and by setting the probability equal to 1.0, the analyst is saying the investment cost of $50,000 is known with certainty and is unrelated to the state of the economy. The returns on this investment are *not* known with certainty as evidenced

FIGURE 9–1
Estimated CFAT schedule

Year	State of economy	Estimated project CFAT (dollars)	Probability
0.............	Any state	−50,000	1.0
1.............	Bad	20,000	0.2
	Average	25,000	0.6
	Good	30,000	0.2
2.............	Bad	20,000	0.4
	Average	30,000	0.2
	Good	40,000	0.4
3.............	Bad	10,000	0.4
	Average	20,000	0.2
	Good	30,000	0.4

by the probabilities of all future *CFAT*'s being less than one. In year one if the economy is bad, the estimated project *CFAT* is $20,000 and the associated probability is 0.2. If the economy is average, the estimated project *CFAT* is $25,000 and the probability of this state is, in the analyst's opinion, 0.6. Last, if the economy is good, the project's estimated *CFAT* is $30,000 and the estimated probability of this is 0.2. And so on for the other two years.

Expected CFAT

Given these estimates of *CFAT* and associated probabilities, the analyst now is ready to calculate expected cash flows. Let us slightly alter Equation (9-1) to make it more general and also to put it into symbols more compatible with the problem at hand.

$$\text{Expected } CFAT \text{ in year } t = \overline{CFAT_t} = \sum_{i=1}^{N} p_{ti} \, CFAT_{ti} \qquad (9\text{-}2)$$

where $CFAT_{ti}$ = cash flow after tax in year t of the ith outcome and p_{ti} = probability associated with the ith outcome in year t. Because projects last for several years *each* year has an expected *CFAT*. The expected *CFAT* for year t is denoted by drawing a bar over *CFAT* ($\overline{CFAT_t}$) and equals the weighted probability average of the estimated cash flows in that year:

For year zero:

$$\overline{CFAT_0} = (1.0)(-\$50,000) = -\$50,000$$

For year one:

$$\overline{CFAT_1} = (0.2)(\$20,000) + (0.6)(\$25,000) + (0.2)(\$30,000)$$
$$= \$4,000 + \$15,000 + \$6,000 = \$25,000$$

For year two:

$$\overline{CFAT_2} = (0.4)(\$20,000) + (0.2)(\$30,000) + (0.4)(\$40,000)$$
$$= \$30,000$$

For year three:

$$\overline{CFAT_3} = (0.4)(\$10,000) + (0.2)(\$20,000) + (0.4)(\$30,000)$$
$$= \$20,000$$

This completes the determination of expected cash flows for the project. The calculations may be summarized by listing the calculated $\overline{CFAT_t}$ numbers:

Year, t	0	1	2	3
$\overline{CFAT_t}$	−50,000	25,000	30,000	20,000

If the firm accepts this project it will pay $50,000 (for certain) and in return, it expects to receive $25,000 in year one, $30,000 in year two, and $20,000 in year three.

Both of the two major evaluation techniques described below employ expected cash flows so we will use the calculation procedures just developed in the following analysis.

TWO EVALUATION METHODS

Basically, there are two major competing methods for making risky long-term investment decisions: the *risk adjusted discount rate method* and the *certainty equivalent method*. We will investigate both of these methods and some other procedures used to evaluate risky long-term investment prospects, but we will concentrate first on the risk adjusted discount rate method and the certainty equivalent method since they represent fairly complete decision systems, are most widely used by both theorists and practitioners, and are logically consistent with the firm's goal of stockholder wealth maximization.

Risk adjusted discount rate method

The risk adjusted discount rate method is based on the premise that the riskiness of a project may be accounted for by adjusting the discount rate (cost of capital). Relatively risky projects would have relatively high discount rates and relatively safe projects would be assigned relatively low discount rates. The risk adjusted discount rate may be estimated by procedures developed in the last chapter where we studied the risk adjusted cost of capital. It might also be estimated by other less sophisticated methods. Some companies, for example, have established ranges of discount rates for certain types of frequently encountered projects. An oil company might regularly use a 10-percent discount rate on less risky development oil wells, 15 percent on domestic exploratory wells, and 20 percent on Middle East exploratory wells. The rates presumably reflect the differential risk in the different classes of investments. Once the risk adjusted discount rate is estimated it may be used to evaluate the desirability of the proposed project. Under the risk adjusted discount rate approach the firm uses an expected net present value model to evaluate the project, where the future cash flows are *expected* cash flows and the discount rate is k^*:

$$\overline{NPV} = \sum_{t=0}^{n} \frac{\overline{CFAT_t}}{(1 + k^*)^t} \tag{9–3}$$

where

$\overline{NPV}$ = expected NPV; $\overline{CFAT_t}$ = expected $CFAT$ in year t; and k^* = risk adjusted discount rate.

The accept-reject decision rule is the same as that developed in Ch. 7:

If $\overline{NPV} > 0$,   accept the project.

If $\overline{NPV} < 0$,   reject the project.

Equation (9–3) is consistent with the original valuation Equation (5–1) developed in Chapter 5. Projects are evaluated on the basis of future cash flow projections and an appropriate discount rate. Equation (9–3) emphasizes that future cash flows are expected values of the annual distribution of *CFAT* outcomes, and the discount rate reflects the degree of risk in the project.

Suppose the firm is evaluating the project described in Figure 9–1, which, recall, has the following expected $\overline{CFAT}$ stream: $\overline{CFAT}_0 = -\$50,000$, $\overline{CFAT}_1 = \$25,000$, $\overline{CFAT}_2 = \$30,000$, $\overline{CFAT}_3 = \$20,000$. Assume further that—say, using methods described in Chapter 8—the firm has determined that k^* for this project is 25 percent.

$$\overline{NPV} = -\$50,000 + \frac{\$25,000}{1.25} + \frac{\$30,000}{(1.25)^2} + \frac{\$20,000}{(1.25)^3}$$

$$\overline{NPV} = -\$50,000 + (\$25,000)(0.800) + (30,000)(0.640) + (20,000)(0.512)$$

$$= -\$50,000 + \$20,000 + \$19,200 + \$10,240$$
$$= -\$560$$

Given the expected cash flows and estimated risk adjusted cost of capital, the project's expected net present value is negative and the project would be rejected.

Notice that there is nothing really new in this approach. The only real difference between this evaluation technique and the *NPV* technique we studied in Chapter 7 is that we have explicitly accounted for the fact that future cash flows are not certain and the risk in the project has been related to the discount rate.

Certainty equivalent method

Some financial theorists object to using a risk adjusted discount rate to evaluate risky proposals as was just done. The objection goes like this. There are two important things to account for in the valuation process, the time value of money and risk attitudes. But these two concepts should be logically separated in the valuation process. Specifically, use of a discount rate that lumps together the risk free interest rate and a risk premium is wrong. That is, discounting for the futurity of cash flows should *only* include time value considerations and *not* risk considerations. Adding the risk premium into the discount rate leads to a *compounding* of risk over time, which is a questionable practice.

Proponents of this argument advocate an alternate evaluation method that avoids the problem of including a risk premium in the discount factor. This approach is called the *certainty equivalent method*. Under this evaluation approach the riskiness of the project is handled not by adjusting the discount rate, but by adjusting the expected cash flows:

$$\overline{NPV} = \sum_{t=0}^{n} \frac{\alpha_t \, \overline{CFAT}_t}{(1 + i)^t} \tag{9-4}$$

Where

α_t = certainty equivalent factor for year t ($0 \leq \alpha_t \leq 1$) and i
   = risk free interest rate.

The accept-reject decision rule is the same:

If $\overline{NPV} > 0$,   accept the project.
If $\overline{NPV} < 0$,   reject the project.

Certainty equivalent factors

The certainty equivalent factor, α_t, in any year represents that *CFAT* that investors would be satisfied to receive *for certain* in lieu of the distribution of *CFAT*'s that are possible for that year. In effect, the certainty equivalent factor converts the project's expected *CFAT* for the year into a *certain* amount that investors consider *equivalent* to the project's calculated $\overline{CFAT}$ for the year. The riskier the year's distribution of *CFAT*'s appears to investors, the lower the certainty equivalent factor; the safer the distribution appears, the larger the certainty equivalent factor. At one extreme, if there is *no* risk involved $\alpha_t = 1$. Thus, if a project has only one *possible CFAT* outcome for some year there is no risk involved that year and investors would be unwilling to accept less than the *CFAT* that is sure to occur. But as risk increases, investors will presumably accept a certainty equivalent amount that is less than the calculated expected cash flow. So as risk *increases*, α_t *decreases*.

Suppose that for the example project illustrated in Figure 9–1, certainty equivalents for each year have been determined as follows:

$$\alpha_0 = 1.0;\ \alpha_1 = 0.9;\ \alpha_2 = 0.7;\ \text{and } \alpha_3 = 0.7.$$

There is no risk in the initial investment so $\alpha_0 = 1$. In year one, $\alpha_1 = 0.9$ so that the certainty equivalent cash flow in that year is $(0.9 \times \$25,000) = \$22,500$. Basically this represents the analyst's estimate of what *CFAT* marginal investors (the "market") would accept for certain in lieu of a distribution of *CFAT*'s shown in Figure 9–1 for year one. In year two α_t drops to 0.7 indicating increasing risk. Intuitively this makes sense because the probabilities in year two are relatively larger for the extreme *CFAT* outcomes in comparison to year one when the probability for the average *CFAT* outcome is relatively larger. Notice also that the implication is that the risk in year three is the same as in year two since $\alpha_3 = \alpha_2$. is that the risk in year three is the same as in year two since $\alpha_3 = \alpha_2$.

Evaluating the project by the certainty equivalent method, assume that the risk free interest rate, i, has been determined to be 7 percent. Recall that the risk free interest rate can be approximated by the interest rate on government bonds, which are about as risk free as any financial asset an investor can buy. The expected net present value, $\overline{NPV}$, of the project is found using (9–4):

$$\overline{NPV} = (1.0)(-\$50,000) + \frac{(0.9)(\$25,000)}{1.07} + \frac{(0.7)(\$30,000)}{(1.07)^2} + \frac{(0.7)(\$20,000)}{(1.07)^3}$$

$$= -\$50,000 + \frac{\$22,500}{1.07} + \frac{\$21,000}{(1.07)^2} + \frac{\$14,000}{(1.07)^3}$$

$$= -\$50,000 + \$21,038 + \$18,333 + \$11,424$$

$$= \$795$$

Since $\overline{NPV} > 0$ the project should be accepted. This decision conflicts with the decision reached under the risk adjusted discount rate approach where (with $k^* = 25$ percent) the project $\overline{NPV} < 0$. Proponents of the certainty equivalent method would argue that, given the analyst's estimates, the project should be accepted.

Risk adjusted discount rate versus certainty equivalent

These two approaches to risky project evaluation both have strengths and weaknesses. The risk adjusted discount rate approach is an intuitively appealing method. It seems very logical to apply a higher discount rate to more risky proposals and a lower discount rate to less risky proposals. Also, the theory behind determining the risk adjusted cost of capital is well developed and provides some concrete guidance about how to find risk adjusted discount rates; thus, the method is both plausible and operationally tractable. On the disadvantage side, the use of a risk adjusted discount rate clearly equates discounting for time with discounting for risk. This implies that risk necessarily increases with time since the discount factor for year $t + 1$ is less than the discount factor for year t. Certainty equivalent proponents argue that in some years (such as years two and three in Figure 9–1) risk may be the same. Handling risk by increasing the discount rate necessarily implies that risk increases with time, and instances where risk does not increase with time may not be properly evaluated by the risk adjusted cost of capital method.

Because the certainty equivalent method can properly account for cash flow patterns that do not exhibit increasing risk with time it is a more flexible model and has more generality. And this is the outstanding feature of the certainty equivalent method. On the negative side, the certainty equivalent method is not as intuitively appealing as the risk adjusted discount rate method. It is more difficult to both understand and explain the certainty equivalent adjustment made in the numerator of the expected cash flows. Also, implementation of the approach is more difficult. As opposed to the risk adjusted discount rate approach, which, in addition to expected cash flows, requires estimation of only one other parameter, k^*, the certainty equivalent method requires the analyst to estimate a certainty equivalent factor for *each* year. In the Figure 9–1 example this was no great chore because the project lasted only 3 years, but for long-lived projects, say 20 years, this is a much more arduous task.

In summary, both methods have good and bad features. The essence of the difference between the two methods is that the risk adjusted discount rate method accounts for risk by adjusting the discount rate in the *denominator* of the expected net present value formula, while the certainty equivalent method accounts for risk by adjusting the expected cash flows in the *numerator* of the expected net present value formula.

The careful reader will note that the valuation formula developed in Chapter 5 and used throughout the text is a risk adjusted discount rate method. This fact does not imply that the certainty equivalent method is wrong, but rather this choice reflects the more widespread usage today of the risk adjusted discount rate approach for reasons just described.

OTHER EVALUATION TECHNIQUES

We have now looked at two evaluation methods that are consistent with the goal of the firm and are "complete" methods. By complete we mean that given the required parameter values (such as expected cash flows, project life, and k^* in the risk adjusted discount rate method), a clear-cut investment decision can always be made. We now turn to some other techniques that are either not necessarily consistent with the firm's goal or are not complete.

Payback

Recall in Chapter 7 that one of the reasons payback is used in evaluating projects is because it provides a rough screen for evaluating risk. The firm can crudely account for risk differences by altering payback requirements. Generally this is done by shortening the payback standard for more risky investments. If, for example, a firm normally uses a four-year payback requirement for projects that expand current product lines it may require a three-year payback for a proposed new product line that the firm feels is a riskier investment. Shortening the payback is an analogous concept to raising the discount rate, but for reasons explained in Chapter 7, it is not necessarily consistent with the firm's goal of stockholder wealth maximization.

Decision trees

Some firms use decision trees to evaluate risky proposals. A decision tree illustrates what the sequential outcomes of a risky decision might be. In the investment decision problem the decision tree shows the sequential cash flows and net present value of the proposed project under different possible circumstances.

Suppose, for example, the firm has an opportunity to invest in equipment that will last two years, will cost $100,000 initially (after tax), and has the following estimated possible $CFAT$ pattern. In year one there is a 30-percent chance that $CFAT$ will be $40,000, a 40-percent chance that $CFAT$ will be $60,000, and a 30-percent chance that $CFAT$ will be $80,000. In year two the $CFAT$ possibilities depend on the $CFAT$ that occurs in year one. We say that the year two $CFAT$'s are *conditional CFAT's*: They are conditional upon what happens in year one. Similarly, the associated probabilities for year two $CFAT$'s are *conditional probabilities*. These estimated conditional $CFAT$'s and probabilities are as follows:

If $CFAT_1 = $40,000$		If $CFAT_1 = $60,000$		If $CFAT_1 = $80,000$	
$CFAT_2$ (dollars)	Probability	$CFAT_2$ (dollars)	Probability	$CFAT_2$ (dollars)	Probability
20,000	0.2	70,000	0.3	80,000	0.1
50,000	0.6	80,000	0.4	100,000	0.8
80,000	0.2	90,000	0.3	120,000	0.1

This somewhat complex problem can be illustrated with the decision tree shown in Figure 9–2.

Notice that the decision tree accurately portrays the problem description. That is, the decision tree shows the timing of the cash flows, the possible *CFAT* outcomes in each year (including the conditional nature of the *CFAT* outcomes in year two), and the probabilities associated with these outcomes. Notice also that the tree shows nine distinct *paths*, or *combinations* of *outcomes*, the project could take if accepted. One possibility is that the first year's *realized CFAT* is $40,000 and the second year's *realized CFAT* is $20,000. Inspection of Figure 9–2 shows that this is the worst combination of outcomes that could occur. The firm would have paid $100,000 for a *CFAT* stream of $40,000 and $20,000 in

FIGURE 9–2
Decision tree

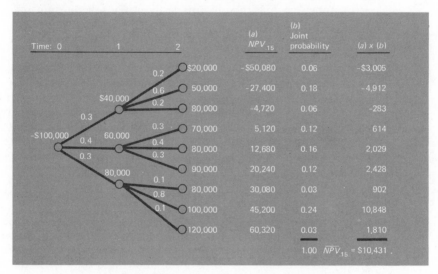

years one and two, respectively. If the firm has determined that an appropriate discount rate for this project is 15 percent, the net present values of the *worst path* is −$50,080. Similarly, by inspection, the *best path* is $CFAT_1 = \$80,000$ and $CFAT_2 = \$120,000$. The net present value at 15 percent of that path is $60,320. Figure 9–2 shows the net present value at 15 percent of each of the nine distinct possible *CFAT* paths in the tree.

Expected net present value

The *expected* net present value of the problem depicted by the decision tree is the expected value of the net present value of all the paths:

$$\overline{NPV} = \sum_{i=1}^{N} p_i\, NPV_i \qquad (9\text{--}5)$$

where

NPV_i = net present value of the ith path; p_i = the probability of the ith path occurring; and N = number of possible paths.

The probability of the ith path occurring is called the *joint probability*. It is equal to the product of the probabilities along the path. For example, the probability of the worst path ($CFAT_1$ = \$40,000 and $CFAT_2$ = \$20,000) is $0.3 \times 0.2 = 0.06$, and the probability of the best path ($CFAT_1$ = \$80,000 and $CFAT_2$ = \$120,000) is $0.3 \times 0.1 = 0.03$. The joint or path probability of each path is shown in Figure 9–2, and the sum of the path probabilities for all possible paths (nine in the example) is 1.0. The last column in Figure 9–2 shows calculation of $\overline{NPV}$, which is the weighted average of the individual path NPVs where the weights are the path probabilities. The sum of these weighted NPVs is $\overline{NPV}$. $\overline{NPV}$ for the example is \$10,431 and the project would be accepted.

This approach has the advantage of visually laying out all possible consequences of investing in the proposed project and makes management aware of the adverse possibilities. Also, the conditional nature of successive years cash flows can be clearly expressed. The primary shortcoming of the use of decision trees is that most problems are too complex to permit a year-by-year depiction. For the two-year project just analyzed there are only nine paths. For the three-year project described in Figure 9–1 there are 27 paths. For a ten-year project of similar construction (where each year's result is followed by three possible outcomes for the next year) there are almost 60,000 paths. Clearly, for long-lived projects the decision tree would be impractical to prepare without substantial simplification.

Simulation

Another method used by corporations to evaluate risky investment proposals is *simulation*. As applied to investment analysis simulation typically involves using computers to determine the distribution of the internal rate of return or net present value. Suppose the firm is considering a risky investment and has estimated probability distributions for initial investment, annual sales, and operating costs, life and salvage value. An example of these estimations is shown in Figure 9–3. Notice that this probabilistic information is stated in terms of the same financial variables we have worked with in the past. For each of these variables the firm has estimated the probability distribution associated with the variable.

The simulation proceeds as follows:

1. Randomly select (sample) a value of each variable from its given distribution.
2. Take these selected values and other given information (tax rate, type of depreciation used, etc.) and calculate the project's *IRR* or *NPV*. Record this value.
3. Repeat steps one and two many times (for example, 1,000 times).
4. Prepare the *IRR* or *NPV* distribution (see Figure 9–3).

The result of this repeated simulation is the distribution of *IRR* as shown in Figure 9–3 (alternatively it could be a *NPV* distribution). This distribution demonstrates several things. First, it shows the *expected IRR*, $\overline{IRR}$. Second, it shows the probability of *IRR* being less than zero or less than some established hurdle rate. From the information used to prepare the distribution the analyst can also determine the standard deviation of the project's *IRR*, σ_j, which is part of the covariance term, cov_{jm}, used in determining project risk.

It used to be that a simulation could only be performed for major projects because they were so expensive. Today, some companies routinely perform simulations on almost all proposals. One of the main advantages of simulation is that it systematically explores many possible outcomes associated with the project rather than just the outcome associated with

FIGURE 9–3
Simulation approach

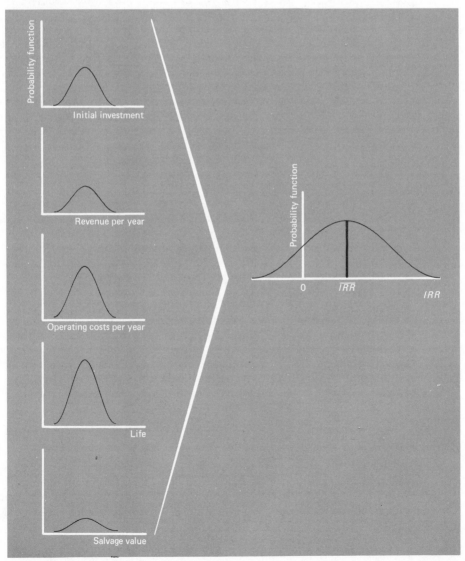

expected values. Consequently, it identifies possible extremely bad outcomes that might happen if the project is accepted. For projects that involve large investments this would be very useful information.

SENSITIVITY ANALYSIS

All of the evaluation methods we have discussed involved estimating three general classes of project parameters: expected cash flows, discount rate, and project life. These parameters are only *estimates* of what will occur in the future and are subject to error. Presumably, more experienced financial analysts will make better estimates of the future than less experienced analysts, but given that the future is always uncertain, there will always be estimation errors. One way to systematically investigate the effect of estimation errors is through *sensitivity analysis*. Sensitivity analysis provides information regarding how sensitive the performed calculation results are to estimation errors. In the context of net present value investment decision making, sensitivity analysis provides information regarding the sensitivity of the calculated $\overline{NPV}$ to possible estimation errors in expected cash flows, the discount rate, and project life.

Suppose, for example, that a proposed project has an estimated initial cost (after tax) of \$75,000 and an estimated, constant, expected *CFAT* stream of \$20,000 per year for seven years. The estimated cost of capital for the project is 15 percent. Then:

$$\overline{NPV} = -\$75,000 + (\$20,000)(ADF_{.15,7})$$
$$= -\$75,000 + (\$20,000)(4.160)$$
$$= -\$75,000 + 83,200$$
$$= \$8,200$$

The analyst's recommendation would be to accept the project. Now consider this question: What if the analyst overestimated expected annual *CFAT* by \$3,000 per year? That is, what if expected *CFAT* is \$17,000 per year?

$$\overline{NPV} = -\$75,000 + (\$17,000)(4.160)$$
$$= -\$4,280$$

If the analyst overestimates expected *CFAT* by \$3,000 per year the project will turn out to be a poor project for the firm because it will have negative expected net present value. Similarly, the analyst can determine the sensitivity of $\overline{NPV}$ to estimation errors in the other variables: life and discount rate. A sensitivity analysis would be particularly helpful on projects that are large and will therefore have a substantial impact on the firm.

SUMMARY

A conspicuous element of all investment decisions is risk, and the firm is never really sure of the future consequences of its current investment decisions. In this chapter we pulled together elements from several chapters to analyze investment decision making under risk.

An important part of many risky investment decision models is determining expected cash flows. Determining expected cash flows begins with relating future cash flows to general economic conditions. Once CFAT outcomes for each year have been estimated the expected CFAT for year t, $\overline{CFAT}_t$, can be calculated:

$$\overline{CFAT}_t = \sum_{i=1}^{N} p_{ti}\, CFAT_{ti}$$

These expected cash flows are used in the two most widely used evaluation methods: the *risk adjusted discount rate method* and the *certainty equivalent method*.

In the risk adjusted discount rate method the firm adjusts for the riskiness of the project by adjusting the discount rate: The riskier the project, the higher the discount rate. Under this approach the firm calculates an expected net present value using expected cash flows and the risk adjusted discount rate:

$$\overline{NPV} = \sum_{t=0}^{n} \frac{\overline{CFAT}_t}{(1 + k^*)^t}$$

This approach is intuitively appealing and is consistent with the valuation framework developed in Chapter 5. In theory, projects with $\overline{NPV} > 0$ should be accepted and should lead to increased stockholder wealth. There is some dissatisfaction with this approach, however, because it handles risk by increasing the discount rate. This implies that risk increases with time and for some projects this may not be true. This criticism has led to an alternative investment decision model, the *certainty equivalent method*.

The certainty equivalent approach accounts for risk by adjusting the expected cash flows downward. Certainty equivalent factors, α_t, which take on values from zero to one, are multiplied by $\overline{CFAT}_t$ to transform the risky cash flows into *certain* cash flows that are *equivalent* in desirability. The greater the risk, the lower α_t is. This method also uses an expected NPV formulation where the discount rate is the riskless interest rate (government bond rate):

$$\overline{NPV} = \sum_{t=0}^{n} \frac{\alpha_t\, \overline{CFAT}_t}{(1 + i)^t}$$

This approach is more flexible in that it can handle projects where the risk is not increasing, but it is also more cumbersome since an α_t must be estimated for each year of the project's life. This method is also consistent with the general concept of valuation presented in Chapter 5.

Payback is another risky investment evaluation technique. For riskier projects the required payback is shortened. However, this is not a good evaluation method because it has little to do with the firm's goal.

Decision trees and *simulation* are also used by some firms. They are useful because they reveal the bad outcomes as well as the expected value outcomes. Both methods can be used to determine information needed in the risk adjusted discount rate and certainty equivalent methods, so they are supplemental rather than competing alternatives.

All these methods involve estimation of future project parameters (such as cash flows), and since the future is always unknown these estimates will always be erroneous to some extent. If the project is large relative to the firm and there are substantial adverse estimation errors, the firm may find itself in trouble. Consequently, the firm may wish to perform a sensitivity analysis on the project to see what effect estimation errors of expected cash flows, life, and discount rate will have on expected *NPV*. The result of this sensitivity analysis may lead the firm to reject an otherwise acceptable project or to spend resources to gather more reliable project information prior to accepting the project.

QUESTIONS

1. Define the following terms and phrases.
   a. Expected *CFAT*.
   b. Risk adjusted discount rate.
   c. Certainty equivalent factors.
   d. Decision trees.
   e. Expected net present value.
   f. Simulation.
   g. Sensitivity analysis.

2. In comparing the risk adjusted discount rate method to the certainty equivalent method:
   a. What similarities are there between the two methods?
   b. Explain the fundamental conceptual difference between the two methods.
   c. Explain the comparative advantages and disadvantages of each.

3. Explain why payback is frequently said to be an effective risk screening device.

4. a. What should be the relationship between a project's risk adjusted discount rate and its beta?
   b. In what sense is k_j^* (from Chapter 8) a risk adjusted discount rate?

5. What is the principal advantage of using simulation analysis on capital budgeting problems?

6. An analyst who favors use of the risk adjusted discount rate argues that he cannot think of a practical "real world" example where risk would decrease over time. Therefore, he argues, there is no real advantage offered by the certainty equivalent method, which claims that it can better handle such problems. Try to think of at least one example of a real world problem where project risk does decrease over time.

7. "To some degree, simulation and sensitivity analysis provide similar information to the financial analyst, although simulation is a more comprehensive form of analysis." Comment on this statement.

8. Barker-Boardman, Inc., uses the certainty equivalent method to evaluate new investment proposals. Currently three potential investments are being analyzed by the firm's financial staff. Each is expected to last five years, and analysts have estimated the following certainty equivalent factors for the proposed projects:

	Year				
Project	1	2	3	4	5
A	0.9	0.8	0.7	0.6	0.5
B	0.5	0.4	0.4	0.3	0.1
C	1.0	1.0	1.0	1.0	1.0

a. Rank the three projects from most risky to least risky. Justify your rankings.
b. What do the certainty equivalent factors for project C imply about the riskiness of the project's cash flows?
c. Would the three projects be discounted at the same interest rate? Explain.

PROBLEMS

1. The Meggison Mining Company is considering two mutually exclusive investment prospects. Projects A and B have expected cash flows after tax as shown below:

t	A (dollars)	B (dollars)
0	−250,000	−350,000
1	75,000	50,000
2	75,000	55,000
3	75,000	65,000
4	75,000	75,000
5	75,000	80,000
6	75,000	70,000
7		60,000
8		60,000
9		60,000
10		60,000

The company uses the risk adjusted discount rate method of evaluating risky projects and selects the appropriate discount rate by determining the project payback and using the following table:

Project payback	Discount rate
Less than 1 year	0.06
1 to 5 years	0.08
5 to 10 years	0.10
Over 10 years	0.12

Which project should Meggison invest in?

2. Amalgamated–Great Southern is evaluating two mutually exclusive investment possibilities. Each proposal costs $3,000 and is expected to last three years. Estimated operating cash flows for the proposed projects depend on the kind of economic climate that prevails each year and look as follows:

Economic Climate	Probability	CFAT per year (dollars) A	B
Bad.....................	0.2	2,400	0
Average	0.6	3,000	3,000
Good	0.2	3,600	7,500

Amalgamated has decided to evaluate the riskier project at $k = 10$ percent and the less risky project at $k = 8$ percent.

a. Calculate the expected annual operating cash flow for each project.

b. Determine the expected net present value of each project if Amalgamated equates risk with the standard deviation of annual operating cash flows after tax.

c. What investment decision action should Amalgamated take with respect to these two projects? Justify your answer.

3. Norris Broadcasting uses the certainty equivalent approach in evaluation of uncertain investments. For a new project under consideration the following data have been determined:

Year	Expected CFAT (dollars)	Certainty equivalents
0..............	−100,000	0.9
1..............	75,000	0.7
2..............	75,000	0.5
3..............	75,000	0.3
4..............	75,000	0.2

The firm's cost of equity capital is 20 percent; its cost of debt is 10 percent, and the U.S. government bond rate is 7 percent. Should the project be accepted? Justify your answer with appropriate calculations.

4. Page Venture Capital Co. uses the certainty equivalent approach in evaluation of uncertain investments. For a new project under consideration the following data have been determined.

Year	Expected CFAT (dollars)	Certainty equivalents
0..............	−50,000	1.0
1..............	30,000	0.8
2..............	30,000	0.7
3..............	30,000	0.6
4..............	30,000	0.5

What risk free interest rate was used if the expected net present value of the project — according to Page's calculations — is $16,906?

5. Firm X uses the certainty equivalent method to evaluate risky investment projects, while firm Y uses the risk adjusted discount method. The data below pertain to a proposed five-year investment project. Evaluate the project from both firms' standpoint, determining if the project is acceptable.

Future CFAT estimates:

Year	CFAT (dollars)	Probabilities	α
0	−6,000	0.8	
	−8,000	0.2	0.8
1	2,000	0.7	
	3,000	0.3	0.7
2	2,000	0.7	
	3,000	0.3	0.7
3	3,000	0.6	
	4,000	0.4	0.6
4	4,000	0.5	
	5,000	0.5	0.5
5	2,000	0.4	
	3,000	0.6	0.4

Current financial data

Expected market rate of return.................... 11%
High-grade bond interest rate.................... 9
Long-term government bond rate.............. 6
Interest rate on Firm Y Bonds.................... 10

Firm Y estimates that the risk of the proposed project is 20 percent greater than the risk of the market index (β_m).

6. The Barne's Equipment Company is considering an investment proposal whose cash flows after tax are dependent upon the state of the economy. The following estimates have been prepared.

Year	State of economy	$CFAT_t$ (dollars)	Probability
0..............	Any state	−11,000	1.0
1..............	Bad	4,700	0.1
	Average	5,000	0.8
	Good	5,400	0.1
2..............	Bad	4,400	0.15
	Average	5,000	0.8
	Good	5,400	0.05
3..............	Bad	3,200	0.1
	Average	4,000	0.8
	Good	4,400	0.1
4..............	Bad	4,400	0.05
	Average	4,500	0.9
	Good	4,600	0.05

The company uses the certainty equivalent method of evaluating risky investments and selects the certainty equivalent factors according to the following system:

1. Calculate the average $CFAT$ for each year, $\overline{CFAT_t}$:

$$\overline{CFAT_t} = \sum_{i=1}^{n} (CFAT_{ti})(p_{ti})$$

2. Calculate the standard deviation of $CFAT$ for each year, σ_t:

$$\sigma_t = \sqrt{\sum_{i=1}^{n} (CFAT_{ti} - \overline{CFAT_t})^2(p_{ti})}$$

3. For each year, determine $\sigma_t/\overline{CFAT_t}$.
4. Find α_t by using the following chart:

$\sigma_t/CFAT$	α_t
0.00 to 0.009.........................	1.0
0.01 to 0.029.........................	0.9
0.03 to 0.049.........................	0.8
0.05 to 0.069.........................	0.7
0.07 to 0.089.........................	0.6
Greater than 0.089.................	0.3

If the risk free interest rate is 6 percent, should Barnes make this investment?

7. A proposed investment project is expected to cost $200,000 initially after all tax considerations have been determined. The subsequent expected $CFAT$s for the project are $100,000 per year, and the estimated life of the investment is four years. The firm has also determined that the appropriate risk adjusted discount rate for this proposal is 10 percent.

a. Determine the expected net present value of the project.
b. If all other estimates stay the same, determine the project's $\overline{NPV}$ if:

(1) The initial cost were 50 percent higher than originally estimated.

(2) The expected annual *CFAT* were 50 percent lower than originally estimated.

(3) The risk adjusted discount rate were 50 percent higher than originally estimated.

(4) The project's life were 50 percent shorter than originally estimated.

c. To which of the four estimation errors in (b) is the $\overline{NPV}$ of the project more sensitive to? Justify your answer.

8. Griffen Printing Company is evaluating a new plate-making process which they may purchase. The company has made the following estimates of the cash flows after tax associated with this proposal and intends to use a decision tree to get a clearer picture of the possible outcomes of this investment, which has an expected life of two years.

$CFAT_1$	Probability
$5,000	0.5
$6,000	0.5

	$CFAT_2$	Probability
If $CFAT_1 = \$5,000$	$ 4,000	0.4
	$ 6,000	0.6
If $CFAT_1 = \$6,000$	$ 8,000	0.7
	$10,000	0.3

The equipment costs $10,000 and the company uses a 10-percent discount rate for this type of investment.

a. Prepare a decision tree for this investment proposal, showing the net present value of all possible outcomes and their associated probabilities.

b. What net present value will the project yield if the worst outcome is realized? What is the probability of this occurring?

c. What net present value will result if the best outcome occurs? What is its probability?

d. What is the project's expected net present value?

e. Suppose the company defines failure as the situation where an investment has a net present value less than zero. What is the probability of failure for this proposal?

SELECTED BASIC REFERENCES

Grayson, C. J. "The Use of Statistical Techniques in Capital Budgeting," pp. 90–132 in *Financial Research and Management Decisions*. New York: John Wiley & Sons, 1967, ed. by A. A. Robichek.

Haley, C. W., and L. D. Schall. *The Theory of Financial Decisions,* New York: McGraw-Hill Book Co., 1973, pp. 179–90.

Hertz, D. B. "Risk Analysis in Capital Investment," *Harvard Business Review* (January–February 1964), pp. 95–106.

Magee, J. F. "How to Use Decision Trees in Capital Investment," *Harvard Business Review* (September–October 1964), pp. 79–96.

Weston, J. F. "Investment Decisions Using the Capital Asset Pricing Model," *Financial Management* (Spring 1973), pp. 25–33.

SELECTED ADVANCED REFERENCES

Hespos, R. F., and P. A. Straussman. "Stochastic Decision Trees for the Analysis of Investment Decisions," *Management Science* (August 1965), pp. 244–59.

Robichek, A. A., and S. C. Myers. "Conceptual Problems in the Use of Risk-Adjusted Discount Rates," *Journal of Finance* (December 1966), pp. 727–30.

Rubinstein, M. E. "A Synthesis of Corporate Financial Theory," *Journal of Finance* (March 1973), pp. 167–81.

Tuttle, D. L., and R. H. Litzenberger. "Leverage, Diversification and Capital Market Effects on a Risk Adjusted Capital Budgeting Framework," *Journal of Finance* (June 1968), pp. 427–43.

CAPITAL STRUCTURE AND DIVIDEND POLICY

10

LEVERAGE AND CAPITAL STRUCTURE

In the previous set of four chapters we investigated the subject of long-term investment decisions. Once the firm has decided which investments it will undertake, it must decide on how to finance them. This and the subsequent five chapters are concerned with long-term financing topics. The present chapter takes an overview of the effects on stock price of using financial leverage, where financial leverage refers to the use of fixed charge financing sources, such as debt. The next chapter, Chapter 11, takes a close look at dividend and retained earnings policies. Chapters 10 and 11 are more theoretically oriented than the four following chapters, which entail the study of long-term capital markets and the different kinds of long-term financing sources. Most of the details of long-term financing are deferred to Chapters 12 through 15.

The decision to select a particular financing plan is called the financing decision, and logically, the firm should select that financing plan that maximizes stockholder wealth. One procedure that seems consistent with this goal is to employ that capital source with the lowest cost of capital. Recall that we studied cost of capital in Chapter 8. We investigated cost of capital theory from a "what does it mean" and "how is it calculated" standpoint. However, our investigation was made under the presumption that the firm's capital structure – the composition of the firm's long-term financing – did not change. The decision to invest in new assets requires new financing, and this new financing may or may not change the firm's capital structure. That is, the firm's *current* capital structure reflects the historical financing decisions made by the firm, and the firm's *future* capital structure will reflect current and future financing decisions. If, for example, the firm begins to rely more heavily on debt financing than it has in the past, the firm's capital structure will be more heavily weighted with debt than previously. Unfortunately, while it is very difficult to determine capital costs when the capital structure remains relatively stable, it is even more difficult to determine capital costs when the capital structure is changing. There is, in fact, considerable controversy surrounding cost of capital calculations when capital structure changes.

The overriding concern from a valuation perspective is the effect that the firm's financing decisions have on stock price. In this chapter we continue the valuation theme by investigating the relationship between stock price and capital structure. The main question of interest here is whether the firm can *increase* the price of its stock by choosing some best financing plan or, alternatively stated, by choosing some best capital structure.

To answer this question we must first formally introduce the concept of *leverage*. Leverage refers to acquiring assets that have *fixed* costs — costs that are not related to the amount of revenue generated by the asset — and employing financing sources that have fixed costs. Leverage associated with investment (asset acquisition) activities is called *operating* leverage, and leverage associated with financing activities is called *financial* leverage. While we are mainly concerned with financial leverage it will enhance our study to investigate the subject of operating leverage first.

OPERATING LEVERAGE

Leverage refers to the fulcrum principle. To lever means to convert one force into a larger second force. When a mechanic applies a wrench to a nut he gains mechanical leverage as the wrench converts the force in his arm into a larger force at the point of contact of the wrench and nut. In finance, we usually refer to leverage as the magnification of profit by the employment of assets and liabilities that have fixed costs. The employment of *assets* with fixed costs leads to a discussion of *operating leverage*, which we take up now. *Financial leverage* is discussed later.

Operating leverage shows the relationship between percentage changes in sales and percentage changes in earnings before interest and taxes (*EBIT*). Operating leverage thus reflects the possibilities of magnifying gains and losses in the firms *EBIT* level by changes that may occur in sales. This magnification possibility comes about because in employing assets the firm incurs certain *fixed costs*, costs that are unrelated to the sales volume created by the assets.

In the short run, the costs associated with a particular project or the firm as a whole entity can be divided into *variable* costs and *fixed* costs. Variable costs are that portion of the firm's costs that are related to the firm's sales level. As sales change so will variable costs. Typically, we assume a linear relationship between sales and variable costs so that as sales change, variable costs change in a proportionate amount. This means that the *variable cost ratio* (variable costs/sales) is constant with respect to changes in sales. However, the variable cost ratio is usually constant only over some *relevant range* of sales. If, for example, current sales are $10 million and the variable cost ratio is 0.65, the relevant sales range over which the variable cost ratio is constant might be considered as from $9 to $11 million. Within this range, for every $1 change in sales there will also be a $0.65 change in variable costs. As sales increase over

$11 million or fall below $9 million the variable cost ratio of 0.65 will change as the firm's cost-sales relationships change. Examples of variable cost items are materials costs, direct labor costs, and repair and maintenance expenses. These costs will tend to rise and fall as sales rise and fall.

Fixed costs are those costs that are independent of the sales level in the short run and over the relevant sales range. As sales change within this range, fixed costs will remain constant. Fixed cost items are depreciation, indirect labor costs, and overhead expenses, such as office supplies, office rental, light and heating bills, and executive and staff salaries. In the short run and within the relevant sales range, these costs are considered fixed. Outside the relevant sales range the firm may have to hire or fire more staff or change plant size to a new scale. Also, we are obviously only discussing the short-run time period here, since in the long run *all* costs are variable. Given enough time the firm can change plant size and hire or fire personnel. Actually, even in the short run, the firm can change some of its fixed costs, such as salaries, in response to temporary sales fluctuations. These costs are called *semivariable* costs.

The fixed costs we have been discussing are *operating* fixed costs. Interest is another fixed cost, but it is a fixed cost associated with financing investments. Operating leverage is only concerned with the operating fixed costs, so we ignore interest charges. Interest charges do enter the analysis of *financial* leverage, which is discussed below.

Degree of operating leverage

Operating leverage is quantitatively described by defining the *degree of operating leverage*, *DOL*:

$$\text{Degree of operating leverage} = DOL = \frac{\text{Percent change in } EBIT}{\text{Percent change in sales}}$$

That is:

$$DOL = \frac{\Delta EBIT/EBIT}{\Delta \text{Sales}/\text{Sales}} \qquad (10\text{--}1)$$

where

$\Delta EBIT$ is change in *EBIT*; *EBIT* is current *EBIT*; ΔSales is change in sales; Sales is current sales.

The degree of operating leverage measures the effect of a percentage change in sales on the percentage change in *EBIT*. The greater the degree of operating leverage, the more operating leverage the firm has.

Suppose that AB Co. currently has the sales, cost, and *EBIT* data shown in the top of Figure 10–1. The question of interest here is: What is the firm's degree of operating leverage? That is, what will happen to *EBIT* if sales change? First of all, we must divide expenses into fixed and variable components. Cost accountants have various techniques for doing this, and we will presume that the results of that analysis for the AB Co. are as shown in Figure 10–1 below the current operating statement. Notice that the AB Co. has $25,000 of fixed costs and $63,000 of variable costs at the current $100,000 sales level. The variable costs are composed of a large portion of the cost of goods sold and a small portion of selling expenses. The firm's variable cost ratio is 0.63. For every dollar that sales change, variable costs will change by $0.63. Fixed costs are composed of costs of goods sold, selling expenses, general and administrative and depreciation expenses. These costs will remain constant within a relevant range of sales changes. Suppose that sales increase by 10 percent to $110,000. AB's new operating statement in Figure 10–1 shows that *EBIT* will increase to $15,700. Based on these calculations the firm's degree of operating leverage is determined to be 3.1.

FIGURE 10–1
Degree of operating leverage calculation for the AB Co.

Current operating statement

Sales...	$100,000
Cost of goods sold.................................	70,000
Selling	10,000
General and administrative.......................	5,000
Depreciation	3,000
EBIT	$ 12,000

Variable costs			*Fixed costs*	
Cost of goods sold = (0.60)(sales)......	$60,000	Cost of goods sold......	$10,000
Selling expenses = (0.03)(sales)........	3,000	Selling expenses	7,000
Total variable costs	$63,000	General and adminis-	
		trative.................	5,000
Variable cost ratio.................. 0.63		Depreciation............	3,000
		Total fixed costs	$25,000

Operating statement if sales increase by 10 percent

Sales...	$110,000
Cost of goods sold.................................	76,000*
Selling	10,300†
General and administrative.......................	5,000
Depreciation	3,000
EBIT	$ 15,700

$$\text{Degree of operating leverage} = \frac{\Delta EBIT/EBIT}{\Delta sales/sales} = \frac{(\$15,700-\$12,000)/\$12,000}{(\$110,000-\$100,000)/\$100,000} = 3.1$$

* Cost of goods sold = (0.60)(sales) + $10,000 = (0.60)($110,000) + $10,000 = $76,000.
† Selling expenses = (0.03)(sales) + $7,000 = (0.03)($110,000) + $7,000 = $10,300.

An alternate and frequently easier way to calculate the degree of operating leverage is from a formula that can be derived from (10–1):

$$DOL = \frac{S - V}{EBIT} \tag{10–2}$$

where

S = current sales; V = current variable costs; and $EBIT$ = current *EBIT*. Referring to the AB Co. example in Figure 10–1, note that $S = \$100,000$; $V = \$63,000$; and $EBIT = \$12,000$. Therefore:

$$DOL = \frac{\$100,000 - \$63,000}{\$12,000} = 3.1$$

This calculation formula gives the same answer as (10–1) but is a computational shortcut.

The meaning of the 3.1 degree of operating leverage result is that, from the base sales of $100,000, for every 1-percent change in sales within the relevant range, there will be a 3.1-percent change in EBIT in the same direction as the sales change. If sales increase by 10 percent, as in the example, EBIT will increase by (10 percent × 3.1) = 31 percent. Similarly, if sales decrease by 10 percent, EBIT will decrease by 31 percent. This magnification of EBIT caused by sales changes is what operating leverage is all about. The operating fixed charges act as a fulcrum and cause operating leverage. The larger the degree of operating leverage, the greater the magnification of sales changes into EBIT changes. If AB Co.'s current sales were $100,000, but current variable costs were $55,000 and current fixed costs were $33,000 (leaving current EBIT at $12,000, as before), the company's degree of operating leverage would be:

$$\text{Degree of operating leverage} = \frac{\$100,000 - \$55,000}{\$12,000} = 3.8$$

The only difference here is that fixed costs are higher relative to variable costs. Other things equal, the higher the fixed costs relative to variable costs, the more operating leverage in the firm. We must be very careful to note, however, that these conclusions are based on the assumption that future operating conditions will be approximately the same as past operating conditions. That is, within the relevant sales range, fixed costs will remain constant in the short run, and the ratio of variable costs to sales will stay approximately the same.

Operating leverage and business risk

From a purely mechanical perspective, the degree of operating leverage shows the percentage change in EBIT that will occur for a 1-percent change in sales. However, the degree of operating leverage is also related to the business risk inherent in the firm. Business risk refers to the risk inherent in the firm's investments and is associated with the operating characteristics of the firm. Let

$$R = \text{The rate of return on assets (before interest and taxes)} = \frac{EBIT}{\text{Total assets}}$$

Then business risk may be defined as:

$$\text{Business risk} = \text{Cov}_{Rm} = \rho_{Rm}\sigma_R\sigma_m \qquad (10\text{–}3)$$

where

Cov_{Rm} = covariance between the firm's R and the market index rate of return; ρ_{RM} = correlation between R and the market index rate of return; σ_R = standard deviation of R; and σ_m = standard deviation of the market index rate of return.

Consistent with our earlier work on risk (Chapter 4), business risk is defined as a covariance term where the covariance is measured with the market index. Business risk is thus conceptually associated with how the rate of return on the firm's income stream prior to interest charges and taxes (R) covaries with the market. The higher this covariance the greater the firm's business risk. Business risk is determined by the kinds of investments the firm makes and is reflected in the type of business the firm is in. Utility companies, for example, own assets whose return on assets covaries less with the market, year in and year out, than mobile home companies. Accordingly, we say that the utilities have less business risk than the mobile home companies.

The firm's operating leverage is related to σ_R in Equation (10–3). The greater the firm's operating leverage, the greater will be the standard deviation of R (σ_R) and, therefore, the greater the firm's business risk (Cov_{Rm}). An example will illustrate why increased operating leverage causes σ_R to be higher.

Consider two firms, the AB Co. and the CD Co., that have the following current financial data.

	AB Co.	CD Co.
Sales	$100,000	$100,000
EBIT	12,000	14,000
Total assets (TA)	100,000	100,000
DOL	3.1	5.0
R = EBIT/TA	12 percent	14 percent

Notice that the firms have the same sales and total asset levels, but CD has a greater *DOL* than AB, which means that CD has more operating leverage than AB. This higher degree of operating leverage has contributed to a higher *EBIT* and before interest and tax rate of return on assets (R) for the CD Co.

Now suppose that management in both companies estimates that, with no increase in assets, future annual sales will either decrease 10 percent, remain the same, or increase 10 percent. The associated probabilities of these outcomes are 0.25, 0.50, and 0.25, respectively. Given this information, Figure 10–2 shows that the CD Co., which has more operating leverage, has the higher σ_R, and Equation (10–3) shows that the higher σ_R, the higher the covariance with the market. Thus, operating leverage is directly related to business risk. The greater the firm's operating leverage, the greater its business risk.

It must be noted, however, that just because one company has a higher σ_R than another company it does not necessarily mean the first company has more business risk. We must also consider the correlation coefficient, ρ_{Rm}. Continuing the example from Figure 10–2, if ρ_{Rm} for the AB Co. is

FIGURE 10–2
Operating leverage and σ_R

AB Co.   DOL $= 3.1$
Current $EBIT = \$12,000$
Total assets $= \$100,000$

p	Percent Δ in sales	Percent Δ in EBIT*	New EBIT† (dollars)	R‡ (percent)	$p\,(R - \mu_R)^2$
0.25.........	-10	-31	8,280	8.3	3.42
0.50.........	0	0	12,000	12.0	0
0.25.........	10	31	15,720	15.7	3.42
				$\mu_R = 12.0$§	6.84

$$\sigma_R = \sqrt{6.84} = 2.6 \text{ percent}$$

CD Co.   DOL $= 5.0$
Current $EBIT = \$14,000$
Total assets $= \$100,000$

p	Percent Δ in sales	Percent Δ in EBIT*	New EBIT† (dollars)	R‡ (percent)	$p\,(R - \mu_R)^2$
0.25.........	-10	-50	7,000	7	12.25
0.50.........	0	0	14,000	14	0
0.25.........	10	50	21,000	21	12.25
				$\mu_R = 14$§	24.5

$$\sigma_R = \sqrt{24.5} = 4.9 \text{ percent}$$

* Rearranging the definition of DOL, percent Δ in $EBIT = (DOL)$ (Percent Δ in sales)
† The new $EBIT$ = Current $EBIT$ + (Current $EBIT$) (Percent Δ in $EBIT/100$)
‡ R = new $EBIT$/Total assets
§ $\mu_R = \sum_{i=1}^{3} p_i R_i$

0.9 and ρ_{Rm} for the CD Co. is 0.3, then the business risk for AB Co. is greater than the business risk for CD Co. Recall that:

$$\text{Business risk} = \rho_{Rm}\sigma_R\sigma_m$$

Therefore,

$$\text{AB business risk} = (0.9)(2.6)\sigma_m = 2.34\ \sigma_m$$

$$\text{CD business risk} = (0.3)(4.9)\sigma_m = 1.47\ \sigma_m$$

The value of σ_m is always positive so that in this simple example, AB Co. has more business risk than CD Co., regardless of the size of σ_m. Thus, even though AB's σ_R is less than CD's, AB may have more business risk. This requires a lower ρ_{Rm} value for AB than for CD.

The more important point in this section, however, is the conclusion that if the firm increases its operating leverage, σ_R will increase, and *other things equal,* this increases the firm's business risk.

Break-even analysis

Operating leverage is frequently analyzed in conjunction with *break-even analysis.* Break-even analysis is also concerned with the relationships between sales, costs, and *EBIT,* but the emphasis is more on determining the sales level that must be achieved to exactly break even on *EBIT.* The sales level that corresponds with a *zero EBIT* level is called the *break-even sales level.*

There are several ways we could determine the break-even sales level, the least sophisticated and most tedious method would be a trial-and-error solution. We could pick a sales level, go through the cost calculations involved in Figure 10–1, and calculate *EBIT.* Whenever we chose a sales level that resulted in *EBIT* = 0, we would be finished. This process might take several trials, however. A more efficient and less tedious approach is to algebraically solve for breakeven sales.

Let

$$S^* = \text{breakeven sales (dollars)}$$
$$F = \text{fixed costs (dollars)}$$
$$v = \text{variable costs/sales}^1 \text{ (dollar/dollar)}.$$

Now:

$$EBIT = \text{sales} - \text{variable costs} - \text{fixed costs}$$
$$= S - (v)(S) - F$$
$$= S(1 - v) - F$$

But at break-even: $EBIT = 0$ and $S = S^*$; therefore, at break-even:

$$0 = S^*(1 - v) - F$$

and

$$S^* = \frac{F}{1 - v} \tag{10-4}$$

Recall from the AB Co. example in Figure 10–1 that $F = \$25{,}000$ and $v = 0.63$. The break-even sales level for AB is therefore:

$$S^* = \frac{\$25{,}000}{1 - 0.63} = \$67{,}568$$

AB's sales would have to drop below \$67,568 before the firm would have a negative *EBIT* level.

We may also graphically see the break-even point and the relationships between sales, costs, and *EBIT* through a break-even chart. Figure 10–3 is a break-even chart for the AB Co. and displays the relationships

---

[1] v is the variable cost ratio (the ratio of variable costs to sales). In contrast, V [from Equation (10–2)] is *total dollars* of variable cost.

FIGURE 10–3
Break-even EBIT chart

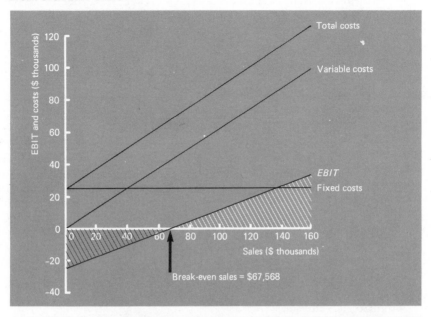

Sales (dollars)	Fixed costs (dollars)	Variable costs (dollars)	Total costs (dollars)	EBIT (dollars)
0	25,000	0	25,000	−25,000
50,000	25,000	31,500	56,500	−6,500
75,000	25,000	47,250	72,250	2,750
100,000	25,000	63,000	88,000	12,000
125,000	25,000	78,750	103,750	21,250
150,000	25,000	94,500	119,500	30,500

Fixed costs = $25,000
Variable costs = (0.63)(Sales)
Total costs = $25,000 + (0.63)(Sales)
EBIT = Sales − Total costs

between sales levels and (1) fixed costs, (2) variable costs, (3) total costs (variable plus fixed costs), and (4) *EBIT*. By definition, fixed costs are constant for all sales levels, and variable and total costs increase as sales increase. *EBIT* also increases as sales increase. Notice that at sales levels above break-even, the firm's *EBIT* is positive, and *EBIT* is negative below the break-even sales level.

Break-even analysis limitations While break-even analysis is a useful technique we must be careful to note some important limitations. Figure 10–3 implies that over the range of sales from 0 to $160,000, fixed costs are indeed constant, and variable and total costs and *EBIT* are all linear functions of the sales level. But recall the earlier discussion in this chapter on the concept of the "relevant range" of sales. This is the range of sales level over which we might reasonably expect fixed costs to be actually fixed, and where there might be stable linear relationships between variable costs, *EBIT*, and sales. Certainly over the wide array of sales possibilities shown for the firm in Figure 10–3, it is questionable that the linear relationships shown really do exist. More likely, the relationships are nonlinear, which means we must regard the linear break-even sales calculation from Equation (10–4) with some skepticism.

Another difficulty with break-even analysis is the categorization of costs into fixed and variable components. It is extremely difficult to classify some costs into these categories. Many costs appear to be *semivariable* because they are partly fixed and partly variable. The presence of these hard-to-categorize costs are unfortunately all too common. Furthermore, there is the problem of the long run versus the short run. In the long run *all* costs are variable. But there is no general agreement on how long the short run may be for a particular situation. This means that a break-even chart may not be a very reliable representation of the relationships between sales, costs, and *EBIT*, since it is inherently unstable over time.

FINANCIAL LEVERAGE

As we just saw, operating leverage is caused by investing in assets that have fixed costs. There is another kind of leverage the firm can employ: *financial leverage*. Financial leverage is created when the firm finances with sources of capital that have fixed charges that must be met. The major sources of fixed charge financing are debt (interest payments and principal repayments), preferred stock (preferred dividend payments), and leases (lease payments). These *financing* fixed costs provide the same magnification effect on the firm's earnings per share (*EPS*) that *operating* fixed costs have on the firm's *EBIT*. While all three fixed charge sources of long-term capital are important, much of our discussion in the remainder of the chapter will focus on *debt* financing. The more fixed charge financing the firm uses, the more financial leverage it will have.

Degree of financial leverage

The degree of financial leverage, *DFL*, is defined as the percentage change in *EPS* divided by the percentage change in *EBIT*:

$$\text{Degree of financial leverage} = DFL = \frac{\text{Percent change in } EPS}{\text{Percent change in } EBIT}$$

$$DFL = \frac{\Delta EPS/EPS}{\Delta EBIT/EBIT} \qquad (10\text{--}5)$$

where

$$\Delta EPS = \text{change in earnings per share}$$
$$EPS = \text{current earnings per share}$$

$$\Delta EBIT = \text{change in } EBIT$$
$$EBIT = \text{current } EBIT.$$

The degree of financial leverage reflects the leverage in the firm that is solely due to the firm's financing policy, and the effect of financial leverage is to magnify changes in $EBIT$ into *larger* changes in EPS.

Suppose, for example, that two companies, Conservative, Inc., and Balanced Co. are alike in all respects except that Conservative is an all equity company (it has no long-term debt) and Balanced has a long-term debt to equity ratio of 1:1. Current financial data for the two companies are shown in the top portion of Figure 10–4. Notice that both companies have the same total asset and current liabilities levels and both have the same $EBIT$ of \$1.5 million. However, the presence of debt (and therefore the fewer number of common shares outstanding) in Balanced Co. result in it having a higher EPS level than Conservative Co. Now suppose that both firms anticipate a 20-percent increase in $EBIT$. As the calculations in the bottom of Figure 10–4 show, the degree of financial leverage is 1.0 for Conservative and 1.36 for Balanced. Balanced Co. has a larger degree of financial leverage because it has debt in its capital structure.

FIGURE 10–4
Degree of financial leverage example

	Current Financial Data		
Conservative, Inc.		**Balanced Co.**	
Total assets...............	$12,000,000	Total assets...............	$12,000,000
Current liabilities	2,000,000	Current liabilities	2,000,000
Common		Long term debt	
(1,000,000 sh)..........	10,000,000	(8 percent)..............	5,000,000
		Common (500,000 sh) ...	5,000,000
EBIT.........................	$ 1,500,000	EBIT.........................	$ 1,500,000
Tax (T = 0.4)..............	600,000	Interest	400,000
Net income .... $	900,000	EBT..........................	1,100,000
EPS	$0.90	Tax (T = 0.4)..............	440,000
		Net income .... $	660,000
		EPS	$1.32
Assume EBIT Increases 20 Percent			
EBIT.........................	$ 1,800,000	EBIT.........................	$ 1,800,000
Tax (T = 0.4)..............	720,000	Interest	400,000
Net income .... $	1,080,000	EBT..........................	1,400,000
EPS	$1.08	Tax (T = 0.4)..............	560,000
		Net income .... $	840,000
		EPS	$1.68

$$DFL = \frac{(\$1.08 - \$0.90)/\$0.90}{(\$1,800,000 - \$1,500,000)/\$1,500,000} = 1.00$$

$$DFL = \frac{(\$1.68 - \$1.32)/\$1.32}{(\$1,800,000 - \$1,500,000)/\$1,500,000} = 1.36$$

The degree of financial leverage for Conservative is 1.0, which means that a 1-percent change in the company's *EBIT* will result in a 1-percent change in its *EPS*. This is illustrated in the Conservative, Inc., example: a 20-percent increase in Conservative's *EBIT* from the $1.5 million level causes Conservative's *EPS* to also increase by 20 percent. There is no magnification of the *EPS* in this case. Firms that do not use fixed charge financing will have no financial leverage, and their *DFL* will equal one. In contrast, Balanced Co.'s degree of financial leverage is 1.36, which indicates that for every 1-percent change in the firm's *EBIT*, the company's *EPS* will change 1.36 percent. In the Balanced Co. example, *EBIT* increased by 20 percent and *EPS* increased by (20 percent times 1.36) 27.2 percent. This magnification of *EPS* is due solely to the firm's use of debt and illustrates what is meant by financial leverage: Changes in *EBIT* are levered (magnified) into larger changes in *EPS*. And leverage is a two-way street. If both companies had 20-percent *decreases* in *EBIT* from the $1.5 million level, Conservative would suffer a 20-percent decrease in *EPS* while Balanced would suffer a more severe 27.2-percent decrease.

An alternate formula for calculating the degree of financial leverage, which is often easier to use, may be derived from Equation (10–5):

$$DFL = \frac{EBIT}{EBIT - I - L - d/(1 - T)} \tag{10–6}$$

where

I = Interest payments (dollars)
L = Lease payments (dollars)
d = Preferred dividend payments (dollars)
T = Tax rate.

Unlike interest and lease payments, preferred dividends are not tax deductible. Therefore, a dollar paid in preferred dividends is more costly to the firm than a dollar paid in interest or lease payments. Dividing any preferred dividend paid in Equation (10–6) by $(1 - T)$ accounts for this fact of life and puts interest, lease, and dividend payments on an equivalent basis.

Applying equation (10–6) to the two companies in Figure 10–4 gives the following results:

	Conservative, Inc.		Balanced Co.
EBIT	$1,500,000	*EBIT*	$1,500,000
I	0	*I*	$ 400,000
L	0	*L*	0
d/(1 − *T*) ...	0	*d*/(1 − *T*) ...	0
DFL	$\dfrac{\$1,500,000}{\$1,500,000 - 0} = 1.00$	*DFL*	$\dfrac{\$1,500,000}{\$1,500,000 - \$400,000} = 1.36$

Of course, these answers agree with the previous calculations.

COMBINED LEVERAGE

We have now seen that there are two kinds of leverage. *Operating leverage* is defined as the percentage change in *EBIT* per percentage change in sales. *Financial leverage* is defined as the percentage change in *EPS* per percentage change in *EBIT*. Putting these two elements together we define the firm's *degree of combined leverage, DCL*, as the percentage change in *EPS* per percentage change in sales:

$$\text{Degree of combined leverage} = DCL = \frac{\text{Percent change in } EPS}{\text{Percent change in sales}}$$

The degree of combined leverage is simply the product of the degree of operating leverage times the degree of financial leverage:[2]

$$\text{Degree of combined leverage} = \begin{pmatrix} \text{Degree of} \\ \text{operating} \\ \text{leverage} \end{pmatrix} \times \begin{pmatrix} \text{Degree of} \\ \text{financial} \\ \text{leverage} \end{pmatrix}$$

That is:

$$DCL = (DOL)(DFL) \qquad (10\text{--}7)$$

Thus, if a firm has a degree of operating leverage of 1.25 and a degree of financial leverage of 1.15, the degree of combined leverage will be 1.25 times 1.15 = 1.44. This means that for every 1-percent change in sales the firm's *EPS* will change 1.44 percent.

We can also derive a calculation formula for *DCL* in terms of the basic factors that determine combined leverage. Recall that:

$$\text{Degree of operating leverage} = \frac{S - V}{EBIT}$$

and:

$$\text{Degree of financial leverage} = \frac{EBIT}{EBIT - I - L - d/(1 - T)}$$

Therefore:

$$DCL = (DOL)(DFL)$$
$$= \left(\frac{S - V}{EBIT}\right)\left(\frac{EBIT}{EBIT - I - L - d/(1 - T)}\right)$$

and

$$DCL = \frac{S - V}{EBIT - I - L - d/(1 - T)} \qquad (10\text{--}8)$$

---

[2] This expression for the degree of combined leverage is consistent with the definition because:

$$\text{Degree of combined leverage} = \begin{pmatrix} \text{Degree of} \\ \text{operating} \\ \text{leverage} \end{pmatrix} \times \begin{pmatrix} \text{Degree of} \\ \text{financial} \\ \text{leverage} \end{pmatrix}$$
$$= \left(\frac{\text{Percent change in } EBIT}{\text{Percent change in sales}}\right)\left(\frac{\text{Percent change in } EPS}{\text{Percent change in } EBIT}\right)$$
$$= \frac{\text{Percent change in } EPS}{\text{Percent change in sales}}$$

Suppose, for example, that the firm's current sales level is $8,000,000, variable costs at this sales level are $4,500,000, *EBIT* is $2,500,000, annual interest payments are $400,000, lease payments are $200,000, preferred dividends are $50,000, and the tax rate = 50 percent. Then:

$$DCL = \frac{\$8,000,000 - \$4,500,000}{\$2,500,000 - \$400,000 - \$200,000 - \$50,000/0.5} = 1.94$$

The degree of combined leverage is approximately two, so for every 1-percent change in sales from the present $8 million level, this example firm's *EPS* will change in the same direction by approximately 2 percent. This two-to-one magnification is the result of both operating and financial leverage.

The firm's degree of combined leverage is a useful piece of information because it roughly describes the effect that sales changes will have on *EPS*. We must be careful to realize the approximate nature of this calculation, however. If the anticipated sales change is beyond the "relevant range" of sales described earlier in the chapter, the variable cost ratio may change, and if the time period is too long, fixed costs may change. In such cases the degree of operating leverage and hence the degree of combined leverage estimates may no longer be very accurate.

The *DCL* can also be used in assessing the approximate effects of new investment and financing plans on *EPS*. If, for example, the firm begins to invest heavily in riskier assets than usual, the firm's operating leverage will increase. If the firm's financing policy remains relatively constant (that is, if the firm finances the new investments with approximately the same proportions of debt, leasing, preferred, and equity capital as used in the past) financial leverage will remain fairly constant. The effect of increased operating leverage and unchanged financial leverage will result in increased combined leverage since *DCL* = (*DOL*)(*DFL*). The firm may consciously choose instead to finance the new investments with more equity than it has used in the past. This would decrease financial leverage and would compensate for the increased operating leverage caused by the new riskier investments the firm is acquiring.

FINANCIAL LEVERAGE AND CAPITAL STRUCTURE

We have seen how operating leverage and financial leverage interact to determine combined leverage. We now turn our attention to a more in-depth look at financial leverage. Recall that financial leverage is caused by financing investments with capital sources that have *fixed* charges: debt, preferred stock, and leases.

In the beginning of this book (in Chapter 1) we saw that there were three fundamental financial management decision areas: (1) the investment decision area, (2) the financing decision area, and (3) the dividend decision area. The broad question we address in the remainder of this chapter is concerned with the second of these areas. Specifically we will consider the very important question: Is there a "best" way to finance assets? By "best" we mean in the context of stockholder wealth maximization. We could alternatively phrase the question: Is there some optimal method of financing that will maximize stockholder wealth?

A financing plan merely refers to how the firm raises capital to pay for the assets it has acquired. The sum total of the financing effected to date by the firm is revealed in the firm's present capital structure. The capital structure, which is shown in the company's balance sheet, shows how much long-term debt, preferred stock, and common stock the firm has issued. The relative proportions of these long-term sources of capital constitute the capital structure. Another way of expressing the financing question is: Is there some optimal capital structure that will maximize stockholder wealth?

The question of optimal capital structure has relevance in decisions about financing new investments and in decisions about recapitalizing the firm. Unless the firm finances new investments over the long run in the same approximate proportions as it has financed its old assets, the firm's capital structure will obviously change. If the firm currently has an optimal capital structure, it will choose to finance new investments by a financing mix that is approximately equivalent to the current financing mix. If the current capital structure is not optimal, the firm should finance new assets in such a manner that the capital structure will be moved toward the optimal position. Moreover, if the present capital structure is not optimal, the firm should give serious consideration to recapitalizing, perhaps exchanging debt for equity or equity for debt so that an optimal position can be attained.

This all presumes, of course, that there is such a thing as an optimal capital structure. Some financial theorists argue that there is not. We'll analyze these issues in the remainder of this chapter.

Effect of financial leverage on EPS

We have seen that, other things the same, the more debt in the firm's capital structure, the more financial leverage there is in the firm. We now turn our attention to the effect that financial leverage has on the firm's *EPS*.

Suppose a new firm, the Tyro Co., is just now incorporating, and the firm is contemplating how it should be capitalized. That is, it is considering alternate financing plans. The firm needs $100,000 of long-term capital to begin operations, and after some consideration it has narrowed the choice to two alternate financing plans:

Plan 1 – Sell 1,000 shares of common stock at $100 per share.
Plan 2 – Sell 500 shares of common stock at $100 per share and borrow $50,000 from the bank at 5-percent interest.

Plan 1 is an all equity plan. If the firm adopts it there will be no long-term debt in the firm. The company's long-term debt to equity ratio would be zero. Plan 2 involves the sale of equal amounts of debt and equity ($50,000 each), and the firm's long-term debt/equity ratio would be one.

Let's now look at the effect that these plans would have on Tyro's *EPS*. Actually, the effect depends on the relationship between the before tax cost of debt and the rate of return on assets before interest and taxes. The before tax cost of debt is merely the cost of debt without any tax considerations. In the Tyro example it is the stated interest rate, 5 percent. The rate of return on assets before interest and taxes is equal to *EBIT*/total assets [(*EBIT*/*TA*)]. Most companies' *EBIT* will be heavily influenced by general economic conditions. If the economy is strong, *EBIT* will be favorable; if the economy is weak, *EBIT* will be unfavorable; if the economy is about average, *EBIT* will be about average. Tyro estimates that if the economy is weak, *EBIT* will only be $4,000; if the economy is about average, *EBIT* will be $6,000; and if the economy is strong, *EBIT* will be $8,000. These estimates imply that Tyro's *EBIT*/*TA* will be ($4,000/$100,000) = 4 percent in a weak economy, 6 percent in an average economy, and 8 percent in a strong economy. In comparison, the before tax cost of debt is 5 percent. We may now look at what Tyro's *EPS* would be next year in each of the two financing plans and for the estimated market conditions. Figure 10–5 shows these results.

In a weak economy Tyro's *EPS* is higher under the all equity plan. However, in either an average or strong economy, *EPS* of the 50-percent equity–50-percent debt plan (Plan 2) is higher. Actually, Plan 2 will result in higher *EPS* than Plan 1 so long as *EBIT*/*TA* is greater than the before tax cost of debt of 5 percent. We can see this result more clearly by preparing an *EBIT-EPS chart*. This chart is constructed by plotting *EPS* against *EBIT* for the two plans. Figure 10–6 shows this construction. There is a straight-line relationship between *EPS* and *EBIT* for each

FIGURE 10–5
Effect of financial leverage on EPS for the Tyro Co.

	Economic conditions (dollars)		
	Weak	Average	Strong
Plan 1: All equity (*LT* debt/equity = 0):			
EBIT.............................	4,000	6,000	8,000
Interest.........................	0	0	0
EBT	4,000	6,000	8,000
Tax (*T* = 0.5)................	2,000	3,000	4,000
Net income...................	2,000	3,000	4,000
No. shares common........	1,000	1,000	1,000
EPS.............................	2.00	3.00	4.00
Plan 2: 50-percent equity–50-percent debt (*LT* debt/equity = 1):			
EBIT.............................	4,000	6,000	8,000
Interest*.........................	2,500	2,500	2,500
EBT	1,500	3,500	5,500
Tax (*T* = 0.5)................	750	1,750	2,750
Net income...................	750	1,750	2,750
No. shares common........	500	500	500
EPS.............................	1.50	3.50	5.50

Interest = (0.05)($50,000) = $2,500.

FIGURE 10–6
EBIT-EPS chart

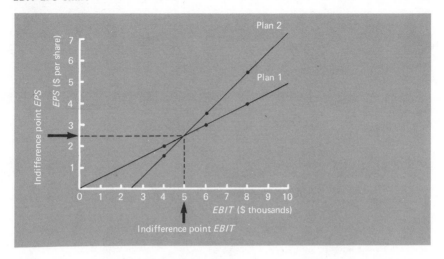

plan, and we can determine these straight lines by plotting the *EPS* and *EBIT* results from Figure 10–5.

Indifference point EBIT-EPS analysis The *EBIT-EPS* chart shows two important things. First, for either plan the straight line shows what *EPS* would result from a given *EBIT*. Under Plan 1, for example, if *EBIT* equals $2,000, the Plan 1 line indicates that *EPS* will be $1 per share. A quick calculation like that done in Figure 10–5 verifies this. So the *EBIT* chart graphically relates *EBIT* levels to *EPS* levels for either plan.

Second, Figure 10–6 shows that above some critical level of *EBIT*, Plan 2 always results in a higher *EPS* than Plan 1. The reverse is true below this critical level of *EBIT*. This critical level of *EBIT* occurs at the intersection of the two straight lines, and we call this intersection the *EBIT-EPS indifference point*. It's called the indifference point because at that *EBIT* level, the *EPS* of the two plans are equal. At *EBIT* levels above break-even *EBIT*, Plan 2 (the plan that uses some debt) always provides higher *EPS*, and at *EBIT* levels below break-even *EBIT*, Plan 1 always provides higher *EPS*. From the graph this break-even *EBIT* is seen to be $5,000. At *EBIT* = $5,000, *EPS* under both plans is $2.50 per share.

Now notice that when *EBIT* = $5,000, *EBIT/TA* = $5,000/$100,000 = 5 percent. Also, recall that the before tax cost of debt for Tyro is 5 percent. So for all levels of *EBIT* such that *EBIT/TA* is greater than 5 percent, Plan 2 will result in higher *EPS*. This is what was meant in an earlier statement that the effect of financial leverage on *EPS* depends on the relationship between the before tax cost of debt and the *EBIT* rate of return on assets.

We can also algebraically solve for *EBIT* at the indifference point. By definition:

$$EPS = \frac{(EBIT - I - L)(1 - T) - d}{N} \qquad (10\text{--}9)$$

where

N = number of shares of common stock.

Expressions for Tyro's EPS under Plans 1 and 2 are:

Plan 1: $EPS = \dfrac{(EBIT - 0)(0.5) - 0}{1,000} = 0.0005\ EBIT$

Plan 2: $EPS = \dfrac{(EBIT - \$2,500)(0.5) - 0}{500} = 0.001\ EBIT - \$2.50$

The indifference point is where the EPS under the two plans are equal. Equating the two EPS expressions and letting $EBIT^*$ equal the indifference point $EBIT$:

$$0.0005\ EBIT^* = 0.001\ EBIT^* - \$2.50$$
$$EBIT^* = \$5,000$$

Effect of financial leverage on financial risk and expected EPS

The question of interest here is whether there is an optimal capital structure for the firm or not. To answer this question we need to take a deeper look at the impact of financial leverage on stock price. We will do this in a stepwise fashion. First, in this section we will investigate how financial leverage affects the firm's *expected EPS* and financial risk. Then we will use these findings in the next section to relate expected *EPS* and financial risk to stock price.

Let's pick up the Tyro example again. Suppose that the company feels that the estimated *EBIT* outcomes of \$4,000, \$6,000, and \$8,000 are equally likely. This implies that probabilities of each are one third. We can now prepare the following probability functions for the two financing plans:

EBIT (dollars)	p_i	EPS (dollars per share)	
		Plan 1	*Plan 2*
4,000	1/3	2.00	1.50
6,000	1/3	3.00	3.50
8,000	1/3	4.00	5.50

We may now calculate the expected $EPS(\mu_{EPS})$ and standard deviation of $EPS\ (\sigma_{EPS})$ for each plan using Equations (4–1) and (4–3) developed back in Chapter 4:

$$\mu = \Sigma \; p_i x_i$$
$$\sigma = \sqrt{\Sigma \; p_i(x_i - \mu)^2}$$

where, in this case, $x = EPS$ and i is a subscript denoting three different outcomes.

For Plan 1, the all equity plan:

$$\mu_{EPS} = \frac{1}{3}(\$2) + \frac{1}{3}(\$3) + \frac{1}{3}(\$4) = \$3 \text{ per share}$$
$$\sigma_{EPS} = \sqrt{\frac{1}{3}(\$2 - \$3)^2 + \frac{1}{3}(\$3 - \$3)^2 + \frac{1}{3}(\$4 - \$3)^2}$$
$$= \$1.15 \text{ per share}$$

For Plan 2:

$$\mu_{EPS} = \frac{1}{3}(\$1.50) + \frac{1}{3}(\$3.50) + \frac{1}{3} \; (\$5.50) = \$3.50 \text{ per share}$$
$$\sigma_{EPS} = \sqrt{\frac{1}{3}(\$1.50 - \$3.50)^2 + \frac{1}{3}(\$3.50 - \$3.50)^2 + \frac{1}{3}(\$4.50 - \$3.50)^2}$$
$$= \$1.63 \text{ per share}$$

In reexamining Tyro's two proposed financial plans we observe that there are two effects of financing with debt. That is, there are two effects of financial leverage:

1. Expected earnings per share (μ_{EPS}) increases.[3]
2. The standard deviation of earnings per share (σ_{EPS}) increases.

These two conclusions have important valuation implications. First, the firm's ability to pay dividends is directly related to its expected earnings per share (μ_{EPS}). The greater μ_{EPS} the greater the firm's future expected dividends will be. The reason that debt financing causes expected earnings per share to be larger is that debt is a cheaper source of capital than equity. Since debt is a safer investment—from an investor's standpoint—than common stock, the required rate of return (cost of capital) on debt is lower than on stock. This difference causes expected EPS (and hence expected dividends) to be greater under debt financing.

Increases in the firm's μ_{EPS} level are desirable, *other things equal.* Notice, however, that other things are *not* equal in this financial leverage example. The standard deviation of earnings per share (σ_{EPS}) also increases as financial leverage increases. This increase in σ_{EPS} will also cause investors' standard deviation of rate of return on the stock (σ_f) to increase. The total financial management risk in the firm equals the covariance between the rate of return on the firm's stock and the rate of return on the market index, Cov_{fm}. That is,

$$\text{Cov}_{fm} = \rho_{fm}\sigma_f\sigma_m \tag{10-10}$$

where

σ_f = standard deviation of rate of return on the firm's stock;
σ_m = standard deviation of rate of return on a market index of wealth
ρ_{fm} = correlation of stock and market index rates of return.

As Equation (10–10) shows, the greater σ_f is, the greater Cov_{fm}, and the greater the risk associated with the common stock will be.

---

[3] It is possible for μ_{EPS} to be lower under the debt financing plan than the all equity financing plan. This would occur whenever the cost of borrowing is greater than the expected rate of return on proposed projects.

In the Tyro example, σ_{EPS} under Plan 2, where debt is used, is greater than σ_{EPS} under Plan 1, where debt is not used. Consequently, σ_f will be larger under Plan 2. Assuming ρ_{fm} is the same under both plans and since σ_m is independent of the choice of financing plan, we see that Cov_{fm} is greater under Plan 2 and there is thus more risk involved in Plan 2. This extra risk introduced into the firm is solely due to financial leverage, and we conclude that financial leverage increases the stockholders' risk.

EFFECT OF CAPITAL STRUCTURE ON STOCKHOLDER WEALTH

Repetitively choosing financing plans for new investment implies choice of a capital structure. In choosing among capital structures we encounter the usual tradeoff between risk and return. If the firm tries to increase its expected earnings per share (and hence stockholders' wealth) by employing financial leverage, the financial risk of the firm will also increase.

Now, the fundamental question of interest here is still the one we asked earlier: Can the firm increase the price of its common stock by choosing an optimal capital structure? That is: Is there an optimal capital structure? The answer to this question depends on the nature of the risk-return tradeoff involved in debt financing. We just saw that when debt is used to finance investments, the expected return and risk to stockholders both increase. But, do expected return and risk increase at the same rate? If they do not, there may be an advantage to financing investments with debt. Specifically, if, by using debt financing, expected return increases more than risk increases, then stock price will increase. What we need to investigate next is the nature of the risk-return tradeoff caused by debt financing.

Dividend valuation model

To address the issue of the debt financing risk-return tradeoff let's go back to the dividend valuation model developed in Chapter 5 (Equation [5–5]).

$$P_0 = \sum_{t=1}^{\infty} \frac{D_t}{(1 + k_e)^t}$$

where

D_t is the expected dividend per share in period t; and
k_e is the required rate of return or cost of equity capital.

The dividend valuation model expresses the current price of the stock, P_0, as a function of future expected dividends and the cost of equity capital. We can use this model to investigate the debt financing risk-return tradeoff and, ultimately, to assess the effect that capital structure has on stock price.

For simplification assume that the expected dividend stream is constant for a very long time ($n \to \infty$). Recall from Chapter 5 that these assumptions reduce (5–5) to a simpler expression [Equation (5–6)].

$$P_0 = \frac{D}{k_e}$$

where

D is the constant expected dividend per share. Assume further that the firm has a 100-percent dividend payout. That is, the firm pays out all earnings as dividends. This means that the constant expected dividends per share equals the firm's expected earnings per share (μ_{EPS}).

We are now prepared to begin the analysis. We will see that there is considerable controversy about the effect of capital structure on stock price. To fully understand and highlight this controversy it will be useful to separate the analysis into two parts. First, we will ignore taxes. Under this obviously unrealistic assumption we will see that some finance theorists argue that there is no such thing as an optimal capital structure. Second, we will introduce taxes into the analysis and see that much of the controversy about an optimal capital structure disappears.

Optimal capital structure controversy: no taxes

Suppose that the Bradley Manufacturing Co. is an all equity firm (no long-term debt). It has the following financial data:

Number of shares of common stock = 1,000,000 shares.
Current stock price = $P_0 = \$10$.
Expected $EBIT = \$1,000,000$ per year (for a very long time).
Dividend payout ratio = 1.0.

Since Bradley has no debt there are no interest changes, and since there are no taxes:

Expected net income = $1,000,000.
Expected $EPS = \$1$.
Expected dividend per share = $1.

Since expected dividends per share are constant for a very long time we can rearrange equation (5–6) to find the company's cost of equity capital, k_e.

$$k_e = \frac{D}{P_0} = \frac{\$1}{\$10} = 0.10$$

If there is an advantage to debt financing and Bradley changes its capital structure to include some debt, its stock price should increase. Suppose that Bradley borrows $5 million at 8 percent and uses this money to buy back half of its stock at the current market price of $10 per share. It will now have the following financial data:

Capital structure

Common stock	500,000 shares
Long term debt (8 percent)	$5,000,000
Expected *EBIT*	$1,000,000
Interest...	400,000
Expected net income............................	$ 600,000
Expected *EPS*......................................	$1.20
Expected dividend per share..................	$1.20

Just as in the Tyro example, the use of debt increases expected *EPS* and the expected dividend per share on the common. In Bradley's case, the expected dividend increases by 20 percent (from $1.00 per share to $1.20 per share). From Equation (5–6) we know that the greater *D* is, other things equal, the greater P_0 will be:

<table>
<tr><td align="center">*Before recapitalization*</td><td align="center">*After recapitalization*</td></tr>
<tr><td align="center">$P_0 = \dfrac{\$1.00}{0.10} = \$10$ per share</td><td align="center">$P_0 = \dfrac{\$1.20}{k_e}$</td></tr>
</table>

We are interested in knowing what P_0 will be *after* recapitalization. The answer to this question depends on how k_e is affected by the recapitalization. We know that the recapitalization creates financial leverage and financial risk. k_e is a function of financial risk, and the greater the financial risk the greater k_e. However, if k_e does not increase as much as the expected dividend increased, P_0 will increase.

There are two principal theories as to how k_e and P_0 are affected by financial leverage in a taxless environment. One is called the *traditional* theory and the other the *net operating income* theory.[4]

Traditional theory   The traditional theory asserts that, within the range of prudent financial leverage positions, up to some particular point, as financial leverage increases (as the firm's capital structure includes a larger percentage of debt financing) the firm's expected dividend will increase proportionately *more* than the firm's cost of equity capital. That is, up to some particular point:

$$\text{Percent } \Delta \text{ in } D > \text{Percent } \Delta \text{ in } k_e$$

In the Bradley example, if we assume that $5 million of debt financing is within this prudent range of financial leverage positions, the traditional theory argues that k_e will increase by less than the 20-percent increase in *D*. There is no exact assertion in the traditional theory as to what the precise percentage increase in k_e will be—only that it will be less than the percentage increase in *D*. Suppose the percentage increase in k_e is 15 percent, raising k_e to 0.115. Then:

$$P_0 = \frac{\$1.20}{0.115} = \$10.44$$

According to this theory, the firm's expected dividends increase here more than k_e will increase. That is, k_e increases as investors observe increased financial risk, but up to some point, this increase in k_e is not as large as the increase in *D*. Consequently, P_0 will increase.

To continue this theory, when the firm reaches financial leverage positions that are *too* risky, k_e will increase proportionately more than *D* does, and the stock price will start to decline. That is, *beyond* a certain financial leverage position, P_0 will start to drop as:

$$\text{Percent } \Delta \text{ in } k_e > \text{Percent } \Delta \text{ in } D$$

These arguments imply that there is some optimal capital structure at which P_0 will be maximized. This means that stockholders' wealth is a

---

[4] There is a third theory called the *net income theory* that has been convincingly refuted by financial research. This theory argues that k_e does not increase with increasing financial leverage.

function of the firm's capital structure, and to maximize stockholders' wealth the firm should seek out its optimal capital structure.

Typically, financial leverage is portrayed as a long-term debt to equity ratio or some variant (such as long-term debt to total capital). The relationship between k_e and financial leverage under the traditional theory is graphically shown in Figure 10–7. Up to the optimal capital structure k_e increases with increasing financial leverage, but beyond the optimal capital structure k_e begins to increase more rapidly as the firm is viewed by investors as being overextended debtwise. This overextension raises the specter of bankruptcy.

This relationship between k_e and financial leverage causes the relationship between stock price, P_0, and financial leverage to be some-

FIGURE 10–7
k_e versus financial leverage traditional theory: No taxes

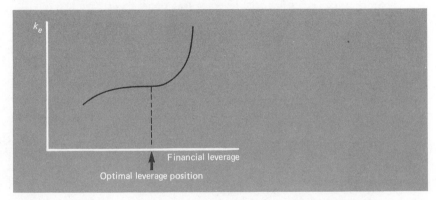

thing like that shown in Figure 10–8. Up to the optimal capital structure, P_0 increases as percent ΔD > percent Δ in k_e. Beyond the optimal capital structure position, P_0 decreases as percent Δk_e > percent ΔD.

In summary, under the traditional approach, there is an optimal capital structure. Up to the optimal debt/equity ratio the firm can and should employ the cheaper financing source: debt. Beyond the optimal capital structure the firm has employed too much debt. Debt is no longer cheaper than equity.

Net operating income theory The second major theory relating capital structure and stock price is the net operating income (NOI) theory. In a taxless world, this theory argues that there is no advantage to debt financing by the firm. That is, stock price is independent of financial leverage. According to the NOI argument, as the firm adds debt, k_e increases at *exactly* the same rate as the expected dividend increases:

$$\text{Percent } \Delta \text{ in } k_e = \text{Percent } \Delta \text{ in } D$$

Going back to the Bradley Manufacturing Co. example, if D increases 20 percent from $1.00 per share to $1.20 per share, k_e will also increase 20 percent from 0.10 to 0.12. So P_0 *after* recapitalization will equal

($1.20/0.12 =) $10, the same value as *before* recapitalization ($1.00/0.10 = $10). If this theory is true, then – in a taxless world – there is no such thing as an optimal capital structure. Investors are presumed to fully understand that increases in expected dividends caused by the firm's increased use of financial leverage also result in increased financial risk. The response of investors to the increased financial risk they are exposed to by the company's financing actions is to raise their required rate of return (k_e) *exactly* the same amount as the expected dividend increase. The important assumption in the *NOI* theory is that investors raise k_e in *exactly* the same proportion that expected dividends increase. Thus, the tradeoff between increased return (higher expected dividends) and increased risk (higher k_e) is linear. The gains that accrue

FIGURE 10–8
Stock price versus financial leverage traditional theory: No taxes

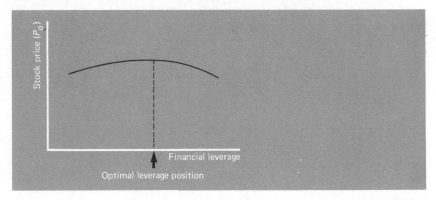

to the stockholders because of increased expected dividends are *exactly* offset or washed out by the increased required rate of return on the common stock (k_e) attributable to the higher degree of risk in the stock.

The relationships between k_e and financial leverage and between P_0 and financial leverage under the *NOI* theory are shown in Figures 10–9 and 10–10, respectively. k_e is a straight-line function of financial leverage, and P_0 is independent of financial leverage.

The *NOI* theory of capital structure has several important implications. First, the theory implies that the *real* costs of debt and equity are equal. This means that even though we calculate costs of debt (k_i) and equity (k_e) – as was done in Chapter 8 – that show $k_e > k_i$, these results are deceiving. Finance theorists frequently call these calculated costs of capital *explicit* costs of capital. There are also *implicit* costs of capital. Implicit costs of capital are the changes in the cost of one source of capital caused by financing with another source. The *real* cost of capital would equal the sum of its explicit and implicit costs. Thus, the real cost of debt financing would equal the *explicit* cost of debt plus the *implicit* cost of debt, where the implicit cost of debt equals the increase in the

FIGURE 10–9
k_e versus financial leverage NOI theory: No taxes

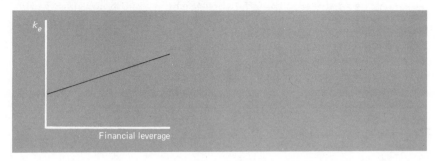

cost of equity that occurs when the firm finances with debt. The *NOI* theory argues that when the implicit cost of debt financing is properly accounted for, the *real* costs of debt and equity are the same when there are no taxes.

The second implication of the *NOI* theory is that – in a taxless world – it is a matter of indifference as to how the firm finances its investments in the long run. There may be short-run circumstances that would lead the firm to issue new debt (the stock market may be temporarily depressed) or new equity (the bond market may be temporarily saturated or depressed), but in the long run there is no reason for the firm to prefer debt financing over equity financing.

In one of the classic articles in the finance literature, professors Modigliani and Miller demonstrated a behavioral model that showed why – in a taxless world – there would be no preference for debt financing by the firm and, therefore, no optimal capital structure.[5] Modigliani and Miller showed that because stocks in the same risk class were perfect substitutes for one another, investors would perform "switching" operations (buying and selling stocks that are perfect substitutes for one another)

FIGURE 10–10
Stock price versus financial leverage NOI theory: No taxes

---

[5] See the Modigliani and Miller article referenced in the Advanced References at the end of the chapter.

whenever firms with the same operating characteristics, but with different capital structures had different stock values. These switching operations assure that the *NOI* theory would hold in a taxless world.

The effect of the Modigliani and Miller thesis is to emphasize that investors can arrange their own personal capital structures in a way that maximizes their total wealth and the firm need not concern itself with searching for an optimal capital structure. The firm need not borrow on the investors' behalf when investors can borrow themselves, if they so choose. Therefore, in a taxless world, the firm's financing decision is an unimportant long-run decision according to the *NOI* theory.

Optimal capital structure: with taxes

When taxes are introduced into the analysis some of the controversy about optimal capital structure vanishes. Both the traditional and *NOI* theories then acknowledge existence of an optimal capital structure. There are, however, still some differences between the two theories.

The substance of the traditional theory is largely unchanged with the addition of taxes. Up to the optimal capital structure position, k_e does not increase as fast as expected dividends (earnings) increase; therefore P_0 increases. Beyond the optimal capital structure P_0 declines as k_e increases faster than D increases.

The optimal capital structure in the *NOI* theory is similar in a *qualitative* sense to the optimal capital structure in the traditional theory, but *NOI* proponents argue that there are still significant *quantitative* differences. According to the *NOI* theory, the *only* advantage of debt financing is the tax deductibility feature of the interest payments on the firm's debt. This alone, says this theory, causes debt financing to be advantageous. And *NOI* theorists also argue that this advantage is usually smaller than believed.

Nonetheless, when bankruptcy possibilities are considered in conjunction with the tax deductibility of interest payments, the *NOI* optimal structure looks qualitatively much like the traditional theory. As financial leverage is increased, the firm's expected dividends increase by more than k_e increases (solely because of the interest deductibility says the *NOI* theory), so P_0 rises (but not by much according to *NOI* proponents). As the firm increases its financial leverage, the probability of bankruptcy grows, and beyond some leverage position (the optimal capital structure) k_e rises faster than D, so P_0 will drop as the firm overextends itself. At the extreme, the firm could fail and P_0 would plummet.

In summarizing this material, we started out by asking: Is there an optimal capital structure? After much debate there appears to be an uneasy agreement that there is an optimal capital structure that results from the interplay of the tax deductibility of debt interest charges and the increasing probability of bankruptcy as the firm adds financial leverage. There is very little compelling theory today, however, that will guide the firm toward identifying the optimal capital structure. This unresolved issue will probably be one of the major research topics in finance in future years.

SUMMARY

We began this chapter with a discussion of *operating leverage.* Operating leverage refers to the firm's use of assets with fixed costs. The higher the ratio of the firm's fixed costs to its variable costs (or, alternatively, the higher the ratio of the firm's fixed costs to its total costs), the more operating leverage the firm has. The effect of operating leverage is to magnify any changes in the firm's sales into larger changes in the firm's *EBIT*. The *degree of operating leverage* (*DOL*) measures the firm's present operating leverage position and is defined as the percentage change in *EBIT* divided by the percentage change in sales.

Operating leverage is directly related to *business risk*. Business risk refers to the risk associated with the firm's investments in aggregate, and is approximately measured by the covariance between the firm's *EBIT* rate of return and market rate of return. The greater the firms operating leverage, the greater its business risk. Operating leverage is frequently studied in the context of *break-even analysis*, which shows the relationship between sales and (1) costs and (2) *EBIT*. While break-even analysis is a popular and useful analytic technique, we also saw that there are many practical limitations regarding its use.

Financial leverage refers to the use of financing that involves fixed charges. The major sources of long-term fixed charge financing are debt, preferred stock, and leasing. The greater the usage of fixed charge financing, the greater the firm's financial leverage. The *degree of financial leverage* (*DFL*) measures the firm's financial leverage position, and is defined as the percentage change in *EPS* divided by the percentage change in *EBIT*. *DFL* shows the magnification of *EPS* changes relative to *EBIT* changes. Financial leverage is also reflected by the firm's long-term debt to equity ratio or some variant such as the long-term debt to total assets ratio. These capital structure measures of financial leverage show the relative usage of debt financing by the firm.

The greater the firm's use of fixed charge financing, the greater its financial leverage and the greater its financial risk. Financial risk refers to the extra covariability between firm and market index rates of return caused solely by financing with capital that has fixed charge obligations. The greater the firm's financial leverage, the riskier the stock becomes. At the same time, however, increased use of financial leverage will usually increase the firm's expected earnings per share. Financial leverage thus leads to both greater expected earnings per share (and therefore greater expected dividends) and increased financial risk.

The increased financial risk in the firm caused by increased financial leverage manifests itself in a higher cost of equity capital, k_e. This increase in k_e partially offsets the gains to the stockholders caused by increased *EPS*. But in a world where interest payments are tax deductible, this offsetting is not complete up to some particular leverage position, and it appears advantageous (to the stockholders) to have the firm finance with debt up to some point.

Beyond this debt limit it is disadvantageous for the firm to finance with debt. The foregoing implies the existence of an *optimal capital structure,* that is, a debt/equity financing ratio that will optimize stock-holder wealth. And, both the traditional and *NOI* theories of capital structure agree that—when taxes are properly accounted for—there is some optimal capital structure for the firm. Guides for finding this optimal position are not well spelled out in the finance literature but entail balancing out the tax deductibility gains of debt financing with the expected costs of possible bankruptcy.

QUESTIONS

1. Define the following terms and phrases:

a. Operating leverage.	*f.* Break-even sales level.
b. Financial leverage.	*g.* Degree of financial leverage.
c. Degree of operating leverage.	*h.* Degree of combined leverage.
d. Business risk.	*i.* Capital structure.
e. Variable cost ratio.	*j.* Optimal capital structure.

2. An analyst is comparing the operating leverage of two similar firms. If all operating data for the two companies were identical except for the differences listed below, which company would have the greater amount of operating leverage in each instance?

   a. Company A has a lower sales level than Company B.

   b. Company B has a higher *EBIT* level.

   c. Company A has a higher variable cost ratio.

3. Suppose that X Co. has a higher degree of operating leverage than Y Co. Which company has the greater amount of business risk? Explain your answer.

4. Other things equal, what is the effect on a firm's break-even sales level if:

   a. Costs unrelated to sales volume increase?

   b. The variable cost ratio increases?

   c. Prices on all the firm's products were lowered with no increase in sales volume?

5. Carol Smith, a new junior analyst with the Western Mexico Import-Export Co., has completed preparing a break-even *EBIT* chart for the company. She is preparing to present this chart to her boss and is interested in making a good impression. She has some nagging doubts, however, about how accurately and realistically the chart reflects what the firm's *EBIT* would be for particular sales levels. While she is thus skeptical of some of the work she has done, she is really not sure why she is skeptical. If she comes to you to talk about the problem, what could you tell her about the validity of her break-even chart?

6. Other things equal, what effect would the following changes have on a firm's degree of combined leverage? Explain your answer.

      a. The firm's *EBIT* level increases.
      b. Sales price increases, but volume remains the same.
      c. Fixed operating costs decline.

7. In comparing the financial leverage of two companies, A and B, with the same amount of assets and *EBIT*, we notice that A has a greater amount of debt (and more interest charges) than B.
      a. Other things equal, which company would have the greater amount of financial risk? Why?
      b. Suppose that even though A has more debt financing, greater interest charges and the same amount of assets and *EBIT* as B, B still has a larger calculated degree of financial leverage. Explain whether this is possible or not.

8. Financial leverage is generally thought to have two effects on the firm's earnings per share. Identify these two effects and explain why they occur.

9. In the simplified world of "no taxes," there are two competing theories that purport to describe how stock prices are related to capital structure.
      a. Identify these two theories.
      b. Briefly describe these two theories.
      c. What main impact does including taxes have on the debate?

PROBLEMS

1. Consider the following operating information about companies H and I.

	H	I
Sales	$10,000,000	$12,000,000
Fixed costs	3,000,000	6,000,000
Variable costs	5,000,000	3,000,000

      a. Find the break-even sales level for each company.
      b. Find the degree of operating leverage for each company.

2. First Chance Corporation has the following balance sheet and income statement information:

Balance Sheet

Assets:		Claims:	
Cash and securities	$ 50,000	Current	$ 50,000
Accounts Receivable	8,000	Mortgage (5 percent)	200,000
Inventory	150,000	Common ($10 par)	278,000
Net fixed assets	430,000	Retained earnings	110,000
Total	$638,000	Total	$638,000

Income Statement

Sales	$80,000
Operating expenses (including $20,000 depreciation)	40,000
EBIT	40,000
Interest	10,000
Lease payments	2,000
EBT	28,000
Taxes (40 percent)	11,200
Net income	$16,800

a. Compute degree of operating, financial, and combined leverage at the current sales level if all operating expenses other than depreciation are variable costs.
b. If total assets remain at the same level, but sales increase by 5 percent, what will net income be?
c. Calculate current earnings per share and earnings per share for the situation described in (b).

3. The Long and Mansfield Pencil Co.'s most recent balance sheet follows:

Balance Sheet
(thousands of dollars)

Assets		Claims	
Current assets	$ 250	Current liabilities	$ 200
Net fixed assets	750	Long-term debt	400
		Common stock ($10 par)	300
		Retained earnings	100
Total assets	$1,000	Total claims	$1,000

The company's total assets turnover ratio is 2.0, its fixed operating costs are $800,000, and its variable operating cost ratio is 30 percent. Interest charges are $50,000 and the income tax rate is 40 percent. The firm makes no lease payments.
a. Determine the firm's most recent earnings per share.
b. Find Long and Mansfield's (1) degree of operating leverage, (2) degree of financial leverage, and (3) degree of combined leverage at the present sales level.
c. What would earnings per share be if sales (1) increased 10 percent, (2) decreased 10 percent?
d. In comparison to the current year's sales level, management feels there is a 20-percent chance that next year's sales will be 10-percent less, a 60-percent chance that sales will be 10-percent greater, and a 20-percent chance that sales will remain at the same level. Calculate next year's expected earnings per share.

4. Incomplete balance sheets of the Caldwell Glass Company and the Diamond Bottling Works are presented below. Notice that both companies have the same number of common shares outstanding.

	Caldwell	*Diamond*
Total assets	$120,000,000	$100,000,000
Claims on assets:		
Current liabilities.............................	$ 20,000,000	$ 20,000,000
Long-term debt (7 percent)	—	—
Preferred stock (8 percent)..................	—	—
Common stock (5,000,000 shares).........	40,000,000	40,000,000
Total claims on assets...............	$120,000,000	$100,000,000

a. Complete each company's balance sheet if the ratio of long-term debt to total assets for Caldwell and Diamond are 0.2 and 0.4, respectively.

b. Caldwell has $1 million in lease payments and its *EBIT* is $22 million. Diamond has no lease payments and an *EBIT* of $15 million. Calculate *EPS* for Caldwell and Diamond at their current levels of *EBIT* if each company's tax rate is 40 percent. Assume no interest charges on current liabilities. (Note: lease payments are deductible for tax purposes just like interest charges.)

c. Calculate *EPS* for each company if *EBIT* were to decline by 10 percent.

d. Determine each company's degree of financial leverage using Equation (10–5). (Round off your answer to one decimal place.) Verify your results by calculating *DFL* using Equation (10–6). How do you account for these results given Diamond's greater use of debt?

e. Each company's analysts estimate that next year's *EBIT* could change from their current levels as shown below.

Percentage change in EBIT	*Probability*
−5	0.3
0	0.4
5	0.3

Calculate expected *EPS* and the standard deviation of *EPS* given these estimates.

f. Based on the results of (e), which company has the greater amount of financial management risk, everything else equal? Explain your answer.

5. Mrs. Stone, a rich industrialist, is considering the purchase of one of two lamp manufacturing companies. The Malls Lamp Co. is more automated in its production process while the Rattray Lamp Co. relies more heavily on labor to produce its products. Stone's financial staff

has developed financial information about the two companies which is presented below. Both companies have total assets of $500,000.

Current Operating Statements	*Malls*	*Rattray*
Sales......................................	$1,000,000	$1,000,000
Cost of goods sold	750,000	750,000
Selling expenses........................	80,000	80,000
Administrative expenses..............	30,000	50,000
Depreciation	40,000	30,000
EBIT	$ 100,000	$ 90,000

Cost Breakdowns		
Variable costs		
Cost of goods sold	$300,000	$600,000
Selling expenses.....................	50,000	50,000
Total variable costs	$350,000	$650,000
Fixed costs		
Cost of goods sold	$450,000	$150,000
Selling expenses.....................	30,000	30,000
Administrative expenses...........	30,000	50,000
Depreciation	40,000	30,000
Total fixed costs	$550,000	$260,000

a. Prepare an operating statement for each company assuming that sales increase by 15 percent. Assume that for this size sales increase that fixed costs are constant and that variable costs are a linear function of sales.
b. Determine each company's degree of operating leverage using Equation (10–1). Verify your results by calculating each company's *DOL* using Equation (10–2).
c. Stone's analysts believe that next year's sales for each company might change as follows:

Percentage change in sales	Probability
−10%	0.2
0............................	0.6
10............................	0.2

Given these estimates, calculate the expected rate of return on assets before interest and taxes (μ_R), and standard deviation of rate of return on assets before interest and taxes (σ_R) for each company.
d. Based on the results of part (c), under the following circumstances, which company would have the greatest amount of business risk?
1. ρ_{Rm} (Malls) = ρ_{Rm} (Rattray) = 0.9
2. ρ_{Rm} (Malls) = 0.4; ρ_{Rm} (Rattray) = 0.9
   Explain your answer.

6. Anderson Electronics is currently making substantial new investments in minitransistors. They plan to finance this investment with either a new stock issue (100,000 shares) or with new 8-percent debt. Total financing required is $500,000. The firm's preexpansion income statement is as follows:

Sales	$1,500,000
Operating costs	1,000,000
EBIT	500,000
Interest	100,000
EBT	400,000
Tax ($T = 0.5$)	200,000
Net income	200,000
EPS (200,000 shares)	$1/sh.

Anderson estimates that EBIT after the new investment will be $500,000 or $600,000 or $800,000, with associated probabilities of 0.3, 0.5 and 0.2.
   a. Determine the EPS for both plans under each EBIT possibility.
   b. Calculate expected EPS and the standard deviation of EPS for each plan.
   c. If the correlation between Anderson stock and market index rates of return is essentially the same under the two plans, which plan has more financial risk? Explain your answer.

7. Bobrow Ceramic Fixtures is an all equity company (there is no long-term debt outstanding). The company has 500,000 shares of common outstanding, currently selling at $10 per share. Current earnings per share (EPS) is $1/share, and the company's policy is (and will be) to pay out all earnings as dividends to stockholders. Bobrow needs to raise $5 million for new investment purposes and is considering two alternative financing plans (ignoring floatation costs):
   Plan A: Sell 500,000 shares of stock at $10 per share.
   Plan B: Sell $2 million in 5-percent bonds and 300,000 shares of stock at $10 per share.
   a. If after the expansion Bobrow anticipates earning $2.5 million before interest and taxes (EBIT) for the foreseeable future, calculate EPS and dividends per share under each plan. The tax rate is 40 percent.
   b. Assume the conditions given in (a) and that furthermore, the cost of equity is estimated to be 10 percent if Plan A is adopted and 11 percent if Plan B is adopted. Estimate the market price of the stock under both plans.
   c. Assume that you and another financial analyst on Bobrow's corporate planning staff are presenting your results to several of Bobrow's top executives.
      (1) How would you explain the anticipated increase in stock price over the current $10 price if Plan A is adopted?
      (2) How would you explain the further anticipated increase in stock price (over that of Plan A) if Plan B is adopted?

(3) One of the executives asks how a *third* alternative financing plan, namely, issuing $5 million in debt, would compare with the other plans. Your colleague, Jane Brown, responds that that plan was considered. However, it was estimated that the coupon rate on the debt would go up to 6 percent, and that the estimated stock price would be $11 per share. As she talks she signals to you to calculate the *EPS* result for this case. Do this and also determine what cost of equity is implied in the calculation of the $11 stock price.

(4) How would you justify using different costs of equity capital for the three different plans?

(5) Based on all these calculations, which plan do you recommend? Why?

8. Jarvis, Inc., a manufacturer and retailer of pianos and organs, is planning to expand its assets by 30 percent. All financing for this expansion will come from external sources, and the company is considering three alternative financing plans.

Plan I: Issue debt (8-percent interest rate)
Plan II: Issue preferred stock (10-percent dividend rate)
Plan III: Issue common stock

The company's current price/earnings ratio (stock price divided by earnings per share) is ten, the marginal tax rate = 40 percent, and Jarvis has the following current balance sheet and income statement data.

Balance Sheet		Income Statement	
Total assets..................	$1,000,000	Sales	$2,000,000
Claims:		Operating costs	1,700,000
Current liabilities	$ 250,000	*EBIT*	$ 300,000
Bonds, 4 percent	250,000	Interest	10,000
Common ($1 par)	348,000	*EBT*	$ 290,000
Retained earnings	152,000	Tax (0.40)..................	116,000
Total	$1,000,000	Net income	$ 174,000

a. Determine the firm's current earnings per share and current stock price.

b. Ignoring floatation costs, how many shares of common stock must be issued if Plan III is implemented?

c. Ignoring floatation costs, and assuming that *EBIT*/sales after the expansion will be the same as before the expansion, calculate earnings per share at the following sales levels for all three financing plans: (*1*) $1.5 million, (*2*) $2.5 million, (*3*) $3.5 million.

d. Use Equation (10–9) to determine break-even *EBIT* levels between (*1*) Plans I and II, (*2*) Plans I and III, and (*3*) Plans II and III.

e. Assume that the stock's P/E ratio is expected to stay at ten if the stock plan is used and is expected to drop to nine if either the debt plan or the preferred plan is used. Determine the market price of the stock for all situations in part (*c*).

f. If the probabilities associated with the three sales outcomes given in (*c*) are 0.2, 0.4, and 0.4, respectively, determine the expected value of earnings per share and stock price for each of the three plans.

g. Given all these estimates, which plan would you advise Jarvis to adopt? Why?

SELECTED BASIC REFERENCES

Helfert, E. A. *Techniques of Financial Analysis.* 3d ed. Homewood, Ill.: Richard D. Irwin, Inc., 1972, chapter 6.

Hunt, P. "A Proposal for Precise Definitions of 'Trading on the Equity' and 'Leverage,'" *Journal of Finance* (September 1961), pp. 377–86.

Solomon, E. *The Theory of Financial Management.* New York: Columbia University Press, 1963, chapter 8.

SELECTED ADVANCED REFERENCES

Baxter, N. D. "Leverage, Risk of Ruin, and the Cost of Capital," *Journal of Finance* (September 1967), pp. 395–404.

Hamada, R. S. "The Effect of the Firm's Capital Structure on the Systematic Risk of Common Stocks," *Journal of Finance* (May 1972), pp. 435–52.

Modigliani, F., and M. Miller. "The Cost of Capital, Corporation Finance, and the Theory of Investment," *American Economic Review* (June 1958), pp. 261–97.

RETAINED EARNINGS AND DIVIDEND POLICY

I n the following four chapters we will investigate various aspects of intermediate and long-term *external* financing sources. We begin this chapter by studying the use of retained earnings as a source of capital. Since dividends equal earnings minus retained earnings, the study of retained earnings is closely related to dividend policy. We look at dividend policy in some detail in this chapter.

INTERNAL FINANCING

For most companies, internal funds provided from operations for any year are approximately equal to retained earnings (undistributed earnings) plus depreciation charges. These internal funds are an important source of financing for firms. As Figure 11–1 shows, internally provided funds have historically been the main source of financing for U.S. firms. The percentage has varied, but since World War II, approximately 60 percent of all funds used by U.S. business firms have been internally provided funds.

Recall that depreciation charges represent noncash charges allocated against earnings to reflect the declining economic value of the firm's fixed assets. Figure 11–2 shows retained earnings and depreciation charges for U.S. corporations since World War II. Notice that since 1950, depreciation has been the larger of the two internal financing components.

DIVIDEND POLICY

As noted above, the cash flow in any year for a firm is approximately equal to its earnings (net income) plus depreciation. If depreciation charges are used as intended – to replace worn out fixed assets – the firm's main financial management decision regarding internal financing

FIGURE 11–1
Internal financing as a percentage of total (nonfarm and nonfinancial) business financing

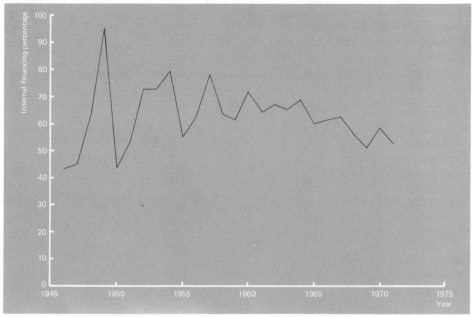

Source: Economic Report of the President, 1973.

FIGURE 11–2
Components of internal financing for U.S. corporations

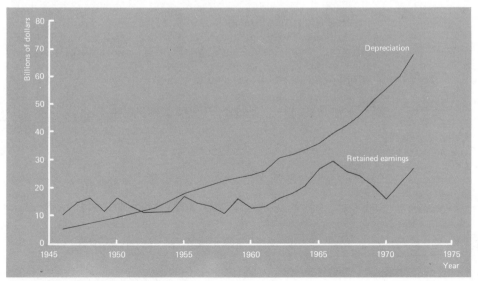

Source: Economic Report of the President, 1973.

concerns how much of its earnings to keep and how much to pay out as dividends to common stockholders. We call this decision the *dividend decision*.

Dividend payout ratio

Dividend policy actually refers to two things: the *level* of dividends and the *stability* of dividends paid. In *absolute* terms, dividend levels are indicated by their dollar amount. A $3 per share dividend this year for DEF, Inc., for example, is a clear statement of DEF's current dividend levels in absolute terms. In *relative* terms, dividend levels are indicated by *dividend payout* ratios.

$$\text{Dividend payout} = D/E = \frac{\text{Dividends per Share}}{\text{Earnings per Share}}$$

Because different firms have different earnings levels, it is very difficult to compare dividend policies among companies by comparing dollar dividend levels. The dividend payout ratio facilitates comparison by describing how much of each dollar's worth of earnings is returned to stockholders as dividends.

Suppose, for example, that ABC Co. and DEF, Inc., are currently paying $0.20 per share and $3.00 per share annual dividends, respectively. However, it is not possible to compare dividend policies of these two firms only on the basis of this information about dividends/share. If ABC earns $0.40 per share and DEF $6.00 per share, both companies have 0.5 payout ratios, and are similar in the sense of the *relative level* of their dividend payments: Both companies are paying out half of their earnings to common stockholders.

Dividend stability

Dividend stability refers to the steadiness or lack of variability of the stream of dividends. There is no universally accepted measure of dividend stability although the *coefficient of variation* of the dividend stream has been used as a measure of dividend *instability*.

Let D_t = dividend payment in period t; then

$$\text{Coefficient of variation of dividend stream} = \frac{\sigma_D}{\mu_D} \qquad (11\text{--}1)$$

where

$$\mu_D = \text{Average dividend payment}$$

$$\mu_D = \sum_{t=1}^{n} D_t/n \qquad (11\text{--}2)$$

and

$$\sigma_D = \text{standard deviation of dividend payments}$$

$$\sigma_D = \sqrt{\sum_{t=1}^{n} (D_t - \mu_D)^2/n} \qquad (11\text{--}3)$$

Suppose, for example, that ABC and DEF have the following dividend histories:

	Dividend	
Year	ABC *(dollars per share)*	DEF *(dollars per share)*
1	0.13	2.90
2	0.08	2.80
3	0.04	2.90
4	0.15	3.00
5	0.20	3.00
μ_D	0.12	2.92
σ_D	0.06	0.07
Coefficient of variation	0.50	0.02

The smaller the coefficient of variation, the more stable the dividend. Thus, DEF's dividend stream is considerably more stable than ABC's. This is also readily seen by inspection of the two dividend streams.

The coefficient of variation of the dividends is merely the standard deviation (recall Chapter 4) of dividends divided by the average dividend. Dividing by average dividends puts the variability measure on a *relative* basis much as the dividend payout puts the level of dividends on a relative basis. The coefficient of variation thus permits comparison of dividend instability among companies. Notice that if we only compared standard deviations of ABC and DEF dividend streams, ABC would appear to be more stable because its σ_D is lower. But this is because DEF's *level* of dividends is much higher. The coefficient of variation accounts for the difference in magnitudes of dividend levels. Relative to its average dividend, DEF has the more stable dividend stream.

We should qualify this kind of analysis, however, by emphasizing that dividend instability is *most* important in the sense of *downward* variability of dividends. A rising dividend over time exhibits variability but is hardly of much concern. Thus, the dividend sequence $1, $2, $3 and the dividend sequence $3, $2, $1 have the same coefficient of variation, yet the former appears to be more attractive. We will see below that most firms strive for relatively stable dividend patterns that increase over time.

Alternative dividend policies

The words "dividend policy" imply some sort of long-range plan for distributing dividends to common stockholders. There are many such plans that an imaginative financial manager could establish, but most can be described by one of the following three categorizations.

Stable dividend/share policy   One plausible dividend policy is to maintain a relatively stable dividend payment. This policy results in a dividend stream that is fairly constant, with dividend increases when earnings increase, and dividend decreases only when the firm can no longer support the present level of dividends. Selection of a stable dividend per share policy implies that the dividend payout (D/E) will fluctuate as earnings fluctuate.

Selection of a stable dividend per share policy is usually coupled with a long range "target" D/E ratio. As earnings per share grow over time, the firm will raise dividends per share in accordance with the target D/E ratio. Suppose, for example, the firm has decided on a stable dividend/share policy and has established a target D/E ratio of 0.4. Suppose, further, that earnings over the past few years have been fairly constant at $2.00 per share with only minor fluctuations. Under these conditions the firm would pay $0.80 per share in dividends. Now suppose the company's earnings begin to grow and over the next few years average about $3.00 per share. As this growth in earnings is realized, the firm will begin to gradually increase the dividends to the level of about $1.20 per share.

The range of possible target D/E ratios is from one, where all earnings are paid out, to zero, where all earnings are retained. The firm may also pay a dividend when a loss is incurred. This is discussed further below. Relatively high target D/E ratios may require the firm to seek outside capital frequently, while relatively low target D/E ratios will provide a greater amount of internal financing. Some companies, such as General Motors, have relatively low D/E ratios and pay an annual "extra" dividend at the end of the year. The size of this extra dividend is usually dependent on how well the firm fared in the year. However, many financial theorists would argue that regular "extra" dividends are eventually considered by investors to be part of the firm's normal annual total.

Constant payout ratio policy   An alternate dividend policy is to pay out a fixed amount of each year's earnings. That is, the firm attempts to keep a constant payout ratio. When the firm keeps a constant payout ratio, dividends per share will fluctuate with earnings per share. As earnings per share increase, dividends per share will also increase. Likewise, when earnings per share decrease, dividends per share will also decrease. Actually, very few U.S. companies appear to have adopted this kind of dividend policy.

Residual dividend policy   A third alternate dividend policy is to treat dividends as a residual decision that is subservient to the investment decision. A firm that treats dividend decisions in this fashion would pay out dividends whenever it had more earnings than were needed for financing new investments and would pay no dividends when it needed all of its earnings for investment purposes. Under this approach, growth companies with large financing needs would be expected to pay small or no dividends, and mature companies with few attractive investment opportunities would be expected to pay out most or all of their earnings. If a firm follows this policy it would have no target payout ratio, and its dollar dividend and dividend payout ratio would fluctuate as its earnings and investment plans fluctuate.

DIVIDEND POLICY CONTROVERSY

In recent years there has been considerable debate among finance scholars about the importance of dividend policy. Some argue that dividend policy has a strong influence on stock price while others argue that dividend policy has no influence on stock price. The controversy centers on the question of what *level* of dividends the firm should pay. That is, is it advantageous to have a particular payout ratio? Two principal theories have been advanced in this debate. They are sometimes called the "Bird in the Hand" (*BIH*) theory and the "Perfect Markets" theory.

"Bird in the hand" theory

The "bird in the hand" (*BIH*) theory asserts that the firm's dividend policy is very important and has a strong influence on the firm's stock price. According to this argument, investors prefer high dividend payout (*D/E*) ratios, and other things equal, firms with relatively high *D/E* ratios will have relatively high stock prices. Conversely, firms that have relatively low *D/E* ratios will have relatively low stock prices.

The basic tenet of the *BIH* theory is that the dominant feature of the investment environment is uncertainty. Moreover, the *BIH* theory notes that uncertainty usually increases with time. If the firm makes an investment, it is usually more certain what cash flows will result in the early years of the investment than in later years. Since the firm ultimately looks to its cash flows to pay dividends, this increasing uncertainty over time implies that the more distant in the future an expected dividend is, the more uncertain it is. Therefore, goes the argument, since investors are risk averse, they will prefer receipt of current *certain* dividends to the *expected* receipt of increased riskier *future* dividends. That is, investors will prefer a bird in the hand to two in the bush.

It's important to note that we are not talking about the time value of money preferences of investors here. We have already seen (in Chapter 3) that any rational investor would prefer a dollar of dividends today rather than a dollar of dividends at some time in the future. The question here is: Would an investor prefer a dollar of dividends today over *more* than a dollar of dividends in the future? By retaining the dollar rather than paying it out as current dividends, the firm expects to pay larger future dividends since the firm expects to earn a rate of return on the dollar of current retained earnings. The question here then, is whether investors prefer the *certain* current dollar of dividends to the *expectation* of increased future dividends.

The *BIH* theory argues that investors prefer current dividends because of the uncertainty of the expected future dividends. This conclusion has a strong dividend policy implication: *Investors prefer and firms should maintain high D/E ratios*. According to the *BIH* theory, firms that pay out relatively large proportions of their earnings (and thus have high *D/E* ratios) will be following a dividend policy that will maximize their firm's stock price.

Perfect market theory

The perfect market theory asserts that investors are indifferent about the firm's dividend policy. More precisely, *given* the firm's investment policy (that is, given the firm's decision to make certain investments), investors do not really care whether the firm has a high or low payout ratio.

According to this theory, if the firm's payout ratio is too low, an investor can sell a portion of his stock to increase his current income from the stock. Similarly, if the firm's payout ratio is too high, and an investor is receiving more current income than he wishes (he would prefer the firm to invest more on his behalf), he may always reinvest the dividend proceeds by purchasing more stock. Suppose, for example, that an investor owns 100 shares of Mayer Co. that sells for $10 per share. The company is earning $0.50 per share and it pays a $0.20 per share dividend. Our hypothetical investor will receive a $20 dividend for the year. Now suppose that he would prefer a $30 income from his investment in Mayer. He can obtain this higher income by selling one share of Mayer for $10, which together with his $20 dividend will give him $30 income.[1] Now suppose, instead, that he desires only a $10 income from Mayer. He can purchase one share of Mayer for $10, which subtracted from his $20 dividend will give him the desired $10 current income. This example shows that the investor can arrange his own "dividend" stream by buying or selling small amounts of the firm's stock.

The basis of this theory is that capital markets are "perfect" and investors are "rational." Let's examine these terms. Perfect capital markets are markets where there are no imperfections such as "friction" costs. Examples of friction costs are transaction costs that investors pay to buy and sell securities, floatation costs that firms pay to sell new securities in the market, and tax differentials on dividend income versus capital gains income. The rational investors assumption means that investors prefer more income to less, but also that investors are indifferent as to how they receive their income. Specifically, rational investors are presumed to be indifferent between dividend income and income obtained from sale of their stock.

These assumptions lead to the conclusion that dividend policy is irrelevant. If investors can buy and sell stock without cost and there are no tax differentials between dividend income and income obtained from the sale of stock, then investors should be indifferent between dividend income and capital gains income, and there would be no such thing as a best dividend policy that firms should follow.

It is clear, however, that these assumptions are not perfectly descriptive of conditions in today's capital markets. Transaction costs associated with investors buying and selling securities do exist, and there are floatation costs and differential taxes. In advocating the unimportance of dividend policy's influence on stock price, the perfect market theory asserts that these friction costs, while present, will not necessarily cause investors to prefer *high* dividend payout ratios. However, before we assess

---

[1] This example is not meant to imply that the investor is invading his original principal. He is forming his increased dividend through a capital gain on his stock sale.

the impact of these capital market imperfections we need to further examine the debate between the *BIH* and perfect market theories.

Dividend policy irrelevance

The perfect market theory concludes that dividend policy is irrelevant. That is, there is no *optimal* dividend policy, in the sense that there is no particular dividend payout ratio that will maximize stock price. Recall the basic dividend valuation model (Equation 5–5) developed back in Chapter 5:

$$P_0 = \sum_{t=1}^{\infty} \frac{D_t}{(1 + k_e)^t}$$

It may at first seem paradoxical to argue that dividend policy has no effect on P_0 since (5–5) clearly shows that P_0 is a function of future dividend payments. But actually, we can construct a simple example that illustrates the main point that the perfect market theory asserts: *Given the firm's investment policy, dividend policy is irrelevant.*

Notice that the firm's choice of dividend policy could affect P_0 through two different ways. First, dividend policy could affect P_0 through rearrangement of the dividend stream. That is, the choice of the firm's dividend payout ratio may cause the *pattern* of dividends to be such that P_0 is maximized by choice of a particular payout ratio. Second, dividend policy could affect P_0 because the cost of equity capital, k_e, is related to dividend policy. Since investors, in aggregate, determine what k_e is, if investors prefer high dividend payouts, they may respond favorably to companies that comply with their preferences. If this is true, then P_0 could possibly be maximized by choosing a dividend policy that minimizes k_e.[2] Let's look at the effect of rearranging the dividend stream first.

Rearrangement of dividend stream Obviously, more dividends are preferred to less according to Equation (5–5). But what would cause the dividend stream to increase? The answer is the fruition of investment opportunities. That is, successful investments will cause future dividends to increase. The perfect market proponents argue that it is *only* a successful investment program that will cause the firm's dividend stream to grow in the future and that *given* the firm's investment policy, dividend policy doesn't affect P_0 via the dividend stream per se. The dividend policy only *rearranges* the stream of dividends. We can illustrate this point with an example.

Suppose the Miller Co. is an all equity company (no long-term debt) with 100,000 shares of common outstanding. The company expects to earn about $100,000 per year on its present set of assets. The company normally pays out all earnings as dividends. Therefore, its expected dividend from present operations is about $1 per share each year. The firm's stock is selling at $10 per share and the cost of equity capital (k_e) is 10 percent. Now suppose Miller needs $100,000 next year for new investments that will return $10,000 per year for an indefinitely long period of

---

[2] Recall from Chapter 3 that as the discount rate (k_e) decreases, present value (P_0) increases.

time. Assume further that the firm has decided to finance the investment with equity. It does not wish to issue any debt.

There are two completely different financing alternatives available to Miller:

Plan 1: Maintain the $1 per share dividend and issue $100,000 of new stock to finance the investments.

Plan 2: Omit the next year's dividends and finance the investments with the $100,000 of retained earnings.

There are also intermediate financing plans, such as paying $50,000 in dividends in the coming year and issuing $50,000 of new stock. However, the two extremes represented by Plans 1 and 2 will illustrate the point adequately. Notice that under either plan, the investment takes place at the end of year one, and annual earnings beginning in year two will be $110,000 per year.

Plan 1: Sales price of new stock issued = $10 per share.[3]

$$\text{Number of new shares of stock required} = \frac{\$100,000}{\$10 \text{ per share}}$$
$$= 10,000 \text{ shares}$$

$$D_1 = \$1 \text{ per share}$$

Subsequent dividends per share $(D_2 \ldots D_\infty) = \$110,000/110,000$ shares $= \$1$ per share.[4]

Now recall the dividend valuation model:

$$P_0 = \sum_{t=1}^{\infty} \frac{D_t}{(1 + k_e)^t}$$

Therefore:

$$P_0 = \sum_{t=1}^{\infty} \frac{\$1}{(1.10)^t} = (\$1)(ADF_{.10, \infty}) = (\$1)(10)$$

$$P_0 = \$10 \text{ per share}$$

Plan 2: $D_1 = 0$. Subsequent dividends per share $(D_2 \cdots D_\infty) = \$110,000/100,000$ shares $= \$1.10$ per share.
Therefore:

$$P_0 = 0 + \sum_{t=2}^{\infty} \frac{\$1.10}{(1.10)^t} = (\$1.10)(ADF_{.10, \infty})(DF_{.10,1})$$

$$P_0 = (\$1.10)(10)(0.909)$$

$$P_0 = \$10 \text{ per share}$$

The important point here is that the theoretical current price of the firm's stock is $10 per share under either of the two extreme plans. That

---

[3] This calculation ignores any floatation costs associated with the issue.

[4] This calculation assumes Miller will maintain its policy of paying out all earnings in subsequent years. The 110,000 shares in years two and onward are the sum of the original 100,000 shares plus the additional 10,000 shares issued in year one.

is, all the firm has accomplished in choosing one dividend plan over the other is to rearrange the dividend stream. In particular, there is no enhancement of current stock price by choosing a high dividend payout ratio (as was done in Plan 1) in year one.

Change in the discount rate   Opponents of the perfect market theory argue that the example just presented does not embody the notion that investors prefer high current dividends because it does not reflect the increasing uncertainty of future dividends. To understand this criticism we can compare the expected dividend streams of Plans 1 and 2 in the example from a slightly different perspective. It's very informative to *net* the expected dividend streams from the competing plans:

Expected dividend payments (dollars per share)

	D_1	$D_2, D_3, D_4 \cdots D_\infty$
Plan 2	0	1.10
Plan 1	1.00	1.00
Plan 2 − Plan 1	−1.00	0.10

The difference between the two plans is clearly illustrated here. A decision to finance the new investments with retained earnings means giving up a $1 per share dividend in year one, but also results in increasing expected future dividends by $0.10 per share. The *BIH* theory contends, however, that the future increases in dividends (of $0.10) will be riskier since they are deferred to the (riskier) future. Specifically, the *BIH* theory asserts that the firm's cost of equity capital, k_e, will be larger under Plan 2 than under Plan 1 to reflect the increased riskiness of the Plan 2 dividend stream. Suppose, for example, that k_e remains at 10 percent if the Miller Co. opts for dividend Plan 1, but increases to 12 percent if Plan 2 is chosen. These assumptions imply the following current stock prices for Miller:

$$\text{Plan 1: } P_0 = \sum_{t=1}^{\infty} \frac{\$1}{(1.10)^t} = \$10$$

$$\text{Plan 2: } P_0 = 0 + \sum_{t=2}^{\infty} \frac{\$1.10}{(1.12)^t} = (\$1.10)(ADF_{.12,\infty})(DF_{.12,1}) = \$8.19$$

Since k_e is assumed to be higher under Plan 2, stock price declines. The principal point argued here by the *BIH* theory is that low D/E ratios cause risk to increase and this is manifested by k_e increasing. Therefore, k_e and D/E are inversely related. The *BIH* theory argues that firms that have relatively high D/E payouts will have relatively low k_e values, which will enhance stock price. Firms that have relatively low D/E ratios will have relatively high k_e values, which will depress stock price.

The perfect market theory denies the inverse relationship between k_e and D/E, asserting instead, that there is *no* relationship between k_e

and D/E. Many empirical studies have attempted to resolve the issue, but unfortunately, results are, in the main, inconclusive.

Principal points of debate

No one would argue with the validity of the perfect market theory if its assumptions were true. Indeed, much of the debate about the importance of dividend policy has revolved around the realism of the assumptions of the perfect market theory.

BIH theory arguments   The *BIH* theory questions two key assumptions of the perfect market theory: (1) that future dividends are no more risky than current dividends and (2) that transaction costs associated with investors arranging their own "dividend" stream are negligible.

Resolution of uncertainty. *BIH* proponents argue that since uncertainty increases with time, current dividends are less risky than (larger) deferred dividends. Consequently, investors will, on balance, favor firms that have relatively high D/E ratios.

Existence of transactions costs. *BIH* proponents criticize the perfect market theory for ignoring the existence of transactions costs. Recall the earlier Mayer Co. example where the firm paid a \$0.20-share dividend. According to the perfect market theory, if an investor didn't think this dividend high enough, he could always sell a portion of his stock and thus make his own "dividend." Similarly, if an investor felt the dividend were too high, he could always reinvest a portion of it. *BIH* theorists argue that this would be true *if*, as the perfect market theory assumes, there were no transaction costs involved. However, since investors have to pay brokerage fees, they lose a portion of their capital by buying and selling securities to arrange their own dividend stream.

Perfect market theory arguments   Proponents of this theory agree that their assumptions are not perfectly realistic, but they maintain that the realism of the assumptions of a theory is not an adequate test of the validity of the theory. Since *any* theory is an abstraction from reality, it will never be perfectly descriptive of reality, and the appropriate test of the theory is whether its predictions are consistent with observed behavior in the real world. This puts the burden of proof on empirical testing of the theory. While we noted above that results from the empirical tests are mixed, perfect market proponents argue that those tests that have been properly performed definitely support the perfect market theory.

Perfect market proponents also point out that, while it is wrong to test a theory on the realism of its assumptions, the inclusion of more realistic assumptions in the perfect market theory would lead investors to prefer *low* dividend payouts rather than high ones. Specifically, the acknowledgment of different tax rates on dividend income and capital gains, and the presence of floatation costs would cause investors to prefer *low* dividend payout policies by firms.

Differential taxation rates. Dividends are taxed at the ordinary income tax rate while capital gains are taxed at a lower rate. This would cause many investors to prefer that the firm retain most of its earnings so that investors would not have to pay the higher tax rate. Some investors would not be affected by the differential tax rates. Up to $100 of dividends ($200 for a couple filing jointly) are exempted from taxation, and small investors whose total dividend income (from all sources) does not exceed this $100 ($200 joint) limit would not be caused to prefer low dividend payouts. Similarly, institutional investors, such as pension funds, are exempt from taxes on dividend income and have no reason to prefer low dividend payouts. But there are clearly many investors whose high tax rates cause them to prefer low dividend payouts.

Floatation costs. The perfect market theory also assumes no floatation costs (the costs incurred by the firm when it issues new securities) exist. If this assumption were relaxed, perfect market proponents point out that investors would be led to prefer *low* dividend payouts. Suppose, for example, that the investment needs of the firm cause it to require $1 million of new equity money each year for the next five years, and the company also expects to earn $1 million in each of those years. Suppose, further, that the firm currently pays out 50 percent of its earnings. If the firm maintains this policy during the coming five years it will need to sell about $500,000 of new stock each year. Alternately, the firm could cut its dividend to zero, finance internally, and have no need to issue new stock. But recall from Chapter 8 that the cost of retained earnings is less than the cost of common stock. Therefore, rational investors should prefer that the company retain the earnings. That is, investors would prefer a lower dividend payout given the existence of floatation costs.

Clientele theory

Who is right and who is wrong in the dividend policy debate? There is no unanimity on the importance of dividend policy and its impact on stock price. Both sides have their strong supporters. However, there seems to be a growing belief among many finance scholars that a "clientele effect" exists with respect to dividend policy preference by investors.

The clientele theory explicitly acknowledges that investors have reasons for preferring particular payout ratios. Some will prefer high payout ratios. This group would include some institutional investors and many small investors, all of whom receive dividend income tax free. It would also include investors (such as retired people) who need the current income for living expenses and who do not wish to sell even a small portion of their stock, either because of the transactions costs involved or because they feel adversely about "living off capital." Other investors will prefer low dividend payouts. This group would include those individuals whose income tax rates are high enough to cause them to prefer capital gains over dividends. It would also include those investors who are averse to seeing the firm issue more common stock.

So there are clearly reasons for some individuals preferring high payout ratios and others preferring low ones. The clientele theory says that the former group will be attracted to high payout firms and the latter group to low payout firms. Therefore, neither high payout nor low payout firms will command a premium in the sense that the firm's stock price

will be affected by its dividend policy. Only if there were some fundamental change in the underlying preferences of investors in aggregate
would dividend policy influence stock price.

Notice that this theory is consistent with the perfect market theory.
The firm chooses whatever dividend policy it wishes, and it accumulates
an ownership clientele that approves of that policy. Notice also, however,
that this theory implies that once the firm has selected a target dividend
policy that it may be harmful (to stock price) to radically deviate from it.
If the firm has a relatively low payout, for example, switching to a high
payout may cause the old clientele to sell their stock and seek out relatively low dividend payers. While it is true that a new clientele would be
attracted, the transactions costs involved in this change of owners group
would be expected to have an adverse effect on stock price.

OBSERVED DIVIDEND PRACTICES

While there is considerable disagreement as to whether there is such
a thing as an optimal dividend policy, there are certain dividend policy
practices that many U.S. firms follow.

Level of dividends

First of all, most major U.S. corporations regularly pay cash dividends.
Figure 11–3 shows what percentage of companies listed on the New York
Stock Exchange paid cash dividends over the period from 1930 to 1970.

Even in the depression years about half of the firms on the New York
Stock Exchange paid cash dividends, and since World War II the percentage of cash dividend payers has been mostly in the 80-percent to
90-percent range. We should note that the New York Stock Exchange
contains the largest U.S. companies, but this only emphasizes the main

FIGURE 11–3
Percentage of New York Stock Exchange firms paying cash dividends

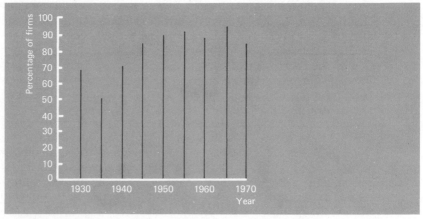

Source: New York Stock Exchange Fact Book (1973).

FIGURE 11-4
Average U.S. corporate dividend payout ratio

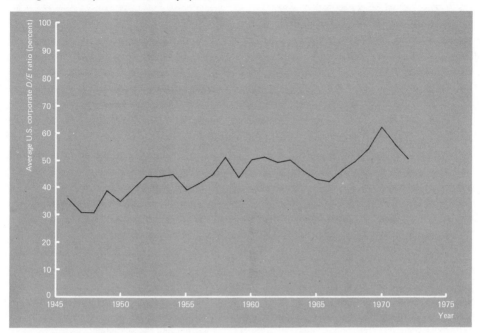

Source: Economic Report of the President, 1973.

point that most major U.S. corporations usually pay some kind of cash dividend.

We can also observe what approximate level of dividends are being paid. Figure 11–4 shows the percentage of earnings that have been paid out as dividends by all nongovernment U.S. corporations from 1945 to 1972. This diagram illustrates that the average D/E ratio for U.S. corporations has ranged between 30 percent and 60 percent in the postwar years. Since the 1950s, the average U.S. D/E ratio has been mainly between 40 and 50 percent.

Figure 11–4 is limited in the sense that it only shows the *average* U.S. corporation D/E ratio. It is also instructive to look at the distribution of D/E ratios on a company-by-company basis. Recall that Figure 11–3 showed what fraction of New York Stock Exchange firms paid *any* cash dividend. Figure 11–5 shows a distribution of D/E ratios of the largest 500 U.S. industrial firms in 1967. About two thirds of these companies were in the "middle ground" (30 to 70 percent) D/E ratio range. The most popular D/E ratio was between 46 and 50 percent. There were also 39 zero dividend payers and 12 100-percent dividend payers.

Stability of dividends

Another common dividend practice among major U.S. firms is the observance of a fairly stable dividend per share policy. Regardless of

FIGURE 11–5
Distribution of D/E ratios of Fortune 500 companies in 1967

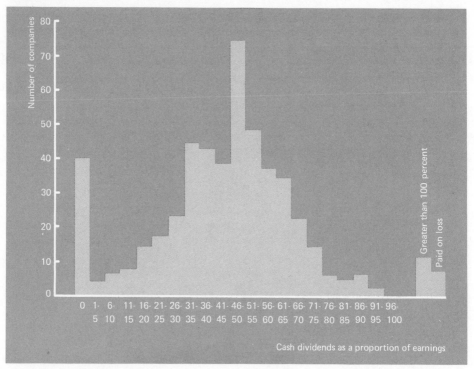

Source: "A Case for Dropping Dividends," by Carol J. Loomis, *Fortune Magazine* (June 1968). *Robert Rosenthal for Fortune Magazine.*

whether or not investors actually prefer stable dividends per share, firms seem to operate as if investors preferred this stability. Actually, most firms seem to favor a policy of establishing a nondecreasing dividend per share stream over time. The firm will raise its dividend per share as earnings per share increase over time, but firms seem to be especially careful not to raise dividends per share above a level that can safely be sustained in the future. This cautious "creep up" of dividends per share results in a flat dividend per share pattern during fluctuating earnings per share periods, and a rising "step function" pattern of dividends per share during rising earnings per share periods. Figure 11–6 illustrates a typical dividend per share pattern under these conditions.

As earnings per share fluctuate up and down in the years 19+0 through 19+2 the example firm maintains its dividend per share at $0.40. In the third quarter of 19+3, after earnings per share have increased substantially and the firm's management feels the long-term earnings prospects look good, the dividends are increased to $0.50 per share. In later periods, dividends are further stepped up to $0.60 per share and $0.75 per share. This increase in dividends per share lags the increase in earnings per share and is usually tied to the long-term target D/E ratio discussed earlier in the chapter.

FIGURE 11–6
Typical nondecreasing dividend per share pattern

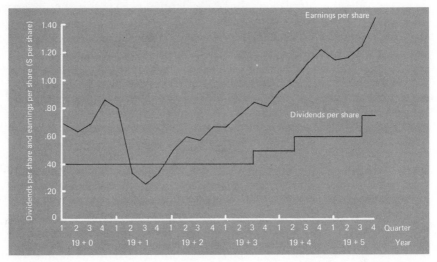

FACTORS INFLUENCING DIVIDEND POLICY

A firm's dividend policy is a function of many factors. We have already discussed some, including the possible existence of an "optimal" D/E ratio and management's preference for a nondecreasing dividend pattern. There are also other factors that influence dividend policy. These factors can be broadly categorized as pertaining to: (1) legal constraints, (2) control issues, and (3) investment and financing considerations.

Legal constraints

Management does not have complete discretion regarding how large a dividend it may pay to common stockholders as there are several kinds of legal constraints the firm must satisfy.

Capital impairment rules   Statutes have been enacted in most states that limit the amount of cash dividends the firm may pay. In most states, cash dividends paid may not exceed current net income plus cumulative retained earnings. That is, the firm may not impair the common stock capital account by paying a regular dividend that would reduce the dollar amount of the common stock capital account. The intention of this kind of law is to protect the claims of preferred stockholders and creditors. Without the protection of the capital impairment rule, preferred stockholders and creditors could have their preference positions eroded by common dividends that are effectively liquidation proceeds.

Indenture constraints   Bond indentures often contain provisions (covenants) that restrict the amount of dividends the firm may pay without approval of the bond trustee. These indenture constraints can effectively limit the firm's dividend policy.

Illegal accumulation   Since dividends are taxed at the investor's ordinary income tax rate, which is higher than his capital gains tax rate, there is clearly some incentive for firms not to pay cash dividends. To prevent firms from restricting dividends solely to allow stockholder avoidance of ordinary tax rates on the dividends, the Internal Revenue Service prohibits unwarranted retention of earnings. The Internal Revenue Service is empowered to *force* the firm to pay dividends when unwarranted earnings retention can be established.

Insolvency   Insolvency is defined two different ways (see Chapter 22). A firm is insolvent in the *bankruptcy* sense when its liabilities exceed its assets. A firm is insolvent in the *equity* sense when it is unable to pay its bills. If the firm is currently insolvent in *either* sense, it is prohibited from paying dividends; nor may it pay a dividend that would *cause* insolvency in either sense.

Control issues

Dividend policy may be strongly influenced by stockholder or managerial control motives. If a controlling group of stockholders either cannot or does not wish to purchase new shares of common stock, the firm's only source of new equity money will be retentions. This may impel the firm to maintain a low D/E ratio to insure an adequate supply of new equity money. The firm's dividend policy may also be dictated by the income tax status of its controlling owners. If these owners have high tax rates they may prefer that earnings be plowed back into the firm rather than paid (and taxed) as dividends.

Occasionally, however, firms whose dividend payout is low have been the target of takeover bids by other companies, who promise a higher dividend to stockholders if the takeover is successful. This kind of situation may cause the incumbent management to immediately raise the dividend payout to disarm the acquiring company of a powerful psychological weapon.

Investment and financing considerations

Another set of factors that can influence dividend policy relate to the firm's investment needs and financing opportunities.

Investment needs   Many firms appear to establish their dividend policy on the basis of their foreseeable investment needs. Firms that have abundant investment opportunities, for example, often prefer to retain a large fraction of their earnings for several years. This causes the dividend payout to be relatively low. Analysts frequently describe such firms as "growth" companies. Likewise, firms that have fewer investment opportunities are often observed to have low retention rates and relatively high D/E ratios. Notice that this is the residual dividend policy discussed earlier.

Earnings stability   The stability of the firm's earnings stream also frequently affects dividend policy. In general, the more stable the company's income stream, the higher its D/E ratio is. This effect is linked to the fact that firms are reluctant to reduce dividends and tend to set dividend levels that they can be reasonably sure of meeting. Firms that have relatively stable earnings over time are more confident that a relatively high dividend payment level can be safely maintained and are thus more likely to choose a relatively high D/E ratio policy. Public utility companies are good examples of firms that have relatively stable earnings patterns and relatively high D/E ratios.

Capital market access   Another factor that can strongly affect dividend policy is the extent to which the firm has access to the capital markets. If a firm is not financially strong enough or big enough to be able to issue bonds to investors, it can still lease assets and borrow through term loans at banks. Thus, most firms have access to the *debt* segment of the capital market. However, only the largest few thousand or so U.S. companies have access to the *Public equity* segment of the capital market where new public common stock is issued. This places a heavier than normal burden of new equity capital financing on retained earnings. Consequently, firms with limited access to equity capital markets tend to have lower dividend payout ratios, reflecting their heavier reliance on retained earnings as a source of equity capital.

A somewhat different, but related point, pertains to the decision to pay a minimum dividend. Many financial institutions are prohibited by their state charter from buying stock in companies that pay no dividends. Since these financial institutions play a major stock purchasing role in today's capital markets, some firms that would otherwise choose to pay no dividends pay a minimum dividend to qualify for the list of securities that financial institutions may purchase.

STOCK DIVIDENDS AND STOCK SPLITS

In addition to or in lieu of paying *cash dividends*, firms may pay *stock dividends*. A stock dividend is a small distribution (a dividend) of shares of stock to current owners. Closely related to stock dividends are *stock splits*, which are larger distributions of new shares to current owners and are for other than dividend purposes. There is no real financial difference between stock dividends and stock splits, but they are treated differently for accounting purposes, and the motive for declaring stock dividends is usually different from the motive for declaring a stock split. Because the two are so similar, it is somewhat difficult to distinguish between them, but the New York Stock Exchange classifies any distribution of shares greater than or equal to 25 percent of current shares outstanding as a stock split, and any smaller percentage distribution as a stock dividend.

Reasons for stock dividends and splits

While stock dividends and splits are, for practical purposes, very similar, they are typically undertaken for different reasons. Stock dividends are frequently paid by companies that feel it is important that they have a track record of dividends, but need the cash generated from operations for investments, and do not wish to raise external capital to pay cash dividends. Many firms considered to be "growth" companies pay small (2 to 5 percent) regular stock dividends. Other firms that are not considered growth companies sometimes choose to pay stock dividends in lieu of cash dividends because they are experiencing cash flow difficulties yet wish to maintain their dividend record.

Stock splits are typically undertaken to keep the firm's stock price in a "popular" trading range. Many financial executives feel that there is a "best" stock price range (some propose a range from about $10 per share to about $50 per share) for common stocks to trade in. Stocks that sell in this range are supposed to attract a broader array of investors because of favorable brokerage fee schedules and because more investors can afford to buy round lots (100-share increments) of the stock. If the stock price gets to be, say, $90, the firm could split the stock three for one (issuing three new shares for each old share) and cause stock price to be about $30 per share.

Accounting treatment

Current accounting practices treat stock splits and stock dividends quite differently. An example illustrates this. Assume that the ABC Co. has the following current data:

Common stock ($10 par; 1,000,000 shares) $10,000,000
Paid in surplus* 10,000,000
Retained earnings 30,000,000
    Equity $50,000,000

Current stock price = $100 per share

> * Paid in surplus is the excess over par that common stock is sold for. A share of $10 par value stock that is sold for $30, for example, will increase paid in surplus by $20.

Stock dividend   Now assume that ABC pays a 2-percent stock dividend. This will result in an equity rearrangement that is illustrated by the following calculations:

$$\text{Number of new shares issued} = (0.02)(1,000,000 \text{ shares}) = 20,000 \text{ shares}$$

$$\text{Market value of stock dividend} = (20,000 \text{ shares})(\$100 \text{ per share}) = \$2,000,000$$

$$\text{Increase in common stock account} = (20,000 \text{ shares})(\$10 \text{ per share}) = \$200,000$$

$$\text{Increase in paid in surplus account} = \$2,000,000 - \$200,000 = \$1,800,000$$

$$\text{Decrease in retained earnings} = \text{Market value of stock dividend} = \$2,000,000$$

The new equity position is therefore:

```
Common stock ($10 par; 1,020,000 shares) ........ $10,200,000
Paid in surplus.............................................  11,800,000
Retained earnings .........................................  28,000,000
    Equity ..............................................  $50,000,000
```

Since this transaction is a payment of a dividend, the market value of the dividend, $2 million, is deducted from retained earnings and is allocated between common stock and paid in surplus accounts. Notice it is only a *rearrangement* of the equity account since total equity is still $50 million.

Stock split   Referring back to the original ABC equity position, suppose that the company splits its stock four for one. The only changes in the equity statement are that the par value of each share of stock is one fourth of its original value, and there are four times the number of common shares outstanding. The total value of the individual accounts do not change. The new equity statement is:

```
Common stock ($2.50 par; 4,000,000 shares)...... $10,000,000
Paid in surplus.............................................  10,000,000
Retained earnings .........................................  30,000,000
    Equity ..............................................  $50,000,000
```

Effects on stockholder wealth

Theoretically, a stock split or dividend is, in itself, valueless. If there are no changes in the firm's earning power or risk characteristics that accompany a stock dividend or split, there should be no change in stockholder wealth at the time of the stock dividend or split. Suppose, for example, that the firm's stock price is $50 per share, there are one million shares outstanding, and the firm decides to split the stock two for one. The total stockholders' wealth before the split is $50 million. After the split, if there is no change in the firm's profitability or risk, each of the two million shares of stock should be worth about $25 per share, which results in a total stockholders' wealth of $50 million.

If, however, the firm's profitability and/or risk changes or is perceived to change, the total market value of the firm's shares will change. One of the most closely watched variables at the time of a stock split is the dividend rate. If, in the above example, the presplit cash dividend were $2 per share and were raised to $1.10 per share at the time of the split, the stock price would probably be worth more than $25 after the split.[5] In general, if the firm increases *total* cash dividends (the number of shares times the cash dividend per share), the total market value of the firm's shares will usually increase. Similarly, if the firm reduces its total cash dividends, the total market value of the firm's shares will usually decrease. These changes in the market value of the firm's stock are

---

[5] The change from a $2 per share to $1.10 per share is a *raise* in dividends because there are twice as many shares after the split. An investor who owns ten shares before the split would receive $20 in dividends. He would receive (20 × $1.10) = $22 in dividends after the split.

caused by the information content in the dividend change. An increased cash dividend is usually interpreted by investors as an indication of good times ahead, and a decrease in cash dividends has the opposite interpretation. Consequently, the market usually reacts favorably to a stock split accompanied by an increase in cash dividends and unfavorably to a stock split accompanied by a decrease in cash dividends. However, stock splits (and stock dividends) themselves appear to be recognized as valueless by investors.

STOCK REPURCHASES

Stock repurchases refer to the firm buying its own stock. Repurchased stock is called *treasury stock*. From time to time there has been intense repurchase activity among U.S. corporations, and recent years have been no exception. In the late 1960s and early 1970s, treasury stock was being acquired at a rapid pace. Not surprisingly, stock is normally repurchased during poor stock market periods when stock prices are low.

Methods of stock repurchasing

There are three methods of stock repurchase. First of all there is a *tender offer*. The company advertises that it stands ready to buy a stated number of its shares at a stipulated price that is set above the current market price of the stock (to entice stockholders to tender their shares). The firm then repurchases stock under this arrangement. Sometimes the tender will be oversubscribed (more shares are tendered than the firm agreed to take). In these instances the firm may either prorate its purchases or agree to take all the shares. In 1972 Teledyne made a tender offer for one million shares and shareholders tendered 8.9 million shares, more than a quarter of the company's total shares outstanding. Teledyne bought all of the 8.9 million shares tendered.

A second method of acquiring treasury stock is by buying it in the stock market just as an investor would purchase stock. Kraftco Corp. purchased about a million shares of its stock in this *open market purchasing* fashion. An extremely large number of firms have repurchased stock through a program of regular stock market purchases in recent years. However, there are restrictions on how much buying activity a firm can engage in relative to a firm's normal stock trading volume. For many firms, these restrictions make this repurchase alternative too slow.

The third approach to repurchasing stock is to buy large blocks of stock from major institutional investors, such as mutual funds or insurance companies. This alternative has the advantage of a speedy transaction, such as tender offers, but is less expensive since there is no similar markup over current stock price.

Effect of stockholder wealth

In principle, there should be no effect on stockholder wealth in a "fair" stock repurchase arrangement. "Fair" refers here to the assumption that management is not acting on information that, if publicly known, would cause the value of the stock to be revalued upward. In fact, a fair stock repurchase arrangement may be logically equated to a cash dividend. An example will illustrate this.

Suppose Folk, Inc. has the following financial data:

Number of shares outstanding .... 2,000,000 shares
Net income per year (assumed constant)......... $5,000,000 per year
D/E 1.0
Cost of equity, k_e 0.10

For simplicity, presume that Folk pays an annual dividend and that the next dividend is a full year away. Then:

$$\text{Dividends per share} = \text{Earnings} = \frac{\$5,000,000}{2,000,000 \text{ shares}} = \$2.50 \text{ per share}$$
$$\text{per share}$$

and,

$$P_0 = \sum_{t=1}^{\infty} \frac{\$2.50}{(1.10)^t} = (\$2.50)(ADF_{.10,\infty}) = (\$2.50)(10)$$

$$P_0 = \$25 \text{ per share}$$

Now suppose that in lieu of distributing the $5 million earnings as dividends, Folk decides to buy back $5 million of its stock via a tender offer at $27.50 a share. What effect would this have on stockholder wealth? We can answer this question by performing the following analysis:

$$\text{Number of shares repurchased} = \frac{\$5,000,000}{\$27.50 \text{ per share}} = 181,818 \text{ shares}$$

$$\text{Number of shares remaining} = 2,000,000 - 181,818 = 1,818,182 \text{ shares}$$
$$\text{Future dividends per share} \quad = \frac{\$5,000,000}{1,818,182 \text{ shares}} = \$2.75 \text{ per share}$$

Assuming k_e remains at 10 percent,

$$P_0 = 0 + \sum_{t=2}^{\infty} \frac{\$2.75}{(1.10)^t} = (\$2.75)(ADF_{.10,\infty})(DF_{.10,1}) = (\$2.75)(10)(0.909)$$

$$P_0 = \$25.$$

There is no effect on P_0 in this example of omitting the dividend and substituting an equivalent stock repurchase plan. Why? Under the dividend alternative, earnings per share and dividend per share stay at $2.50 per share and the next dividend is one year in the future. Under the repurchasing alternative, the next year's dividend is omitted, but future dividends and earnings per share will increase to $2.75 (because there are fewer shares outstanding), which means the stock price at the end of year one is expected to be $27.50. Thus, the repurchase plan substitutes a $2.50 capital gains for the $2.50 dividend omitted.

We assumed in this analysis that: k_e does not change, there are no preferences for a particular form of income (dividend income versus capital gains income), and the firm uses only the amount of the usual dividend to repurchase stock (that is, the firm does not pay a premium to repurchase stock). Under these conditions, repurchasing stock has no real effect on stockholder wealth. It is merely an alternate way of distributing profits.

If these conditions do not fairly approximate real world conditions then there will be some effect on P_0 of repurchase plans. Some financial theorists argue that stock repurchasing has an inherent advantage over dividends in that the capital gains expected to accrue to remaining shareholders are taxed at a lower rate than dividends. But there is an offsetting transaction cost feature of brokerage fees incurred by stockholders and the firm. There is also the question of whether some stockholders may not really prefer dividend income for whatever reason.

Reasons for repurchasing[6]

Several reasons have been suggested to explain the rapid growth of share repurchase activity among U.S. firms since the early 1960s.

Controlling the equity base The two most important reasons for stock repurchases given by surveyed firms were: (1) to *shrink* the equity base and (2) to *avoid increasing* the equity base. Many firms reach a life cycle stage where their investment needs are outstripped by the cash generating capacity of their current investments. These firms feel they should cut back their equity base. This equity shrinkage also increases earnings per share as we saw in the example above. Other firms in similar life cycle positions buy back equity today with the intention of reissuing it in the future as investment needs begin increasing again. This practice allows the firm to avoid increasing the equity base.

Repurchase as an investment Another frequently heard reason for stock repurchases is that it represents a good investment opportunity. Many firms publicly announced in the 1970s that they were repurchasing their stock because it was seriously undervalued. However, many of these firms saw their stock become even *more* undervalued in following months. Grumman Corp., for example, repurchased almost a half million shares in the early 1970s at an average price of about $19 per share. In early 1975 Grumman's stock was selling for only about $10 per share. However, these corporations usually argue that these *temporary* aberrations are unimportant, as the stock is repurchased for the *long run*.

Repurchases to support the stock price Some firms repurchase stock to support their stock price. In 1973 International Telephone and Telegraph publicly announced it would buy up to 2 million shares of its stock to support the stock price. A common form of stock price support has been to buy large blocks of stock put up by sellers to ensure that no "overhang," or supply imbalance, unduly depresses stock price. We should note, however, that no amount of support by the firm will keep the stock price propped up if the market decides the stock is overvalued.

---

[6] This section is based on an article that surveyed 20 companies that actively repurchased their stock in the mid-1960s plus about 100 finance professionals and academicians. See the Guthart article in the Basic References at the end of the chapter.

Eliminating small stockholders It is fairly expensive for the firm to service small stockholders' accounts. Each shareholder is entitled to receive all proxy materials, annual reports, and other pertinent mailing information sent to owners, and a dividend check must be mailed regardless of whether the stockholder owns 10 or 10,000 shares. Consequently, it is more expensive to have many small shareholders as opposed to fewer, larger shareholders. Many firms have repurchased stock to eliminate stockholders who own less than 100 shares in an attempt to reduce these service costs.

Stock option and retirement plans Most companies have stock option plans for their executives and also employee stock purchase plans that are a part of the company's retirement program. Implementation of these programs motivates many such companies to regularly purchase their stock.

Financing merger activities Many companies use treasury stock to finance their merger and acquisition activities (see Chapter 21). This may require that the firm actively buy back its own stock to assure that it has sufficient equity to pursue all the profitable expansion plans it intends. However, there are some fairly rigid accounting standards that must be met with respect to using buy-back shares in mergers. Because of the tax advantage, most companies try to merge under a "pooling of interest" merger arrangement that involves swapping shares of stock (see Chapter 21). However, the Securities and Exchange Commission (SEC) no longer allows companies to use a large amount of recently repurchased stock in a pooling of interest merger. The SEC now requires that the repurchased shares be held at least two years before such use is allowed. In 1974, Marlennan Corp., which was accumulating repurchased stock for merger purposes, announced the discontinuance of their repurchase plans because of this ruling.

Caveats of stock repurchasing

While there are many apparent reasons for buying treasury stock, many of these reasons obviously are open to criticism. In addition to the questions raised above, the firm must be mindful of the legal and moral issues involved. One of the most obvious is the question of conflict of interest. There have been instances where much of the tendered stock was from the firm's executives. If the stock price should subsequently fall, nontendering stockholders may be properly suspicious that the executives possessed inside knowledge that the fall was coming and "got out while the getting was good." This is a special case of the more general issue of how to perform the stock repurchase so that *all* investors have similar access to information regarding the future prospects of the firm and also have equal opportunity to participate in the buy-back plan.

SUMMARY

Dividend policy is usually described in terms of the *level* and *stability* of the stream of dividends paid by the firm. The level of dividends refers to the dollar per share amount in the absolute sense, and to the dividend payout ratio in the relative sense. One measure of dividend instability is the coefficient of variation of the dividend stream.

An important aspect of dividend policy is the debate about an optimal payout level. One theory, the "bird in the hand" (*BIH*) theory, argues that since investors are risk averse and since risk increases with time, investors will prefer relatively high dividend payout ratios over relatively low ones. Even though relatively low dividend payout ratios will contribute to larger future growth in dividends and growth in the stock price, investors are presumed, in the *BIH* theory, to prefer a certain dividend now to an uncertain increase in future dividends and stock price. They prefer a bird in the hand to two in the bush. This preference implies that an optimal corporate dividend policy would be to establish as high a *D/E* ratio as the firm can maintain.

The perfect market theory argues that rational investors are indifferent between dividend income and capital gains income and will therefore be indifferent between relatively high and relatively low corporate payout ratios. This implies there is no optimal dividend payout ratio that will maximize stock price.

There is no consensus today about which of these two theories more nearly reflects investors' dividend preferences, but a variant of the perfect market theory called the clientele theory has gained considerable attention in recent years. This theory argues that there are compelling reasons for some investors preferring low payout ratios and others preferring high ones. Consequently, investors with strong preferences will tend to acquire stocks of companies whose dividend policies match up with these preferences. This theory implies that there is no such thing as an optimal payout ratio but that once a firm selects a target payout ratio, the firm should probably not radically depart from the policy because of the relatively high cost of replacing one clientele with another.

Most firms are observed to pay some cash dividend, and most firms seem to prefer a nondecreasing, stable dividend per share pattern over time. In part, these practices seem to reflect management's perception of investor preferences. Other factors that influence dividend policy are legal constraints, control issues, and investment and financing considerations.

Stock dividends are an alternative to cash dividends, and stock splits are closely related to stock dividends. Stock dividends and splits are theoretically valueless in and of themselves and have no real economic impact on stockholder wealth. However, stock splits are often accompanied by cash dividend changes which do affect stockholder wealth because of their information content concerning the future profitability of the firm.

While a stock repurchase plan is logically equivalent to a cash dividend, it is usually undertaken for other reasons. Firms engage in stock buy-backs to control the equity base, as an investment outlet, to support the stock price, to eliminate small investors, to supply option and retirement fund needs, and to finance merger activities. Repurchases may be made through tender offers, open market purchasing, or through large block purchases from a financial institution.

QUESTIONS

1. Define the following terms and phrases:
    a. Dividend payout ratio.
    b. Dividend policy.
    c. Stock dividends.
    d. Stock splits.
    e. Stock repurchase.
    f. Treasury stock.
    g. Tender offer.

2. Most U.S. business firms are observed to be reluctant to *cut* dividends per share. What would this observed behavioral phenomenon of managerial reluctance to reduce dividends per share imply about the pattern of the firm's dividends per share and dividend payout ratio over time?

3. With respect to the Bird in the Hand dividend theory:
    a. Briefly describe the theory, including the main premise the theory rests on.
    b. Indicate what "optimal" dividend policy (if any) is implied by this theory.
    c. Identify and discuss the purported weak points of this theory according to the "perfect market" theory.

4. With respect to the perfect market dividend theory:
    a. Briefly describe the theory, including the main premise the theory rests on.
    b. Indicate what "optimal" dividend policy (if any) is implied by this theory.
    c. Identify and discuss the purported weak points of this theory according to the "Bird in the Hand" theory.

5. Explain the clientele theory and how it fits into the dividend policy controversy.

6. What effect would the following conditions be expected to have on the firm's dividend policy? Explain your answer.
    a. The company has recently borrowed a substantial amount of money. The loan agreement carries a very restrictive dividend covenant.
    b. The firm is declared legally insolvent.
    c. A new group of stockholders has gained controlling interest in the firm by steadily buying the company's stock over time. They indicate that their income levels (and hence tax rates) are so high that they are averse to receipt of ordinary income.
    d. The company has recently "gone private" by buying back all stock held by minority stockholders. There are now only three stockholders in the firm. Also, the firm plans to remain privately held.
    e. The firm has had several loss years in a row but has continued to pay a small dividend. Cumulative retained earnings are now zero.

    f. The company has identified several exciting new investment opportunities that will require large amounts of new capital.

7. What probable effects would the following situations have on dividend payout ratios, *in general?*
   a. Interest rates decrease.
   b. There is a gradual reduction in new investment opportunities.
   c. A reduction in ordinary income tax rates and an increase in capital gains tax rates occur.
   d. A widely publicized finding by a prestigious study of the National Bureau of Economic Research reveals that most "blue chip" (very high quality) stocks have a payout ratio of about 0.5.

8. Explain the main difference between a stock split and a stock dividend from:
   a. An accounting treatment standpoint
   b. The New York Stock Exchange standpoint
   c. An economic standpoint

9. In theory, a stock split, in and of itself, is worth nothing. However, after a recent stock split, shareholders of the XYZ company notice that their wealth in XYZ stock (their number of shares times the prevailing stock price) is greater than before the split. How would you explain to them that a stock split is valueless?

10. Describe what is meant by a "fair" stock repurchase.

PROBLEMS

1. Scott Supersports, a mass merchandiser of athletic equipment, has the following current financial data taken from the firm's balance sheet:

Common stock ($5 par)	$ 500,000
Paid in surplus	200,000
Retained earnings	450,000
Equity	$1,150,000

   a. Determine what the equity accounts would look like if Scott's stock is selling for $20 per share and the company pays a 10-percent stock dividend.
   b. Repeat part (*a*) if the company splits the stock two for one.
   c. Determine what Scott's new stock price should be for both (*a*) and (*b*), other things equal.
   d. What do we mean by "other things equal" in part (*c*)?

2. Rework parts (*a*), (*b*), and (*c*) of problem 1 for the situation where Scott's stock is selling for $10 per share.

3. A five-year-old company that has never paid common dividends is now reaching the point where it feels it is earning enough to justify doing so. A portion of the anticipated income statement for the coming year is shown below:

```
EBIT ............................... $5,800,000
Interest........................      400,000
EBT ...............................  $5,400,000
Tax (50%).......................    2,700,000
Net income.....................    $2,700,000
EPS (3,000,000 shares) 0.90 per share
```

The firm's management is considering continuing to pay no dividends or paying either a $0.20 per share or a $0.40 per share dividend, which it would expect to maintain in the foreseeable future. However, although the company could begin paying a dividend, it still has a substantial need for investment funds in the next few years. For the coming year, the firm will need about $5 million in equity funds for new investment purposes.

a. Which of the three proposed dividend levels would be considered optimal according to the "bird in the hand" and "perfect market" theories? Explain your answer.

b. Suppose that the firm decided to continue to pay no dividends. How could an investor who owns 100 shares create her own $0.20 per share dividend, assuming the stock sells for $10 per share?

c. Ignoring floatation costs, how many total dollars of external equity financing would be required under each of the three plans?

4. a. Given the following dividend per share information, calculate the coefficient of variation of dividends for each company.

			Year			
Company	1	2	3	4	5	6
A	$2.00	2.00	3.00	3.00	4.00	4.00
B..........	6.00	6.00	6.25	6.25	6.50	6.50
C	1.00	4.00	1.75	1.00	2.50	2.00

b. Rank the three stocks for dividend stability according to the coefficient of variation of dividends. What difficulties does Company A present in this ranking?

c. Other things equal, which company's stock price do you think would have performed best during this period? Why? Which stock price do you think would have performed worst? Why?

5. Alpha-Alpha and Beta-Beta are two companies in the space technology industry. They are close competitors and their asset composition, capital structure, and profitability records have been very similar for several years. The primary difference between the companies from a financial management perspective is their dividend policy. Alpha-Alpha tries to maintain a nondecreasing dividend per share series, while Beta-Beta maintains a constant dividend payout

ratio equal to 1/6. Their recent earnings per share, dividend per share, and stock price history are as follows:

	Alpha-Alpha			Beta-Beta		
Year	EPS	DPS	Stock price range	EPS	DPS	Stock price range
19+7	$3.79...	$0.50	$31–43	$4.00...	$0.67	$26–39
19+6	3.20...	0.50	30–40	3.40...	0.57	28–36
19+5	4.00...	0.50	27–42	4.05...	0.68	22–45
19+4	2.55...	0.45	21–27	2.45...	0.41	16–24
19+3	2.01...	0.40	14–22	2.05...	0.34	7–16
19+2	1.48...	0.40	11–16	1.40...	0.23	5–13
19+1	1.86...	0.40	15–18	1.90...	0.32	12–16

In all calculations below that require a stock price use the average of the two prices given in the stock price range.

a. Determine the dividend payout ratio (D/E) and price to earnings ratio (P/E) for both companies for all years.
b. Determine the average D/E and P/E for both companies over the period 19+1 through 19+7.
c. The management of Beta-Beta is puzzled as to why their stock has historically not performed as well as Alpha-Alpha's, even though the Beta-Beta profitability record is slightly better. The past three years are particularly puzzling to Beta-Beta's managers. As a financial consultant, how would you explain this phenomenon?

6. Northeastern Seafood Products is in in the midst of some dividend policy planning. The company's net income this past year was $12 million and the board of directors paid a $0.40 dividend on 15 million shares. The President would like to increase dividends, if possible, but there are two complicating factors. First, Northeastern is vigorously expanding its canning capacity and has decided to use internally generated funds to accomplish this. The company's board has considered and rejected any external financing plans for this purpose. The expansion is expected to take about five years. This veto on externally financed expansion strongly affects the dividend policy question, particularly when considered in light of the second complicating factor. Northeastern's board is proud of its long record of nondecreasing dividend per share payments. The firm has not had a dividend reduction since 1939, and the board will veto any proposed dividend increase that is so large that it couldn't be sustained.

Given this background information, Northeastern's finance staff has prepared an estimate of the firm's net income for the next few years along with a schedule of estimated amounts of retained earnings needed to implement the coming expansion. As shown below, the firm's net income is rising and the need for retained earnings peaks out in three years.

	(Millions of dollars)	
Year	*Net income*	*Needed retained earnings*
1..................	13	5
2..................	14	6
3..................	17	10
4..................	18	8
5..................	25	5

  a. Assuming the firm can always profitably employ any "extra" retained earnings over and above the coming expansion needs, and being mindful of the board's desires, determine how much of a dividend per share increase, if any, the company could make at present?

  b. At what point in the future would a (possibly further) increase in dividends appear feasible?

  c. If the net income and required retained earnings figures in the schedule shown above are only expected values, which may not be realized, what (qualitative) impact might this have on your answers to (*a*) and (*b*)?

7. The J. M. Betty Company, an electrical contracting firm, is in the process of formulating some long range plans. The firm is considering the following new investment proposals for the coming year:

Project	*Initial cost (dollars)*	*Present value of future CFAT's (dollars)*
A..............	300,000	336,000
B..............	100,000	108,000
C..............	100,000	120,000
D..............	200,000	230,000
E..............	200,000	190,000
F..............	300,000	330,000

The company currently has 100,000 shares of common stock outstanding. The board of directors has decided to not sell any new common stock but to finance new investments with either internal equity or by selling 30-year $1,000 mortgage bonds.

The company's earnings and dividend record for recent years is shown below.

Year	Net income (dollars)	Dividends per share (dollars)
19+6 (current).............	500,000 (expected)	—
19+5.........................	390,000	2.00
19+4.........................	410,000	2.00
19+3.........................	400,000	1.50
19+2.........................	295,000	1.50
19+1.........................	300,000	1.50

a. Determine which projects should be accepted and the size of J. M. Betty Company's capital budget for the current year.
b. What will be the probable dividend per share if Betty continues its present dividend policy?
c. How many bonds will the company expect to have to sell if they pay the dividend determined in (b)? (Ignore floatation costs.)
d. What will be expected dividends per share if the firm pays dividends according to the residual dividend policy?
e. How many mortgage bonds will the company expect to have to sell if they pay the dividend determined in (d)? (Ignore floatation costs.)

8. Consider the following information about the Allison Manufacturing Company:

Year	Net income (dollars)	Capital expenditure budget (dollars)
1.............	1,000,000	500,000
2.............	800,000	600,000
3.............	1,200,000	1,200,000
4.............	1,300,000	500,000
5.............	1,300,000	-0-
6.............	500,000	100,000

In year 0, the company earned $1 million and paid dividends of $1 per share on the 500,000 shares outstanding.
a. Determine the company's dividend per share for each year: (1) using a residual dividend policy, assuming that the capital budget will be financed using internal equity; (2) using a constant payout ratio policy with D/E of 0.6; (3) using a constant dollar per share policy with a target D/E of 0.5, and no change in dividends unless net income has changed by at least 5 percent in the same direction for two successive years.
b. Which policy would result in the highest average dividend over the six-year period?

c. Which policy would result in the most stable dividend per share pattern over the six-year period? (Determine this answer by a visual inspection of the dividend patterns.)

SELECTED BASIC REFERENCES

Guthart, L. A. "Why Companies Buy Their Own Stock," *Financial Analyst's Journal* (March–April 1967), pp. 105–10.

Loomis, C. J. "A Case for Dropping Dividends," *Fortune Magazine* (June 1968).

Porterfield, J. T. S. *Investment Decisions and Capital Costs*. Englewood Cliffs, N.J.: Prentice-Hall, Inc., 1965, chapter 6.

SELECTED ADVANCED REFERENCES

Elton, E. J., and M. J. Gruber. "The Effect of Share Repurchases on the Value of the Firm," *Journal of Finance* (March 1968), pp. 135–50.

Gordon, M. J. "Dividends, Earnings and Stock Prices," *Review of Economics and Statistics* (May 1959), pp. 99–105.

Lintner, J. "Distribution of Income of Corporations Among Dividends, Retained Earnings and Taxes," *American Economic Review* (May 1956), pp. 97–113.

Miller, M. H., and F. Modigliani. "Dividend Policy, Growth and the Valuation of Shares," *Journal of Business* (October 1961), pp. 411–33.

INTERMEDIATE AND LONG-TERM FINANCING DECISIONS

12

INTERMEDIATE AND LONG-TERM FINANCING

When the firm has decided to undertake capital investments it must decide how to finance them. The firm may look either internally or externally for financing. Internal financing refers to cash flow generated by the firm's normal operating activities. In the last chapter we discussed dividend policy and its complement, retained earnings. External financing refers to capital provided by parties external to the firm. In this chapter we analyze how to estimate intermediate and long-term financing requirements and we investigate some of the important aspects of acquiring external intermediate and long-term capital. In the following three chapters we study specific sources of external intermediate and long-term capital.

ESTIMATING FINANCING REQUIREMENTS

Estimating how much financing the firm will need is an important planning problem. For one thing, it takes time to arrange the external financing. If the firm needs, say, $5 million, it will take a few months to arrange things. Therefore, it is very crucial that the firm estimate its financing requirements accurately. Also, accurate financing requirements estimation can reduce the costs associated with acquiring new funds. These costs are called *floatation costs* and are discussed later in the chapter. One way the firm can hold these costs down is to limit the number of times they are incurred. There will be less total floatation costs, for example, if the entire $5 million is raised at one time, rather than raising part at one time and the remainder later. There may be, of course, compelling reasons for deferring part of the financing. If, for example, interest rates are expected to drop during the year, the firm might choose to defer as much financing as it can. But, in general, floatation costs can be reduced by concentrating financing efforts, and this further emphasizes the need for accurate estimation of financing requirements.

Procedures for estimating future financing requirements are varied and some are very sophisticated. Our analysis here will focus on a fairly simple approach that relates asset levels to sales levels. At the outset we should note that capital investments (investment in fixed or long-term assets) cause the firm to increase its investment in current assets also. As the firm increases its fixed asset base, sales would be expected to increase. Increased sales will require the firm to maintain a higher cash level to ensure ready payment of bills incurred in producing the new sales. Increased sales also cause the firm to increase its accounts receivable level since a large part of most sales are on credit. In addition, inventory levels will increase as the firm's stock of raw and purchased materials, work in process, and finished goods increase with rising sales. At the same time accounts payable and accrual accounts will increase, but the net result is an increase in net working capital (current assets less current liabilities).

Usually, firms will finance long-term investments (plant and equipment) with intermediate and long-term financing.[1] The way that short-term assets (working capital) are financed depends on the expected permanency of the increased working capital. If the buildup of working capital is temporary (perhaps because of seasonal sales patterns), the financing is usually short-term. If the increase in working capital is relatively permanent (for example, because of the expansion of plant capacity), the financing is usually a combination of intermediate and long-term financing and increases in selected current liabilities (accounts payable and accruals) that will also be relatively permanent. Thus, long-term investment decisions also create a need for financing relatively permanent increases in net working capital. The example below illustrates this point more clearly.

A financing requirements example

The need for new financing arises because of the firm's investment activities. The firm may be preparing to undertake new investments, or replace older investments, or recent investments may be coming into fruition. The firm needs capital to purchase fixed assets, and as we just saw, net working capital requirements will also increase to support the higher sales level. Also, the firm may incur financing requirements because of a new sales promotion campaign or because of product price or quality changes that cause sales to increase.

Most financing requirements analyses revolve around a sales forecast. Asset levels are related to sales, and estimated increases in sales can be used to predict financing requirements. A good way to look at this procedure is through an example. Figure 12–1 shows current balance sheet

---

[1] The distinctions between short-term, intermediate-term, and long-term financing are not clear-cut. Short-term usually means a period of time less than a year. Intermediate-term typically means a period of time longer than a year but shorter than five to ten years. Anything longer is long-term financing. A lengthier discussion is presented below.

and income statements for Hamlin Co. that we can use to study the financing requirements calculations.

Hamlin is preparing to undertake a major expansion of its plant of $5 million and also plans to spend about $2 million to replace some of its older equipment. In total, Hamlin plans to spend about $7 million on new plant and equipment in the coming year.

FIGURE 12–1

HAMLIN CO.
Financial Statements
Balance Sheet

Assets:		Claims on Assets:	
Cash*	$ 1,200,000	Accounts payable*	$ 8,000,000
Accounts receivable*	15,400,000	Accruals*	3,500,000
Inventory*	16,600,000	Notes payable	4,600,000
Total current assets	$33,200,000	Total current liabilities	$16,100,000
Net fixed assets	$21,600,000	Bonds	$ 6,100,000
		Preferred stock	$ 4,000,000
		Common stock	8,500,000
		Retained earnings	20,100,000
Total assets	$54,800,000	Total claims	$54,800,000

Income Statement

Net sales	$81,800,000
Costs and expenses:	
Cost of goods sold	$54,400,000
Selling and administrative†	17,000,000
Interest	6,200,000
Total costs and expenses	$77,600,000
Income before taxes	$ 4,200,000
Taxes	1,700,000
Net income	$ 2,500,000
Dividends	$ 500,000

* These items normally change with sales changes.
† Included in selling and administrative expenses are $2 million of depreciation charges.

The expansion of fixed assets will cause the firm to increase current asset accounts to support the new production level. Some of this increase in current assets will be financed by fairly automatic increases in current liabilities. However, some of the increase in current assets must be financed through other means. Figure 12–1 also shows what asset and asset claims items normally will be affected by increases (and decreases) in sales. All of the short-term assets will be affected. Changes in net fixed assets are primary *causes* of sales changes. On the asset claims side, accounts payable and accruals will change in the same direction as sales. The other asset claims items (notes payable, bonds, preferred stock, and common stock) will not automatically change with sales changes. They are the *discretionary* financing accounts. Indeed, one of the aims of this analysis is to determine how much discretionary financing the firm needs to facilitate its investment plans.

Estimating future sales levels

To begin the analysis we first estimate what increase in sales will be generated by the new investment. This estimate could be obtained several ways. If we presume that the firm has performed its investment analysis of the new expenditures, we can estimate the sales associated with these investments by taking the revenue estimates from the investment analysis work sheets (recall our previous work in Chapter 6). Hamlin's capital budgeting staff has prepared the following estimates:

Annual new sales from $5 million plant expansion $25,000,000
Annual sales gain from $2 million replacement investment*........... 1,000,000
　　　Total annual sales increase $26,000,000

* The fact that the sales increase from the replacement investment is very low relative to the sales increase from the plant expansion does not imply that the replacement investment is economically unattractive. Typically, replacement projects are economically desirable because they reduce costs.

The larger component of the sales increase comes from the plant expansion. The $1 million sales gain from the replacement expenditure is the difference between the sales generated by the new and old equipment.

Another frequently used method for estimating sales increases uses the fixed assets turnover ratio. Recall from Chapter 2 that fixed assets turnover equals sales divided by fixed assets. The firm's present fixed assets turnover is ($81,800,000/$21,600,000) 3.8. Net fixed assets should increase by about $5 million due to the new investment.[2] Turning the fixed assets turnover ratio around and solving for the amount of new sales generated by an additional $5 million of fixed assets, we get

$$\text{Sales increase} = \left(\begin{array}{c}\text{Fixed assets}\\\text{turnover}\end{array}\right)\left(\begin{array}{c}\text{Fixed assets}\\\text{increase}\end{array}\right)$$
$$= (3.8)(\$5,000,000)$$
$$= \$19,000,000$$

This estimate is considerably lower than the previous estimate because the $26 million figure obviously has a much higher implied fixed assets turnover ratio. In the following analysis we will use the $26 million forecast of sales increase.

Changes in net working capital

Next we determine the increases in current asset and liability accounts that will accompany the anticipated sales increase. We can make these estimates by relating levels of these accounts to sales levels. We do this by dividing these accounts by current sales. The current sales and

---

[2] The increase in net fixed assets equals new investment in fixed assets ($7 million) less depreciation for next year (about $2 million based on last year's income statement), assuming that the replaced equipment was fully depreciated.

those current liabilities that are automatically affected by sales are shown in Figure 12–1 by an asterisk. Figure 12–2 shows these relevant accounts as a percent of current sales.

Figure 12–2 shows that, on average, every dollars worth of sales requires 1.5¢ worth of cash, 18.8¢ worth of accounts receivable, and 20.3¢ worth of inventory. In total, every dollar of sales requires about 40.6¢ of current asset "support." Now, if sales increases by a dollar, the firm will need to invest 40.6¢ in current assets to support this increase. However, Figure 12–2 also shows that there are offsets or automatic sources of funds that will partially finance the increase of 40.6¢ of current assets. Every dollar increase in sales will, on average, cause current liabilities to increase by about 14.1¢. This automatic rise in current liabilities reduces the need for financing caused by sales increases.

The difference between 40.6 percent and 14.1 percent represents the net requirement for financing the buildup in current assets for each dollar of sales increase.

FIGURE 12–2
Current assets and selected current liabilities as percent of sales

Assets:		Liabilities:	
Cash...............................	1.5%	Accounts payable............	9.8%
Accounts receivable............	18.8	Accruals........................	4.3
Inventory..........................	20.3		
Total	40.6%	Total	14.1%

$$\begin{matrix} \text{Hamlin's net working capital requirement} \\ \text{per dollar of sales increase} \end{matrix} = 0.406 - 0.141 = 0.265$$

For every dollar increase in sales, the firm will have to spend about 26.5¢ to build up net working capital to support this higher sales level.

The total financing needed to increase net working capital is the per dollar net working capital requirement times the sales increase. Assuming that sales will increase by $26 million (recall our earlier calculations):

$$\begin{matrix} \text{Hamlin's total net working} \\ \text{capital requirement} \end{matrix} = (0.265)(\$26,000,000) = \$6,890,000$$

$$\approx \$7,000,000$$

Hamlin will thus need to increase its net working capital by about $7 million to support its new investment in fixed assets.

Total financing requirement

We can now estimate the total financing requirement for Hamlin. The total financing requirement is the sum of the new capital investment activities (this includes both the plant expansion and replacement investments) and the net working capital increase.

$$\text{Hamlin's total financing requirement} = \$7,000,000 + \$7,000,000$$

$$= \$14,000,000$$

All total, Hamlin will need about $14 million to carry out its expansion and modernization plans. Notice also that about half of this requirement is for building up net working capital to support the increase in sales that will accompany the investment plans. Typically, the investment in plant and equipment will precede (in time) the buildup in net working capital. This causes the financing requirements to have important timing elements that should be considered. In our analysis we assume that Hamlin's need for $14 million financing occurs within the same year and we don't attempt to account for timing differences.

Internal financing availability

At this point, Hamlin has estimated how much financing it needs for its investment plans for next year. As we said at the beginning of this chapter, the firm may look either internally or externally for financing. Internal financing refers to cash flow provided from operations, and external financing refers to securing outside capital by borrowing, leasing, issuing new stock, etc.

First, let's estimate how much internal financing is available for Hamlin. We assume at the outset that, while Hamlin will invest about $14 million this year, the company will generate no sales and, therefore, no cash inflow from the new investments this year. Recall from Chapter 6 that this is the standard "pattern" in investment problems: a cash outlay at time zero, followed by cash inflows in later periods. This means that internal financing that will be available for this increased investment can only come from *current* operations. An approximate measure of cash flow from operations is the sum of net income plus noncash charges that were deducted as expenses to calculate net income. The principal component of noncash charges for most companies is depreciation. Therefore:

$$\text{Cash flow from operations} = \text{Net income} + \text{Depreciation}$$

We have already assumed that the new investment will not affect this year's cash flow. If we further assume that this year's cash flow will be approximately the same as last year's, we can use Figure 12–1 to help estimate internal cash flow.

$$\text{Hamlin's cash flow from operations} = \$2,500,000 + \$2,000,000$$

$$= \$4,500,000$$

Notice (from Figure 12–1) that, like most firms, Hamlin is currently paying common dividends. Assuming the dividends will be continued at the present $500,000 level, only the retained earnings portion of net income for the coming year, $2,000,000, will be available for use in financing. Internal financing available equals cash flow from operations minus dividends.

$$\frac{\text{Internal}}{\text{financing available}} = \frac{\text{Cash flow}}{\text{from operations}} - \text{Dividends}$$

For Hamlin:

$$\frac{\text{Internal}}{\text{financing available}} = \$4{,}500{,}000 - \$500{,}000 = \$4{,}000{,}000$$

During the coming year, Hamlin thus expects to generate about $4 million from internal operations that can be used to finance its new investments. Notice that it takes a full year to produce this $4 million and therefore this money will not be available at the first of the year. However, as we noted earlier, the firm will not need the entire $14 million of financing at time zero. The investment in plant will come first, followed by the buildup in working capital. This gives the firm some time to generate internal funds. Suppose, for example, the firm doesn't need the full $4 million expected to be provided by present operations until the end of nine months. Ignoring seasonal patterns in profit, the firm should have earned three fourths of its expected internal financing, about $3 million. The remainder ($1 million) can be borrowed for a short period. Short-term negotiated sources of financing are covered in Chapter 20. When the remainder of the profit is earned the firm can liquidate the loan.

External permanent financing requirement

Permanent financing refers to intermediate and long-term financing. The firm's external permanent financing requirement is the difference between its total financing requirement and its internal financing available:

$$\frac{\text{External}}{\substack{\text{permanent financing} \\ \text{requirement}}} = \frac{\text{Total}}{\text{financing requirement}} - \frac{\text{Internal}}{\text{financing available}}$$

For Hamlin:

$$\frac{\text{External permanent}}{\text{financing requirement}} = \$14{,}000{,}000 - \$4{,}000{,}000$$

$$= \$10{,}000{,}000$$

What we have done to this point is illustrate how the firm might go about determining its external financing needs. In the example, Hamlin needs to raise about $10 million externally. In the remainder of this chapter we introduce the concept of capital markets, where the firm may secure intermediate and long-term capital. In subsequent chapters we systematically investigate the main features of these capital sources.

CAPITAL MARKETS

The firm may acquire external capital from three related markets: the short-term market, the intermediate-term market, and the long-term market. The suppliers of short-term financing are a collection of individuals, corporations, and financial institutions who provide capital to qualified borrowers for short periods of time, where short is usually defined as less than a year. Similarly, intermediate and long-term capital suppliers are individuals and companies who provide capital to qualified applicants for periods of time longer than a year. The distinction between "intermediate" and "long" periods of time is arbitrary, but the duration of intermediate financing is typically described as being no longer than five to ten years. Financing that involves longer periods is called long-term financing. Term loans made by banks and financial leases (both discussed in Chapter 14) are the most common form of intermediate capital available to business firms. On the long-term side, firms sell common and preferred stock (Chapter 13), bonds (Chapter 14), and "hybrid" securities, such as convertible securities (Chapter 15), to obtain long-term capital.

Markets are places where things are bought and sold, and capital markets are a set of markets where suppliers of capital offer cash to those who need intermediate and long-term capital (demanders) in return for pieces of paper (securities) that obligate the demanders of capital to make future payments to the suppliers. Capital markets include both *impersonal* and *customer* markets. In impersonal or open markets there is no *direct* negotiation between capital suppliers and capital demanders, but rather intermediaries—such as investment bankers (discussed below)—arrange for the sale of securities. When the firm sells common or preferred stock or bonds it usually operates in the impersonal capital market. In the customer market there is direct negotiation between borrower and lender. When the firm makes a term loan at a bank or leases an asset or places debt privately with an insurance company, it is operating in the customer capital market. It is also important to emphasize that *capital* markets deal with intermediate and long-term funds as opposed to *money* markets, which are markets for short-term funds. In the block of four chapters that we are now beginning we only deal with capital markets.

Intermediate and long-term financial instruments

Our attention now is directed toward identifying the sources of intermediate and long-term capital and the advantages and disadvantages of the firm's using these alternative sources of capital. The list of alternative sources of external capital is as follows:

1. Common stock
2. Debt
   a. Bonds
   b. Term loans

3. Other
    a. Preferred stock
    b. Convertible securities
    c. Warrants
    d. Leases

To get an approximate idea of the volume of new external financing involved in U.S. capital markets consider Figure 12–3. It shows the vol-

FIGURE 12–3
Gross proceeds of new corporate issues: 1950–1973

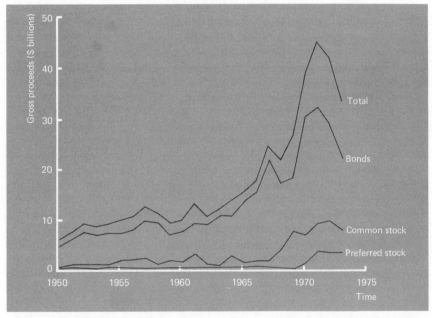

Source: *Federal Reserve Bulletin.*

ume of common stock, preferred stock, and bonds issued in the years since 1950. Convertible securities are included in the preferred stock (convertible preferred) and bonds (convertible bonds). Warrants, term loans, and leases are not shown.

As Figure 12–3 shows, the use of external capital has increased dramatically since 1950, particularly so since 1965. It also shows that business firms rely more heavily on debt that on new common and preferred stock. However, internal funds (retained earnings and depreciation allowances), not shown in Figure 12–3, provide an even larger percent of the total capital requirements of the firm. These internal funds provide a strong equity base that permits the firm to acquire debt financing in the capital markets.

Capital suppliers

There are many different groups or economic agents who supply capital to the firm. First, there are *individuals*. Many individuals and families regularly save a portion of their income and directly provide capital to corporations by buying the firm's stocks and bonds. Additionally, individuals *indirectly* provide capital to corporations through *financial institutions*. Basically, there are three types of such financial intermediaries: (1) deposit institutions (banks, both commercial and mutual savings, and savings and loan associations), (2) investment companies (mutual funds), and (3) contractual institutions (insurance companies and pension funds).

Deposit institutions make term loans and lease equipment to corporations through their commercial lending operations, and they also — through their trust departments — purchase common stock and debt from corporations. In addition, they provide considerable capital to federal, state, and local government agencies by purchasing government debt issues, and they provide mortgage money through real estate loans. These latter activities are not of major interest to us since we are concerned with the *corporate* sector of the U.S. economy.

Investment companies collect capital from individuals by selling shares and then invest this capital in marketable securities. Some companies invest primarily in government securities, but the vast majority of investment companies invest in stocks and bonds of corporations. Mutual funds have widely different investment goals ranging from capital appreciation (growth funds) to stable income generation (income funds), but the major emphasis in the majority of funds is in purchasing common stock. Mutual funds are particularly important economic agents in the secondary security markets described below.

Insurance companies collect insurance premiums from individuals and reinvest a portion of the premiums. Insurance companies have been one of the more active groups in buying corporate securities — mainly debt — via *private placements*. Private placements are security issues placed with a buyer through direct negotiation between company and buyer. There is no public offering of the securities. This is discussed more fully below.

METHODS OF ACQUIRING EXTERNAL CAPITAL

Recall that intermediate-term financing has a maturity of one year to about five to ten years and long-term financing maturity is anything beyond that. There are two major means of acquiring intermediate-term capital: through term loans and lease financing. On the long-term side there are three channels open to the firm. First, the firm may use an investment banker to sell securities via a *public offering*. Second, it may place a *privileged subscription* with a special group of stockholders. Last, it may make a *private placement* with (typically) some large financial institution. These methods of acquiring external capital are all discussed in detail below, but first we should note the role that security markets play in aiding firms in acquiring external capital.

Role of Security Markets

Security markets are markets where financial assets such as stocks and bonds are bought and sold. These markets may be characterized in different ways, but from the firm's standpoint there is a particularly important distinction between *primary* and *secondary* markets.

When the firm sells securities it does so in the primary market. The primary market is also called the *new issues* market because the firm issues its new securities through this market. In actuality, the primary market is constituted of firms who wish to issue securities (and thereby procure capital) on one side, and a collection of individual and institutional investors who will buy the newly issued securities (and thereby provide capital to the firms) on the other side. This collection of capital seekers (firms) and capital providers (investors) "constitute" the primary market. As we will see below it is frequently necessary to have middlemen (investment bankers and brokers) to bring the buyers and sellers together.

Once the firm has sold the securities, they may then be traded (bought and sold) among investors. An original buyer of newly issued General Electric stock, for example, may decide after holding the stock two years that he needs the money for other purposes or that the stock no longer suits his investment goals. Since the firm will only buy back securities under stipulated conditions that rarely match most individuals' selling decisions, the investor must find another investor to purchase his stock. When one investor sells a security to another it is through the *secondary* market. By definition, security transactions through the secondary market do not involve the firm in any financial transaction. The only effect on the firm is that ownership of a financial instrument the firm previously issued is changed. If John Brown sells 100 shares of General Electric common to Sam Jones, General Electric's stock ownership files will be changed, and future dividend checks and other stockholder mailings will be sent to Jones rather than to Brown.

Because we are interested in the firm's acquisition of *new* capital we are interested in this group of chapters in the *primary* markets. However, the secondary markets are essential to the operation of the primary markets. Suppose, for example, that Mr. Brown lives in Seattle and Mr. Jones in Tulsa. Without some means of bringing unacquainted sellers and buyers together there would obviously be a very limited secondary market. Mr. Brown would have to personally find a buyer and negotiate a sale with him. In most instances this would involve a costly and time-consuming search for Mr. Brown. Similarly, it would be difficult for Mr. Jones to find a seller. The probable result of such an arrangement would be that neither would invest as much in corporate securities as they would in an arrangement where there was a convenient, well-functioning secondary security market. This means that General Electric and other companies would have more difficulty in issuing securities in the primary market because new issue buyers would have trouble reselling these securities.

The obvious conclusion of this simplified discussion is that well-developed secondary markets are crucial to the success of the primary market where the firm operates. It will behoove us to briefly describe the major features of the secondary U.S. markets before proceeding to our development of the primary market channels that the firm utilizes. Secondary markets are characterized by their accessibility to the public at large. Anyone who possesses the necessary capital may purchase securities in secondary markets. These markets are of two general types: *registered exchanges* and *over-the-counter markets.*

Registered exchanges   Registered exchanges are physical marketplaces established specifically for the trading (buying and selling) of securities. They are auction markets in that prices of securities are determined by competitive bids of buyers and sellers. For a company to have its securities traded on a registered exchange it must be *listed* on the exchange. To be listed the firm must meet the *listing requirements* of the exchange. These are specified by each of the several exchanges but generally require that the firm keep the investing public apprised of its activities and meet certain standards of corporate size that effectively grants the listing priviledge to the larger U.S. corporations. These size requirements vary across exchanges but mainly relate to the number of shares and shareholders the company has and the size of the company's net income and asset base. The most stringent listing requirements are imposed by the most prestigious exchanges.

The most prestigious U.S. exchange is the New York Stock Exchange and the next most prestigious is the American Stock Exchange. Both exchanges have trading facilities for common and preferred stocks, bonds, and some high-quality warrants of the major companies in the United States. There are also several *regional* exchanges such as the Midwest Stock Exchange, the Pacific Coast Stock Exchange, and the Boston Stock Exchange. These exchanges specialize in providing secondary markets for some of the more important regional companies.

Over-the-counter markets   Securities not traded on a registered exchange are said to be traded *over-the-counter.* Unlike the exchanges, the over-the-counter market has no physical trading facility but is a far-flung collection of security broker-dealers who participate in arranging transactions in unlisted securities. While the over-the-counter market does provide a secondary market for securities, only a few thousand unlisted securities have active secondary markets. Primary markets for unlisted companies will not be as readily available as for companies that are listed.

Use of investment bankers

Unlike investment decisions, which the firm continually makes, most firms only periodically arrange for long-term external financing. Since the potential suppliers of long-term capital are spread across the country and since most firms don't raise long-term capital frequently enough to become expert at it, firms usually turn to financing experts when they seek long-term capital. These experts in procuring long-term capital are *investment bankers.* They are specialists in being middlemen between seekers of capital (firms) and suppliers of capital (investors). U.S. firms use investment bankers extensively when issuing new securities.

In performing this middleman service of bringing firms and investors together the investment banker performs three functions:

1. Advisory function.
2. Underwriting function.
3. Marketing function.

The compensation the investment banker receives for performing these functions is called the *spread*. The spread is the percent of gross sale proceeds that the investment banker receives. We discuss this further below.

Advisory function   Because investment bankers are experts in selling securities, an important part of their service to client firms is providing advice during the planning stage before any securities are issued. This advice typically covers all aspects of the issue:

1. What kinds of securities to sell (bonds, stocks, or . . . ?).
2. The price of the new security.
3. The nonprice features. (For example, on a bond issue, the maturity, coupon interest rate, provision for sinking fund, etc.).
4. The issuing date.

Since most firms are only infrequent users of the capital markets the investment banker's advisory function is very important to the firm.

In some instances the investment banker doesn't provide advice. Arrangements between investment bankers and issuing firms are of two types. The *negotiated* bid is an arrangement where the firm selects an investment banker or group of investment bankers at the beginning of the planning stage and negotiates and works with the banker to decide what kind of securities to issue and all other associated details of the planned issue. In such an arrangement the investment banker provides advice and counsel. The other arrangement is through *competitive* bids. The firm decides before approaching any investment bankers what kind of securities it will issue and other associated details, and then asks investment bankers to bid on the issue. The firm then takes the best offer. In competitive bids the firm does not use the investment banker as an advisor.[3] Most state public utilities are required by law to secure competitive bids, and the Interstate Commerce Commission requires railroads to issue new securities through competitive bids. The theory behind requiring competitive bids is that it results in lower costs to the issuing firm. However, this advantage is offset by the fact that the firm loses the expert advice of the investment banker. A security sale planned without the help of an investment banker may turn out to be relatively unattractive to investors, and what the firm saves on advisory expenses may be more than offset in losses to the firm because of low net proceeds that result from a relatively unattractive security issue. Preparing the details of a security issue without the aid of investment bankers is somewhat analagous to preparing a will without a lawyer, and firms that are not required to seek competitive bids prefer the negotiated offering arrangement.

---

[3] Some firms will use an investment banker for advisory purposes and then preclude that particular investment banker from bidding on the issue.

Underwriting function The underwriting function is essentially an insurance function since the investment banker bears the risk of price declines of the securities while they are being issued. Once the details of the security issue have been worked out, the firm sells the issue to the investment banker, who will then sell the securities to investors. That is, the firm receives its money *before* the investment banker sells the securities to the public. The sequential nature of this process means that the investment banker will own the securities until they can be resold. Many issues are sold out the very day they are first offered to the public, but some issues may take from a week to a month to be marketed. Conceivably it could take longer. If the price of the securities declines during the time between when the investment banker buys them and when it finishes reselling them, the investment banker can suffer a loss. Thus, the investment banker underwrites the issue by bearing the risk that investors (the market) may not like the issue. This underwriting function ensures the firm from a loss should the issue not be well-received by the market. Since the investment bankers are experts at floating securities (selling new issues) most issues are successful, but investment bankers are not infallible, and errors in judgment and consequent losses do occur. Some of these losses are large.

Investment bankers naturally attempt to protect themselves from such losses. They very carefully analyze any proposed security issue offered them. Basically, they are trying to predict what investor response will be at the time of issue. Issues usually fail to receive a good investor response either because the firm or the capital market is unhealthy. The capital market may be in good condition with considerable activity, and with most issues being marketed successfully, but the particular firm in question could be financially or operationally weak, or the type of security being floated by the firm may be unattractive to investors. The new issue could be a failure, in the sense that the underwriters take a loss or cannot resell all the securities. It is, of course, much easier for large, financially strong firms (such as those on the New York Stock Exchange) to get investment banking backing. The other worry is that the market could be unreceptive to new issues. If the investment community is jittery about the future and unreceptive to new securities, investment bankers may hesitate to underwrite any but the very strongest companies' securities. Market conditions affect the willingness of investment bankers to underwrite securities, and frequently firms postpone new issues until market conditions become more favorable.

Investment bankers also protect themselves by forming *syndicates*. The underwriting syndicate spreads out the risk of failure over several investment bankers. Underwriting syndicates are, in fact, a good example of the advantages of diversification. One of the investment banking firms oversees the underwriting syndicate and is called the underwriting manager. Often there are two or more comanagers. Another form of protection for the underwriters is the so-called *best efforts* arrangement where the investment bankers do not actually buy the new securities from the issuer but only agree to sell as many of the securities as they can at the agreed price. The risk of not selling all the securities is consequently borne by the issuer, not the investment bankers. No underwriting function is performed by the investment bankers in such situations. Most frequently, best efforts arrangements involve securities of smaller, more risky firms that the investment banking community would not agree to underwrite. Occasionally, particularly strong firms will issue securities through a best efforts offering if they are very confident that the new issue will be well-received by the market. This arrangement spares them the expensive underwriting costs.

Finally, many contracts between investment bankers and firms contain *out clauses* that permit the cancellation of the banker's agreement to arrange the sale if market conditions turn bad. Such clauses protect the investment bankers from extremely adverse conditions, such as a temporary collapse in the new issues market.

Historically, the investment banking industry has been a competitive industry, and there are about 50 firms that managed or comanaged at

FIGURE 12–4
Major U.S. investment bankers in 1973

Rank and Underwriter	Number of issued managed or comanaged	Dollar volume (billions of dollars)
1. Merrill Lynch, Pierce, Fenner & Smith	135	7.2
2. Salomon Brothers	119	6.6
3. First Boston Corp.	86	5.6
4. Blythe Eastman Dillon	95	5.3
5. Goldman, Sachs	68	4.9
6. Lehman Brothers	65	4.8
7. Kidder, Peabody	60	4.5
8. Halsey, Stuart	63	4.4
9. Morgan Stanley	40	3.9
10. White, Weld	51	3.6

Data source: *Institutional Investor.*

least $100 million of new issues in 1973. Like other industries, investment banking has its leaders. Figure 12–4 shows the top ten investment banking firms in 1973 based on dollar volume of total new issues managed or comanaged.

Marketing function The third major function investment bankers perform related to new security issues is the marketing of the securities. Except in best efforts arrangements the investment banking group buys the securities from the issuer and then resells (markets) the securities through distribution channels it has arranged. Securities are usually sold through a *selling group* established by the investment banking syndicate expressly for the purpose of marketing the securities to investors. This selling group is composed of the sales organization of the underwriters, and also *dealers,* who are specialists in marketing new issues. Sales achieved through the underwriters will receive a full commission, and large investment banking firms have well-developed sales organizations that are a regular part of the selling group team. The dealers receive only a sales commission for their efforts. This commission is less than the underwriting commission because the dealers are not exposed to underwriting risk. The underwriters actually own the securities until they are all sold, while the dealers are only concerned with selling the securities.

In a negotiated offering the underwriting syndicate assembles the selling group even before the Securities and Exchange Commission has approved the sale of the securities. A preliminary prospectus outlining the features of the new security issue is sent out to investors. Because the new issue has not yet been approved by the Securities and Exchange Commission no offering date or price is shown on the prospectus. In addition, a prominently displayed statement, printed in red ink, is stamped on the prospectus that clearly indicates the prospectus is only an information circular and not an offer to sell securities to investors. The stamped red ink statement on the prospectus has led investors to call the prospectus a *red herring*.

Once the issue has been approved, the selling group begins marketing the securities. If the group has properly done its homework prior to approval, and the market and the new issue under consideration are healthy, the issue will be fully subscribed (completely sold) relatively quickly. However, if something goes wrong, the issue could be very hard to sell.

Privileged subscriptions

Instead of selling new securities to the general public the firm may sell the new securities to its current security holders. That is, the firm offers the new securities to its existing security holders on a right of first refusal basis. The vast majority of such arrangements are concerned with offering new common stock to current common holders. Many corporations have discretion over whether a new stock issue will be sold to the general public or to existing common stockholders, but in most companies the common stockholders have the legal right (called the *preemptive right*) to have the right of first refusal to buy any newly issued common stock. New common issues that are offered first to existing shareholders are called *privileged subscriptions* or *preemptive right issues*.

We discuss preemptive right issues in detail in the next chapter, but we can present the preliminary information here. The preemptive right provides protection of the stockholders' control position. If new stock were sold to the outside public it would decrease current stockholders' proportional ownership. Priviledged subscriptions preserve the current stockholders' proportional ownership because current owners are given the right to buy the same percentage of new stock as their percentage holdings of old stock. As we will see in the next chapter those stockholders who do not wish to buy new shares can sell their *rights* (the preemptive right to buy new shares) in the market. To a lesser extent, new securities that are convertible into common (such as convertible preferred stock, convertible bonds and warrants, all discussed in Chapter

15) are sometimes offered to current common owners on a priviledged basis. Occasionally, nonconvertible preferred or bonds will be offered to common owners, but such instances are rare.

Firms usually rely less heavily on investment bankers when issuing new securities via a rights offering. When firms do use investment bankers to underwrite the issue it is usually on a *standby* basis, where the underwriting syndicate agrees to buy all unsold shares at a stipulated price.

Private placements

As an alternative to either selling securities to the public or through priviledged subscriptions the firm may consider *private* or *direct* placement of securities with one or more financial institutions, such as life insurance companies or pension funds. Many different kinds of securities are placed privately, but the most common private placement involves debt.

Figure 12–5 shows the gross amounts of privately and publicly placed bonds issued by U.S. corporations from 1950 to 1973. Up until about 1966 the volume of private and public issues were fairly equal. After 1966 the public market became relatively the more important of the two markets, but private lenders have supplied between $4 and $10 billion per year to U.S. corporations and are still a very important source of long-term capital.

Many firms do not use investment bankers in arranging private placements but rather work directly with the lending financial institutions. Dealing directly with the lender saves the firm all of the investment banking fees. However, many other firms prefer to use investment bankers in arranging private placements. Use of investment bankers offers two main advantages to the borrowing firm. First, the investment bankers have a much wider range of contacts among financial institutions than the borrowing firms do. Consequently, the investment banker has better knowledge of *when* financial institutions have money available, *which* institutions are ready to lend, and *what kind of securities* they would be most interested in. Most firms need external capital only infrequently and therefore don't regularly cultivate these business associations as investment bankers do. The investment banker can help in guiding the firm to the most likely institution. Second, since the investment banker is also intimately aware of conditions in the public issues market he can provide comparative information the firm may use in evaluating terms offered by the financial institutions. If the offer is way out of line with the public market, the investment banker will apprise the firm that it might do better elsewhere. Also the investment banker can suggest to the two negotiating sides ways to resolve differences that block agreement. The total costs of using an investment banker to help locate a lender and of using his advisory skills are usually around 0.5 percent of the sale proceeds and rarely exceed 1.5 percent. The big saving, of course, is the absence of underwriting expenses.

There are two primary advantages of private placements in comparison to public offerings:

1. Speed of transaction.
2. Reduced floatation costs.

The speed advantage refers to the fairly rigid timetable that public offerings must adhere to. A proposed public issue must be registered with the proper authorities, which (if it's a federal registration) requires a minimum 20-day wait before it may be marketed. Frequently the waiting period is much longer (from 40 to 60 days), and during this waiting period market conditions may change and impair the success of the new issue. Mobil Oil planned a $300 million debenture sale in 1972, and after registration with the Securities and Exchange Commission, but *before* issuing, the U.S. Treasury announced a substantial budget deficit. Market interest rates increased, causing Mobil to withdraw their planned issue. Direct placements are exempt from registration so there is no comparable waiting time. This speed of transaction advantage eliminates some of the uncertainty regarding the timing of the new issue.

Direct placements also have lower floatation costs than public place-

FIGURE 12–5
Gross proceeds of new public and private corporate bond issues 1950–1973

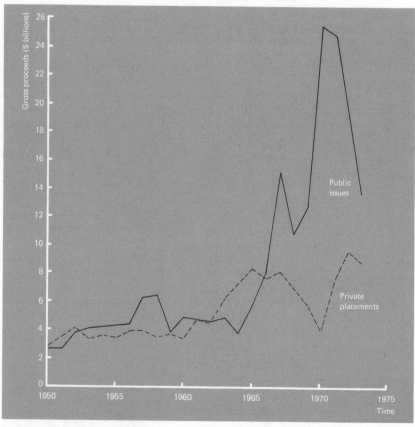

Source: *Federal Reserve Bulletin.*

ments. This mainly occurs because of the lack of underwriting expenses, but there are also small savings on registration fees. If the investment banker is not used there is also the saving of the agency fees associated with a public issue.

The major *disadvantage* of private placements is the higher interest cost (or dividend cost if stock is involved). Financial institutions charge higher interest rates than a comparable publicly issued security would yield, and they also frequently demand an equity "kicker" or "sweetener," such as warrants. This gives the lender some chance to share in any capital appreciation on the stock if it should do well.

Term loans and leasing

Recall that private or direct placements are nonpublic sales of long-lived securities (stocks and bonds) to financial institutions. Private placements result in the firm receiving long-term capital. Term loans and leasing are methods of raising *intermediate-term* capital without going to the public. In effect, they are forms of intermediate-term direct placements, as the firm directly negotiates with the lender or lessor to secure needed financing.

Term loans Term loans are loans granted to the firm, mainly from commercial banks. The loan is a debt instrument which makes the bank a creditor of the firm. The firm arranges the loan directly with the bank without the help of a middleman. This is a very important source of capital to all firms, but it is a particularly important source to smaller firms who frequently can't raise capital elsewhere because of their size. We will investigate term loans in some detail in Chapter 14.

Lease financing In a lease arrangement the firm does not actually "purchase" an investment it has decided to make, but rather obtains the use of the asset by leasing it from the asset's owner (the lessor). Effectively, the firm is renting the asset. There are two kinds of leases, distinguished mainly by the ease with which the lease can be cancelled. An operating lease (good examples are vehicle rental and data processing equipment) is cancelable before the end of the contract, while a *financial* lease is usually not cancelable prior to the end of the contract. A wide variety of capital equipment that U.S. corporations used to purchase is now being leased through a financial lease arrangement. Airlines, for example, used to purchase all their airplanes but now lease many of them.

Leasing has become an important form of intermediate-term financing for U.S. businesses, and we will study the various aspects of lease financing in Chapter 14.

FLOTATION COSTS

Flotation costs are composed of two components:

1. Underwriter's spread.
2. Issue expenses.

The spread includes all compensation paid for investment banking services provided: advising, underwriting, and selling. The spread is a percentage cost defined as:[4]

$$\text{Underwriter's spread} = \left[\frac{\left(\substack{\text{Gross sales}\\\text{proceeds}}\right) - \left(\substack{\text{Net sales}\\\text{proceeds}}\right)}{\left(\substack{\text{Gross sales}\\\text{proceeds}}\right)}\right] \times (100) \qquad (12\text{-}1)$$

In April 1973, Eli Lilly and Co. issued 950,000 shares of new common stock through an underwriting team managed by Morgan Stanley and Co. The underwriters paid Lilly $74,908,153 and sold the securities for $77,187,500.

$$\text{Underwriter's spread} = \left(\frac{77,187,500 - 74,908,153}{77,187,500}\right)(100)$$

$$= 2.953 \text{ percent}$$

The underwriting spread is the larger of the two components of flotation costs. Issue expenses include legal fees, printing costs, registration fees, and taxes.

Flotation costs are mainly determined by the size of the issue and the risk associated with the issue. Figure 12–6 shows flotations costs for debt, preferred stock, and common stock during the period from 1963 to 1965. These costs presume full underwriting services are provided by investment banking syndicates.

Figure 12–6 illustrates the point that flotation costs are determined by size of the issue and the type of security issued. For all three security forms the flotation cost decreases as size of issue increases. It is important to note that flotation cost is expressed as a *percent* of gross proceeds so that it is percentage cost that is decreasing as size of issue increases. It would cost the firm more total dollars to market $50 million of securities as opposed to $30 million worth of securities, but the percentage cost would be reduced. This is partly because of the fixed component of flotation costs. Certain flotation costs are fixed costs, and these costs, expressed as a percent of gross proceeds, will naturally fall as issue size increases. Thus, if fixed costs are, say, $50,000, when expressed as a percentage of gross proceeds, these fixed costs are much higher in a $500,000 security issue ($50,000/$500,000 = 10 percent) than in a $50,000,000 security issue ($50,000/$50,000,000 = 0.1 percent). A second reason that larger issues have smaller percentage flotation costs is that larger firms tend to sell securities in larger blocks, and these larger companies are thought to be safer. Consequently they are charged less by the investment bankers for the underwriting (risk bearing) and selling functions the investment bankers' perform for the firm.

The second point that Figure 12–6 shows is that common stocks have higher flotation costs than preferred stocks, which in turn have higher flotation costs than debt. This reflects the relative riskiness of the se-

---

[4] The spread can also be calculated on a per security basis by dividing both gross and net sales proceeds by the number of securities issued.

curity forms. From an investor's standpoint, debt is the safest security to own and common stock the riskiest. This means that the underwriter is exposed to the most risk in marketing common stocks and the least risk in marketing debt. The underwriter passes on these relative risks to the firm in the form of relative flotation costs: highest costs for common and lowest costs for debt.

Needless to say there are other factors that influence flotation costs. If firms try to float securities in periods of market uncertainty, such as

FIGURE 12–6
Flotation costs 1963–1965

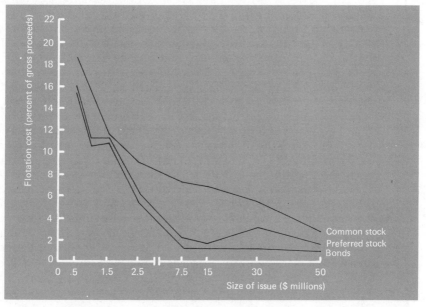

Sources: *Cost of Flotation of Registered Equity Issues 1963–1965* (Washington, D.C.: U.S. Government Printing Office, 1970) and *Investment Banking and the New Issues Market* by Irwin Friend et al. (Cleveland: World Publishing Company, 1967).

the mid-1974 period, for example, they may find they face higher flotation costs since underwriter risk increases in such periods. The data depicted in Figure 12–6 are somewhat dated, but the two main points are still valid: percentage flotation costs decrease with issue size and increase with the riskiness of the security type.

GOVERNMENT REGULATION

After the collapse of the securities markets in 1929 it became evident that there were many instances of misrepresentation concerning new security issues. Up to 1933, security issues were regulated only by state agencies, but the quality of the regulation was adjudged spotty and ineffective. Today both the primary and secondary security markets are regulated by state and federal agencies, but the more important regulation is at the federal level.

Federal regulation

The Securities Act of 1933 pertained to the regulation of new security issues. This act requires issuers to provide prospective investors full and truthful information about the company and the new securities being sold. The act is frequently referred to as the Truth in Securities Act. The reasoning behind the act is that a fully informed investor can make enlightened judgments about the risk and return characteristics of the new securities. The Securities and Exchange Commission (SEC) enforces the Securities Act, and while the SEC requires full and truthful information concerning new issues, it does not pass judgment on the investment quality of the new securities. Issues are not barred from sale because they are speculative, for example. So long as there is, in the SEC's judgment, full and truthful disclosure of the nature of the security and of the issuing company, the SEC is satisfied. Investors may then evaluate the new securities in terms of their own propensities for risk taking.

In enforcing the Securities Act the SEC requires a registration statement be filed by the firm that states in detail all the particulars concerning the firm and the proposed new issue. The SEC then has 20 days (in busy times longer periods are taken) to evaluate the registration statement. During this *cooling off period* the firm issues the *red herring* preliminary prospectus described earlier. If the SEC does not object to the new issue within the proscribed period the firm is free to begin selling the securities. Final versions of the prospectus must be given each security purchaser at or prior to sale. This final prospectus stipulates the price of the security and date of sale. If the SEC does *not* approve the registration statement, the issuer is required to satisfy the SEC's objections or else the issue may not be sold.

Certain kinds of corporate security issues are exempt from SEC regulation:

1. Nonpublic sales are exempted. Nonpublic sales are either priviledged subscriptions or private placements.
2. Short-term notes and bills whose maturity does not exceed nine months are exempted.
3. Small issues are exempted. If the total value of the sale does not exceed $300,000, the issue is not regulated by the SEC.
4. Intrastate offerings are exempted. Intrastate offerings are where all purchasers live in the same state where the firm is incorporated.
5. Securities of federally regulated companies (such as railroads, banks, airlines, and public utilities) are exempted from SEC regulation. Regulation of new securities of such companies is administered by the appropriate regulatory agency (in the public utilities case, for example, the Federal Power Commission).

The SEC has the power to bring both civil and criminal charges against violators of the Securities Act. The SEC also regulates the secondary market for securities and has similar powers there.

State regulation

Individual states regulate securities issued in their state through so-called *blue sky* laws, which are aimed at preventing fraudulent promotion and sales practices. Most states do not attempt to regulate new issues that are federally regulated, but there is considerable variability in other aspects of state regulation. Some states, for example, attempt to adjudge the investment quality of the new issue. There is also considerable variability in the regulatory zeal of the various state agencies. The basic intent of the state regulatory statutes, however, is the same as at the federal level: to promote full and truthful disclosure of information to investors.

SUMMARY

The decision to invest in fixed assets creates intermediate and long-term financing needs for the firm to pay for these fixed assets and the concomitant increase in net working capital. In this chapter we began the study of intermediate and long-term financing sources.

First, we investigated ways of estimating the firm's intermediate and long-term financing requirements. Our procedure was predicated on the firm's capital expenditure plans. The estimation procedure included both the cost of new fixed assets and the increase in net working capital necessary to support the sales increase caused by the new fixed assets. Once the total financing requirement was determined we estimated how much internal financing would be available.

We then began the study of alternate sources of external intermediate and long-term financing. The markets for these funds are collectively called the *capital markets*. Capital markets include *impersonal* markets, where there is no direct negotiation between the firm and capital suppliers, and *customer* markets, where there is direct negotiation. Capital suppliers include individual investors and financial institutions (banks, insurance companies, investment companies, and pension funds). The list of alternate forms of raising external intermediate and long-term capital includes common and preferred stock, bonds, term loans, leases, convertible securities, and warrants. External capital is raised in *primary* capital markets and we discussed the important role that *secondary* capital markets play in enhancing the ability of the firm to raise external capital. Firms whose securities are not traded on a registered exchange have more difficulty in issuing new securities to the public.

Firms rely heavily on investment bankers to market new securities. Investment bankers provide advice and counsel, underwrite security issues, and distribute (sell to the public) the new securities. The fee they receive for these services is the *spread*.

In lieu of marketing new securities to the general public, the firm may sell them to current security holders. The most common form of such a sale is the *privileged subscription* or *preemptive rights issue*, where the firm offers new common stock to current stockholders. Another alternative to public sales is the *private placement* where the firm directly sells securities to one or more financial institutions. Debt is most frequently used in such placements. Private placements offer the advantage of speed of transaction and reduced floatation costs, but interest costs are higher. *Term loans* from commercial banks and *leasing arrangements* are other forms of raising capital through direct negotiations.

Floatation costs are composed of the underwriter's spread and issue expenses, and are higher (on a percentage basis) for smaller issues than for larger ones. Also, floatation costs for common stock sales are higher than floatation costs for preferred stock, which, in turn, are higher than floatation costs for debt.

QUESTIONS

1. Define the following terms and phrases:
   a. Net working capital.
   b. Fixed assets turnover.
   c. Cash flow from operations.
   d. Internal financing available.
   e. Private placements.
   f. Privileged subscriptions.
   g. Investment banker.

2. Suppose that a firm's investment plans for the next two or three years have been fairly well decided, as the firm knows about how much its capital investment will be over that period. Other things equal, how would the following factors affect how much external permanent financing the firm would need to implement its investment plans? Briefly explain your answer:
   a. The firm's cash flow from operations increases.
   b. The firm's board of directors decided to increase dividends next year.
   c. The firm's inventory turnover ratio increases because of better inventory control.
   d. The company's collection period increases because of a decision to sell merchandise on credit to customers that are slower paying than other customer groups the firm sells on credit to.
   e. Floatation costs increase because of increased market uncertainty.

3. Breipohl Electronics is in the process of diversifying its investment base. For the next few years the company expects that the most substantial part of its new investment activities will be the purchase of tracts of undeveloped land. These lands will be held from five to ten years and then sold to developers. Historically, when the firm has increased its fixed assets by 1 percent, it has had to increase net working capital by 0.5 percent. However, the financial analyst in charge of estimating Breipohl's expected external permanent financing requirement for the coming year has estimated only a 1-percent net working capital increase for the year even though there is a planned 6-percent increase in the firm's fixed assets, mainly in new land purchases. A colleague reviewing the analyst's work asks for a justification of this deviation from the firm's usual net working capital estimation guidelines.

Assuming there have been no increases in asset management efficiency in the company, why do you suppose the analyst's forecast of the net working capital increase is so low here?

4. As sales increase some current liabilities accounts are also expected to increase automatically. Explain why notes payable are not usually expected to automatically increase with increasing sales.

5. What advantages would a firm expect to gain from listing its stock on a major stock exchange?

6. For many years many public utilities were required to issue new securities through competitive bid arrangements. Recently, however, it was proposed that utilities be permitted to issue new securities through a negotiated bid. Given that the regulatory agencies are concerned with holding down floatation costs when the utilities issue new securities, why do you suppose this proposal was made?

7. Many planned issues of new securities are cancelled or postponed before the sale actually takes place. Sometimes this withdrawal takes place at the last minute, even though considerable effort and expense has already been expended. List some factors that could cause withdrawal of new securities issues.

8. Whenever possible, many firms prefer to place new securities, particularly debt, with private lenders rather than engaging in a public sale. What advantages and disadvantages do private placements offer over public sales?

9. Occasionally, a legislator will criticize the common practice of forming underwriting syndicates and selling groups to handle new securities issues. If you were a securities industry spokesman, what economic justifications would you cite for defending these practices?

10. Briefly explain the primary purpose of state and federal securities regulation laws.

PROBLEMS

1. Tarheel Furniture has just published its balance sheet as shown:

Balance Sheet
(millions of dollars)

Assets:		Claims:	
Cash and securities	4.2	Accounts payable	$ 6.1
Accounts receivable	7.5	Accruals	3.6
Inventory	10.3	Notes payable	1.5
Property and equipment	20.5	Long-term notes	8.6
		Preferred stock	5.0
		Common stock	12.4
		Retained earnings	5.3
Total assets	$42.5	Total claims	$42.5

Tarheel begins a major expansion of its plant facilities this year and will need to increase its net working capital to accommodate the new sales anticipated by the expansion. The increase in plant will be $5 million and the firms fixed assets turnover is about 2.5.

a. Determine the firm's current sales level.

b. Determine the anticipated sales increase.

c. Estimate the amount of extra net working capital needed because of the expansion.

d. If anticipations are realized, show the balance sheet entries for those current asset and current liabilities accounts that are affected by the expansion.

2. The North Iowa Match Co. is attempting to do some long range forecasting. Basically, it is trying to estimate how much financing it will need during the next five years. North Iowa's balance sheet for last year is shown below. The company's sales were $2.5 million last year.

Balance Sheet
(thousands of dollars)

Assets:		Claims:	
Cash............................	$ 158	Accounts payable	$ 188
Accounts receivable..........	201	Notes payable......................	20
Inventory........................	250	Accruals	107
Total current assets...	609	Total current liabilities	315
Net fixed assets................	873	Bonds	100
		Common stock.....................	800
		Retained earnings	267
Total assets	$1,482	Total claims	$1,482

Estimate North Iowa's total financing requirement in the coming five years assuming that sales will increase by 10 percent per year and that *all* assets and the relevant claims accounts keep their present relationship to sales.

3. Bey Paperboard is committed to spend about $6 million over the next three years to expand their production facilities, replace their aging truck fleet, and to build up working capital to support these plans. The treasurer for Bey, Ms. Willard, further estimates that these planned expenses will be about $2.5 million per year for the next two years, and then $1 million in the third year. Ms. Willard also has estimated the following income statement items for the next three years:

	Year 1	Year 2	Year 3
Sales...................	$45,000,000	$46,000,000	$48,000,000
Depreciation	1,000,000	1,000,000	1,200,000
Net income..........	1,500,000	1,600,000	1,800,000

Bey's board of directors plans to maintain a 40-percent common dividend payout ratio during this expansion period.

In each of the three years, estimate Bey's:
a. Cash flow from operations.
b. Internal financing available.
c. External permanent financing requirement.
d. What is the significance of the answer for Year 3 in part (c)?

4. As a corporate planning analyst for West Fabrics, you have been assigned the task of estimating how much external permanent financing the company will need to secure this coming year. From the director of the firm's Capital Investment Department you have determined that West will spend about $5 million on new capital investment this year and about $4 million on replacement capital expenditures. You also have a copy of West's balance sheet and income statements for last year:

Balance Sheet (millions of dollars):		Income statement (millions of dollars):	
Current assets	$ 20	Sales	$90
Net fixed assets	80	Costs*	75
Total	$100	EBIT	15
Payables and accruals.........	$ 1.5	Tax (40%)	6
Preferred stock	10	Net income	$ 9
Common stock..................	50	Pfd. dividends	1
Retained earnings	25	Available for common...........	8
Total	$100	Common dividends	$ 2

* Includes $5 of depreciation.

The firm expects to pay the same common dividend this coming year as was paid last year, and all turnover ratios should remain fairly constant. Also, this year's depreciation charges should be about the same as last year's.
a. Estimate this year's fixed assets level.
b. Use the fixed assets turnover ratio to estimate this year's sales increase.
c. Determine the increased net working capital required to support the higher sales level.
d. Determine West's total financing requirement.
e. Assuming this year's cash flow will be approximately the same as last year's, estimate West's (1) cash flow from operations and (2) internal financing available.
f. Estimate the external permanent financing requirement.

5. Several financial analysts for Monroe Associates have been working on projections of next year's financing needs for the company. Monroe's investment plans have been pretty well set. The company plans to invest about $8 million in plant renovation and new equipment. In the past year the firm's sales were $260 million, and Monroe carried $56 million of current assets and $30 million of accounts payable and accruals.

The analysts have made their projections on the basis of what would happen if a "good" year occurred and what would happen if a "bad" year occurred. Regardless of the kind of year Monroe has, however, the company will pay a $2 million common dividend and a $1.5 million preferred dividend. Depreciation charges are $4 million. Some other data that Monroe's analysts have estimated are shown below.

Type of economic climate	Bad	Good
Probability............................	0.5	0.5
Sales	$260,000,000	$300,000,000
Profit margin.........................	2 percent	2.5 percent

a. Determine Monroe's expected (expected value) total financing requirement.
b. Accepting the estimates of all financial data as valid, what is the maximum amount of total financing required next year?
c. Determine the expected (expected value) of external financing required.
d. What is the maximum amount of external financing that Monroe should need?

6. Determine the underwriters spread in each of the following situations:
   a. Gross sales proceeds = $2,500,000
       Net sales proceeds   = $2,300,000
   b. Common stock is sold to investors for $20 per share. The firm receives $18.50 per share.
   c. 7.5 million shares of common sold.
       Gross sales proceeds = $62,500,000
       Net sales proceeds   = $8 per share

7. Clark Dental Supply is preparing to issue new bonds through its investment banker. Clark needs to net $40 million from the sale to facilitate its investment plans.
   a. Determine how much total debt (in dollars) Clark must issue if the underwriter's spread is 2.60 percent and issue expenses are $100,000. (Round *up* the answer to the nearest $10,000.)
   b. How many $1,000 bonds will be issued if the bonds are priced to sell at (1) $1,000 each? (2) $900 each? (3) $1,100 each?

8. Pinches Automotive Parts is preparing to issue some new stock. The firm's investment banker proposes two alternatives to Pinches:
   Plan I: The investment banker will guarantee (underwrite) the sale of 500,000 shares at a price of $2 per share under the market price of Pinches present stock on the last day of registration.
   Plan II: The investment banker will sell the new stock on a best efforts basis for a fixed fee of $500,000. The sale price will be fixed at a price of $1 per share under the prevailing Pinches stock price on the last day of registration. Pinches assumes that 95 percent of the shares would be sold under such an arrangement.

The estimated probability distribution of Pinches stock price on the last day of registration is:

Price	$30	$31	$32	$33
Probability	0.1	0.1	0.5	0.3

a. For each plan determine:
    (1) The expected net proceeds to Pinches.
    (2) The expected percentage underwriting spreads [use Equation (12–1)].
    (3) The maximum net proceeds to Pinches.
    (4) The minimum net proceeds to Pinches.
b. Which plan is better if the firm wants to minimize its expected percentage underwriting spread?
c. Which plan is better if the firm wants to maximize the probability of raising at least $15 million?

9. The Larcker Logging Company is in the process of determining its capital budget and external capital financing needs for 19+1. Toward that end, they have prepared the following estimates on six prospective investments and other related financial data.

Project	Description
A	Replace chain saws with water-jet cutting tools. Cost, $300,000. Expected life, eight years. Expected CFAT $63,-000 per year. Standard deviation of returns, 0.26. Correlation with market index rate of return, +1.0.
B	Market sawdust as insulation material. Cost, $200,000. Expected life, six years. Expected CFAT, $38,936 per year. Standard deviation of returns, 0.13. Correlation with market index rate of return, +0.5.
C	Install a forest fire prevention system. Cost, $100,000. Expected life, five years. Expected CFAT, $30,236 per year. Standard deviation of returns, 0.25. Correlation with market index rate of return, +0.78.
D	Purchase logging rights in adjacent national forest. Cost, $200,000. Expected life, nine years. Expected CFAT, $39,590 per year. The risk of this project is approximately equal to the company's overall level of risk.
E	Institute an ecology-oriented marketing program. Cost, $200,000. Expected life, three years. Expected CFAT, $85,061 per year. $\alpha_1 = \alpha_2 = \alpha_3 = 0.95$.
F	Adopt a computerized tree harvesting model. Cost, $300,-000. Expected life, 2 years. Expected CFAT, $170,178 in year one, and $225,400 in year two. $\alpha_1 = .95$, $\alpha_2 = .90$.

Each project's initial cost includes the net working capital requirement for the project. The last year's cash flows include recovery of the net working capital. The risk free interest rate is 0.06, the market index rate of return is 0.10, and the standard deviation of the market index rate of return is 0.13. Larcker's average cost of capital is 10 percent.

Projects A, B, and C are to be evaluated using the risk adjusted discount rate method. Project D should be evaluated at the average cost of capital. Projects E and F are to be evaluated using the certainty equivalent approach.

Other relevant financial data for last year (19+0) are:

Sales	$16,000,000
Profit margin	4 percent
Depreciation	$500,000
Dividend	$2.00 per share
Number of common shares	500,000

a. Determine which projects Larcker should accept. What is the total size of this new investment capital budget?

b. What is Larcker's total financing requirement?

c. Assuming that sales, profit margin, and depreciation for 19 + 1 are the same as for 19+0, estimate Larcker's cash flow from operations for 19+1.

d. Determine Larcker's 19+1 external permanent financing requirement assuming that the firm continues to pay a dividend of $2 per share.

e. To what level would dividends per share have to be reduced if the company wants to avoid using external financing?

SELECTED BASIC REFERENCES

McKeon, J. J. "Structure of Corporate External Financing," *Financial Analysts Journal* (September–October 1969), pp. 25–28.

Polakoff, M. E., et al. *Financial Institutions and Markets*. Boston: Houghton Mifflin, 1970.

SELECTED ADVANCED REFERENCES

Cohan, A. B. *Private Placements and Public Offerings: Market Shares since 1945*. Chapel Hill, N.C.: University of North Carolina Press, 1961.

Van Horne, J. C. *The Function and Analysis of Capital Market Rates*. Englewood Cliffs, N.J.: Prentice-Hall, Inc., 1970.

13

PREFERRED STOCK AND COMMON STOCK

In this chapter we further study preferred stock and common stock as a means of raising external long-term funds. Both are *legal* ownership securities, but we will see that for many purposes, preferred stock is more like debt than equity.

PREFERRED STOCK

There are several features that characterize preferred stock as a financial instrument. Some of these major features are common to virtually all preferred stocks. Other features are somewhat rare.

Priority status

Preferred stock is distinguished from common stock by the seniority position of preferred stockholders relative to common holders with respect to claims on the firm's income and assets. Preferred stockholders have a prior claim on the firm's income, in that the firm must pay the preferred dividends first. Preferred stockholders also have a prior claim on the firm's assets in the event the firm is dissolved. If, for example, the firm is declared bankrupt (see Chapter 22), the preferred stockholders have a claim on the proceeds of the sale of the firm's assets that is prior to that of the common holders. However, the preferred claim is behind the firm's creditors' (such as bond holders') claims. Preferred stock's priority position makes it a safer investment than common stock. In return for this prior claim status, preferred stockholders give up their voting rights as owners and their right to share in any exceptionally good profits the firm may realize. Essentially, preferred holders have a less risk but (historically) less profitable form of stock. They are trading away higher financial returns for greater safety.

Fixed income status

Preferred stockholders receive dividends that are contractually stipulated. These dividends are stated either as a percent of *par value* or in dollar terms. Par value represents the face or nominal amount of each preferred share. When the preferred dividend is stated as a percent of par value the dollar amount of the dividend is determined by multiplying par value times the percent. For example, Grolier preferred stock has a 5-percent dividend and par value is $50 per share. The annual Grolier preferred dividend is therefore $2.50 per share.[1] Many preferred stocks have either no par value or a nominal (frequently $1 per share) value. For these stocks, and even for many preferred stocks with meaningful par values, dividends are stated simply in dollar terms. For example, Merck and Co.'s no par preferred stock has a stated $3.50 dividend and B. F. Goodrich's $1 par preferred stock has a $7.85 dividend.

Preferred stocks are called *fixed income* securities because they offer an expected constant (fixed) income to investors who purchase them. An investor who buys Goodrich preferred stock expects to receive $7.85 per share each year until he either sells the stock to another investor or the company redeems (buys back) the stock. There is no guarantee the company will actually pay the preferred dividend each period it is due, but barring difficulty the firm will honor its commitment.

The other major class of fixed income securities is debt (bonds), which also offers an expected constant income to investors (see Chapter 14). In this regard preferred stock is similar to debt. Together with its priority feature, the fixed income aspect of preferred stock creates *financial leverage* (recall Chapter 10) which magnifies earnings per share increases and decreases. This similarity to debt results in preferred being called a *hybrid* or *quasi-debt* security. This simply means that preferred stock has features that are much like debt features, and preferred's effect on the firm's common stock is much the same as with debt. So, from the common stockholder's viewpoint, preferred stock looks almost like debt. It is not exactly like debt from the common stockholder's view because, unlike with debt, should the firm not make a scheduled preferred dividend payment the preferred stockholders cannot force the firm into bankruptcy. Also, from the creditors perspective, the preferred looks like equity. Since the creditors have a priority position to preferred holders both with respect to income claims and asset claims, preferred stock plays the very same role as common stock: It serves as an equity cushion should the firm fail and enhances the chances that creditors will be able to recover their full investment. Thus, preferred stock is considered as equity by some investors and as debt by others. It is a hybrid security.

Cumulative dividends

The cumulative dividend feature is a protective device for preferred stockholders. When the firm fails to pay a scheduled preferred dividend

---

[1] Like common stock, preferred stock usually pays a quarterly dividend. In the Grolier case this would amount to $0.625 per share each quarter.

an *arrearage* is created. A cumulative dividend feature requires that all arrearages must be paid before any *common* dividends are paid. Since preferred stockholders can neither force the firm to pay scheduled preferred dividends nor force the firm into bankruptcy because of omitted dividends, the cumulative dividend feature allows the preferred holders to block the payment of common dividends. If, for example, the preferred stock is supposed to pay a $3 per share annual dividend but has omitted four years of preferred dividends, there is a $12 per share arrearage, and common dividends may not be paid until this arrearage is paid off.

As an alternative to paying off the arrearage the firm may choose to try and negotiate a settlement with its preferred stockholders. Suppose, for example, that a $100 par 7-percent preferred is in arrears by $35. The firm might consider that this arrearage is too large to pay off in its current financial position. Suppose further that the preferred stock is selling in the market at $70 per share and that the firm's common stock is selling for $30 per share. The firm might consider offering, say, three shares of common for each share of preferred outstanding. For each share of preferred stock the preferred holders would be exchanging $70 worth of preferred for $90 worth of common. Some preferred holders may balk at such a swap, arguing that their preferred stock is worth $135 ($100 par plus $35 arrearage). However, if it seems unlikely that the firm can or will pay the arrearage, many preferred holders will agree to the compromise. Such an arrangement requires a vote of the preferred holders. If the vote is favorable, the firm can perform the exchange and is free to begin paying common dividends again. Of course the additional new shares of common stock issued will decrease (dilute) earnings per share. If the preferred stock is noncumulative the firm can pay common dividends even if there are preferred arrearages. However, most preferred stock has the cumulative feature.

Retirement provisions

Preferred stock has no fixed maturity date, but there are several provisions that may be included in the preferred agreement that provide for retirement of an outstanding issue.

Convertibility   A convertibility feature permits preferred stockholders to convert their shares of preferred into shares of common. Preferred stocks that permit this are called *convertible preferred*. Convertible securities (bonds as well as preferred stocks) are discussed in Chapter 15.

Call feature   The call feature allows the firm to buy back the preferred stock at a *call price* stipulated when the preferred is first sold. The call price is set above the initial sale price of the preferred (creating a *call premium*). The call premium is the difference between call price and par or face value. For example, Merck and Co.'s preferred has a par value of $100 per share, but the call price is $102 per share. Usually the firm agrees not to call the preferred for a period of at least two or three years after issue. The firm would only exercise its call option when the market price of the preferred stock is above the call price, for if the market price of the preferred were *below* the call price, the firm could attempt to buy the outstanding preferred stock. The company could purchase preferred stock in the open market and/or it could make a *tender offer* where it publicly advertises to buy preferred stock at a stipulated price (set above the current market price).

Sinking fund   A sinking fund provision requires the firm to set aside a certain amount of money to sequentially retire the issue. The money is used to either purchase preferred stock in the open market (if the preferred's market price is below call price) or to call the preferred (if market price is above call price). In either situation the amount of preferred outstanding is decreased.

Participation feature

The participation feature gives the preferred owners the right to share in unusual profits earned by the firm. The participation formula is clearly spelled out, and formula details vary with the particular issue. The most common formula provides preferred owners an extra dividend equal to the amount of the common stock dividend that exceeds the regular preferred dividend. Thus, if a participating preferred stock has a $7.50 dividend and the firm pays a common dividend of $9.00, the preferred would receive an extra $1.50 ($9.00 − $7.50) per share. Such features are very rare, however.

Voting rights

Preferred stocks frequently possess *contingent* voting rights. Voting rights are contingent in that they only vest when the firm is in arrears on preferred dividends by a specified amount. The New York Stock Exchange will only list preferred stocks that provide contingent voting rights after the firm has accumulated the equivalent of six quarters of arrearages. Contingent voting rights give the preferred owners (as a group) either the same voting privilege as common stockholders or the right to elect a stipulated number of directors.

Advantages of issuing preferred stock

By advantages we mean advantages to the firm and, ultimately, the common stockholders. Basically, there are four purported attractive features about preferred stock.

Leverage with no default risk   Preferred dividends are a prior, fixed obligation relative to earnings, which creates financial leverage, but if the firm omits a dividend payment or a sinking fund payment, the preferred stockholders cannot force the firm into bankruptcy. That is, there is no default risk as there is with debt. Firms make every effort to meet their preferred obligations on schedule, and failure to do so will adversely affect the common stock price, but the consequences are not as severe as when the firm misses scheduled debt charges.

Cash flow flexibility   Because preferred has no maturity date (unlike debt) and because of the firm's discretionary power to omit scheduled preferred obligations, the firm has some flexibility with regards to cash flow. If cash flow is particularly low the firm may choose to omit a preferred dividend, for example. Also, the firm can choose to retire preferred when it has sufficient financial resources to do so, as opposed to having to meet a contractual maturity date that may occur at a time when its financial resources are limited.

Preservation of stockholder control In comparison to issuing new common stock, preferred stock does not diminish the current stockholder's control position. Frequently the financing choice is between new common or new preferred because the firm feels it cannot safely service more debt. Issuing preferred increases the equity base but does not dilute the control (proportionate ownership) position of current common owners because preferred carries no normal voting rights.

Tax advantage in mergers and acquisitions In recent years many firms have effectively used convertible preferred stock in their merger and acquisition activities. This practice has been very popular because of the structure of U.S. tax laws. If the common stockholders of a company that is being acquired sell their stock for cash or exchange it for bonds of the acquiring company, they will incur an immediate capital gains tax on the difference between the price received on their stock and their original cost basis. However, if the acquiring firm issues convertible preferred stock to the common owners of the acquired firm, the transaction is exempt from the capital gains tax described above. The tax is deferred until the preferred is sold. We discuss this and other aspects of merger and acquisition activity more fully in Chapter 21.

Disadvantages of issuing preferred stock

Many finance people argue that while preferred stock is perceived by common stockholders as being debt (because preferred dividends are paid before common dividends), preferred has none of the advantages of debt. Unlike interest payments on debt, preferred dividends are not tax deductible. At today's 48-percent tax rate a dollar of interest expense costs the firm only $0.52 after tax, while a dollar of preferred dividends costs a dollar after tax. This results in the cost of debt being less than the cost of preferred (recall Chapter 8). Since preferred is viewed as debt by the stockholders but does not have the tax deductibility advantage of debt, many firms consider preferred to be one of the worst kinds of financing alternatives available.

COMMON STOCK

The common stockholders are the owners of the firm. We established in Chapter 1 that the goal of the firm was to maximize common stockholders' wealth, and the emphasis throughout this book is on making financial management decisions that are consistent with that goal. In this portion of the chapter we investigate what rights common stockholders have and the advantages and disadvantages of the firm issuing new common stock. Recall that common stock has no maturity date.

Prerogatives of common stockholders

Common owners basically have two sets of prerogatives:

1. Claim prerogatives.
2. Control prerogatives.

Claim prerogatives describe the common stockholder's claim on the firm's income and assets. Common stockholders are *residual* owners, which means that their claims on the firm's income and assets are residual claims. That is, they are last in line to receive either normal income or asset dissolution proceeds. Control prerogatives describe what rights the common stockholders have with respect to selecting the firm's board of directors, examining the firm's books, voting on certain major issues – such as proposed mergers – and maintaining their proportionate ownership.

Claim prerogatives

As noted above, the common stockholder is a residual claimant. This residual ownership claim may be thought of as having two distinct aspects. First, there is the *income* claim in normal times when the firm is viewed as a going concern. Second, there is the *asset* claim when the firm is contemplating dissolution for reasons of failure, or of acquisition by or merger with another company, or simply discontinuance of the firm.

Income claims With the firm as an ongoing entity, the common stockholder's income claim is through the dividend paid by the firm. The residual status of this claim is clear. The firm must first pay its operating expenses, that is, the expenses associated with performing its basic operating activities. The firm next pays its interest expenses and its tax liabilities. If the firm has preferred stock outstanding, it must also pay preferred dividends. The resultant residual, the firm's *earning available for common*, are available for distribution to the common stockholders as dividends. Thus, the common owners are at the end of a long line of income claimants. Moreover, the firm is not obligated to pay earnings out as dividends. It may decide to retain either all or a portion of earnings for investment purposes. Although we presume that the firm will adopt a dividend policy with the best interests of the stockholder in mind, common stock dividends are not mandatory, and the firm's management has discretionary power over dividend policy. This further emphasizes the residual status of the common owner's income claim.

This residual claimant status helps explain why common ownership is risky even when the firm is viewed as an ongoing entity. If the firm experiences poor or even mediocre earnings results, there is really nothing left for the common stockholder, and the common stock price and stockholder wealth will suffer. On the other hand, however, if the firm experiences good earnings results, the common owners' residual claimant position works to their advantage because they are the sole recipient of the favorable residual profits. In good times the firm's common stock price will increase and stockholders' wealth will increase. Since the mid-1920s rates of return on common stock investments in major U.S. companies have averaged about 9 percent per year, which is higher than the rates of return on investment in these same companies' bonds or preferred stock.[2] However, investments in common stock have also been riskier. Common stock ownership is thus characterized by high expected return and high risk relative to fixed income investments.

Asset claims Dissolution can occur because of failure, business combination, or through a decision to terminate the business by selling all assets. Common stockholders are also residual claimants with respect to the firm's assets in dissolution. All other claimants are in front of the common stockholders. In business combination and termination proceedings the stockholders typically receive some sort of proceeds from sale of assets. However, in bankruptcy proceedings, the residual status of the common position usually means that common owners receive nothing in either a liquidation or reorganization.

Control prerogatives

Corporate control has different meanings to different people, but a general definition is that corporate control means having the power to determine the broad policies of the firm. From a financial perspective, control means having the power to establish the major financial management policies of the firm. Control of the routine operations of the firm naturally rests with the firm's management, but major decisions, like issuing new common stock or debt or making a major investment are approved by the company's board of directors. Consequently, control may be more narrowly defined as the power to elect a majority of the firm's directors. This power is *legally* vested in the common stockholders. If management ignores the owners' interests, the owners can always vote the management out of office. Such happenings are rare, but prolonged periods of poor profitability can and do lead to replacement of management, if not by the firm itself, then by irate stockholders.

The control prerogatives of the common stockholders are principally their voting rights and their right to preserve their proportionate ownership position. We will look at both of these privileges in some detail. In addition, the common owners have the right to examine the firm's books. This latter right is important in cases where stockholders are attempting to overthrow the firm's management, but gaining access to the books usually requires a law suit where the stockholders must show a valid reason for examining the books. Similarly, stockholders have the right to secure the names and addresses of fellow stockholders to seek support for such activities. These rights are very important where battles for control of the firm are waged, but in normal times are unimportant privileges.

---

[2] In the most recent decade, however, common stock rates of return have been much lower.

Voting rights

Normally, there are two kinds of proposals that must be voted on by common owners. First, any change in the corporation's charter must be voted on. An example of such a change would be to increase the number of shares authorized by the firm. Authorized shares represent the maximum number of shares the firm may issue. However, the firm does not need stockholder approval to issue authorized but unissued shares. Similarly, any business combination proposal that would change the charter, such as a merger, requires stockholder approval. Second, the election of directors of the board requires a stockholder vote.

Electing directors

Directors are elected at the firm's annual meeting; however, in large corporations only a relatively few stockholders attend the meeting. To ensure that all bona fide stockholders are allowed to exercise their voting privilege, *proxies* are used. A proxy is a written authorization that empowers another to vote for the signer. Prior to the annual meeting the firm's management will solicit proxies from the stockholders for director candidates that management has nominated. In normal times when things are proceeding smoothly for the company, the stockholders will return their signed proxies and the nominated candidates will be elected. There are other times, however, when a group of stockholders may wish to elect directors that have not been nominated by the firm. This situation may arise because the firm's profitability has declined and some of the stockholders feel that the candidates proposed by management will do little to improve conditions.

Alternatively, there may be a takeover bid by some outsiders who wish to gain control of the firm. Or some group of stockholders may wish to place a member of their group on the board of directors to champion their interests. These situations lead to occasionally rigorous battles for votes called *proxy fights*. Accordingly, it is interesting to examine the nature of the election procedures.

The key point to remember in director elections is that stockholders receive one vote per share of stock for each board vacancy. If, for example, Battle Co. is electing four new board members and you own 100 shares of their common stock, you get (100 × 4) 400 votes in the election. There are two kinds of voting plans used in electing directors: *majority* voting and *cumulative* voting. These methods are best explained with an example.

Assume that Battle Co.'s charter provides that the company shall have four elected board members with elections held annually. Management has nominated four candidates: A, B, C, and D, and there are 1,000 shares of common outstanding. Assume further that a dissident minority of stockholders has nominated their own slate of candidates: W, X, Y, and Z. Let us further presume that the dissident group, realizing its minority status, would be satisfied to capture one of the four positions. How many shares would a minority group need to elect one of their men? The answer depends on the method of voting employed.

Majority voting   First, notice that with four vacancies and 1,000 shares outstanding there are a total of 4,000 eligible votes. Under majority voting, stockholders may cast no more votes for any one candidate than they have shares. Thus, if you own 100 shares of Battle, you receive (100×4) 400 votes, but you may cast no more than 100 votes for any one candidate. This system of casting no more than one vote per share per candidate favors the voting majority, in that the majority can ensure that *all* of its candidates will be elected. The minority will be shut out! Suppose, for example, that the majority group controls proxies for 700 shares and the minority group controls proxies for the other 300 shares. The majority would cast a vote for A, B, C, and D for each share they control and the minority group would cast a vote for W, X, Y, and Z for each share they control. If all shares are voted, the election results will be as follows:

				Candidate					
	A	B	C	D	W	X	Y	Z	Total
Majority votes	700	700	700	700	0	0	0	0	2,800
Minority votes	0	0	0	0	300	300	300	300	1,200
Total votes...	700	700	700	700	300	300	300	300	4,000

All the majority candidates are elected and the minority group is shut out even though they own 30 percent of the firm's stock. The majority can shut out the minority so long as they control more than 50 percent of the vote.[3] Because the majority can control all directorships with substantially less than 100-percent ownership, cumulative voting has come into widespread usage.

Cumulative voting   A cumulative voting system does not restrict the number of votes a stockholder may cast for any one candidate to the number of shares he owns: the only restriction is the number of *votes* he owns. A stockholder may cast *all* of his votes for only one candidate if he chooses. Looking at the previous Battle Co. example, let us continue, assuming that the minority group is primarily interested in not being shut out. They would consider it a victory if they elected one of their men. How many shares must they control to insure election of one board member?

The answer to this question is given by a formula that determines the minimum number of shares the minority group must control to guarantee election of any given number of directors:

$$\text{Minimum number of shares needed to elect a desired number of directors} = \frac{\left(\begin{array}{c}\text{Total shares}\\\text{outstanding}\end{array}\right)\left(\begin{array}{c}\text{Number of}\\\text{directors desired}\end{array}\right)}{\left(\begin{array}{c}\text{Total number of}\\\text{directors to be elected}\end{array}\right) + 1} + 1$$

---

[3] This presumes all majority group members exercise their vote. Many stockholders never take time to vote and a fairly strong and well-organized minority group can win an election.

Or, put more compactly in symbols:

$$r = \frac{(S)(d)}{D+1} + 1 \tag{13–1}$$

In the example:

$$r = \frac{(1{,}000)(1)}{4+1} + 1 = 201 \text{ shares}$$

Thus, to elect one director the minority group needs to control at least 201 shares. Since they control 300 shares they should be able to get one person in. Notice that in order to elect *two* directors ($d = 2$) they must control:

$$r = \frac{(1{,}000)(2)}{4+1} + 1 = 401 \text{ shares}$$

This means that the minority can gain 50-percent representation on the board with only 40.1 percent (401/1,000) of the shares.

Actually, the minority group may be able to elect directors with fewer shares than are indicated by Equation (13–1). In Equation (13–1), S is defined as total shares *outstanding*. Not all stockholders exercise their vote, and a more realistic definition of S is total shares *voting*. Suppose, for example, that only 95 percent of the firms 1,000 shares are voted. Then the number of minority shares required to elect one director is:

$$r = \frac{(950)(1)}{4+1} + 1 = 191 \text{ shares}$$

If the minority group has a rough approximation of how many shares it controls, it can determine the maximum number of directors it can elect by rearranging Equation (13–1) to solve for d.

$$d = \frac{(r-1)(D+1)}{S} \tag{13–2}$$

If we assume that the minority owns 300 shares of stock and that only 95 percent of the total stock will be voted, the maximum number of minority directors that can be elected is:

$$d = \frac{(299)(5)}{950} = 1.57$$

Since fractional directors are not permitted we round down and find that with 300 shares and 95-percent voting turnout the minority group can elect at most one director.

We can also note that the company can thwart the intent of cumulative voting procedures by either reducing the size of the board or only electing a *portion* of the board each year. In the Battle example, suppose that directors are elected for two-year terms and that the terms are staggered so that two directors are elected each year. To elect one director the minority group must now control (assuming a 95-percent vote):

$$r = \frac{(950)(1)}{2+1} + 1 = 317.67 = 318 \text{ shares}$$

If the minority group controls only 300 shares, they will be unsuccessful in their efforts.

Cumulative voting is a somewhat controversial voting method intended to provide minority representation on boards of directors. Most states permit it if the corporation chooses to use it; some states require it, and some forbid it. Cumulative voting is only used in voting for directors.

Preemptive rights

A preemptive right is a provision in the company's charter that grants the stockholder the right to purchase new common stock the firm issues in the same proportion as his current ownership. Thus, if a stockholder owns 10 percent of the firm's common stock, a preemptive right would give him the opportunity to buy 10 percent of new common issued. He may, of course, decline to exercise his right. A right is an option to buy shares of common stock at a specified price (called the *subscription price*) during a specified period of time, usually two to four weeks.

Offering terms and procedures One of the key features to remember in a rights offering is that each share of current stock receives one right. If there are 4 million shares of ABC Co. common outstanding, and the company has a rights issue, there will be 4 million rights issued. This guarantees proportionate ownership protection. If a stockholder owns 40,000 shares of ABC common, which represents a 1-percent ownership position, he will receive 40,000 rights, which will entitle him to buy 1 percent of the new stock issued.

The recipients of the rights are the firm's current stockholders, and they have three alternatives with respect to their rights:

1. Exercise the rights and buy new stock.
2. Sell the rights.
3. Do nothing.

Option one permits them to maintain proportionate ownership, which is the primary purpose of the rights offering. Option two permits stockholders to sell their rights should they not desire to maintain their ownership percentage. As we will see below, only the third option will hurt the current stockholders.

The *subscription price* is the price at which new stock is sold in a right issue. It is set below the current market price to ensure that the new shares of common will be sold. If the stock's market price ever got below the subscription price, investors would buy stock on the secondary market rather than new common stock through the rights issue. The subscription price determines how many shares of new common stock will be issued. Let's look at an example. The ABC Co. has 4 million shares of common stock outstanding with a market price of $60 per share. It needs to raise $20 million for investment purposes and has decided to sell new common through a rights issue. ABC's management has set the subscription price at $40 per share. Knowing this information we can readily determine: (1) the number of new shares of common that ABC will issue, (2) the number of rights required to buy a new share, and (3) the cost of a new share to investors.

(1)
$$\text{Number of new shares issued} = \frac{\text{New funds raised}}{\text{Subscription price}}$$

$$= \frac{\$20,000,000}{\$40 \text{ per share}} = 500,000 \text{ shares}$$

ABC is raising $20 million by selling stock at a price of $40 per share. This requires the firm to issue 500,000 new shares of stock. The number of shares of stock outstanding after the rights issue is closed will therefore be (4,000,000 + 500,000) 4,500,000 shares.

(2)
$$\frac{\text{Number of rights}}{\text{per new share}} = \frac{\text{Number of rights issued}}{\text{Number of new shares}}$$

$$= \frac{4,000,000 \text{ rights}}{500,000 \text{ shares}} = 8 \text{ rights per share}$$

Since there are 4 million rights issued, and a half million new shares will be sold, it will take eight rights to claim a new share of stock. Recall the investor who owns 40,000 shares of ABC stock, which is 1 percent of the company's original 4 million shares. He will receive 40,000 rights. These rights will entitle him to buy (40,000/8) 5,000 shares of new stock, which is 1 percent of the 500,000 new shares.

(3)
$$\text{Cost of a new share} = \frac{\text{Subscription}}{\text{price}} + \frac{\text{number of rights}}{\text{per new share}}$$

$$= \$40 + 8 \text{ rights}$$

The total cost of a new share of stock is the subscription price plus the number of rights per new share required. A stockholder who wishes to exercise his rights will remit this total cost to the firm. In the ABC case, this is $40 + eight rights per new share. In the example of the investor who owns 40,000 shares of ABC, he has the opportunity to buy 5,000 new shares at $40 per share. If he chooses to exercise all his rights he must remit $200,000 + 40,000 rights to ABC.

Value of rights and stock

Should a stockholder not wish to exercise all or a part of his rights he may sell them. Until the time they expire rights are sold on the secondary market just like the firm's stock. This leads to the valuation question of what the rights will sell for (what they are worth) on the market. Closely related to this issue is the question of the value of the stock, both before and after the rights issue.

In the valuation work we are preparing to do there are three distinct values to consider:

1. market value of "stock rights on."
2. market value of "stock ex rights."
3. market value of rights.

The reason for there being three valuation entities arises from the procedures of the rights issue. These procedures are probably best explained by an example.

ABC Co. announces on April 5 that all "holders of record" as of May 10 will have rights mailed to them on May 30.[4] All rights must be exercised by June 30. May 10 is the holder of record date, but it takes some time to transfer stock ownership. Suppose Mr. Brown owns 2,000 shares of ABC stock. If he sells his 2,000 shares of ABC stock on May 9 to Mr. Smith, for example, there would not be enough time to replace Brown's name with Smith's on the company's records, and while Smith actually owns the ABC stock on May 10, Brown would be the holder of record as of May 10, and ABC would send Brown the 2,000 rights. These rights can subsequently be sold in the market and thus are worth something. To avoid such problems the securities industry has worked out the following procedure. Four trading days before the holder of record date the stock sells *ex rights*. That is, the buyer of the stock is clearly notified that he is buying the stock *without* (ex) the rights attached. In the ABC case, if a sale is made on or prior to May 6, the buyer buys the stock *rights on* (with rights attached) since there will be enough time to get the buyer's name on the ownership record before the holder of record date. Any stock sale made between May 7 and June 30 (the expiration date of the rights) is made *ex rights* (without rights attached). When Smith buys on May 9 he receives the stock ex rights. The rights trade on the market as a separate security while they are in existence. The timing of this procedure is shown in Figure 13–1.[5]

FIGURE 13–1
Important dates of ABC's rights issue

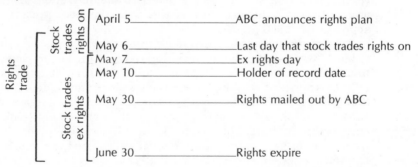

In addition to showing the important dates associated with ABC's rights issue, Figure 13–1 also shows how the stock is "divided" on the ex rights day into two distinct parts: the stock ex rights and the rights. As we will see immediately below, the market price of a share of stock

---

[4] A "holder of record" is anyone shown on the firm's ownership records as owning (holding) the stock.

[5] As Figure 13–1 shows, the rights are actually traded in the market *before* they are physically issued by the firm. They are traded in such instances on a *when issued* basis.

rights on is approximately equal to the sum of the market price of a share of the same stock ex rights plus the market price of the rights required to buy one new share of stock.

Value of stock rights on When a firm declares it is selling new stock through a rights issue (or through a direct sale to the public) investors are generally aware that something is "going on" at the company. Either the company is undertaking new major investments and needs the new capital to finance these investments or the firm is refinancing: retiring one form of capital and replacing it with another. Typically the firm releases information as to why new stock is being issued. Investors (the market) will evaluate this new information, and the value of the stock may increase if the market feels that the firm has uncovered some profitable new investments. Alternatively, the stock price may stay at approximately the same level, or even drop if the market evaluates the new information adversely. In any event, opinions about value may change as new information is released to the market.

Referring back to Figure 13–1, we may safely assume that any new information concerning the events leading to the ABC rights issue has been digested by the market between April 5, the announcement date, and May 6, the day before the ex rights day. For illustrative purposes, assume that ABC stock sold for $60 per share before April 5 and on May 6 is still selling for $60 per share. There have been some relatively minor fluctuations over that time period as the ABC stock price ranged from $59\frac{1}{2}$ to $60\frac{3}{8}$, but basically, the stock has been steady. Evidently, investors' opinions about the value of the stock have not changed given the new information they received about ABC's $20 million investment plans.

The stock price prior to the ex rights date is called the *stock price rights on*. It is what the stock is worth in the market on any given day prior to the ex rights day. In the ABC case, the stock price rights on is approximately $60 per share.

Value of stock ex rights Any stock transaction among investors prior to May 7 will transfer the forthcoming rights to the buyer. However, any transaction made on May 7 or later (up to the June 30 expiration date) will not transfer the rights to the buyer. Since the rights have value — they permit the owner to buy shares of new stock at a bargain price (the subscription price) — the market price of the outstanding stock will fall on the ex rights date. This decline in stock price merely reflects that the rights, which have value, are no longer transferred to the buyer. Thus, the stock price ex rights will normally be lower than the stock price rights on. Of course, if some "good news" about the company is received by the market around the ex rights date, or if the stock market rises substantially on the ex rights date, the stock price ex rights could exceed the stock price rights on.

The question we address here is: What is the value of the stock ex rights? We can answer that question two ways. First, we can consider what is really happening to the firm's equity position. Let's do this by continuing the ABC example. Before the rights offering, recall that ABC has 4 million shares of common outstanding. Before the ex rights date these shares are selling for $60 per share. Recall further that ABC is issuing 500,000 new shares through the rights issue at a price of $40 per share. The ex rights stock price will be approximately equal to the weighted average of these prices, where the weights are the relative numbers of old and new shares. At the end of the rights issue there will be 4.5 million shares outstanding, and the stock price ex rights should theoretically reflect the mixture of old and new stock weighted for percentages of this total 4.5 million shares. Under this approach the stock ex rights should be:

$$P_x = W_o P_o + W_s P_s \qquad (13\text{--}3)$$

where

P_x = stock price ex rights, P_o = stock prices rights on, P_s = subscription price, W_o = number of old shares per number of total shares; and W_s = number of new shares per number of total shares.

In the ABC example:

$$P_x = \left(\frac{4,000,000}{4,500,000}\right)(\$60) + \left(\frac{500,000}{4,500,000}\right)(\$40)$$
$$P_x = (0.889)(\$60) + (0.111)(\$40) = \$53.34 + \$4.44$$
$$P_x = \$57.78$$

That is, the ABC stock price ex rights should be approximately $57.78.

Equation (13–3) requires that we know the weights W_o and W_s and hence the number of old and new shares. This information may not be immediately available, and many analysts prefer and are more familiar with an alternate formula, which gives the same answer as (13–3):

$$P_x = \frac{(P_o)(N) + P_s}{N + 1} \qquad (13\text{--}4)$$

where

N = number of rights required to buy one new share of stock. Recall that for the ABC example, $N = 8$.

$$P_x = \frac{(\$60 \times 8) + \$40}{8 + 1} = \$57.78$$

We must emphasize that these calculations only represent approximations of theoretical calculations. New information about the company may become available during the rights issue, or market conditions may change, or the formula calculations may be poor approximations.

Value of rights The third value we consider is the value of the rights themselves. The rights have value because they permit investors to buy stock at the subscription price, which is lower than the market price of the stock ex rights. In the ABC issue, an investor can buy one share of new stock for $40 plus eight rights. But this stock is theoretically worth $57.78 after the ex rights date. This implies that the eight rights together must be worth ($57.78 − $40) $17.78. Consequently, each right must be separately worth ($17.78/8) $2.22. And, this makes intuitive sense. On the ex rights date the stock price drops $2.22 from the rights on price of $60 to the ex rights price of $57.78. And this drop of $2.22 is exactly the value of the right. What has occurred, *in effect,* is that the stock value has been split into two parts, the stock ex right and the right itself, and the summed value of these two parts equals the original value of the stock ($57.78 + $2.22 = $60).

There are also formulas for calculating the value of the rights. Since the rights trade on the market both before and after the ex rights date there are two separate formulas, one for calculating the value of a right when the stock is selling rights on and one for calculating the value of a right when the stock is selling ex rights.

When the stock is selling rights on, the value of a right, R_o, is:

$$R_o = \frac{P_o - P_s}{N + 1} \tag{13-5}$$

For ABC:

$$R_o = \frac{\$60 - \$40}{8 + 1} = \$2.22$$

When the stock is selling ex rights, the value of a rights, R_x, is:

$$R_x = \frac{P_x - P_s}{N} \tag{13-6}$$

For ABC:

$$R_x = \frac{\$57.78 - \$40}{8} = \$2.22$$

These answers all agree and are all subject to the previous warning about either a reevaluation of the firm's stock by investors reacting to new information or changing market conditions. The calculations for stock and rights values are all only approximations under the assumption that future conditions in the market will be approximately the same as current conditions.

Effect of rights issue on stockholder wealth

Given the firm's goal of stockholder wealth maximization, and the fact that a rights issue causes stock price to decline on the ex rights date (from $60 to $57.78 in the ABC case), it may seem at first glance that the rights issue has a detrimental effect on stockholder wealth. Actually, the stockholder should not be harmed, unless he is negligent and lets the rights expire. Recall that a stockholder has three options with regards to his rights: (1) he may exercise them and buy new stock, or (2) he may sell them, or (3) he may do nothing and let them expire. Only in the last case will the stockholder be harmed.

Figure 13-2 illustrates these conclusions. It shows what happens to an investor who owns eight shares of ABC stock worth $480 before the rights issue. He receives eight rights, which is just enough to buy one new share. If he exercises the rights the current value of his original wealth remains at $480 although he now has increased his total investment in ABC to $520. If he sells the rights he likewise protects the current value of his original wealth, but he has decreased his investment in ABC to $462.24. Only if he does nothing has he lost money, and the expected loss would be the value of the rights, $17.76. In almost every

FIGURE 13–2
Effect of rights issue on stockholder wealth

Alternative 1: Exercise the rights

Tenders 8 rights + $40 for 1 new share

Owns 9 shares at $57.78 per share	= $520
Less $40 investment cost	= −40
Current value of original wealth	= $480

Alternative 2: Sell the rights

Sell 8 rights at $2.22 per right	= $ 17.76
Owns 8 shares at $57.78 per share	= 462.24
Current value of original wealth	= $480.00

Alternative 3: Do nothing

Owns 8 shares at $57.78 per share	= $462.24
Current value of original wealth	= $462.24

Assumptions: An investor has eight shares of ABC stock. Original wealth of the investor = 8 shares at $60 per share = $480.

rights issue some stockholders, because of negligence, neither exercise nor sell their rights.

Setting the subscription price

One of the decisions the firm's management must make in a rights issue is what the subscription price should be. Obviously the subscription price should be set below the current market price of the common, otherwise investors would prefer to buy the less expensive "old" stock on the secondary market rather than "new" stock via the rights issue. The new stock would never be sold, and the firm would have failed to raise new capital. So the subscription price is always set below the current stock price. How much below? If the firm sets the subscription price too close to the current stock price, a drop in stock price, for whatever reason, could cause the stock price to be below subscription price and the issue would fail. The safe thing is to set the subscription price well below current stock price. Some argue that this is a questionable practice, because by setting a low subscription price, the number of new shares increases and the firms earnings per share are diluted. Consequently, the stock price declines more than it otherwise would. While this is a somewhat popular view there seems to be no evidence to support it. The more important issue is ensuring that the rights issue is fully subscribed, and this is heavily influenced by the size of the spread between market price and subscription price: The larger the spread, the more probable that all rights will be exercised.

Advantages and disadvantages of rights issues

There are two primary advantages to issuing common stock through a rights issue. First, the stockholders' control position is protected, as they can maintain their proportionate ownership if they wish. This has most meaning in firms where there is a struggle for control. In normal times, if the firm sells stock directly to the public rather than through a rights issue, an investor can always maintain his percentage ownership position by either buying new stock when it is issued or else by buying stock on the open market. It would only be in stress times that an investor may have trouble in buying stock. In such times the preemptive rights privilege protects proportionate ownership positions. A second advantage to selling new stock through a rights issue is the lower floatation cost. In comparison to a straight public issue, the rights issue has a lower floatation cost because there is usually no underwriting fee in the rights issue, although many rights issues do have *standby* underwriting arrangements where investment bankers will buy all unsubscribed shares. The less sure the firm's management is that most of the rights will be exercised, the more likely they will seek out a standby underwriting arrangement. The standby arrangement increases floatation costs as it incurs underwriting fees.

The primary disadvantage of a rights issue is that it creates losses to forgetful stockholders. Some firms overcome this by selling the rights of these negligent shareholders at the end of the rights sale and remitting the proceeds to them.

Advantages and disadvantages of common stock financing

As we have seen, when new common stock is issued it may be placed privately, it may be sold to the public through an underwriter, or it may be sold through a preemptive rights offering. Whatever the mode of issue, the end result is that there is new common stock outstanding. In comparison to other forms of long-term financing there are certain advantages and disadvantages of issuing common stock.

Advantages   One advantage of issuing new common stock is that, unlike interest payments, the firm is not required to pay common dividends. This is most crucial when the firm's cash flow levels are low. A skipped interest payment may lead to bankruptcy, but a skipped dividend payment will not. To be sure, stockholders will be unhappy with an omitted or reduced dividend, and the stock price will suffer, but the resulting decline in stock price would not be as severe when a dividend is cut as when an interest payment is not met. So the fact that dividend payments are not legal obligations gives the firm some flexibility, which is particularly important in difficult times.

In the same context, since common stock has no maturity date there is no obligation to ever redeem the stock. Firms occasionally do repurchase stock (See Chapter 11), but they do so when they have the cash available, at a time of their own choosing. Debt, on the other hand, does have a maturity date, and the firm must have cash for redemption on that date. If the firm cannot meet its redemption obligation it may be forced into bankruptcy. The fact that common stock has no maturity date adds flexibility to the firm's cash flow management operations. If the firm chooses to repurchase stock, it can do so under favorable conditions, at its discretion.

Last, addition of common stock to the firm's capital structure enhances the *future* borrowing capacity of the firm. Creditors prefer to
lend to firms with substantial equity bases, and new common stock increases this base. Future financing needs may come at a time when stock
prices are depressed to such low levels that management would not wish
to sell stock. But at the same time, debt financing may be very costly and/
or hard to get because the firm has too much debt relative to its equity
base. At such times the firm may well wish it had financed earlier with
equity when it had the chance.

Disadvantages Most new common issues, even when accomplished
through a rights issue, bring in new owners. The old owners may feel
this control dilution is a disadvantage, although as long as their right to
proportionate ownership is protected this would not seem an important
criticism.[6] Another frequent stockholder complaint is that since there
now are more shares outstanding the earnings per share will be less and
stock price will decline. But this is a short-sighted view. The funds received by the stock sale are invested by the firm, and presumably these
investments have positive expected net value. By definition such investments should *increase* stock price. Of course, if the investments turn
out bad, the stock price will suffer, but *not* because new stock was issued.
Stock price will suffer because the investments turn out bad.

It is true, however, that it is more expensive to issue stock than alternate long-term instruments. We saw in Chapter 12 that floatation
costs associated with common stock are high because of the risk involved. Also, we saw in Chapter 8 that equity has the highest explicit
cost of capital. The practice of *underpricing* new stock (setting the
selling price below current market price of the outstanding stock) further
increases this cost.

SUMMARY

In this chapter we continued our study of long-term financing sources.
Preferred stock and common are both legal equity-ownership instruments, but the differences between the two are perhaps more important
than the similarities.

Preferred stock has a *priority* status over common with respect to
income and asset claims. This makes preferred stock a safer security.
Preferred is similar to debt in that it is a fixed income security. Because
of this similarity to debt, preferred is called a *hybrid* security. Unlike
creditors, however, preferred stockholders cannot force the firm into
bankruptcy. Preferred holders main protection is the *cumulative dividend* clause. While preferred has no maturity date, the firm can provide
for retirement of preferred stock in future years by issuing the stock as
convertible preferred or by calling the stock at its *call price* or through a
sinking fund arrangement. The purported advantages of preferred stock
are that it offers leverage with no default risk, it provides cash flow

---

[6] An exception might be where original owners cannot raise the money to maintain their
desired percentage ownership. Figure 13–2 illustrates that to keep a proportionate ownership
position the investor must *increase* his total investment in the firm.

flexibility, it does not dilute stockholder control, and it affords tax advantages in business combination activities. Offsetting these advantages is the fact that common stockholders view preferred as being equivalent to debt, but preferred dividends are not tax deductible like interest charges. That is, preferred looks like debt, but costs more.

Common stockholders have only a residual claimant position both with regard to income claims and asset claims. The primary control prerogatives of common owners are their right to elect the board of directors and their right to maintain proportionate ownership. In electing directors two methods are employed in the United States. *Majority* voting limits the number of ballots an investor may cast for any one candidate to the number of shares he owns. Under majority voting it is very difficult for a minority group to elect any directors. *Cumulative* voting allows stockholders to cast all their votes for one candidate and makes it easier for minority groups to elect directors.

New common shares may be issued by a public sale through an investment banker, by a private placement, or via a *preemptive rights* issue. A preemptive rights issue gives current stockholders the right of first refusal to buy new stock and preserve their ownership percentage. Stockholders may exercise their rights and buy new stock or sell the rights or do nothing. Stock price will decline because of a rights issue, but only if stockholders are negligent and let their rights expire will they suffer a loss in wealth. The possibility of negligence is the primary disadvantage of a sale of new stock through rights, and the primary advantages are ownership protection and lower issue costs.

The main advantages of issuing new common (regardless of the means of doing so) are cash flow flexibility (since common dividends are not mandatory and common stock has no maturity date) and the enhancement of future borrowing capacity. The major disadvantage of common stock financing is its higher explicit cost of capital.

QUESTIONS

1. Define the following terms and phrases:
   a. Cumulative dividend feature.
   b. Call feature.
   c. Participation feature.
   d. Cumulative voting.
   e. Preemptive rights.
   f. Stock price rights on.
   g. Stock price ex rights.

2. Nine months ago Zeigler Products missed its regularly scheduled $2 per share preferred quarterly dividend payment because of severe cash flow problems. Three months later Zeigler missed another payment. Three months ago Zeigler was able to pay the regularly scheduled preferred dividend but was still in arrears two quarterly payments. Today, Zeigler not only paid its scheduled $2 per share preferred quarterly dividend but made up the arrearage by paying an additional $4 per share to preferred stock holders.

In announcing the extra payment Zeigler's president noted that its preferred stockholders have been "made whole again. Their loss is completely recouped." As a Zeigler preferred stockholder do you agree with this statement? Explain your answer.

3. Reilly Breweries issued some $100 par preferred stock five years ago. The stock has a call price of $104 per share. Reilly is now interested in retiring the stock. Indicate whether the company should attempt to buy back the stock in the open market or exercise the call feature if the current market price of the preferred is:
   a. $90
   b. $110
   c. $102
   d. $104

4. Preferred stock is frequently called a "hybrid" security. Explain what this means.

5. Many financial markets experts view preferred stock as an inferior financing alternative to debt.
   a. Explain their reasons for this conclusion.
   b. Discuss rebuttals to their position.

6. At the annual stockholders meeting an irate investor complains that the recent sale of stock via a rights issue sorely depressed the company's stock price. He loudly asks the treasurer to explain why the subscription price was set so low. As treasurer, how would you answer this question?

7. A company incorporated in a state where there is no requirement to use preemptive rights when common stock is sold is preparing to issue some new common stock. Management is deliberating about the good and bad features of a rights offering as opposed to a public offering of stock. How would the following circumstances influence the firm's choice? Explain your answer.
   a. The firm only reluctantly decided to sell new stock in the first place because the stock price is low relative to its historical level and to management's opinion of the "true" value of the stock.
   b. Two opposing groups of shareholders, who have entirely different views of how the firm should be managed, each own substantial amounts of stock. Either group would probably sue management if it thought that there were an inequitable distribution of shares.
   c. It would be advantageous to broaden the ownership of the stock by having more investors owning shares.
   d. The president of the firm would insist on a relatively high subscription price if a rights issue is employed.
   e. Current floatation costs are viewed as being very high by historical standards.

8. A dissident minority stockholder group is meeting to discuss their chances for placing a candidate on the firm's board of directors at the upcoming election. The firm's charter requires a cumulative

voting procedure, but a quick calculation indicates that the dissident group does not own a large enough percentage of the total shares outstanding to assure a successful election. Several members of the group point out, however, that they may still be in good shape.

a. What voting phenomenon are they counting on in making this assessment?

b. If the group is unwilling to be content with their chances of winning despite the phenomenon noted in (*a*), what action could they take to absolutely assure their success?

9. What are the main advantages and disadvantages of financing investments with common stock in comparison to debt or preferred stock?

PROBLEMS

1. Simkowitz Mobile Homes has an issue of 4-percent, $100 par preferred stock outstanding. However, the stock is two and one-half years in arrears on its dividends, and the preferred is selling for about $60 per share. Because of the arrearage, Simkowitz cannot pay common dividends and the common is trading for $6 per share. In the last few months the company's operations and financial affairs have been markedly improved, and the financial staff has been assigned the task of designing a plan to allow Simkowitz to pay common dividends. The staff has come up with two alternate plans.

Plan I: On the next quarterly preferred dividend date, make the scheduled dividend payment and also pay off the arrearage in full.

Plan II: Attempt to negotiate a settlement with the preferred stockholders. The company would swap ten shares of common plus $5 cash for each share of preferred.

If Plan I is adopted and the arrearage is paid in full, Simkowitz estimates that the preferred stock's price would increase to $70. At the same time, expectations of resumed common dividends would cause the common stock price, in Simkowitz's opinion, to increase to $8 per share. If Plan II is chosen, there is a 50–50 chance that the preferred stockholders would approve the swap. If the swap is approved, Simkowitz estimates that the firm's common stock will sell for $9 per share. If the swap is not approved, the firm will go ahead and pay the arrearage in full.

a. Calculate the amount of arrearage owed and the per share regularly scheduled preferred dividend due on the next payment date.

b. Assuming Simkowitz's estimates are reasonably accurate, which plan is better (1) from the common stockholders' viewpoint? (2) from the preferred stockholders' viewpoint?

c. Since preferred stockholders do not have access to Simkowitz's estimates but only have today's observed market prices, would they prefer that the arrearage be made up or a swap of ten shares of common plus $5 cash for their preferred?

2. The 5 percent, $100 par preferred stock of Rutgers Portland Cement has the following participation clause. If the total (aggregate) dollar amount of common dividends paid in any year ever exceeds the total (aggregate) dollar amount of preferred dividends paid in that year, the preferred stock is entitled to a participating dividend equal to 30 percent of the total (aggregate) dollar excess (over the total dollar preferred dividend) paid to the common. Determine the participating dividend per share the preferred stock would receive under the following conditions:

Situation	Number of shares common	Common dividend per share	Number of shares preferred
a...............	2,000,000	$3.00	1,000,000
b...............	2,000,000	$2.00	500,000
c...............	10,000,000	$2.50	2,000,000
d...............	5,000,000	$0.80	1,000,000

3. A proxy fight is in full swing at Red Flag Flour and Milling, and a dissident group of stockholders is contesting management's board of directors nominees.

   a. If there are 2 million shares outstanding, determine how many shares the dissident group must control to achieve their election objectives under the following conditions:

Situation	Election objectives (no. directorships desired)	Expected percentage of shares voted	Kind of voting	No. of board vacancies
1	1	100	cumulative	3
2	3	90	cumulative	3
3	3	90	majority	3
4	2	80	cumulative	4

   b. If there are 10,000 shares outstanding, determine the maximum number of directors the dissident group may elect assuming cumulative voting under the following conditions.

Situation	No. shares controlled	Expected percentage of shares voted	No. of board vacancies
1	1,800	100	4
2	1,800	80	4
3	1,800	80	3
4	3,000	80	5

4. Krogh Insurance Co. has four vacancies on its board of directors. A dissident group of stockholders is interested in capturing two of these vacancies. If cumulative voting is permitted, what is the critical percent of share ownership that the dissident group must exceed to guarantee that their two directors are elected?

5. Barnstormers, Inc., has common stock selling for $50 per share on the New York Stock Exchange. The company is planning a pre-emptive rights issue that will allow current stockholders to buy one new share at a price of $40 for every four shares held. Determine:
    a. The approximate value of the stock rights on.
    b. The approximate value of the stock ex rights.
    c. The approximate value of a right.

6. D and E Research Labs, Inc. has common stock selling for $20 per share. The company has 5 million shares currently outstanding and plans to issue 4 million new shares through a rights issue.
    a. What must the subscription price be to establish an $18 per share ex rights stock price?
    b. How many rights must be presented to buy one share of stock during the rights issue?
    c. What is the theoretical value of each right?
    d. What must an investor present to the firm to purchase a new share of stock? (That is, what is the cost of a new share?)
    e. What is the approximate market value of the answer to part (*d*)? How does this compare with the ex rights stock price?

7. New York Copper and Zinc (NYCZ) is preparing to raise $30 million through a rights issue. The firm needs the funds to finance new mineral deposit purchases. After public announcement of the deposit purchases NYCZ's stock price bounced around some, but has now steadied at about $35 per share. There are 10 million shares outstanding. Currently, NYCZ's financial staff is attempting to set the subscription price on the new stock. They have proposed two plans: Plan A's subscription price is $30. Plan B's price is $15.
    a. Assuming that both plans would be successful (in that all new shares were fully subscribed), determine the number of new shares issued under each plan.
    b. How many rights will be issued under each plan and how many rights will be required to purchase a new share of stock?
    c. What should be the ex rights price of the stock in each plan?
    d. What should be the value of a right in each plan?
    e. Which plan is preferable from a stockholder wealth maximization standpoint? Why?
    f. Which plan is preferable from the standpoint of ensuring that the issue will be fully subscribed? Why?
    g. Which plan would you recommend to NYCZ? Why?

8. The M. J. Lane Air Freight Company announced a rights offering on November 1, 19+0, for the purpose of raising $1.6 million to purchase new cargo carrying helicopters. The offer is made to holders of record on December 1, 19+0. The company currently has 1.4 million shares of common stock outstanding which is trading at $12 per share. The subscription price of the new stock has been set at $8 per share.
    a. Determine:
        (1) The number of new shares that must be sold.
        (2) The number of rights required to purchase one share.

        (3) The value of one right.

        (4) The ex rights price of the stock.

   b. On November 3, 19+0, the president of the M. J. Lane Company receives a phone call from an irate stockholder who owns 1,000 shares of stock. The stockholder maintains that he will suffer a loss in wealth due to the offering of new shares at a price lower than the current market price. The president assures the stockholder that the rights offering will not cause a wealth loss if the stockholder takes appropriate action. In addition, he promises to send the stockholder some data which will illustrate this point.

       Prepare a statement showing the effect of the rights issue on the stockholder's wealth assuming:

        (1) He exercises as many rights as possible and sells the rest.

        (2) He sells all of the rights.

        (3) He fails to do anything.

   c. Are there any "real world facts of life" that might lend support to the stockholder's claim? Explain.

SELECTED BASIC REFERENCES

Donaldson, G. "In Defense of Preferred Stock," *Harvard Business Review* (July–August 1962), pp. 123–36.

Elsaid, H. H. "The Function of Preferred Stock in the Corporate Financial Plan," *Financial Analysts Journal* (July–August 1969), pp. 112–17.

Fisher, D. E., and G. A. Wilt, Jr. "Nonconvertible Preferred Stock as a Financing Instrument, 1950–65," *Journal of Finance* (September 1968), pp. 611–24.

SELECTED ADVANCED REFERENCES

Bildersee, J. S. "Some Aspects of the Performance of Non-Convertible Preferred Stocks," *Journal of Finance* (December 1973), pp. 1187–1201.

Duvall, R. M., and D. V. Austin. "Predicting the Results of Proxy Contests," *Journal of Finance* (September 1965), pp. 467–71.

Nelson, J. R. "Price Effects in Rights Offerings," *Journal of Finance* (December 1965), pp. 647–60.

Stevenson, R. A. "Retirement of Non-Callable Preferred Stock," *Journal of Finance* (December 1970), pp. 1143–52.

14

DEBT AND LEASES

By accounting precepts the firm's liabilities are divided into short-term and long-term claims, the usual distinction between the two being that the former are due within a year while the latter are not. However, in financial literature there is frequently a finer distinction made among long-term liabilities. Finance often distinguishes between intermediate-term and long-term credit claims, where intermediate-term — somewhat ambiguously — usually connotes a period of time ranging from five to ten years. Because of this ambiguity and because of the fundamental similarity between intermediate and long-term liabilities, we will study both together in this chapter.

There are three major kinds of long- and intermediate-term credit financing available to the firm:

1. Bonds.
2. Term loans.
3. Leases.

These sources of creditor financing will be fully discussed below, but it is worth noting that in the standard finance taxonomy, bonds are usually considered a long-term source of capital, and term loans and leases are intermediate-term sources of capital.

BONDS

"Bond" is a generalized name given to long-term promises the firm issues to lenders, the nature of the promise being that the firm will pay bond principal and interest on specified dates in the future. Bonds are thus essentially long-term promissory notes.

There are many kinds of bonds and alternate ways to classify them. One particularly useful classification scheme uses the specific security feature of the bond. Bonds are either *secured* or *unsecured.* A secured bond has specific assets of the firm pledged as collateral. If the firm should default on scheduled payments, an appointed trustee can seize the specified collateral on behalf of the secured bondholders. Unsecured bonds have no specific assets pledged as collateral, and holders of these bonds are thus *general* creditors of the firm. If the firm should default, unsecured bondholders would look to those assets of the firm that are not pledged elsewhere to satisfy their claims.

Secured bonds

Mortgage bonds While any assets the firm owns may, in theory, be pledged as collateral, lenders frequently prefer the firm's fixed assets, particularly the land and buildings. *Mortgage bonds* are (most commonly) bonds with mortgages on the firm's fixed assets.

Sometimes the firm will support two bond issues with the same property. If one of such issues has a favored position it is called the *first* mortgage bonds. The less favored bonds are *second* mortgage bonds. First mortgage bonds have priority should default occur, and second mortgage holders cannot receive payment until all first mortgage claims are satisfied. Many bondholders prefer to own first mortgage bonds and tend to look somewhat suspiciously at seconds.

Equipment trust certificates Equipment trusts are not actually bonds but are leases secured by equipment. They work as follows. The firm orders equipment from a manufacturer and sells equipment trust certificates to investors to pay for the equipment. A trustee is established, who, on behalf of the investors, holds title to the equipment that secures the certificates. The firm makes periodic lease payments to the investors through the trustee. When the certificates mature they are retired (redeemed) by the firm and the trustee passes title to the equipment to the firm. Should the firm fail to meet its lease payment obligations, the trustee may seize the equipment on behalf of the investors. Equipment trust certificates have been extensively and successfully used by railroads in financing their railroad car purchases. Equipment trust certificates are also frequently used to finance the purchase of buses, trucks, and aircraft.

Many mortgage bonds have an *after acquired clause* which pledges *future* assets acquired by the firm to the bond issue. This creates future financing difficulties for the firm because the future assets that will be acquired are already pledged to a previous bond. However, since under an equipment trust certificate the firm does not actually buy assets but rather leases them, the assets leased cannot be pledged to the prior bond issue under its after acquired clause. Therefore, the firm can effectively pledge the new assets to the new lenders.

Collateral trust bonds Many firms own stocks and bonds of other corporations including their own subsidiaries. These marketable securities may be used to secure bonds of the issuing firm, and such bonds are called *collateral trust bonds.* The quality of the security is obviously dependent on the quality of the pledged stocks and bonds.

Unsecured bonds

Unsecured bondholders are general creditors of the firm. Unless the indenture agreement specifies otherwise (see the discussion of subordinated debentures below), the unsecured bondholders have an equal claim with other general creditors on the firm's unpledged assets.

Debentures *Debentures* are bonds that have no specific collateral pledged to them. They are unsecured long-term promissory notes. While asset security is important, in the final analysis it is the firm's earning power that mainly determines the attractiveness of bonds, since few investors would buy bonds of a company where the probability of default is very high. Consequently, many debentures enjoy high investment ratings and compare favorably with secured bonds. From the firm's standpoint, the main advantage of issuing debentures rather than secured bonds is that it preserves future borrowing capacity. Because no specific assets are pledged as security to debentures, other general creditors (such as suppliers and banks) will not have the priority of their claim status on the firm's assets impaired and will be more willing to extend credit.

Subordinated debentures If the firm's earning position is particularly strong, it may be able to sell *subordinated debentures.* These are debentures that are subordinated (or inferior to) in asset claim priority to some specified senior debt. This means that in event of failure, the subordinated debenture holders' claims will not be honored until the specified senior debt claims have been completely satisfied.

The subordination usually refers to outstanding mortgage bonds or other debentures, but it may also refer to bank credit or even all other senior debt. Because of the inferiority of the subordinated debentures' asset claim position, they receive lower investment ratings by bond rating services. That is, they are risky relative to other kinds of bonds, and only companies with substantial earning power could hope to persuade investors to buy them. As with straight debenture bonds, the main advantage to the firm of issuing this type of debt is that it preserves the firm's borrowing capacity with respect to other lenders.

Income bonds The other bonds we have discussed have mandatory interest schedules the firm must meet, but *income bonds* receive interest only when the firm has sufficient earnings to pay the interest. In bad times the firm could be forced into bankruptcy by failure to pay a scheduled interest payment on the normal kind of bond, but interest payments can be skipped with income bonds. These bonds are somewhat rare and are typically issued to creditors when a firm is reorganized under bankruptcy proceedings. The firm is trying to get back on its feet, and income bonds permit the firm some breathing room. There is usually a *cumulative clause* that permits income bondholders to recover omitted interest payments, and income bonds are senior in claim to subordinated debt and preferred and common stockholders.

Bond features

Some of the features associated with bonds we have already discussed. Basically, bonds are long-term, fixed income, creditor financial instruments.

Indenture agreement   The indenture agreement, known as the *trust* or *bond* indenture is a lengthy contract that establishes all the terms of the loan and the relationships between (1) the borrowing firm, (2) the bondholders, and (3) the indenture trustee. The indenture trustee is a disinterested third party, usually a trust company or bank, appointed to represent the interests of the bondholders. Because ownership of publicly held bonds of large corporations is diffuse, the trustee, who acts on behalf of all bondholders, can efficiently perform certain necessary functions. The major duties of the trustee are:

1.   To ascertain that all legal requirements pertaining to the bond issue have been satisfied by the issuing firm.
2.   To ensure that the firm meets all scheduled interest and principal payments and all other promises agreed upon in the trust indenture.
3.   To take appropriate action to protect the interests of the bondholders should the firm fail to comply with the trust indenture articles.

In effect, the trustee acts as legal representative, watchdog, and conservator for the bondholders.

Income claims   Bondholders are legal creditors of the firm and therefore have a prior claim on the firm's income relative to preferred and common stockholders. The firm must pay its interest obligations to bondholders before any dividends are paid. This income claim is a contractual obligation the firm must meet, and failure to do so can force the firm into bankruptcy.[1]

The amount of the interest payment is determined by the face value of the bond (usually $1,000 per bond) and the coupon rate (an annual interest rate). Typically, interest is paid semiannually. If, for example, a $1,000 bond has an 8-percent coupon rate and pays interest semiannually, bondholders will receive $80 per bond each year in two $40 payments (one each six months) during the bond's life. At maturity, the bondholder will receive the principal (face value). In the above example, bondholders would receive $1,000 per bond at maturity. The situation when bonds are redeemed prior to maturity is discussed below.

Asset claims   Bonds also have prior claim on the firm's assets relative to preferred and common stock. The exact nature of the priority status depends on the type of bond. Secured bonds look to the assets pledged to them. If their claim is still not satisfied, they then become general creditors with claims equal to, but not superior to, other general creditors. Subordinated debt claims, however, cannot be satisfied until the senior debt to which they have been subordinated is satisfied. Illustrations of these and other asset claims are given in Chapter 22.

---

[1] An exception to the mandatory, scheduled interest payment is the case of *income* bonds (discussed above) where interest is paid only if there are sufficient earnings to pay interest. Even in this case, though, interest payments have priority over dividends.

Maturity and redemption Unlike preferred and common stock, bonds have a specified *maturity* date. On the maturity date the firm pays the bondholders the principal of the bond plus any remaining interest due and redeems the bonds. In many instances, however, the bonds do not remain outstanding until the maturity date. Early redemption may be accomplished either by use of a *sinking fund* or through a *call provision*.

Sinking fund. A sinking fund is an actual cash reserve set up to provide early retirement of the bonds. The fund is usually under the control of the aforementioned indenture trustee. Periodic payments are made by the firm to the sinking fund and the payments can be used to retire some of the outstanding debt. Usually, the firm is permitted to use the sinking fund payments to retire bonds in the cheapest manner. The firm may either buy back bonds in the market or use the call provision. If interest rates have risen since time of issue, the market price of bonds will be below their face value. In such times the firm will prefer to use the sinking fund payment to buy bonds in the market. If interest rates have fallen substantially since time of issue, the market price of bonds will be substantially above their face value, and the firm will prefer to call the bonds, paying a premium over face value. This *call premium* is discussed below. Bonds so chosen for early retirement are selected by lottery.

In contrast to the methods described above, some sinking funds invest the periodic payments made by the firm into other securities, such as government bonds, and then use the accumulated investment proceeds to retire the firm's bonds at maturity. One of the main reasons that bondholders require a sinking fund provision is that it compels the firm to regularly set aside a portion of the principal repayment for the retirement of the debt. If no such payment were set aside, the firm would be required to pay off the entire debt principal at maturity. A large maturity date payment is called a *balloon payment*. If the maturity date came during bad economic times for the company, the firm could possibly have difficulty in making payment and the bondholder's principal would be jeopardized. A sinking fund mitigates this problem.

Call provision. The call provision enables the firm to prematurely retire debt by buying it back at a stipulated *call price*. The call price is above the bond's face value, the difference being the *call premium*. If interest rates have fallen, the firm may wish to call the outstanding debt and reissue new debt at a lower interest rate, thereby effecting interest savings in future years. This operation is called a *refunding* and is discussed in detail below. Since interest rates have fallen, investors who hold the bonds can only invest their proceeds from the refunding in bonds offered at lower interest rates. The call premium is intended to compensate them for this loss. Typically the call premium amounts to one year's interest. An 8-percent bond may, for example, have a call price of $1,080 per bond. Obviously, the call provision can work to the disadvantage of bondholders in times of high interest rates, since if rates subsequently fall, the bonds can be recalled. To protect the bondholders some indenture agreements stipulate that the bonds cannot be called for a specified number of years.

Convertibility   Many bonds have a convertible feature. This permits the bondholder to convert his debt into shares of common stock. In effect, this grants the bondholder a "piece of the action" if the common stock price should do well. Convertible securities are discussed in Chapter 15.

Bond refunding

Bond refunding refers to calling in outstanding bonds and issuing new bonds. There are several reasons why firms might refund. The most frequent reason is that interest rates have fallen, and refunding will be at a lower interest rate, resulting in lower interest payments. A second reason is that the outstanding bonds have restrictive covenants that inhibit the firm's financial operations. This may be because the firm issued the bonds during a period of tight money or when the firm was experiencing difficulties. The indenture agreement may restrict the firm from issuing new debt, for example. If the firm now needs new debt financing and feels itself strong enough to issue it, were there no restrictions, the firm may wish to consider refunding to clear the way for more new debt.

A third reason for refunding relates to the way bond repurchases by the firm are treated for accounting reporting purposes. Any difference in principal arising from the early retirement of debt must be flowed through *current* earnings. This procedure has led some firms to refund bonds when interest rates have *risen*. When interest rates rise, bond prices fall, and the firm can refund its old bonds at prices below face value. The difference between purchase price and face value is then reported — less expenses — as pretax earnings. For firms with poor earnings records this permits a big boost to current earnings. United Brands in 1973 performed just such a refund, calling in some of their $5\frac{1}{2}$ percent convertible debentures and issuing new $9\frac{1}{8}$ percent nonconvertible debentures. However, this reason for refunding is highly suspect. The firm is committed to higher interest payments and must pay all issuing expenses associated with refunding. In such instances refunding may be merely a method of artificially increasing current earnings.

The above discussion does not mean, however, that it would never be economically desirable to refund when interest rates have risen. If interest rates rise and the firm refunds, the firm must repay all refunding expenses now and make higher interest payments in the future. However, the firm will issue fewer new bonds in the refunding operation than there are old bonds (since old bond prices fell due to the interest rate rise). This means a less expensive bond redemption in the future. If this future saving is great enough, it may make the refunding attractive, even though interest rates have risen.

In analyzing bond refunding we will concentrate on the more common economic reason of issuing new bonds to take advantage of a lower interest rate. In this sense, bond refunding is actually a specialized investment problem. There is an initial outlay of funds required to call in the bonds outstanding, and there are cash inflows in later periods because of interest savings. Since refunding is an investment problem we need to know the usual investment data: (1) all cash flows after tax associated with the investment, (2) the appropriate discount rate, and (3) an appropriate evaluation criterion to use. We will use net present value to analyze the refunding problem.

The mechanics of refunding are straightforward. The firm issues new bonds, takes these proceeds plus cash and retires (buys back) the old (outstanding) bonds. The refunding problem is best analyzed with an example.

Newton Tire Co. is considering refunding its old bonds. Interest rates have dropped since Newton issued the bonds ten years ago and the company is interested in knowing if it would be economically advantageous to refund now. Pertinent data are as follows:

Old bonds

Amount	$100,000,000
Remaining life...............................	20 years
Coupon rate	9 percent
Call price.....................................	$1,070 per bond
Unamortized floatation costs	$1,500,000

New bonds

Amount	$100,000,000
Life...	20 years
Coupon rate	8 percent
Floatation costs	$2,000,000

Other data

Tax rate	40 percent
Overlap on bonds...........................	1 month

The one-month overlap refers to the common practice of issuing the new bonds between 30 to 60 days *before* the old bonds are redeemed. The firm is depending on the proceeds of the new bonds to help pay for the redemption of the old bonds. However, if the firm planned to issue new bonds simultaneously with the redemption of its old bonds, but bond market conditions were bad and the new bond issue was delayed—as occasionally happens—the firm would be in dire straits to find the money to pay off its old bonds. To protect itself from this possibility firms usually issue the new bonds at least a month or so prior to the redemption of the old bonds. Consequently, the firm will have both bonds outstanding during this "overlap" period.

Should the firm refund? To answer this question we must first determine the relevant cash flows associated with the refunding. Notice that the refunding is actually a replacement problem. The firm replaces one set of bonds with another. This means that the cash flows in the refunding problem are *changes* in cash flow incurred by replacing the old bonds with new bonds.

Initial investment We first calculate the initial investment before tax consequences are incorporated in the analysis:

Before tax calculations:

Repay old bond principal $100,000,000
Pay call premium (7% of principal).............. 7,000,000
$107,000,000
Overlap interest on old bonds* 750,000
$107,750,000
Less: net proceeds of new bonds† .... −98,000,000
Before tax initial investment......... $ 9,750,000

* Overlap interest equals one month's interest on the old bonds. That is, over-lap interest = $1/12 \times 0.09 \times \$100,000,000 = \$750,000$.
† Net proceeds of new bonds equal sale price minus floatation costs: $100,000,-000 − $2,000,000 = $98,000,000.

As these calculations illustrate, the net proceeds from the sale of the new bonds are used to offset the amount of money the firm needs to redeem the old bonds.

We turn now to tax considerations. First, the overlap payment, being interest, is tax deductible. Second, the firm gets to expense the call premium for tax purposes. The last tax consideration in the initial investment concerns the unamortized floatation costs associated with the old bonds. Floatation costs incurred with issuing bonds are amortized over the life of the bonds, and the firm gets a tax deduction against ordinary income each year equal to the amount of the amortized cost. When bonds are retired early the unrecovered or unamortized floatation costs may be expensed at time of refunding. Accordingly, the tax calculations are as follows:

Tax deductible expenses:

Overlap interest on old bonds .... $ 750,000
Call premium on old bonds 7,000,000
Unamortized floatation costs on old bonds......... 1,500,000
Total tax deductible expenses................. $9,250,000

Tax savings:

Tax savings = (T)(Total tax deductible expenses)
= $(0.40)(\$9,250,000) = \$3,700,000$

After tax calculations:

Before tax initial investment............................ $9,750,000
Less tax savings.. −3,700,000
After tax initial investment*.................... $6,050,000

* That is, $CFAT_0 = -\$6,050,000$

Because the firm can deduct for tax purposes the overlap interest, the unamortized floatation costs, and call premium of the outstanding bonds (a total of $9.25 million dollar in the example), it creates a tax savings ($3.7 million). The resultant after tax initial investment is the amount of money the firm must pay to effect the refunding.

Annual interest savings   There are alternate equivalent ways to determine the annual interest savings from issuing the new bonds. Our approach will be to separately calculate the after tax annual cost of servicing the old bonds and the new bonds, and then to net these figures. This difference represents the annual after tax interest savings attained by issuing the new bonds. Each separate calculation has two parts, the before tax interest cost and the tax considerations. Both the annual interest payments and the amortization of floatation costs discussed above are tax deductible, which create tax savings.

Old bonds:
  Before tax annual interest (0.09)($100,000,000)............$9,000,000 per year
  Tax deduction:
    Interest.. $9,000,000
    Amortized floatation costs*.............   75,000
      Total tax deductible expenses $9,075,000
  Tax savings (0.4)($9,075,000) ....   −3,630,000 per year
    Annual after tax interest payments ..... $5,370,000 per year
New bonds:
  Before tax annual interest (0.08)($100,000,000)............$8,000,000 per year
  Tax deduction:
    Interest.. $8,000,000
    Amortized floatation costs†   100,000
      Total tax deductible expenses $8,100,000
  Tax savings (0.4)($8,100,000) ....   −3,240,000 per year
    Annual after tax interest payments ....$4,760,000 per year

Annual after tax   Annual after tax   Annual after tax
interest savings = interest payments − interest payments
              on old bonds   on new bonds
          = $5,370,000 − $4,760,000
          = $610,000 per year

  * Amortized floatation costs = $1,500,000/20 = $75,000 per year.
  † Amortized floatation costs = $2,000,000/20 = $100,000 per year.

By refunding the firm will save itself $610,000 per year for 20 years. This is the direct result of a lower interest rate on the new bonds.

Net present value of refunding   The evaluation of refunding is a net present value problem. In the example, the firm must pay an initial investment of $6,050,000 to achieve an interest saving of $610,000 per year for 20 years. Therefore:

$$NPV = -\$6,050,000 + \sum_{t=1}^{20} \frac{\$610,000}{(1 + k)^t}$$
$$= -\$6,050.000 + \$610,000 \ ADF_{k,20}$$

Recall that $ADF_{k,20}$ is the annuity discount factor for k percent for 20 years. The next question we face is: What should k, the discount rate, be?

In Chapters 8 and 9 we developed the idea that the discount rate for a project should reflect the risk inherent in that project. For projects where cash flows are fairly certain, the project's risk will be relatively low and the discount rate will therefore be low. Bond refunding is a good example of this. Unlike most projects the firm undertakes, the cash flows associated with the bond refunding are known with a large degree of certainty because they represent interest savings that, barring failure of the firm, are certain. Therefore, the discount rate that is appropriate for the refunding net present value calculation is a low discount rate that is near the so-called risk free interest rate. k is, in fact, the cost of debt we discussed in Chapter 8. Recalling the approximation formula for the cost of debt [Equation (8–3)]

$$k = \frac{(1 - T) I}{(1 - f) B_0}$$

where

T = tax rate, I = annual interest payment on new bonds, B_0 = sale price of bonds, f = floatation costs (percent), and

$$k = \frac{(0.6)(80)}{(0.98)(1000)} = 0.049 \approx 5 \text{ percent}$$

Thus, the appropriate discount rate for the refunding problem is approximately 5 percent. The final step is to calculate the net present value of refunding

$$
\begin{aligned}
NPV &= -\$6{,}050{,}000 + \$610{,}000 \; ADF_{.05,20} \\
&= -\$6{,}050{,}000 + (\$610{,}000)(12.462) \\
&= -\$6{,}050{,}000 + \$7{,}601{,}820 \\
&= \quad \$2{,}051{,}820
\end{aligned}
$$

If net present value is positive, the firm should refund, and if negative, the firm should keep its outstanding bonds. In the example the decision should be to refund. Another alternative is to *wait* to refund. If interest rates keep dropping the firm may prefer to wait and achieve further interest savings. However, predicting future interest rates is a difficult task, and many financial managers would prefer to refund before a favorable opportunity disappears.

Advantages and disadvantages of financing with debt

There is one primary advantage to financing with debt: It's cheaper than any other capital source. This is because debt is the safest security an investor can buy, and also because of the tax deductibility of interest charges. A secondary advantage of financing with debt is that it does not dilute stockholder control since debt is a creditor instrument.

The major disadvantage of financing with debt is the increased risk added to the firm. Financing with debt adds financial leverage to the firm, which magnifies earnings fluctuations. We saw in Chapter 10 that financial leverage causes the cost of equity, k_e, to increase. A different aspect of increased risk caused by the addition of debt is the increased probability of bankruptcy. As the firm finances with debt it increases its fixed charge obligations, and should the firm not be able to meet these commitments, it may fail. Another disadvantage of debt financing is the occasionally stringent covenants written into the bond indenture. If the covenants are so strict that the firm has difficulty in arranging new future debt financing the firm's activities may be hampered.

TERM LOANS

Recall our earlier discussions on debt maturity. Short-term loans mature within a year; intermediate-term loans have maturities longer than a year, but shorter than about ten years; long-term loans have maturities longer than about ten years.[2] In this context, *term loans* have intermediate-lived maturities. Term loans are also characterized by the placement of the loan with a private lender as opposed to a public sale. The lender is most commonly a bank or insurance company. Term loans are therefore intermediate-lived, private placements of debt.

Features of term loans

The basic features or characteristics of term loans are: (1) maturity, (2) the direct negotiation with the lender, (3) collateral, (4) restrictive provisions, and (5) the repayment schedule.

Maturity As discussed above, term loan maturities vary from 1 to 15 years. Banks, one of the country's major term lending groups, have historically been active in supplying three-year to five-year term loans. Only in recent years have banks made term loans greater than five years. Longer lived term loans are usually made by insurance companies. Occasionally a bank and an insurance company will make a cooperative term loan, the bank making the shorter maturity portion of the loan (say five years) and the insurance company making the longer portion (say from five to ten years).

Direct negotiations As opposed to a public sale of bonds, a term loan is a private placement of debt. The firm and the lender negotiate directly. Consequently, there is no need for an investment banker in the negotiations. Occasionally, firms do use investment bankers to locate potential term lenders. This is particularly true when the lender is an insurance company. When the lender is a bank the firm usually does the seeking itself. If the amount of debt to be borrowed is large, one bank may serve as the agent or manager for a group of lenders.

Collateral Term loans frequently involve collateral. As with other important features of the loan, whether or not the firm is required to provide collateral depends upon economic factors, and the decision to require collateral is resolved during negotiations. The lender's attitude toward collateral is directly related to how safe he feels the loan is. Other things equal, the lender is more apt to require collateral from a small firm than a large one. Lenders are also more likely to be able to negotiate a collateral provision if money is relatively tight, since borrowers will

---

[2] The maturity of an "intermediate"-lived loan is actually very vague. While everyone agrees that it is longer than one year, many view loans with maturity greater than *five* years as being long-term debt. Others consider any loan with maturity less than 15 years as intermediate-term. So the description above that identifies ten years as being the dividing line between intermediate-term and long-term is only a rough generalization.

have more difficulty in arranging loans elsewhere. Firms that have a relatively large amount of debt outstanding, or have relatively low cash flow projections for the future, will be required to pledge assets to the loan. As opposed to short-term lending, where lenders look mainly at the firm's current assets and current liabilities to determine the safety of their loan, term lenders look more toward the firm's future earning power (the cash flow stream) over the life of the loan. The riskier this projected cash flow stream the more likely that collateral will be required. Most frequently, collateral takes the form of plant, equipment, land, stocks, and bonds.

Restrictive provisions To further protect itself the lender may attempt to add restrictive provisions to the loan. These provisions involve negotiation, and the composition of the final set of provisions indicates the relative strengths of borrower and lender. If the firm's position is relatively strong, it may successfully negotiate the loan with few onerous restrictions. If the firm's position is relatively weak, it may find it can only acquire the loan under very stringent terms. Of course, if the firm is too weak it won't receive the loan under any conditions. Also, the lender may feel the firm is creditworthy, but the firm and lender cannot come to agreement about terms; the firm will seek money elsewhere. In addition to the commonplace requirement that the firm provide quarterly and annual financial statements, the following provisions are most commonly found in term loans.

Asset control provisions. Even if a loan is secured by collateral the lender is interested in the firm maintaining its asset base. Should the firm default and the collateral not be sufficient to pay off the loan, the lender will become a general creditor and will look to the firm's *other* assets for satisfaction. There are two main asset control provisions. First, the firm may be required to maintain some specified minimum net working capital (current assets minus current liabilities) position. This requirement may be stated either in terms of the minimum dollars of net working capital or in terms of a minimum current or quick ratio. Second, the firm may be enjoined from selling fixed assets in excess of some specified dollar amount without the lender's approval.

Liability control provisions. To protect its investment the lender will attempt to restrict the firm from acquiring new liabilities. Almost always the lender will demand a negative pledge clause where the firm agrees not to pledge assets purchased by the loan to others. Many loan agreements also restrict the amount of new debt the firm may issue since this reduces the term lender's position as a general creditor. Also, the lender will usually attempt to restrict the amount of leasing agreements the firm can enter into. Specifically, sale and leaseback arrangements (these are discussed below) are prohibited.

Cash flow control provisions. The lender will also attempt to restrain the cash outflow of the firm. These provisions may relate to restrictions on cash dividends paid to stockholders, salaries and bonuses paid to officers of the company, and major fixed asset purchases.

Management control restrictions. The lender provides the loan on the expectation that the firm's management will be at least as competent in the future as it is at the time of the loan. To assure itself that these conditions will likely be met, the lender may insist on key-man insurance on the firm's top executives. At the extreme, the lender may require that named key executives maintain their association with the firm during the life of the loan.

Payment schedule

The *payment schedule* specifies when interest payments and principal repayments are due. Because term loans are relatively long-lived the lender looks to the long-run earning power of the firm to service the loan. A common principal repayment plan that is consistent with this "pay as you earn" concept is to *amortize* the loan. An amortized loan is one where periodic payments are made to reduce the loan balance. This is by far the most common type of principal repayment plan in the United States today. It avoids the necessity of having a large end of life repayment, called a *balloon payment*. The amortization schedule includes both interest and principal payments, and usually this schedule is set up to make *equal* periodic amortization payments.

Suppose, for example, that the firm negotiates a $30,000 six-year term loan that charges 10 percent on the unpaid balance. The loan will be amortized over the life of the loan through six equal year end payments, the last coming at the maturity date. What is the repayment schedule?

This question is actually right out of Chapter 3. Recall from the *capital recovery* section in that chapter (Equation 3–21):

$$R = \frac{V_o}{ADF_{i,n}}$$

where

R = periodic equal payment, V_o = current sum of money, and $ADF_{i,n}$ = annuity discount factor for i percent for n periods.

Therefore:[3]

$$R = \frac{\$30,000}{ADF_{.10,6}} = \frac{\$30,000}{4.355} = \$6,889$$

That is, if the firm pays $6,889 to the lender at the end of each year for six years, the lender will recover his investment plus 10-percent interest over the loan period. A portion of this annual payment is interest and a portion is principal recovery. Since the periodic payment is constant, the portion of $6,889 that is interest will drop as the loan balance declines. We can readily determine that portion of the annual payment that is interest payment and that portion that is principal repayment since we know the interest rate, initial loan balance, and the annual amortization payment. This separation into interest and principal payment is important for income tax purposes since interest is tax deductible, but principal repayment is not. These calculations are shown in Figure 14–1.

---

[3] In this example, R actually equals $6,888.63, but we have rounded to the nearest whole dollar. This causes a slight rounding error in the work presented in Figure 14–1.

FIGURE 14–1
Example loan amortization schedule

Year	(1) Loan balance at beginning of year	(2) Total loan payment	(3) Interest payment $[0.10 \times (1)]$	(4) Principal payment $[(2)-(3)]$	(5) Loan balance at end of year $[(1)-(4)]$
1........	$30,000	$ 6,889	$ 3,000	$ 3,889	$26,111
2........	26,111	6,889	2,611	4,278	21,833
3........	21,833	6,889	2,183	4,706	17,127
4........	17,127	6,889	1,713	5,176	11,951
5........	11,951	6,889	1,195	5,694	6,257
6........	6,257	6,883*	626	6,257	0
		$41,328	$11,328	$30,000	

* The last loan payment is slightly different from the equal payments made in the earlier years. This is to compensate for rounding errors by making the last principal payment exactly pay off the last year's loan balance.

Cost of term loans

The firm figures the cost of term loans the same way it determines the cost of capital for any source of financing. Interest charges are tax deductible, and we use the same concepts developed in Chapter 8. The interest rate on term loans is usually about one-half to one percent above the *prime rate*, which is the rate that banks charge their best corporate borrowers for short-term loans (see Chapter 20). Sometimes the stated term interest rate is analagously tied to the Federal Reserve rediscount rate, which is the rate the Federal Reserve system charges member commercial banks on short-term loans. Interest rates on term loans may be *fixed* or *variable*. A fixed interest rate commits the firm to one contractual interest rate over the life of the loan. A variable rate permits the interest rate to be changed at designated points in time should money market conditions warrant the change. Usually, the interest rate of a variable rate term loan will be tied to the prime rate.

In addition to interest charges, the firm must pay for the legal preparation of the loan documents, and for a loan or commitment fee from the bank. These costs are a form of floatation costs and are relatively small compared to floatation costs associated with underwriting expenses. Assume in the example in Figure 14–1 that these floatation costs are $150. The cost of capital for this term loan is found by equating the net proceeds received from the loan with the present value of the after tax payments made to the lender. The most complete calculation of k_i, the cost of borrowing, would use the definitional Equation (8–2) from Chapter 8:

$$B_o(1-f) = \sum_{t=1}^{n} \frac{B_t + (1-T)I_t}{(1+k_i)^t}$$

where

$B_0 (1 - f)$ = net proceeds received, B_t = principal repayment in year t, T = tax rate, and I_t = interest payment in year t.

However, we can get a reasonably good approximation of k_i by using a variant of shortcut Equation (8–3) from Chapter 8:

$$k_i = \frac{(1 - T)}{(1 - f)} \text{ (Interest rate)} \tag{14-1}$$

where

$1 - f$ = the *percentage* net proceeds received and Interest rate = the *stated* annual interest rate charged.

In the example problem, $(1 - f)$ = \$29,850/\$30,000 = 0.995, the interest rate is 10 percent and we assume that T = 40 percent. Therefore

$$k_i = \frac{(0.6)(0.10)}{0.995} = 0.0603 \approx 6 \text{ percent}$$

An additional factor that influences these calculations is the bank's requirement that the firm keep compensating balances. This practice raises the cost of term loans. Compensating balances are also required in short-term loans, and we discuss this practice in detail in Chapter 20. Any other restrictive covenants placed on the firm by the lender would also effectively increase the cost of the loan.

Sources of term loans

Commercial banks   Commercial banks are the primary providers of term loans. To many in finance, term loans are synonymous with bank loans. Because banks receive much of their loanable funds from demand deposits (checking accounts kept at banks) that can be drawn down quickly by depositors, banks prefer to make term loans for relatively short periods of time, usually no longer than three to five years. They will, however, provide longer loans under some conditions.

Insurance companies and pension funds   These financial institutions provide the bulk of the longer term loans (five to ten years and sometimes longer) to corporations. This is because the liabilities of these institutions are longer lived than banks' demand deposits, so they can seek out longer lived assets (loans).

Commercial finance companies   Commercial finance companies are firms that lend to other firms. In comparison with banks and insurance companies this source of term loans is expensive. Most firms will only seek out a commercial finance company loan when all other sources fail, and frequently it is a sign of weakness to borrow from a commercial finance company. For many marginal companies with either poor or nonexistent records of success, however, commercial finance companies are an extremely important source of term lending.

Government sources These are state and federal agencies that specialize in providing loans to small businesses. These agencies serve as a last possible source of borrowing for many marginal firms. A well-known federal lending agency is the Small Business Administration (SBA). The SBA prefers to lend jointly with private lending institutions, but on smaller loans may be the sole lender. At the state level, some states have active state development authorities that use public funds in loan guarantee programs aimed at bringing industry into the state. City and county governments have used tax exempt industrial aid bonds to attract industry. This is actually a form of leasing where the municipality builds the facility and leases it to the firm. The removal of the tax exempt status of all such issues over $5 million dollars has apparently drastically reduced the use of these bonds however.

Advantages of term loans

In comparison to equity financing, term loans have the usual debt advantage of the tax deductibility of interest payments. That is, debt has a lower cost of capital, up to a point. There are several other advantages to the firm of using term loans in comparison to issuing bonds. First, there are all the advantages associated with directly negotiated debt. The placement is faster, which protects the firm from the possible deterioration of conditions in the bond market. Floatation costs of directly placed loans are also less. Another important direct negotiation feature is the personal nature of the relationship between borrower and lender. In public bond issues there is an impersonal relationship between the firm and its many bondholders. Should the firm encounter financial problems, it will have great difficulty in arranging any necessary leniencies from the bondholders because the borrower-lender relationship is impersonal. Because this relationship is personal in term lending, the firm should be able to negotiate more readily with the lender. This does not mean that the negotiations necessarily will be satisfactory however. Term lenders are mostly financial institutions with significant financial expertise, and they will vigorously protect their investment. The personal nature of the relationship merely provides the firm more access to try and negotiate around the difficulty.

A second advantage to term borrowing relates to the so-called matching principle. Most firms prefer to match up the maturities of assets and asset claims. If the firm invests in an asset with an expected life of five years it will normally seek financing that will last about five years also. If the firm decides to borrow to buy the asset, it can readily arrange a five-year term loan, but five-year bonds would not be very well-received. The time period is too short. And most lenders prefer not to make short-term loans (less than one year) for fixed asset purchases by the firm. So term loans facilitate the investment-financing match up.

A third advantage of term borrowing pertains to smaller firms. As we have noted earlier, smaller firms have limited access to the bond market and depend on term loans to substitute for this source of capital that is closed to them.

Disadvantages of term loans

In comparison to equity money, term loans have the usual disadvantage: Debt money is riskier. Recall from Chapter 10 that adding debt increases the firm's cost of equity capital, k_e. Furthermore, if the firm cannot service the debt, the firm will fail. In addition, term loans usually have fairly stringent restrictions or loan provisions. We discussed these various restrictive provisions above. In periods of tight money, term lenders also frequently demand "equity sweeteners" as part of the loan agreement.

LEASE FINANCING

The firm makes investments to enhance stockholder's wealth. Once attractive projects are identified, the firm considers alternate methods of financing them. In making an investment, however, the firm need not *own* the asset: The firm basically wishes to acquire the *services* of the asset rather than the asset itself. Thus, the firm can consider *renting* the asset rather than *buying* it. A prominent form of renting assets is through *leasing*. Leasing represents a method of asset employment without purchase, and the use of lease financing has grown substantially since the 1950s. Prior to 1950 most leases pertained to real estate (buildings and land). Today, a wide variety of fixed assets, from airplanes to office equipment, can be leased. Leasing has become a very important form of intermediate-term financing. In a lease arrangement, the *lessor* is the asset owner; he receives the rent payments. The *lessee* is the asset user; he pays rent to the lessor. In the following discussion the firm is the lessee.

Types of leases and features

There are two basic kinds of leases: *operating leases* and *financial leases*.

Operating leases   A good example of an operating or service lease is a lease for telephone service. An operating lease is usually characterized by the following features:

1. The lease is cancelable on notice by the lessee prior to the expiration of the lease.[4]
2. The lessor provides service, maintenance, and insurance for the asset.
3. The sum of all the lease payments the lessee makes do not necessarily fully provide for the recovery of the asset's cost.[5]

For operating lessors to make a reasonable profit they typically offer leasing services that are not peculiar to one kind of industry. That is,

---

[4] Typically, operating leases have renewal options that permit the lessee to renew the lease on the expiration date.

[5] That is, the asset is not fully amortized over the life of the lease. The lessor looks to leasing the same asset to subsequent lessees or to selling the asset to fully recover his investment and expected profit.

they offer services that many different kind of lessees can use. Good example's are office rentals, computer leasing, and truck and car fleet leasing.

Financial leases As opposed to operating leases, financial leases typically have the following features:

1. The lease is *not* cancelable by the lessee prior to its expiration date.
2. The lessor may or may not provide service, maintenance, and insurance of the asset.[6]
3. The asset is fully amortized over the life of the lease.

Because the financial lease involves a noncancelable agreement by the firm to acquire the services of an asset, a decision to enter into a financial lease is an important commitment and merits special attention. We will restrict attention in the remainder of this chapter to financial leases.

There are two kinds of financial lease arrangements; they are distinguished only by who originally owned the asset. First, in a *sale and leaseback* arrangement, the firm sells an asset it currently owns and then leases the same asset back from the buyer. The firm receives cash from the sale and will make periodic lease payments to the lessor over the life of the lease. This arrangement allows the firm to continue using the asset but also provides cash for the firm. If the firm is in need of cash and either chooses not to or is unable to secure cash from other sources, the sale and leaseback arrangement can be of great help.

A second financial lease arrangement is the *direct* lease. Under this arrangement, the firm will lease an asset it did not previously own. If, for example, the firm has decided to lease some new equipment it will arrange to lease the as yet unpurchased equipment from a willing lessor. The firm will simultaneously sign the lease agreement with the lessor and order the equipment from the manufacturer. The lessor will pay for the equipment, which is sent to the firm. The firm will make periodic lease payments to the lessor just as in the sale and leaseback arrangement.

Sources of lease financing

There are basically three kinds of companies that provide lease financing. First, many equipment manufacturers provide leasing: Most typically, these durable goods manufacturers will establish subsidiary (called "captive") leasing or credit companies. One of the main reasons that manufacturing companies provide lease financing is to encourage the use of their product. A second source of lease financing comes from financial institutions: banks, bank holding companies, and life insurance companies. These institutions are heavily involved in longer term financial leases. From the standpoint of these institutions, leases are merely an alternate form of secured lending. A third source of lease

---

[6] Financial leases that require the lessor to service, maintain, and provide insurance for the asset are called *maintenance* or *gross* leases. Financial leases that require the lessee (firm) to pay for these costs are called *nonmaintenance* or *net* leases.

financing is independent leasing companies, who provide much of the direct leasing contracts to business.

Lease or borrow?

Finance theory asserts that corporate investment and financing decisions are separate decisions. That is, the firm first makes an accept-reject decision on a proposed investment, then it determines how the asset will be financed. In this context, since leasing is a form of financing, the decision to lease an asset is only made *after* the firm has made an accept-reject decision concerning the acquisition of the asset. If the investment is rejected, there is no need for a subsequent financing decision. But if the investment is accepted, a subsequent financing decision is necessary. It is at this point that the firm would consider leasing the asset rather than buying it. In comparing leasing with alternate financing plans, many financial analysts argue that the only truly appropriate comparison is with *debt* financing. The reasoning for this argument goes like this. Since lease financing is equivalent to debt financing (albeit "off balance sheet" debt financing), if the firm leases the asset, it has effectively committed itself to debt financing. Therefore, to properly compare leasing to purchasing, we must use an equivalent financing alternative. The only equivalent financing alternative is borrowing. Hence, the comparison of interest in leasing is lease-vs.-borrow.

While many financial analysts subscribe to this position there is a competing theory that views the leasing decision as a lease-vs.-*buy* comparison. The crux of this argument is that under the lease-vs.-borrow analysis the firm would never consider a lease until the project had passed the accept-reject decision. But, goes this argument, assets that are rejected in such analyses may be acceptable under a lease arrangement if the leasing terms are more favorable than purchasing terms. Deferring the leasing decision until the standard investment decision is made may cause the firm to reject proposals that are actually desirable. Such anomalies would be inconsistent with the firm's goal.

There is no unanimity today regarding which method of analysis is correct. Our approach here will be the lease-vs.-borrow method. This presumes that the investment decision has already been resolved with an accept conclusion and the firm is now interested in comparing leasing and borrowing financing alternatives. This analysis entails a cost comparison of leasing and borrowing, and we will illustrate this comparison with an example.

The firm has previously decided that a project that costs $10,000 should be accepted. The expected life of the asset is five years and the firms tax rate is 40 percent. The asset is expected to have zero salvage value. The firm can arrange a maintenance financial lease (the lessor pays all maintenance costs) on the asset for $2,700 per year. Alternatively, the firm can buy the asset and arrange an 8-percent term loan that will require annual payments to the bank of $2,504 per year.[7] Under this

---

[7] The equal annual payment of a $10,000, 8-percent loan over five years is found by the method discussed in the term loan section of this chapter: $R = \$10,000/ADF_{.08.5} = \$2,504$.

latter alternative, operating costs (borne by the firm) will be $100 per year. We are now prepared to evaluate the two alternatives.

Leasing costs As with other financial management problems the firm must make, the lease or borrow decision requires analysis of relevant tax considerations. The entire lease payment is tax deductible. Therefore:

$$\begin{array}{l}\text{Annual after tax} \\ \text{lease payment}\end{array} = (1-T)\left(\begin{array}{l}\text{Annual before tax} \\ \text{lease payment}\end{array}\right)$$
$$= (0.6)(\$2,700)$$
$$= \$1,620 \text{ per year}$$

We are now prepared to find the present value of this stream of costs. Because these lease costs are relatively certain the appropriate discount rate should reflect that relative certainty. The appropriate rate is the firm's cost of borrowing, k_i. We may find this (approximate) rate in the same manner as we did earlier in the chapter in the term loan analysis. Recall Equation (14–1):

$$k_i = \frac{(1-T)}{(1-f)} \text{ (interest rate)}$$

Using the 8-percent term loan rate as the interest rate and assuming that floatation costs are negligibly small (that is, that $f \approx 0$); we see that

$$k_i = (0.6)(0.08) = 0.048 \approx 5 \text{ percent}$$

Now, the leasing cost equals the present value of the after tax lease payments:

$$\begin{array}{l}\text{Present value of} \\ \text{after tax lease} \\ \text{payments}\end{array} = (\$1,620)(ADF_{.05,5}) = (\$1,620)(4.329)$$
$$= \$7,013$$

Borrowing costs In comparing borrowing to leasing we must also consider the tax aspects of the problem. In addition, we must consider any incremental operating costs incurred because of the decision to purchase the asset rather than lease it. The $100 per year operating costs are additional costs of owning rather than leasing in the example. The tax deductible costs of owning include the interest on the loan, depreciation on the asset, and operating costs. Because only the interest portion of the loan payment is tax deductible we must first prepare a loan amortization schedule as was done in Figure 14–1. The loan amortization schedule for the current example is shown in Figure 14–2.

The loan amortization schedule is a necessary step in determining the cost of borrowing since it splits the total annual loan payment into tax deductible interest payments and nontax deductible principal payments. Next, we determine the after tax cash outflow schedule associated with the borrowing alternative. We assume that the asset is depreciated using the straight-line method. The after tax cash flow and subsequent present value calculations (using $k = 0.05$) are shown in Figure 14–3.

FIGURE 14–2
Loan amortization schedule

Year	(1) Loan balance at beginning of year	(2) Total loan payment	(3) Interest payment [0.08 × (1)]	(4) Principal payment [(2) − (3)]	(5) Loan balance at end of year [(1) − (4)]
1.........	$10,000	$ 2,504	$ 800	$ 1,704	$8,296
2.........	8,296	2,504	664	1,840	6,456
3.........	6,456	2,504	516	1,988	4,468
4.........	4,468	2,504	357	2,147	2,321
5.........	2,321	2,507*	186	2,321	0
		$12,523	$2,523	$10,000	

* The last loan payment is slightly different from the equal payments made in the earlier years. This is to compensate for rounding errors by making the last principal payment exactly pay off the last year's loan balance.

FIGURE 14–3
Cost of borrowing calculations

Year	(1) Loan payment	(2) Interest	(3) Operating costs	(4) Depreciation*	(5) Tax savings†	(6) After tax costs‡	(7) PV.05
1.......	$2,504	$800	$100	$2,000	$1,160	$1,444	$1,375
2.......	$2,504	664	100	$2,000	1,105	1,499	$1,360
3.......	$2,504	516	100	$2,000	1,046	1,558	1,337
4.......	$2,504	357	100	$2,000	983	1,621	1,334
5.......	$2,507	186	100	$2,000	914	1,693	1,327
							$6,733

* Annual depreciation = $10,000/5 = $2,000 per year.
† Tax savings = (T) [(2) + (3) + (4)] = (0.4) [(2) + (3) + (4)].
‡ After tax costs = (1) + (3) − (5).

As Figure 14–3 shows, the present value of pertinent costs associated with borrowing is $6,733, which is less than the present value of leasing costs, $7,013. Based on this analysis the firm should buy the asset rather than lease it.

Advantages of leasing

Despite the fact that leasing is frequently more expensive than borrowing, there has been a substantial increase in the volume of leasing in recent years. In investigating the factors that influence choice in a lease or buy decision we must be careful to distinguish between *per-*

FIGURE 14-4
Perceived advantages of leasing (1968 survey of 30 manufacturers)

		Rating by percentage of surveyed firms		
		High	*Medium*	*Low*
1.	Conserves working capital	53	32	15
2.	Shifts obsolescence risk to lessor	47	37	16
3.	Eliminates equipment disposal problem	47	32	21
4.	Preserves credit capacity	42	37	21
5.	Encourages trying new equipment	37	37	26
6.	Avoids restrictive covenants in bank loan	32	37	31
7.	Eliminates maintenance problems	16	42	42
8.	Permits greater flexibility in use	5	68	42
9.	Low cost	5	21	74
10.	Tax advantage	5	20	75

Source: George L. Marrah, "To Lease or Not to Lease," *Financial Executive* (October 1968).

ceived advantages and disadvantages of leasing and *actual* advantages and disadvantages. Our discussion will be based on Figure 14-4, which shows the results of a 1968 small (30 firm) sample survey regarding perceived advantages of leasing.

Among the perceived advantages of leasing, the most prominent are the first four: conserving working capital, shifting risk of obsolescence, eliminating the equipment disposal problem, and the preservation of credit capacity.

Conserving working capital The notion that lease financing is advantageous because it conserves working capital refers to the fact that the firm may be able to arrange 100-percent financing in a lease arrangement so that no cash is required to purchase the asset. In comparison, borrowing frequently requires a down payment. This point seems valid for small firms that have limited access to other sources of financing and would have to finance internally otherwise. It is also a valid reason for lease preference in times of tight money. Not surprisingly, there is increased demand for leasing in such times. For large companies in normal times, however, other forms of outside capital are available, and the firm could arrange 100-percent financing *in effect* from these sources. In addition, many lease arrangements also require a payment at time zero.

Shifting obsolescence risk If equipment purchased today becomes obsolete in the future because of the development of better equipment, its future market value will be impaired. The rationale for the purported advantage of shifting obsolescence risk to the lessor is that since the firm does not own the asset, the risk of equipment obsolescence caused by future technological advances has been effectively shifted to the lessor. This would be true if the lessor did not pass on the expected costs of obsolescence to the lessee by charging higher lease payments. If we presume (as seems likely) that lessors are no less enlightened than lessees, then there is certainly no merit to the contention that a lease arrangement shifts the risk of equipment obsolescence to the lessor.

Elimination of equipment disposal problem   This seems a mere convenience advantage rather than an economic one. There is little reason to think that the lessee can salvage the asset for less than the lessor. Even if the equipment has *negative* market value (nuisance value) at disposal time, the lessor may be counted on to pass this expected cost on to the lessee.

Preservation of credit capacity   Some firms feel that even though leasing is equivalent to borrowing, because it commits them to a schedule of fixed payments, some creditors do not perceive leasing as being equivalent to debt. These firms argue that by leasing assets rather than buying

FIGURE 14–5
Off balance sheet financing effect of lease financing

	Standard reporting practices	Capitalization of leases
Assets:		
Current assets	$ 500,000	$ 500,000
Fixed assets	2,500,000	3,000,000
Total assets..............	$3,000,000	$3,500,000
Current liabilities:	$ 250,000	$ 250,000
Long-term debt.................	750,000	1,250,000
Equity	2,000,000	2,000,000
Total claims.............	$3,000,000	$3,500,000

them and paying with debt, they can preserve their future borrowing capacity. This argument refers to the "off balance sheet" nature of lease financing. Since the firm does not own the leased asset, under current accounting practices neither the asset nor the companion lease liability must appear in the body of the balance sheet.[8] The effect of this accounting practice is to understate the indebtedness position of the firm. Suppose, for example, the firm has a balance sheet as shown in the left-hand panel of Figure 14–5. The firm's reported debt-equity ratio is ($1,000,000/ $2,000,000) = 0.5. However, the firm also has $500,000 of leased assets as shown by the balance sheet in the right-hand panel of Figure 14–5. This alternate balance sheet has capitalized the lease payments to reflect asset and liability values. Now the firm's debt-equity ratio is ($1,500,000/$2,000,000) = 0.75.

---

[8] While many accountants and financial analysts have argued for requiring the firm to report lease obligations in the balance sheet, currently the firm is only required to report lease obligations in a note in its financial statements. Frequently, however, these notes are terse and it is difficult to determine the degree to which the firm is committed to financial leases.

Since leases are equivalent to debt, but leased asset and liability values do not appear on the balance sheet, the firm indebtedness position is understated. A good example of this phenomenon is found in the airline industry, which has extensively leased airplanes in recent years. Figure 14–6 shows the ten major domestic airlines' long-term debt/total capital ratio's calculated with and without capitalization of leases. In seven of the ten airlines there is an increase in the firm's indebtedness position, and five of these increases (the first five) are substantial ones.

FIGURE 14–6
Effect of lease capitalization on airline long-term debt/total capital

Airline	Without lease capitalization	With lease capitalization
American	53.9%	60.3%
Eastern	73.2	77.2
TWA	63.0	66.8
United	52.7	58.0
Braniff	65.8	69.1
Continental	62.0	62.0
Delta	38.7	38.7
National	25.7	27.4
Northwest	17.2	17.2
Western	63.2	65.5

Source: Richard D. Gritta, "The Impact of the Capitalization of Leases on Financial Analysis," *Financial Analysts' Journal* (March–April 1974).

In comparison to debt financing, lease financing will also make the firm's return on assets and times interest earned higher because the firm's asset levels and fixed charges are both understated.

While off balance sheet financing understates the firm's indebtedness position, it is extremely doubtful that creditors (and stockholders) are unaware of the firm's real indebtedness position. The fact that most indenture agreements written recently limit the firm's subsequent leasing activity as well as its borrowing activity underscores creditors' awareness of the effect of leasing on the firm's ability to meet its fixed charge obligations. Consequently, it is extremely doubtful that leasing really preserves the firm's credit capacity.

Disadvantages of leasing

In discussing the disadvantages of lease financing we must continue to distinguish between perceived and actual disadvantages. Figure 14–7 shows the results of the survey alluded to earlier in Figure 14–4. The most prominent perceived disadvantages are the high interest cost, increased fixed obligations, and the fact that the firm does not build up any equity in a leased asset. This last point particularly refers to leasing an asset, such as land, whose residual value is substantial.

FIGURE 14–7
Perceived disadvantages of leasing (1968 survey of 30 manufacturers)

	Disadvantages	Rating by percentage of surveyed firms		
		High	*Medium*	*Low*
1.	High cost..	70%	21%	8%
2.	Increased fixed obligations...........................	68	27	5
3.	Does not build an equity.............................	53	26	21
4.	Objectionable clauses and limitations	31	47	22
5.	Curtails lessee's freedom in using equipment ...	21	37	42
6.	Difficult to get improvements	16	37	47
7.	Reluctance to absorb obsolescence loss..........	10	63	27
8.	Tax disadvantages......................................	5	53	42
9.	Difficult to finance improvements..................	5	47	48
10.	Found to use inferior supply items................	0	37	63

Source: George L. Marrah, "To Lease or Not to Lease," *Financial Executive* (October 1968).

High interest cost As with other sources of financing, leases have a cost of capital, which is that discount rate that equates the initial cost of the asset with the present value of the stream of after tax lease payments the firm must make. Generally, the cost of leasing is higher than the cost of debt, which is thought to be a comparable financing alternative to leasing. This higher cost reflects, in part, the lessor charging the lessee for inventory costs, overhead costs, and a passing of the risk of obsolescence back to the lessee. Of course, the cost of leasing need not always be higher than borrowing costs. Occasionally, individuals in personal income tax brackets higher than the firm's marginal tax rate form partnerships to purchase equipment through borrowing, and then lease the equipment. Their very high tax rates make the depreciation tax shields associated with the equipment and the interest tax shields associated with their borrowing worth more to these individuals than to the firm. To the extent that these partnerships are willing to pass along some of this tax gain to the lessee in the form of lower periodic lease payments, the cost of leasing may be less than the cost of debt.

Increased fixed obligations The notion that a major disadvantage of leasing is the increase in the firm's fixed obligations implies a comparison of leasing and equity financing. In comparison with other debt financing, lease financing is really no different in this respect. However, it is true that, like other debt financing, leasing increases the firm's fixed obligations and makes the firm riskier both with respect to earnings covariability and the possibility of bankruptcy.

In regard to the bankruptcy issue, if the firm defaults on its lease payments prior to any declaration of bankruptcy, the lessor will reclaim the asset. If the firm enters bankruptcy prior to the breach of a lease, the strength of the lessor's claim on his asset is dependent upon the nature of the asset and the outcome of the bankruptcy proceeding. If the asset leased is personal property, such as equipment, the lessor's full claim on the asset is senior. If the asset is real property, such as land or buildings, however, the lessor has a claim equal at most to three year's lease payments if the firm is reorganized, and at most only one year's lease payments if the firm is liquidated.

Loss of residual value Since the firm only leases the asset, when the lease expires the firm has no equity investment; the lessor has title to any residual value. For many assets, particularly equipment, this loss should be relatively unimportant. Most equipment's economic value depreciates over time, and salvage values are not substantial. However, in the case of real property, which frequently appreciates over time, the loss to the firm of the assets' residual value may be substantial. Offsetting such losses is the futurity of the residual value. Leases on real property are typically long, and the present value of the loss of residual value may not be large because of the long futurity. Lessees are oftentimes given the first option to buy a leased asset at fair market value, which gives the firm an opportunity to retain an asset, such as land, that is essential to the firm's operations.

SUMMARY

In this chapter we have investigated long-term debt (bonds), intermediate-term debt (term loans), and leasing as sources of financing. These alternatives encompass the main sources of financing for the firm's long-term (more than one year) investments. While the maturity range of these claims is broad—from 1 to 10 years or so on term loans and leasing, to as much as 30 or more years on bonds—they have several common features. They all represent fixed charge financing. This means the firm is committed to future fixed charges when it employs these sources. Fixed charge financing is less expensive than equity financing, but it also involves more risk. In Chapter 10 we saw that fixed charge financing raises the firm's cost of equity (k_e). Debt financing also increases the probability of failure since the firm may experience times when it is difficult to service its fixed charges.

Two particularly interesting problems that were studied in this chapter were the bond refunding problem and the leasing problem. Bond refunding—exchanging one bond issue for another—most frequently occurs during periods of falling interest rates. In such situations, the firm may wish to issue new debt with a lower coupon rate than its currently outstanding bonds. This possibility of interest savings is analyzed as a long-term investment problem. The firm incurs an initial investment to effect the refunding, and compares this cost with the present value of future after tax interest savings. The leasing problem refers to the question of whether it is more profitable to lease an asset rather than purchase it. While there is considerable controversy over the details of the analysis of a leasing decision, the analysis we used basically involves a comparison of leasing costs and the costs of financing with a comparable source of debt financing: borrowing.

QUESTIONS

1. Define the following terms and phrases:
    a. Mortgage bonds.
    b. Debentures.
    c. Subordinated debt.
    d. Term loan.
    e. Collateral.
    f. Loan amortization schedule.
    g. Operating lease.
    h. Financial lease.

2. In many instances the firm may choose to redeem bonds before their maturity date. Identify and discuss ways that the firm may accomplish early redemption.

3. Far West Trucking has some 6-percent coupon rate bonds outstanding that mature in about 20 years. Current interest rates are 8 percent, and Far West is talking about refunding its bonds. What motives can you identify for Far West refunding at this time? Discuss these motives.

4. Double Eagle Mfg. is preparing to issue new bonds. In a preliminary discussion, Sherr and Johnson, the firm's Chicago investment bankers, and the firm talk about the need for and the desirability of arranging a call feature and a sinking fund provision for the bond.
    a. Explain which of these two features would be considered desirable from the firm's standpoint and why. From bond investors' standpoint and why.
    b. Qualitatively, how would the omission of the call feature affect the bond's desirability from investors' viewpoint? What effect would omission of the call have on the bond's yield (and hence cost of capital), other things equal?
    c. Repeat part (*b*), only from the standpoint of omitting the sinking fund provision.

5. How should the following expectations on the firm's part affect its willingness to include a sinking fund provision and its insistence to include a call feature on a new bond issue?
    a. Interest rates are expected to rise.
    b. Fairly serious cash flow problems are expected for the next ten years.
    c. Interest rates are expected to fall.

6. What are the primary differences between the firm acquiring debt money from a bond issue and a term loan? What advantages does term borrowing have over issuing bonds?

7. Cargo National Bank is willing to make a term loan to Golden Bear Soft Drinks but insists on certain restrictive provisions to protect the loan. A list of potential problems the firm faces follow. Indicate for each problem what restrictive provision the bank would probably impose.

    a. The current officers are key men to the firm's success and would be difficult to replace.

    b. The collateral on the loan may not be sufficient to pay off the loan if the firm defaulted.

    c. The firm appears to be relying more and more on debt financing.

    d. The firm is having severe profitability and cash flow problems.

8. What is the main theoretical disagreement between lease-borrow and lease-buy proponents?

9. List the major *perceived* advantages and disadvantages of leasing in comparison to borrowing. Which of these might be classified as *actual* advantages and disadvantages?

PROBLEMS

1. KMJ Co. has the following amortization schedule on a five-year term loan.

Year	Interest payment	Principal payment
1..................	$35	$65
2..................	29	71
3..................	23	77
4..................	16	84
5..................	8	92

    a. What is the amount of the loan?

    b. Determine the before tax rate of return the lender is receiving.

    c. Using Equation (14–1) determine the after tax cost of borrowing to KMJ if its tax rate is 30 percent and the lender charged KMJ $7 to process the loan.

2. Allemagne West & Co. has added a new sales division to the firm. This addition will require the use of about 50 cars for the new division's traveling salesmen. Allemagne has priced these cars at $4,000 each. However, a car leasing firm has offered Allemagne a financial lease arrangement on the cars. The lease would be for three years, and Allemagne would make annual year end payments of $81,-833 during the life of the lease.

    a. What before tax rate of return would Allemagne be paying on the lease?

    b. Repeat part (*a*) assuming that the lease payments must be made at the *beginning* of each year.

3. The Id Co. currently has an issue of 6-percent bonds worth $30 million outstanding whose call price is $1,050. Remaining life of the bonds is 20 years. The company is contemplating refunding with a new $30 million issue of 5-percent, 20-year bonds. Sale price of the new bonds is expected to be $980 per bond and issue costs are $100,-000. The effective tax rate for Id is zero percent, and no overlap interest payments are planned. Should the Id Co. refund the old issue?

4. East Topeka Carpet Mart (ETCM) has just had a $1,000 three-year term loan application approved by a local bank. At the end of each year ETCM will pay an agreed upon amount of principal plus 7-percent interest on the loan balance that was outstanding at the beginning of each year. The bank has offered ETCM three alternate amortization schedules:

   Plan A: The loan is amortized by equal annual payments.
   Plan B: $600 principal is paid at the end of the first year, $300 principal is paid at the end of the second year, and the remainder of the loan is retired at the end of year three.
   Plan C: No principal payment is made at the end of the first year, while principal payments of $500 are made at the end of each of the second and third years.

   a. Prepare a loan amortization schedule showing yearly interest, principal and total payments for each plan. Note that an interest payment must be paid each year under each plan.
   b. Determine the total amount of undiscounted dollars paid in interest under each plan.
   c. Use Equation (14–1) to determine the explicit cost of term borrowing for each plan, assuming that floatation costs are negligible and that ETCM's tax rate is 29 percent.
   d. Rank order the plans from economically most to least desirable. Explain your rankings.
   e. What cash flow circumstances at the company level could cause ETCM to prefer one plan over the other two?

5. Shaw Airlines is attempting to decide whether to lease or buy new aircraft. The company has already decided the new planes are desirable, and their total cost is $15 million. The company plans to keep the planes five years, after which they are expected to be valueless. If the planes are leased, there will be a $4 million lease payment every year. If the planes are bought, the firm will take out a 10-percent term loan that will be amortized over the life of the planes in equal payments. Operating costs would be about $500,000 per year if the planes are purchased. The company uses straight-line depreciation and the tax rate is 40 percent. Determine which method of financing is better. (In working the problem round all numbers to the nearest thousand dollars.)

6. Craig Craftsmen Builders needs the use of $300,000 worth of equipment for four years. At the end of that period the equipment will have estimated zero salvage value. The manufacturer of the equipment has offered to finance the sale of the assets; the loan would be paid off in four equal year-end payments of $88,574 each. Assume that Craig would use straight-line depreciation. Alternatively, Craig may lease the equipment from a life insurance company. End of year payments would be $90,000 per year for four years. Assume that the equipment's economic desirability has already been verified and that Craig's tax rate is 30 percent.
   a. Determine the appropriate discount rate to be used in the analysis. (Round up to the nearest whole number discount rate.)

    b. Determine whether the asset should be leased or purchased.

7. Central Oklahoma Gas & Light currently has one thousand $1,000 par value 8-percent bonds outstanding with a remaining life of five years. Interest rates have declined in recent months and Central figures it could replace these bonds with new five-year 6-percent notes. A financial analyst for Central has been assigned the task of determining if it would be advantageous to refund. The analyst has gathered the following pertinent financial data:

> Floatation costs on new notes $50,000
> Sale price of new notes .... $1,000 each
> Unamortized floatation costs of old bonds........... $10,000
> Call premium on old bonds............................... 8 percent
> Tax rate .... 33 percent

Determine if a refunding should be made assuming no overlap interest payments are made.

8. Brown Drugs and Pinet Pharmacy Supplies are both in the packaged drugs industry. Their recent balance sheets are shown below. However, while Brown includes capitalized financial leases in its balance sheet, Pinet does not.

Balance sheets
(dollars in millions)

Assets:	Brown	Pinet
Current assets......................	18	46
Fixed assets.........................	52	130
Total	70	176
Claims:		
Current liabilities..................	11	36
Long-term debt.....................	16	20
Equity................................	43	120
Total	70	176

    a. Calculate debt-equity and long-term debt-equity ratios for both companies, using the reported accounting information. Which company has more financial leverage based on these calculations?

    b. What effect does the difference in their accounting procedures with respect to leases have on comparative analyses such as those in (*a*) above?

    c. A security analyst is attempting to find out how much leased assets Pinet would have to be using to have the same long-term debt-equity ratio as Brown (counting leases as debt). Perform this calculation.

9. The Cooper Barrel Company has outstanding a $10 million issue of first mortgage bonds that pay 11-percent interest annually. The bonds

have a remaining life of 20 years and are callable upon payment of a call premium equivalent to one year's interest payment. The firm has determined that, since market rates of interest have fallen to 9 percent, it would be profitable to refund the issue.

a. Determine the price at which Cooper could buy back the bonds on the open market.

b. Determine the call price of the bonds.

c. Would you recommend that Cooper call the old bonds or attempt to buy them back in the open market? Explain your answer.

SELECTED BASIC REFERENCES

Bowlin, O. D. "The Refunding Decision: Another Special Case in Capital Budgeting," *Journal of Finance* (March 1966), pp. 55–68.

Gritta, R. D. "The Impact of the Capitalization of Leases on Financial Analysis," *Financial Analysts Journal* (March–April 1974), pp. 47–52.

Middleton, J. W. "Term Lending – Practical and Profitable," *Journal of Commercial Bank Lending"* (August 1968), pp. 31–43.

Vanderwicken, P. "The Powerful Logic of the Leasing Boom," *Fortune Magazine* (November 1973).

SELECTED ADVANCED REFERENCES

Ang, J. S. "The Two Faces of Bond Refunding," *Journal of Finance* (June 1975), pp. 869–74.

Johnson, R. W., and W. G. Lewellen. "Analysis of the Lease-or-Buy Decision," *Journal of Finance* (September 1972), pp. 815–23.

Schall, L. D. "The Lease-or-Buy and Asset Acquisition Decisions," *Journal of Finance* (September 1974), pp. 1203–14.

15

CONVERTIBLE SECURITIES
AND WARRANTS

In the previous chapters we have dealt with various long-term securities that are all similar in that once they are issued, their legal ownership status remains the same throughout their life. A conventional bond, for example, is a creditor financial instrument throughout its life just as common stock is an owner instrument throughout its life. There are other financial instruments, however, whose ownership status changes or is at least potentially changeable. These financial instruments are convertible securities and warrants.

CONVERTIBLE SECURITIES

Convertible securities are bonds and preferred stocks that may be converted into shares of common stock of the same company. Basically, then, a convertible is simply a senior security with an option to convert into common stock. An owner of a Celanese Corporation convertible bond, for example, may convert his bond into ten shares of Celanese common stock. And the owner of a Halliburton Co. convertible bond may change his bond into 7.63 shares of Halliburton common stock. In either case the number of shares of common stock received is determined by the conversion terms.

Conversion terms

When a convertible security is issued it has clearly designated *conversion terms* that establish how many shares of common stock will be exchanged for the convertible security and the effective price that is being paid for the common stock being received in the exchange. These conversion terms may be stated in either of two ways:

1. Conversion ratio = The number of shares of common stock received per convertible security.

2. Conversion price = The effective price paid for the common stock upon conversion.

Knowledge of either one of these two quantities permits us to calculate the other because they are related:

$$\text{Conversion ratio} = \frac{\text{Par value of convertible security}}{\text{Conversion price}} \qquad (15\text{--}1)$$

An example will help illustrate these terms. Suppose that the Tuggle Co. sells $1,000 par value convertible bonds. These bonds are convertible into Tuggle common stock at $50 per share. The conversion price is $50 and the conversion ratio is ($1,000/$50) or 20 to 1, which means that each bond may be converted into 20 shares of Tuggle stock. The higher the conversion price is set, the lower the conversion ratio and the fewer shares of new stock that the convertible issue will ultimately be exchanged for. In the Tuggle example, if the firm were issuing $10,000,000 of bonds there would be ($10,000,000/$1,000) or 10,000 bonds sold, which one day would be converted into (20 × 10,000) or 200,000 shares of common. If, however, the conversion price were set at $62.50, the conversion ratio would be ($1,000/$62.50) or 16, and there would be only (10,000 × 16) or 160,000 new shares upon conversion. The advantage of having fewer shares is that it means higher earnings per share for the *current* stockholders. The more shares created by conversion the more dilution in future earnings per share.

Mechanics of issuing convertibles

When a company issues convertible securities it receives the proceeds of the sale less floatation costs, as in the case with nonconvertible (straight) preferred or bonds. This one-time receipt of proceeds is the cash inflow the firm receives from the capital source. In return, the firm pays preferred dividends (if the convertible is a preferred stock issue) or interest payments (if the convertible is a bond issue) up until the convertible securities are converted into common stock. Whenever an investor converts he receives shares of common stock (in accordance with the conversion terms) in exchange for surrendering his convertible securities. No cash changes hands! The investor merely exchanges one form of security (debt or preferred stock) for another (common stock). He no longer receives preferred dividends or interest payments, but he receives common dividends. His position becomes the same as any other common stockholder. The firm has a one-time receipt of funds and makes payments to convertible holders in the form of preferred dividends or interest payments until conversion, and then common dividends thereafter.

Valuation of convertibles

Because of the possibility of conversion there are two values that the convertible investor is concerned with: the convertible's *market value* and its *conversion value*.

Conversion value The conversion terms specify how many shares of common the convertible can be exchanged for. This ratio and the current market price of the common stock determine what the convertible's conversion value is.

$$\text{Conversion value} = \left(\begin{array}{c}\text{Conversion} \\ \text{ratio}\end{array}\right)\left(\begin{array}{c}\text{Common} \\ \text{stock price}\end{array}\right) \qquad (15\text{-}2)$$

The conversion value is simply the amount of money the convertible would be worth if it were converted into common stock now. In the Tuggle example, the conversion ratio is 20 to 1. If the common stock is selling for $40 per share, the conversion value of one convertible bond is (20/1 × $40) or $800. If the common stock were currently selling for $45 per share, the conversion value would be $900 per bond.

Market value Until all the convertible securities are either converted or called back (retired), they may be bought and sold in the market by investors, just like straight preferred stocks or bonds. The price at which the convertible is selling for is called its *market value*. At time of issue, the market value is approximately equal to the par value of the security.

The market value of the convertible is a function of two things: its value as a *straight* senior security and its value as common stock. If the common stock price is substantially below conversion price there will be little interest in conversion. The conversion privilege will be worth little and the convertible will have a market value that is roughly equal to its value as a senior security *without* any conversion option (that is, its value is a straight senior security). As the common stock price approaches the conversion price, however, conversion becomes increasingly possible and the market value of the convertible security becomes more and more dependent on the value of the common stock. In effect, the common stock "pulls" the convertible with it. We discuss this phenomenon below.

Conversion premiums The conversion premium is the difference between the convertible's market value and its conversion value. The premium is *positive* whenever market value is greater than conversion value, and the premium is *negative* whenever market value is less than conversion value. Premiums are frequently expressed as percentages.

$$\begin{array}{c}\text{Percentage} \\ \text{conversion premium}\end{array} = \left(\frac{\text{Market value} - \text{Conversion value}}{\text{Conversion value}}\right) \times 100$$

$$(15\text{-}3)$$

Price movements Figure 15-1 illustrates the relationships between stock price, conversion value and market values, and conversion premiums.

This figure shows several things. First, it reinforces our understanding of how conversion values are calculated. Conversion value is simply the conversion ratio (20 in the example) times the stock price. Next, notice that the conversion price is a benchmark for explaining the market value fluctuations (price movements) of convertibles. When a convertible is first issued, the conversion price is typically set between 10 and 20 percent above the current common stock price. So long as the common price gets no closer to the conversion price, the market value of the convertible is largely determined by its senior security features (interest yield, safety, etc.). So when the Tuggle stock price dropped down to 35½, although the conversion value dropped by $130, the bond's *market* value was largely unaffected.[1] Since the common stock is far below the conversion price of $50 there is little chance of conversion (no one would be interested in converting a $980 bond into stock worth $710). As the stock price begins to approach the conversion price, however, conversion becomes feasible and the convertible's market value begins to rise also. This is because the conversion value acts as a floor for the bond's market value. Notice in Figure 15–1 that the market value

FIGURE 15–1
Example of relationship between stock price and conversion premiums
(The Tuggle Co. issues 30-year 7-percent bonds at $1,000 [par value] on Dec. 15,19+0 that are convertible into Tuggle common at $50 per share)

Date	Stock price	Conversion value	Market value	Conversion premium	Percent conversion premium
12/30/+0	$42	$ 840	$ 998	$158	19
12/30/+1	35½	710	980	270	37
12/30/+2	45	900	1,050	150	17
12/30/+3	50	1,000	1,150	150	15
12/30/+4	53	1,060	1,205	145	14
12/30/+5	62	1,240	1,370	130	10

is always greater than the conversion value; that is, the conversion premium is always positive. If the market value were ever *less* than conversion value there would be *arbitrage* possibilities for investors. Arbitrage means to buy and sell the same securities in different markets to take advantage of unequal prices. Suppose, for example, that when the stock price was $50 (and therefore conversion value = $1,000) the convertible's market value was $980. There would be a −$20 premium and a chance for arbitrage profits by investors. Ignoring transaction costs (brokerage fees and taxes) the simplest form of arbitrage would be to buy the convertible for $980, convert into 20 shares of stock, and sell the stock for $1,000 (20 × $50 per share), yielding an instantaneous $20 profit. As more and more investors (technically they are called arbitragers) competed to buy the convertible and sell the stock they would create an upward pressure on the market value (price) of the convertible and a downward pressure on the stock price. This competition to make an arbitrage profit would eventually cause the convertible's market value

---

[1] The drop in the bond's market value from $998 to $980 indicates that interest rates were rising slightly during this period.

to be at least as large as its conversion value.[2] This means that the convertible shouldn't sell for less than its conversion value. If it did, arbitragers would step in and perform the operations just described.

So the conversion value acts as a floor for the market value, which explains why the market value rises once the stock price approaches the conversion price. In fact, for every dollar the stock rises above the conversion price, the convertible will increase by an amount approximately equal to the *conversion ratio times one dollar*. In Figure 15–1, for example, as the stock price increases from $50 to $53 the convertible rises $55 from $1,150 to $1,205, which is *approximately* $60 ($3 × 20). The market value did not increase the full $60 because of the positive premium on the convertible. Positive premiums exist because investors view convertibles as extremely attractive financial instruments. When they buy convertibles they receive a senior security with all of its income and asset preference features *plus* the speculative appeal of sharing in the price appreciation if the stock does well and rises above conversion price. As a result, investors are attracted to convertibles and bid up the price (market value), causing a positive premium over the conversion value. However, as the stock price continues to rise above the conversion price, the conversion premium will begin to erode. This is mainly because of the symmetric nature of the price movements of the convertible. When the common stock price is greater than the conversion price, as stock price increases the convertible's market value increases by an amount approximately equal to the conversion ratio times the dollar increase in the stock price. But when stock price is greater than conversion price and stock price *decreases,* the convertible will also *decrease* by an amount approximately equal to the conversion ratio times the dollar decrease in the stock price. So the convertible becomes riskier as the stock price continues to increase and consequently the conversion premium decreases.

Advantages of issuing convertibles

Instead of issuing convertible securities the firm obviously may issue nonconvertible bonds and preferred stock or it may issue common stock. Why then do firms issue convertible securities? There are three principle reasons. Convertibles provide delayed equity financing, they enhance the marketability of the basic senior security, and they are frequently useful in financing mergers and acquisitions.

Delayed equity financing   The most commonly stated reason for issuing convertible securities is because the firm really wants to issue equity capital but feels the time is not right for such an issue. Frequently, the firm feels its stock price is too low to justify issuing common stock. That is, the firm feels its stock price is temporarily depressed from its "true" level. In comparison to the number of shares the firm would have to issue if the price were *not* depressed, the firm must issue more shares to get

---

[2] Occasionally, there are instances reported in the newspapers where a convertible's market value is less than its conversion value. But these discrepancies are so small that arbitrage (by an average investor) would be unprofitable after paying transaction costs.

the same amount of capital from the market. But conversion prices are usually set from 10 to 20 percent higher than the common stock price at the time the convertibles are issued, which means that the convertible securities will convert into fewer shares of common than if the firm went ahead and sold stock at today's depressed price. If, for example, a firm can issue common stock at only $20 per share currently, but can issue a convertible security that will convert at $25 per share, the firm will ultimately have 25 percent fewer new shares outstanding if it chooses the convertible route. Essentially, the firm has made a deferred equity sale at the higher $25 per share price. And this is what the conversion price really means. It is the *effective* price the firm receives for the common stock. It is as if the firm were issuing common *at the conversion price* at some date in the future, except that it receives the funds that it needs for investment *now*. By reducing the number of common shares that will ultimately be outstanding the firm reduces the potential dilution in earnings per share that could occur, reduces the total dollar dividend payment the firm must pay in the future, and also keeps to a minimum any possible dilution of control caused by issuing new shares.

Marketability reasons The next most frequently cited reason for issuing convertible securities is that the convertibility feature makes the securities more marketable. If the firm has already decided to issue a senior security, attaching the conversion privilege facilitates the sale (in the extreme case the underwriter may even insist that the issue be convertible). First of all, the convertibility feature broadens the range of possible buyers for the issue since those investors who are primarily attracted to equity securities may now be interested also. A closely allied reason is that it lowers the cost of the issue. Convertible securities have traditionally paid lower dividend and interest rates than similar quality straight senior securities because the conversion privilege is presumably worth something to the investor: It acts as a "sweetener" to the bond or preferred issue. Not only does the purchaser get a security that is senior to the common stock, but if the common stock does well it will pull the convertible along with it.

Financing mergers and acquisitions In the 1960s, convertible preferred stock was frequently used in mergers for several reasons. Many growth-oriented conglomerate firms built what appeared to be hugely successful earnings records through the use of the then widespread and permissive accounting practice of "pooling of interest." This provided immediate earnings growth to the acquiring firm.[3] The use of convertible preferred also provides the basis for a tax-free exchange of the common stock of the acquired company for the convertible preferred stock of the acquiring firm. This defers taxes for the stockholders of the acquired firm. Last, the use of convertible preferred allows firms time to reconcile extremely different dividend policies. If the acquired firm were paying a much larger common dividend, for example, the acquiring firm could continue this rate through a preferred payment but would not have to radically raise the dividend rate on its own common immediately. Issuing

---

[3] Today's tax laws and accounting practices no longer encourage the use of convertible preferred stock in mergers and acquisitions (see Chapter 21).

convertible preferred allows the acquiring firm time to work up to a higher dividend rate on its common.

Disadvantages of issuing convertibles

There are some aspects of convertibles that discourage their use. Foremost is the prospect of an *overhanging issue.* If the convertibles were issued primarily as a delayed equity financing scheme, but the price of the common stock fails to increase enough to permit conversion, no conversion will occur and the issue is said to be overhanging. If the market value of the convertible is below the convertible's call price the firm cannot force conversion by calling the issue so it is stuck with the convertible. The effect of the overhanging issue is detrimental to attempts to obtain *any* kind of external long-term capital. It would be very difficult for the firm to issue *another* convertible as the market would be very skeptical of any prospects of conversion given the current overhanging issue. It may also be difficult to get a *straight* senior security issued except on very unfavorable cost and indenture terms because of the current difficulties. If the firm were highly levered to begin with and were counting on conversion to create more debt capacity, it may be impossible to float any form of senior securities. And common stock will still be very unattractive because of its depressed price.

Another disadvantage to issuing convertible securities is the potentially adverse reaction of the common stock. This has two aspects. At time of issue the convertible, being a senior security, imposes a fixed charge in front of the earnings stream, making the common stock riskier. Also, the convertible will be converted some day, which ultimately means a dilution of earnings per share. This double effect of increased risk and future dilution may depress the stock price, which is contrary to the firm's goal.

When convertibles are converted

A decision to convert the senior securities into common stock is made for two different reasons. While the investor technically "makes" the conversion decision, that is, he has the conversion option, in one instance he may voluntarily do so while in the other instance the firm essentially forces him to convert. In *either* case the convertible security holder converts because there is an economic advantage to converting. This economic advantage is the trigger that causes conversion to occur.

Voluntary conversions Investors voluntarily convert for several reasons. If the firm is doing well, the common dividends will probably be steadily increased and there will be a spread between the common dividends and the fixed convertible dividends or interest payments. Even allowing for the extra risk on the common, this spread will induce many investors to convert. Also, if the common price is increasing, the convertible price will also increase and this lessens the downside protection (defensive value) of the convertible, making it more risky and less desirable to hold. Another reason for voluntary conversion occurs when the conversion privilege is about to expire and the common stock is selling above the conversion price. Many convertibles have a scheduled expiration of the conversion privilege, and on that date the convertible will be worth less than its previous conversion value, and this induces conversion. Many convertibles have no expiration date however. Last, if the firm is in a power struggle for control, opposing parties will buy up the convertibles and convert to increase their voting strength.

Forced conversions   The firm can induce investors to convert by exercising the *call provision* of the convertible. As with ordinary bonds and preferred stock, the call provision permits the firm to retire a security by buying it back from investors at the *call price*. Unlike calls on ordinary senior securities, however, very few convertibles are *actually* bought back by the firm. Instead, the call forces conversion into common stock. If the purpose of the call is to force conversion, the firm will issue the call only when the convertible's conversion value is safely above the call price. When the call is announced the convertible investor must choose between: (1) converting into common, (2) selling the convertible at its market value (to someone who will convert into common), or (3) allowing the firm to call the convertible back at the call price. Rather than accept the lower call price, investors will opt for (1) or (2) depending on whether they wish to hold the firm's common or not.[4] By exercising the call provision the firm is said to have *forced* conversion.

Another way to force conversion is to include an *acceleration clause* in the convertible. This clause provides that on designated future dates the conversion price increases (accelerates). When the conversion price increases the conversion ratio decreases and the convertible's conversion value decreases. Since the conversion value provides a floor for the convertible's market value the market value will decrease also. Rather than suffer this drop in market value investors will convert.

Conversion policy

Conversion policy refers to the decision rule the firm uses to influence conversion once the conversion value exceeds the call price. One common policy is to force conversion whenever the conversion value of the convertible is approximately 20 percent greater than the call price. There is usually a 30-day period or so from the time the call is announced to the exercising of the call and the 20-percent cushion ensures that should the firm's stock price unexpectedly decline in this 30-day period, it would have to drop approximately 20 percent – a severe drop in 30 days – before conversion would become unprofitable. Should the stock drop by *more* than 20 percent, investors would sell the convertible back to the firm at the call price rather than convert and the firm would have to find the cash to buy these securities back. The purpose of the call would have been defeated. Another policy is to encourage conversion by raising common dividends to the point that convertible owners would rather hold the common even allowing for its riskier nature. A third policy is one of no action on the firm's part to precipitate conversion.

---

[4] While it would appear that any rational investor would not accept the call price, because of investor negligence there is usually a small fraction of convertibles that must be redeemed by the firm.

Presumably, the firm's conversion policy is dictated by the reason the convertibles were issued in the first place. Firms that force conversion probably issued convertibles expressly for the purpose of delayed equity financing and are now completing their original plan by replacing the senior securities with common stock. They may also be clearing the way for a new senior security issue. Firms that have no explicit conversion policy probably issued the convertibles for marketability reasons.

WARRANTS

A warrant is an option to buy a specified number of shares of common stock at some specific price during a designated time period, usually five years. An owner of a Capital Mortgage Investment Co. warrant, for example, may purchase one share of Capital's common stock at $20 per share by exercising the warrant prior to November 23, 1979. The number of common shares per warrant, the price paid per share, and the time period during which this option privilege can be exercised are terms of the warrant that are designated on the warrant.

Warrant terms

Option price The firm is obligated to sell common stock to its warrant holders at the warrant's *option price*, regardless of the current market price of the stock. The option price is thus a guaranteed price at which warrant holders may opt to buy stock. In the Capital Mortgage Investment Co. example, the option price is $20.

Exercise ratio A warrant's exercise ratio specifies how many shares may be purchased per warrant (at the option price). This is an effective exchange ratio that is similar to the conversion ratio of convertible securities. The exercise ratio for Capital Mortgage is 1 to 1: one share of stock per warrant.

Expiration date Most warrants have expiration dates that run from about four or five years to ten years. On the expiration date the warrant terminates and it can no longer be used to purchase common stock. Some warrants have no expiration date and are called *perpetual* warrants. Occasionally the expiration date is extended. Capital Mortgage's warrants originally expired in November, 1974, but were extended five years to November 23, 1979.

Detachable versus nondetachable warrants Warrants are frequently issued by attaching them to another security (such as a bond). In these cases the warrants may either be detachable or nondetachable. A *detachable* warrant may be separated from the bond and sold by itself. This feature is very attractive to investors. If the warrant price appreciates substantially because the stock price has increased significantly, the bondholder may sell the warrant and still hold the bond. The detachability feature gives the investor considerable flexibility. A *nondetachable* warrant cannot be sold separately from the bond and may only be separated from the bond when the warrant is exercised. If the warrant is nondetachable and if the bond is sold before the warrant is exercised, the warrant, being nondetachable, goes along with the bond to the buyer.

Mechanics of issuing warrants

When a company issues warrants it receives as an initial cash inflow the proceeds of the sale less flotation costs. (But if the warrants are attached to another security, such as bonds, it may be difficult to identify the cash inflows associated *solely* with the warrants.) There are no cash outflows to the warrant holders however; they receive no dividend or interest income during the life of the warrant. When a warrant is exercised by an investor the following exchange takes place: The investor surrenders the warrant to the firm *along with* a cash payment equal to the option price times the exercise ratio and the firm returns to the investor the number of common shares per warrant that is stipulated on the warrant. If the option price were $25 and the exercise ratio were 6/1, the investor would surrender the warrant and $150 in return for six shares of stock. From that point on, the new common stock is treated like the old common and receives whatever dividend is declared. At the expiration date (if there is one), if the common stock price is selling *above* the warrant's option price any remaining warrants will be exercised; if the common is selling *below* the option price the remaining warrants are worthless and will not be exercised. In either event the warrant issue is terminated. In recent years many firms have extended the life of their warrants when it appeared that they would expire unexercised.

Warrant valuation

Unlike convertibles, warrants have no value independent of the common stock; that is, a warrant is merely an option to buy common stock. In discussing how warrants are valued and how this value changes as the common stock price changes there are two elementary terms to define.

Market value   The market value of a warrant refers to the price that the warrant trades for in the market and is exactly analogous to the price of any other security, such as the common stock price, for example. A warrant has a market value or price, and this value is determined through competitive market forces as investors buy and sell the warrants.

Theoretical value   Since a warrant is merely an option to buy a specified number of shares of common (determined by the exercise ratio) at some specified price (the option price), the theoretical value of a warrant—which is an elegant way of saying "what the warrant should be worth"—is determined by the price of the common stock, the warrant's option price, and the warrant's exercise ratio.

$$\text{Theoretical value} = \text{Exercise ratio} \times (\text{Stock price} - \text{Option price})$$
$$(15\text{-}4)$$

If the exercise ratio on Bell Industries warrants is four shares of common per warrant, the option price is $30 per share and the common stock is selling for $50 per share: The theoretical value of the warrant is 4 × ($50 − $30) = $80. This answer is no more than a common sense solution to evaluating the warrant. Suppose, for example, an investor wanted to buy four shares of Bell stock. Forgetting the transaction costs involved, it would cost him $200 (4 × $50) to buy the stock directly. However, an alternate way to acquire the stock would be to buy one warrant (since one warrant controls four shares of stock) and exercise it. Let's figure out what he would pay for the warrant, forgetting again the transaction costs. Once he owns the warrant, to get the stock he must present the warrant plus $120 (4 × $30). But notice this is $80 less than he would have had to pay to buy the stock directly. So, it should be worth (have a *theoretical value* equal to) what an investor can buy stock for *without* the warrant minus what he can buy stock for *with* the warrant. In our example: $80.

There is one instance where this formula definition of warrants is not valid. When the stock price is less than the option price, applying the formula would give a *negative* theoretical value. This is a nonsense answer, so we define a warrant's theoretical value to be zero when the stock price is less than the option price.

Premiums   A premium exists if the warrant's market value is not equal to its theoretical value. Premiums may be stated in either dollar or percentage terms, but for comparison purposes they are best stated as percentages:

$$\text{Percent premium} = \left(\frac{\text{Market value} - \text{Theoretical value}}{\text{Theoretical value}}\right) \times 100 \quad (15\text{--}5)$$

There are two kinds of premiums possible: positive and negative. The premium is positive whenever the warrant's market value is greater than its theoretical value, and the premium is negative whenever the warrant's market value is less than its theoretical value. However, negative premiums are rarely seen because of arbitrage opportunities. As we have already seen, if the exercise ratio were 4/1, the option price were $30, and the stock were selling for $50, the theoretical value of the warrant is $80. If the warrant market value were less than $80, say $75, arbitragers would buy the warrant (for $75) exercise (paying the firm 4 × $30 = $120) and then sell the stock (for 4 × $50 = $200). An arbitrager would have made an instantaneous $5 profit by buying stock for $195 ($75 + $120) and selling immediately for $200. As arbitragers competed for this profit the warrant market value would be bid up to the point where market value equals theoretical value. Occasionally, you may observe negative premiums on warrants in the financial news, but these will be very small, and some calculations will show that the arbitrage profit is insufficient to pay the transaction costs incurred in performing the arbitrage. So the theoretical value of a warrant acts as a floor for the market value, effectively precluding large negative premiums.

Positive premiums on warrants, however, are the general rule. That is, warrants are typically priced *above* their theoretical value. Figure 15–2 shows some typical relationships that exist between the stock price and the warrant's theoretical and market values.

As Figure 15–2 shows, when the stock price is not above the option price the warrant's theoretical value is zero. When the stock price increases, the theoretical value can be found using Equation (15–4). Notice, however, that the market value is always greater than the theoretical value so there are positive premiums. Why do positive premiums exist? Because of leverage possibilities. If, for example, an investor buys

FIGURE 15–2
Example of relationship between stock price and warrant values and premiums (Bell Industries has issued warrants with an exercise ratio of 4/1 and an option price of $30. The following are theoretical and market values of the warrants at some selected stock prices)

Stock price	Theoretical value	Market value	Dollar premium	Percent premium
$25	$ 0	$ 2	$ 2	*
30	0	5	5	*
40	40	50	10	25
60	120	125	5	4

* Since the theoretical value is zero, the percent premium is undefined.

the stock at $30 and the stock subsequently goes to $40, the investor has made a [($40 − $30)/$30 × 100] 33⅓ percent return. Alternatively, had he bought the warrants (selling for $5 when the stock sells for $30), he would have made a [($50 − $5)/$5 × 100] 900 percent return (since the market value of the warrants increased to $50 when the stock went to $40). These numbers show why warrants are attractive to investors: The gains of the stock are magnified in the warrants. This means that warrants offer the investor *leverage*, the amount of which can be calculated as follows:

$$\text{Warrant leverage} = \frac{\text{Percent return on warrants}}{\text{Percent return on stock}} \qquad (15\text{–}6)$$

Using the example numbers above, we see that the warrant leverage is 900 percent/33 percent = 27. Because this leverage is appealing to many investors, there is competition to own the warrants, and this competition bids up the market value (price) of the warrants so that the warrant's market value exceeds its theoretical value. This causes a positive premium to exist.

As the common stock price increases beyond the option price, however, the percentage premium decreases. There are two reasons for this. First, the leverage potential decreases as the stock price increases. An investor who buys the stock at $40 and sells the stock at $60 makes a 50-percent return while an investor who buys the warrants at $50 and sells at $125 makes a 150-percent return. The warrant still offers leverage, but the warrant leverage ratio has gone down to three. And the warrant leverage ratio keeps dropping as the common stock price rises farther above the option price so that as the common price increases the warrant offers *relatively* less leverage, and since the premiums are caused by the leverage possibilities, the premiums decline. Another reason for the declining premiums is the increased risk in the warrants should the stock price drop. An investor who buys the stock at $60 and sees the price drop to $30 loses 50 percent of his investment. But an investor who buys a warrant at $125 and sees the warrant drop to $5 loses 96 percent of his investment. Leverage is a two-way street: It magnifies both the gains *and* the losses and the potential percentage loss increases as the stock price rises above the option price. This increased risk exposure also causes the premium to decline.

A summary of warrant valuation is shown graphically in Figure 15–3. The dotted line represents the warrant price and the solid line represents the theoretical value of the warrant. The theoretical value is zero until the stock price rises above the option price. The warrant price is shown above the theoretical value, indicating the presence of positive premiums regardless of the common stock price. In dollar terms, this premium is

FIGURE 15–3
Market and theoretical values of a warrant

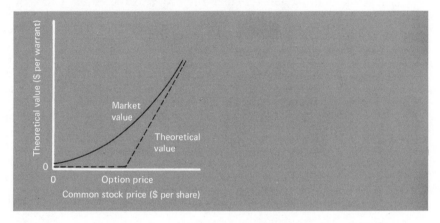

largest when the common is trading around the option price. The premium declines as the common price rises above the option price and it also declines as the common price falls substantially below the option price. This latter phenomenon occurs because the warrants become less valuable as the possibility of exercising them becomes more remote. If the common stock were hopelessly stuck below the conversion price and the warrants were about to expire there would be almost no chance of exercising the warrants and they would become worthless. This would mean that the lower left-hand segment of the warrant price curve (the dotted line) would be pushed down toward the horizontal axis.

Advantages of warrant financing

Marketability of senior securities The most commonly stated reason for issuing warrants is that once the firm has decided to issue bonds or preferred stock the warrant serves to "sweeten" the senior instrument. This need to add an equity sweetner may arise for two reasons. First, the firm may feel that the interest rate (on bonds) or the dividend yield (on preferred) is unacceptably high on the *straight* senior security, so warrants are attached to induce investors to accept a lower return. Second, the underwriters may feel the issue will not be fully subscribed unless there is an equity sweetner and will insist that warrants be included in the financing package. Of course an alternative to issuing warrants in either of these two cases is to make the bonds or preferred stock convertible, which is another form of equity sweetening.

Financing mergers and acquisitions Mergers and acquisition attempts invariably hinge on the tax liabilities incurred by the stockholders of the acquired company. This induces the acquiring company to arrange financing of the purchase in a manner that is acceptable to these stockholders and warrants provide one way of "tailoring" the financing package. If an acquisition can be classified as an installment sale, a bond-warrant package can provide a substantial tax savings for the stockholders of the acquired firm. In addition, the warrants provide these stockholders a chance to share in any realized equity gains later on by exercising the warrants.

Delayed equity financing As with convertibles, warrants provide for delayed equity financing. By setting the option price above the common stock price prevailing when the warrants are issued, the firm is effectively setting up a delayed sale of equity at the conversion price. This presumes, however, that the warrants will eventually be exercised, which occasionally does not occur.

Delayed capital inflow Another advantage of warrant financing is the fresh inflow of capital to the firm when the warrants are exercised. In contrast the conversion of convertible securities where the convertible holder merely exchanges his convertible security for new common stock, the warrant holder exchanges his warrant *plus cash* for the new common. The firm may be planning on receiving this delayed capital inflow.

Disadvantages of warrant financing

Effect on future financing Attaching warrants to senior securities may limit the firm's future financing flexibility. Since warrants do not have call provisions, exercising of the warrants is entirely at the discretion of the investor. In the past, many warrant issues have been hard to retire because warrant owners chose to sell the warrants to other investors rather than exercise them. So long as the warrants are outstanding, however, the firm may have difficulty in raising new equity capital. This is because when the warrants *are* exercised there will be more common shares outstanding and earnings per share will be diluted. This potential dilution makes any new equity issue hard to sell.

Outstanding warrants influence future financing in another way. Many investors view warrants as a sign of weakness, feeling that the firm had to issue the warrants to market the senior securities. This apprehension may mean that the firm will have problems in raising new capital because of investor suspicion, resulting in higher costs and/or restrictive indentures.

Common stock reaction When warrants are issued the common stock price may be depressed. First, there is the expected earnings dilution that will occur sometime in the future. Next, there is the possibility of dilution of control, particularly if the common stock the warrants control comprise a sizeable number of new common shares.

When warrants are exercised

As with convertibles, the exercise privilege belongs to the warrant holder, not the firm. The warrants would only be exercised when the common stock price exceeds the option price since it would always be less expensive to buy the stock on the market otherwise. A warrant holder may decide to exercise his option because of the dividend being paid on the common (the warrants receive no dividends). But the warrant can always be sold to other investors and there may be little voluntary exercising. Unlike convertibles, warrants have no call provision, so technically the firm cannot force the investors to exercise. However, a *flexible option price* and the expiration date are features that allow the firm to effectively force exercising.

The warrant's option price may be either fixed or flexible. If it is fixed, the option price never changes during the life of the warrant. Flexible option prices, however, provide for changes in the option price. The most common feature is to provide an acceleration clause in the warrant that permits the firm to increase the option price at some pre-specified date. If the common stock is selling *above* the option price, but the option price is about to be stepped up by the acceleration clause, this will precipitate exercising. On the step-up date the warrant holder will suffer in immediate capital loss since his option is not as valuable as it was and he will prefer to exercise his warrant (even if it means immediately selling the stock) rather than take this loss. If, for example, a warrant with a 1/1 exercise ratio has an option price of $15 per share that will be stepped up to $18 per share and the common is selling for $30 per share, the theoretical value changes from $15 to $12 on the step-up date, and the warrant's market value will drop also. A second kind of flexible option price clause allows the firm to *lower* the option price. If the common stock is selling for *less* than the option price and the firm feels it needs to retire the warrants to clear the way for new financing, a provision that allows the firm to temporarily *reduce* the option price will induce exercising. Temporarily reducing the option price makes the warrant temporarily more valuable, and warrant holders will be willing to exercise before the higher option price is reinstated. It is as if the firm were offering a special "sale" to its warrant holders. This is a fairly new idea, and firms hope that they do not have to resort to it, since the common being purchased through the warrants in this manner is underpriced. Nevertheless, it is a way to force retirement of the warrants.

The last form of effective exercising comes about when the expiration date is imminent. If the common price is above the option price, the warrants will be exercised since they will be worthless after the expiration date. Of course, if the common price is below the option price the warrants will not be exercised.

SUMMARY

Convertible securities are either bonds or preferred stocks that may be converted into shares of common stock of the issuing company. The terms of conversion specify the conversion ratio – how many shares of common each convertible may be exchanged for – the conversion price – the effective price paid for the common on conversion – and the time period during which conversion may take place. On conversion no cash changes hands; the convertible holder merely returns the convertible security to the firm and receives common stock. The relationship between conversion value – what the convertible is worth if conversion were made now – and the convertible's market value typically involves a positive premium since convertible securities offer investors all the advantages of holding a senior security plus the possibility of leverage should the common stock prosper. The advantages of issuing convertibles are that they provide delayed equity financing, they enhance the marketability of the underlying senior security, and they are frequently useful in financing mergers and acquisitions. The main disadvantages are the effect on future financing of an overhanging issue and the potentially adverse reaction of the common stock.

A warrant is an option to buy a specified number of shares of common stock at a specified price during a designated time period. The terms of this option include the option price – the price at which warrant holders may buy common stock – the exercise ratio – the number of shares of common that may be purchased for each warrant owned – and the expiration date of the warrant. When warrants are exercised the warrant owner surrenders his warrant plus a cash payment equal to the option price times the exercise ratio and the firm gives the investor the stipulated number of shares per warrant. The relationship between the warrant's theoretical value – what the warrant should be worth – and its market value usually involves a premium that reflects the relationship between stock price and option price and the nearness of the expiration date. Warrants usually carry positive premiums because of leverage possibilities. The major advantages of issuing warrants are the enhanced marketability of the senior securities, their use in mergers and acquisitions, their effective delayed equity financing nature, and the fact that they provide a delayed capital inflow. Warrants are disadvantageous in that they sometimes limit future financing flexibility and potentially can cause adverse common stock reactions.

QUESTIONS

1. Define the following terms and phrases:
   - *a.* Convertible security.
   - *b.* Conversion ratio.
   - *c.* Conversion price.
   - *d.* Conversion value.
   - *e.* Conversion premium.
   - *f.* Warrant.
   - *g.* Option price.

      h. Exercise ratio.
      i. Theoretical value of warrant.
      j. Warrant leverage.

2. Explain in what sense the conversion price of a convertible preferred stock is an "effective common stock price."

3. The right to convert a convertible security ultimately rests with the investor. However, the firm can include provisions when a convertible security is first issued that will effectively cause conversion. Explain these provisions.

4. Basic Products has an issue of $100 par convertible preferred stock with a 5-to-1 conversion ratio. What effect should the following circumstances have on the number of shares of Basic's preferred outstanding if the common stock is selling for about $25 per share?
    a. The conversion ratio is scheduled to decrease soon due to the acceleration clause.
    b. The conversion privilege is soon scheduled to expire.
    c. A dividend increase on the common is declared.
    d. Repeat parts (*a*) through (*c*) if the common stock is selling for $17 per share.

5. Cook-Patterson wants to retire its convertible bonds. These $1,000 face value bonds have a call price of $1,050 and a 10-to-1 conversion ratio. Assuming zero premium, would it be better for Cook-Patterson to buy the bonds back in the open market or exercise the call option if the price of common stock is:
    a. $90?
    b. $120?
    c. $105?
    d. $104?

6. A firm is preparing to float a new bond issue. The firm's investment banker says that current bond market conditions are such that either the bond will have to be convertible or five-year warrants will have to be attached. In deliberating about these two alternatives, which would be more compatible with the following situations?
    a. There is a stong possibility that the firm will need external financing in about five years.
    b. The firm's long-range plans anticipate a major financing push in about seven to eight years, and this could be jeopardized by any overhanging issues.
    c. The firm does not have any real desire to issue new equity in the foreseeable future.

7. In recent years, several firms that issued warrants were facing imminent expiration dates on the warrants where there was no hope of them being exercised. What situation must exist for there to be no hope of the warrants being exercised?

8. If the firm wants to be able to force the exercising of its warrants by investors, what provisions can be made when the warrants are issued? Briefly explain how these provisions work.

9. Describe those advantageous and disadvantageous features that are common to both convertible securities and warrants.

PROBLEMS

1. Carlson Soap has an issue of $100 par value convertible preferred outstanding. Determine the conversion price, conversion value, and percent conversion premium for this issue under the following conditions:

Condition	Conversion ratio	Common stock price	Preferred stock price
a................	10/1	$20	$225
b................	10/1	5	51
c................	4/1	30	140
d................	1/1	85	87

2. Determine the theoretical value and the percent premium on a warrant with a 1-to-1 exercise ratio and an option price of $15 per share and the following additional information:

Condition	Common stock price	Market price of warrant
a....................	$25	$13
b....................	20	9
c....................	15	3
d....................	10	1

3. Hudson Bancorp is preparing to issue some $100 par convertible preferred stock. Assuming the stock sells at par, the initial conversion premium is expected to be 25 percent. The current market price of Hudson's common is $5 per share. Determine the preferred's:
   a. Initial conversion value
   b. Conversion ratio
   c. Conversion price

4. The Kirk Slugger Baseball Bat Co. earns $2 per share on its common stock and has a *P/E* ratio of ten. The company plans to offer 5-percent 20-year convertible bonds ($1,000 face value) with a conversion price of $25 per share.
   a. What is the conversion ratio?
   b. What will be the initial conversion value of the bond if the common stock stays at its present price level and the bonds sell at face value?
   c. What is the initial percent conversion premium?
   d. Suppose after two years that the common stock price drops and interest rates on comparable quality bonds increase to 6 percent. What should be the price of the Kirk convertible bonds?

5. The Merrit Corporation currently has an *EBIT* level of $20 million. The firm has 10 million shares of common stock outstanding and no interest bearing debt. The firm's tax rate is 60 percent and Merrit's common stock *P/E* ratio is ten. To finance new investments, the company plans to issue $5 million worth of $1,000 par value, 8-percent convertible bonds. The conversion price on the bonds will be set at 25 percent above current stock price.
   a. Determine the conversion ratio.
   b. Calculate how many shares of new stock will be issued if all the bonds are converted.
   c. If Merrit's *EBIT* increases by $1 million next year because of the new investments, determine the firm's earnings per share for next year with conversion (and therefore no interest charges) and without conversion.
   d. Assuming the firm's *P/E* ratio increases to 12, what would the stock price be in part (c) assuming no conversions had occurred?

6. Nantell Corp. plans to issue $40 million of convertible 10-percent 30-year bonds. The bonds will have a 40-to-1 conversion ratio and are expected to sell initially at their face value of $1,000. Nantell's most recent income statement is:

EBIT	$50,000,000
Interest	5,000,000
EBT	$45,000,000
Tax (0.4)	18,000,000
Net income	$27,000,000
EPS (30 million shares)	0.90

   a. Determine the conversion price, initial conversion value, and initial conversion premium of the bonds, assuming Nantell's common has a 20-to-1 *P/E* ratio.
   b. How many shares of common will eventually be issued if all bonds are converted?
   c. The new investments being financed by these bonds should bring in no additional *EBIT* in the coming year. If the firm's present assets will earn the same $50 million *EBIT* as last year, determine next year's *EPS* (assuming no conversions are made).
   d. The firm wants to convert the bonds at the earliest possible moment. It plans to issue a call on the bonds whenever their conversion value is 20 percent greater than the bond's call price of $1,100 per bond. In years subsequent to next year *EPS* is expected to begin increasing by $0.20 per year (for example, *EPS* in year 2 is expected to be $0.20 greater than the *EPS* calculated in part (c), *EPS* in year 3 will be $0.20 larger than year 2 *EPS*, and so on). Assuming that the common stock's *P/E* ratio remains at its present level, determine how long it will be (in what year) before Nantell can call the bonds.

7. Deville Bros. Wines is preparing to issue $3 million in new long-term bonds. Deville is either going to make the bonds convertible or attach warrants to the bonds. If the bonds are made convertible, they will carry a 7-percent interest rate, while if warrants are attached the bond will carry a 9-percent interest rate. Deville has $10 million in assets.

   a. Deville anticipates earning 10 percent on its assets before interest and taxes, the company's tax rate is 40 percent, there are no interest charges on current liabilities, and there are currently 200,000 shares of common stock outstanding. Determine earnings per share under each plan prior to either conversion of any bonds or exercising of any warrants.

   b. Repeat part (a) for each plan assuming that earnings before interest and taxes will be 20 percent of assets.

   c. If the P/E ratio on the common is 20, determine the *expected* common stock price for both plans if there is a 50-percent chance that EBIT will be $1 million and a 50-percent chance that EBIT will be $2 million. Which plan is better? Why?

   d. Repeat part (c) assuming that the expected P/E ratio under the convertible plan is 20 and the expected P/E ratio under the warrant plan is 22.

8. Hagan Trucking has decided to issue $3 million worth of bonds. After the bonds have been issued, the claims portion of the balance sheet will look as follows:

Current liabilities	$ 1,000,000
Long-term bonds	3,000,000
Common stock ($10 par)	2,000,000
Paid in surplus	2,000,000
Retained earnings	2,000,000
Total Claims	$10,000,000

Hagan has been advised by its investment banker that the bonds should either be convertible or should have warrants attached. If the bond is made convertible, the conversion ratio will be 25/1. If warrants are used, the holder of a $1,000 par value bond may buy ten shares of stock at $42 per share.

   a. Determine how many shares of new stock would ultimately be used in each of the two plans assuming either complete conversion or complete exercising of all warrants.

   b. Prepare balance sheets for both plans that are consistent with part (a). Assume that current liabilities and retained earnings stay constant.

   c. If EBIT = $2.5 million, the company's current liabilities have no interest charges, the long-term debt has a 6-percent interest rate, and the tax rate is 40 percent, determine EPS for both plans consistent with part (a).

SELECTED BASIC REFERENCES

Hays, S. L., and H. B. Reiling. "Sophisticated Financing Tool: The Warrant," *Harvard Business Review* (January–February 1969), pp. 137–50.

Miller, A. B. "How to Call Your Convertible," *Harvard Business Review* (May–June 1971), pp. 66–70.

Pinches, G. E. "Financing with Convertible Preferred Stock, 1960–67," *Journal of Finance* (March 1970), pp. 53–64.

SELECTED ADVANCED REFERENCES

Shelton, J. P. "The Relation of the Price of a Warrant to the Price of Its Associated Stock," *Financial Analysts Journal* (May–June and July–August 1967), pp. 143–51 and 88–99, respectively.

Weil, R. L., Jr., et al. "Premiums on Convertible Bonds," *Journal of Finance* (June 1968), pp. 445–63.

section six

SHORT-TERM INVESTMENTS

16
Working capital management

17
Management of cash and marketable securities

18
Receivables and inventory

WORKING CAPITAL
MANAGEMENT

In Chapters 6 through 9 we investigated the principles of long-term investment analysis, and in Chapters 10 through 15 we studied sources of intermediate and long-term financing. In this and the next four chapters we turn our attention to a new subject: management of the firm's current assets and current liabilities. Recall that current assets are mainly cash, marketable securities, accounts receivable, and inventory, while current liabilities are mainly accounts payable, notes payable, and accruals. The management of current assets and liabilities is called *working capital management.*

Actually, the title "working capital management" is a misnomer, since financial analysts and executives usually define working capital as current assets, and define *net* working capital as current assets minus current liabilities. However, when we speak of working capital management, we usually mean the management of *both* current assets and current liabilities.

In the following two chapters we study the management of specific kinds of current assets: cash and marketable securities, accounts receivable, and inventory. After completing these chapters on short-term investments, we will investigate management of the firm's current liabilities (short-term financing) in Chapters 19 and 20.

Our purpose in this chapter then is to address the broader questions associated with working capital management. There are three fundamental questions involved:

1. Why should the firm invest in current assets?
2. What level of current assets should the firm carry?
3. How should the firm finance its current assets?

THE NEED FOR CURRENT ASSETS

Business firms are supposedly interested in enhancing stockholder wealth, and this requires the steady generation of profits by the firm. This, in turn, requires a successful sales program by the firm, and current assets are necessary to ensure the smooth functioning of the sales program. At the heart of this need for current assets is the *operating cycle*.

Operating cycle

The operating cycle refers to the length of time necessary to complete the following cycle of events:

1. Convert cash into inventory.
2. Convert inventory into receivables.
3. Convert receivables into cash.

If it were possible to instantaneously traverse the operating cycle, the firm would need no current assets. But since an instantaneous operating

FIGURE 16–1
Operating cycle

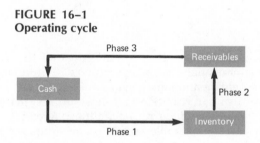

cycle is impossible, the firm must necessarily invest funds in current assets. The firm needs cash to pay bills that are not perfectly matched by current cash inflows, and many firms hold marketable securities (such as short-term government notes) to have funds available to meet emergencies that may arise. Firms carry inventory to ensure they do not run out of products to sell, and firms issue their customers credit (hold accounts receivable) for competitive sales reasons.[1] An adequate level of current assets assures a smooth, uninterrupted sales process, thus enhancing stockholder wealth maximization.

The operating cycle is shown schematically in Figure 16–1. In Phase 1, cash is used to produce inventory. For manufacturing firms, this phase would start with the purchase of materials and would conclude with the manufacturing process delivering goods to inventory. Some nonmanufacturing firms (wholesalers and retailers) would not have a manufacturing portion of this phase but would have a direct conversion of

---

[1] If a company does not provide its customers credit, competitors who do provide credit terms may capture sales from the firm.

cash into inventory. In addition, some service firms may have no Phase 1 since they have no inventory. In the second phase of the cycle the inventory is converted into receivables as sales are made to customers. Firms that have no credit terms (cash and carry firms) would have no Phase 2 since they sell only for cash. The last phase of the operating cycle, Phase 3, sees the receivables being collected, and the operating cycle is complete. The firm has moved from cash to inventory, to receivables, to cash again.

Permanent and temporary current assets

The operating cycle thus creates a need for current assets. At first glance it might appear that this need is reduced as the operating cycle ends. However, that conclusion is naive and leads us to distinguish between *permanent* and *temporary* current assets. So long as we envision the firm as a going concern, it is obvious that the firm will have a con-

FIGURE 16–2
Permanent and temporary current assets

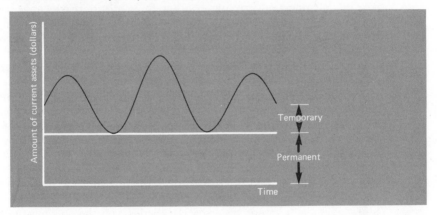

tinuous need for some minimum level of current assets. This minimum level is, in effect, every bit as permanent as the firm's fixed assets. We call this minimum level "*permanent* current assets." Any amount over and above the permanent current assets level we refer to as *temporary* current assets. Both kinds are created to facilitate the sales process through the operating cycle, but temporary current assets are carried by the firm to meet liquidity needs that are expected to last only temporarily. We discuss some of these needs below. Figure 16–2 illustrates the basic distinction between permanent and temporary current assets. The permanent level stays fairly constant during the two years shown, while temporary current assets fluctuate over the time period.[2]

---

[2] Of course, if the firm's need for permanent current assets increased or decreased over the period, the permanent current assets line would not be perfectly horizontal as shown in Figure 16–2.

Determinants of current assets changes

In determining the optimal level of current assets to maintain, which we discuss below, the firm should always be cognizant of two problems: the problem of having *too much* current assets, and the problem of having *too little*. Balancing these two kinds of costs will play an important part in determining optimal levels for the various classes of current assets. Suppose, for the moment, however, that the firm is at some satisfactory level of current assets. What factors would cause the firm to *change* this level? There are three primary reasons: (1) changes in levels of sales and/or operating expenses, (2) policy changes, and (3) changes in technology.

Sales and operating expense changes   As sales increase the firm must keep larger amounts of cash, accounts receivable, and inventory on hand to facilitate this increase. Similarly, as operating expenses rise (even without a sales increase) there is a requirement to keep more funds tied up in current assets. The opposite effect occurs when sales or operating expenses decline: The need for current assets will decline.

There are typically three reasons for sales and/or operating expense changes. First, there may be long-run trends at work. If, for example, the cost of an important raw material (such as oil) increases over time, the firm may be required to keep larger amounts of capital tied up in inventory. Secular trends would mainly affect the firm's need for permanent current assets.

A second source of change is *cyclical change* in the economy. All economies inevitably go through up and down periods, and these conditions will influence current asset levels, both permanent and temporary. A third source of change is the presence of *seasonality* in sales patterns. Because of their line of business, many firms have peak sales seasons, which cause peak cash, inventory, and receivables needs. Seasonality is the main source of variation in the firm's temporary current asset level.

Policy changes   A second major cause of changes in the level of current assets is policy changes instituted by management. If a company has had an historically conservative current asset policy—it keeps relatively high levels of current assets for its sales, volume—a conscious managerial decision to have a less conservative policy will have an obvious impact on the firm's level of current assets.

Technological changes   Another important factor that can cause changes in current asset levels is technological change. If a brewery company finds a way to speed up the brewing process, for example, it can reduce its operating cycle duration and lower the firm's commitment of funds to current assets by decreasing its investment in goods in process.

OPTIMAL LEVELS OF CURRENT ASSETS

The optimal level of current assets is that level that is most consistent with the goal of stockholder wealth maximization. Actually, since current assets comprise several categories, we will need to study the determination of optimal levels of *each* category of current assets. This will be done in the following two chapters. Before we address these issues, however, it will be helpful to discuss the basic idea of an optimal level of current assets.

Current assets, sales, and fixed assets

As sales increase, there is a need for increased levels of cash, inventory, and receivables. A firm invests in fixed assets for the same reasons it invests in current assets, and as the firm expands its sales volume, there will be a need to increase investment in fixed assets as well as in-

FIGURE 16–3
CA/TA ratio versus current asset managerial philosophy

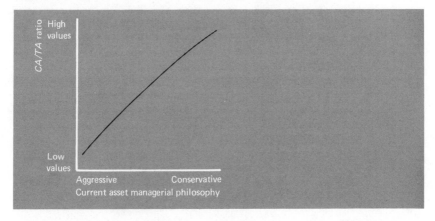

vestment in current assets. The levels of sales, current assets, and fixed assets are thus all related.

One useful way to express the firm's level of current assets is to relate current assets to the total amount of assets the firm has employed. Dividing current assets by total assets gives the *CA/TA* ratio:

$$CA/TA \text{ ratio} = \frac{\text{Current assets}}{\text{Total assets}} \qquad (16\text{–}1)$$

The higher the *CA/TA* ratio, the larger the relative investment in liquid (current) assets. As we will see below, there is a tradeoff between the profitability (return) and risk associated with holding liquid assets.

If we were to envision a plot of the *CA/TA* ratio for any firm against possible managerial philosophies regarding current asset policy, we would obtain something akin to Figure 16–3. Generally speaking, the higher a firm's *CA/TA* ratio, the more conservative that firm's current asset policy, and the lower a firm's *CA/TA* ratio, the more aggressive that firm's current asset policy. However, a low *CA/TA* ratio may also indicate the firm has a liquidity problem.

Industry norms

We must be careful not to compare apples and oranges, however. The nature of some industries dictates relatively high or low *CA/TA* ratios, and it is usually most meaningful to compare firms that are in similar lines of business.

Figure 16–4 shows 1973 *CA/TA* ratios for firms from six different industries. Of the six industries, two each are in retailing, wholesaling, and manufacturing. Generally, wholesalers and retailers, by the nature of their business, have higher *CA/TA* ratios than most other kinds of companies. Manufacturing companies tend to have somewhat lower *CA/TA* ratios. Although they are not shown, service company *CA/TA* ratios tend to be even lower, and transportation and utility companies have the lowest *CA/TA* ratios. Notice also, that even though manufacturers tend to have smaller *CA/TA* ratios than retailers, there are exceptions. The drug industry which is a manufacturing industry, had a higher average *CA/TA* ratio in 1973 than the grocery store industry, which is in retailing.

FIGURE 16–4
Current asset/total asset ratios (CA/TA) for samples of firms in six industries (1973)

Industry	General classification	Average industry CA/TA ratio
Discount stores	Retailing	84%
Grocery stores	Retailing	62
Automotive parts and supplies	Wholesaling	88
Scrap and waste materials	Wholesaling	71
Petroleum refining	Manufacturing	44
Drugs	Manufacturing	71

Source: Annual reports of sample companies.

Risk-return and current assets

In deciding upon the proper current asset level to carry (and hence, the proper *CA/TA* ratio), management must evaluate the risk-return tradeoff alluded to above. For any particular sales level or range of sales levels, in general, the greater the firm's *CA/TA* ratio, the lower the firm's risk and return. Conversely, the smaller the firm's *CA/TA* ratio, the greater the firm's risk and return. Risk in this sense is not the usual covariance form of risk we have discussed many times previously but rather alludes to a kind of *failure risk* we discussed at the end of Chapter 4.

If the firm maintains a relatively high level of current assets (a high *CA/TA* ratio), it will have sufficient cash to pay all its bills as they come due and it will have sufficient inventory to fill all sales orders.[3] Therefore,

---

[3] We have not discussed in this chapter the *composition* of current assets. This is done in Chapters 17 and 18.

the firm will have relatively less risk of experiencing a cash stockout (not having sufficient cash to pay bills) or an inventory stockout (losing orders for lack of inventory). There is a cost associated with maintaining this comfortable liquid position however. The firm will have a considerable amount of money tied up in current assets, and to the extent that this investment is idle, the firm's profitability will suffer.

Suppose, on the other hand, the firm maintains a relatively low level of current assets for its sales and fixed asset levels. The firm's profitability will improve as less resources are tied up in idle current assets. But the firm will now be exposed to greater risks of cash and inventory stockouts.

A risk-return example   This tradeoff between risk and return lies at the heart of the determination of an optimal level of current assets, in ag-

FIGURE 16–5
Current asset risk-return example—Summex Company data

Fixed Assets   = $100,000
Expected *EBIT** = $30,000 per year
Current assets under:
   Plan A: $100,000 (conservative)
   Plan B: $ 75,000 (moderate)
   Plan C: $ 50,000 (aggressive)

	Anticipated Results		
	A	*B*	*C*
Current assets......................	$100,000	$ 75,000	$ 50,000
Fixed assets..........................	100,000	100,000	100,000
Total assets	$200,000	$175,000	$150,000
EBIT/total assets	15 percent	17 percent	20 percent
Current assets/total assets........	0.50	0.43	0.33

* Recall that *EBIT* is earnings before interest and taxes.

gregate, and in the individual components of current assets. The following example further illustrates this tradeoff. The Summex Co. is considering three different levels of investment in current assets. One plan is fairly conservative, another moderate or middle of the road, and the third is fairly aggressive. The level of fixed assets in the three plans is the same. The details and the effect of these differing levels of investment in current assets is shown in Figure 16–5.

As Figure 16–5 shows, profitability—measured here by *EBIT*/total assets—is highest under the aggressive plan (*C*) and is progressively lower under the moderate (*B*) and conservative (*A*) plans. That is:

$$\frac{\text{Return of}}{\text{Plan C}} > \frac{\text{Return of}}{\text{Plan B}} > \frac{\text{Return of}}{\text{Plan A}}$$

FIGURE 16–6
Tradeoff between cost of liquidity and cost of illiquidity

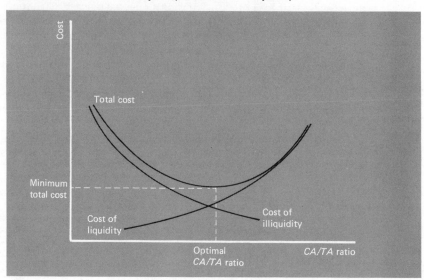

Notice also, however, that measuring insolvency risk by the CA/TA ratio:

$$\frac{\text{Risk of}}{\text{Plan C}} > \frac{\text{Risk of}}{\text{Plan B}} > \frac{\text{Risk of}}{\text{Plan A}}$$

Not surprisingly, the greater the risk, the higher the rate of return, and the lower the risk, the lower the rate of return.

The cost tradeoff   Another way to think of the risk-return tradeoff is in terms of the *cost* to the firm of having a particular CA/TA ratio. There are really two different kinds of costs involved. First, there is the *cost of liquidity*. If the firm carries too much liquidity (excessive amounts of current assets), the firm's rate of return on total assets will suffer. Funds tied up in idle cash and excess inventory earn nothing, and receivables levels that are too large also reduce the firm's profitability. As the firm's CA/TA ratio increases, the cost of liquidity increases, and this is manifested in a progressively lower rate of return on assets.

Second, there is the *cost of illiquidity,* which is the cost of having too little invested in current assets. If the firm carries too little cash, it may not be able to pay bills promptly as they mature. This may cause the firm to pay exorbitant interest rates to procure emergency funds; it may also cause the firm's credit rating to deteriorate, even to the point that the firm may have difficulty obtaining credit. At the extreme, there is the danger of insolvency (see Chapter 22). If the firm's inventory level is too low, sales may be lost because the firm can only fill orders with unacceptable delays, and customers who switch to competitors may never come back. Additionally, excessively low receivables levels may be symptomatic of a credit policy that is so tight that sales are impaired. All of these problems involve costs, and these costs increase as the firm's CA/TA ratio declines.

In selecting an optimal level of current assets (and an optimal *CA/TA* ratio) the firm must balance these two costs, seeking a minimum cost position. This concept is illustrated in Figure 16–6. As the firm's *CA/TA* ratio increases, the cost of liquidity increases, but the cost of illiquidity declines. As the firm's *CA/TA* ratio decreases, the cost of liquidity decreases, but the cost of illiquidity increases. The total cost of maintaining a particular working capital policy is the sum of these two costs, and the firm is interested in finding the minimum point of the total cost function. Figure 16–6 indicates a minimum level on the total cost function and an associated optimal *CA/TA* (and therefore optimal current assets) position.

FINANCING CURRENT ASSETS

Investment in current assets requires financing, as does investment in fixed assets. When we began investigating long-term and intermediate-term financing in Chapter 10 we briefly studied how increasing sales levels caused increased needs for current assets, which, in turn, required financing. At the time, we made no distinction between permanent and temporary current assets, nor did we distinguish among alternate types of financing available for current asset expansion. We are now prepared to address the question of financing current assets.

Short-term versus long-term financing

If we classify financing sources by maturity, there are two major categories: short-term and long-term.[4] The primary categories of short-term financing are accounts payable, accruals, and notes payable. We study these and other short-term financing sources in Chapters 19 and 20. We studied the several long-term financing sources in Chapters 10 through 15.

Our attention in this portion of the chapter is directed to the pros and cons of financing current assets with either short-term or long-term financing. The material we covered in Chapters 10 through 15 make it clear that there are substantial differences in the features of the various long-term sources of financing. Our work in Chapters 19 and 20 will support a similar conclusion for short-term financing sources. Consequently, it is obviously a crude abstraction to speak of "short-term" versus "long-term" financing as if each of these categories contained financing alternatives that have homogeneous features. However, the various short-term sources of financing do share some fundamental risk and return features as do the several long-term sources of financing. Since the choice of a current assets financing plan ultimately reduces down to a risk-return tradeoff, it seems helpful to contrast short-term versus long-term financing in a general way despite the fact that there are important differences among short-term financing sources and among long-term financing sources. So let us pursue this point.

---

[4] In this simplified two-category classification we are including intermediate-term financing with long-term financing.

Cost considerations   Most typically, the cost of short-term financing is less than the cost of long-term financing. At one extreme, accruals and accounts payable are almost free (see Chapter 19). Even ignoring these two sources, the cost of short-term borrowing is usually less than the cost of long-term borrowing, which is considered the least cost of all the long-term financing alternatives (see Chapter 8).

The relationship between the maturity of debt and its cost is called the *term structure of interest rates.* The term structure of interest rates can be displayed in a *yield curve.* The yield curve relates the debt's maturity (length of time the money will be borrowed) to its cost (its interest rate). The yield curve has taken on several shapes in past years,

FIGURE 16–7
Term structure of interest rates

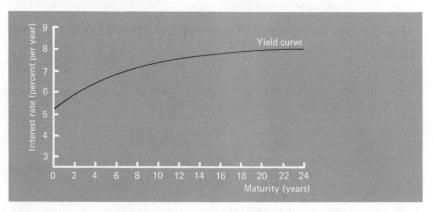

but the most common is the *upward sloping* yield curve shown in Figure 16–7. In this figure, interest rates increase with time; the longer the maturity of the debt, the greater the interest rate. The increase in interest rates is usually most pronounced in the shorter lived maturities (as shown in Figure 16–7), which emphasizes the cost differential between short-term and long-term interest rates. It is usually cheaper to borrow short-term rather than long-term.

The yield curve has taken other shapes in the past. Sometimes the yield curve has sloped *downward,* as short-term rates have been higher than long-term rates. However, the most common shape, historically, has been upward sloping such as shown in Figure 16–7, which is consistent with the phenomenon of long-term rates being higher than short-term rates. Figure 16–8 verifies that since 1950, in most years the long-term interest rate has exceeded the short-term rate.[5] The early 1970s have provided some striking exceptions however.

One of the most frequent explanations given for the fact that long-

---

[5] There is actually no such thing as "the" long-term or short-term rate. There are *many* such rates. The rates shown in Figure 16–8 are representative examples. The long-term rate shown is the Aaa Moody's bond interest rate, and the short-term rate is the prime commercial rate (see Chapter 20). These rates are for comparable, high-quality corporate debt obligations.

term interest costs are more than short-term interest costs is the *liquidity preference theory*. This theory says that since lenders are risk averse, and risk generally increases with length of lending time (because it is more difficult to forecast the more distant future), most lenders would prefer to make short-term loans. These lenders—says the theory—can only be induced to lend for longer periods of time by granting them higher interest rates. Hence, the usual upward sloping yield curve.

While they are not the most common cases, yield curves also slope downward and are sometimes flat. To explain these kind of yield curves, most economists appeal to the *expectations theory* of the term structure

FIGURE 16–8
Short-term versus long-term interest rates

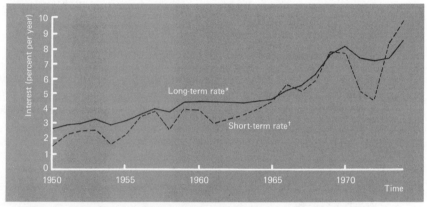

* High-quality (Aaa) bonds.
† High-quality (prime) commercial paper (four to six months)
Source: Economic Report of the President, 1975.

of interest rates. This theory asserts that yield curves reflect investors' expectations of future short-term interest rates. Downward sloping yield curves are explained as situations where future short-term interest rates are expected to decline; flat yield curves are explained as situations where future short-term interest rates are expected to be about the same as they are now. The typical effect of higher long-term financing costs relative to short-term financing costs is to make the rate of return on equity higher when the firm chooses short-term financing. Thus, from a *return* standpoint, short-term financing is usually (but not always) preferable.

Risk considerations   The other major consideration in comparing short-term versus long-term financing is that short-term financing involves more risk. If the firm uses long-term financing to build up current assets, there will be less risk involved in renewing the borrowing. This is most evident in financing permanent current assets. Recall that permanent current assets refers to that minimum level of current assets that the firm requires to continue as a successful ongoing company. Suppose the firm finances its permanent current assets with short-term debt. As the short-term debt matures the firm must arrange new short-term borrowing. This periodic refinancing exposes the firm to the possibility that there may be times when it is difficult to borrow new money, particularly if the firm is experiencing hard times. At the extreme, the firm may be unable to acquire new financing and will face the prospect of disruption of its operating activities, or possibly even failure. If the firm finances with long-term debt instead, there will be fewer refunding occasions. This means that there will be less risk of failure in a long-term financing plan (relative to a short-term financing plan), other things equal.

Therefore, while we saw above that short-term financing is usually less costly than long-term, short-term financing also typically involves more risk. We have a risk-return tradeoff involved in the choice between short-term and long-term financing of current assets. The more short-term financing used, the greater the firm's profitability but the more risk placed upon the firm.

Financing needs

At any point in time the firm may be described as having a need for financing. This need is the sum total of financing needed for the firm's investment in current and fixed assets. Figure 16–9 shows a diagram of

FIGURE 16–9
Financing needs

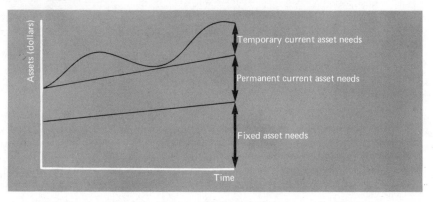

the firm's financing needs. Note that consistent with our discussion earlier in the chapter (see Figure 16–2), current asset requirements are divided into permanent and temporary components.

Alternate financing plans

The current asset financing plan may be readily related to the broader issue of the financing plan for *all* the firm's assets. The firm has a wide variety of financing policies it may choose, and the fact that short-term financing usually is less costly but involves more risk than long-term financing plays an important part in describing the degree of aggressiveness or conservatism of the firm's financing policy.

In comparing financing plans we should distinguish between three different kinds of financing: long-term financing, *negotiated* short-term financing, and *spontaneous* short-term financing. We have studied long-term financing in detail in previous chapters, and this encompasses cash flow from operations, common and preferred stock, bonds, leases, and term loans. Negotiated short-term financing refers to those sources of short-term credit the firm must arrange in advance to obtain. These sources are covered in Chapter 20 and include short-term bank and finance company loans, commercial paper, and factoring receivables.

Spontaneous short-term financing refers to those sources of short-term funds that the firm may acquire almost automatically without formal negotiation. The major forms of short-term spontaneous financing are trade credit (accounts payable) and accruals (wages and taxes), and we discuss these sources in Chapter 19. Since spontaneous short-term financing is almost free, most firms will attempt to finance current assets with trade credit as much as possible; therefore, spontaneous financing will increase and decrease as the firm's need for financing current assets increases and decreases. Because spontaneous short-term financing is so desirable we may safely assume that the firm will always use it to the fullest extent possible. Consequently, we will omit spontaneous short-term financing and that portion of current assets supported by it from the following discussion of the relative desirability of long-term versus short-term financing. That is, the choice of financing plans discussed immediately below will abstract from spontaneous short-term financing and related short-term assets. In effect, we focus on the negotiated sources of financing (both long-term and short-term) available to the firm.

A matching approach[6] One financing plan involves matching; it involves matching the expected life of assets purchased with the expected life of the financing raised to pay for the assets. The rationale for matching is that since the purpose of financing is to pay for assets, when the asset is expected to be relinquished, so should the financing be relinquished. Arranging financing for longer periods than the assets require (such as long-term financing for short-term assets) is costly because the financing is not needed for the full period. Similarly, arranging financing for shorter periods than the assets require (such as short-term financing for long-term assets) is also costly in that there will be extra transaction costs involved in continually arranging new short-term financing. Also, there is always the risk that new financing cannot be obtained in times of economic difficulty.

Under a matching approach, fixed assets and permanent current assets would be financed with long-term financing, and temporary current assets would be financed with short-term financing.[7] Figure 16–10A shows the firm's investment and financing patterns over time under a matching plan. As the firm's fixed asset and permanent current asset

---

[6] Matching is also called "hedging."

[7] Recall that we are not including spontaneous short-term financing and the current assets supported by spontaneous short-term financing in this and the following discussions.

FIGURE 16–10
Financing plans

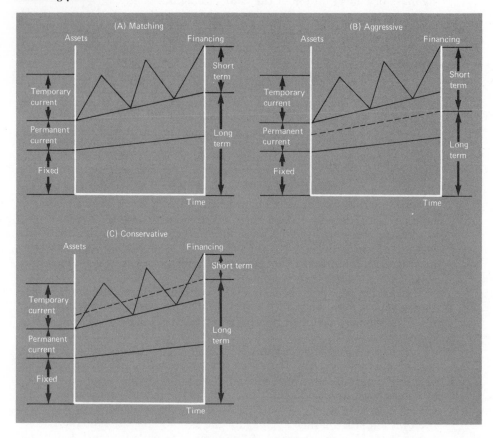

levels increase, the long-term financing level also increases. When temporary current asset levels increase, short-term negotiated financing increases, and when the firm has no temporary current assets, it also has no short-term negotiated financing.

Aggressive approaches The firm's financing plan is said to be aggressive if the firm uses more short-term negotiated financing than is needed under a matching approach. Figure 16–10B illustrates this situation. The firm is no longer financing all its permanent current assets with long-term financing. Such plans are said to be aggressive because they involve a relatively heavy use of (riskier) short-term financing. The more short-term financing used relative to long-term financing, the more aggressive the financing plan. Some firms even finance part of their long-term assets with short-term debt, which would be a highly aggressive plan.

Conservative approaches Conservative financing plans are those plans that use more long-term financing than is needed under a matching approach. Figure 16–10C illustrates this approach. The firm is financing a portion of its temporary current assets requirements with long-term financing. Also, in periods when the firm has no temporary current assets, the firm has excess (unneeded) financing available that will be invested in marketable securities. These plans are called conservative because they involve relatively heavy use of (less risky) long-term financing.

A financing risk-return example The tradeoff between risk and return involved in financing may be demonstrated with a simple example. To expedite our discussion we may think of the risk involved in the financing mix as being measured by the following ratio:

$$CF/TF \text{ ratio} = \frac{\text{Current financing}}{\text{Total financing}} \qquad (16\text{--}2)$$

This ratio relates how much of the firm's total financing is *current* financing, where current financing is the sum of all the firm's current liabilities.[8] Our previous discussions about risk imply that the greater the firm's CF/TF ratio, the more risk the firm has. Now consider the following example.

A newly formed company, Bovee Printing, Inc., is considering three alternate financing plans described below. One, Plan A, makes relatively heavy use of long-term financing and thus is a conservative plan; another, Plan B, is a matching plan, and the third, Plan C, is more aggressive in that it makes relatively heavy use of short-term financing. The company will use payables and accruals to the fullest extent possible, and will have the same net worth and *EBIT* under each of the three plans. The basic financing alternatives are as follows:

Plan	Short-term debt (6 percent)	Long-term debt (10 percent)
A (conservative)	$100,000	$400,000
B (matching)	300,000	200,000
C (aggressive)	500,000	0

All other data and the results of the analysis showing the effect of the choice of financing plan on risk and return are shown in Figure 16–11.

Earnings per share and return on equity are highest under the aggressive plan and lowest under the conservative plan. The Plan B results are between these extremes. That is,

Return under Plan C > Return under Plan B > Return under Plan A

Notice also, however, that financing risks (measured here by the CF/TF ratio) are similarly ordered:

$$\frac{\text{Risk of}}{\text{Plan C}} > \frac{\text{Risk of}}{\text{Plan B}} > \frac{\text{Risk of}}{\text{Plan A}}$$

---

[8] The ratio is conceptually similar to the CA/TA ratio [Equation 16–1)], which measures how much of the firm's total assets are current assets.

FIGURE 16–11
Financing risk-return tradeoff example — Bovee Printing, Inc.

	(Conservative) Plan A	(Matching) Plan B	(Aggressive) Plan C
Current assets	$ 400,000	$ 400,000	$ 400,000
Fixed assets	600,000	600,000	600,000
Total assets	$1,000,000	$1,000,000	$1,000,000
Payables and accruals	$ 100,000	$ 100,000	$ 100,000
Short-term debt (6%)	100,000	300,000	500,000
Current liabilities	$ 200,000	$ 400,000	$ 600,000
Long-term debt (10%)	400,000	200,000	0
Equity (10,000 shares)	400,000	400,000	400,000
Total financing	$1,000,000	$1,000,000	$1,000,000
EBIT	$ 120,000	$ 120,000	$ 120,000
Interest	46,000	38,000	30,000
EBT	74,000	82,000	90,000
Tax (40%)	29,600	32,800	36,000
Net income	$ 44,400	$ 49,200	$ 54,000
EPS*	$4.44 per share	$4.92 per share	$5.40 per share
Return on equity†	11.1 percent	12.3 percent	13.5 percent
CF/TF‡	0.2	0.4	0.6

* EPS = Earnings per share.
† Return on equity = Net income/Equity.
‡ CF/TF = Current financing/Total financing.

Thus, we have an example of the financing risk-return tradeoff described above. Heavier reliance on cheaper short-term financing provides greater returns but is riskier.

Interaction of current asset and current financing levels The *CA/TA* ratio measures the relative liquidity of the firm's asset structure, and other things equal, the greater the *CA/TA* ratio, the less risky and also the less profitable the firm will be. Similarly, the *CF/TF* ratio measures the relative liquidity of the firm's financial structure, and other things equal, the greater the *CF/TF* ratio, the more risky and profitable the firm will be. In describing a firm's working capital policy we should bear in mind that, at the broadest level, working capital policy has these two dimensions — relative asset liquidity (*CA/TA*) and relative financing liquidity (*CF/TF*) — which may reinforce or offset one another. Thus, a working capital policy that selects a high *CA/TA* ratio (which decreases risk and return) combined with a low *CF/TF* ratio (which also decreases risk and return) will cause the firm to be fairly conservative and to be characterized by low risk and low return. Another example of this interaction is where the firm chooses to offset a somewhat risky illiquid asset structure (a low *CA/TA* ratio) caused by the firm's line of business with a conservative financing policy (a low *CF/TF* ratio). This discussion illustrates one of the main features of working capital management: the interaction effect between asset and financing mixes. It is an important point to remember. Our work in the following four chapters will necessarily focus on isolated aspects of current asset and current liability management. But these two topics are fundamentally related, and both are also related to the long-term investment and financing decisions the firm makes.

SUMMARY

Working capital management refers to the management of the firm's current assets and the financing of those assets. Like fixed assets, current assets are needed to smoothly facilitate the sales process. The need for current assets is related to the firm's *operating cycle*, which is the length of time necessary to convert cash to inventory, inventory to receivables, and receivables to cash. The two primary working capital policy questions are deciding what level of current assets to invest in and how to finance current assets.

The different components of current assets are each thought to have optimal levels that, in aggregate, determine the firm's optimal level of current assets. In general, the greater the level of current assets, the less profitable and the less risky the firm will be. Relatively heavy investment in current assets is less profitable because funds are tied up in idle assets. A heavy investment in current assets also means the firm is less prone to suffer cash and inventory stockouts and is less likely to lose sales because of an overly restrictive credit policy. Relatively low investment in current assets can lead to profitability increases, as less resources are idle, but risk increases as cash and inventory stockouts are more likely, and lost sales due to restrictive credit policies are also more likely. The choice of an optimal level of current assets thus involves a risk-return tradeoff.

The choice of a financing plan for supporting the firm's current assets also involves a risk-return tradeoff. Since accounts payable and accruals are "free" sources of financing, the firm will use them to the fullest extent possible. With regard to the remaining financing, if the firm makes relatively heavy use of short-term borrowing, the firm will be more profitable (since short-term borrowing costs are usually less than long-term borrowing costs). But the firm will also be riskier (since short-term debt must be refinanced more frequently and there is the danger of being unable to refinance). On the other hand, if the firm makes relatively light use of short-term financing, the opposite effects will occur: The firm will be both less profitable and less risky.

Working capital management is therefore concerned with *both* the choice of a current asset level and the financing of this chosen level. The two problems are interrelated and the risk-return tradeoffs involved in each may be used to reinforce or to offset each other. In the next two chapters (17 and 18) we investigate the current asset management problem in more detail, and in the following two chapters (19 and 20) we further investigate the subject of short-term financing.

QUESTIONS

1. Define the following terms and phrases:
   a. Working capital management.
   b. Permanent current assets.
   c. Temporary current assets.
   d. Yield curve.
   e. Negotiated short-term financing.
   f. Spontaneous short-term financing.

2. Describe what effects the following situations would have on the firm's level of current assets:
   a. The company's inventory management skills increase because of a successful training program.
   b. Most economists agree that there will be a "liquidity crunch" in the next few months and that cash will be a scarce commodity.
   c. The firm has just finished its peak sales season.
   d. Management believes that the company's return on assets is too low and that the firm needs to manage all assets more efficiently.

3. At a financial analysts meeting in Denver, treasurers from two companies, Ollie Mae Pies and Derrington Equipment, present and discuss financial information from their companies to the analysts. Derrington has the lower CA/TA ratio and the higher CF/TF ratio. However, the analysts conclude that Derrington has less working capital management risk than Ollie Mae. How could you explain this finding?

4. Classify the following as either spontaneous or negotiated sources of short-term financing:
   a. Accounts payable
   b. Notes payable
   c. Commercial paper
   d. Accrued taxes

5. Explain the advantage of a matching financing plan relative to a financing plan that extensively uses:
   a. Long-term financing
   b. Negotiated short-term financing

6. Mary Green, an analyst, is comparing two companies, A and B, that are in the same industry. The analyst makes several comparisons of interest, including an assessment of the firms' working capital policy. In writing up her report, she notes that A has a greater current asset to total asset ratio than B.
   a. Other things equal, what effect would this finding probably have on the analyst's assessment of the relative risk and return of the two companies?

    b. In summarizing her report, she concludes that A's working capital management policy seems to be more aggressive than B's. Is this conclusion necessarily inconsistent with the information given in the problem? Explain.

7. Explain why many economists argue that short-term borrowing costs are usually less than long-term borrowing costs.

8. Assume that a firm has decided to use no new long-term financing in the near future. Other things equal, how would the following events affect the firm's CA/TA and CF/TF ratios?
   a. The collection period increases.
   b. Inventory turnover decreases.
   c. The firm retires a small portion of its long-term debt by buying it back on the open market with cash.

PROBLEMS

1. Pratt-Lyons anticipates an $800,000 sales volume next year. Normally, for every dollar in sales the firm generates, $0.15 in earnings before interest and tax will result. Pratt-Lyons fixed asset investment is $1 million and the company will maintain current assets at one of three levels: (I) $200,000, (II) $250,000, or (III) $300,000. The firm's tax rate is 30 percent, the annual interest charge is $20,000, and the firm has $850,000 equity in its capital structure. Determine for each of the three plans:
   a. CA/TA ratios
   b. $EBIT/TA$ ratios
   c. Return on equity (see Chapter 2)
   d. Rank the plans from most risky to least risky and from most profitable to least profitable. Indicate the basis of your rankings.

2. Financial data for several firms in the same industry are shown below:

	Financial data (millions of dollars)		
	A	*B*	*C*
Cash and securities	2	3	4
Accounts receivable	4	4	4
Inventory	8	9	10
Fixed assets	20	20	20
Accounts payable	3	3	3
Wages and taxes payable	1	1	1
Notes payable	6	5	4
Long-term debt	6	9	12
Preferred stock	6	6	6
Common equity	12	12	12

a. Determine *CA/TA* and *CF/TF* ratios for all three firms.
b. Assume that *CA/TA* and *CF/TF* ratios measure current asset and current liability managerial philosophies, respectively. Rank the firms from most aggressive to least aggressive with respect to current asset and current liability management philosophies.
c. Combine your answers to (*a*) and (*b*) to rank the three companies' working capital management philosophy from most aggressive to least aggressive.
d. Assume that the tax rate = 50 percent and that *EBIT* is 20 percent of fixed assets for each firm. Also assume that notes payable have 6-percent interest costs and that long-term debt will have 7-percent interest costs. Calculate net income for each company.
e. Are the results from (*d*) consistent with part (*c*)? Briefly explain.

3. The information listed below pertains to Poindexter's, a department store chain: (Recall that a list of financial ratios is presented in the Summary of Chapter 2).

Annual sales	$73,000,000
Fixed assets turnover........	4
Inventory turnover...........	2
Current ratio	1.5
Collection period............	30 days
Total financing	$64,000,000

a. Fill in the following balance sheet:

Cash and securities	_____	Current liabilities	_____
Accounts receivable	_____	Long-term claims	_____
Inventory	_____		
Fixed assets	_____		
Total	_____	Total	_____

b. Determine Poindexter's *CA/TA* and *CF/TF* ratios.
c. Poindexter's financial staff is convinced that the firm could be more aggressive in the management of its inventory. Assuming that any decrease in current assets would result in an equal dollar decrease in the level of current liabilities, redetermine the *CA/TA* and *CF/TF* ratios if the firm's inventory turnover increases to 2.5.
d. In what ways do the inventory and financing decisions made by Poindexter in part (*c*) affect working capital risk?

4. Holcomb Enterprises has the abbreviated income statement shown below. The firm's comptroller has suggested that the firm is keeping too much inventory and cash. Furthermore, a $200,000 reduction in inventory and cash would allow the firm to forego renewing a $200,000 note payable that matures soon. That is, the firm would reduce both its current assets and current liabilities by $200,000.

```
EBIT ............................... $2,600,000
Interest............................    450,000
EBT ...............................  2,150,000
Tax (0.4) ..........................    860,000
Net income ...................... $1,290,000
EPS (2,000,000 shares) ......... $0.645 per share
```

a. Determine the price of the stock if Holcomb's *P/E* ratio is 10.
b. If the $200,000 note to be renewed has a 10-percent interest rate determine the interest saving the firm would realize by adopting the comptroller's suggestion.
c. Assuming that *EBIT* is unaffected by the reduction in current assets and current liabilities, determine *EPS* if the comptroller's suggestion is adopted. Determine the new stock price if the *P/E* ratio remains at 10.
d. An analyst argues that *EBIT* may suffer because the firm may lose some sales due to low inventory levels if the suggestion is adopted. The analyst estimates the probable loss in *EBIT* at $30,000. Determine the *EPS* if the analyst's forecast is accurate. Assuming a *P/E* ratio of 10, estimate stock price.
e. If there is a 50-50 chance that the $30,000 *EBIT* loss would occur, calculate the expected price if the comptroller's suggestion is adopted. Based on this calculation would you agree with the recommended change?

5. Holsinger Computer is in the process of estimating how much short-term borrowing it will need to do over the next two years. A company analyst has estimated the firm's current assets levels for each quarter of the next two years. These estimates are shown below.

	Estimated current assets (millions of dollars)
Year 1	
Quarter 1.....................	10
Quarter 2.....................	13
Quarter 3.....................	10
Quarter 4.....................	9
Year 2	
Quarter 1.....................	11
Quarter 2.....................	15
Quarter 3.....................	12
Quarter 4.....................	10

a. Each year's permanent current asset level is defined by Holsinger as the minimum of the estimated quarterly current asset levels for that year. What are Holsinger's permanent current asset levels in Year 1 and Year 2?

b. Using the answers from part (*a*), determine the firm's anticipated temporary current asset levels in each quarter.

c. Ignoring any spontaneous short-term financing considerations, how much short-term negotiated financing will Holsinger need each quarter if the company adopts a matching financing plan?

d. Holsinger is also considering taking out a two-year term loan to finance its temporary current asset needs. If this plan were followed, Holsinger would borrow an amount today equal to the maximum amount of short-term negotiated financing needs estimated. How large a term loan would be needed under this plan?

e. If Holsinger takes out the two-year term loan described in (*d*) it will pay 8-percent annual interest, with one fourth of the interest due each quarter. If the matching plan described in (*c*) is used, Holsinger expects to pay 7-percent annual interest during the first year and 8.5-percent annual interest during the second year. Each quarter's actual interest is one fourth of the annual rate times the loan amount outstanding. Determine the interest that would be paid each quarter under each plan.

f. Which plan appears more costly? Which plan entails more risk? Explain your answers.

6. For planning purposes analysts with Crites Engineering prepare a simplified balance sheet such as the one shown below in part (*a*). The balance sheet is not only simplified, but it is also labeled somewhat differently. It is, in fact, specifically prepared to distinguish between permanent and temporary current assets and between spontaneous and negotiated short-term financing. Assume that you are a Crites analyst attempting to estimate future financing needs. You have been provided estimates of permanent and temporary current asset and fixed asset levels for the next three years and you also have the following instructions:

1. Each one dollar increase (decrease) in current assets will cause spontaneous short-term financing to increase (decrease) by $0.50.

2. After spontaneous short-term financing has been exhausted, permanent current asset increases will be financed by long-term debt.

3. After spontaneous short-term financing has been exhausted, temporary current asset increases will be financed by negotiated short-term financing (borrowing).

4. The firm will never carry more negotiated short-term financing than needed to finance that portion of temporary current assets not covered by spontaneous short-term financing.

5. Any increase in fixed assets will be financed by new long-term debt.

a. Use these guidelines to fill in the blanks in the financing section of future balance sheets shown below:

	Present balance sheet (millions of dollars)	Estimated future balance sheets (millions of dollars)		
	19 + 0	19 + 1	19 + 2	19 + 3
Temporary current assets............	2	4	6	4
Permanent current assets	14	14	14	16
Fixed assets	20	20	20	22
Total assets....................	36	38	40	42
Spontaneous short-term financing	8	—	—	—
Negotiated short-term financing	1	—	—	—
Long-term debt........................	12	—	—	—
Equity	15	15	15	15
Total financing...............	36	38	40	42

 b. Basically, what kind of financing policy is Crites using?

7. Litzenberger and Associates, Inc., is an economic advisory service firm located in San Francisco. The firm has recently experienced vigorous growth and finds that it needs to expand its asset base by about $10 million; this will bring total assets to the $60 million level. The firm's financial planning staff has been doing some research on how best to raise the $10 million and has reached some tentative conclusions. First of all, the staff feels that the financing maturity should only be about five years long as it is very likely that the firm's asset base will shrink back in about five years when some of the company's government contracts expire. This pretty much rules out common stock, preferred stock, and long-term bonds.

 Two debt plans have been suggested. Plan I calls for a five-year term loan from an insurance company at a 8-percent interest rate. Plan II calls for borrowing short-term and then renewing the loan annually during the entire five-year period. Since the short-term loan would be renewed in the future the firm does not know now what interest rates will prevail at times of renewal. Litzenberger's staff estimates, however, the average interest rate under Plan II will be a function of the firm's average annual *EBIT* level. The average annual *EBIT* level will, in turn, be considerably influenced by the economic conditions prevailing. Litzenberger's estimates of economic conditions, probability of occurrence, average annual *EBIT* levels, and average short-term interest rates are:

Economic conditions	Probability	Average annual EBIT	Average short-term interest rates (percent)
Good	0.2	$9 million	5
Average.................	0.6	6 million	6
Bad	0.2	3 million	10

In addition to this new debt, Litzenberger also has $10 million of 6-percent bonds that will be outstanding for another 15 years. There are no preferred shares and 3 million shares of common stock outstanding. The company's present tax rate is 40 percent.

a. Determine *EPS* for both plans under each possible economic outcome.

b. Determine expected *EPS* for both plans.

c. The financial staff estimates that if Plan I is adopted the stock's *P/E* ratio will be about 30/1 as it is now. Which plan would be preferable from an expected stock price standpoint if the *P/E* ratio were estimated to be 25/1 if Plan II were chosen?

d. What reason would probably be given for a drop in the *P/E* ratio if Plan II were adopted?

SELECTED BASIC REFERENCES

Cossaboom, R. A.   "Let's Reassess the Profitability-Liquidity Tradeoff," *Financial Executive* (May 1971), pp. 46–51.

Walker, E. W.   "Towards a Theory of Working Capital," *Engineering Economist* (January–February 1964), pp. 21–35.

Welter, P.   "How to Calculate Savings Possible through Reduction of Working Capital," *Financial Executive* (October 1970), pp. 50–58.

SELECTED ADVANCED REFERENCES

Knight, W. D.   "Working Capital Management-Satisficing vs. Optimization," *Financial Management* (Spring 1972), pp. 33–40.

Smith, K. V.   "State of the Art of Working Capital Management," *Financial Management* (Autumn 1973), pp. 50–55.

Van Horne, J. C.   "A Risk-Return Analysis of a Firm's Working Capital Position," *Engineering Economist* (Winter 1969), pp. 71–88.

17

MANAGEMENT OF CASH AND MARKETABLE SECURITIES

I n the previous chapter we introduced the general concepts associated with managing the firm's current asset and liability positions. In this chapter we look in more detail at the problems involved with managing two very important components of current assets: cash and marketable securities. Cash includes currency the firm has in its till and, more importantly for modern businesses, checking accounts kept at commercial banks. Marketable securities come in many forms and will be discussed later, but their main characteristic is that they represent "near cash" in that they may be readily sold. Hence marketable securities serve as a backup pool of liquidity that provides cash quickly when needed. Marketable securities also provide a short-term investment outlet for excess cash and are also useful for meeting planned outflows of funds.

MOTIVES FOR HOLDING CASH AND MARKETABLE SECURITIES

Economists have historically discussed motives for holding *cash*. However, given the "near cash" status of marketable securities, we may conveniently include them in the discussion also.

Transactions motive

One of the primary reasons for holding cash and marketable securities is to enable the firm to meet all its bills as they come due. This reason is referred to as the *transactions motive*. If the firm's cash receipts and cash payments were perfectly synchronized so that whenever the firm had to pay out $X, $X in cash receipts were forthcoming, there would be no need to hold cash or marketable securities for transactions reasons. However, cash inflows and outflows are never fully synchronized. Some days, cash receipts will exceed cash payments, and other days, cash payments will exceed cash receipts. To ensure that the firm can pay its bills

429

on days that cash payments exceed cash receipts, the firm will maintain a positive cash balance that can be used to finance any such requirement. Firms may also keep marketable securities for transactions purposes. A commonplace example of investment in marketable securities for transactions reasons would be the purchase of securities whose maturity coincides with a scheduled dividend payment by the firm. Mainly, however, the transactions motive refers to holding *cash* to meet anticipated bills whose timing is not perfectly synchronized with cash receipts.

Precautionary motive

In addition to the fact that anticipated cash inflows and outflows are not perfectly synchronized, there is also the possibility that large unanticipated net cash outflows may occur. There are many reasons why the firm could experience unanticipated net cash outflows. Several bills may be presented for cash settlement earlier than expected. Or cash receipts the firm was anticipating from previous sales could be unexpectedly delayed, or the customer may be unhappy with the merchandise and may cancel the sale. These and similar needs cause firms to keep cash and marketable securities for precautionary reasons. Marketable securities play an especially important role here. Because precautionary liquidity reserves are not *expected* to be utilized, the firm will attempt to earn some positive rate of return on funds kept for precautionary reasons. This leads the firm to invest such funds in highly liquid, safe, marketable securities. Most financial theorists argue that relatively little *cash* is held for precautionary reasons, but rather most precautionary balances are held in the form of marketable securities.

Speculative motive

Another reason sometimes given for holding cash and marketable securities is the speculative motive. This motive actually covers a wide array of things. From time to time the firm may have an opportunity to purchase material at a cut-rate price, provided it can pay cash immediately. There is also the chance to speculate on interest rate movements by buying securities when interest rates are expected to decline.[1] The firm can also delay materials purchasing, holding cash on the anticipation that materials prices will decline in the near future. While some firms do engage in such speculation, most firms do not seem to regularly hold cash and securities for speculative reasons.

Compensating balances

Modern businesses depend on commercial banks for many services, which are discussed below. While some of these services are paid for by direct fees, others are paid for indirectly by the firm keeping *compensating balances* at the bank. Compensating balances are minimum checking account levels that the firm agrees to maintain at the bank. Com-

---

[1] Recall that when interest rates decline, financial securities, such as bonds, rise in price.

pensating balances are also maintained by the firm in conjunction with bank loans (see Chapter 20). Because the firm has agreed to keep the compensating balance above some specified minimum amount, the bank can safely loan this balance to other customers, thereby earning a rate of return on the balance. This is what is meant by the firm paying an *indirect* fee. The services motive seems to be the dominant reason today that firms keep large levels of cash.

MANAGING THE CASH FLOW

When the firm makes a sale, it would like to collect the receipt in cash as quickly as possible. Conversely, when the firm makes a purchase, it would like to delay payment as long as possible. Thus, in managing its cash flow, the firm attempts (within legal and moral bounds) to speed up cash collections as much as possible, and it attempts to slow cash disbursements as much as possible.

Speeding up cash collections[2]

Speeding up cash collections refers to reducing the time interval from the time that a customer places a payment check in the mail to the time that the firm has use of the money. Within this time interval there are two main sources of delay: (1) the transit time and (2) the time spent in "processing" the check.[3] The sum of the checks written by customers that are not yet useable by the firm is called *deposit float,* and the longer the delay in converting customers' checks to useable funds, the greater the firm's deposit float. With respect to collections, efficient cash management is aimed at reducing the firm's deposit float by reducing transit and processing times. There are several techniques available for doing this.

Decentralized collections One way to reduce the mailing time is to decentralize the collection points. Suppose, for example, that a firm whose headquarters is in Boston makes sales all over the country. A check written by a customer in San Francisco may take four days to arrive in Boston. If the firm had a collection center in Los Angeles or San Francisco, however, the mailing time would be reduced. By setting up judiciously chosen decentralized collection centers around the country, the Boston firm can reduce mailing time and, hence, deposit float. There are two principal methods of establishing a decentralized collection network: through *lock boxes* and *field collections.*

Lock boxes. In a lock box arrangement, the firm bills its customers with instructions to mail payments to a post office box in a designated city. The firm authorizes a local bank (called a *concentration bank*) to collect checks from the box — usually several times a day — and to deposit the checks in the firm's bank account. At time of deposit the clear-

---

[2] This discussion is based on an article by Frederick W. Searby referenced in the back of this chapter.

[3] Technically, the firm does not have use of a deposited check until the check is "processed" or "cleared" through the banking system.

ing process begins.[4] The firm does not handle the checks under the lock box arrangement, which is one of its attractive features. However, the bank charges the firm for this service, either through direct fees or the requirement that the firm keep compensating balances at the bank. In determining whether a lock box arrangement is worthwhile, the firm must compare the marginal gains from speeding collections with these costs. These comparisons are usually complex problems. The firm will also want to compare the cost of a lock box system with the field collection system.

Field collections. In this system the firm collects its payments itself, typically through field sales offices or the like. Payments received by the field agents are recorded and then deposited at a local bank (called a *field depository bank*). Like lock boxes, this system has the advantage of placing collection centers close to the customers, thereby reducing mailing transit time. In comparison to a lock box system, under a field collection arrangement the firm must internally process the checks before deposit, while in a lock box arrangement the bank does the processing for the firm.

Bank gathering system components It is typical for firms to use three kinds of banks in gathering cash receipts:

1. Field depository banks.
2. Regional concentration banks.
3. Central bank.

Field depository banks are those banks into which field collections are channeled. These banks are more likely to be smaller banks since many field offices will be in smaller cities. Many firms have several dozen field collection agents and field depository banks. Some firms have hundreds. *Regional concentration banks* are normally those banks where the firm has a lock box arrangement. Because these arrangements are relatively expensive, the firm will normally have relatively few concentration banks. The *central bank* is the control bank for the system. This bank assists the firm in transferring funds between banks. The firm's disbursement accounts are also usually handled through its central bank.

In selecting banks to be part of its gathering system, the firm should keep the following two criteria in mind. First, the banks should be capable of handling the firm's collection needs. Preferably, the bank should belong to the Federal Reserve System, and the bank should be equipped to rapidly receive and transfer funds for the firm (this is discussed further below). Second, the banks should be competitive on pricing of their services, whether in the form of direct fees or compensating balances.

Rapid transfer of funds Once deposits have been made to a bank, the firm is interested in being able to quickly transfer surplus funds (funds above any required minimum compensating balance) to its disbursement

---

[4] This processing amounts to presenting the check back to the writer's (customer's) bank and having that bank accept the check, which signifies the writer has sufficient funds to cover the check.

accounts, which are usually in the firm's central bank. There are several ways to transfer funds more rapidly than by mail.

Wire transfers. The quickest means of transferring is by wire (telegram). Funds may be transferred in a matter of minutes, and many firms have arranged for standing instructions with their concentration and field depository banks to automatically wire any surplus funds to the central bank. Wiring is fairly expensive, however, and wiring very small amounts of money would be uneconomical.

Depository transfer checks. Field collection agents use these to speed deposits made at field depository banks to concentration banks. The field agent simultaneously deposits the daily receipts at the local field depository bank and mails a depository transfer check to a concentration bank or the central bank. The depository transfer will begin the check clearing process upon receipt by the concentration or central bank rather than wait for the field depository bank to begin the clearing process. Depository transfer checks are obviously not as fast as wire transfers but are very inexpensive. They are typically used with small sums of money, where it is uneconomical to use wire transfers.

Special handling. Occasionally, the firm may receive payment of a very large sum of money in a location where wire facilities are not available. If the sum is large enough, there may be economic justification for some sort of special handling. It is not uncommon, for example, for a firm to send an agent by plane to pick up the check personally, fly it back, and deposit it at the firm's central bank. Suppose, for example, a $2 million check is paid to the firm in a South American city, and it would take five days for the check to arrive at the firm's central bank by mail. Suppose further that the firm can fly an employee to pick up the check in one day for $500 total cost. That is, by special handling, the check's transit time can be reduced by four days. Assume now that the going annual interest rate is 5 percent, which is about (5/365) or 0.0137 percent per day. At that interest rate, $2 million would draw daily interest of ($2,000,000 × 0.000137) $274. Four days' interest would be (4 × $274) or $1,096. Therefore, the firm could save about $600 by dispatching an agent to pick up the check.

Slowing cash disbursements

While the firm is interested in collecting cash as rapidly as possible, it is interested in disbursing cash as slowly as possible, subject to the constraint that the firm's credit standing is not impaired. While there are several techniques for legally slowing disbursements, the firm should always be cognizant of the fact that whatever slows down its disbursements also slows down the cash collection of those being paid. The firm's suppliers and creditors may object to practices that blatantly slow the firm's disbursements.

Avoidance of early payments Firms that do not pay promptly will tend to have relatively poor credit ratings. This can create difficulties in securing ample trade credit, so there are definite advantages to making payments on time. However, there are no real advantages — unless a cash discount is offered (see Chapter 19) – to paying early. If a payment is due on the 30th of the month, the firm should not pay *prior* to the 30th.

Centralized disbursement accounts   While collections can be speeded up by a decentralized collection network, disbursements can be slowed by maintaining centralized accounts. Regional bills will be paid by the firm's central bank, which may not be closely located to the regional payee. This increases transit time. Some firms have even set up systems where there are two main disbursement accounts, one on each coast. East Coast bills are paid with checks drawn on the West Coast bank, and West Coast bills are paid with East Coast bank checks. This is a very aggressive arrangement. Another advantage of centralized disbursement accounts is that fewer checking accounts need be maintained, which leads to a smaller total cash balance for the firm.

Bank drafts   When a check issued by the firm is presented to the bank, the firm's checking account is immediately reduced. However, a bank draft, which is an order drawn by the firm upon its bank to pay a third party, must be sent back to the firm by its bank before payment is made. This extra transit time further delays disbursement.

Playing the float   The firm's *actual* bank balance is usually greater than the balance shown on the firm's records; the difference is referred to as *payment float* and is caused by transit and processing delays. If the firm's money managers can accurately estimate when checks will be cleared, they can invest the payment float during the float period, earn a few days' interest, and synchronize the deposit with the anticipated clearing. Some firms have apparently managed to keep *negative* bank balances through careful synchronizations.

CASH BUDGETING

Planning for and controlling the use of cash are extremely important tasks within the firm. Failure to properly anticipate cash flows can lead to idle cash balances (and a lower rate of return) on one hand, and to cash deficits (and possible failure) on the other. The cash budget is a device to help the financial manager plan for and control the use of cash.

A cash budget is basically a work sheet used to show cash inflows, outflows, and cash balances over some projected time period. One of the main purposes of the budget, in fact, is to estimate the firm's cash balance in future time periods. The time horizon of a cash budget is fairly short, seldom longer than a year. Many firms' cash budget time horizon is only three to six months long. Within this time framework, the firm will forecast cash inflows and outflows and cash balances, typically on a monthly or weekly basis. Additionally, most firms use *daily* cash budgets for the next one or two weeks to keep close control of imminent cash flows and balances.

Elements of the cash budgeting system

There is a wide variety of cash budgeting systems. Many are set up to handle *all* cash flows, regardless of their nature. On the other hand, many

FIGURE 17–1
Major cash flow components of cash budget

Cash inflows	*Cash outflows*
Operating:	Operating:
Cash sales	Payroll payments
Receivables collections	Payables payments
	Capital expenditures
Financial:	
Interest receipts	Financial:
Sale of marketable securities	Tax payments
Issuance of new securities	Dividend payments
	Interest payments
	Redemption of securities
	Loan repayments
	Purchase of marketable securities

firms prefer to prepare two separate cash budgeting systems, one handling *operating* cash flows and balances, and the other handling *financial* cash flows and balances. Figure 17–1 illustrates the major categories of cash flows included in the cash budget. Numerous other items appear on the budget also.

A cash budgeting example

An example will help illustrate the preparation of a cash budget. Lessig Boxes is a small manufacturer of cardboard containers. In early January, Mary Smith, the company's comptroller, who manages the firm's working capital, prepares to update the firm's cash budget. The comptroller routinely uses a three-month time horizon because she feels this is about as far ahead as she can accurately forecast cash flows. The period is subdivided into monthly periods. Currently, the comptroller is attempting to estimate cash flows and end-of-month cash balances for the months of January, February, and March.

Sales work sheet In attempting to make these estimates, the comptroller begins her analysis with a *sales work sheet*. This work sheet is illustrated in Figure 17–2. The starting point of the work sheet is the recording of sales for the past two months (November and December) and the projection of sales for the coming three months.

From past experience, the comptroller has noticed that about 10 percent of all sales are cash sales, while 90 percent are credit sales. Although the firm's policy on credit sales (see Chapter 18) is to grant 30 days' time from date of sale for customers to pay their bills, a large portion of credit customers do not pay their bills until during the second month after the sales. Specifically, past experience leads the comptroller to expect that, given present credit policies, about 10 percent of any month's sales will be cash sales, about 50 percent will be credit sales that will be collected during the subsequent month, and the remaining 40 percent will be collected during the second subsequent month.

Using these expected sales lag and percentage data, and the sales estimates shown in Figure 17–2, Lessig's comptroller can estimate cash sales and receivables collections for the coming three months in the planning horizon. These estimates are also shown in Figure 17–2. To check the comptroller's arithmetic, notice that collection of the $450,000 estimated January sales is spread over a three-month period: 10 percent ($45,000) will be collected as cash sales in January, 50 percent ($225,000) will be collected in February, and the remaining 40 percent ($180,000) will be collected in March. These three items sum to $450,000.

Accounts payable are also related to the sales volume, reflecting the ordering of material and supplies in anticipation of future sales. Lessig's production schedule is such that the company orders material and supplies on the basis of next month's sales forecast. On average, the cost of

FIGURE 17–2

LESSIG BOXES
Sales work sheet
(thousands of dollars)

	Nov.	Dec.	Jan.	Feb.	Mar.
Past sales	$480	$450			
Estimated future sales			$450	$500	$500
Estimated sales-related receipts:					
Cash sales (10 percent of current month sales)			$ 45	$ 50	$ 50
Receivables collections					
50 percent of last month sales			$225	$225	$250
40 percent of sales from two months ago			192	180	180
Total receivables collections			$417	$405	$430
Estimated sales-related expenditures:					
Payables payments (50 percent of current month sales)			$225	$250	$250

these orders runs about 50 percent of sales. The firm receives 30 days' credit from its suppliers so payments on accounts payables are made in the month that the sales occur. For example, based on the forecast of a $500,000 sales level in February, the firm will order $250,000 worth of material and supplies in January. However, the $250,000 cash disbursement will not be made until February. The sales work sheet shows that estimated cash payments on the firm's payables each month will be 50 percent of that month's estimated sales.

After preparing the sales work sheet, the comptroller is ready to prepare the cash budget. The cash budget has three parts: the estimated cash inflows section, the estimated cash outflows section, and the estimated cash surplus or shortage position section. Lessig's cash budget is shown in Figure 17–3.

Estimated cash inflows The estimated cash inflows section itemizes all anticipated cash inflows for each month in the planning period. Included here are the estimates of cash sales and cash receivables collections determined from the sales work sheet. Lessig also has some interest receipts, $150,000 of marketable securities that mature in February, and a small amount of other cash receipts.

Estimated cash outflows Similarly, the estimated cash outflows section itemizes all anticipated cash disbursements during the planning period, including the estimated payables payments determined from the sales work sheet. Another major cash expenditure item is payroll. In addition, Lessig has minor capital expenditure payments scheduled in January

FIGURE 17–3

LESSIG BOXES
Cash Budget
(thousands of dollars)

Estimated Cash Inflows:	January	February	March
Cash sales..	$ 45	$ 50	$ 50
Receivables collections............................	417	405	430
Interest receipts......................................	3	3	2
Sale of marketable securities.....................	0	150	0
Other cash receipts.................................	10	15	13
Total Cash Inflows.........................	$ 475	$ 623	$ 495
Estimated Cash Outflows:			
Payroll payments....................................	$ 230	$ 220	$ 240
Payables payments	225	250	250
Capital expenditures	20	10	100
Tax payments	75	0	0
Dividend payments.................................	0	60	0
Interest payments	0	0	4
Repayment of loan	0	0	200
Other cash disbursements	20	20	20
Total Cash Outflows	$ 570	$ 560	$ 814
Estimated net cash flow for month	$ −95	$ 63	$−319
Estimated Cash Surplus (Shortage):			
Beginning-of-month cash balance	$1,050	$ 955	$1,018
Estimated end-of-month cash balance*........	955	1,018	699
Less: minimum cash balance	1,000	1,000	1,000
Estimated Cash Surplus (Shortage) ....$	−45	$ 18	$−301

* Beginning-of-month cash balance plus estimated net cash flow for month.

and February, and a major capital expenditure of $100,000 planned in March. The company also has a quarterly income tax payment of $75,000 to make in January and a $60,000 quarterly cash dividend payment to make to the company's common stockholders. Also, the company is repaying a $200,000 loan in March and has other cash disbursements of about $20,000 per month during the planning period.

The difference between estimated cash inflows and outflows is the estimated net cash flow for the month. As Figure 17–3 shows, estimated net cash flows for the three months are: $−95,000, $+63,000, and $−319,000, respectively. The large negative estimated net cash flow for

March is caused by the $100,000 capital expenditure and the repayment of the $200,000 term loan.

Estimated cash surplus or shortage position   The last section of the cash budget shows the calculation of the estimated cash surplus or shortage position of the firm, given the estimated net cash flows for the planning period. Included in these calculations is the firm's minimum cash balance level. This minimum cash balance represents that level of cash ($1 million here) that Lessig does not want to go below. We discuss the determination of the minimum cash balance level later in this chapter.

At the end of December, when the planning period begins, Lessig has a cash balance of $1,050,000. If the firm were to make no working capital corrections during the planning period, the firm's estimated end-of-month cash balance would be $955,000 in January, $1,018,000 in February, and $699,000 in March. That is, relative to the desired $1 million minimum cash balance, the firm would have a $45,000 cash shortage at the end of January, an $18,000 cash surplus at the end of February, and a $301,000 cash shortage at the end of March.

Balancing the cash budget   The cash budget shown in Figure 17–3 is incomplete in the sense that it does not include the effect of any financial management actions the cash manager may take to eliminate the anticipated cash surpluses and/or shortages. For this reason, the cash budget shown in Figure 17–3 is usually called an *unbalanced* cash budget. There are many solutions for balancing the budget. The simplest is to borrow the amount of any cash shortage and invest the amount of any cash surplus. In the example, Lessig would borrow $45,000 in January, invest $18,000 in February, and borrow $301,000 in March.[5] Notice also that there are some complications even in this simple solution. First, these new borrowing and investing plans will entail interest cash flows that should be included in the cash budget. Second, if the amounts borrowed and invested mature *within* the planning period, the repayment of any loan principal and the receipt of any investment principal must also be included in the cash flow section of the budget. If, for example, Lessig borrows $45,000 in January for 30 days to cover its estimated January cash shortage, the $45,000 loan repayment and attendant interest payments must be included in the February estimated cash outflows section. Thus, even simple solutions to balancing the cash budget entail some complicating factors that cause the preparation of a *revised* or *balanced* cash budget.

What makes the cash budget problem particularly difficult and challenging is the vast array of ways to balance the budget. There are dozens of ways that the firm could go in attempting to balance the cash budget, and each has interactive effects on estimated cash flows. At one extreme, the firm may choose to reduce cash outflows by delaying payment on its accounts payable (see Chapter 19). Another alternative is to attempt to speed up cash inflows by applying pressure on those credit customers

---

[5] The planned investment and borrowing in February and March, respectively, would only be *planned* actions, since when the comptroller prepares her updated cash budget at the beginning of February, she may well have new expectations of estimated cash inflows and outflows based on events that transpired in January. These new expectations could affect the estimated cash surplus or shortage positions.

who are slow payers (see Chapter 18). A third alternative is to sell in January the $150,000 of marketable securities maturing in February, and there are many other alternatives.

The point is, in addition to estimating how large a cash surplus or shortage is anticipated in the near future, there is also the associated problem of what actions to take to balance the cash budget. There are many competing alternatives, and the choice involves considering all the dimensions of working capital management. Actually, the choice can also involve long-term decisions. For example, Lessig may even want to consider postponing its $100,000 March capital expenditure because of the large cash outflow anticipated in that month. Usually, however, the cash flows associated with long-term investment decisions are taken as given, and the cash manager is charged with the responsibility of arranging the firm's working capital in such a way that a satisfactory cash balance is maintained and the firm's long-term investment plans are unimpeded.

ESTIMATING OPTIMAL CASH LEVELS

Estimating optimal cash levels is an extremely important short-term financial management task. If the firm keeps too much cash on hand, it suffers an opportunity cost in that resources are tied up in a nonearning asset. On the other hand, if too little cash is held, the firm will continually incur the costs of raising cash on short notice, and at the extreme, the firm may fail if it cannot find the needed cash. Planning for the optimal cash level to maintain begins with a projection or estimation of future net cash flows over a near-term planning period. This period, usually a month or less, is normally shorter than the cash budget planning period discussed above.

Known versus random cash flows

First, the firm should separate anticipated cash flows into *known* and *random* categories. Known cash flows are those cash outflows and inflows that are reasonably foreseeable; the size and timing of these cash flows are known with some degree of certainty. A previously declared dividend that will be paid in two weeks is an example of a known cash outflow. Random cash flows are those outflows and inflows whose size and timing are estimated with less precision. Cash sales is a good example of a random cash inflow. A list of the major known and random cash flows looks like the following:

Major known cash flows	*Major random cash flows*
Proceeds from issuing new securities	Cash sales
Payroll payments	Receivables collections
Capital expenditures	Payables payments
Tax payments	
Dividend payments	
Interest receipts and payments	
Loan repayments	

The random cash flows require a different sort of planning than the known cash flows. Since the firm knows when a major known cash outflow will occur and how much it will be, arrangements can be made to meet the scheduled outflow. If, for example, a $200,000 tax payment is scheduled on January 15, the firm will arrange to have cash on hand on that date. Because the size and timing of random cash flows are much less predictable, the cash management problems associated with this type of cash outflows and inflows are more difficult. In the following analysis, we address only the random cash flow components.

Net cash flow distribution

Let us assume for illustration purposes that the near-term planning period is a month, and that net cash flow per day is the relevant unit of

FIGURE 17–4
Distribution of daily net cash flows

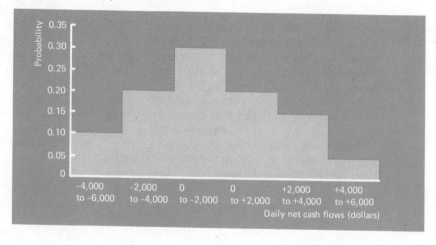

interest. Past net cash flow records can be of great value to the cash manager in estimating the future net cash flow activity of the firm.

Consider the problem facing Bob Jones, the cash manager for the Kelso Co. He is preparing to estimate how much cash the firm should plan on maintaining during the coming month of November. He has compiled a chart of net cash flows and the frequency with which these net cash flows have occurred during the November months for the past two years. This chart, called a *histogram*, is actually a simple kind of probability distribution (see Chapter 4) and is shown in Figure 17–4.

The vertical axis of the probability distribution shown in Figure 17–4 is relative frequency, which is one way to express probability. Relative frequency is a percentage that shows the number of times a particular outcome occurred divided by the total number of outcomes. As an example of interpreting Figure 17–4, notice that 20 percent of Kelso's daily net cash flows for the past two Novembers were between $–2,000 and $-4,000. For computational purposes below, we will make use of the *midrange* (The value midway between the interval endpoints) of such intervals ($-3,000 in this illustration). To the extent that this historical distribution reflects the future, it can be used as an indicator of the distribution of *future* net cash flows. Kelso's cash manager feels that this upcoming November's net cash flow distribution will be very similar to the distribution shown in Figure 17-4, as the firm's sales level is at approximately the same level that it has been in the past. Because of the seasonal nature of the firm's business, Kelso's cash manager has not included data from other months. If there were no seasonal cash flow elements involved, the firm could use data from other months in preparation of Figure 17-4.

Two motives for holding cash

Recall from our earlier discussions that there are four motives for holding cash and securities: transactions, precautionary, speculative, and compensating balances motives. Of these, many economists argue that speculative liquidity balances are usually unimportant because most firms do not regularly keep cash or securities for speculative reasons. In addition, most firms keep their precautionary liquidity balances in the form of marketable securities. We discuss this topic below. Cash balances are thus usually held for transactions and compensating balances reasons. We can investigate how the firm can estimate its optimal cash balances held for these two reasons by continuing the Kelso example.

Transactions balances[6]

The main problem in determining how much cash to hold for transactions purposes involves a cost tradeoff between too much and too little cash. If the firm keeps too much cash there is an opportunity cost suffered, which is the amount of foregone return the firm could have earned by investing the cash in some productive asset. At some point, the firm will want to invest excess cash in short-term interest-earning assets, such as marketable securities. This will incur a transfer cost. On the other hand, if the firm keeps too little cash, there will be a need to sell some securities or borrow (say, from a bank), which also incurs a transfer cost each time this is done. The transfer cost includes brokerage fees. Part of this cost will also be for time and expenses of arrangements, long-distance calls, clerical expenses incurred, and other expenses attributable to the cash manager's efforts during the transfer.

Figure 17-5 shows a picture of how the firm's transactions cash balance fluctuates as the firm's net cash flows randomly fluctuate. When the transactions cash balance hits zero, the firm must either sell some marketable securities or borrow to restore the cash balance to level z. At the other extreme, when the cash balance has grown to level h, the

---

[6] This section is based on an article by Merton H. Miller and Daniel Orr referenced in the back of this chapter.

firm will want to reduce the cash balance back to level z by investing $h - z$ amount of dollars in marketable securities.

The firm's transactions cash balance problem becomes a search for the optimal values of z and h that will minimize the total expected cost of cash management. Total expected cost of cash management is the sum of opportunity costs plus transactions costs. The procedure for solving this problem involves some complex mathematics, but the solution

FIGURE 17–5
Behavior of daily cash balances over time

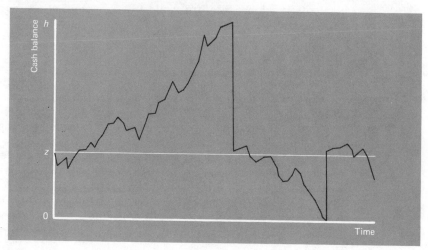

has been worked out in the Miller and Orr article referenced in Footnote 6.[7] For the optimal cash balance *return point*, z:[8]

$$z = C \sqrt[3]{\sigma^2} \tag{17-1}$$

where

$\sigma^2 =$ variance of daily net cash flows and $C = \sqrt[3]{273.75(b/i)}$,

where

$b =$ transfer cost (dollars), and $i =$ annual interest rate (percent per year).

For the optimal *maximum* cash balance, h:

$$h = 3z \tag{17-2}$$

If the firm follows this kind of policy, its *average* cash balance for transactions purposes, M_T, will be:

---

[7] Actually, the equations we discuss immediately below, (17–1), (17–2), and (17–3), apply to the special case where there is a 0.5 probability of an increase in the daily cash balance and a 0.5 probability of a decrease in the daily cash balance. Optimal z and h values for other situations are presented in the Miller and Orr article.

[8] The symbol, $\sqrt[3]{\ }$, stands for cube root. Equation (17–1) was derived from an equation in the Miller and Orr article.

$$M_T = \frac{h + z}{3} \tag{17-3}$$

Notice that the optimal cash return point is a function of the transfer cost (b), the opportunity cost (i), and the variance of the daily net cash flows (σ^2). To simplify the computational work, several values of C are presented in Figure 17–6. To find C we merely need to know the values of the transfer cost and the annual interest rate. If, for example, the transfer cost is $30 and the annual interest rate is 9 percent, then $C = 45.0$.

FIGURE 17–6
Selected values of C

Transfer cost b (dollars)	Interest rate, i (percent per year)						
	4	5	6	7	8	9	10
30	59.0	54.8	51.5	49.0	46.8	45.0	43.5
40	64.9	60.3	56.7	53.9	51.5	49.5	47.8
50	69.9	64.9	61.1	58.0	55.5	53.4	51.5

The variance of the daily net cash flows, σ^2, can be related to the daily net cash flow distribution, such as the one shown in Figure 17–4. To calculate σ^2:

$$\sigma^2 = \sum_{j=1}^{n} p_j (x_j - \mu)^2 \tag{17-4}$$

where

n = the number of net cash flow intervals, p_j = the probability of the jth net cash flow interval, x_j = midrange value of the jth cash flow interval, and μ = expected daily net cash flow.

$$\mu = \sum_{j=1}^{n} p_j x_j \tag{17-5}$$

Now let us apply this analysis to the Kelso problem. Kelso's cash manager estimates the transfer cost and the interest rate, respectively, as:

$$b = \$40$$
$$i = 7\%.$$

From Figure 17–6, these numbers imply that $C = 53.9$. Using Figure 17–4, the cash manager also gathers the following information pertaining to the six net cash flow intervals:

	Interval					
	1	2	3	4	5	6
p_j......	0.10	0.20	0.30	0.20	0.15	0.05
x_j......	$-5,000	$-3,000	$-1,000	$1,000	$3,000	$5,000

This information is used to calculate the expected daily net cash flow, μ, which is then used to calculate σ^2, the variance of daily net cash flows:

$$\mu = (0.10)(\$-5,000) + (0.20)(\$-3,000) + (0.30)(\$-1,000)$$
$$+ (0.20)(\$1,000) + (0.15)(\$3,000) + (0.05)(\$5,000)$$
$$\mu = \$-500$$

and

$$\sigma^2 = (0.10)(\$-4,500)^2 + (0.20)(\$-2,500)^2 + (0.30)(\$-500)^2$$
$$+ (0.20)(\$1,500)^2 + (0.15)(\$3,500)^2 + (0.05)(\$5,500)^2$$
$$\sigma^2 = 7,150,000$$

Solving now for the optimum cash balance return point for transactions purposes, we get

$$z = (53.9)(\sqrt[3]{7,150,000})$$

To find the value inside the cubic radical, look at Figure 17–7, which shows some selected values of σ^2 and associated cube roots. Not all possible σ^2 values are shown in this figure, but we can approximate σ^2 values not specifically shown.[9] Using Figure 17–7, we find by interpolation that:

$$\sqrt[3]{7,150,000} \approx 194$$

Therefore:

$$z = (53.9)(194) = \$10,456$$
$$z \approx \$10,500$$

and:

$$h = 3z = (3)(\$10,500)$$
$$h = \$31,500.$$

To handle its transaction cash needs, Kelso should never carry more than $31,500 during the planning period (November). Whenever the cash balance reaches $31,500, the firm should transfer $21,000 into marketable securities or a savings account. When the cash account is exhausted, Kelso should transfer $10,500 from marketable securities or from its savings account into the cash account.

---

[9] The answer need not be approximated, as it is possible to get an exact solution. Figure 17–7 is presented to help those who do not have a calculator that takes cube roots and who do not know how to solve for cubic roots mathematically.

FIGURE 17–7
Selected values of $\sqrt[3]{\sigma^2}$

σ^2 (millions)	$\sqrt[3]{\sigma^2}$	σ^2 (millions)	$\sqrt[3]{\sigma^2}$	σ^2 (millions)	$\sqrt[3]{\sigma^2}$
0.1	46.4	6	181.7	40	342.0
0.5	79.4	7	191.2	50	368.4
1	100.0	8	200.0	60	391.5
2	126.0	9	208.0	70	412.1
3	144.2	10	215.4	80	430.9
4	158.7	20	271.4	90	448.1
5	171.0	30	310.7	100	464.2

The firm's average transactions cash balance from following this policy will be:

$$M_T = \frac{\$10,500 + \$31,500}{3} = \$14,000$$

Compensating balances

Some finance studies have found that most firms keep much larger cash balances than are necessary for purely transactions needs. These are compensating balances held for services motives and to satisfy loan agreements. The amount of the compensating balance depends on the amount of services provided and the amount of loans outstanding, and the actual compensating balance the firm will be required to maintain will be the subject of negotiation between the firm and the bank. Obviously, the firm would like to keep as small a compensating balance as possible, and the bank would like to set the compensating balance as large as possible. Where the balance is finally set will depend on the negotiating strengths of the two parties.

Minimum compensating balances are usually established in one of two ways. First, there may be an *absolute* minimum balance requirement. Under this arrangement, the firm's bank account may not go below the stipulated absolute minimum amount without penalty. The other arrangement is to have a minimum *average* balance. In this situation, the firm need only keep its average bank balance above the stipulated minimum. Suppose, for example, the minimum compensating balance is established at $400,000. If this is an *absolute* minimum, the firm's checking account can never be less than $400,000. If, on the other hand, the $400,000 is a minimum *average* balance, the firm's checking account can be less than $400,000 on any given day so long as the average daily balance for some agreed period of time (such as a month) is not less than $400,000.

Optimal cash balances

We are interested in determining *optimal* cash balance levels. While the firm's cash balance will not be constant over time, we can investigate what the optimal *average* cash balance for the firm should be over a designated time interval. Additionally, we will determine what the optimal *minimum* and *maximum* cash balances should be. The firm's minimum and maximum cash balances are the lowest and highest levels, respectively, that the firm would permit its total cash account to reach during the current planning period. Also, we will establish the optimal cash return point for the total cash balance. The size of these optimal values will depend on whether the firm's compensating balance requirement is established as an *absolute* minimum or as a minimum *average*. This point can be best illustrated with an example.

Suppose that, using techniques described earlier, the Cubic Co. decides that for *transactions* purposes, its optimal cash return point is $z = \$150,000$, which implies that:

$$\text{Maximum transactions cash balances} = h = 3z = \$450,000$$

and

$$\text{Optimal average transactions cash balance} = M_T = \frac{h+z}{3} = \$200,000$$

Furthermore

$$\text{minimum transactions cash balance} = \$0.$$

Assume also, that the Cubic Co. must keep a $400,000 compensating balance. The questions here are: What will be Cubic's optimal minimum, maximum, and average cash balances, and the optimal cash return point? The answers depend on the type of compensating balance requirement.

The absolute minimum compensating balance case   The amount of cash held for transactions reasons will fluctuate, but the *total* cash balance should never fall below the minimum compensating balance level ($400,000 in this example). That is, when there is an *absolute* minimum compensating balance requirement, that requirement becomes the firm's minimum cash balance level. For the Cubic Co. example, minimum cash balance = $400,000.

Establishing the minimum cash balance determines the other cash balance results also:

$$\text{Cash return point} = \text{Minimum cash balance} + z$$
$$= \$400,000 + \$150,000 = \$550,000$$

$$\text{Maximum cash balance} = \text{Minimum cash balance} + h$$
$$= \$400,000 + \$450,000 = \$850,000$$

$$\text{Average cash balance} = \text{Minimum cash balance} + M_T$$
$$= \$400,000 + \$200,000 = \$600,000$$

Notice that in each of these calculations the basic building block is the amount of the minimum cash balance. Cubic merely adds the appropriate transactions requirements in each instance to the minimum cash balance, which was determined by the compensating balance arrangement. Cubic's total cash balance will not be allowed to go below $400,-000, and when that level is reached, the treasurer will place $150,000 into the cash account, building it up to $550,000. Whenever the cash account reaches the upper limit of $850,000, the treasurer will invest $300,000 in marketable securities, reducing the cash account back to $550,000. The average cash balance over the planning period should be $600,000.

The minimum average compensating balance case In the previous example, the absolute minimum compensating balance requirement established the minimum cash balance level for the firm. In the example here, however, the compensating balance is stated as an *average* rather than an inviolable minimum. Since the firm will keep an average balance for transactions reasons also, the average transactions balance may be used to help meet the compensating balance requirement.

When there is an *average* minimum compensating balance requirement, the firm's average cash balance will be the *larger* of the average compensating balance requirement and the average transactions balance needs. Therefore, in the Cubic example, where the former is $400,000 and the latter is $200,000: Average cash balance = $400,000.

However, the $200,000 average transactions balance may be simultaneously used to satisfy the compensating balance requirement. The firm's optimal *minimum* cash balance would therefore be $200,000, the difference between the average cash balance and the average transactions need:

$$\text{Minimum cash balance} = \$400,000 - \$200,000 = \$200,000$$

The optimal cash return point and maximum cash balance are determined by adding the relevant transactions needs to the optimal minimum cash balance:

$$\text{Cash return point} = \text{Minimum cash balance} + z$$
$$= \$200,000 + \$150,000 = \$350,000$$

$$\text{Maximum cash balance} = \text{Minimum cash balance} + h$$
$$= \$200,000 + \$450,000 = \$650,000$$

The firm's optimal minimum, maximum and average cash balances and the cash return point are all $200,000 lower than in the absolute minimum compensating balance case because part of the compensating balance requirement is covered with transactions balances. Since the lower cash balances mean better profitability, an average compensating balance arrangement would be preferred by the firm.

In instances where the average transactions needs are greater than the minimum average compensating balance, there will be no need to hold cash purely for compensating balances reasons because all of this need will be covered by the firm's transactions balances. The average cash balance, the maximum and minimum cash balance, and the cash return point would all be determined solely by the transactions needs of the firm.

INVESTMENT IN MARKETABLE SECURITIES

The management of the investment in marketable securities is an important financial management responsibility because of the close relationship between cash and marketable securities. One important aspect of this responsibility is determining the amount of marketable securities to hold. Another major aspect of the problem of investment in marketable securities is deciding which securities should the firm invest in? That is, what should be the composition of the firm's portfolio of securities. A vast array of types and maturities is available, and the financial manager must choose among these alternatives.

Security features

In choosing a portfolio of marketable securities the firm will be particularly interested in the safety of the securities, their marketability, and their maturity. Differences in these features are the primary determinants of the yield differences among securities, and differences in these features also explain why firms select certain kinds of securities for short-term investments.

Safety Other things equal, the firm would like to receive as high a yield on its investment in marketable securities as is possible. However, as we have seen repeatedly, seeking higher rates of return leads to accepting larger amounts of risk. Since the firm keeps marketable securities for precautionary reasons and to meet known, scheduled outflows of cash, the firm will tend to invest in very safe marketable securities. Firms tend to buy the highest yielding marketable securities they can find subject to the constraint that the securities have an acceptable risk level. Risk in this context refers to risk of failure (recall Chapter 4). However, failure can have more than one meaning here. At one extreme, a security could default: The issuer fails to redeem the security as per the contract. In a less severe sense, the price of the security could fall at a time when the firm needs to liquidate the security (perhaps to replenish the cash account). If the firm sells the security for less than the needed amount, this too is a kind of failure. To minimize these possibilities firms tend to restrict their marketable securities investments to certain classes of "safe" financial instruments (described below), accepting the relatively low yields that accompany such investments as an unavoidable consequence.

Maturity The longer the maturity of a security the more possibility for price fluctuations prior to its maturity. Since downside price fluctuations are undesirable for safety reasons, the firm will prefer short-lived securities. At the long end of the maturity spectrum, firms prefer marketable securities whose remaining life is no greater than six to nine months. At the short end of the spectrum, firms can and do invest funds overnight.

Marketability Marketability refers to how readily the security can be liquidated into a cash position prior to maturity. Highly marketable securities are those where there is an active secondary market of many buyers and sellers. This ensures that securities can be liquidated quickly and that there need be no major price concessions made to facilitate the sale. Firms tend to purchase securities that are highly marketable so that when money is needed, the securities can be quickly converted into cash. Acceptable securities that have restricted marketability (see below) tend to have very short maturities.

Kinds of marketable securities

There are many kinds of marketable securities that firms invest in. For the most part, however, they are characterized as being very safe, short-lived, and highly marketable.

U.S. Treasury securities   Treasury securities are issued by the U.S. government. The market for these securities is the largest and most liquid sector of the U.S. money markets. U.S. Treasury securities include bills, certificates, notes, and bonds. All are thought of as default risk free since they have the full financial backing of the U.S. government. The primary differences among these securities are their initial maturities.

Security	Usual initial maturity
Treasury bills...........................	91 days to 182 days
Treasury certificates	9 to 12 months
Treasury notes	1 to 5 years
Treasury bonds	over 5 years

The government also sells tax anticipation bills that mature at tax payment time. Because Treasury securities are so safe and so readily marketable, they tend to have lower yields than other marketable securities. U.S. Treasury securities have historically been the most widely used marketable securities by corporations.

Federal agency securities   In recent years, many U.S. government agencies have raised funds by issuing securities. These securities have maturities ranging from one month to several years and have been widely purchased by corporations because of their high degree of marketability and relative safety. Secondary markets for these securities are strong, although not equal to the Treasury securities market. The securities are guaranteed by the agencies themselves rather than the U.S. government. Their slightly lower marketability and safety in comparison to Treasury securities causes agency securities to have slightly higher yields. Some prominent examples of agency issues are: Federal Intermediate Credit Banks, Federal National Mortgage Association, Federal Land Banks, Federal Home Loan Banks, Government National Mortgage Association, and Banks for Cooperatives.

Bankers' acceptances   Bankers' acceptances are "time drafts" used to facilitate trade that are drawn on and accepted by banks. They have been particularly useful in export-import businesses, and the mechanics of acceptances are discussed in Chapter 20. Since acceptances are guaranteed by the participating bank, they are as safe as that bank's guarantee. The secondary market for acceptances is an active one, with New York the primary market. Primary participants are banks and five principal "dealers." Initial maturities are usually no longer than 180 days, and yields are usually higher than on similar maturity Treasury securities. Bankers' acceptances are normally issued in units of $25,000 or more.

Commercial paper Commercial paper refers to unsecured promissory notes issued by companies to raise short-term financing. This subject is covered in more detail in Chapter 20. When a firm invests in commercial paper it is essentially lending to the issuing company. Commercial paper is rated as to its safety, which is dependent on the financial strength of the issuing company. The highest quality paper is rated "prime 1." Yields on commercial paper are related to rating and maturity, and initial maturities usually range from five days to nine months. There is no active secondary market for commercial paper, so most purchasers will hold the paper until maturity. However, issuing firms and dealers will often agree to repurchase paper prior to maturity, at a discount, on request. The combination of limited marketability and extra risk causes commercial paper yields to exceed Treasury security yields. Commercial paper is usually issued in units of $25,000 or more.

Negotiable certificate of deposit A certificate of deposit (CD) refers to a specified amount of money placed in a bank that will receive a stated amount of interest for a stated amount of time. Banks have effectively used CD's to induce business firms to invest their short-term funds with them. The safety of the CD's is guaranteed by (and hence is related to the strength of) the issuing bank, and CD's may be sold prior to maturity. A fairly strong secondary market has developed for CD's issued by banks in New York, Chicago, and other major financial center cities. Yields on CD's tend to exceed Treasury security yields. Major banks normally issue CD's in denominations of $500,000 or more, but smaller banks issue CD's in smaller denominations. This effectively means that the highest quality CD's are only available to large firms.

Repurchase agreements Repurchase agreements, or "repos," consist of the purchase of short-term securities by an investor from a government bond dealer, and the subsequent *repurchase* of the securities by the dealer. Government bond dealers are agents who actively buy and sell government securities, and they have used the repo technique to help them finance their large inventories of government securities. Offering packages of safe government securities with a guaranteed repurchase enables dealers to procure funds from the corporate sector of the economy. The firm receives a specified interest rate on the arrangement, which is basically a short-term loan to the dealer, and the repurchase date is arranged to suit the needs of the firm. There is no active secondary market for repos, but maturities are very short, ranging from one day to a few weeks. Since most repos involve Treasury securities, yields on repos are competitive with Treasury security yields.

SUMMARY

In this chapter we have investigated several aspects of the problem of managing the firm's most liquid assets, cash and marketable securities.

Firms primarily hold cash and securities for transactions, precautionary, speculative, and compensating balances motives.

An important aspect of cash management is the conscious speeding up of cash collections and slowing down of cash disbursements. Cash budgeting is also an important cash management task and is closely related to the major issue of determining optimal cash balance levels. We developed procedures to estimate optimal maximum, minimum, average, and return cash balances, accounting both for the transactions and compensating balances requirements of the firm.

With respect to management of the firm's portfolio of marketable securities, the majority of securities is held for precautionary reasons and to meet scheduled cash outflows, and these securities are usually characterized by the qualities of very short maturity, very low risk, and high marketability. The most widely used such securities are U.S. Treasury obligations.

QUESTIONS

1. Define the following terms and phrases:
    a. Transactions motive.
    b. Compensating balances.
    c. Playing the float.
    d. Cash budgeting.
    e. Minimum cash balance.
    f. Maximum cash balance.

2. Identify in each of the following situations which of the four motives for holding cash explains the increase in cash described:
    a. The bank requires that the firm increase its checking account level before a current loan is renewed.
    b. The Vice President–Controller directs that the cash balance be built up to allow the firm to take advantage of some possible merger opportunities that are expected to arise within the next few months.
    c. Cash balances increase as a cyclical increase in sales begins.
    d. The firm's new management orders that the checking account level be permanently raised to make the chance of a cash stockout less likely.

3. Contrast deposit float and payment float.

4. Other things equal, what effect would the following events have on the average cash balance that the firm keeps for transactions purposes? Explain your answer.
    a. Interest rates increase
    b. It becomes more expensive to transfer funds from cash to securities and vice versa
    c. The variability of daily net cash flows increases

5. In the transactions cash balance model, contrast the average cash balance and the return point.

6. Compare the cost and the speed of collection of wire transfers, depository transfer checks, and special handling procedures.

7. Explain the difference between an unbalanced cash budget and a revised cash budget.

8. Treasury bills are the most widely used marketable security by U.S. businesses, yet Treasury bills have the lowest yield of any marketable security. Why do you suppose they are used so extensively?

9. The Federal National Mortgage Association and the Government National Mortgage Association both issue marketable securities that investors, including firms, can buy. Yields on the securities of these two federal agencies are higher than Treasury bill yields.
   a. What does this yield difference indicate about the risk difference between agency issues and Treasury bills?
   b. What causes this risk difference?

PROBLEMS

1. Lacey's Stores has annual sales of $73 million. The company uses a centralized billing system, and, on average, the firm's deposit float is about five days' worth of sales. A financial consultant has suggested that Lacey should consider going to a field collection system. This would reduce deposit float to about three days' worth of sales.
   a. Assuming uniform sales during the year (365 days), determine the firm's average sales per day.
   b. Calculate the average dollar value of deposit float under the centralized billing system and the field collection system.
   c. If money can be risklessly put to work (even for periods as short as a day) at 6-percent annual interest, determine whether Lacey should change to a field collection period if the cost of the field collection system will be $40,000 per year.
   d. Repeat part (c), assuming deposit float would be reduced to two days worth of sales and that the riskless interest rate is 7 percent per year.

2. Shannon Kentucky Stables has just completed the sale of some thoroughbred horses to a wealthy businessman in Africa. The buyer has indicated that he will pay the bill of $1.6 million by check on the 13th of the month. If sent through the mail, there is a 20-percent chance the check will arrive by the 19th, a 60-percent chance it will arrive by the 20th, and a 20-percent chance it will arrive by the 21st. Alternatively, Shannon can send a courier to pick up the check. Airfare is $1,000, and other expenses (including time not spent on other duties by the courier) are about $200 per day. If all goes smoothly the courier would be gone two days. But there may be disruptions in the courier's schedule. For example, the African businessman may wish to entertain the courier, and reluctance to accept the invitation may appear rude and would jeopardize any possible future sales.

Such a disruption would probably cause a one-day delay, and there is a 50–50 chance that the disruption would occur.

    a. Determine the expected cost of sending a courier after the money.

    b. Determine the expected opportunity cost savings the firm would realize by sending a courier and reducing transit time if the current annual interest rate on money lent risklessly for short periods of time is 6 percent.

    c. What recommendations would you make about sending a courier?

3. Redwood Aussie Products is preparing a sales work sheet for the coming six months. Monthly sales for the next three months (April, May, and June) are anticipated to be $70,000. Sales are then anticipated to rise to $80,000 in July before falling to $60,000 in August and $50,000 in September. The firm has no cash sales; 20 percent of any month's sales are collected in the following month, 30 percent the next month, 40 percent the next month, and 10 percent four months after the initial sale. Payables for a given month are 40 percent of the previous month's sales and 20 percent of the current month's sales level. Sales data on the past four months are: December, $50,000; January, $50,000; February, $60,000; and March, $70,000.

    a. Set up a sales work sheet for the next six months showing estimated sales related cash receipts and expenditures.

    b. Determine Redwood's sales related net cash flow for each month.

4. Kleiner Kub Drugs' analysts are preparing a cash budget for the months of October, November, and December. Estimated sales for those months are $830,000, $860,000, and $900,000, respectively. Sales in the just completed month of September were $840,000. Kleiner has a small chain of downtown drugstores, and about 70 percent of sales are cash, the other 30 percent are credit sales collected the month following the sale. Kleiner's settles its payables, which run at about 40 percent of sales, one month after the sales month.

Payroll expenditures for Kleiner for the coming three months are expected to be $300,000 per month. Also, Kleiner has capital expenditure cash payments scheduled equal to $50,000 in November and $200,000 in December. A previously declared dividend of $80,000 is to be paid in October, and miscellaneous expenditures are estimated to be $10,000 per month. Also Kleiner has a $400,000 note payable due in November.

    a. Prepare a sales work sheet for Kleiner for the next three months.

    b. Assuming that the October 1 cash balance was $500,000 and that Kleiner has a minimum absolute cash balance requirement of $500,000, prepare a cash budget for Kleiner for the next three months. The last line of the budget should show the estimated cash surplus or shortage for each month.

    c. As the cash manager for the firm, explain to the president the reason for the existence of any occurrences of estimated cash shortages that appear imminent.

d. Suppose that Kleiner lends any surpluses at 8 percent per year for one month and borrows for three months at 10 percent per year when there are cash shortages. Make the necessary changes to your cash budget prepared in (b) to make it balance. Assume that interest is paid at the *end* of any borrowing or lending period.

5. The manager of the cash desk for Krider, Shulenberger & Associates is preparing to estimate the transactions balances needs for the firm for the next few weeks. Ignoring all other motives for holding cash, determine the optimal cash balance return point, the maximum cash balance, and the average cash balance expected if the following conditions exist:

Situation	Variance of daily net cash flows (dollars)	Transfer cost (dollars)	Annual interest rate (percent)
a........................	7,000,000	30	10
b........................	7,000,000	30	5
c........................	10,000,000	40	7
d........................	40,000,000	50	6
e........................	1,000,000	50	10

6. The cash and securities manager at Mueller-Northwestern Co. has estimated the firm's optimal average *transactions* cash balance will be about $12 million during the next few weeks.
   a. Determine the company's optimal transactions cash return point and the maximum transactions cash balance.
   b. If Mueller-Northwestern has a $15 million absolute minimum compensating loan balance agreement with its bank, determine the firm's *total:* (1) minimum cash balance, (2) cash return point, (3) maximum cash balance, and (4) average cash balance.
   c. Repeat part (b) if the bank agreement calls for a minimum average compensating balance.
   d. Repeat part (c) if the company's minimum average compensating balance is $10 million.

7. Ms. Harshaw is a working capital analyst with Kissinger & Co., a certified public accounting firm. The company is preparing to enter into its annual negotiation with its banker regarding how large a compensating bank balance Kissinger must maintain to support its loan and open line of credit from the bank. Harshaw has collected daily net cash flow frequency data for the past two years as shown below. These data are thought to be representative of the daily net cash flow frequencies Kissinger will experience during the coming year. Harshaw has also estimated the cash-to-securities or securities-to-cash transfer cost to be $50. An economist at the bank told Harshaw that the average short-term interest rate during the coming year would be about 7 percent.

Daily net cash flow frequency data

	Interval			
	1	*2*	*3*	*4*
Range of daily net cash flow.......	−$10,000 to $0	$0 to $5,000	$5,000 to $10,000	$10,000 to $15,000
Probability	0.2	0.4	0.2	0.2

a. Determine the anticipated variance of the daily net cash flows for the coming year.

b. Determine the optimal cash balance return point for transactions purposes and the maximum and average transactions cash balances. (Round all your answers to the nearest thousand dollars.)

c. If there is a $20,000 absolute minimum cash balance required after negotiations, what would be the firm's average cash balance?

d. Would Kissinger prefer the $20,000 minimum cash balance requirement or a $40,000 minimum average cash balance? Explain your answer.

SELECTED BASIC REFERENCES

Money Market Instruments. Cleveland: Federal Reserve Bank of Cleveland, 1970.

Searby, F. W. "Use your Hidden Cash Resources," *Harvard Business Review* (March–April 1968), pp. 71–80.

Stancill, J. McN. *The Management of Working Capital.* Scranton, Pa.: Intext Educational Publishers, 1971, chapters 2 and 3.

SELECTED ADVANCED REFERENCES

Baumol, W. J. "The Transactions Demand for Cash: An Inventory Theoretic Approach," *Quarterly Journal of Economics* (November 1952), pp. 545–56.

Miller, M. H., and D. Orr. "A Model of the Demand for Money by Firms," *Quarterly Journal of Economics* (August 1966), pp. 413–35.

Orgler, Y. E. *Cash Management.* Belmont, Calif.: Wadsworth Publishing Co., Inc., 1970.

18

RECEIVABLES AND INVENTORY

In Chapter 16 we took an overview of current asset and current liability management, and in Chapter 17 we investigated various aspects of managing two components of current assets: cash and securities. In this chapter we take up the subject of the two remaining major components of current assets: receivables and inventory. The two chapters immediately following will be concerned with short-term financing topics. Taken together, these five chapters constitute the topic of working capital management.

RECEIVABLES

There are several categories of receivables. If the firm makes a short-term loan to its officers, employees, or stockholders, a receivable is created, which will show up in the *sundry assets* account under the current assets caption. Other forms of receivables are *notes* and *acceptances receivable*. These are short-term promissory instruments of indebtedness that reflect obligations owed the firm. All of these kinds of receivables are distinguished by their *out of the ordinary* nature, in that they do not arise from the normal sales efforts of the company. A note receivable, for example, may be created when the firm sells some of its fixed assets to another firm and does not receive immediate cash payment.

The most common and most important form of receivables is *accounts receivable*, which is debt owed the firm by customers arising from sale of the firm's goods or services in the *ordinary* course of business. When the firm makes an ordinary sale and does not receive cash payment, the firm grants trade credit and creates an account receivable, which it expects to collect in the near future. In the United States, most ordinary business sales are credit sales, so most business firms have substantial investments in receivables. In fact, for all U.S. business firms in aggregate, receivables represent the largest component of current assets investment. Most credit sales are made on *open account*, without any formal acknowledgment of debt obligation through a financial instrument. Our interest in this portion of the chapter will be on the analysis of investment in accounts receivable.

The need for accounts receivable

Like any other form of asset, accounts receivable must be managed efficiently to enhance successful accomplishment of the firm's goal of stockholder wealth maximization. The firm grants trade credit because it expects the investment in receivables to be profitable. The immediate impact of granting trade credit shows up in the firm's sales level, and the motivation for investment in receivables may be either oriented toward *sales expansion* or *sales retention*. Sales expansion motivated investment in receivables refers to granting more trade credit to enable sales to present customers to increase and/or to attract new customers. This need for accounts receivable is growth-oriented. Sales retention motivated investment in receivables refers to granting trade credit to protect the firm's sales from competitors' sales programs. If, for example, the competition affords customers better credit terms (we discuss credit terms below), the firm may choose to match these terms to protect its sales. This is a defensive motive.

Credit policy: an overview

The expression "credit policy" refers to those policy decisions made by the firm that will affect the amount of trade credit (investment in receivables) it will grant. Although general economic conditions and industry practices have strong impacts on receivables levels, the firm's investment in receivables is also affected by credit policy decisions made by management. While the firm has no control over general economic conditions, and typically little control over industry-wide economic conditions, the firm can influence its own destiny through its credit policy decisions. Moreover, the firm can obviously change its credit policies in response to changing economic conditions.

Generally speaking, any firm's credit policy may be broadly defined as being somewhere in the range of "tight" (or "restrictive") to "loose" (or "expansive"). Firms with tight credit policies tend to sell on credit only to those customers who have the highest quality credit ratings. That is, relatively tight credit policies imply relatively high credit standards. Firms with loose credit policies tend to sell on credit to a broader array of customers, including customers with relatively low credit ratings. Obviously, tight and loose are vague, qualitative terms that have meaning only in a relative sense. But they are useful terms in describing differences between firms' credit policies, and in describing differences between alternate policies the firm may be considering.

Credit policies can have a major impact on the firm's sales, costs, and profitability. Other things equal, firms with relatively loose credit policies will tend to have higher sales levels than firms with relatively tight credit policies. Loose credit policies stimulate sales because the potential customer base is broadened. At the same time, however, firms with relatively loose credit policies will tend to have higher costs than firms with relatively tight policies. Thus, as with most financial management decisions, the decision to commit funds to accounts receivable (that is, the decision to grant trade credit) involves a tradeoff. Certain benefits will accrue to the firm from establishing a particular trade credit policy, and certain costs will be incurred. The firm's problem is to compare the costs and benefits involved to determine its *best* level of receivables. The costs and benefits to be compared are *marginal* costs and benefits. That is, the firm should only consider the incremental benefits and costs that result from a change in the receivables policy.

Benefits of extending trade credit

The benefits of extending trade credit are attributable to increased sales. As the firm relaxes its credit standards, it increases the population of potential customers who may purchase the firm's goods and services on credit. This increased volume of revenues will increase the profit of the firm and add to the market value of the firm's stock, provided the increased sales are not economically overshadowed by the increased costs associated with producing the new sales.

Since uncertainty is a pervasive fact of life, anticipated sales increases from credit extension or relaxation can only be estimated. One convenient way to depict the impact of credit granting on the firm's sales outlook is to estimate the distribution of sales under different credit policies. These distributions may be related to possible economic conditions. Consider the following example. A firm forecasts three different economic outlooks for the next year together with associated estimated probabilities of occurrence. Given these projections, the firm estimates next year's sales levels under each of the possible economic conditions and proposed credit policies:

Economic		Sales if credit policy is		
conditions	Probability	Tightened	Unchanged	Loosened
Bad year	0.25	$400,000	$500,000	$600,000
Average year	0.50	500,000	600,000	700,000
Good year	0.25	600,000	700,000	800,000

Notice that the effect of tightening the firm's credit policy in this example is to reduce next year's sales by $100,000 for any given economic conditions, and the effect of loosening the firm's credit policy is to increase next year's sales by $100,000 for any given economic conditions. This is consistent with our discussion above. Tightening credit constricts sales, and loosening credit expands sales. Whether or not a loosening (or

a tightening) of credit policy is desirable depends on a complete cost/
benefit analysis, which we will perform later.

Costs of extending trade credit

Basically, there are five categories of costs involved in extension of
trade credit decisions:

1. Bad debt losses.
2. Production and selling costs.
3. Administrative expenses.
4. Opportunity cost of funds.
5. Cash discounts.

Bad debt losses   Bad debt losses are those sales the firm cannot collect
on. One important determinant of the size of bad debt losses is general
economic conditions. As the economy worsens, more customers will fail
to pay, and bad debt losses will increase. The important *discretionary*
determinant of the size of a firm's bad debt losses is the quality of customer credit accounts. As the firm loosens its credit policy and sells to
less reliable customers, bad debt losses will increase. Conversely, as the
firm tightens its credit policy by more selective choice of its credit customers, bad debt losses will decrease. It's worth emphasizing, however,
that the firm should not let its trade credit policy be oriented toward minimizing bad debt losses. That is, the firm should not myopically focus on
the size of bad debt losses (or any other cost). If the sales gains from
credit relaxation create profits that are greater than associated costs,
including additional bad debt losses, then credit relaxation is financially
desirable.

The effect of bad debt losses is to reduce the amount of sales revenue
received. Suppose, for example, that the firm expects sales to be $40
million and also anticipates that bad debt losses will be 2 percent of sales.
Then bad debt losses will be (0.02 × $40,000,000) or $800,000 and *net*
sales will be $39,200,000.

Production and selling costs   Since the decision to extend or expand
credit is expected to lead to increased sales, the additional production
and selling costs incurred in the sales expansion are properly included
as costs associated with the credit granting decision. As noted earlier,
only the *incremental* or *marginal* costs should be included. That is,
only the *variable* production and selling costs should be included. If,
for example, the firm expects that by relaxing its credit policy, sales will
be increased by 100,000 units and variable production and selling costs
will be $8 per unit, then the additional production and selling costs as-
sociated with the credit relaxation are $800,000.

Administrative expenses   Any additional administrative expenses incurred in extending or relaxing credit should also be included in the cost
calculations. Generally speaking, there are two major kinds of such expenses. First, any incremental *credit checking* expenses should be included. The firm will either perform the investigative credit function
itself or pay an outside agency for the service. Second, *collection costs*
associated with increased sales from credit granting or extension are a

relevant cost consideration. These costs are monies the firm expends to collect accounts receivable that are tardy. For both of these cost categories, the emphasis again is on *incremental* or *marginal* costs. If the firm can increase its sales and accounts receivable with increases in neither credit checking nor collection costs, there should be no administrative expenses charged to the receivables increase. This would tend to occur when the firm's credit department is operating below capacity.

Cost of funds   The increased level of accounts receivable is an investment in assets, just like the purchase of machinery. And, just as we require the investment in machinery to earn enough to cover the cost of capital the firm must pay to acquire the machinery, so should the investment in receivables earn enough to cover the cost of obtaining funds to increase receivables. We account for this concept by charging a cost of funds to the investment in receivables. In dollar terms, the cost of funds is the product of the variable cost of the increased investment in receivables times an appropriate opportunity cost (cost of capital). Suppose, for example, that increasing receivables $100,000 by relaxing trade credit results in increased production and selling costs of $75,000 and increased administrative expenses of $5,000. Assume further that the opportunity cost of funds is 15 percent. Then the cost of funds of the additional investment in receivables is ($80,000 × 0.15) or $12,000 per year. That is, it will cost the firm $12,000 per year to raise funds to pay for the additional investment in receivables.

Cash discounts   Many firms offer cash discounts as inducements for customers to pay their bills early.[1] Cash discounts are discussed in more detail below and in Chapter 19, but the main idea is that if payment is made by a certain date (called the *discount date*), the buyer can pay less than the full amount of the invoice. Suppose, for example, a firm offers its customers a 2-percent discount if they pay their bills by the discount date. Suppose, further, that $30 million of the firm's sales are expected to be paid by the discount date. The cost to the firm will be ($30,-000,000 × 0.02) or $600,000 per year. What the firm gets in return is an acceleration of its receipts and a reduced level of receivables. The firm may also realize a higher level of sales because of the effective price decrease, although that is not the usual intent of the cash discount.

Credit policy decisions

Establishment of optimal credit policies first requires identification of the credit granting decision framework. There are three major subcomponents to the credit policy area:

1. Credit terms.
2. Credit standards and credit analysis.
3. Collection policy.

---

[1] A *cash* discount is different from a *quantity* discount. Both are price discounts, but the latter is a price concession made to large quantity purchasers.

Credit terms

Credit terms are a specification of the conditions under which the firm extends credit to its customers. There are two important parts: the *credit period* and any *cash discount terms* offered.

Credit period   The credit period is the length of time the firm extends credit on a sale; it is usually stated in terms of a *net date*. If, for example, the firm's credit terms are "net 30," the firm expects payment 30 days from date of invoice.[2] Credit periods tend to be fairly uniform within an industry, but firms can and do lengthen their credit period to stimulate demand. However, longer credit periods cause higher levels of receivables also.

Cash discounts   The second important part of the firm's credit terms is the *cash discount* offered, if any. Recall from the earlier discussion on trade credit costs that many firms offer cash discounts to induce customers to pay their bills early. If a discount is offered, the credit terms will reflect the *amount* of the discount and the discount *period*, which is the length of time the discount is offered. If a customer foregoes the cash discount, he is expected to pay his bill by the net date.

A complete specification of the firm's credit terms, thus, has three parts: (1) the amount of discount, (2) the discount period (or date), and (3) the credit period (or date). One of the most common credit combinations in the United States is a 2-percent discount if the invoice is paid within 10 days; otherwise the invoice must be paid by the 30th day. Notice that the discount is 2 percent, the discount period is 10 days, and the credit period 30 days. The terms are compactly written as "2/10, net 30." If there were a 3-percent discount, a 15-day discount period and a 60-day credit period, the terms would be 3/15, net 60. Any customer who pays by the 15th day receives a 3-percent discount. All other customers are expected to pay the full amount of the bill by the 60th day.

An example   Suppose, for example, a firm currently offers net 30 credit terms, and is considering changing to 3/15, net 60 terms to stimulate demand. Estimated financial data relevant to this proposed change are as follows:

Present sales	$ 90,000,000 per year
Estimated increased sales	10,000,000 per year
Total sales	100,000,000 per year
Estimated total sales that would take discount.....	30,000,000 per year
Estimated increased receivables.......................	8,000,000
Estimated increased costs:	
1. Bad debt losses	1 percent of increased sales
2. Production and selling costs...................	75 percent of increased sales
3. Administrative expenses	5 percent of increased sales
4. Opportunity cost	10 percent of increased investment in receivables
5. Cash discounts.....................................	3 percent of total sales that take discount

[2] Actually, there are several ways to state the net date. These are discussed in Chapter 19.

Are the new credit terms desirable? That is, is the profit from the extra sales greater than the increased costs incurred in changing the credit period? Let's perform the cost/benefit analysis.

		Dollars per year
Increased sales...............................		$10,000,000
Increased costs.................................		
1. Bad debt losses.........................	$ 100,000	
2. Production and selling costs	7,500,000	
3. Administrative expenses	500,000	
4. Opportunity cost*	640,000	
5. Cash discounts	900,000	
		9,640,000
Increased annual profit		$ 360,000

* Opportunity cost is 10 percent of the increased investment in receivables. The increased investment in receivables is increased receivables times the sum of production, selling, and administrative costs as a percent of sale. Therefore, opportunity cost = (0.10)[($8,000,000)(0.75 + 0.05)] = $640,000.

The increased sales generated by relaxing the credit terms is greater than the sum of the increased costs, so the relaxation is desirable and should be undertaken. Of course, there may be alternate credit terms that are even more desirable. It may be, for example, that 3/15, net 90, or simply net 60 (no discount) would increase profitability even more. The point is, the firm's credit managers should attempt to find the best credit terms possible. One thing the firm must be very careful of, however, is the competition's reaction to such moves. If the firm's competitors relax *their* credit periods to protect their sales, the firm's increased sales could be substantially lower than predicted, and the firm may suffer a loss from its credit relaxation decision.

Credit standards and analysis

Establishment of credit standards will determine what kind of customers the firm will make credit sales to. This, in turn, will have an impact on sales and receivables levels. If the firm has relatively loose credit standards, sales and receivables levels will be relatively high. Conversely, if the firm has relatively tight credit standards, sales and receivables levels will be relatively low. Credit standards are frequently depicted in terms of the "three C's" of credit: (1) *character* (the willingness of the customer to pay), (2) *capacity* (the ability of the customer to pay), and (3) *conditions* (the present economic conditions).

Credit risk classes Credit standards are typically stated in terms of what *risk class* of customers the firm will extend trade credit to. Customer credit ratings are frequently designated by the estimated "financial strength" (net worth) and the credit rating as supplied by credit rating agencies. An example of such a rating scheme is shown in Figure 18–1. This shows the rating key of Dun and Bradstreet, a prominent credit rating service. Any company's rating has two parts: (1) an estimated finan-

FIGURE 18-1
Dun and Bradstreet rating key

	Estimated financial strength		High	Good	Fair	Limited
			Composite credit appraisal			
			High	Good	Fair	Limited
5A	Over	$50,000,000	1	2	3	4
4A	$10,000,000 to	50,000,000	1	2	3	4
3A	1,000,000 to	10,000,000	1	2	3	4
2A	750,000 to	1,000,000	1	2	3	4
1A	500,000 to	750,000	1	2	3	4
BA	300,000 to	500,000	1	2	3	4
BB	200,000 to	300,000	1	2	3	4
CB	125,000 to	200,000	1	2	3	4
CC	75,000 to	125,000	1	2	3	4
DC	50,000 to	75,000	1	2	3	4
DD	35,000 to	50,000	1	2	3	4
EE	20,000 to	35,000	1	2	3	4
FF	10,000 to	20,000	1	2	3	4
GG	5,000 to	10,000	1	2	3	4
HH	Up to	5,000	1	2	3	4

Source: Courtesy of Dun & Bradstreet, Inc.

cial strength and (2) a composite credit appraisal. If, for example, a company is rated CC2, Figure 18-1 shows that its net worth is estimated to be between $75,000 and $125,000, and its composite credit rating, according to Dun and Bradstreet is "good."

Based on such information, many firms classify current and potential customers into *risk classes* that reflect the payment promptness and the bad debt losses of the customers. A firm may find, for example, that in recent years, its customers tend to fall into four risk classes, with average collection period and bad debt loss experience as follows:

Risk class	Credit rating*	Average collection period†	Bad debt loss (percent)
1	All credit 1 ratings	30 days	0
2	5A2 to DD2 ratings	45 days	1
3	EE2 to DC3 ratings	60 days	2
4	All others	120 days	5

* Credit rating refers to Dun and Bradstreet ratings shown in Figure 18-1.
† Average collection period = (Accounts receivable)(365)/Sales.

Evaluating receivables management

In Chapter 1 we noted that the control function is an important part of the financial management area. This idea also applies to receivables, and the firm should continually check on how well it manages its investment in receivables.

Average collection period In Chapter 2 we defined the average collection period as:

$$\text{Average collection period} = \frac{(\text{Accounts receivable})(365)}{\text{Sales}} \quad (18\text{--}1)$$

One method of evaluating the accounts receivable management is to compare the firm's average collection period to the firm's stated credit terms. If terms are 2/10, net 30, and the average collection period is 60 days, something certainly seems wrong. Also, the time pattern of the average collection period should be analyzed to see if there have been major changes that would indicate difficulties in receivables management. Last, the firm can compare its average collection period to that of competitors who offer similar credit terms. If the firm's average collection period is substantially different, an explanation should be sought.

Aging schedule The average collection period is an aggregate indicator of receivables management. The *aging schedule,* which shows what volume and percentage of the accounts receivable have been outstanding for various lengths of time, is a more refined measure of receivables management. An example of an aging schedule might look like the following:

Period outstanding	Amount of accounts receivable outstanding	Percentage of total accounts receivable
Less than 30 days	$2,500,000	62.5
30 days to 60 days	1,000,000	25.0
60 days to 90 days	300,000	7.5
90 days to 180 days	160,000	4.0
Over 180 days	40,000	1.0
Total	$4,000,000	100.0

If significant amounts of accounts receivable have been outstanding more than the firm's stated credit terms, they will be clearly identified by an aging schedule. Thus, the aging schedule is extremely helpful in identifying to what extent the firm has receivables problems. It gives management considerably more information than the average collection period.

INVENTORY

Generally speaking, inventory is composed of assets that will be sold in the future in the normal course of the firm's business operations.

There are several kinds of inventory. *Raw materials* inventories are those input materials used in the firm's product that have been purchased but have not yet been utilized. Depending on the nature of the business, raw materials may range from basic industrial supplies (such as oil, paper, and rubber) to finished parts that are purchased for inclusion in the product (such as transistors for radios). *Goods in process* inventories are partially completed products. They represent goods that require further work before sale is possible. An example would be an automobile that is only halfway through the assembly line. *Finished goods* inventories are those products *ready* for sale that have not yet been sold, for example, an automobile just off the assembly line. By their nature, manufacturing firms have substantial levels of all three kinds of inventories, while retail and wholesale firms have very high levels of finished goods inventories.

A fourth kind of inventory, *supplies*, refers to materials regularly used by the firm but not *directly* in the production process, such as office and plant cleaning materials (soap, brooms, etc.), light bulbs, fuel, and the like. While these materials do not fit the general definition of inventory in that they will not be sold later as product, they are obviously necessary to the production and/or selling process. Supplies are usually not a large component of the firm's total inventory.

The need for inventory

As with any other asset, the firm invests in inventory to enhance the successful accomplishment of its goal of maximization of stockholder wealth. Moreover, for most firms, the investment in inventory is a substantial one. Why do firms maintain substantial inventory levels? The reason is that maintaining inventory allows the firm to independently perform the key activities of: (1) purchasing, (2) production, and (3) selling. Without substantial stocks of inventory, the first two activities would be completely controlled by the firm's sales schedule. If sales increased, the purchasing and production activities would also have to increase. Similarly, if sales decreased, purchasing and production activities would have to decrease.

There are, however, compelling reasons for not *rigidly* tying the firm's purchasing and production schedules to its sales activities. On the purchasing side, the firm may be able to obtain significant cost savings (through *quantity discounts*) by purchasing in larger quantities than needed for a particular sales level. Or the firm may wish to purchase raw materials before an announced or anticipated price increase. On the production side, many firms have seasonal sales patterns where they need to build substantial finished goods inventories prior to the peak sales season. Failure to stockpile such inventories may mean lost sales during the peak season. The basic function of inventories, then, is to uncouple the purchasing, production, and selling activities so that each may operate at its most efficient rate. In the long run, the purchasing and production activities are, and should be, tied to the firm's sales activity. But in the short run it is debilitating to force these three activities to be rigidly related. Inventories permit this desired short-run relaxation so that each activity may be pursued in an optimal manner.

Financial management of inventory

While inventories thus permit the uncoupling of the purchasing, production, and selling functions, the firm can all too easily maintain excessive inventory levels. As we will see below, determination of optimal inventory levels requires a comparison of the costs and benefits of holding inventory. As with any other kind of asset, the upper level financial management officers of the firm and, ultimately, the chief executive officer of the firm have final responsibility for inventory management. However, functional area managers in the purchasing, production, and sales departments typically have considerable managerial control of various inventories. Unfortunately, because of the nature of their jobs, these functional area managers may not view inventory management from a financial management perspective. The purchasing department, for example, may focus too much on quantity discounts offered for large purchases, which can lead to raw materials inventories that are much larger than optimal. Production managers may encourage excess inventory accumulation by their desire to minimize production problems. Likewise, sales and marketing departments will prefer large finished goods inventories so that all sales orders can be filled promptly.

These functional area pressures for large inventories are pervasive facts of life. And, inventories are necessary to permit a smooth functioning of the purchasing, production, and sales efforts that is consistent with the firm's goal. But, just as too little inventory is undesirable, so is too much inventory. From a financial management viewpoint, there must be a balancing of the costs and benefits of holding inventories. We turn to this issue next.

Benefits of holding inventory

We have already noted that the basic benefit from inventory stocks is the uncoupling of short-run purchasing, production, and sales activities. This benefit has several effects that should be clearly identified. First, on the purchasing side, quantity discounts may be advantageously taken. Also, expectations about rising or falling supply costs may be used to help hold down purchasing costs. Acquisition costs may also be reduced through inventory purchasing, since fewer orders need be made. On the production side, production runs may be accomplished more efficiently since inventory permits least cost production scheduling. The sales effort is also enhanced because lost sales are less likely since an adequate inventory of finished goods reduces the possibility of a stockout.

Inventory costs

Costs associated with inventory decisions may be classified into three broad categories:

1. Acquisition costs.
2. Carrying costs.
3. Stockout costs.

These costs are important elements of the optimal inventory level decision, which is analyzed below. As in other cost/benefit analyses, an important thing to bear in mind is that only marginal costs should be included in the analysis. That is, allocation of costs to inventory that are not actually affected by inventory level decisions should be avoided.

Acquisition costs Acquisition costs are the actual dollar costs of acquiring inventory. They encompass costs incurred in some or all of the following activities: requisitioning, purchase ordering, setting up, trucking, receiving, and storage placement. The more frequently acquisitions of inventory are made, the higher the firm's acquisitions costs. From a different perspective, if the firm keeps relatively large inventory levels, there will be a fewer number of acquisitions made, and acquisition costs will be relatively small. So, acquisition costs decrease with increasing inventory size.

Carrying costs Carrying costs are those costs (both out of pocket and opportunity) that are related to holding a given quantity of inventory. Major carrying cost categories are: opportunity cost of funds, insurance, taxes, storage, and obsolescence risk. As opposed to acquisition costs, inventory carrying costs and inventory levels move in the same direction. If inventory levels increase, for example, carrying costs would also increase.

Stockout costs Stockout costs are costs related to running out of inventory. The stockout cost categories are: lost sales, less efficient production, and "emergency" procurement costs. In general, these components are more difficult to estimate than acquisition or carrying costs because they are either hypothetical (such as lost sales) or are contingent upon other events (such as emergency procurement costs, whose size may depend on the inventory level of the firm's suppliers at the time of a stockout). Inventory levels and stockout costs move inversely to one another. As inventory levels increase, for example, expected stockout costs would decrease, as there is less chance for an inventory shortage.

Optimal inventory policies

In managing its inventory, the firm should establish operating policies that are consistent with the goal of stockholder wealth maximization. Particular attention must be given to three problem areas that comprise the heart of inventory control: (1) the classification problem, (2) the order quantity problem, and (3) the order point problem.

The classification problem The classification problem refers to the task of identifying *which* inventories the firm should spend the most effort on in controlling. Even modest-sized manufacturers, retailers, and wholesalers may have several hundred items in inventories. The purpose of classification techniques is to identify those items that, valuewise, are most important to the firm. It is seldom justified, for example, to keep the same degree of inventory control on all items that the firm inventories. Rather, the firm will usually be well-advised to emphasize control on those items whose market value are most important. Some studies have shown that for the average manufacturer, the inventory breakdown between number of items and inventory value looks approximately as follows:

Group	Number of items (percent)	Inventory value (percent)
A......................	15	70
B......................	30	20
C......................	55	10
	100	100

Source: Arthur Snyder, "Principles of Inventory Management," *Financial Executive* (April 1964).

While Group A is least important in terms of the number of items, it is by far the most important from a value standpoint. Because of its importance, the firm should direct most of its inventory control efforts to group A items. Groups B and C should not be ignored, but they do not warrant the special inventory control attention that group A receives. This system is frequently called the *ABC inventory classification,* and the first task of inventory management is to properly classify inventory items into one of the three categories.

The order quantity problem   One of the key inventory problems the firm must resolve is how much inventory to add when inventory is replenished. If the firm is purchasing raw materials or finished goods, the issue is how much inventory to buy on each replenishment. If the firm is planning a production run, the issue is how much production (which will become inventory) to schedule. Problems like these are called *order quantity problems.* There are several ways to attack them, ranging from fairly simple to very sophisticated, and most methods are oriented toward a cost minimization procedure. The presentation here will focus on one of the simpler methods. While our analytical method is not very sophisticated relative to many inventory management techniques, it nonetheless captures the main elements of the inventory order quantity problem.

The task is to determine the optimal order quantity for estimated demand levels of inventory and estimated costs of (1) acquisition, (2) carrying, and (3) stockouts associated with different inventory levels. For the moment, let us ignore stockout costs, which we will account for below. Let us assume that the demand for the inventory is known with certainty and is steady (constant) over some relevant planning horizon. Assume, also, that ordering and carrying costs are constant over the range of possible inventory levels being considered. Given these assumptions, the inventory level over time would look like that shown in Figure 18–2. Beginning inventory is at level Q and is used up steadily until it reaches zero, when inventory is restored to level Q again.

FIGURE 18–2
Inventory level over time

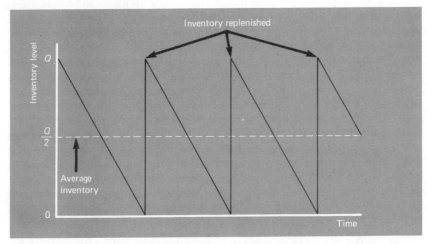

Given the assumptions we have made, the optimal or *economic order quantity (EOQ)* will be that level of inventory that minimizes the total cost associated with inventory management. Since we are not considering stockout costs here, total cost equals carrying cost plus acquisition cost:

$$\text{Total cost} = \text{Carrying cost} + \text{Acquisition cost} \qquad (18\text{--}2)$$

Now, the carrying cost is the average number of units in inventory times the carrying cost per unit. Figure 18–2 shows that the average inventory is $Q/2$. Therefore:

$$\text{Carrying cost} = (\text{Average inventory})(\text{Carrying cost per Unit})$$

$$= \frac{QC}{2} \qquad (18\text{--}3)$$

where

$$Q = \text{order quantity (units)}$$
$$C = \text{carrying cost per unit (dollars per unit).}$$

The acquisition cost is the number of acquisitions of inventory made during the planning period times the cost per acquisition. If D is total demand or total usage over the planning period, and inventory is replenished in lots of size Q at each ordering, there will be D/Q number of inventory acquisitions during the planning period. Therefore:

$$\text{Acquisition cost} = (\text{Number of acquisitions})(\text{Cost per acquisition})$$

$$= \frac{DA}{Q} \qquad (18\text{--}4)$$

where

D = total demand (units), A = cost per acquisition (dollars per acquisition).

Substituting (18–3) and (18–4) into Equation (18–2), we get

$$\text{Total cost} = \frac{QC}{2} + \frac{DA}{Q} \qquad (18\text{–}5)$$

Written this way, the total cost function reflects the tradeoff between carrying costs and acquisition costs in determining the optimal order quantity. Figure 18–3 also graphically shows this tradeoff. As Q in-

FIGURE 18–3
Cost tradeoff and EOQ

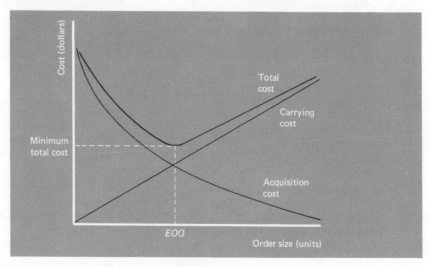

creases, carrying costs increase since the average inventory level increases. But acquisition costs decrease, since a larger average inventory means there will be fewer acquisitions. Similarly, as Q decreases, carrying costs decrease while acquisition costs increase. Figure 18–3 also shows that at the optimal order quantity (*EOQ*) total cost is minimized. It is this optimal order quantity we are trying to determine.

Mathematically, we find the *EOQ* by differentiating Equation (18–5) with respect to Q, setting this differential equal to zero, and solving for the optimal value of Q, *EOQ*. Without presenting the mathematics, the answer to this exercise is:

$$EOQ = \sqrt{\frac{2DA}{C}} \qquad (18\text{–}6)$$

Notice that the greater the total demand for the item, D, the greater the *EOQ* value. Notice, also, that as C, the carrying cost, increases, the lower *EOQ* will be, which means the firm would keep lower average inventories. And, as acquisition costs increase, the EOQ will also increase, which will result in fewer acquisitions.

Consider the following example. Pichler Bros. Wholesalers sells TV sets to retail outlets in the Midwest. The company's inventory planning period is six months, and estimated demand over this period is 18,000 sets. Acquisition costs are $200 per order and carrying costs are $20 per set during the six months. Using Equation (18–6), the optimal order quantity is:

$$EOQ = \sqrt{\frac{(2)(18,000)(200)}{20}} = 600 \text{ sets}$$

That is, each time Pichler orders TV sets from the manufacturer, it should order in lots of 600 units. Notice that this implies that the average

FIGURE 18–4
Inventory level over time with safety stock

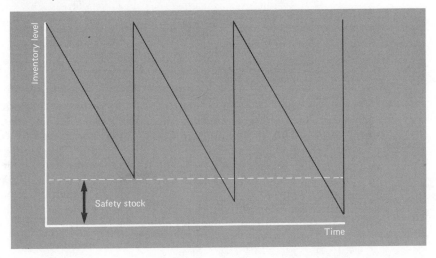

inventory during the planning period will be (600/2) or 300 sets. We can also determine how many orders will be placed during the six-month planning period. There will be (18,000/600) 30 orders, or about one per week. Also, we can calculate the total cost of inventory management during the period from Equation (18–5);

$$\text{Total cost} = \frac{(600)(20)}{2} + \frac{(18,000)(200)}{600}$$

$$= \$12,000$$

While the model we have investigated is only a simple one, it does provide reasonably good guidance regarding the difficult decision of how much inventory to order or to produce. The most limiting assumption of the model is that demand is known with certainty. Since demand is almost never known with certainty, firms carry *safety stocks*.

Safety stocks We determined the *EOQ* by balancing off acquisition and carrying costs. In the analysis, however, we ignored uncertainty. The presence of uncertainty creates a need for inventory safety stocks so that if demand is greater than anticipated, the firm will have an inventory buffer. The acknowledgment of uncertainty and the addition of safety stock changes the inventory level diagram shown in Figure 18–2 to a diagram like Figure 18–4. The usage rate is not completely known so that the inventory buffer is used to reduce stockout possibilities.

Determining the optimal level of safety stock involves comparing stockout costs and the cost of carrying *additional* inventory in excess of the average inventory determined in the *EOQ* calculations.

Acknowledging the fact that demand is never known with complete certainty, suppose the Pichler Bros. Company estimates that if *no* safety stock were carried, it would face the following stockout prospects:

Size of stockout if no safety stock is carried	Probability
0	0.6
100 units	0.3
200 units	0.1
	1.0

Based on this probability distribution of possible stockout sizes, Pichler is considering three different safety stock levels: Plan A, no units; Plan B, 100 units; and Plan C, 200 units. Recall that the carrying cost from the *EOQ* calculation above is $20 per unit. The company also estimates that the stockout cost is about $80 per unit. For Pichler Bros. this latter cost is mainly composed of lost profit from unfilled current orders and lost profit from *future* sales to customers who switch wholesalers because of dissatisfaction created by the current stockout. In summary, then, the firm's cost estimates are:

Carrying cost = $20 times excess inventory

Stockout cost = $80 times amount of shortage

The *conditional cost* for any plan should the need for a particular safety stock arise is the sum of carrying and stockout costs:

Conditional cost = Carrying cost + Stockout cost   (18–7)

Consider, for example, the consequences of Pichler's inventory manager choosing to carry a safety stock of 100 units, Plan B. The conditional cost incurred will depend on the need for safety stock that arises. Calculation of conditional costs are shown in Figure 18–5. Since there are three demand levels forecasted, there are three conditional costs. If demand for safety stock is zero (if there is no need for inventory in excess of the level that Pichler would normally carry for *EOQ* reasons) the firm will incur a $2,000 carrying cost, but there will be no stockout costs. The conditional cost for the demand level of no safety stock units is therefore $2,000. At the other extreme, if demand for safety stock is 200 units, there will be no carrying costs, but there will be an $8,000 stockout cost,

FIGURE 18–5
Calculation of conditional costs for inventory Plan B (safety stock = 100 units)

	Demand for safety stock		
	0 units	100 units	200 units
Excess inventory*...............	100 units	0 units	0 units
Carrying cost†....................	$2,000	$0	$0
Amount of shortage‡..........	0 units	0 units	100 units
Stockout cost§...................	$0	$0	$8,000
Conditional cost‖...............	$2,000	$0	$8,000

* Excess inventory = Amount that safety stock exceeds demand level.
† Carrying cost = ($20)(Excess inventory).
‡ Amount of shortage = Amount that demand level exceeds safety stock.
§ Stockout cost = ($80)(Amount of shortage).
‖ Conditional cost = Carrying cost + Stockout cost.

and the conditional cost will be $8,000. Finally, if demand is for 100 units of safety stock, the conditional cost is zero, as Pichler will have fortuitously held just the right amount of safety stock.

Conditional costs for all three plans are shown in Figure 18–6 in a matrix that relates the different demand levels and the safety stock sizes provided by the alternate plans. The right-hand column of Figure 18–6 also shows the *expected* cost of each plan. The formula for expected cost (recall Chapter 4) is given at the bottom of Figure 18–6. Using that formula, the expected cost of Plan B, for example, is:

$$\text{Expected cost}_B = (0.6)(\$2,000) + (0.3)(\$0) + (0.1)(\$8,000)$$
$$= \$2,000$$

FIGURE 18–6
Conditional and expected costs for different safety stock plans

		Conditional costs Demand for safety stocks			
Plan	Size of safety stock	0 units	100 units	200 units	Expected costs*
A.......	0 units	$0	$8,000	$16,000	$4,000
B.......	100 units	2,000	0	8,000	2,000
C.......	200 units	4,000	2,000	0	3,000
Probability.........		0.6	0.3	0.1	

* Expected cost $= \sum_{i=1}^{n} p_i c_i$

where n = number of demand levels, p_i = probability of the ith demand level, and c_i = conditional cost if the ith demand level occurs.

The least cost plan is B, which Pichler would presumably prefer. The next best plan is C, and the worst plan is A.

The order point problem   In addition to determining *how much* inventory to order, the inventory manager must determine *when* to order inventory. This is called the *order point* problem. The order point is stated in terms of the inventory level at which an order should be placed. One method for determining the order point is:

$$\text{Order point} = (EOQ)(P\text{-}L) + \text{safety stock} \qquad\qquad (18\text{-}7)$$

where

$$EOQ = \text{economic order quantity}$$
$$P = \text{procurement time fraction}$$
$$L = \text{lead time fraction.}$$

FIGURE 18–7
Basic components of inventory problem

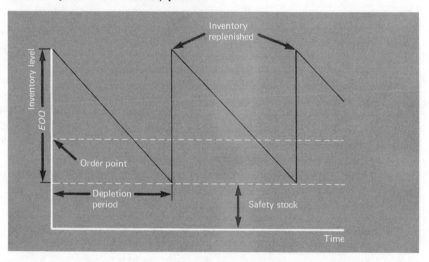

To help understand this method, consider Figure 18–7. This figure shows the basic components of the inventory management problem that we have been developing. A safety stock is maintained, and when inventory is replenished in *EOQ* lot sizes, the inventory level is *EOQ* + safety stock. Figure 18–7 also shows the order point and the depletion period. The *depletion period* is the length of time taken for inventory to be reduced from the level *EOQ* + safety stock to the safety stock level. That is, it is the length of time within which the *EOQ* amount of inventory is "used up" in the firm's normal business activity.

Procurement time is the total time normally needed to procure (or produce) new inventory. It encompasses the time span from the point when a decision to order inventory is made to actual receipt of the inventory. *P*, the *procurement time fraction,* is the procurement time expressed as a fraction of the depletion period. Lead time is the amount of time normally taken to release items from inventory. It is the time span from receipt of order to shipment from inventory. *Lead time fraction, L,* is lead time expressed as a fraction of the depletion period. Let's look at an example.

Suppose that an oil refining company has determined that its *EOQ* amount of crude oil is 2 million barrels. The firm also keeps a 200,000 barrel safety stock, and the depletion period is five days. Procurement and lead times are four and two days, respectively. The optimal order point, given these data are:

$$\text{Order point} = (2,000,000)(0.8 - 0.4) + 200,000$$
$$= 1,000,000 \text{ barrels}$$

Whenever the inventory of crude oil gets as low as 1 million barrels, the refiner should order another 2 million barrels.

This method we have developed is one of several that may be employed. It has the advantage of being simple and straightforward, but like any other technique we must be cognizant of its shortcomings. One particular thing that the inventory manager must be watchful of is that ordering the *EOQ* amount of inventory when the order point is reached may not always be desirable. This problem arises when the inventory is reduced significantly below the order point. Suppose, for example, that inventory in the previous example is 1,200,000 barrels and an order for 600,000 barrels is received. This will reduce inventory to 600,000 barrels and trigger the ordering of new inventory. But if only the 2 million barrel *EOQ* amount is ordered, this ignores the fact that the inventory was significantly below the order point when new inventory was ordered. The result would be more frequent stockouts. To avoid this problem the refiner should boost the inventory order by the difference between the order point and the inventory level when the order is placed (in the example, 400,000 barrels). This example illustrates that, while mathematical techniques and rules are devised to provide helpful guidance, managers must always be aware of possible limitations of the model and analysis being used.

Evaluating inventory management

For many companies inventory represents a substantial investment, and the degree to which the firm successfully accomplishes its goal of stockholder wealth maximization is importantly related to how well inventory is managed. It is clear, therefore, that reliable inventory evaluation techniques are important to the firm.

One widely used method of evaluating inventory management is the practice of analyzing the inventory turnover ratio. The inventory turnover ratio was introduced in Chapter 2. Recall that

$$\text{Inventory turnover} = \frac{\text{Sales}}{\text{Inventory}} \qquad (18\text{--}8)$$

Presumably, the higher the inventory turnover, the more efficiently inventory is managed, and the lower the turnover, the less efficient the inventory management. Recall also from Chapter 2 that inventory turnover only has meaning when compared to competitors' ratios and/or with the firm's inventory ratios in previous years. The analyst must also bear in mind that there may be perfectly logical reasons for low inventory turnover ratios that may not be apparent solely from the financial data. Also, extremely *high* inventory turnover ratios may be an indication of future problems: Inventory levels may be too low to support future sales.

Another method of evaluating inventory management and control is a detailed breakdown of inventory costs. This breakdown should be complete in the sense that *all* relevant costs are accounted for, whether acquisition, carrying, or stockout. Also, the cost breakdown should only reflect *marginal* costs, as we have emphasized before. As with turnover ratios, costs have meaning only in a comparative sense.

SUMMARY

While there are several kinds of receivables, the most important kind for most firms is accounts receivable. Investment in accounts receivables is made by granting trade credit and is motivated by sales expansion or sales retention reasons. However, granting trade credit involves several kinds of costs. These include bad debt losses, production and selling costs, administrative expenses, the cost of funds, and any cash discounts offered. Sales gains made by changes in credit policy must be compared against these costs in determining optimal credit policies. The main features of credit terms offered are the credit period and cash discount terms, and the firm's credit policy formulation begins with establishment of credit standards. Individual credit applicants may then be compared against these standards using the cost/benefit principle. The final aspect of credit policy is the firm's collection policy.

The primary purpose of keeping inventory is to permit "uncoupling" of the purchasing, production, and sales activities, allowing each to proceed at its optimal pace. Establishment of optimal inventory policies involves balancing off acquisition, carrying, and stockout costs, and there are several parts of the optimal inventory policy issue. First, the classification problem requires identification of the most important inventoried items. Then, optimal order quantity (*EOQ*) and inventory safety stocks must be determined. Last, there is the order point problem of when to replenish inventory. Like accounts receivable management, inventory management is an important topic since many firms must maintain substantial investments in inventory.

QUESTIONS

1. Define the following terms and phrases:
    a. Credit policy.
    b. Bad debt losses.
    c. Credit terms.
    d. Aging schedule.
    e. Acquisition costs.
    f. Carrying costs.

   g. Stockout costs.
   h. EOQ.
   i. Safety stocks.
   j. Order point.

2. What probable effects would the following changes have on the level of the company's accounts receivables?
   a. The firm changes its credit terms from 2/10, net 30 to 3/10, net 30.
   b. Interest rates increase.
   c. Production and selling costs associated with the firm's product decline.
   d. The economy worsens and the country slips into a mild recession.

3. In assessing how well the firm's receivables are being managed what advantage does the aging schedule offer in comparison to the average collection period calculation?

4. At a staff meeting the controller criticizes the credit manager for what appears to be a deterioration in the management of the firm's receivables. The controller points out that bad debt losses have increased considerably lately and that the collection period has also increased. Describe under what conditions this criticism may be unjustified.

5. Lemmer Cereals is attempting to determine its EOQ level for grain. Would the following events tend to raise or lower this EOQ? Explain your answer.
   a. Purchase ordering costs increase.
   b. Storage insurance rates increase.
   c. Interest rates decrease.
   d. Trucking costs decrease.
   e. Sales decrease.

6. Explain the purpose of the ABC inventory classification scheme.

7. Other things equal, what effect would the following circumstances have on the order point for an inventoried item?
   a. The depletion period decreases.
   b. Safety stock levels are lowered.
   c. The amount of time normally required to release items from inventory decreases.
   d. Procurement time increases.

8. Sea W, a wholly owned subsidiary of Park, Ltd., makes a heavy-duty fishing reel. As part of routine inventory control, Park receives a monthly report on inventory turnover ratios of all its subsidiaries. For the past few months Sea W's inventory turnover ratio has been high and has steadily increased. Sea W's management is proud of its performance, but Park's inventory control manager is somewhat concerned with the situation. What do you suppose is bothering the inventory control manager?

PROBLEMS

1. A firm currently offers net 30 credit terms and is considering chang-
    ing to net 60 terms. Neither set of terms includes a cash discount.
    The firm does not contemplate selling to lower quality customers,
    but if the change is made, the firm believes that more sales can be
    made to current customers and to new customers of the same general
    credit caliber. Because there will be no relaxation of credit quality,
    the percentage bad debt losses on the new sales should stay the same
    as on current sales, 3 percent. Incremental production, selling, credit
    checking, and collection costs are $0.90 per dollar of sales and are
    expected to remain constant over the range of anticipated sales in-
    creases. The relevant opportunity cost for receivables is 15 percent.
    Current credit sales are $36.5 million, and the current level of ac-
    counts receivable is $4 million. If the change in credit terms is made,
    credit sales are expected to increase to $42 million, and the firm's
    receivables level will increase also. The firm's credit manager esti-
    mates that the new credit terms will cause the firm's collection pe-
    riod to increase by 30 days. In the following work, round all answers
    to the nearest thousand dollars.

    a. Determine the present collection period and the collection period
        under the proposed credit terms change.
    b. What level of accounts receivable is implied by the new collec-
        tion period?
    c. Determine the increased investment in accounts receivable if
        the new credit terms are adopted.
    d. Are the new credit terms desirable? Show all work.

2. Meadows Equipment rents drilling equipment to small drilling con-
    tractors in south Texas. Each year the company has about $60,000
    of hard-to-collect accounts. Meadows gets competitive bids at the
    beginning of the year from Houston collection agencies and then
    determines which agency will handle the company's business for
    the year. This year two agencies, Quick Find and Acme, have sub-
    mitted bids. Quick Find's bid is $9,400 plus 50 percent of the amount
    collected, while Acme's bid is $15,200 plus 25 percent of the amount
    collected. Based on past experience, Meadows assesses the likelihood
    of collections as the same regardless of which bid is accepted.
    Meadows estimates collection possibilities as:

Amount collected...	$10,000	$20,000	$30,000	$40,000	$50,000
Probability............	0.3	0.3	0.2	0.1	0.1

    a. Determine the expected amount that will be collected this year.
    b. Determine the expected bad debt losses for this year.
    c. Determine the expected cost of each bid. Indicate which bid is
        most desirable on an expected cost basis.
    d. What is the probability of collection costs exceeding the amount
        collected under each bid?

3. Rao's, an electrical appliance wholesaler, is considering extending trade credit on terms of 4/10, net 30 to some new customers that previously Rao sold to only on a cash-before-delivery basis. The credit manager at Rao's has argued that these customers actually comprise two credit groups. Group I firms are financially stronger and would have lower collection periods and lower bad debt losses. Also, Rao's credit manager feels that the sales, collection period, bad debt loss, discount behavior, and collection costs for the two groups will be strongly influenced each year by economic conditions. The credit manager's estimates of the situation are shown below. In total, incremental production and selling costs associated with expanding sales are $0.80 per dollar of sales. The opportunity cost of money tied up in receivables investment is 15 percent.

	Economic outlook		
	Bad	Average	Good
Probability	0.3	0.5	0.2
Group I			
Sales per year	$2 million	$2.5 million	$3 million
Collection period.......................	50 days	35 days	25 days
Bad debt losses/sales.................	6 percent	3 percent	2 percent
Percent taking discount..............	40 percent	60 percent	70 percent
Checking and collection			
costs/sales...........................	15 percent	10 percent	5 percent
Group II			
Sales per year	$3 million	$5 million	$6 million
Collection period.......................	100 days	50 days	40 days
Bad debt losses/sales.................	10 percent	8 percent	6 percent
Percent taking discount..............	10 percent	40 percent	50 percent
Checking and collection			
costs/sales...........................	20 percent	15 percent	10 percent

a. Determine the increase in receivables and the increased investment in receivables for each group under each possible economic outlook. (Round answers to nearest thousand dollars.)
b. Determine the increased annual profit or loss for each group under each possible economic outlook. (Round all costs to nearest thousand dollars.)
c. Calculate the expected annual profit or loss for each group.
d. What action would you recommend to Rao relative to these two groups? Explain your answer.

4. The Burr Co.'s credit department has divided up its credit applicants into five categories, A through E. Currently, Burr sells on open account to categories A, B, and C, but not D and E. The projected annual sales and costs of each category for three different kinds of economic climates, shown below, have been estimated by a credit analyst who is attempting to assess the success of current credit

terms. Projected sales for categories D and E are on the basis of "what if" the firm extends credit to those two categories.

		Annual sales (millions of dollars)			Annual costs (millions of dollars)	
Category	Bad	Average	Good	Bad	Average	Good
A	6.1	7.2	8.0	6.9	7.1	7.3
B	5.0	5.4	6.8	5.3	5.6	5.8
C	9.4	12.2	15.0	10.0	11.6	13.6
D	2.6	2.8	3.1	2.8	2.8	3.0
E	5.2	5.2	7.0	5.5	5.4	6.0
Probability ...	0.3	0.4	0.3	0.3	0.4	0.3

  a. Determine the annual profit or loss from each category for each possible economic climate.
  b. Determine the expected annual profit or loss for each category.
  c. What is the probability of an annual loss for each category?
  d. Burr's current policy is to entend credit only to firms in those categories that have an expected annual profit and where the probability of an annual loss is less than 50 percent. If Burr maintains this policy, which of the categories would Burr extend credit to? What would the expected annual profit from total credit sales be?
  e. If Burr changes their credit policy to eliminate the probability constraint, which categories would Burr extend credit to? What would the expected annual profit be?

5. Assuming uniform usage of inventory and no safety stock, determine in each following instance (1) *EOQ* and (2) total inventory management cost (round to nearest whole number):

Situation	Demand (units)	Carrying cost ($/unit)	Acquisition cost ($/order)
a	800	5	100
b	800	10	40
c	200,000	1	25
d	100	50	400
e	100	50	50

6. H. Frank and Son (HF&S) is an office supply company. Among their important inventoried items is white $8\frac{1}{2} \times 11\frac{3}{4}$ paper pads. HF&S has already estimated its *EOQ* level of pads but is attempting to estimate the safety stock level. HF&S orders pads monthly and the monthly carrying cost is about $0.45 per box. This mainly represents the opportunity cost of funds tied up in inventory. Stockout costs, estimated to be $6 per box, are mainly attributable to lost current and future sales. After some checking of past records, HF&S estimate that if *no* safety stock were maintained there would be a 20 percent

chance of a 2,000-box stockout, a 30-percent chance of a 1,000-box stockout and a 50-percent chance of no stockout. However, since HF&S only have storage area for 1,500 boxes of safety stock at most, they are considering holding a safety stock level of either 1,500 boxes or 1,000 boxes.

    a. Prepare a table (such as Figure 18–5) showing conditional costs for both the 1,500-box and 1,000-box plan for all three stockout possibilities.

    b. Calculate expected costs for each plan. On the basis of expected costs which plan do you recommend?

    c. For an extra $50 per month HF&S can rent enough storage space from a camera shop next door to stock an extra 500 boxes. Would it be worthwhile to do this? Show your work.

7. An aircraft manufacturer purchases titanium wire coils to use as fasteners on airplanes. The manufacturer's estimated demand for these coils during the coming planning period is 500 coils. Acquisition costs are $500 per order; carrying costs are about $50 per coil. The safety stock is set at 20 percent of the *EOQ* level. The rate of usage is 5 coils per day, procurement time is 15 days, and lead time is about 3 days.

    a. Determine the *EOQ* inventory level.

    b. Determine the safety stock level.

    c. Determine the order point.

SELECTED BASIC REFERENCES

Davis, P. M. "Marginal Analysis of Credit Sales," *Accounting Review* (January 1966), pp. 121–26.

Niemeyer, R. D. "Inventory Control," *Management Services* (July–August 1964), pp. 25–31.

Snyder, A. "Principles of Inventory Management," *Financial Executive* (April 1964), pp. 16–19.

Soldofsky, R. M. "A Model for Accounts Receivable Management," *Management Accounting* (January 1966), pp. 55–58.

SELECTED ADVANCED REFERENCES

Eilon, S., and J. Elmaleh. "Adaptive Limits in Inventory Control," *Management Science* (April 1970), pp. 533–48.

Schiff, M., and Z. Leiber. "A Model for the Integration of Credit and Inventory Management," *Journal of Finance* (March 1974), pp. 133–40.

Shapiro, A. "Optimal Inventory and Credit Granting Strategies under Inflation and Devaluation," *Journal of Financial and Quantitative Analysis* (January 1973), pp. 37–46.

SHORT-TERM FINANCING

19

SPONTANEOUS SOURCES
OF SHORT-TERM
FINANCING

In Chapters 10 through 13 we looked at intermediate and long-term sources of funds available to the firm. In this and the next chapter we look at short-term sources of funds. Recall that the distinction between short-term and other kinds of financing is usually whether the repayment is to be made within one year or not.

In general, there are two broad classes of short-term funds: *spontaneous* sources and *negotiated* sources. The former refers to sources of funds that arise (more or less) automatically and don't require much formal arrangement by the firm. In a sense these sources "seek out the firm." The negotiated sources require (more or less) intensive effort by the firm to obtain them. The firm must negotiate for these funds. That is, the firm must "seek out the funds." This chapter covers the spontaneous sources of short-term funds, and the next chapter covers the negotiated sources of short-term funds. In describing spontaneous sources we divide them into two categories: *trade credit* and *accruals*.

TRADE CREDIT

Trade credit refers to the credit that sellers grant their customers during the ordinary course of business. Most purchases made by the firm do not have to be paid immediately, and this deferral of payment is a short-term source of funds called trade credit.

Use of trade credit

Trade credit is a major source of funds for U.S. business firms. Traditionally, trade credit has provided from approximately 5 to 25 percent of the firm's financing. This range is, of course, very large, and the extent that a firm uses trade credit is determined mainly by the kind of business (industry) the firm is in and the size of the firm. Wholesale and retail companies have historically been heavy users, as have manufacturers. Also, smaller companies tend to rely on trade credit more than larger ones. Smaller companies are typically financially weaker and are consequently less able to secure funds from negotiated sources that comprise the capital and money markets. Trade credit can be obtained very readily by any firm with a reasonable financial record, and this easy accessibility, together with the smaller firm's competitive disadvantage in acquiring negotiated sources of funds, causes smaller firms to be heavier users of trade credit than larger firms. This dependence on trade credit by smaller companies is particularly important during tight money periods when raising funds from negotiated sources is difficult for all companies, but particularly so for smaller ones.

Open account

In an open account credit sale the seller ships the merchandise to the buyer, but the buyer never *formally* acknowledges the debt. That is, the buyer signs no legal instrument of any kind stating that he owes the seller any money. Open account trade credit appears on the buyer's books as accounts payable. The seller is willing to grant open account trade credit because he thinks that the buyer's general credit worthiness is sufficiently good to run the risk that there may never be any payment or that payment may be late. The seller's confidence in entering this kind of arrangement usually comes from checking the credit worthiness of the buyer and/or the history (if any) of previous business transactions with the buyer (see Chapter 18). Because open account transactions are the most widely used type of trade credit, a firm would be in trouble if its credit rating deteriorated to the point where it was difficult to get open account trade credit. Any other form of short-term funds would be more difficult to obtain and probably would carry unfavorable restrictions on the firm's future financing activities.

Trade notes payable and trade acceptances

When the buyer signs a promissory note to obtain trade credit, it shows up on his balance sheet as *trade notes payable*.[1] The note will have a specified future payment date and is usually used when the seller is less sure that the buyer will pay for the delivered goods. While this is a more formal arrangement than the open account, it is actually no more legally binding. It does, however, document the debt and, when presented for collection through a bank, gives the seller more leverage in forcing collection. Trade notes payable are also used routinely in some industries where the merchandise is extremely expensive, as with furs and jewelry.

A *trade acceptance* is another way to get formal acknowledgment of the debt the buyer owes the seller for the delivered goods. The seller draws a bank draft (trade acceptance) on the buyer. This draft is a legal

---

[1] Other notes payable that are not trade notes payable, are notes issued to banks, employees, officers, and stockholders.

instrument proclaiming that the buyer will pay the bank the amount of the bill on some specified future date. The seller sends the merchandise after the buyer signs the draft; on the due date the bank asks for payment and forwards this payment (less a service fee) to the seller. There are several advantages to the seller of using trade acceptances. As with notes payable, the seller has forced the buyer to acknowledge in writing that a debt exists. More importantly, the seller has employed the bank to make collection, and most companies would be much more hesitant about not promptly paying an acceptance to the bank than about not promptly paying an open account trade credit to the supplier. So a trade acceptance enhances prompt payment. Last, if the buyer has a reasonably good credit rating, the trade acceptance may be sold at a discount (for less than face value) to investors. That is, the trade acceptance is marketable, so the supplier can receive immediate payment by selling the acceptance (at a discount). Most of these advantages to the supplier, however, are disadvantages to the buyer, and competition among suppliers for sales has caused the use of trade acceptances to be somewhat rare in recent years. There is also the problem of time, effort, and cost involved in dealing with both acceptances and notes.

Credit terms

The expression "credit terms" refer to the conditions under which credit is granted. By definition, credit implies a deferred payment date; unless the supplier permits a delayed payment there is actually no credit being extended. Consequently, the familiar COD (cash on delivery) and the less familiar CBD (cash before delivery) are not really credit sales because no delayed payment date is offered the buyer. There are three main parts to the credit terms that summarize the sales arrangement between buyer and seller: the net date, the cash discount, and the discount date. We also discussed these topics in Chapter 18.

Net date Recall from the previous chapter that the *net date* or due date is the date by which the supplier expects net payment. Most typically the net date is 30 days from either the arrival of the goods (AOG) or from the end of the following month (EOM). If, for example, a shipment of goods arrived on September 12, the AOG net date would be October 12, and the EOM date would be October 30. Of course, the buyer may pay for the goods sooner than the net date, but he is not obligated to do so. Similarly, he may decide to pay *after* the net date, a practice which we discuss below.

Cash discount and discount date To encourage speedy payment of the bill the supplier frequently offers the buyer a *cash discount.* This discount can only be taken if the buyer pays the bill by a certain date, the *discount* date, which is earlier than the net date. If the bill is not paid by the discount date, the right to take the cash discount is lost and the buyer is expected to pay for the merchandise by the net date. The cash discount is expressed as a percent so that a 2-percent discount means the buyer who avails himself of the cash discount only pays $0.98 for each dollar owed. The discount date, like the net date, is stated in terms of days from some starting point.

The three major items of the credit terms—net date, cash discount, and discount date—are usually stated as follows: x/y, net z, where x is the cash discount (percent), y is the discount date (days), and z is the net date (days). Consider the following two examples of credit terms and their interpretation:

Credit terms	Interpretation
2/10, net 30*	A 2-percent cash discount is allowed if the bill is paid by the 10th day. If the discount is not taken, the full amount of the bill is due by the 30th day.
3/15, net 60	A 3-percent cash discount is allowed if the bill is paid by the 15th day. If the discount is not taken, the full amount of the bill is due by the 60th day.

* These are the most common credit terms in the United States.

If the buyer wishes to take the cash discount, he must pay the bill—less the discount—by the discount date. A buyer of $1,000 worth of merchandise who is offered terms of 2/10 net 30, for example, may pay $980 any time up to the tenth day. There is no advantage to paying *before* the tenth day, however. If the discount is not taken, $1,000 is due by the 30th day. In effect, the $980 is the "cash price" of the merchandise, and the firm is receiving ten days of free credit on the $980.

Cost of trade credit

In discussing the cost of trade credit it is important to distinguish between *explicit* and *implicit* costs, and between *standard* and *non-standard* uses of trade credit. By explicit costs we mean those costs whose dollar value can be readily measured. Implicit costs are costs that are more difficult to determine. A good example of an implicit cost is the cost of deterioration of the firm's credit rating. If the firm's credit rating were to slip—because of financial difficulties—it would be extremely difficult to to put a dollar value on the cost of this deterioration, but there clearly is a cost. We classify this and other hard to measure costs as implicit costs.

We make another distinction between standard and nonstandard uses of trade credit. By standard use of trade credit, we mean those situations where the firm pays off the trade credit exactly on time. There are two such possibilities. If a cash discount is offered, paying on time means paying on the discount date. If a cash discount is not offered, paying on time means paying on the net date. Nonstandard use of trade credit means *not* paying on time. If a cash discount is offered, but not taken, or if the full bill is not paid by the net date, the firm is making nonstandard use of trade credit. Figure 19–1 shows a cross classification of standard-vs.-nonstandard uses and explicit-versus-implicit costs. Our discussion will address each of the four cells in the figure.

FIGURE 19–1
Trade credit use and costs

	Standard use	Nonstandard use
Explicit costs	None	Cost of foregoing cash discount
Implicit costs	Costs passed on to buyer by seller for: 1. Carrying costs 2. Credit checking 3. Bad debt losses	Cost of paying late

Standard use – explicit costs The northwest cell of Figure 19–1 shows there are no explicit costs to the firm associated with the standard use of trade credit. That is, if the firm pays its suppliers exactly on time, taking all cash discounts on their discount date and paying all other bills on the net date, there are no explicit or visible dollar costs to the firm of using trade credit. But this does not mean that there are no trade credit costs to the firm. It only means there are no *explicit* costs.

Standard use – implicit costs There are always invisible or hidden costs associated with standard trade credit use. To better see these, consider John Jones, the supplier. Some credit sales will result in bad debt losses to him. He also has to pay for the funds used to produce his product; consequently, he can scarcely afford to grant credit (funds) to his customers costlessly. In addition, the credit granting procedure usually involves some credit checking operation, which either the supplier will perform himself (by maintaining a credit department) or by purchasing the information from a credit checking agency. The supplier will try to cover all of these costs. He does this by pricing his product higher than he would if there were only *cash* sales. How successful he is depends largely on how competitive his industry is. The aggregate demand for his product and the competition for sales among sellers will determine how much of these costs can be passed on to the buyer as implicit costs. While this is true in the *aggregate*, the individual buyer cannot reduce the implicit cost passed on to him by the seller.

Nonstandard use – explicit costs The firm incurs an explicit cost when it foregoes any cash discount offered. We have already seen that if the firm takes the cash discount by the discount date there are no explicit costs involved. However, if the firm fails to take the discount, it incurs a substantial explicit cost. An easy way to examine this cost is to put the decision to take the discount or not in a capital budgeting framework. On the discount date the firm may: (*a*) take the discount or (*b*) forego it and pay the full amount of the bill on the net date.[2] Let's look at an example.

---

[2] The full amount of the bill may be paid *after* the net date, but we consider this possibility below.

Suppose the terms on a $100 credit sale are 2/10, net 30. The firm is faced effectively with a capital budgeting problem with the following cash flows:

Day	(a) Take discount	(b) Forego discount	(c) (a) − (b)
10...................	−$98		−$98
30...................		−$100	+100

Column (c) shows that by paying the $98 on day 10 ($t_0$) the firm avoids paying (saves) $100 on day 30 ($t_1$). The $98 is like an investment and the $100 is like a cash inflow. Considering the 20-day interval from day 10 to day 30 as one period, the interest rate (internal rate of return) the firm is paying when it foregoes the discount is found by the usual method (from Chapter 7) for a one period capital budgeting problem:

$$\$98 = \frac{\$100}{1 + i}$$

Solving for i, we get

$$i = \frac{2}{98} = 2.04 \text{ percent}$$

But this rate of return is for a 20-day period, and there are $(365/20) = 18.25$ such 20-day periods in a year. Therefore:

$$\text{Explicit annual cost of foregoing cash discount} = (2.04)(18.25) = 37.2 \text{ percent}$$

The purpose of the above discussion was to explain *why* the annual cost of foregoing the cash discount in this problem was about 37 percent. When working problems there is no reason to proceed step by step through the analysis. We simply calculate the annual cost in the following manner:

$$\text{Explicit annual cost of foregoing cash discount} = \left(\frac{\text{Percent cash discount}}{100 \text{ percent} - \text{Percent cash discount}}\right)\left(\frac{365}{N}\right) \quad (19\text{–}1)$$

where

$N = $ number of days between net date and discount date. In the example:

$$\text{Explicit annual cost of foregoing cash discount} = \left(\frac{2}{98}\right)\left(\frac{365}{20}\right) = 37.2 \text{ percent}$$

The firm may reduce the large explicit cost of foregoing cash discounts by not paying the full amount of the bill by the net date. Equation (19–1) may be generalized to include payment on dates other than the net date.

$$\begin{matrix} \text{Explicit} \\ \text{annual cost} \\ \text{of foregoing} \\ \text{cash discount} \end{matrix} = \left(\frac{\text{Percent cash discount}}{100 \text{ percent} - \text{Percent cash discount}}\right)\left(\frac{365}{N'}\right) \quad (19\text{-}2)$$

where

N' = number of days between discount date and date the bill is paid.

Suppose the firm doesn't pay the $100 bill in the example until day 40, 10 days *after* the net date. Then:

$$\begin{matrix} \text{Explicit annual cost of} \\ \text{foregoing cash discount} \end{matrix} = \left(\frac{2}{98}\right)\left(\frac{365}{30}\right) = 24.8 \text{ percent}$$

By stretching out the payment date, N' increases, and the explicit cost of foregoing the cash discount is reduced; the longer the firm stretches the payment date, the lower the explicit cost.

Nonstandard use – implicit costs Failure to pay trade credit on time is called "*stretching the payables.*" As we just saw, this practice reduces the explicit cost of foregoing cash discounts, but it increases the implicit cost. This implicit cost arises because of the possible deterioration of the firm's credit rating. If, for example, a firm became known as a slow payer, its suppliers may offer less favorable trade credit terms (they may even stop granting credit), particularly in times of tight credit. Less favorable credit terms mean increased costs to the firm, and it is these costs we identify as implicit costs associated with stretching the payables. The size of these implicit costs depends mainly on the competitive conditions that exist between buyers and suppliers. A firm can more successfully stretch its payables if it is a dominant buyer rather than if it is one of many buyers. But the main point is that stretching the payables is not costless; the supplier will attempt to pass all costs associated with such practices on to the buyer.

Determinants of credit terms

There is considerable variation evident in credit terms in U.S. industry, ranging from liberal to stringent. In general, there are three broadly defined determinants of credit terms.

General economic conditions When money and credit are tight, that is, difficult to obtain, credit terms will be more stringent. Suppliers will have more difficulty in procuring funds themselves and may be more reluctant to continue offering credit at the same terms. In extreme cases, suppliers may not be able to offer credit at all to their slow payers. It is for such reasons that most firms try to keep a good credit rating.

Industry factors Another important determinant of credit terms is the prevailing practice in the industries in which the buyer and seller operate. In the first place, the credit period is a function of the durability of the commodity. Perishable items such as food have fairly short credit periods, while nonperishable items such as manufactured goods have longer credit periods. Another industry factor is the nature and relationship of buyer and seller competition. These are classical economic demand and supply conditions. If there is vigorous competition for sales by a large number of sellers, there will be more liberal credit terms. On the other hand, if there are few sellers and many buyers, credit terms will be less liberal. The buyer's industry also strongly influences the amount of risk involved in granting credit and, consequently, the credit terms. Failure rates are not the same in all industries, and companies in high failure rate industries will receive less favorable credit terms.

Company factors   In addition to general economic and industry considerations, certain factors are unique to the company. One such factor is the financial strength of the buyer and seller. If the buyer is financially strong, it is more likely to get liberal credit terms because there is less risk that the supplier will not be paid. Similarly, if the seller is financially strong, it is more able to acquire funds and thus can offer more liberal credit terms. Another consideration is the *relative* financial strength of the buyer and seller. Relatively weaker buyers *need* more liberal terms but will be generally unable to *command* more liberal terms unless there is strong sales competition among suppliers. Perhaps the dominant company consideration is the buyer's credit history. Firms that have been prompt payers in the past are more likely to have liberal credit terms extended to them than firms that are slow payers.

Advantages of trade credit

Availability   The most obvious advantage of trade credit is availability. It is, by definition, a spontaneous source of short-term funds. Except for firms in financial trouble, trade credit is an almost automatic source, and there are no negotiations or special arrangements required to obtain the credit. This availability is particularly important to smaller companies who may have difficulty getting funds elsewhere.

Flexibility   Another advantage of trade credit is its flexibility. If the firm's sales increase, causing its purchases of goods and services to increase, trade credit will increase also. Consequently, the firm will have met this need for funds readily. Likewise, if the firm's sales should decrease, causing purchasing needs to drop, trade credit will decrease automatically. This flexibility means that the firm can secure needed funds easily in periods of increased purchasing and can readily reduce its level of funds acquisition in periods of decreased purchasing.

Less restrictive terms   When the firm *negotiates* for short-term funds (see Chapter 20), it may have restrictions imposed on its financial activities by the lenders. Restrictions may also be placed on trade credit in some instances, but this is far less common. In general, trade credit terms are much less restrictive than those of negotiated sources of funds. In addition, failure to meet accounts payable on time (stretching the payables) has less severe consequences and is a more common practice than late payment on a loan.

ACCRUALS

There is an even more automatic source of short-term funds than trade credit. Many obligations the firm incurs are not paid immediately: Such deferred payment arrangements are called *accrued expenses* or *accruals*. Since – by definition – accruals permit the firm to receive some service before paying for it, accruals are a form of short-term funds supplied to the firm. If the liability required immediate payment – instead of a deferred one – funds would have to be directed to paying off the liability. The main components of accrued expenses are wages, interest, and taxes. These expenses are usually nonpostponable and will vary with the firm's level of operations. An important point about accrual financing is that it is provided at no cost to the firm.

Accrued wages

From an accounting viewpoint, the firm incurs a liability at the instant the labor is furnished. But employees are paid afterward, usually at some fixed interval like two weeks or a month. In effect, the firm's employees are supplying the firm with short-term funds by receiving deferred wages and salaries. Obviously, the longer this payment interval, the greater the amount of funds provided by the employees.

Accrued income taxes

While the government has a percentage tax claim on each dollar the firm earns, the bulk of these taxes are only paid *after* profits have accumulated. This, too, is a deferred payment of an obligation the firm has, and is a form of short-term capital provided to the firm. Corporate income taxes are calculated annually but are paid quarterly during the year the income is earned. In earlier years, income taxes were not paid until *after* the year in which income was earned, which means that the government no longer supplies as much short-term funds to U.S. industry as it previously did.

Accrued interest payments

Another accrual results from the institutional practices associated with interest payments. The firm has a contractual obligation to repay interest on its borrowings, but while the firm has continuous use of the borrowed funds, interest payments are made periodically at the *end* of agreed upon time periods. This deferred, rather than continuous, payment of interest also provides short-term funds to the firm.

SUMMARY

In this chapter we have looked at *spontaneous* sources of short-term funds that the firm can acquire. These funds are almost automatic in the sense that companies don't usually have to negotiate with the supplier for the funds. There are two main spontaneous sources: *trade credit* and *accruals*.

Trade credit is the major spontaneous source of funds and refers to suppliers "carrying" the buyers by accepting deferred payment on sales.

There are several types of trade credit. An *open account* arrangement is where the buyer never formally acknowledges the liability incurred to the seller; open accounts are granted to companies with reasonably good credit ratings. *Trade notes payable* and *trade acceptances* are more formal trade credit arrangements where the buyer formally acknowledges the liability.

Credit terms specify the conditions of the credit sale. The *net date* is the date that payment is expected, and if a *cash discount* is given, there is also a *discount date*, which is prior in time to the net date. Cash discounts must be taken by the discount date. The most common credit terms are 2/10, net 30, which means a 2-percent cash discount is allowed if the bill is paid by the 10th day, otherwise the full bill is due by the 30th day.

There are two kinds of costs associated with trade credit. *Explicit costs* are costs whose dollar value can be readily determined. All other costs are *implicit costs*. We also made a distinction between *standard* and *nonstandard* uses of trade credit. The former refers to the practice of paying trade credit exactly on time, the latter refers to paying late. The standard use of trade credit has no explicit costs but does have implicit costs: charges passed on for recovery of bad debt losses, hidden carrying costs, and credit checking expenses. Nonstandard trade credit usage has explicit costs when cash discounts are passed up and has implicit costs (of credit deterioration) when the bill is not settled by the net date. In particular, we saw that the cost of foregoing cash discounts can be prohibitively large.

The major determinants of credit terms are general economic conditions, industry factors, and company factors. The main advantages of trade credit are its ready availability, the flexibility it offers the firm, and the less restrictive terms associated with trade credit. The other spontaneous source of short-term funds the firm has is *accruals*. Like trade credit, these involve deferred payment of a liability, and they arise because of the U.S. business practice of paying some continuously occurring liabilities at fixed deferred time intervals. There are three major components of accruals: wages, income taxes, and interest.

QUESTIONS

1. Define the following terms and phrases:
   a. Spontaneous short-term funds.
   b. Negotiated short-term funds.
   c. Trade acceptance.
   d. Cash discount.
   e. Stretching the payables.
   f. Accruals.

2. What main advantage does the use of trade notes payable have over open account sales? What main disadvantage?

3. A new firm is considering how best to set up credit terms and one important feature is how quickly the customers will pay their bills.

Three credit terms plans have been suggested: plan A, 3/10, net 40; plan B, 2/5, net 30; and plan C, 3/10, net 50.

Other things equal, which of these three plans would encourage speediest customer payment habits? Which would encourage slowest customer payment habits? Explain your answers.

4. Even when the firm's credit terms are such that the explicit annual cost of foregoing the cash discount is high, many customers still forego the discount. If we were to survey these customers, what reasons might they give to explain their actions?

5. What effect does stretching the payables have on the cost of trade credit?

6. In what sense are accruals "a more automatic source" of short-term funds than trade credit?

7. The XYZ Company operates in an industry where the typical credit terms are 3/10, net 60. Mr. A, a credit analyst with XYZ, thinks that if the company changed its credit terms to 3/10, net 75, the company's sales would increase significantly. Ms. B, another analyst with XYZ, argues that this sales increase would only be temporary and that in the long run the firm could not increase its sales level by the suggestion made by Mr. A. "Why?" asks A. "Because," says B, ". . . ." Give her answer.

8. If credit sales were outlawed, what would probably happen to the overall level of invoice prices? Explain your answer.

9. Two firms, X and Y, both buy raw goods from the same supplier, who offers them credit on 2/10, net 30 terms. When X is short of cash it foregoes the discount and often stretches the payables. When Y is short of cash it borrows for 30 days from the bank at a rate that is usually between 10 and 15 percent. X thinks Y foolish to borrow at these rates to take advantage of a 2 percent discount. How would you explain Y's "foolishness" to X?

PROBLEMS

1. Determine the annual percentage interest cost of foregoing the cash discount if the firm pays on the net date, given the following terms of trade:
   a. 2/5, net 20.   d. 1/30, net 31.
   b. 5/2, net 30.   e. 3/15, net 45.
   c. 2/5, net 30.   f. 3/30, net 60.

2. a. Re-do problem 1 assuming that the firm pays ten days after the net date.
   b. What are the two effects of stretching payables?

3. In each instance in problem 1, the buyer firm is receiving "free credit" for a period of time stated in the credit terms listed.
   a. How long is the credit period in each part of problem 1?

    b. If the invoice is for $500, determine for each part of problem 1 the "cash price" of the invoice.

4. Boarsback, a small retail leathercrafts store, has periodic cash flow problems that create payments difficulties for the firm when it is billed by its leather supplier. Over lunch one day, Mr. Goulet, the owner of Boarsback, who is untrained in finance, tells you that he has two alternatives when these difficulties arise. He can borrow from a local commercial lending company or he can forego the trade discount his leather supplier offers him. Because of his somewhat shaky financial position the owner would never attempt to stretch the payables for fear that the supplier would cease offering trade credit to him.

    Which of the two alternatives available would you recommend to him if the following conditions prevail:

Situation	After tax cost of loan from commercial lending company	Credit terms
a	15%	2/10, net 50
b	18	2/15, net 60
c	20	3/10, net 60

5. Last year Harvey's, Inc., had sales of $20 million. Last year's annual report shows Harvey's current liabilities as:

Accounts payable	$1,000,000
Accruals	800,000
Notes payable	500,000
Total current liabilities	$2,300,000

    Assuming that negotiated short-term financing remains constant and assuming that the relationships between sales and all spontaneous sources of short-term credit remain constant, what would this year's current liabilities accounts look like if:

    a. Sales = $22,000,000.
    b. Sales = 25,000,000.
    c. Sales = 18,000,000.

6. Knapper Knickers Company is experiencing some temporary cash flow problems. The company has been refused further short-term loans from financial institutions, and because of this Knapper has decided to forego cash discounts from its clothing suppliers. Presently, Knapper is taking the cash discount; payables to these suppliers account for about 80 percent of Knapper's total accounts payable. Credit terms from these suppliers are 2/10, net 20. Annual clothing purchases by Knapper are about $200,000.

    a. Determine Knapper's present level of accounts payable to its clothing suppliers.

    b. Determine Knapper's present total level of accounts payable.

    c. Determine Knapper's new levels of clothing suppliers accounts payable and total accounts payable if Knapper pays its clothing supplier payables on the net date.

    d. Repeat part (c) assuming that Knapper stretches it's clothing supplier payables by ten days.

SELECTED BASIC REFERENCES

Brosky, J. J. *The Implicit Cost of Trade Credit and Theory of Optimal Terms of Sale.* New York: Credit Research Foundation, 1969.

Seiden, M. H. *The Quality of Trade Credit,* Occasional Paper No. 87. New York: National Bureau of Economic Research, 1964.

20

NEGOTIATED SOURCES OF SHORT-TERM FINANCING

In Chapter 19 we investigated short-term sources of financing that were spontaneous (automatically available), provided the firm is not in trouble. In this chapter we study short-term sources of financing that require negotiation on the firm's part to obtain. As in Chapter 19, we are studying short-term financing possibilities, where "short-term" denotes repayment of the financing within a year.

SHORT-TERM BANK LOANS

A commercial bank receives money through customer deposits into checking accounts (demand deposits) and savings accounts (time deposits), and lends these funds to individuals (by consumer loans), to businesses (by commercial loans), and to governments (by buying government securities). A short-term bank loan is a business loan from a commercial bank that will be repaid within one year. Short-term bank loans are not as important a source of short-term financing in the United States as trade credit but are the dominant source of negotiated short-term financing. In fact, bank loans play a similar role to trade credit. Whenever the firm's short-term financing needs increase, the first place the firm turns to is trade credit. Trade credit is readily expandable and serves as a financing reserve. Likewise, whenever the firm has a short-term need for funds that can't be satisfied with trade credit and internally generated funds, the firm usually turns first to bank credit. So bank credit also serves as a financing reserve. The main difference between these two forms of financing reserves is the negotiation effort the firm must make to secure bank credit.

Negotiating a bank loan

Selecting a bank   When a firm engages in financial transactions with a bank, it establishes a banking *relationship* or *connection*. Large firms, because of the size of their short-term financing needs and/or because of their diversified geographical operations, may have connections with several banks; small firms will normally deal with only one bank. The first step in the process of establishing this relationship is to choose among the competing banks. From the firm's standpoint, the following questions need to be answered:

1. Are the bank's loan costs competitive with other banks?
2. Is the bank large enough to service the firm's expected borrowing needs?
3. Are the bank's lending policies consistent with the firm's borrowing needs? That is:
    a. Does the bank have conservative or liberal lending policies?
    b. Does the bank understand and is it prepared to help with borrowing needs that are peculiar to the type of business the firm is in?

Good bank relationships   Good bank relationships involve keeping the bank happy. Mainly, this means keeping the bank well informed on the firm's operations and financial position, and being honest with the bank about the use of the borrowed funds. Specifically, the firm's management should:

1. Establish business friendships with some of the bank officers. This includes having these officers personally visit the firm to become more familiar with its operations. Banking relationships are no different than any other relationships, and personal friendships between bank and company officers will help the firm in securing future credit.
2. Provide the bank full information on the firm's current operations and financial position. In particular, notify the bank of any major changes in the firm's operations or financial status and why they occurred. Banks are also very interested in any future cash flow projections made by the firm.
3. Comply with the loan agreement. Use the loan proceeds only for the purpose they were intended, and meticulously observe all loan restrictions and covenants.

Loan analysis

The bank's analysis of the loan application is primarily directed to an appraisal of the firm's integrity, the intended use of the loan, and the repayment prospects.

Borrower integrity   The bank lends money on the expectation of repayment. While the bank has legal recourse to recapture its investment, loan defaults are not profitable to the bank. In assessing the likelihood of default, the bank will make a judgment on the character, or willingness to pay, of the applicant firm. It's for exactly this reason that the firm should cultivate business friendships with the bank, since this is one of the best ways the firm can establish a reputation for integrity.

Intended use of the loan proceeds   One of the first questions the bank will ask the firm is why it needs the loan. There are exceptions, but most short-term loans are granted for short-term uses of the money. The most common uses of short-term funds are for inventory expansion and for financing accounts receivables, and the bank will usually prefer these kinds of short-term loan applications. The bank will look less favorably on speculative uses of the money (even if for short periods) and long-term uses of the money since banks prefer to make long-term loans for long-term uses.

Repayment prospects   Obviously, a loan won't be granted unless the bank is reasonably certain of repayment. So the banker will carefully investigate the prospects of repayment. This involves determining the sources of repayment and the possible timing of repayment. Banks look favorably on *self-liquidating* loans: loans used to acquire assets that will pay themselves off, such as loans for inventory or accounts receivable expansion. For example, a loan granted to finance expanded accounts receivables will look primarily to collection of those receivables for its repayment. However, banks make loans for many investment proposals that are not self-liquidating. In these instances the bank will normally look to the long run profitability or earning power of the firm. Another source of repayment is the infusion of new *permanent* capital into the firm either in the form of debt or equity.

To protect itself against the prospect of default on the loan, the bank may require *collateral* – pledging of assets to settlement of the loan. This is discussed in more detail below. The bank will also be impressed by financial contingency plans formulated for possible trouble situations. These plans assure the bank that the company has given thoughtful consideration to the possibility that its investments may be disappointing and has formulated plans for repayment of the loan should this situation develop.

Reasons for loan rejections

In general, banks reject commercial loan applications for three reasons: (1) either the company is a poor credit risk, and/or (2) the loan is inconsistent with the bank's *overall* loan policy, and/or (3) the bank is prohibited from making the loan because of federal or state banking regulations.

Poor credit evaluation   A poor credit evaluation is the most common explanation for loan denial. One of the most common reasons for a poor credit evaluation is that there is insufficient owner's equity in the firm. Debt holders view equity as a cushion or protection for their loans to the company. If the firm should fail, the greater this equity cushion, the more likely the debt holders are to recover their entire loan, since debt holders get first claim on the firm's assets. Other factors that cause loan rejection because of a poor credit evaluation are an inferior earnings record, questionable managerial talent, insufficient collateral, and a poor or nonexistent (a new firm) credit history.

Inconsistency with bank's loan policy This is the next most common reason for loan rejection. Among the inconsistencies are: the requested loan duration is too long, there is no established deposit relationship with the bank, the bank doesn't handle the type of loan requested, and the bank's portfolio (its total collection of loans) already has enough loans of the kind requested.

Loan rejections for regulatory reasons Occasionally a loan may be rejected because of state or federal banking restrictions. This usually happens when the loan is too large for the bank to handle. Banks are specifically prohibited from lending more than 10 percent of their assets to any one applicant, and a large loan application may exceed the bank's legal loan limit.

Types of short-term bank loans

There are essentially two kinds of *short-term* bank loans: *single loans* and *line of credit arrangements.*

Single loans A *single loan* or a *transaction loan* is one that is negotiated and administratively handled by itself (singly). The loan is for a specified use, a promissory note is signed to document the indebtedness, and the loan is repaid in a single (lump sum) payment on the due date stated on the promissory note. The loan may be renewed, but once again it is handled by itself just as described above. This type of loan is used most often by borrowers who have infrequent needs for short-term bank loans.

Line of credit Many firms use short-term bank loans so frequently that the single loan is administratively cumbersome. They use instead a *line of credit* arrangement. This is a relatively informal agreement between the bank and the company that permits the company to borrow up to some specified maximum amount from the bank. The result of this arrangement is that the firm minimizes its negotiation effort. In addition, the firm secures a very flexible source of financing from the bank: The firm does not actually use or "draw down" its line of credit until it needs to, and when the firm does need the money the process is more automatic than with a single loan. Actually, the bank is not legally committed to honor the line of credit agreement, but except for situations where the firm or bank has encountered financial difficulties, it almost always does. The line of credit arrangement is periodically reviewed, commonly after the firm's annual report is published so that the bank can use this audited report in analyzing the firm's position.

The most common use of the line of credit is to arrange seasonal financing needs. The firm will estimate its peak seasonal cash needs, add a safety factor, and ask the bank for a line of credit. If, for example, the firm estimates it will need $200,000 cash to expand its inventories and accounts receivables during its peak season in September, it will probably add a safety margin, say $25,000, and ask for a line of credit of $225,000.

Short-term loan features

The particulars or features of the loan will vary depending on the financial strength of the borrower, the loan policies of the bank, and general credit conditions. In this section we will look at the major features of short-term bank loans.

Collateral   If, after receipt of a loan, the borrowing company should run into difficulty and not be able to pay off the loan (that is, should the firm default on the loan), the bank would like to have some protection. This is accomplished by requiring the firm to put up *collateral* before the loan is granted. Collateral refers to assets that the firm pledges to turn over to the bank should default occur. Some firms are financially strong enough that the bank feels the loan is safe without requiring collateral, but the riskier the loan looks to the bank, the more likely that collateral will be required. Any assets may be pledged, but short-term loans are most usually secured by short-term assets: cash, securities, accounts receivable, and inventories. If the loan is unsecured (that is, if no collateral is required) the bank merely becomes a general creditor, and its claims in case of firm bankruptcy are the same as other general creditors. We'll discuss collateral from the broader perspective of both bank and nonbank lenders at the end of this chapter.

Compensating balances   Compensating balances refer to some minimum balance the borrower must keep in its checking account with the lending bank.[1] Typically, compensating balances run from 10 to 20 percent of the loan, and these balances are stated in terms of a minimum monthly average or an absolute minimum balance. If, for example, the firm borrowed $400,000 and were required to keep a 10-percent minimum average compensating balance, then the firm's checking account must have a monthly average of at least $40,000. The bank requires compensating balances for two reasons. First, compensating balances raise the effective interest rate the bank earns on the loan because the firm does not have the use of the entire amount of the loan. (This point will be elaborated below when we look at the cost of loans.) A second reason the bank requires compensating balances is for safety. The bank has the *right of offset* against the firm's checking account balances should the loan default. This means that the bank can recover the firm's checking balance without sharing this balance with the firm's creditors, which offers the bank some protection even when the loan is unsecured. The percent of the loan required as compensating balances fluctuates with money market conditions; in times of tight money when credit is hard to get, the percent will go up, and the reverse is true when credit is loose.

Cleanup clause   When the bank extends a line of credit to the firm it is expressly granting *short-term* credit to help the firm meet emergencies or seasonal financing needs. A credit line is *not* extended for *permanent* financing purposes. One way the bank has of ensuring that the credit line is being used as intended is to have a debt *cleanup clause* in the loan agreement. This clause requires that the firm be completely "out of debt"

---

[1] See the earlier discussion on compensating balances in Chapter 17.

to the line of credit for one or more months. If the firm is unable to comply with this clause, the bank will infer that the line of credit is being used as permanent capital by the firm and may suggest that the firm secure long-term capital for its long term-needs.

Cost of short-term bank loans

Short-term bank loans merely represent a particular kind of financing source for the firm and, like all the other financing sources we have looked at, cost the firm something. As before, we express this cost in *effective annual percentage* terms. Three things determine the firm's cost of short-term loans: the stated or *nominal* interest rate, the way that the bank collects the interest, and the firm's tax rate.

Nominal interest rates The nominal interest rate is the annual interest rate stated on the loan agreement. It is similar to the coupon rate on a bond. As we will see, however, this is rarely equal to the *effective* annual interest rate. The nominal interest rate the firm pays depends on the general credit conditions prevailing in the economy and the credit worthiness of the applicant firm.

Prime rate The *prime rate* is the nominal interest rate that banks charge to their most credit worthy corporate borrowers. It is the lowest interest rate the bank charges and, like other interest rates, is determined by supply and demand conditions in the marketplace for funds. When the economy is expanding, firms will need funds to make investments, and this competition for funds will bid up interest rates. When the economy is contracting, lenders will bid down interest rates because there is less demand for funds. The prime rate tends to fluctuate with other interest rates, and these fluctuations reflect general economic conditions. As with other interest rates, the prime rate also increases in periods of inflation and decreases in periods of deflation. The list of firms that qualify for the prime rate is not necessarily a stable one. Since high prime rates reflect the relative scarcity of short-term bank loan funds available, as the prime rate increases, banks may reduce the number of firms that qualify for the prime rate even though the credit worthiness of the newly excluded firms hasn't changed. Similarly, as the prime rate decreases, the list of firms that qualify for prime rate loans may expand.

Credit worthiness Firms that don't qualify for prime rate loans are generally considered less credit worthy by the bank. Consequently, they are charged a higher interest rate. Thus, the prime rate serves as a benchmark for short-term bank loan rates. All other loans are made at a rate equal to the prime rate plus some additional risk premium. This premium will increase as the perceived credit worthiness of the firm decreases. In general, smaller firms pay larger interest rates than larger firms since smaller firms fail more often and are hence riskier. Interest rates on these riskier loans will typically range from about 0.25 to 0.5 percent greater than the prime rate on very large loans ($1 million and larger) and from 1.5 to 2 percent over the prime rate on very small loans (under $10,000).

Effective interest rates The effective interest rate is the actual annual interest rate of the loan. It is the (before tax) annual rate of return that the lender is earning (and the borrower is paying) on the loan. To understand how the effective interest rate is calculated we must first look at how the bank determines the dollar interest on the short-term loan. The bank figures *simple* interest on the loan.

$$I = (P)(i)(t) \tag{20-1}$$

where

I = interest (dollars),
P = loan principal (dollars),
i = nominal interest rate (percent per year), and
t = time (years).

Once the interest is determined, we can easily calculate the *effective* interest rate:[2]

$$r = \left(\frac{I}{P_o}\right)(m) \tag{20-2}$$

where

r = effective interest rate (percent per year)
P_o = net loan proceeds
m = the number of time periods per year.

Multiplying by m in Equation (20-2) serves to *annualize* the interest rate.

Now the cost of the short-term loan to the borrowing firm is lower than the effective interest rate because the interest payments (as on long-term debt) are tax deductible. Therefore:

$$k = (1 - T)(r) \tag{20-3}$$

where

k = cost of short-term loan
T = tax rate.

Suppose, for example, that the Crescent Entertainment Co. has negotiated a 180-day, $200,000 loan with the Fourth National Bank. The nominal interest rate is 8 percent, and the interest and principal are due on the maturity date. What is the cost of the loan if Crescent's tax rate = 50 percent?

$$I = (\$200,000)(0.08)\left(\frac{180}{365}\right) = \$7,890$$

$$r = \left(\frac{\$7,890}{\$200,000}\right)\left(\frac{365}{180}\right) = 8 \text{ percent}$$

$$k = (0.5)(8) = 4 \text{ percent}$$

---

[2] This is actually only an approximation of the effective interest rate. The exact determination of the effective interest rate would require a compound interest solution whenever the loan was for less than one year. See Chapter 3.

The mechanics of this loan are simple. The firm receives $200,000 net loan proceeds at the time of the loan and pays the bank back $207,890 later. In this simplified example the nominal and effective interest rates are equal because the loan principal, P, and the net loan proceeds, P_o, are equal. However, commercial banks discount loans and require compensating balances, and these practices raise the effective interest rate and, therefore, the cost on bank loans.

Discounting loans   Discounting a loan means to collect the interest at the *start* of the loan rather than at the *end* of the loan. Consider the Crescent Entertainment example again, only assume that the interest must be paid at the beginning of the loan. That is, the loan is discounted. To find the cost of the loan:

$$I = (\$200,000)(0.08)\left(\frac{180}{365}\right) = \$7,890$$

$$P_o = \$200,000 - \$7,890 = \$192,110$$

$$r = \left(\frac{\$\ 7,890}{\$192,110}\right)\left(\frac{365}{180}\right) = 8.33 \text{ percent}$$

$$k = (0.5)(8.33) = 4.17 \text{ percent}$$

The firm receives $192,110 net loan proceeds at the time of the loan and pays the bank back $200,000 six months later. The total dollar amount of interest ($7,890) is the same as in the earlier example, but by charging the interest at the *start* of the loan, the bank reduces the net loan proceeds, which means the firm has less proceeds to work with over the life of the loan ($192,110 instead of $200,000) and, consequently, is paying a higher effective interest rate and a higher cost. Discounting loans causes the effective interest rate to be larger than the nominal interest rate, thereby increasing the cost of short-term borrowing.

Compensating balances   We discussed compensating balances earlier, and stated that one reason banks require them is to increase the effective yield on loans. Suppose that in the Crescent Entertainment example, in addition to an 8-percent discount, the bank requires a 10-percent compensating balance on the loan. Now

$$\text{Interest} = (\$200,000)(0.08)\left(\frac{180}{365}\right) = \$7,890$$

$$\text{Compensating balance} = (\$200,000)(0.10) = \$20,000$$

$$\text{Net loan proceeds} = \$200,000 - \$7,890 - \$20,000 = \$172,110$$

$$r = \left(\frac{\$\ 7,890}{\$172,110}\right)\left(\frac{365}{180}\right) = 9.30 \text{ percent}$$

$$k = (0.5)(9.30) = 4.65 \text{ percent}$$

In comparison to the previous example, the effective interest rate and cost have been increased by requiring a 10-percent compensating balance. This is because $20,000 is now tied up in the firm's checking account, reducing the net loan proceeds from $192,110 to $172,110. And the bank is charging Crescent interest on this unusable $20,000. Of course, if Crescent already had $20,000 in its Fourth National checking account it would use that money as its compensating balance and get use of the full $192,110, reducing the effective interest rate and cost back to their previously determined levels.

EURODOLLAR LOANS

Another kind of bank loan that international companies are increasingly using involves the Eurodollar market. Eurodollars are dollars deposited in banks outside of the United States. These banks may be either foreign owned banks or U.S.-owned banks located in a foreign country (a foreign branch of a U.S. bank). The name implies these dollars are held in banks in European countries, but actually Eurodollars refers to dollar deposits held by a bank located in *any* foreign country. From a more general standpoint, Eurodollars are part of the Eurocurrency market, where Eurocurrency refers to any national currency held in banks outside of that nation. As an example, British pounds on deposit in a French bank would be part of the Eurocurrency market.

The Eurocurrency market is simply a pool of funds available for lending to qualified borrowers. These borrowers are mainly international business firms and governments, but noninternational business firms also use the Eurocurrency market. This market has grown greatly since the early 1960s, and Eurodollars have played a dominant role in the Eurocurrency market, mainly due to the U.S. dollar's designated role as an international currency exchange standard and the U.S. balance of payments deficit that accumulated dollars overseas in the 1960s.

The mechanics of obtaining a Eurodollar loan are varied, but in simplest form parallel the procedures in getting a U.S. bank loan. U.S. firms can apply directly for a straight bank loan in Eurodollars from a bank outside the United States for a fixed term at a fixed interest rate. Such loans are unsecured and have maturities from overnight (one day) to about five years. Short-term loans are normally issued from one day to six months. Interest rates on these loans are very volatile but are roughly comparable to the U.S. prime rate.

OPEN MARKET LOANS

Open market loans refer to the impersonal national and international money market, where funds are borrowed and lent for periods of one year or less. The primary feature of this market is the negotiable feature of the financial instrument that is created because of the loan. This means that while the loan may be initially made by one party, such as a bank, the resultant debt is negotiable: It may be resold to investors on the open market.

Commercial paper

Commercial paper is a form of unsecured promissory note that firms issue to raise short-term money. The commercial paper market is a "blue chip" market, as only the largest, most prestigious, and most credit worthy U.S. companies can issue commercial paper. The reason for the exclusion of lesser companies from issuing paper is the lending motive of the lenders in this market (the *buyers* of the commercial paper). These lenders are mainly other businesses, insurance companies, pension funds, and banks, and they are primarily interested in investing excess cash for a short time without exposing themselves to any appreciable risk of loss (see Chapter 17). This motive translates into a demand for only very high-quality commercial paper from a select group of credit worthy firms. Consequently, there are only a few hundred firms that can issue commercial paper.

The paper is issued either through a *dealer* or via *direct placement*. A dealer is a special agent that handles (for a fee) commercial paper and whose role is much like the investment banker. Dealers may either buy the paper outright from the firm, or they may sell the paper on commission. An alternative to the dealer market is direct placement of the paper to investors. This route has been particularly used by large sales finance companies such as General Motors Acceptance Corporation.

Maturity and use   Maturities on commercial paper run from about five days to nine months and are sold in denominations of $5,000 minimum with larger denominations in multiples of $5,000. While use of commercial paper is small compared to short-term borrowing from commercial banks, the dollar volume of commercial paper has substantially increased since World War II. This increase was accentuated by tight money conditions in the late 1960s when banks were unable to meet the demand for short-term funds from large corporations.

Cost   The cost (annual percent) or interest yield of commercial paper is determined by the same supply and demand factors that determine other interest rates. Usually, the interest yield on commercial paper is from 0.5 to 1.5 percent or so under the commercial bank prime rate. The firm pays no interest on the paper but sells the paper at a discount from face value, with the difference between selling price and redemption at face value providing the investor his return, which is designated as interest. If, for example, four-month paper were sold by the firm at $97.50 net,[3] the effective (before tax) interest rate, r, to the firm would be $[(2.50/97.50)(12/4)]$ 7.69%. Accounting for the tax deductibility of interest, the cost of commercial paper, k, is:

$$k = (1 - T)(r)$$

If $T = 40$ percent, $k = (0.6)(0.0769) = 4.61$ percent.

Advantages and disadvantages   Foremost of the advantages of using commercial paper is its low cost. The effective interest rate on paper is lower than the bank's prime rate, which is a *nominal* rate. Recalling how the bank increases the effective yield on a loan underscores just how much cheaper commercial paper is. A second major advantage is the availability of commercial paper during periods of tight bank credit. This reason has, in fact, led many companies into the commercial paper market.

---

[3] Because commercial paper is usually sold in multiples of $5,000, the $97.50 net means the firm receives $0.975 net on each collar of paper sold.

The main disadvantage of using commercial paper stems for the impersonal nature of the paper market. If the firm encounters financial difficulties and can't redeem its paper, there will be no extensions of time forthcoming from the investors who hold the firm's paper. Banks are inclined to help the firm work things out in time of distress, but the paper market is completely impersonal.

Banker's acceptances

Banker's acceptances are an important form of short-term financing for firms in the import-export trade. A banker's acceptance essentially amounts to credit extended from a foreign bank. As an example, consider a California company that wants to import $75,000 worth of Japanese radio components. The American company first gets the Japanese company to grant it 60-days credit from the shipment date. Then the American company arranges a line of credit letter through its California bank for the Japanese company. The Japanese company ships the equipment and then presents a 60-day draft on the California bank to its Japanese bank. Then the Japanese bank pays the Japanese company. The draft is then forwarded to the California bank and, if all paper work is in order, becomes a banker's acceptance, which is a $75,000 debt that the California bank owes the Japanese bank. At the end of 60 days the California importer pays the bank, which in turn pays the acceptance. In the interim, the Japanese bank could sell the acceptance on the open market just as in the case of commercial paper. The final owner of the banker's acceptance will present it to the California bank for payment. Interest rates on banker's acceptances are approximately equal to the prime rate that banks charge their best domestic customers.

SECURED LOANS

Short-term loans may be divided into two groups: (1) unsecured loans where no collateral (security) is put up by the firm and (2) secured loans. The intent of the security is to give the lender some protection should the loan default. In general, the riskier the loan, the more likely that the lender will require the firm to provide security. Therefore, the interest rates on secured borrowing are usually greater than interest rates on unsecured borrowing. Any of the firm's assets may be used as collateral: current assets—either financial (stocks and bonds) or nonfinancial (accounts receivable and inventory)—or long-term assets (plant and equipment). Many firms don't have substantial amounts of financial assets; also long-term assets are normally used as security for long-term loans. Consequently, our development of secured lending will be directed toward the use of accounts receivable and inventory as security.

Lending agents

Commercial banks   As we saw earlier in this chapter, banks frequently make unsecured loans when the loan looks safe enough. When the loan looks too risky to make on an unsecured basis, the bank will require that collateral be pledged.

Finance companies   Finance companies are specialized lending agents. There are three kinds of such companies: *consumer finance* or personal finance companies (such as Household Finance Corporation) lend to consumers for a wide variety of consumer purposes. *Sales finance* companies specialize in buying installment loan contracts that retailers have made with consumers. That is, the sales finance company buys the accounts receivable created by the sale of an item such as a car, boat, TV, etc., on an installment contract. They also finance certain retailer's inventories, for example, car dealers. *Business finance* or commercial finance companies specialize in lending to business firms. Only sales finance and business finance companies lend to businesses.

Factoring receivables

One way the firm can acquire short-term financing is to sell its accounts receivables to a company that specializes in buying accounts receivable. These specialized companies are called *factors*, and this procedure is called *factoring*.[4]

Procedure   There are two ways the firm may use factoring: (1) as a continuous process or (2) on an ad hoc basis. Typically, factoring is a continuous process, but the procedure is similar in both instances. Under a normal factoring arrangement, when the firm receives a credit sales order, it forwards the order to the factor who performs a credit check. If the factor refuses to factor the order, the firm may well refuse to sell the goods on credit. But if the factor approves the order, the goods are shipped with instructions to pay the factor directly. The factor pays the firm (in advance of payment by the customer) the amount of the receivable less a commission, less interest on the advance (since the firm is receiving payment before the factor collects from the customer), and less a reserve the factor sets aside for bad debt losses. The size of this reserve depends on the factor's opinion of the quality of the receivable. With high-quality receivables the factor may advance 80 percent or so of the invoice to the firm (keeping a 20-percent reserve). With lower quality receivables there may only be a 50-percent advance. The factor owns these receivables and cannot look to the firm to cover any bad debt losses. The factor is said to have purchased the receivables *without recourse*. When the customer pays for the shipment the factor will remit the reserve to the firm. There are variations on this procedure. Some firms, for example, don't take advances on the order but wait for payment until the customer remits to the factor.

Cost   There are essentially two cost components involved in factoring: (1) the commission and (2) the interest on any advance paid to the firm. Depending on how risky the factor feels the receivables are, the commission will usually be between about 1 and 3 percent of the invoice. The interest rate, on the advance will depend on the prevailing interest

---

[4] Sometimes these companies are called "old line factors" to distinguish them from factors who lend to the firm using receivables as collateral but who don't *buy* the receivables outright.

rate levels. It will normally be from 4 to 6 percent higher than the prime rate, which merely reflects that such loans are not of the same quality as prime rate loans.

Advantages and disadvantages   Essentially, factors perform three functions for the firm: (1) credit checking, (2) financing, and (3) risk bearing. Firms need not use all three services, but to the extent they do, factoring offers a convenient packaging of services. Moreover, once the factoring arrangement has been established it provides very flexible financing. As sales grow – assuming no deterioration in the quality of receivables – additional financing through factoring is readily available.

There are two principal disadvantages. First, there is the administrative burden of the necessarily constant shuffle of information between the factor and the firm. This, together with the factor's commission has led some firms to reject factoring as too expensive. Second, there has been a long-standing reluctance to use factoring because it has been traditionally perceived to be a sign of financial weakness. This perception is apparently changing in view of recent periodic tight credit situations, and more firms now view factoring as a normal means of securing short-term financing.

Pledging receivables

Pledging receivables refers to using accounts receivables as collateral for a loan, but where – unlike factoring – the legal ownership of the receivables remains with the firm. In essence the lender is buying the receivables *with recourse;* if the receivables turn out to be uncollectable, the lender can turn to the firm to make good the loan. Except that receivables are normally paid directly to the firm under this arrangement, the procedures, costs, and good and bad features are much the same.

Inventory loans

Inventory is another common source of loan collateral. It meets one of the primary conditions for short-term collateral because it is fairly liquid. Consequently, banks and finance companies willingly accept most standard types of inventories as collateral. Extremely unusual inventory (because it may be difficult to convert into cash) or perishable inventory will be less acceptable as security. In obtaining a loan based on inventory the points of negotiation are what percent of inventory value the lender will make the loan on, what the cost is, and what kind of control the lender expects.

Percent of inventory value   The lender will loan from about 40 to 90 percent of the value of the inventory, depending on the quality and liquidity of the inventory. As with any collateral, the lender is concerned with converting the assets to cash should the loan fail. Consequently, the percent loan offered by the lender depends on the answers to questions like: What could the assets be sold for? How quickly could they be sold? Are they perishable? etc. Because such questions have judgmental answers, the percent loan offered by competing lenders may vary considerably, and the firm may find it worth its while to shop around.

Cost The cost of inventory loans has two parts: (1) an interest rate and (2) a service charge. The service charge is imposed because the lender frequently has substantial costs associated with keeping tabs on the inventory to make sure his loan is indeed backed up by some collateral. These costs are directly related to the kind of legal security or control the lender and borrower negotiate.

Legal control Banks and finance companies are not equipped to physically keep the inventory themselves. Therefore, they need a system to hold the firm accountable for the inventory. Basically, there are two systems, one entrusting the collateral goods to the firm, the other entrusting them to an independent third party.

Borrower entrustments Borrower entrustments are in the form of either a *blanket lien* or a *trust receipt*.

Blanket lien. This is an all-inclusive lien that gives the lender recourse to *all* the firm's inventories. This arrangement will be unsatisfactory from the firm's standpoint if it only wants to pledge a portion of its inventory. It is also unsatisfactory from the lender's standpoint because there is no real control over the inventory. If inventory is reduced because of sales, for example, the collateral is also reduced.

Trust receipt. A trust receipt is a pledge by the firm that it will keep the *identified* inventory as collateral for the lender until its sale, at which time the proceeds of the loan will be returned to the lender. This form of entrustment is commonly used where the inventory is easily identifiable, as with cars. Like blanket liens, however, this offers the lender incomplete control since inventory counts can be, and occasionally are, frauded.

Independent third party entrustments Independent third parties are warehouse storage companies. These are special agents whose functions are to: (1) attest to the physical presence of inventory and (2) control the flow of inventory. There are two common forms of warehouse arrangements.

Terminal warehouse. A terminal warehouse is a public warehouse, where, for a fee, goods may be stored. Under a terminal warehouse receipt loan, inventory may be removed from storage only on approval of the lender. Therefore, the lender has good control over the loan collateral. There is an obvious unsatisfactory aspect to this arrangement from the firm's standpoint however. Inventory must be physically moved from the firm's production and/or storage facilities to the warehouse. To alleviate this problem a second kind of warehousing arrangement has developed: field warehousing.

Field warehouses. A field warehouse is an arrangement that establishes a warehouse on the firm's property. The warehousing company physically sets off the pledged inventory in an area that can be controlled (this may be done with a fence or by using a temporary building), and the warehousing agent polices this inventory, releasing any or all of it only on directions from the lender.

OTHER SOURCES OF SHORT-TERM FINANCING

Private lenders

Private lenders also provide short-term capital, although as a percent of total short-term financing this is a small factor. Primarily, these sources are used by small businesses. We can classify these lenders into two groups. *Personal* private lenders include family and friends. *Impersonal* private lenders include individuals, usually found in larger cities, who make loans to businesses. In this latter group, interest rates are *extremely* high, and sometimes organized criminal elements are behind the operation. Consequently, this is frequently not a desirable source of financing.

Customer advances

Some companies have obtained short-term financing by getting customers to make advance payments. Sometimes these payments are made because the customer is fearful that if no advance is given, the company will fail, and the ordered goods may be difficult to acquire elsewhere. Other arrangements are more a matter of a standard industry practice. Aircraft manufacturing companies, for example, have traditionally received progress payments from the airline companies as plane construction proceeds.

Special supplier credit

In the previous chapter we discussed trade credit provided by suppliers. Under certain situations, the firm may obtain *special credit* from its suppliers by negotiation. The most obvious situation is in a financial emergency. In such a crisis time the firm may attempt to get supplier approval to let the firm delay payment without any increase in price of future purchases or diminution of future credit terms. At the extreme, the firm may be negotiating with its suppliers to prevent seizure of the purchased goods. A different kind of scenario involves negotiating for credit terms that are more favorable than would be usually granted. This most normally occurs when the firm promises large quantity purchases and/or is bargaining on the basis of taking its business elsewhere.

SUMMARY

In this chapter we have analyzed those short-term sources of financing that the firm must negotiate for. The most prominent such source is bank loans, and there are several important aspects to choosing a bank. The firm must decide if the bank is large enough for its needs, if the bank is cost competitive, and if the bank's lending policies are consistent with the firm's borrowing needs. Having chosen a bank, the firm needs to maintain good bank relationships. We saw also that the bank's loan analysis is mainly concerned with the firm's integrity, the intended use of the loan, and the repayment schedule. Loans are rejected most usually because of a poor credit evaluation. Other reasons are because the loan is inconsistent with the bank's loan policy and because of regulatory restrictions. There are basically two kinds of bank loans: *single loans* and the *line* of *credit*, and the main features of bank loans are *collateral, compensating balances,* and the *debt* cleanup clause. Regarding the cost of bank loans, the *prime rate* is the bank's lowest *nominal* rate (the stated annual rate), but banks can increase the *effective interest rate* (the actual annual rate) by *discounting* the loan (taking the interest out at the beginning of the loan) and by requiring compensating balances.

We briefly investigated *Eurodollar* loans. Eurodollar loans are loans made by banks (both foreign and U.S.) that are located outside of the United States. These loans are like regular U.S. bank loans and are most usually used by companies that have international operations. We also looked at *commercial paper*, which is a form of unsecured promissory note issued by a few hundred of the most credit worthy U.S. firms, and *banker's acceptances*, which are another kind of unsecured promissory note issued through banks to finance short-term import-export trade.

We next looked at *collateral*, assets pledged to the lender in case of loan default. Collateral on short-term loans may be any kind of assets, either current or fixed, but most frequently it is either the firm's accounts receivables or its inventory. Receivables are either *factored* – sold outright to a company (factor) that specializes in buying accounts receivable – or may be *pledged* as collateral. When receivables are factored, the firm is not responsible for uncollectable receivables, but when the receivables are pledged, the firm must "make good" uncollectable receivables. In inventory loans the main points of negotiation are on what percent of inventory value the lender will make the loan, what the cost is, and what kind of control the lender intends to exert on the inventory. There are basically two kinds of control: *borrower entrustments*, where the lender is depending on the honesty of the borrower; and *third party entrustments*, where the lender is depending on the honesty of a warehousing company. Other sources of financing are private lending, customer advances, and special credit from suppliers.

QUESTIONS

1. Define the following terms and phrases:
    a. Line of credit.
    b. Compensating balance.
    c. Prime rate.
    d. Discounting a loan.
    e. Commercial paper.
    f. Banker's acceptances.
    g. Factoring.

2. Describe the main points of analysis that a bank will perform on a loan application.

3. Explain the reason for including a cleanup clause in a loan agreement.

4. Under what conditions would a firm prefer to seek a single loan from a bank rather than a line of credit?

5. What effect would the following conditions have on the cost of short-term bank borrowing?
   a. Nominal interest rates decrease.
   b. The bank begins the practice of discounting all loans.
   c. The bank lowers its compensating balance requirement.
   d. Tax rates are increased.

6. Explain the advantages and disadvantages to the firm of factoring its receivables.

7. Explain the difference between factoring and pledging receivables.

8. Explain the difference between borrower entrustments and third party entrustments.

PROBLEMS

1. Find the interest payment, effective interest rate, and cost of the following bank loans. Interest and principal are paid at maturity.

Situation	Principal	Term	Nominal interest rate	Firm's tax rate
a	$100,000	180 days	0.08	0.5
b	60,000	90	0.10	0.4
c	75,000	270	0.12	0.48

2. Rework Problem 1 assuming the loans are discounted.

3. Find the interest payment, effective interest rate, and cost of a $150,000, 60-day bank loan when the nominal interest rate is 0.09 and the firm's tax rate is 0.4 under the following circumstances:
   a. Principal and interest paid at maturity, no compensating balance required.
   b. Principal and interest paid at maturity, a 20-percent compensating balance required.
   c. Loan is discounted, no compensating balance required.
   d. Loan is discounted, a 20-percent compensating balance required.

4. The Hopkins Railroad Equipment Company has obtained a one year bank loan of $20,000. The loan is to be repaid in 12 equal monthly installments and bears interest of 12 percent per year.
   a. Determine Hopkins' monthly payment (round to nearest dollar).
   b. Prepare a repayment schedule with the following columns (round to the nearest dollar): (Hint: see Chapter 14.)

Beginning balance	Payment	Interest	Applied to principal	Ending balance

c.   Determine the effective interest rate and the cost of the *average* loan balance assuming Hopkins' tax rate is 0.4.

5.   Allison Sales and Service needs to raise $1 million net in 90 days to finance an expansion of inventory and accounts receivable. The company's analysts are evaluating the merits of obtaining a six-month loan from the bank versus the issuance of six-month commercial paper. Since the company is financially strong, they will be able to borrow from the bank at the prime rate that is in effect when the loan is negotiated.

     If Allison issues commercial paper, they have decided on a direct placement with a local insurance company in order to save on issue expenses. Allison's analysts estimate that the net proceeds of the sale will depend on the prime rate prevailing at the time of issue. The following estimates have been prepared:

Prevailing prime rate	Probability	Proceeds of commercial paper sale* (per $100 of paper)	Probability
		$96.85	0.1
8 percent 0.2		96.75	0.6
		96.60	0.3
		96.60	0.3
8.5 percent........... 0.5		96.00	0.5
		95.80	0.2
		95.35	0.1
9 percent 0.3		95.25	0.7
		95.10	0.2

* Includes issue expenses.

a.   On an expected value basis, how much commercial paper will Allison be required to issue to ensure receiving the $1 million net needed if the prime rate is:
     1.   8 percent?
     2.   8.5 percent?
     3.   9 percent?
b.   Determine the expected effective interest rate of the commercial paper for all three prime rates.
c.   Under what conditions would the firm prefer to issue commercial paper? Under what conditions would the firm prefer to borrow from the bank?
d.   Determine the *overall* expected effective interest rate on the commercial paper sale.
e.   Determine the expected prime rate.
f.   Suppose the firm must decide today whether to borrow from the bank or issue commercial paper. Which should they do? Explain.

6.   The Springate Beverage Company has an immediate requirement for a $30,000 increase in net working capital due to expanded opera-

tions. The company has exhausted its line of credit and is too small to successfully sell commercial paper. Springate's treasurer has been evaluating the possibilities of obtaining the required funds through either factoring accounts receivable or pledging inventory. Springate's receivables can be sold to the Fudge Factor Company, which charges a 2-percent commission on all receivables purchased plus 12 percent interest per year on any funds advanced. The factor requires a reserve of 40 percent of purchased receivables. Springate's treasurer estimates that factoring the receivables will save $750 per month in credit department and bad debt expenses. All sales are credit sales.

The Usury Loan Company has agreed to loan Springate the $30,-000 if the company will pledge its inventory as collateral. Usury will loan up to 80 percent of the value of the inventory in this case because of its liquidity. The interest on the loan will be 14 percent per year and a 1-percent service charge is required. Springate will incur expenses of $100 per month in administering the trust receipt process. The company's sales are $600,000 per year, its average collection period is one month, its inventory turnover is 16 times, and its tax rate is 0.4.

a.   Find the effective interest rate and cost of each source of funds.

b.   Which method should Springate use to raise the $30,000? Why?

SELECTED BASIC REFERENCES

Adler, M. "Administration of Inventory Loans under the Uniform Commercial Code," *Journal of Commercial Bank Lending* (April 1970), pp. 55–60.

Abraham, A. B.   "Factoring – The New Frontier for Commercial Banks," *Journal of Commercial Bank Lending* (April 1971), pp. 32–43.

Rogers, R. W.   "Warehouse Receipts and Their Use in Financing," *Bulletin of the Robert Morris Associates* (April 1964), pp. 317–27.

SELECTED ADVANCED REFERENCES

Baxter, N. D.   *The Commercial Paper Market*. Princeton, N.J.: Princeton University Press, 1964.

Robichek, A. A., et al.   "Optimal Short-Term Financing Decision," *Management Science* (September 1965), pp. 1–36.

Jaffee, D. M., and F. Modigliani.   "A Theory and Test of Credit Rationing," *American Economic Review* (December 1969), pp. 850–72.

section eight

GROWTH AND CONTRACTION

21

BUSINESS COMBINATIONS

To successfully work toward the goal of maximizing shareholder wealth the firm must invest in new assets. These investments cause the firm to grow, and this growth can take place in two ways, internally and externally. *Internal* growth refers to growth caused by investment in projects that the firm develops itself. When an oil company drills an oil well, for example, it is investing in what it hopes is an internal growth project. *External* growth refers to the firm purchasing already existing assets (rather than developing these assets itself). Examples of external growth would be when Oil Company A buys an oil well from Oil Company B, or buys all of Oil Company B.

The means of obtaining external growth are through *business combinations*, which is a phrase that denotes the joining or combining businesses (either in total or in part) and/or the acquisition of other businesses (either in total or in part). As we will see, there are several forms of business combinations, but the common characteristic shared by all combinations is the attempt by the firm to obtain growth through external means.

FORMS OF BUSINESS COMBINATIONS

There is some disagreement on the precise definition of terms relating to external growth because some terms have narrow legal meanings and others do not. Other terms are commonly used interchangeably even when there are legal distinctions between the kinds of combinations. However, there is considerable agreement on the general meaning of the terms.

Legal distinctions[1]

Merger A merger is a combination of two or more existing companies into a single company where only one of the original companies (the

---

[1] Parts of this section (including the figures) are patterned after the Reinhardt article referenced at the end of this chapter.

**FIGURE 21–1
Merger of A into B**

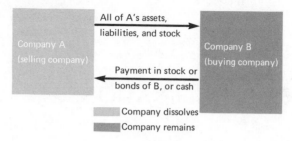

acquiring or buying company) retains its identity. The merged company
or companies are called the acquired or selling companies. Figure 21–1
illustrates the procedure involved in a merger. Company A, the selling
company, is merged into Company B, the buying company. Company A
turns over everything—assets, debts, common stock—to B and then dis-
solves. Company A no longer exists. Company B pays off A's stockholders (we'll discuss alternative payment plans later in the chapter), assumes A's debts, and continues to exist as the same legal (but now larger)
corporation. Sun Oil Company's acquisition of Sunray DX Oil Company
is an example of merger: Sunray DX (the selling company) was merged
into Sun (the buying company) in 1968. Only one company (Sun) sur-
vived, with one common management and ownership.

Consolidation   Consolidation means to combine two or more existing
companies into a *new* (consolidated) firm. In this situation none of the
consolidating firms legally survive (as will be reflected by the name of the
new organization) so there is no designation of buying and selling firms;
all consolidating companies are dissolved and a new corporation appears.

**FIGURE 21–2
Consolidation of A and B into C**

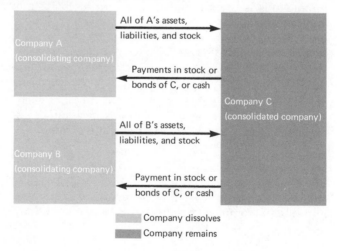

An example of this was the consolidation of Olin Industries and Mathieson Chemical Corporation into Olin Mathieson Chemical Corporation. Figure 21–2 illustrates the transactions involved in a two-company consolidation. The consolidating companies, A and B, dissolve by giving all their assets, liabilities, and stock to the new consolidated company, C, in return for some payment package from C.

Holding company A holding company is a firm that owns (holds) common stock of other companies. By owning enough common stock, the holding company (frequently called the *parent* company) controls the *subsidiary* companies.[2] National Dairy Products Corporation, for example, is a holding company with several subsidiaries, including Kraft Foods Company. Figure 21–3 shows the transactions that take

FIGURE 21–3
Holding company arrangement

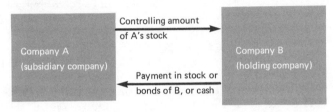

place when a holding company arrangement is set up. Company B, the holding company, buys a controlling interest in A, which then becomes a subsidiary of B. In theory, B would need over 50 percent of A's common to insure control. In reality, effective control can be maintained with a much lower percentage of A's common, sometimes even as low as 5 to 10 percent. This is, in fact, one of the allures of the holding company arrangement.

Acquisition of assets A common feature of mergers, consolidations, and holding company arrangements is that the surviving company purchases the stock of the other companies involved in the combination. In some situations a company may wish only to purchase assets, either all or part of another company. Airline B, for example, may wish to buy some planes from Airline A. Figure 21–4 depicts this arrangement. Company A sells assets to Company B in return for payment in cash, stock, bonds, or whatever. If A sells *all* of its assets, the company may choose to liquidate by paying off its creditors and distributing the residual funds to the stockholders. Alternatively, the selling company may reinvest the proceeds in new assets, or if it received payment in stock, the selling company may simply hold this stock, operating as a holding company.

---

[2] If the parent company owns *all* of the subsidiary's stock, the controlled company is called a *wholly owned subsidiary.*

FIGURE 21–4
Acquisition of A's assets by B

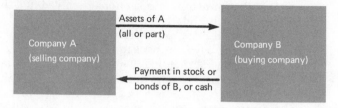

Regulatory distinction

Regulatory agencies that are charged with preventing a significant decline in competition because of business combinations are not so much concerned with the kind of business combination but rather what effect the resultant combination has on competition. Because of this overriding interest in the end result rather than the legal name of the combination, terms like "merger" and "consolidation" tend to be used interchangeably along with the term "acquisition."

Acquisition is a broad term that generally refers to consolidations and/or mergers. The Federal Trade Commission (FTC), one of the federal agencies that watchdogs mergers and consolidation, uses this term to describe any joining together of independently operated businesses under one management. Under this definition there is no real distinction between merger and consolidation. And, in practice there is no real distinction made between terms like merger, consolidation, and acquisition. The terms are used synonymously, and they all allude to the same idea — two or more companies have been formed into one company.

Economic distinction

From an economic distinction there are three kinds of business combinations: (1) vertical, (2) horizontal, and (3) conglomerate.

Vertical   A vertical combination is where a company either combines with a supplier or a customer. That is, one company's output is the other company's input. Merger of a canned goods food processor and a can manufacturer would be a vertical merger.

Horizontal   A horizontal combination occurs when two companies in the same type of business combine. The Sun Oil–Sunray DX Oil merger is an example of a horizontal merger.

Conglomerate   A conglomerate combination is defined as a combination of two corporations in unrelated industries. Merger of RCA and Hertz Rent-A-Car was a conglomerate merger. Conglomerate mergers were fashionable in the 1960s, and many companies aggressively acquired several companies this way. Notable in this group were Gulf and Western and International Telephone.

REASONS FOR BUSINESS COMBINATIONS

Many explanations for business combination activities have been suggested by the business community. We should note at the outset, however, that any proposed combination should be consistent with the firm's
goal of stockholder wealth maximization. We will see that some of the
stated motives for forming business combinations are not necessarily
related to this goal. It is particularly important that external growth opportunities be carefully compared against comparable internal growth
alternatives.

Synergistic operation economies

One of the most common reasons given for the formation of business
combinations is that there are potential synergistic operating economies
to be gained. Synergy means "working together," and this suggested
rationale is predicated on the belief that one combined company is more
efficient than two separate companies, resulting in operating cost savings and increased operating profitability. Simply put, the concept of
operating synergy implies that the worth of the combined companies is
greater than the sum of the worths of the separate companies: $1 + 1 > 2$.
The expected increased operating efficiencies are typically thought to
result from combining sales offices, staff facilities, plants, management,
and the like. In the context of the kind of economic merger accomplished, synergistic operating gains would seem most likely in horizontal
mergers, where there are more opportunities for the elimination of dupli-
cate facilities. At the other extreme, conglomerate mergers would appear to offer the least opportunity to achieve operating economies.

Diversification gains

The diversification motive is one of the most frequently cited reasons
for conglomerate merger activity, which has been at a high level in recent years. The diversification principle says that not all the eggs should
be put into one basket. Some financial theorists have argued that this
implies that the firm should diversify its asset structure by investing in
many different kinds of assets whose cash flows are not perfectly correlated. Conglomerate mergers provide one way to acquire an entirely
different class of assets. Recall from the portfolio theory work in Chapter
4 that the standard deviation of a portfolio may be reduced by adding assets to the portfolio whose returns are not perfectly correlated with the
portfolio's. This reduction in portfolio standard deviation of return implies the new portfolio is less risky than the old portfolio. As applied to
mergers, the case for diversification goes like this: The addition of another company to the existing portfolio of assets will reduce the variability of the firm's earnings if – as is almost always the case – the correlation
between present company earnings and acquired company earnings is
less than +1. This reduction in earnings variability implies the firm is
now less risky than before the merger, and consequently a lower cost

of equity capital (reflecting a less risky investment) is imposed by the "market." Under this argument, there is no requirement that there be operating economies from the combination. The diversification motive stems from a supposed reduction of the cost of equity capital resulting from the reduced risk (variability of earnings) of the firm.

There is strong opposition to the validity of this argument however. The counter-argument goes like this: Investors hold diversified portfolios of stocks; that is, they perform their own diversification and do not need the firm to perform this diversification function for them. If, for example, an investor owned shares of both Company A and Company B and these two companies merged, the investor would not realize any diversification advantages from the combination. He already enjoyed diversification from holding the individual stocks. The majority of current financial theorists seem to support this counter-argument that there is no basis for merging where the motive is to reduce the cost of equity capital (and hence raise the value of the firm) solely on the basis of diversification risk reduction.

Another aspect of diversification is related to the debt capacity of the firm. Recall from Chapter 14 that, up to a point, there is an advantage to debt financing because of the tax deductibility feature of debt interest expenses. And this point of debt usage is set, in part, by the amount of debt that lenders feel is "safe." Given this advantage of debt financing, if the firm could establish that it can safely support more debt, the stockholder's wealth can be increased by doing so. It has been argued that business combinations permit increased debt capacity because of the increased stability of cash flows from the portfolio effect of combining companies. This increased stability means that the combination of two or more firms can safely support a debt level greater than the firms could carry separately.

Taxation advantages

Another suggested reason for combinations concerns the tax effects of mergers and acquisitions. Apparently many mergers and acquisitions are prompted by one of the partners having a tax loss. This tax loss shields the income of the merging partner from taxation, and if the firm with the tax loss were about to lose its tax carry-forward, both companies have an obvious incentive for the proposed combination.

Earnings growth

In past years many companies established very attractive earnings growth rates through their merger and acquisition activities. A large part of this earnings growth was caused by lenient accounting practices permissible in business combinations. Earnings growth in many such instances was illusory, and accounting standards have been recently changed to eliminate potentially deceptive earnings per share calculation procedures. This point is discussed more fully below.

Other reasons

There are other reasons for mergers and acquisitions that are harder to put in a pure economic framework. Apparently, many combinations are inspired by a desire to secure better management. However, this motive makes sense only if the acquiring firm can't hire good management independently of acquiring physical assets as well. Sometimes when a firm is considering a new product line, an important consideration is a manager for that line who knows the market for the product well and there is no one in the present firm who is similarly qualified. From the acquired company's side there are frequently personal reasons for seeking a merger. A key executive may die or reach retirement age, or there may be such a bitter internal dispute with power so evenly split that sale or merger of the company is the only way out of the deadlock.

Disadvantages of business combinations

With all the charisma and glamor associated with mergers and acquisitions it's frequently easy to lose sight of some of the obvious disadvantages of business combinations. First, many mergers and acquisitions just don't work out. Estimates of costs and benefits associated with the acquisition may have been poor ones, and as a result the acquiring firm's earnings are pulled down and the stock price drops. In addition there may be turmoil associated with integrating the firms and friction between the two managements. And there may be problems with dissenting minority stockholders of the acquired firm about the value they received for their stock, as well as vocal dissension about the prudence of the acquisition from some stockholders of the acquiring firm.

Any business combination proposal also should be considered in light of the obvious alternative of *internal* investment, that is, investing directly in the industry that the prospective acquired company is in. Under present antitrust laws, which are designed to discourage reductions in competition, it's easier to make such direct internal investments than to acquire either another firm or its assets. The proposed acquisition may be blocked or delayed so long in court that it becomes unprofitable. Moreover, initial approval of acquisitions or mergers provides no guarantee that the combination is permanent. A divestiture may be enforced at a later (sometimes *much* later) date.

EVALUATING PROPOSED BUSINESS COMBINATIONS

Given the firm's goal of stockholder wealth maximization, a proposal to merge with, or to acquire, or to be acquired by another company should be evaluated in terms of the effect of the combination on stockholder wealth. We will analyze this evaluation from both the acquired and acquiring company perspectives.

Evaluation by the acquired company

Essentially the acquired company is offered an exchange opportunity. The acquired company gives up its stock or assets (depending on the na-

This analysis indicates that Fireside should pay no more than $4,412,033 to acquire Artificial. At any lower price, Artificial is an attractive buy for Fireside.

TERMS OF EXCHANGE

Naturally, both firms in the proposed merger/acquisition will seek the best arrangement (terms) possible for their respective stockholders. This involves negotiation. If the negotiations are successful, the combination will be formed, provided it is legally sanctioned. Frequently, however, negotiations are unsuccessful, and the proposed combination will be called off. The aim of the negotiations is to agree on the *terms of exchange,* which are ratios that indicate what each party receives and gives up by entering into the combination.

Market value exchange ratio

Because the goal of the firm is to maximize stockholder wealth the critical consideration in the terms of exchange is the *market value exchange ratio.* The market value exchange ratio is the market value of the financial assets offered to the stockholders of the acquired firm divided by the market value of the stock of the acquired company. That is:

$$\frac{\text{Market value}}{\text{exchange ratio}} = \frac{\begin{array}{c}\text{Market value of cash and securities offered}\\ \text{to acquired company's stockholders}\end{array}}{\text{Market value of stock of acquired company}} \qquad (21\text{--}1)$$

This ratio directly measures the increase in acquired company stockholder wealth from entering the merger. Market values may be put on either an aggregate or a per share basis.

Suppose the ABC Company, whose common stock sells for $28 per share, has made a merger offer to the XYZ Company whose stock sells for $10 per share. What is the market value exchange ratio if:

a. ABC offers 0.5 shares of common for each share of XYZ?
b. ABC offers $15 cash for each share of XYZ?
c. ABC offers one share of convertible preferred stock worth $95 per share and one share of common for each ten shares of XYZ?

Using Equation (21–1), we see

$$a.\ \text{Market value exchange ratio} = \frac{(0.5)(\$28)}{\$10} = 1.4$$

$$b.\ \text{Market value exchange ratio} = \frac{\$15}{\$10} = 1.5$$

$$c.\ \text{Market value exchange ratio} = \frac{\$95 + \$28}{(10\text{ shares})(\$10\text{ per share})}$$

$$= \frac{\$123}{\$100} = 1.23$$

In each case the market value exchange ratio measures the number of dollars of wealth the XYZ stockholders will receive per dollar of wealth they now have in XYZ stock. Plan (a) is called a *common for common* exchange, plan (b) is a *cash for common* exchange, and (c) is a *combination* plan.

Market value exchange ratios greater than 1.0 reflect *premiums* paid to the acquired company, and obviously, the greater the premium the more attractive the merger/acquisition will appear to the stockholders of the acquired company. Merger/acquisition premiums are commonplace[3] and typically average about 20 percent or so. Theoretically, the acquiring company can afford to offer premiums because of the cost savings it expects to effect. It is very questionable, however, that extremely large premiums are justified. Acquiring companies are all too frequently so eager to consummate the acquisition that they pay exhorbitant premiums with the consequence that the acquisition investment turns out bad. All the acquiring company did was enrich the acquired company's stockholders.

Negotiation limits If the intended acquired company is interested in negotiating, it will seek to arrange the largest merger premium possible.[4] The only market value exchange ratio limit the acquired company sees is the lower limit of 1.0, but the bigger the ratio the better. From the acquiring company's perspective the lower ratio the better, and the upper limit should be set by the investment decision evaluation we developed earlier in this chapter.

Suppose Stettler Sailboats, Inc., has just evaluated Hamman Outboard Motors as a possible acquisition. Stettler estimates that Hamman's assets are worth $2 million. It arrived at this number by present valuing Hamman's cash flows after accounting for some cost savings Stettler thinks it can effect. Hamman has 200,000 shares of stock outstanding that is trading at about $7 per share. What is the upper limit of the market value exchange ratio from Stettler's point of view if:

a. Hamman is an all equity company?
b. Hamman has $300,000 in debt outstanding?

Let's consider these two cases:

a. Market value of Hamman's common $= (200,000 \text{ shares})(\$7 \text{ per share}) = \$1,400,000$

$$\text{Stettler's upper limit of market value exchange ratio} = \frac{\$2,000,000}{\$1,400,000} = 1.43$$

b. Market value of Hamman's common $= \$1,400,000$

$$\text{Market value of Stettler's offer for Hamman's common} = \$2,000,000 - \$300,000 = \$1,700,000$$

$$\text{Stettler's upper limit of market value exchange ratio} = \frac{\$1,700,000}{\$1,400,000} = 1.21$$

---

[3] There would be no normal incentive for a company to let itself be acquired at a discount (market value exchange ratio less than 1.0).

[4] We will see below that in some situations the intended acquired company strongly resists the acquisition under *any* proposed arrangement.

If Stettler buys Hamman for $2 million, the net present value of the "project" will be zero, and Stettler will not have changed the value of its own common stock. If Stettler can negotiate the acquisition for less than $2 million, its stockholder's wealth should be increased. In Case (*a*) this requires negotiating a market value exchange rate of less than 1.43 and in (*b*) of less than 1.21.

P/E ratios

Rightly or wrongly, *P/E* (price/earnings) ratios usually play a key role in merger/acquisition evaluations. The *P/E* exchange ratio is simply the *P/E* ratio of the acquiring company divided by the *P/E* ratio of the acquired company:

$$P/E \text{ exchange ratio} = \frac{P/E \text{ acquiring company}}{P/E \text{ acquired company}} \qquad (21\text{-}2)$$

In particular, the acquiring company looks very hard at this ratio because of its effect on earnings *after* the merger/acquisition. Whenever the *P/E* of the acquiring company is greater than the *P/E* of the acquired company the *P/E* exchange ratio will be greater than 1.0. Many merger oriented companies will not consider acquisitions unless the *P/E* exchange ratio is greater than 1.0. This is because the earnings per share (*EPS*) of the *combined* company will be less than the *EPS* of the acquiring company after the merger whenever the *P/E* exchange ratio is less than 1.0. Consider the following example.

Assume that Aggressive Electronics, Inc., is considering acquisition of two companies, Baker Transistors and Cowden Manufacturing. Financial data for the three companies are as follows:

	Aggressive	*Baker*	*Cowden*
Earnings	$ 1,000,000	$ 200,000	$ 200,000
Number of shares..................	500,000	200,000	100,000
EPS	$ 2.00	$ 1.00	$ 2.00
Market value of stock: Per share ...	$ 40.00	$ 25.00	$ 30.00
Total ...	$20,000,000	$5,000,000	$3,000,000
P/E.............................	20	25	15

Let's find what the *EPS* of Aggressive would be *after* acquisition of Baker and compare this result to what Aggressive's *EPS* would be *after* acquisition of Cowden, assuming the companies are bought for their market value (that is, the market value exchange ratio is 1.0) and they are acquired with common stock. The analysis is as follows:

	Acquisition of	
	Baker	Cowden
Cost	$5,000,000	$3,000,000
No. of Aggressive shares required	$\dfrac{\$5,000,000}{\$40 \text{ per share}} = 125,000$	$\dfrac{\$3,000,000}{\$40 \text{ per share}} = 75,000$
Postacquisition Aggressive data:		
Earnings	$1,200,000	$1,200,000
No. shares	625,000	575,000
EPS	$1.92	$2.08

The effect of acquiring Baker, which has a higher P/E than Aggressive, is to dilute Aggressive's EPS from $2.00 to $1.92. Just the opposite effect occurs when Aggressive buys Cowden, which has a lower P/E: Aggressive's earnings are increased. Of course, it is unrealistic to assume that either Baker or Cowden would be interested in selling to Aggressive at market value: They would require a premium to induce them to sell.

Most acquiring companies are loathe to enter combinations that will result in dilution of current EPS because of the presumed bad effect of this dilution on stock price and stockholder wealth. However, the dilution of current EPS caused by an acquisition may be more than offset by other factors. The acquisition may, for example, lead to increased earnings growth expectations such that the net effect is that the stock price increases. Also, the cost of equity of the combined company may change, which will also affect stock price and stockholder wealth. And the same argument holds for cases where there is an initial earnings *gain* from acquisition (as when Aggressive acquired Cowden). The initial earnings gain may be wiped out by adverse earnings growth or cost of capital changes.

The main point, then, is that an initial earnings dilution or gain may be offset by changes in other factors, and it is a mistake to think that a merger/acquisition looks good or bad from the acquiring company's standpoint solely because its P/E is higher or lower than the acquired company's. The real test of whether the proposed acquisition is a good one from the acquiring company's view is from the present value investment decision analysis we developed earlier.

Book values

Another term that occasionally receives attention in mergers is the book value per share of the companies. There is little to commend book values as being important in merger/acquisition evaluation, however, since book values are simply measures of historical cost, which have little relationship to market values. Usually book value ratios receive attention when the acquired company's market value is less than its book value. This leads some to believe that the company is a good buy. This is not necessarily a proper judgment however. A company is an attractive buy when it can be bought for less than its net present value as we discussed in previous section on merger investment analysis.

FINANCING MERGERS AND ACQUISITIONS

After the decision to enter the business combination has been made, the next step is to decide on a financing plan. A crucial consideration in financing mergers and acquisitions is the tax status of the proposed combination. Business combinations are classified either as *tax free* or *taxable* transactions for purposes of determining the immediate federal income tax liability of the stockholders. If a combination is determined (by the Internal Revenue Service) to be taxable, stockholders who receive new financial assets (cash, stock, bonds, etc.) in return for surrendering their stock must pay federal income tax in the current year on any gains made from the transaction. Combinations ruled to be tax free require no current year tax payment on such gains. Instead, the tax is deferred until the *new* securities are sold by the stockholder. In most situations the selling company will insist on a financing plan that will result in a tax free exchange status. On the other hand, the buying company would prefer a taxable exchange. If the exchange is ruled tax free, any difference between the selling company's book value and the agreed purchase price will be assigned to the buyer's books as nondepreciable good will for tax purposes. This means that there will be more income tax to pay in later years because the depreciation shield will be less than if the transaction were ruled taxable. In a taxable acquisition the acquired assets would be added to the buying company's tangible assets at their purchase price, and the entire purchase price would be depreciable for income tax purposes. There is therefore a basic conflict between tax status preferences of buying and selling companies that must ultimately be resolved by negotiation.

There are many requirements imposed by the Internal Revenue Service that must be met before a combination will be classified as tax free. The two principal requirements are: (1) stockholders who give up stock (as the selling company stockholders would in a merger, or both company's stockholders would in a consolidation) must receive a similar equity position (either common stock or convertible preferred stock) in return and (2) at least 80 percent of the common stock of the selling company must be sold to the buying company.

Payment methods

Payment methods or financing packages are extremely varied. Acquiring firms may use common or preferred stock, convertible securities, cash, straight debt, warrants, or some combination of these securities. Rightly or wrongly, one of the main considerations in determining the financial package has been the effect of the payment method on earnings per share.

Common stock In a *common for common* swap the selling company's stockholders give up their stock in return for common in the buying company. The most obvious advantage of this method of financing is that it is consistent with a tax free exchange. A perceived disadvantage is that issuing stock increases the number of shares outstanding, which may have an adverse effect on earnings per share. When the buying company is purchasing the assets of the selling company rather than the stock, the common stock of the buying company may or may not be distributed to stockholders of the selling company. It depends on whether the selling company intends to liquidate or not.

Convertible securities Convertible debentures and convertible preferred stock were frequently used means of financing conglomerate acquisitions during the 1960s because of the favorable effect on earnings that resulted from use of convertibles to finance acquisitions. Under accounting practices permitted in the 1960s convertibles were not counted as owner's equity financial instruments, even though they would eventually be converted into common stock. Consequently the number of shares the convertibles would eventually be converted into were not included in determining the number of shares the firm had outstanding. This resulted in artificially high earnings per share figures. In the late 1960s the Accounting Principles Board issued an "opinion," which effectively required calculation of earnings per share on a "fully diluted" basis. This fully diluted basis essentially means that the number of shares controlled by the convertibles would be used in determining the number of common shares outstanding and, consequently, earnings per share. These requirements led to a distinction between earnings per share and *fully diluted* earnings per share. The new requirements have also led to a marked decrease in the use of convertible securities as a means of financing mergers and acquisitions.

Cash In a *cash for common* exchange, the selling company stockholders receive cash for their common stock. This results in a taxable transaction. It may also result in a favorable earnings per share figure since the buying firm is picking up new earnings from the acquisition without increasing the number of shares outstanding. This presumes that the buying firm has cash on hand to make the acquisition. If it does not, it must determine how to raise the cash, and one way is to issue stock. In that case the buying firm is effectively engaging in a stock for stock swap but is incurring transactions costs in selling stock to the stock market rather than exchanging stock with the selling company's stockholders.

Accounting policies: Purchase versus pooling of interests

There are two general accounting methods for handling mergers and acquisitions. One is called the *purchase method*, the other the *pooling of interest*, and they have considerably different effects on postcombination *EPS*.

Goodwill, which occurs when the purchase price of the selling company exceeds its book value, is treated substantially different under the two methods. Under the purchase method the excess of the selling company's purchase price over book value is first assigned, to the extent possible, to tangible assets; the remainder is defined as goodwill. Goodwill is depreciable for investor *reporting* purposes but not for *tax* purposes. This means that there will be a depreciation charge against earnings each year for goodwill but no commensurate depreciation tax shield. Under the pooling of interest method the books of the combining companies are simply combined or pooled and there *is* no goodwill created and, consequently, no depreciation of goodwill that will reduce reported earnings.

Another aspect of pooling of interest that made it appear favorable was the previously sanctioned accounting practice regarding acquired assets. Assets acquired at book value under pooling could be resold at market value, and the difference would be reflected in higher profits and earnings. These apparent earnings advantages led to widespread preference for the pooling method along with widespread abuses of the method. The accounting profession has attempted to eliminate what are largely artificial advantages of the pooling method by eliminating some of the obvious enticements and by making it more difficult to qualify for pooling of interest.

ANTITRUST CONSIDERATIONS

Any business combination must be sanctioned either by statute, by legislative acknowledgment, or through approval of a charter. Actions by the various regulatory agencies to deny or block the combination are called antitrust actions. Because of the possibility of such action, either at the state or federal level, the principals involved should assess the likelihood of approval *before* a commitment is made to participate in the proposed combination. The cost involved in pursuing a combination that is blocked or considerably delayed by an antitrust law suit can be so great that a profitable venture is made unprofitable. Moreover, there is no statute of limitations in many antitrust laws, and longstanding combinations can, under certain circumstances, be dissolved. Consequently, the firm should look hard at possible antitrust actions that may arise from a business combination, and this hard look should come early in the analysis. Many firms, in fact, seek an informal advance opinion from antitrust agencies of the possibilities of legal action against the combination before seeking stockholder approval.

Basic antitrust issues

Antitrust laws exist to ensure that markets for goods and services are competitive, so the basic antitrust issue involved in business combinations is: Will competition be reduced because of the combination? The antitrust intent is sometimes interpreted to be anti-bigness, since antitrust actions occur most frequently in cases where one or all principals are large. Actually, antitrust actions are not instigated because of the absolute size of the principals, but rather because of the relative size and number of companies in the industry after the combination. Two basic tenets of competition are: (1) many competitors with (2) none being so large that its actions dominate the market. The real intent of antitrust law as applied to business combinations is to restrain movements away from these tenets.

Assessing the likelihood of antitrust actions is a difficult task because many proposed combinations have such unique features that it's difficult to generalize as to why one merger is approved and another not. Also, laws become more or less restrictive as time passes. In addition there are frequent personnel changes in regulatory agencies; some regulatory personnel are "trust busters" and antimerger oriented, others are more sympathetic to business combinations. But there are some broad guidelines that firms can use to assess the likelihood of regulatory approval.

Reduction of "within" industry competition In general, mergers will be held illegal if *substantial actual* or *potential* competition exists between the principals. Unfortunately, there are no precise standards for measuring what *substantially* means either in terms of market share (percent of total market sales) or dollar volume of business of the principals. Elimination of *actual* competition is most obvious in horizontal mergers (mergers between companies in the same industry). However, not all horizontal mergers are blocked. If there are many competitors in the field, if the market shares of the principals are relatively small, if there are no substantial barriers to entry in the field, and if the number of competitors is not generally declining, there is much less danger of antitrust action. In addition, if a company is in financial distress and is preparing to liquidate, a horizontal combination may receive approval. But, in general, horizontal mergers are viewed with suspicion and are closely analyzed.

Elimination of *potential* competition is a more difficult interpretive issue and cuts across all types of combinations: horizontal, vertical, and conglomerate. The basic guideline here appears to be a judgment by the regulatory agency of the ability of the acquiring company to enter the acquired company's industry as a competitor. Procter and Gamble's proposed merger with Clorox was denied, for example, because Procter and Gamble was considered to be a *potential* competitor of Clorox in the bleach market.

Reduction of "between" industry competition Antitrust actions are also very probable when vertical combinations lessen competition between companies in buyer-seller related industries. Foremost, antitrust theory is concerned with the effect of foreclosing competitors from competitive access to supply or customer markets. If, for example, a shoe manufacturer merged with a large leather processing company, competing shoe manufacturers may be disadvantaged in the supply (of leather) market. If the same shoe manufacturer merged with a retail shoe store, competing shoe manufacturers may be disadvantaged in their customer market.

Antitrust law also specifically prohibits combinations were potential *reciprocal dealing* exists. Suppose a textile fabricator (Company A) buys processed cotton from a cotton mill (Company B) that in turn buys chemicals from a chemical company (Company C) to process raw cotton. If companies A and C were to combine into Company AC, a potential reciprocal dealing opportunity exists. Company AC could insist that

Company B purchase chemicals from it or AC will no longer buy B's cotton. If AC represents a substantial part of B's market, the pressure to agree to this reciprocal deal will be great. But such deals reduce competition between buyers in one industry and sellers in another, and antitrust law prohibits business combinations that create such opportunities.

Regulatory agencies

There are regulatory agencies at both the state and federal level. State agencies regulate *intrastate* commerce and are thus less important to large companies with *interstate* business activities. At the federal level there are many agencies that have antitrust responsibilities. The Antitrust Division of the Department of Justice has the broadest responsibility of the federal agencies. It is charged with enforcing the federal antitrust laws like the Sherman Antitrust Act, the Clayton Act, etc. The Federal Trade Commission (FTC) concentrates on maintaining competition in interstate trade, and the Interstate Commerce Commission (ICC) regulates most transportation (railroad, motorfreight, water, and pipeline) companies. Other agencies are the Federal Power Commission (FPC), which regulates interstate public utilities; the Federal Communications Commission (FCC), which regulates interstate communication companies; and the Securities and Exchange Commission, which regulates interstate public utility holding companies.

CORPORATE TAKEOVER FIGHTS

Negotiations concerning a possible merger or acquisition may be friendly or hostile. In a friendly negotiation a merger/acquisition dialogue takes place between executives of the companies involved, and if no agreement can be reached on the terms of exchange, negotiations are broken off and the proposal for combination is terminated.

Sometimes, however, the buying firm decides to unilaterally pursue the merger/acquisition against the will of the intended selling company: The buying company decides to attempt a *takeover* of the target company. The buying company does this by making a *tender offer*. A tender is an offer made by the buying firm directly to the stockholders of the target firm to sell (tender) their shares of stock, usually for cash, to the buying company. If the buying firm can induce enough target company shareholders to tender their stock, the buying company can gain control of the target company and force the merger/acquisition on the reluctant target company management. The inducement for stockholders tendering their shares comes from setting the tender price well above the current market price of the target's stock. If, for example, the common stock of Target, Inc., is selling for $50 per share, a tender offer may be made at $70 a share. The tender has an expiration date, usually a few weeks, and the stock must be offered within that period.

Sometimes the buying company knows beforehand that the target company's management would be unreceptive to a merger/acquisition proposal, and there are no preliminary negotiations prior to the tender offer. Before legislation that required prior notification of a tender offer, some buying companies made *surprise* (unannounced) tender offers for the target's stock. The target firm's executives would find out about the tender offer when they read about it in the paper!

Target companies

There has been some historical evidence that certain kinds of companies are more likely to be takeover candidates than others. Cash rich companies, for example, attract tender offers because a buying company can readily use the cash. Companies that underutilize debt (that is, have low debt-equity ratios) are also likely targets. Given the tax advantage of debt a buying company may increase its debt capacity greatly by acquiring a low leveraged firm. A third financial indicator that appears to be shared by many takeover targets is a low P/E ratio. As we saw earlier in this chapter there is a presumed magic in buying firms with lower P/E ratios because of immediate *EPS* gains by the buying company. While these and other reasons may be suspect from a normative financial theory standpoint, they do appear to be important in the eyes of the buying company.

Defensive tactics

When a takeover bid is made, the management of the target company must decide whether to actively oppose the takeover or not. If the decision is to fight the raider (buying company), there are several approaches open. However, management of firms acquired by takeovers are commonly discharged, and in fighting the takeover, target company managements frequently appear to be protecting their jobs rather than acting so as to maximize stockholder wealth. This, of course, is inconsistent with the goal of the firm and is in contradiction of management's responsibilities. These kinds of inconsistencies do occur, however, and in evaluating a proposed takeover, stockholders of the target company should attempt to carefully assess just whose interests are being served by management's opposition to the acquisition.

Publicity campaign Typically, the first defensive tactic by the target company is to initiate their own publicity campaign to counter that of the raider. This campaign will typically question the advisability of tendering stock to the raider because of the "true" value of the stock as perceived by the target company's management. If, for example, a tender is made on Target Inc. at $70 per share, and Target's stock is selling for $50 per share, Target's management may issue a statement that, in their opinion, Target's "true" value is much higher, say, $100 per share, and stockholders would be ill-advised to sell at $70 per share.

Stock purchases Another alternative open to the target company is to purchase its own stock on the open market, which soaks up stock available for tendering to the raider. Since the tender offer pulls the stock price up close to the tender price, the target company can expect to pay a price that is fairly close to the tender price on any repurchases. A different approach to this idea is to purchase stock of the raiding company. This tactic would be most effective if the target company is considerably larger than the raider.

Legal tactics There are several legal avenues that target companies have explored to impede takeovers. The most obvious is to build a case against the merger on grounds of infringement of antitrust laws. A second tactic is to encourage stockholders of either the target or raiding company to seek a stockholder's injunction against the takeover because of misrepresentation of value offered in the tender. Last, while the target company is ultimately obligated to provide stockholder lists to the raider, it can delay doing so as long as possible, giving itself more time to fight the takeover.

Defensive mergers As a last resort, some target companies seek out mergers with another, "friendlier" company. This defensive merger tactic is usually undertaken when it is apparent that the raider intends to radically change the company or perhaps intends to fire all of the present management team. Defensive mergers sometimes give the impression that management is more concerned with its own survival than with shareholder wealth maximization, particularly when the offer made by the friendly company is no greater than the raider's.

SUMMARY

Business combinations are of several forms. In a *merger* only the acquiring company retains its corporate identity, while in a *consolidation,* none of the original firms survives—a new entity appears. *Holding companies* are firms that own common stock of other companies. In an acquisition of assets arrangement, all or part of the assets of one company are sold to another. There is also an economic distinction made between *vertical, horizontal,* and *conglomerate* business combinations. Vertical combinations are supplier-customer combinations; horizontal implies within-industry combinations; conglomerate combinations involve firms in unrelated industries. The most common motives for the active formation of business combinations are synergistic operating economies, diversification gains, taxation advantages, and earnings growth potential.

The evaluation of a proposed business combination from the acquired company's standpoint involves comparison of the current market value of its stock against the market value of the proposed package being offered. From the acquiring company's perspective, the evaluation procedure entails computing the present value of the relevant cash flows associated with purchase of the acquired company. This present value represents the theoretical maximum price the acquiring company would offer the acquired company. Other important elements of a proposed combination are the *terms of exchange.* The *market value exchange ratio* shows the premium the acquired firm's stockholders receive. The *P/E exchange ratio* and the *book value exchange ratio* are other commonly used terms of exchange.

The financing of mergers and acquisitions is strongly influenced by the tax status of the combination. Convertible securities have been used advantageously in recent years to preserve the *tax free* status of the combination along with favorable earnings per share effects, although recent accounting practices have reduced illusory earnings per share gains resulting from convertibles. Combinations must be justified to antitrust regulatory agencies, and the main question asked by these agencies is: Will competition be reduced because of the combination? Excepting very peculiar circumstances, if the answer is yes, the combination will probably not be approved.

QUESTIONS

1. Define the following terms and phrases:
   a. Merger.
   b. Consolidation.
   c. Acquisition of assets.
   d. Synergistic gains.
   e. Fully diluted *EPS*.
   f. Pooling of interests.
   g. Tender offer.
2. Many executives cite mergers as an effective way to attain corporate diversification. Discuss the pros and cons of this idea.

3. Companies that engage in merger and acquisitions direct their employees who are involved in the analysis and negotiations and their officers not to buy stock of the target company. One reason for this warning is that the law prohibits "insiders" benefitting from privy information. However, even if there were no such laws the buying company would have another motive for the prohibition on target company stock purchases by employees and officers. What is this other motive?

4. Briefly contrast the purchase method and pooling of interests method of accounting for business combinations.

5. Woolf, Inc., is an aggressive, rapidly growing conglomerate firm that has just made a tender offer to Glitter Co. stockholders. If Glitter's management is against the acquisition, indicate and briefly discuss what actions could be taken to try and block the proposed acquisition.

6. "Many U.S. businessmen feel that federal regulators are against bigness and will block any proposed business combination that leads to or furthers bigness." Comment on this statement.

7. a. What are the main differences among vertical, horizontal, and conglomerate business combinations?
   b. Other things equal, which of the three combinations in (a) is most likely to be blocked for antitrust reasons? Which is least likely? Explain your answers.

8. What is usually the dominant consideration when arranging a financing package for a proposed business combination?

9. Identify and discuss the relative advantages and disadvantages of the following business combination financing plans:
   a. Common for common
   b. Convertibles for common
   c. Cash for common

10. a. Identify several exchange ratios.
    b. Which of these would appear to be most important? Explain why.

PROBLEMS

1. The Mammoth Manufacturing Company is considering the acquisition of the Conway Foundry Company, a small but profitable Western tool manufacturer. Analysts for Mammoth estimate that, with no changes in current operations, Conway's cash flow after taxes will be $1 million next year and will grow at 10 percent a year for the following three years and then remain constant for the foreseeable future. If the acquisition is made, Mammoth will be able to close its present warehouse operation at an annual after tax savings of $200,000 per year. Mammoth expects to lose $175,000 per year after tax on the sales of a line of wrenches that will be discontinued if the tool company is purchased, but expects to add a new line of metric tools contributing $65,000 per year in after tax cash flows. These changes are forecast to persist for the indefinite future.

   What is the maximum price that Mammoth would be willing to pay for Conway if the appropriate discount rate for this venture is 12 percent?

2. Ike and Dewitt Bettor, incorporated consulting engineers, are evaluating the possibility of acquiring the Wright-Waigh Construction Company. Economic analysis indicates that the present value of the cash flows from Wright-Waigh is $1 million.

   The Wright-Waigh Construction Company has 100,000 shares of stock outstanding which are trading at $6 per share. Wright-Waigh has no debt or preferred stock outstanding, and expected earnings available for common are $100,000 per year. Ike and Dewitt Bettor have 200,000 shares of stock outstanding that currently sell for $8 per share. Expected earnings available for Bettor common for the coming year are $400,000.
   a. Determine the upper and lower limits of the market value exchange ratio.
   b. Determine the P/E exchange ratio.
   c. Should Ike and Dewitt Bettor consider this acquisition? Why?
   d. Determine the maximum number of shares Ike and Dewitt Bettor would be willing to offer for each share of Wright-Waigh in a common for common exchange.
   e. What will be the postcombination EPS if the exchange described in (d) is made?

3. Simon Diversified, Inc., is studying the possibility of adding a costume jewelry manufacturing division to the company. After considerable research Simon has identified three possible means of accomplishing this addition. Two of the possibilities would entail acquiring existing costume jewelry manufacturing companies. The two target companies are Magnifico, Inc., and Quality Jewelry.

   If Magnifico were acquired, a Simon analyst estimates that Simon would realize about $400,000 per year in after tax cash flows as a result of the acquisition. Similarly, after tax cash flows of about $200,000 per year would result from the acquisition of Quality Jewelry. The third alternative is for Simon to start its own jewelry lines. The analyst estimates this would create after tax cash flows of about $100,000 per year. In all three instances the anticipated life of the venture is 20 years. The analyst anticipates no termination (salvage) cash flows for any of the three alternatives. Furthermore, the estimated costs of capital for Magnifico and Quality are 16 and 12 percent, respectively. The discount rate for the internally developed jewelry lines is estimated to be 15 percent.

   Both Magnifico and Quality stocks are only infrequently traded, and most of each stock is owned by the management. Most recent quotes on the stocks are $10 per share for Magnifico (150,000 shares outstanding) and $1 per share for Quality (500,000 shares outstanding). However, discussions with managements of the two companies indicate that Magnifico would require a 40-percent premium over the stock's current market price before they agreed to sell out. Quality Jewelry would require a 100-percent premium over current market price. The after tax initial cost of Simon developing jewelry lines on its own is estimated to be $400,000.

   Evaluate the three mutually exclusive alternatives and recommend to Simon what investment action should be taken.

4. American Television is preparing to make Target Soaps a merger offer. American's stock is selling for $30 per share and Target's stock is selling for $50 per share. Determine the market value exchange ratio for each of the following proposed terms of exchange.
   a. American offers 1.6 shares of common plus $5 cash for each share of Target.
   b. American offers nine shares of common for each five shares of Target stock.
   c. American offers a $1,000 face value convertible bond whose estimated market value is $900 per bond for each 16 shares of Target stock.
   d. Ignoring taxes and other possible reasons for preference for a particular *kind* of payments package, which of the three plans is most favorable to Target stockholders? Why?

5. The Mid-West Marble Company is considering four potential merger opportunities for which the financial data are presented below.

	Mid-West Marble Company	A	B	C	D
Net present value		$1,700,000	$475,000	$4,125,000	$5,800,000
Shares common	500,000	200,000	100,000	400,000	300,000
Stock price..............	$10	$8	$3	$6	$12
Debt	$2,000,000	0	$150,000	$1,000,000	$1,400,000
Expected earnings......	$ 500,000	$ 150,000	$ 90,000	$ 500,000	$ 350,000
Stock exchange terms*	—	2.5 for 3	1 for 3	3 for 4	4.25 for 3

* The number of shares of Mid-West stock for merged co. stock proposed by the merged co.

a. Determine the upper limit for the market value exchange ratio for each potential merger.
b. Compare the calculations made in (a) with market exchange ratios implied by the proposed offer from Mid-West to determine which mergers appear feasible.
c. Determine the postcombination *EPS* of the above *feasible mergers*.
d. Which company is the best merger candidate for Mid-West? Explain your answer.

6. Atom Industries, Inc., is negotiating with Young Co. to merge Young into Atom. In assessing the impact that the merger would have, Atom's financial staff has prepared earnings estimates for this year as shown below. As indicated, these estimates are based on three economic outlooks anticipated by Atom's staff. If the merger is undertaken, the market value exchange ratio will be 1.2. Atom currently has 4 million shares of common and Young 2 million. In addition, current stock prices for Atom and Young are $8 and $10, respectively.

		Earnings (millions of dollars)	
Economic outlook	Probability	Atom	Young
Bad	0.3	8	2
Average........................	0.4	10	3
Good...........................	0.3	12	4

Assuming that Atom would finance the acquisition with common stock, determine the postacquisition *EPS* for each of the three economic outlooks and the *expected* postacquisition *EPS*.

7. The ABC Company is in the process of negotiating the terms of an acquisition of the XYZ Company. Evaluation by ABC Company's financial analysts indicate that XYZ has a present value of $12 million. Financial information on the two companies is presented below.

	ABC	XYZ
EBIT	$1,860,000	$890,000
Interest	360,000	140,000
EBT	1,500,000	750,000
Taxes (0.5)	750,000	375,000
Net income	750,000	375,000
Preferred dividends	150,000	-0-
Available to common	$ 600,000	$375,000
EPS	$ 1.50	$ .75
P/E	15	20

Negotiators for ABC and XYZ have narrowed their discussions to two alternative plans for affecting the consolidation.

Alternative I

Trade three shares of ABC common for four shares of XYZ common.

Price of ABC common at time of swap	$23.50	$23.00	$22.50	$22.00	$21.50
Probability	0.1	0.2	0.3	0.3	0.1

Estimated postcombination $P/E = 15$.

Alternative II

Trade $65.00 plus one share of ABC convertible preferred for eight shares of XYZ common.
Dividend on convertible preferred = $5 per share.

Price of ABC convertible at time of swap	$77.00	$76.00	$75.00	$74.00	$73.00
Probability	0.1	0.1	0.5	0.2	0.1

Estimated postcombination $P/E = 14$.

a. Determine the premerger total market value of each company's common stock.
b. Determine the upper limit of the market value exchange ratio assuming that the value of all of XYZ's debt is $3 million.
c. Determine the expected market value exchange ratio of each alternative.
d. Determine (1) the number of shares of common that must be issued under Alternative I. (2) The number of shares of preferred that must be issued under Alternative II.
e. Assuming that XYZ's debt would not be retired, determine:
  1. Expected postcombination earnings per share under each alternative.

2. Expected postcombination stock price under each alternative.
   f. Which alternative should ABC prefer to use? Why?

SELECTED BASIC REFERENCES

Hays, S. L., and R. A. Taussig. "Tactics in Cash Takeover Bids," *Harvard Business Review* (March–April 1967) pp. 135–48.

Heath, J., Jr. "Valuation Factors and Techniques in Mergers and Acquisitions," *Financial Executive* (April 1972), pp. 34–44.

Hexter, R. M. "How to Sell Your Company." *Harvard Business Review* (May–June 1968), pp. 71–77.

Shad, J. S. R. "The Financial Realities of Mergers," *Harvard Business Review* (November–December 1969), pp. 133–46.

SELECTED ADVANCED REFERENCES

Hogarty, T. F. "The Profitability of Corporate Mergers," *Journal of Business* (July 1970), pp. 317–27.

Larson, K. D., and N. J. Gonedes. "Business Combinations: An Exchange-Ratio Determination Model," *Accounting Review* (October 1969), pp. 720–28.

Lewellen, W. G. "A Pure Financial Rationale for the Conglomerate Merger," *Journal of Finance* (May 1971), pp. 521–37.

Nielson, J. F., and R. W. Melicher. "A Financial Analysis of Acquisition and Merger Premiums," *Journal of Financial and Quantitative Analysis* (March 1973), pp. 139–48.

Reinhardt, U. E. *Mergers and Consolidations: A Corporate Finance Approach.* Morristown: General Learning Press, 1972.

22

FINANCIAL DISTRESS

Up to now we have concentrated on the firm as a healthy, ongoing operation. Like people, however, firms can become ill and even die. In this chapter we will look at the firm in *financial distress,* which is a study of the financial side of corporations in trouble.

There are several important terms that will be used frequently in the chapter. *Failure* is a commonly used word in financial distress literature and has two generally accepted meanings. One concept of failure emphasizes the firm's inability to pay its obligations (such as accounts payable and debt interest and principal repayment) as they come due. When a firm cannot meet these obligations it is said to be *technically insolvent.* A second concept of failure is when the value of the firm's liabilities exceed the fair market value of the firm's assets. Under this definition, the firm is a failure whenever its *market* net worth (market value of assets less the value of the liabilities) is negative.[1] While there are thus two definitions of failure, we will use "failure" to apply to both cases, without distinction. This is a common practice.

When a firm fails one of two things may occur. It may either *reorganize* or *liquidate.* A reorganization refers to a recapitalization of the firm. That is, the capital structure is changed with the explicit purpose of reducing the amount of debt in the firm. A liquidation refers to the death of the firm. Assets are sold, creditors (and stockholders, if there is anything left over) are paid off with the proceeds, and the firm is dissolved. If the courts administer the reorganization or liquidation, the firm is said to be *bankrupt,* and the procedures are referred to as bankruptcy procedures. We'll develop these ideas in more detail below.

---

[1] The emphasis here is on *market* net worth as opposed to *book* net worth, which is book value of assets less liabilities.

DISTRESS PLANNING

If performed capably, the financial management tasks of monitoring and planning can substantially lessen any problems that arise during periods of distress.

Causes of failure

Failure is almost always blamed on managerial incompetence. Occasionally a firm may fail because of fraud (as happened with Equity Funding in 1973) or some natural disaster, but these are less common occurrences; managerial incompetence is the main culprit. Incompetence covers several things. Management may make errors in judgment that result in poor financial management decisions. A decision in the early 1900s to keep producing buggy whips or a decision to carry 80 percent of the firm's capital structure as debt when there is a large chance of not servicing the debt are examples of managerial errors on both the operating and financial level. Not planning for contingencies such as a downturn in general business conditions or adverse changes in product demand, or not maintaining adequate working capital are all examples of managerial incompetence. It may seem harsh to equate judgment errors with incompetence, for we all make errors. But if the result of the errors is so severe and irreparable as to cause failure, management has indeed been incompetent. As we will see below, implementation of any major investment or financing plan should be accompanied by a contingency plan that provides for protection for the firm should expectations not be realized. This contingency plan should provide for mobilization of resources to keep the firm from failing.

Signs of failure

In recent years there have been several financial bankruptcy studies that have indicated that financial distress can be predicted by investigating certain key financial ratios. Among these key ratios are:

1. Cash flow/Total debt.
2. Earnings before interest and taxes/Total assets.
3. Cash flow/Total assets.
4. Net income/Total assets.
5. Sales/Total assets.
6. Total debt/Total assets.

Bankruptcy studies have indicated that these ratios tend to be significantly different for healthy firms and for firms headed toward failure. The first five ratios all have some income number divided by total debt or total assets, and failing firms tend to have much lower values for these ratios than nonfailing firms. Also, failing firms tend to have much higher debt ratios (Ratio 6) than nonfailing firms.

To the extent that these and other ratios do have predictive value, management would be remiss in not keeping careful watch on their own ratios in comparison to other firms. Management should also be aware of the time trend in their ratios, as the bankruptcy studies have indicated that these ratios deteriorate as failure approaches.

Contingency plans[2]

Because the firm operates in an uncertain world, judgment and fore-casting errors will occur, and many decisions that looked good at time of inception will lead to unfavorable results. Consequently, the firm needs to carefully plan for contingencies that may arise. Lack of contingency planning simply invites disaster.

Contingency planning covers three distinct stages, all pointed at avoiding failure by maintaining financial mobility. These stages are:

1. Buying time.
2. Mobilizing resources to meet the emergency.
3. Developing strategies for dealing with the emergency.

Buying time Buying time refers to explicitly recognizing the possibility of failure long before it occurs. An unexpected need for funds is frequently fatal because there is insufficient time to react to the crisis. In distress situations time is precious, and contingency planning should start with the firm continually scanning the horizon for trouble. This kind of program keeps the firm alert to changing conditions in the economy, the firm's industry, and in the firm itself. Perhaps the most important part of this continual forecasting by the firm is the explicit inclusion of extremely unfavorable events in the firm's planning. It's not enough, for example, to analyze what will happen to the firm's cash flows if the industry slows down; some of the questions considered should be directed to *catastrophic* slowdowns, because it's the *extremely* unfavorable events that will create financial emergencies.

Mobilizing resources The next step is to identify what resources can be deployed to meet a financial contingency. Figure 22–1 is a work sheet oriented toward identifying resources available to meet such contingencies. There are three general categories of resource mobilization: (1) uncommitted reserves, (2) expense reductions, and (3) asset liquidations.

Within three months or so the firm should be able to increase its cash position in several ways. Extra cash and marketable securities provide a first cushion. Other spontaneous short-term reserves are provided by any unused line of credit and by payables stretching (deferring payment). These sources are spontaneous in that the firm can gain access to them with little effort. Another source of uncommitted reserves is new short-term borrowing; however, the firm must negotiate to secure these funds.

The next category of "within three-month" funds is expense reduction. The firm can cut back production, which reduces variable costs, and/or the firm can reduce the current quarter's dividend. Also, the firm may wish to consider the third category and liquidate inventory and/or receivables.

---

[2] This section is based on Gordon Donaldson's article referenced at the end of this chapter.

Within 12 months even more alternatives are available. The firm can approach the capital markets for either new debt or equity funds. It can deepen the cost reduction program by cutting back on planned capital expenditures, trimming marketing programs (such as advertising and promotion), reducing overhead (by closing or consolidating offices, releasing employees, etc.), and by cutting back research and development expenditures. Last, the firm can sell plant, equipment, and land to raise funds.

FIGURE 22-1
Work sheet for mobilizing resources to meet financial contingencies

		Time lag for obtaining	
Resources		Within 3 months	Within 12 months
I. Uncommitted reserves			
A. Spontaneous			
1. Surplus cash		X	
2. Marketable securities		X	
3. Unused line of credit		X	
4. Stretching payables		X	
B. Negotiated reserves			
1. New short-term borrowing		X	
2. New long-term borrowing			X
3. New equity			X
II. Reduction of expenses			
A. Short-term			
1. Production cut		X	
2. Dividend cut		X	
B. Long-term			
1. Capital expenditure cut			X
2. Marketing program cut			X
3. Overhead cut			X
4. R&D cut			X
III. Liquidation of assets			
1. Inventory and receivables		X	
2. Plant, equipment, and land			X

Figure 22-1 is only meant to be a rough work sheet directed toward mobilizing resources to meet financial distress periods. It may take longer than three months to acquire funds for some entries with a check in the three-month column, and it may take more than one year (or much less) to acquire funds for some of the 12-month entries, depending upon circumstances. The main point is that the work sheet is a useful device in planning for financial emergencies. The firm should make and keep up to date some kind of work sheet such as Figure 22-1, showing how much cash could be raised within what length of time.

Emergency strategies When financial crisis strikes, the firm will need a detailed outline of the sequence of moves that will be taken to alleviate the crisis. That is, the firm needs to prepare a road map of how it will deploy the financial resources listed in Figure 22–1. We call this road map an emergency strategy.

There are a wide range of strategies used. Some emphasize the use of spontaneous uncommitted reserves. Under these approaches the firm uses the most liquid assets available to meet a financial emergency and keeps a rather large stockpile of such assets (such as cash and securities) as a kind of insurance policy. This conservative approach reduces return on investment, and a contrary strategy is to operate with very little liquid reserve. Both of these approaches have drawbacks: one sacrifices return by overemphasizing liquidity – it essentially ignores all aspects of Figure 22–1 except the spontaneous uncommitted reserves portion. The other approach virtually ignores the uncommitted reserves section. Under this latter aggressive policy, any funds required would have to come from the harder to get and slower to procure routes, and the firm may have an inadequate liquid reserve cushion.

In part, the purpose of the work sheet is to point out the time lag necessary to convert resources into cash. If the firm is watchful and sees a major investment or the whole corporate operation is beginning to sour, it can immediately begin a resource mobilization plan. This long-range monitoring will reduce (but not eliminate) the need for liquid resources and will properly lead the firm to considering mobilizing resources that take longer than a few weeks to accomplish.

There are, thus, no hard and fast rules that spell out a "correct" strategy. All crises will not be the same and will not call for identical resource mobilization plans. Left unattended, however, all crises will flirt with the same problem: failure.

FAILURE OF THE FIRM

While failure of the firm is an unpleasant prospect, many thousands of firms fail each year, and knowledge of certain basic facts and procedures about failure is required of financial managers.

Legal rights of claimants

If the firm should fail, the distribution of the remaining value of the company, either in a liquidation or reorganization, will follow a schedule based on the priority of claims on the firm's assets. This priority schedule is as follows:

1. *Priority creditors.* Priority credit claims refer to court costs incurred in administering the liquidation or reorganization of the firm, payment of employee wages,[3] and payment of local, state, and federal taxes.
2. *Secured creditors.* Secured creditors have collateral pledged by the firm to secure the debt. First mortgage bonds are an example of secured debt. The whole purpose of requiring collateral is to ensure a high priority of the debt in case of failure.

---

[3] The employee wages are a priority debt only up to $600 per claimant, and only if the wages were earned within three months of the failure.

3. *General creditors.* All individuals and companies owed money by the failing firm but who have no specified collateral on the loan are general creditors. Normally this mainly includes the firm's debentures and accounts payable. In addition, secured creditors whose claims are not completely satisfied by the assets pledged to their claims have general creditors' rights on the unsatisfied portion of their claims.

4. *Preferred stockholders.* First in line after all creditors have been satisfied are the firm's preferred stockholders; their claims have preference over the common stockholders. Frequently, however, after the creditors have settled there are no assets remaining, and the preferred holders receive neither cash (in a liquidation) or new stocks and bonds (in a reorganization).

5. *Common stockholders.* The firm's common stockholders are last in line; they are the residual claimants on any assets left after all other claimants have been satisfied. Generally, common stockholders receive nothing after the failure.

Out-of-court settlements

When the firm fails there are two ways to resolve or settle the stress problem. One way is to make an *out-of-court* settlement among claimants. The second way is to file for bankruptcy and proceed through an *in-court* resolution of the problem.

Out-of-court settlements are simply agreements among all principals involved that are reached without going to court. There are three kinds of such settlements: extensions, compositions, and assignments.

Extensions When the firm is unable to make payment to its creditors on schedule it will usually approach them and ask for more time. If the creditors agree, they are granting the firm an *extension*. The extension extends the due date and provides for a repayment schedule. Because an extension is somewhat risky—things could get worse instead of better—creditors are hesitant to grant an extension unless they feel the firm is: (1) trustworthy and (2) has a good chance of recovering from its current financial difficulties.

In negotiating for an extension the firm will stress that any other form of settlement will be less satisfactory from the standpoint of the creditor recovering the full amount owed by the firm within a reasonable length of time. This is because other settlements provide either for only a fractional repayment of the debt and/or involve a considerable delay in time, as the courts decide what is a fair and equitable division of the firm's assets. If some creditors involved do not agree to the extension, and their claims are relatively small, the consenting creditors may permit these dissenting creditors to be paid in full to avoid the possibility of a bankruptcy proceeding. If the dissenting creditors' total claims are too large, however, there is little hope of reaching an acceptable extension agreement since the consenting creditors would be afraid of being left on a sinking ship while others get off. Furthermore, the extension agreement will probably include some legal safeguards for the consenting creditors. These safeguards vary from assignment of assets as collateral (explained below), to required approval of some of the operations of the firm, to countersigning disbursement checks.

Compositions   In a composition the creditors agree to receive fractional settlement of their claims. Rather than accept a composition the creditors may force the firm into bankruptcy, but this substantially prolongs the payment date, and there are substantial costs involved in bankruptcy proceedings that may further reduce the amount of payment the creditors eventually receive. Consequently, the creditors will often be better off if they accept a composition. The fraction of payment ultimately decided upon is negotiated by the firm and the creditors and must be agreed to by all creditors involved. As in extensions, dissenting creditors can be paid off in full if their total claims are not too large. If no agreement can be reached with dissenting creditors, they can force the firm into bankruptcy proceedings.

Assignments   An assignment is a liquidation of the firm that takes place without going through court. An assignment is appropriate when it is apparent that there is little hope of the firm recovering from the difficulty it is in, and when all claimants (creditors and stockholders) agree on the terms of the liquidation. Hence, there is no need to have the courts supervise the liquidation. There are technical differences among various kinds of assignments, but the main features of an assignment are: (1) liquidation, carried out (2) without recourse to courts. If all claimants can agree that the assignment is fair, considerable costs can be saved and passed on to the claimants by avoiding bankruptcy proceedings. However, if the claimants can't agree on a fair liquidation, then the firm will be pushed into bankruptcy.

In-court settlements: Bankruptcy

In lieu of an out-of-court settlement the courts may be called upon to supervise the liquidation or reorganization of the failed firm. These in-court settlements are called bankruptcy proceedings. While there are both state and federal bankruptcy laws and procedures, our discussion will be directed toward federal bankruptcy procedures.

Procedure   The basis for federal bankruptcy proceedings is the National Bankruptcy Act. A petition for bankruptcy proceedings may be filed *voluntarily* by the firm or it may be filed by creditors to bring the firm *involuntarily* into bankruptcy. A petition for involuntary bankruptcy proceedings charges that the firm has committed one or more of the six *acts of bankruptcy* within the preceding four months:

1. *Committing fraud while insolvent.*   If the firm tries to transfer assets with the intent of denying creditors access to these assets, or if the firm tries to hide assets, the firm has committed fraud. Committing fraud while insolvent is an act of bankruptcy, and creditors can legally force the firm into bankruptcy.
2. *Preferential disposition of assets while insolvent.*   If, while insolvent, the firm gives undue preference to some creditors over others by transferring title to or permitting seizure of assets that are not legally owned by these creditors, the firm may be forced into

bankruptcy. This protects creditors from not receiving their fair share of the firm's assets.

3. *Failure to remove liens while insolvent.* If, while insolvent, the firm permits a creditor to obtain a lien (a legal right to possess) on any of the firm's assets, and fails to remove the lien within 30 days, the firm may be forced into bankruptcy. This also prevents the firm from giving preferential treatment to some creditors.

4. *Assignment.* Whether or not the firm is insolvent, if it makes an assignment (a voluntary liquidation), the firm may be forced into bankruptcy. This protects dissident creditors from being forced into assignments they feel are unfair to them.

5. *Appointment of a receiver or trustee while insolvent.* If the firm voluntarily accepts the appointment of either a receiver or trustee while insolvent, the firm may be forced into bankruptcy. This protects creditors from having the disposition of the firm's assets administered by someone who may not be impartial and fair.

6. *Written admission of insolvency.* If the firm admits in writing it is unable to meet its due obligations, it may be forced into bankruptcy. When creditors conclude that the only way they will recover what is owed them is through bankruptcy proceedings, and the firm is unwilling to declare voluntary bankruptcy, this affords the creditors a way to force the issue.

Bankruptcy administration   After a petition for involuntary bankruptcy is filed the firm is given a chance to challenge the assertion that it committed an act of bankruptcy as charged. A hearing will be conducted and a decision made as to whether the firm is indeed bankrupt. If the firm is adjudged bankrupt, or if the petition was voluntary, the court will appoint administrators to resolve the bankruptcy.

Referee.   A bankruptcy referee is appointed by the court to oversee the bankruptcy proceedings. In effect, the referee becomes the judge of the proceedings, and his actions and decisions are binding on all parties subject to review of the court. The referee is responsible for notifying all parties affected by the proceedings, for keeping detailed records of all activities and transactions, and for successfully concluding the proceedings.

Receiver.   The receiver in bankruptcy is a short-term custodian assigned by the court to serve as guardian of the firm's assets until a full-time administrator (a trustee) can be appointed by the court to dispose of the firm's assets. Since this latter appointment may take some time, the receiver's primary responsibility is to protect the firm's assets from any further deterioration until the court appoints a trustee.

Trustee.   At the first postbankruptcy meeting of the creditors an election is held to select a trustee in bankruptcy; however, if the creditors cannot agree, or if their choice is unacceptable to the court, the court may intercede and appoint the trustee. The responsibilities of the trustee are: (1) to prepare a list of all the firm's assets and claims on the assets, (2) to conduct an evaluation to determine whether the firm should be liquidated or reorganized, and (3) to carry out either the liquidation or reorganization after the court approves the plan.

EVALUATION OF BANKRUPTCIES

One of the trustee's responsibilities is to decide what should be done with the bankrupt firm. Should it be liquidated or reorganized? The basis for this decision is a comparative evaluation. The trustee will estimate: (1) what the firm could be liquidated for, (2) what the value of a reorganized firm would be, and (3) what price a merger might bring. Because these evaluations are subjective, whatever the decision, there is almost sure to be criticism by some of the interested parties who feel they received less than they deserve.

To guide us through the comparative evaluation, we'll use an extended illustration. Assume that Figure 22-2 is a balance sheet for Spitzer Novelties, a firm recently adjudged bankrupt, and the trustee assigned to the case is facing the problem of deciding what to do with the firm. We'll use this illustration to work through the three alternatives noted above.

FIGURE 22-2

SPITZER NOVELTIES, INC.

Current assets	$1,400,000	
Net long-term assets	4,100,000	
Total Assets		$5,500,000
Accounts payable	600,000	
Notes payable	1,000,000	
Accrued taxes and wages	200,000	
Mortgage bonds*	2,000,000	
Debentures	1,000,000	
Total Liabilities		4,800,000
Preferred stock	600,000	
Common stock	1,000,000	
Retained earnings	(900,000)	
Stockholders' equity		700,000
Liabilities + Stockholders' Equity		$5,500,000

* Mortgage bonds are secured by all the firm's plant and equipment.

Liquidation

Liquidation evaluation begins with the trustee estimating the sale value of the firm's assets. The balance sheet indicates the firm's assets are worth $5.5 million. But balance sheet values are book values, and these may have no close relationship with realizable liquidation values. Liquidations are distress sales in the truest sense, and assets, either current or long term, rarely can be sold for anything other than some fraction of book value in most such situations. Companies in industries with highly specialized inventories and equipment will have particular difficulties since there will be a limited number of prospective buyers.

After considerable time and effort the trustee has prepared the following schedule of projected liquidation values for the firm's assets:

Estimated liquidation proceeds

Cash and securities	$ 100,000
Collection of accounts receivable............	100,000
Sale of inventory	700,000
Sale of plant and equipment	1,200,000
Sale of land.......................................	2,000,000
Total liquidation value.................	$4,100,000

We notice first that there has been a tremendous shrinkage of the value of the assets from what the balance sheet shows. This reflects that some of the accounts receivable are judged to be uncollectable (although the trustee will make every legal effort to collect them), some of the inventory is obsolete, and part of the plant and equipment is old. About half of the value of the firm comes from the land the plant sits on.

The next step is to decide how to distribute the $4.1 million to the claimants if the firm is liquidated. In determining the allocation the trustee will be guided by the *rule of absolute priority*, which says that there is a legally recognized priority of claims beginning with priority creditors and ending with common stockholders. The senior claimants (those high up on the priority ladder) must have their legal claims honored before those of the junior claimants (those low on the priority ladder). Applying the rule to this illustration, the trustee would first satisfy the priority creditors:

Priority creditors	*Claims*	*Distribution*
Bankruptcy costs*............	$ 800,000	$ 800,000
Accrued wages	60,000	60,000
Accrued taxes.................	140,000	140,000
	$1,000,000	$1,000,000

* Legal fees, court costs, and trustee administration costs.

Next, the trustee would turn to the secured creditors' claims: In this example, secured creditors (mortgage bonds) have claims of $2 million and a distribution of $1.2 million. Notice that despite the fact there is $3.1 million remaining after the priority creditors' claims are satisfied, which is more than the $2 million owed the mortgage bonds, only $1.2 million can be earmarked for the bonds as a secured claim. This is because the assets securing the bonds (all the firm's plant and equipment) can only be liquidated for $1.2 million. The remaining portion of the mortgage bond claims ($800,000) will go into general creditors' claims and be paid off, in full if there is enough money or pro rata if there is not. After satisfying the legal claims of the secured creditors there would be $1.9 million remaining ($3,100,000 − $1,200,000) for all other claimants. The trustee would now consider general creditors, who will receive their pro rata share of the remaining $1.9 million.

General creditors	Claims	Pro rata (percent)	Pro rata distribution
Accounts payable ...	$ 600,000	17.6	$ 334,000
Notes payable	1,000,000	29.4	559,000
Mortgage bonds	800,000	23.6	448,000
Debentures	1,000,000	29.4	559,000
	$3,400,000	100.0	$1,900,000

Total general creditor claims amount to $3.4 million, but only $1.9 million is available for distribution, so two things are immediately clear: (1) The general creditors' claims will not be fully honored and (2) preferred and common stockholders will receive *nothing*. There simply are not enough assets to go around, and the big losers under this liquidation plan will be the preferred and common stockholders. In summary, the liquidation plan, including distribution of proceeds and percent recovery of each claimant's claim, is shown in the following table:

Claimant	Claim	Proceeds received	Percent claim received
Accounts payable	$ 600,000	$ 334,000	56
Notes payable	1,000,000	559,000	56
Accrued taxes and wages	200,000	200,000	100
Mortgage bonds	2,000,000	1,648,000	82
Debentures	1,000,000	559,000	56
Preferred stock.................	600,000	0	0
Common stock	100,000	0	0
Bankruptcy costs	800,000	800,000	100
Total......................	$6,300,000	$4,100,000	

There are several interesting points revealed in this liquidation plan. First, the only claimants "made whole" (receiving 100 percent of their claim) are the priority creditors: the bankruptcy administration costs and the accrued taxes and wages accounts.[4] All other creditors would lose part of their principal under this liquidation plan, with the mortgage bond holders in the best position because of the extra protection of their secured claim on the firm's plant and equipment. We emphasize once again that the preferred and common stockholders would receive nothing. It is also worth noting the large bankruptcy costs. Bankruptcy costs are, in general, very high, averaging somewhere around 25 percent of the value of the firm's assets. Going into bankruptcy in this case cost the

---

[4] Usually, the wages claims are not made whole because the owed wages are greater than the legal minimum of $600 per worker.

creditors $800,000. If they could have reached an out-of-court liquidation agreement (an assignment), they could have saved this $800,000. However, it may have been impossible for them to have reached such an agreement.

Reorganization

In addition to estimating how much the firm is worth "dead" (liquidated), the trustee will also estimate how much the firm is worth "alive" via a reorganization. This evaluation requires the trustee to consider both *external* and *internal* reorganization possibilities. An external reorganization would be where the trustee seeks out a merger partner for the bankrupt firm, and an internal reorganization would be a recapitalization of the bankrupt firm, reducing its debt position to a manageable level.

Reorganization, whether internal or external, requires that the proposed plan satisfy both *fairness* and *feasibility* standards. The fairness doctrine primarily requires that the reorganization be consistent with the rule of absolute priority. But the fairness doctrine also requires that the value received by the claimants in the proposed reorganization is satisfactory in terms of risk and return in comparison to other alternative reorganization plans and to possible liquidation. This doctrine can create some difficulty because the financial claims given to various claimants under a reorganization will frequently not be the same kind of claims that the claimants currently have. If, for example, the reorganization is arranged so that debenture holders receive preferred or even common stock, clearly these claimants are not receiving equivalent financial claims to their previous holdings. The crucial test, however, is what alternatives are available. If the only other alternative to the proposed reorganization is liquidation, and the debenture holders will receive less under liquidation than they would under the reorganization, then the reorganization satisfies the fairness standard. In some cases the Securities and Exchange Commission (SEC) will make an independent appraisal of the reorganization and will apprise the court of their opinion of the fairness of the plan. The SEC's role is purely advisory, and the court is not obligated to accept the SEC's conclusion that the plan is unfair; however, the SEC has had a major impact on the valuation process that leads to a proposed plan.

The feasibility doctrine requires that the proposed reorganization results in a firm that would not face the same difficulties as the bankrupt firm. That is, there should be no substantial chance of a repetition of failure. Basically this requires two assurances. First, any and all operating difficulties (like incompetent management personnel, poor inventory management, poor receivables policies, etc.) have been identified and can reasonably be expected to be corrected after the reorganization. This ensures that the fundamental earning power of the reorganized firm will be sufficient to justify its continued existence. Second, the capital structure of the reorganized firm must be arranged such that the firm will not fail because it is top-heavy with debt. This ensures that the reorganized firm will be financially sound. If both of these conditions can be reasonably assured, then the reorganization is said to be feasible.

Internal reorganization An internal reorganization requires the trustee to evaluate the firm as an ongoing enterprise. This means that the trustee must estimate the market value of the reorganized firm. The internal reorganization evaluation process has several steps:

1. Determine if the reorganization is infeasible because of management problems.
2. Estimate the expected cash flows the firm will generate after the reorganization.
3. Estimate the cost of capital for the reorganized firm.
4. Establish a market value for the firm by discounting the expected cash flows at the estimated cost of capital.
5. Establish a feasible capital structure for the reorganized firm.
6. Determine the distribution of new financial claims to the firm's claimants.

None of these steps are easy, but Steps 2, 3, and 4 are particularly difficult because they are so subjective. The question of the feasibility of the reorganization is explicitly considered in Steps 1 and 5. Step 1 directly addresses this question from the managerial side. If the management looks incompetent or is uninterested in reconstructing the firm, there is little hope of a successful reorganization. Consequently, there would be no reason to proceed with a detailed evaluation. Capital structure feasibility is directly considered in Step 5. The trustee must take special care that the proposed structure is not so debt heavy that the reorganized firm will have difficulty meeting its interest obligations.

In further analyzing the internal reorganization procedure let's pick up the Spitzer Novelties illustration again. After careful consideration, including conferences with Spitzer management and inquiries with outside parties concerning their managerial ability, the trustee decides that the current management team is both willing and able to successfully carry out a reorganization. The trustee is also satisfied that all past operating problems that have bothered the company can be resolved. The trustee is then prepared to begin his evaluation, which is shown in Figure 22–3.

As the work sheet indicates, the trustee thinks that sales will be either $3 million, $4 million or $4.5 million. He also has listed his beliefs about the probabilities associated with these sales and the resultant net operating incomes. The expected net operating income is $265,000 per year and the estimated average cost of capital is 10 percent, which leads to an estimated valuation of the reorganized firm of $2,650,000. This figure is considerably lower than the $4,100,000 liquidation value the trustee estimated for the firm, which means that creditors would rather have the firm liquidated than reorganized *internally*. There is still the possibility of a more attractive external reorganization, however.

External reorganization In seeking a business combination partner for the bankrupt firm the trustee keeps two things in mind. First, he will recommend merger over liquidation or internal reorganization only when the value offered to the bankrupt firm from the merger is the largest of the three alternatives. This is in accordance with the fairness doctrine. Second, the trustee must evaluate the feasibility of the proposed merger.

Reorganization may be accomplished internally, where the firm is scaled down and recapitalized, or externally in a merger.

QUESTIONS

1. Define the following terms and phrases.
    a. Technical insolvency.
    b. Priority creditors.
    c. General creditors.
    d. Extensions.
    e. Compositions.
    f. Assignments.
    g. Reorganization.

2. While failure of the firm has a commonly understood meaning there are actually two distinctly different kinds of failure. Identify and contrast them.

3. Marshall Insurance Co. forsees some financial difficulties on the horizon and is making some preliminary resource mobilization plans. Which of the actions listed below are likely to provide funds to Marshall within a three-month period and which are likely to take longer?
    a. Cutting back on a planned capital expenditure
    b. Issuing new bonds
    c. Arranging a term loan at the bank
    d. Selling some marketable securities
    e. Reducing research costs
    f. Factoring receivables
    g. Cutting back production and laying off some production workers
    h. Selling some equipment

4. Generally speaking there are five broad categories of claimants on the failed firm's assets.
    a. Identify these categories and their relative priority.
    b. Which of these five categories do the following groups fall into?
        (1) First mortgage bondholders
        (2) Employees
        (3) Trade creditors
        (4) Government tax authorities
        (5) Convertible preferred stockholders

5. Briefly explain the duties of the following bankruptcy administrators:
    a. Referee
    b. Receiver
    c. Trustee

6. Explain the "fairness" and "feasibility" doctrines with respect to proposed corporate reorganizations.

7. Since bankruptcy counts normally place creditors in a preferred position relative to common stockholders, explain why creditors often prefer some sort of out-of-court settlement to an in-court settlement.

8. In what sense may a creditor be both a secured *and* a general creditor?

PROBLEMS

1. Consider the following financial data about a bankrupt firm that is to be liquidated.

Assets
Current assets................................. $2,000,000
Net long-term assets 8,000,000
    Total Assets.......................... $10,000,000

Liabilities
Accounts payable........................... $ 400,000
Notes payable 1,000,000
Accrued taxes................................ 500,000
Accrued wages 100,000
Mortgage bonds (secured by
  plant and equipment) 4,000,000
Debentures 1,000,000
Subordinated debentures (subordi-
  nated to notes payable) 1,000,000
    Total Liabilities 8,000,000
Preferred stock.............................. 1,500,000
Common stock 3,000,000
Retained earnings........................... (2,500,000)
    Stockholders' Equity............... 2,000,000

    Total Liabilities and
     Stockholders' Equity....... $10,000,000

Bankruptcy costs.... $1,000,000

Proceeds from liquidation
Cash and securities................ $ 100,000
Collection of accounts
  receivable......................... 700,000
Sale of inventory 400,000
Sale of plant and equipment 2,000,000
Sale of land 3,000,000
    Total Proceeds.............. $6,200,000

   a. Determine the distribution of the proceeds assuming the rule of absolute priority and that *all* accrued wages are priority claims.
   b. Assuming that inventory proceeds can be increased, how much larger must these proceeds be before the notes payable holders are made whole in an in-court settlement?
   c. How much must the total proceeds be for all creditors to be made whole:
    (1) With an in-court settlement?
    (2) With an out-of-court settlement?

  d. How much must the total proceeds be for the preferred stockholders to receive $0.25 on the dollar with an in-court settlement?

2. In reference to problem 1, assume that total proceeds increase beyond the original $6.2 million received but that none of these in-
creased proceeds come from increased plant and equipment sales.
How large must total proceeds be to assure the subordinated debenture holders $0.50 on the dollar in an in-court settlement?

3. Prior to reorganization, the Nickel Mining Company had the following capital structure:

Mortgage bonds..................	$1,000,000
Debentures.......................	500,000
Preferred stock	500,000
Common stock	2,000,000
	$4,000,000

Determine the distribution of the new securities under each of the
following reorganization plans assuming the rule of absolute priority.

	(a)	(b)	(c)
Debentures	$ 500,000	$ 500,000	$ 750,000
Income bonds.................	250,000	500,000	500,000
Preferred stock...............	250,000	250,000	500,000
Common stock	500,000	750,000	750,000
	$1,500,000	$2,000,000	$2,500,000

4. Franklin Alexander, trustee in bankruptcy for the Dohme Glass Company, is evaluating the alternatives for resolving the financial difficulties facing Dohme. Alexander has estimated the liquidation value
of the company to be $800,000. However, he has received an offer
from the General Paper and Plastics Company to merge with Dohme.
General Paper and Plastics would pay $900,000 for the company.
Before making his decision, Alexander has decided to determine the
value of Dohme if it were to be internally reorganized. Toward this
end, he has prepared the following estimates.

Probability..................	0.1	0.2	0.4	0.2	0.1
Sales per year..............	$1,000,000	$1,500,000	$2,500,000	$3,000,000	$4,000,000
Cost of goods sold					
per year....................	870,000	1,290,000	2,125,000	2,520,000	3,320,000
Operating expenses					
per year....................	90,000	125,000	175,000	200,000	250,000

Given that the reorganized firm will be fairly risky, Alexander has
estimated a discount rate of 20%.

    a. Determine the expected value of the reorganized firm.

    b. Should Dohme be liquidated, merged with General Paper and Plastics, or reorganized? Why?

5. In reference to problem 4:

Alexander has three alternatives for capitalizing the reorganized firm.

	Capital structure		
	Plan I	Plan II	Plan III
Bonds (14% interest)...............	$ 625,000	$ 400,000	$ 275,000
Preferred stock (16% dividend)...	75,000	100,000	25,000
Common stock ($10 par)	300,000	500,000	700,000
	$1,000,000	$1,000,000	$1,000,000

    a. Determine the probability of insolvency, where insolvency is defined as not being able to meet interest payments.

    b. Which plans are feasible and which are not if Alexander will tolerate no more than a 10-percent chance of technical insolvency?

    c. The capital structure at time of failure for Dohme Glass was as follows:

Debt.............................	$ 750,000
Preferred stock...................	250,000
Common stock	1,000,000
	$2,000,000

Determine the distribution of the new securities under each feasible plan using the rule of absolute priority.

    d. Determine expected earnings per share of common stock under each feasible plan if the tax rate is 50 percent.

    e. If the anticipated *P/E* ratio is five under Plan I and six under Plan II, which plan would the original preferred stockholders favor? Why?

    f. Which plan would you expect the trustee to recommend? Why?

6. C. B. Beall, a financial analyst for the Walrock Manufacturing Company, has received the following memo from his boss, the vice president for finance.

TO: C. B. Beall
FROM: V.P. Finance
SUBJECT: Resource Mobilization Worksheet
I'm concerned about the recent deterioration in some of our financial ratios. In case any problems develop, I'd like to know what resources we could have available within a 3-month and 12-month time period. Please prepare a Resource Mobilization Worksheet using the following points as guidelines:

1. We have no surplus cash, but we do have $5,000 in U.S. Treasury Bills that could be liquidated.
2. As you know, we have a policy of taking trade discounts. I don't want to change this.
3. The money and capital markets and our own circumstances indicate that it won't be possible to obtain any new debt or equity financing. However, we still have $50,000 available from our line of credit with First National Bank.
4. I feel that any liquidity problems that develop would be temporary, so let's not plan for any production cuts or the sale of any plant, equipment, or land.
5. We have a $200,000 dividend payment planned in two months, but I think that can be reduced. You'll have to estimate this.
6. Capital expenditures of $500,000 are planned, but these can probably be cut also.
7. I've talked to Johnson in the lab, and he agrees that we can chop $50,000 from their annual budget with no real difficulty.
8. We're locked in on the marketing budget for the next three months, but for the remaining nine months, I think we can negotiate some reduction from its planned level of $40,000 per month.
9. If we can't have at least $125,000 available within the next three months, plan on getting the balance from the sale of inventories.
10. If we can't have at least $300,000 additional resources available within 12 months, we'll get the balance from a reduction of some overhead costs.

After receiving this memo, Beall made the following preliminary estimates about the possibilities of affecting cuts in the dividend, capital expenditures and the marketing budget.

Dividends					
Percent reduction...........	100	75	50	25	0
Probability.....................	0.05	0.1	0.25	0.4	0.2
Capital expenditures					
Percent reduction...........	50	40	30	20	10
Probability.....................	0.1	0.3	0.3	0.2	0.1
Marketing budget					
Percent reduction...........	50	25	10	0	
Probability.....................	0.1	0.2	0.4	0.3	

Using *expected* reductions, prepare the Resource Mobilization work sheet that Beall will send to the financial vice president.

SELECTED BASIC REFERENCES

DeWitt, N. P. "How to Survive a Corporate Financial Crisis," *Corporate Financing* (March–April 1973), pp. 25–29, 76–77.

Donaldson, G. "Strategy for Financial Emergencies," *Harvard Business Review* (November–December 1969), pp. 67–79.

Krause, S. "Chapters X and XI – A Study in Contrasts," *Business Lawyer* (January 1964), pp. 511–26.

Van Arsdell, P. M. *Corporation Finance.* New York: Ronald Press, 1968, Chapters 48–53.

SELECTED ADVANCED REFERENCES

Altman, E. I. "Financial Ratios, Discriminant Analysis and the Prediction of Corporate Bankruptcy," *Journal of Finance* (September 1968), pp. 589–609.

Beaver, W. H. "Financial Ratios as Predictors of Failure," *Empirical Research in Accounting: Selected Studies,* supplement to *Journal of Accounting Research* (1966), pp. 71–111.

Gordon, M. J. "Towards a Theory of Financial Distress," *Journal of Finance* (May 1971), pp. 347–56.

Walter, J. E. "Determination of Technical Insolvency," *Journal of Business* (January 1957), pp. 30–43.

APPENDIX: TABLES

TABLE A
Compound factors (CF)

Period (n)	Percent (i) 1	2	3	4	5	6	7
1	1.010	1.020	1.030	1.040	1.050	1.060	1.070
2	1.020	1.040	1.061	1.082	1.103	1.124	1.145
3	1.030	1.061	1.093	1.125	1.158	1.191	1.225
4	1.041	1.082	1.126	1.170	1.216	1.262	1.311
5	1.051	1.104	1.159	1.217	1.276	1.338	1.403
6	1.062	1.126	1.194	1.265	1.340	1.419	1.501
7	1.072	1.149	1.230	1.316	1.407	1.504	1.606
8	1.083	1.172	1.267	1.369	1.477	1.594	1.718
9	1.094	1.195	1.305	1.423	1.551	1.689	1.838
10	1.105	1.219	1.344	1.480	1.629	1.791	1.967
11	1.116	1.243	1.384	1.539	1.710	1.898	2.105
12	1.127	1.268	1.426	1.601	1.796	2.012	2.252
13	1.138	1.294	1.469	1.665	1.886	2.133	2.410
14	1.149	1.319	1.513	1.732	1.980	2.261	2.579
15	1.161	1.346	1.558	1.801	2.079	2.397	2.759
16	1.173	1.373	1.605	1.873	2.183	2.540	2.952
17	1.184	1.400	1.653	1.948	2.292	2.693	3.159
18	1.196	1.428	1.702	2.026	2.407	2.854	3.380
19	1.208	1.457	1.754	2.107	2.527	3.026	3.617
20	1.220	1.486	1.806	2.191	2.653	3.207	3.870
25	1.282	1.641	2.094	2.666	3.386	4.292	5.427
30	1.348	1.811	2.427	3.243	4.322	5.743	7.612
40	1.489	2.208	3.262	4.801	7.040	10.286	14.974
50	1.645	2.692	4.384	7.107	11.467	18.420	29.457

Period (n)	Percent (i)						
	8	9	10	11	12	13	14
1	1.080	1.090	1.100	1.110	1.120	1.130	1.140
2	1.166	1.188	1.210	1.232	1.254	1.277	1.300
3	1.260	1.295	1.331	1.368	1.405	1.443	1.482
4	1.360	1.412	1.464	1.518	1.574	1.630	1.689
5	1.469	1.539	1.611	1.685	1.762	1.842	1.925
6	1.587	1.677	1.772	1.870	1.974	2.082	2.195
7	1.714	1.828	1.949	2.076	2.211	2.353	2.502
8	1.851	1.993	2.144	2.305	2.476	2.658	2.853
9	1.999	2.172	2.358	2.558	2.773	3.004	3.252
10	2.159	2.367	2.594	2.839	3.106	3.395	3.707
11	2.332	2.580	2.853	3.152	3.479	3.836	4.226
12	2.518	2.813	3.138	3.498	3.896	4.335	4.818
13	2.720	3.066	3.452	3.883	4.363	4.898	5.492
14	2.937	3.342	3.797	4.310	4.887	5.535	6.261
15	3.172	3.642	4.177	4.785	5.474	6.254	7.138
16	3.426	3.970	4.595	5.311	6.130	7.067	8.137
17	3.700	4.328	5.054	5.895	6.866	7.986	9.276
18	3.996	4.717	5.560	6.544	7.690	9.024	10.575
19	4.316	5.142	6.116	7.263	8.613	10.197	12.056
20	4.661	5.604	6.727	8.062	9.646	11.523	13.743
25	6.848	8.623	10.835	13.585	17.000	21.231	26.462
30	10.063	13.268	17.449	22.892	29.960	39.116	50.950
40	21.725	31.409	45.259	65.001	93.051	132.78	188.88
50	46.902	74.358	117.39	184.57	289.00	450.74	700.23

TABLE A (CF) (concluded)

Period (n)				Percent (i)				
	15	16	17	18	19	20	25	30
1	1.150	1.160	1.170	1.180	1.190	1.200	1.250	1.300
2	1.323	1.346	1.369	1.392	1.416	1.440	1.563	1.690
3	1.521	1.561	1.602	1.643	1.685	1.728	1.953	2.197
4	1.749	1.811	1.874	1.939	2.005	2.074	2.441	2.856
5	2.011	2.100	2.192	2.288	2.386	2.488	3.052	3.713
6	2.313	2.436	2.565	2.700	2.840	2.986	3.815	4.827
7	2.660	2.826	3.001	3.185	3.379	3.583	4.768	6.276
8	3.059	3.278	3.511	3.759	4.021	4.300	5.960	8.157
9	3.518	3.803	4.108	4.435	4.785	5.160	7.451	10.604
10	4.046	4.411	4.807	5.234	5.696	6.192	9.313	13.786
11	4.652	5.117	5.624	6.176	6.777	7.430	11.642	17.922
12	5.350	5.936	6.580	7.288	8.064	8.916	14.552	23.298
13	6.153	6.886	7.699	8.599	9.596	10.699	18.190	30.288
14	7.076	7.988	9.007	10.147	11.420	12.839	22.737	39.374
15	8.137	9.266	10.539	11.974	13.590	15.407	28.422	51.186
16	9.358	10.748	12.330	14.129	16.172	18.488	35.527	66.542
17	10.761	12.468	14.426	16.672	19.244	22.186	44.409	86.504
18	12.375	14.463	16.879	19.673	22.091	26.623	55.511	112.46
19	14.232	16.777	19.748	23.214	27.252	31.948	69.389	146.19
20	16.367	19.461	23.106	27.393	32.429	38.338	86.736	190.05
25	32.919	40.874	50.658	62.669	77.388	95.396	264.70	705.64
30	66.212	85.850	111.07	143.37	184.68	237.38	807.79	2,620.0
40	267.86	378.72	533.87	750.38	1,051.7	1,469.8	7,523.2	36,119.
50	1,083.7	1,670.7	2,566.2	3,927.4	5,988.9	9,100.4	70,065.	497,929.

TABLE B
Annuity compound factors (ACF)

Period (n)	Percent (i)						
	1	2	3	4	5	6	7
1	1.000	1.000	1.000	1.000	1.000	1.000	1.000
2	2.010	2.020	2.030	2.040	2.050	2.060	2.070
3	3.030	3.060	3.091	3.122	3.153	3.184	3.215
4	4.060	4.122	4.184	4.246	4.310	4.375	4.440
5	5.101	5.204	5.309	5.416	5.526	5.637	5.751
6	6.152	6.308	6.468	6.633	6.802	6.975	7.153
7	7.214	7.434	7.662	7.898	8.142	8.394	8.654
8	8.286	8.583	8.892	9.214	9.549	9.897	10.260
9	9.369	9.755	10.159	10.583	11.027	11.491	11.978
10	10.462	10.950	11.464	12.006	12.578	13.181	13.816
11	11.567	12.169	12.808	13.486	14.207	14.972	15.784
12	12.683	13.412	14.192	15.026	15.917	16.870	17.888
13	13.809	14.680	15.618	16.627	17.713	18.882	20.141
14	14.947	15.974	17.086	18.292	19.599	21.015	22.550
15	16.097	17.293	18.599	20.024	21.579	23.276	25.129
16	17.258	18.639	20.157	21.825	23.657	25.673	27.888
17	18.430	20.012	21.762	23.698	25.840	20.213	30.840
18	19.615	21.412	23.414	25.645	28.132	30.906	33.999
19	20.811	22.841	25.117	27.671	30.539	33.760	37.379
20	22.019	24.297	26.870	29.778	33.066	36.786	40.995
25	28.243	32.030	36.459	41.646	47.727	54.865	63.249
30	34.785	40.588	47.575	56.085	66.439	79.058	94.461
40	48.886	60.402	75.401	95.026	120.80	154.76	199.64
50	64.463	84.579	112.80	152.67	209.35	290.34	406.53

TABLE B (ACF) (continued)

Period (n)	Percent (i)							
	8	9	10	11	12	13	14	15
1	1.000	1.000	1.000	1.000	1.000	1.000	1.000	1.000
2	2.080	2.090	2.100	2.110	2.120	2.130	2.140	2.150
3	3.246	3.278	3.310	3.342	3.374	3.407	3.440	3.473
4	4.506	4.573	4.641	4.710	4.779	4.850	4.921	4.993
5	5.867	5.985	6.105	6.228	6.353	6.480	6.610	6.742
6	7.336	7.523	7.716	7.913	8.115	8.323	8.536	8.754
7	8.923	9.200	9.487	9.783	10.089	10.405	10.730	11.067
8	10.637	11.028	11.436	11.859	12.300	12.757	13.233	13.727
9	12.488	13.021	13.579	14.164	14.776	15.416	16.085	16.786
10	14.487	15.193	15.937	16.722	17.549	18.420	19.337	20.304
11	16.645	17.560	18.531	19.561	20.655	21.814	23.045	24.349
12	18.977	20.141	21.384	22.713	24.133	25.650	27.271	29.002
13	21.495	22.953	24.523	26.212	28.029	29.985	32.089	34.352
14	24.215	26.019	27.975	30.095	32.393	34.883	37.581	40.505
15	27.152	29.361	31.772	34.405	37.280	40.417	43.842	47.580
16	30.324	33.003	35.950	39.190	42.753	46.672	50.980	55.717
17	33.750	36.974	40.545	44.501	48.884	53.739	59.118	65.075
18	37.450	41.301	45.599	50.396	55.750	61.725	68.394	75.836
19	41.446	46.018	51.159	56.939	63.440	70.749	78.969	88.212
20	45.762	51.160	57.275	64.203	72.052	80.947	91.025	102.44
25	73.106	84.701	98.347	114.41	133.33	155.62	181.87	212.79
30	113.28	136.31	164.49	199.02	241.33	293.20	356.79	434.75
40	259.06	337.89	442.59	581.83	767.09	1,013.7	1,342.0	1,779.1
50	573.77	815.08	1,163.9	1,668.8	2,400.0	3,459.5	4,994.5	7,217.7

TABLE B (ACF) (concluded)

Period (n)	Percent (i)						
	16	17	18	19	20	25	30
1	1.000	1.000	1.000	1.000	1.000	1.000	1.000
2	2.160	2.170	2.180	2.190	2.200	2.250	2.300
3	3.506	3.539	3.572	3.606	3.640	3.813	3.990
4	5.066	5.141	5.215	5.291	5.368	5.766	6.187
5	6.877	7.014	7.154	7.297	7.442	8.207	9.043
6	8.977	9.207	9.442	9.683	9.930	11.259	12.756
7	11.414	11.772	12.142	12.523	12.916	15.073	17.583
8	14.240	14.773	15.327	15.902	16.499	19.842	23.858
9	17.519	18.285	19.086	19.923	20.799	25.802	32.015
10	21.321	22.393	23.521	24.701	25.959	33.253	42.619
11	25.733	27.200	28.755	30.404	32.150	42.566	56.405
12	30.850	32.824	34.931	37.180	39.581	54.208	74.327
13	36.786	39.404	42.219	45.244	48.497	68.760	97.625
14	43.672	47.103	50.818	54.841	59.196	86.949	127.91
15	51.660	56.110	60.965	66.261	72.035	109.69	167.29
16	60.925	66.649	72.939	79.850	87.442	138.11	218.47
17	71.673	78.979	87.068	96.022	105.93	173.64	285.01
18	84.141	93.406	103.74	115.27	128.12	218.05	371.52
19	98.603	110.29	123.41	138.17	154.74	273.56	483.97
20	115.38	130.03	146.63	165.42	186.69	342.95	630.17
25	249.21	292.11	342.60	402.04	471.98	1,054.8	2,348.80
30	530.31	647.44	790.95	966.7	1,181.9	3,227.2	8,730.0
40	2,360.8	3,134.5	4,163.21	5,529.8	7,343.9	30,089.	120,393.
50	10,436.	15,090.	21,813.	31,515.	45,497.	280,256.	165,976.

TABLE C
Discount factors (DF)

Period (n)	Percent (i)								
	1	2	3	4	5	6	7	8	9
1	0.990	0.980	0.971	0.962	0.952	0.943	0.935	0.926	0.917
2	0.980	0.961	0.943	0.925	0.907	0.890	0.873	0.857	0.842
3	0.971	0.942	0.915	0.889	0.864	0.840	0.816	0.794	0.772
4	0.961	0.924	0.888	0.855	0.823	0.792	0.763	0.735	0.708
5	0.951	0.906	0.863	0.822	0.784	0.747	0.713	0.681	0.650
6	0.942	0.888	0.837	0.790	0.746	0.705	0.666	0.630	0.596
7	0.933	0.871	0.813	0.760	0.711	0.665	0.623	0.583	0.547
8	0.923	0.853	0.789	0.731	0.677	0.627	0.582	0.540	0.502
9	0.914	0.837	0.766	0.703	0.645	0.592	0.544	0.500	0.460
10	0.905	0.820	0.744	0.676	0.614	0.558	0.508	0.463	0.422
11	0.896	0.804	0.722	0.650	0.585	0.527	0.475	0.429	0.388
12	0.887	0.788	0.701	0.625	0.557	0.497	0.444	0.397	0.356
13	0.879	0.773	0.681	0.601	0.530	0.469	0.415	0.368	0.326
14	0.870	0.758	0.661	0.577	0.505	0.442	0.388	0.340	0.299
15	0.861	0.743	0.642	0.555	0.481	0.417	0.362	0.315	0.275
16	0.853	0.728	0.623	0.534	0.458	0.394	0.339	0.292	0.252
17	0.844	0.714	0.605	0.513	0.436	0.371	0.317	0.270	0.231
18	0.836	0.700	0.587	0.494	0.416	0.350	0.296	0.250	0.212
19	0.828	0.686	0.570	0.475	0.396	0.331	0.277	0.232	0.194
20	0.820	0.673	0.554	0.456	0.377	0.312	0.258	0.215	0.178
25	0.780	0.610	0.478	0.375	0.295	0.233	0.184	0.146	0.116
30	0.742	0.552	0.412	0.308	0.231	0.174	0.131	0.099	0.075
40	0.672	0.453	0.307	0.208	0.142	0.097	0.067	0.046	0.032
50	0.608	0.372	0.228	0.141	0.087	0.054	0.034	0.021	0.013

TABLE C (DF) (continued)

Period (n)	Percent (i)								
	10	11	12	13	14	15	16	17	18
1	0.909	0.901	0.893	0.885	0.877	0.870	0.862	0.855	0.847
2	0.826	0.812	0.797	0.783	0.769	0.756	0.743	0.731	0.718
3	0.751	0.731	0.712	0.693	0.675	0.658	0.641	0.624	0.609
4	0.683	0.659	0.636	0.613	0.592	0.572	0.552	0.534	0.516
5	0.621	0.593	0.567	0.543	0.519	0.497	0.476	0.456	0.437
6	0.564	0.535	0.507	0.480	0.456	0.432	0.410	0.390	0.370
7	0.513	0.482	0.452	0.425	0.400	0.376	0.354	0.333	0.314
8	0.467	0.434	0.404	0.376	0.351	0.327	0.305	0.285	0.266
9	0.424	0.391	0.361	0.333	0.300	0.284	0.263	0.243	0.225
10	0.386	0.352	0.322	0.295	0.270	0.247	0.227	0.208	0.191
11	0.350	0.317	0.287	0.261	0.237	0.215	0.195	0.178	0.162
12	0.319	0.286	0.257	0.231	0.208	0.187	0.168	0.152	0.137
13	0.290	0.258	0.229	0.204	0.182	0.163	0.145	0.130	0.116
14	0.263	0.232	0.205	0.181	0.160	0.141	0.125	0.111	0.099
15	0.239	0.209	0.183	0.160	0.140	0.123	0.108	0.095	0.084
16	0.218	0.188	0.163	0.141	0.123	0.107	0.093	0.081	0.071
17	0.198	0.170	0.146	0.125	0.108	0.093	0.080	0.069	0.060
18	0.180	0.153	0.130	0.111	0.095	0.081	0.069	0.059	0.051
19	0.164	0.138	0.116	0.098	0.083	0.070	0.060	0.051	0.043
20	0.149	0.124	0.104	0.087	0.073	0.061	0.051	0.043	0.037
25	0.092	0.074	0.059	0.047	0.038	0.030	0.024	0.020	0.016
30	0.057	0.044	0.033	0.026	0.020	0.015	0.012	0.009	0.007
40	0.022	0.015	0.011	0.008	0.005	0.004	0.003	0.002	0.001
50	0.009	0.005	0.003	0.002	0.001	0.001	0.001	0	0

TABLE C (DF) (concluded)

Period (n)	Percent (i)						
	19	20	25	30	35	40	50
1	0.840	0.833	0.800	0.769	0.741	0.714	0.667
2	0.706	0.694	0.640	0.592	0.549	0.510	0.444
3	0.593	0.579	0.512	0.455	0.406	0.364	0.296
4	0.499	0.482	0.410	0.350	0.301	0.260	0.198
5	0.419	0.402	0.320	0.269	0.223	0.186	0.132
6	0.352	0.335	0.262	0.207	0.165	0.133	0.088
7	0.296	0.279	0.210	0.159	0.122	0.095	0.059
8	0.249	0.233	0.168	0.123	0.091	0.068	0.039
9	0.209	0.194	0.134	0.094	0.067	0.048	0.026
10	0.176	0.162	0.107	0.073	0.050	0.035	0.017
11	0.148	0.135	0.086	0.056	0.037	0.025	0.012
12	0.124	0.112	0.069	0.043	0.027	0.018	0.008
13	0.104	0.093	0.055	0.033	0.020	0.013	0.005
14	0.088	0.078	0.044	0.025	0.015	0.009	0.003
15	0.074	0.065	0.035	0.020	0.011	0.006	0.002
16	0.062	0.054	0.028	0.015	0.008	0.005	0.002
17	0.052	0.045	0.023	0.012	0.006	0.003	0.001
18	0.044	0.038	0.018	0.009	0.005	0.002	0.001
19	0.037	0.031	0.014	0.007	0.003	0.002	0
20	0.031	0.026	0.012	0.005	0.002	0.001	0
25	0.013	0.010	0.004	0.001	0.001	0	0
30	0.005	0.004	0.001	0	0	0	0
40	0.001	0.001	0	0	0	0	0
50	0	0	0	0	0	0	0

TABLE D
Annuity discount factors (ADF)

Period (n)	Percent (i)								
	1	2	3	4	5	6	7	8	9
1	0.990	0.980	0.971	0.962	0.952	0.943	0.935	0.926	0.917
2	1.970	1.942	1.913	1.886	1.859	1.833	1.808	1.783	1.759
3	2.941	2.884	2.829	2.775	2.723	2.673	2.624	2.577	2.531
4	3.902	3.808	3.717	3.630	3.546	3.465	3.387	3.312	3.240
5	4.853	4.713	4.580	4.452	4.329	4.212	4.100	3.993	3.890
6	5.795	5.601	5.417	5.242	5.076	4.917	4.767	4.623	4.486
7	6.728	6.472	6.230	6.002	5.786	5.582	5.389	5.206	5.033
8	7.652	7.325	7.020	6.733	6.463	6.210	5.971	5.747	5.535
9	8.566	8.162	7.786	7.435	7.108	6.802	6.515	6.247	5.995
10	9.471	8.983	8.530	8.111	7.722	7.360	7.024	6.710	6.418
11	10.368	9.787	9.253	8.760	8.306	7.887	7.499	7.139	6.805
12	11.255	10.575	9.954	9.385	8.863	8.384	7.943	7.536	7.161
13	12.134	11.348	10.635	9.986	9.394	8.853	8.358	7.904	7.487
14	13.004	12.106	11.296	10.563	9.899	9.295	8.745	8.244	7.786
15	13.865	12.849	11.938	11.118	10.380	9.712	9.108	8.559	8.061
16	14.718	13.578	12.561	11.652	10.838	10.106	9.447	8.851	8.313
17	15.562	14.292	13.166	12.166	11.274	10.477	9.763	9.122	8.544
18	16.398	14.992	13.754	12.659	11.690	10.828	10.059	9.372	8.756
19	17.226	15.678	14.324	13.134	12.085	11.158	10.336	9.604	8.950
20	18.046	16.351	14.877	13.590	12.462	11.470	10.594	9.818	9.129
25	22.023	19.523	17.413	15.622	14.094	12.783	11.654	10.675	9.823
30	25.808	22.396	19.600	17.292	15.372	13.765	12.409	11.258	10.274
40	32.835	27.355	23.115	19.793	17.159	15.046	13.332	11.925	10.757
50	39.196	31.424	25.730	21.482	18.256	15.762	13.801	12.233	10.962

TABLE D (ADF) (continued)

Period (n)	Percent (i)								
	10	11	12	13	14	15	16	17	18
1	0.909	0.901	0.893	0.885	0.877	0.870	0.862	0.855	0.847
2	1.736	1.713	1.690	1.668	1.647	1.626	1.605	1.585	1.566
3	2.487	2.444	2.402	2.361	2.322	2.283	2.246	2.210	2.174
4	3.170	3.102	3.037	2.974	2.914	2.855	2.798	2.743	2.690
5	3.791	3.696	3.605	3.517	3.433	3.352	3.274	3.199	3.127
6	4.355	4.231	4.111	3.998	3.889	3.784	3.685	3.589	3.498
7	4.868	4.712	4.564	4.423	4.288	4.160	4.039	3.922	3.812
8	5.335	5.146	4.968	4.799	4.639	4.487	4.344	4.207	4.078
9	5.759	5.537	5.328	5.132	4.946	4.772	4.607	4.451	4.303
10	6.145	5.889	5.650	5.426	5.216	5.019	4.833	4.659	4.494
11	6.495	6.207	5.938	5.687	5.453	5.234	5.029	4.836	4.656
12	6.814	6.492	6.194	5.918	5.660	5.421	5.197	4.988	4.793
13	7.103	6.750	6.424	6.122	5.842	5.583	5.342	5.118	4.910
14	7.367	6.982	6.628	6.302	6.002	5.724	5.468	5.229	5.008
15	7.606	7.191	6.811	6.462	6.142	5.847	5.575	5.324	5.092
16	7.824	7.379	6.974	6.604	6.265	5.954	5.668	5.405	5.162
17	8.022	7.549	7.102	6.729	6.373	6.047	5.749	5.475	5.222
18	8.201	7.702	7.250	6.840	6.467	6.128	5.818	5.534	5.273
19	8.365	7.839	7.366	6.938	6.550	6.198	5.877	5.584	5.316
20	8.514	7.963	7.469	7.025	6.623	6.259	5.929	5.628	5.353
25	9.077	8.422	7.843	7.330	6.873	6.464	6.097	5.766	5.467
30	9.427	8.694	8.055	7.496	7.003	6.566	6.177	5.829	5.517
40	9.779	8.951	8.244	7.634	7.105	6.642	6.233	5.871	5.548
50	9.915	9.042	8.304	7.675	7.133	6.661	6.246	5.880	5.554

TABLE D (ADF) (concluded)

Period (n)	Percent (i)						
	19	20	25	30	35	40	50
1	0.840	0.833	0.800	0.769	0.741	0.714	0.667
2	1.547	1.528	1.440	1.361	1.289	1.224	1.111
3	2.140	2.106	1.952	1.816	1.696	1.589	1.407
4	2.639	2.589	2.362	2.166	1.997	1.849	1.605
5	3.058	2.991	2.689	2.436	2.220	2.035	1.737
6	3.410	3.326	2.951	2.643	2.385	2.168	1.824
7	3.706	3.605	3.161	2.802	2.508	2.263	1.883
8	3.954	3.837	3.329	2.925	2.598	2.331	1.922
9	4.163	4.031	3.463	3.019	2.665	2.379	1.948
10	4.339	4.192	3.571	3.092	2.715	2.414	1.965
11	4.486	4.327	3.656	3.147	2.752	2.438	1.977
12	4.611	4.439	3.725	3.190	2.779	2.456	1.985
13	4.715	4.533	3.780	3.223	2.799	2.469	1.990
14	4.802	4.611	3.824	3.249	2.814	2.478	1.993
15	4.876	4.675	3.859	3.268	2.825	2.484	1.995
16	4.938	4.730	3.887	3.283	2.834	2.489	1.997
17	4.988	4.775	3.910	3.295	2.840	2.492	1.998
18	5.033	4.812	3.928	3.304	2.844	2.494	1.999
19	5.070	4.843	3.942	3.311	2.848	2.496	1.999
20	5.101	4.870	3.954	3.316	2.850	2.497	1.999
25	5.195	4.948	3.985	3.329	2.856	2.499	2.000
30	5.235	4.979	3.995	3.332	2.857	2.500	2.000
40	5.258	4.997	3.999	3.333	2.857	2.500	2.000
50	5.262	4.999	4.000	3.333	2.857	2.500	2.000

INDEX

INDEX

This book has been set in 9 and 8 point Primer, leaded 2 points. Section numbers and titles are 24 point Optima Bold. Chapter numbers are 54 point Weiss Series II and chapter titles are 18 point Optima. The size of the type page is 27 by 48 picas.